CCNP: Cisco Internetwork Troubleshooting Study Guide

Exam number (642-831)

OBJECTIVE	CHAPTER NUMBER
TECHNOLOGY	
Identify troubleshooting methods.	1, 3
Explain documentation standards and the requirements for document control.	2, 3
IMPLEMENTATION AND OPERATION	
Establish an optimal system baseline.	2, 3
Diagram and document system topology.	2
Document end system configuration.	3
Verify connectivity at all layers.	3, 4, 5, 6, 7, 8, 10
Select an optimal troubleshooting approach.	3, 4, 5, 6
PLANNING AND DESIGN	
Plan a network documentation system.	3
Plan a baseline monitoring scheme.	3
Plan an approach to troubleshooting that minimizes system downtime.	4, 5, 6, 7
TROUBLESHOOTING	
Use Cisco IOS commands and applications to identify system problems at all layers.	4, 5, 7, 8, 9, 10
Isolate system problems to one or more specific layers.	4, 8
Resolve sub-optimal system performance problems at layers 2 through 7.	5, 8, 9, 10
Resolve local connectivity problems at layer 1.	9, 10
Restore optimal baseline service.	9, 10
Work with external providers to resolve service provision problems.	7, 8
Work with system users to resolve network related end-use problems.	3

NOTE

Exam objectives are subject to change at any time without prior notice and at Cisco's sole discretion. Please visit Cisco's website (http://www.cisco.com) for the most current exam objectives listing.

SYBEX

CCNP:
Cisco Internetwork Troubleshooting
Study Guide

CCNP®:
Cisco Internetwork Troubleshooting
Study Guide

Arthur Pfund

Todd Lammle

San Francisco • London

Associate Publisher: Neil Edde
Acquisitions Editor: Maureen Adams
Developmental Editor: Heather O'Connor
Production Editor: Liz Burke
Technical Editor: Scott Morris
Copyeditor: Carol Henry
Compositor: Craig Woods, Happenstance Type-O-Rama
Graphic Illustrator: Jeff Wilson, Happenstance Type-O-Rama
CD Coordinator: Dan Mummert
CD Technician: Kevin Ly
Proofreaders: Laurie O'Connell, Nancy Riddiough, Emily Hsuan
Indexer: Ted Laux
Book Designer: Bill Gibson
Cover design: Archer Design
Cover photographer: Andrew Ward/Life File

Library of Congress Card Number: 2003109124

ISBN: 0-7821-4295-8

SYBEX

To Our Valued Readers:

Thank you for looking to Sybex for your CCNP certification exam prep needs. We at Sybex are proud of the reputation we've established for providing certification candidates with the practical knowledge and skills needed to succeed in the highly competitive IT marketplace. Sybex is proud to have helped thousands of Cisco certification candidates prepare for their exams over the years, and we are excited about the opportunity to continue to provide computer and networking professionals with the skills they'll need to succeed in the highly competitive IT industry.

We at Sybex are proud of the reputation we've established for providing certification candidates with the practical knowledge and skills needed to succeed in the highly competitive IT marketplace. It has always been Sybex's mission to teach individuals how to utilize technologies in the real world, not to simply feed them answers to test questions. Just as Cisco is committed to establishing measurable standards for certifying those professionals who work in the cutting-edge field of internetworking, Sybex is committed to providing those professionals with the means of acquiring the skills and knowledge they need to meet those standards.

The author and editors have worked hard to ensure that the Study Guide you hold in your hand is comprehensive, in-depth, and pedagogically sound. We're confident that this book will exceed the demanding standards of the certification marketplace and help you, the Cisco certification candidate, succeed in your endeavors.

As always, your feedback is important to us. Please send comments, questions, or suggestions to support@sybex.com. At Sybex we're continually striving to meet the needs of individuals preparing for IT certification exams.

Good luck in pursuit of your CCNP certification!

Neil Edde
Associate Publisher—Certification
Sybex, Inc.

To my parents for helping me become the person I am today.

Acknowledgments

First, I would like to thank my wife Michele for her support during this effort. I would also like to thank the rest of my family for their moral support, especially my parents and grandparents for their words of encouragement and motivation. In addition, thanks to the wonderful group of people at Sybex that helped me get through the process. Especially, thanks to Liz Burke and Heather O'Conner for their assistance. As always, they were a great team to work with!!

Contents at a Glance

Table of Contents

Introduction

This book is intended to help you continue on your exciting new path toward obtaining your CCNP certification. Before reading this book, it is important to have at least read the Sybex *CCNA: Cisco Certified Network Associate Study Guide*, Fourth Edition. You can take the CCNP tests in any order, but you should have passed the CCNA exam before pursuing your CCNP. Many questions in the Cisco Internet Troubleshooting Support (CIT) exam are built on the CCNA material. However, we have done everything possible to make sure that you can pass the CIT exam by reading this book and practicing with Cisco routers.

Cisco Systems's Place in Networking

Cisco Systems has become an unrivaled worldwide leader in networking for the Internet. Its networking solutions can easily connect users who work from diverse devices on disparate networks. Cisco products make it simple for people to access and transfer information without regard to differences in time, place, or platform.

Cisco Systems's big picture is that it provides end-to-end networking solutions that customers can use to build an efficient, unified information infrastructure of their own or to connect to someone else's. This is an important piece in the Internet/networking-industry puzzle, because a common architecture that delivers consistent network services to all users is now a functional imperative. Because Cisco Systems offers such a broad range of networking and Internet services and capabilities, users needing regular access to their local network or the Internet can do so unhindered, making Cisco's wares indispensable.

Cisco answers this need with a wide range of hardware products that are used to form information networks using the Cisco Internetworking Operating System (IOS) software. This software provides network services, paving the way for networked technical support and professional services to maintain and optimize all network operations.

Along with the Cisco IOS, one of the services Cisco created to help support the vast amount of hardware it has engineered is the Cisco Certified Internetworking Expert (CCIE) program, which was designed specifically to equip people to effectively manage the vast quantity of installed Cisco networks. The business plan is simple: If you want to sell more Cisco equipment and have more Cisco networks installed, ensure that the networks you installed run properly.

However, having an extraordinary product line isn't all it takes to guarantee the huge success that Cisco enjoys—lots of companies with great products are now defunct. If you have complicated products designed to solve complicated problems, you need knowledgeable people who are fully capable of installing, managing, and troubleshooting those products. That part isn't easy, so Cisco began the CCIE program to equip people to support these complicated networks. This program, known colloquially as the Doctorate of Networking, has also been very successful, primarily due to its extreme difficulty. Cisco continually monitors the program, making the changes needed to make sure that the program remains pertinent and accurately reflects the demands of today's internetworking business environments.

Building on the highly successful CCIE program, Cisco Career Certifications permit you to become certified at various levels of technical proficiency, spanning the disciplines of network design and support. So, whether you're beginning a career, changing careers, securing your present position, or seeking to refine and promote your position, this is the book for you!

Cisco's Certifications

Cisco has created several certification tracks that will help you become a CCIE, as well as aid prospective employers in measuring skill levels. Before these new certifications existed, you took only one test and were then faced with the lab, which made it difficult to succeed. With the new certifications that add a better approach to preparing for that almighty lab, Cisco has opened doors that few were allowed through before. So, what are these new certifications, and how do they help you get your CCIE?

Cisco Certified Network Associate (CCNA)

The CCNA certification is the first certification in the new line of Cisco certifications and is a precursor to all current Cisco certifications. With the new certification programs, Cisco has created a type of stepping-stone approach to CCIE certification. Now, you can become a Cisco Certified Network Associate for the meager cost of the Sybex *CCNA: Cisco Certified Network Associate Study Guide*, Fourth Edition, plus $125 for the test.

And you don't have to stop there—you can choose to continue with your studies and select a specific track to follow. The Installation and Support track will help you prepare for the CCIE Routing and Switching certification; the Communications and Services track will help you prepare for the CCIE Communication and Services certification. It is important to note that you do not have to attempt any of these tracks to reach the CCIE, but choosing a track is recommended for the best success.

Cisco Certified Network Professional (CCNP)

The Cisco Certified Network Professional (CCNP) certification has opened many opportunities for the individual wishing to become Cisco-certified but who is lacking the training, the expertise, or the bucks to pass the notorious and often-failed two-day Cisco torture lab. The new Cisco certifications will truly provide exciting new opportunities for the CNE and MCSE who don't see an obvious way to advance.

So, you're thinking, "Great, what do I do after I pass the CCNA exam?" Well, if you want to become a CCIE in Routing and Switching (the most popular certification), understand that there's more than one path to the CCIE certification. One way is to continue studying and become a Cisco Certified Network Professional (CCNP). That means taking four more tests in addition to obtaining the CCNA certification.

We'll discuss requirements for the CCIE exams later on in this introduction.

Remember that you don't need to be a CCNP or even a CCNA to take the CCIE lab, but to accomplish that, it's extremely helpful if you already have these certifications.

The CCNP program will prepare you to understand and comprehensively tackle the internetworking issues of today and beyond—not limited to the Cisco world. You will undergo metamorphosis, vastly increasing your knowledge and skills through the process of obtaining these certifications.

What Are the CCNP Certification Skills?

Cisco demands a certain level of proficiency for its CCNP certification. In addition to what's required for the CCNA, you'll need to have the following skills:

- Installing, configuring, operating, and troubleshooting complex routed LAN, routed WAN, and switched LAN networks, and Dial Access Services.
- Understanding complex networking concepts, such as IP, IGRP, Async Routing, extended access lists, IP RIP, route redistribution, route summarization, OSPF, VLSM, BGP, Serial, IGRP, Frame Relay, ISDN, ISL, X.25, DDR, PSTN, PPP, VLANs, Ethernet, ATM LAN emulation, access lists, 802.10, FDDI, and transparent and translational bridging.

To meet the Cisco Certified Network Professional requirements, you must be able to perform the following:

- Install and/or configure a network to increase bandwidth, quicken network response times, and improve reliability and quality of service.
- Maximize performance through campus LANs, routed WANs, and remote access.
- Improve network security.
- Create a global intranet.
- Provide access security to campus switches and routers.
- Provide increased switching and routing bandwidth—end-to-end resiliency services.
- Provide custom queuing and routed priority services.

How Do You Become a CCNP?

After becoming a CCNA, the four exams you must take to get your CCNP are as follows:

Exam 642-801: Building Scalable Cisco Internetworks (BSCI)   A while back, Cisco retired the Routing (640-603) exam and now uses this exam, 642-801, to build on the fundamentals of the CCNA exam. BSCI focuses on large multiprotocol internetworks and how to manage them. The BSCI exam is also a required exam for the CCIP and CCDP certifications, which will be discussed later in this introduction.

Exam 642-811: Building Cisco Multilayer Switched Networks (BCMSN)   The Building Cisco Multilayer Switched Networks exam tests your knowledge of the 1900 and 5000 series of Catalyst switches. You'll also be challenged on your knowledge of switching technology, implementation and operation, planning and design.

Exam 642-821: Building Cisco Remote Access Networks (BCRAN)   The Building Cisco Remote Access Networks (BCRAN) exam tests your knowledge of installing, configuring, monitoring, and troubleshooting Cisco ISDN and dial-up access products. You must understand PPP, ISDN, Frame Relay, and authentication.

Exam 642-831: Cisco Internetwork Troubleshooting Support (CIT)   The Cisco Internetwork Troubleshooting Support (CIT) exam tests you on troubleshooting information. You must be able to document a network; troubleshoot Ethernet LANS and IP networks, as well as ISDN, PPP, and Frame Relay networks. This book covers all the topics you'll need to pass the CIT exam.

An Alternate Plan

If you hate tests, you can take fewer of them by signing up for the CCNA exam and the CIT exam, and then take just one more long exam called the Foundation R/S exam (640-841). Doing this also gives you your CCNP—but beware, it's a really long test that fuses all the material listed previously in this introduction into one exam. Good luck! That said, by taking this exam you get three tests for the price of two, which saves you $125 (if you pass). Some people think it's easier to take the Foundation R/S exam because you can leverage your higher-scoring areas against the areas in which you don't do as well. There is also an option to obtain your CCNP. This is to do three tests: the Composite Exam (642-891), which fuses the BSCI and BCMSN exams, plus the BCRAN and CIT exams.

 Remember that test objectives and tests can change at any time without notice. Always check the Cisco website for the most up-to-date information (www.cisco.com).

Sybex has a solution for each one of the CCNP exams. Each study guide listed in the following table covers all the exam objectives for their respective exams.

Exam Name	Exam #	Sybex Products
Building Scalable Cisco Internetworks	642-801	CCNP: *Building Scalable Cisco Internetworks Study Guide* (ISBN 0-7821-4293-1)
Switching	642-811	CCNP: *Building Cisco Multilayer Switched Networks Study Guide* (0-7821-4294-X)
Remote Access	642-821	CCNP: *Building Cisco Remote Access Networks Study Guide* (0-7821-4296-6)
Support	642-831	CCNP: *Cisco Internetwork Troubleshooting Study Guide.* (0-7821-4295-8)

Also available: *CCNP Study Guide Kit, 3rd Ed.* (0-7821-4297-4); covers all four exams.

Cisco Certified Internetwork Professional (CCIP)

After passing the CCNA, the next step in the Communications and Services track is the CCIP. The CCIP is a professional-level certification.

The CCIP certification gives you the skills necessary to understand and tackle the complex internetworking world of the service provider. You will acquire the knowledge necessary to prepare you for moving forward toward the coveted CCIE Communications and Services certification.

What Are the CCIP Certification Skills?

Cisco demands a certain level of proficiency for its CCIP certification. In addition to what's required for the CCNA, you will need to have the following skills:

- Performing complex planning, operations, installations, implementations, and trouble-shooting of internetworks.

- Understanding and managing complex communications networks—last mile, edge, or core.

How Do You Become a CCIP?

After becoming a CCNA, you must take two core exams and an elective. The core exams are:

Exam 642-801: Building Scalable Cisco Internetworks (BSCI)   A while back, Cisco retired the Routing (640-603) exam and now uses this exam, 642-801, to build on the fundamentals of the CCNA exam. BSCI focuses on large multiprotocol internetworks and how to manage them.

Exam 642-641: Quality of Services (QoS)   This exam tests your knowledge of Quality of Service for internetworks.

Exam 640-910: Implementing Cisco MPLS (MPLS)   This exam tests your knowledge of multiprotocol label switching and its implementation. The Sybex *CCIP: MPLS Study Guide* (ISBN 0-7821-4096-3) covers all the exam objectives.

Exam 642-661: Border Gateway Protocol (BGP)   This exam tests your knowledge of Border Gateway Protocol (BGP). When you complete this exam you should be able to manage a large BGP network.

Cisco's Network Design and Installation Certifications

In addition to the Network Installation and Support track and the Communications and Services track, Cisco has created another certification track for network designers. The two certifications within this track are the Cisco Certified Design Associate (CCDA) and Cisco Certified Design Professional (CCDP). If you're reaching for the CCIE stars, we highly recommend the CCNP and CCDP certifications before attempting the CCIE R/S Qualification exam.

These two certifications will give you the knowledge to design routed LAN, routed WAN, and switched LAN.

Cisco Certified Design Associate (CCDA)

To become a CCDA, you must pass the DESGN (Designing for Cisco Internetwork Solutions) test (640-861). To pass this test, you must understand how to do the following:

- Design simple routed LAN, routed WAN, and switched LAN and ATM LANE networks.

- Use network-layer addressing.

- Filter with access lists.

- Use and propagate VLAN.

- Size networks.

Cisco Certified Design Professional (CCDP)

If you're already a CCNP and want to get your CCDP, you can simply take the ARCH 642-871 test. If you're not yet a CCNP, however, you must take the CCDA, CCNA, BSCI, Switching, Remote Access, and CID exams.

CCDP certification skills include:

- Designing complex routed LAN, routed WAN, and switched LAN and ATM LANE networks.
- Technical knowledge beyond the base level of CCDA.

CCDPs must also demonstrate proficiency in the following:

- Network-layer addressing in a hierarchical environment.
- Traffic management with access lists.
- Hierarchical network design.
- VLAN use and propagation.
- Performance considerations: required hardware and software; switching engines; memory, cost, and minimization.

Cisco's Security Certifications

Quite a few Cisco security certifications are available. All of the Cisco security certifications also require a valid CCNA.

Cisco Certified Security Professional (CCSP)

You have to pass five exams to get your CCSP. The pivotal exam is the SECUR. Here are the exams you must pass to call the CCSP yours:

Exam 642-501: Securing Cisco IOS Networks (SECUR)   This exam tests your understanding of such concepts as basic router security, AAA security for Cisco routers and networks, Cisco IOS Firewall configuration and authentication, building basic and advanced IPSec VPNs, and managing Cisco enterprise VPN routers. Sybex can help you pass the SECUR exam with the *CCSP: Securing Cisco IOS Networks Study Guide* (ISBN 0-7821-4231-1).

Exam 642-521: Cisco Secure PIX Firewall Advanced (CSPFA)   This exam challenges your knowledge of the fundamentals of Cisco PIX Firewalls, as well as translations and connections, object grouping, advanced protocol handling and authentication, authorization, and accounting, among other topics. You can tackle the CSPFA exam with the help of Sybex's *CCSP: Secure PIX and Secure VPN Study Guide* (ISBN 0-7821-4287-7).

Exam 642-511: Cisco Secure Virtual Private Networks (CSVPN)   The CSVPN exam covers the basics of Cisco VPNs; configuring various Cisco VPNs for remote access, hardware client, backup server, and load balancing; plus IPSec over UDP and IPSec over TCP. Again, using the Sybex *CCSP: Secure PIX and Secure VPN Study Guide* (ISBN 0-7821-4287-7), you'll approach the CSVPN exam with confidence.

Exam 642-531: Cisco Secure Intrusion Detection System (CSIDS)   The CSIDS exam will challenge your knowledge of intrusion detection technologies and solutions, and test your abilities to install and configure ISD components. You'll also be tested on managing large-scale deployments of Cisco IDS sensors using Cisco IDS management software. Prepare for the CSIDS exam using Sybex's *CCSP: Secure Intrusion Detection and SAFE Implementation Study Guide* (ISBN 0-7821-4288-5).

Exam 9E0-131: Cisco SAFE Implementation (CSI) This exam tests such topics as security and architecture fundamentals, SAFE Network design for small and medium corporate and campus situations, and SAFE remote-user network implementation. You can take advantage of Sybex's *CCSP: Secure PIX and Secure VPN Study Guide* (ISBN 0-7821-4287-7) for help with this exam.

Cisco Firewall Specialist

Cisco Security certifications focus on the growing need for knowledgeable network professionals who can implement complete security solutions. Cisco Firewall Specialists focus on securing network access using Cisco IOS Software and Cisco PIX Firewall technologies.

The two exams you must pass to achieve the Cisco Firewall Specialist certification are Securing Cisco IOS Networks (SECUR) and Cisco Secure PIX Firewall Advanced (CSPFA).

Cisco IDS Specialist

Cisco IDS Specialists can both operate and monitor Cisco IOS Software and IDS technologies to detect and respond to intrusion activities.

The two exams you must pass to achieve the Cisco IDS Specialist certification are Securing Cisco IOS Networks (SECUR) and Cisco Secure Intrusion Detection System (CSIDS).

Cisco VPN Specialist

Cisco VPN Specialists can configure VPNs across shared public networks using Cisco IOS Software and Cisco VPN 3000 Series Concentrator technologies.

The exams you must pass to achieve the Cisco VPN Specialist certification are Securing Cisco IOS Networks (SECUR) and Cisco Secure Virtual Networks (CSVPN).

Cisco Certified Internetwork Expert (CCIE)

Cool! You've become a CCNP, and now your sights are fixed on getting your Cisco Certified Internetwork Expert (CCIE) certification. What do you do next? Cisco recommends a *minimum* of two years on-the-job experience before taking the CCIE lab. After jumping those hurdles, you then have to pass the written CCIE Exam Qualifications before taking the actual lab.

There are four CCIE certifications, and you must pass a written section and a lob portion for each certification. As can be seen from below, most of the CCIE certifications require only a single test, but one requires multiple:

CCIE Communications and Services (Exams 350-020, 350-021, 350-022, 350-023) The four CCIE Communications and Services written exams cover IP and IP routing, optical, DSL, dial, cable, wireless, WAN switching, content networking, and voice.

CCIE Routing and Switching (Exam 350-001) The CCIE Routing and Switching exam covers IP and IP routing, non-IP desktop protocols such as IPX, and bridge- and switch-related technologies.

Sybex can help you pass the CCIE Routing and Switching exam with the *CCIE: Cisco Certified Internetworking Expert Study Guide,* Second Edition (ISBN 0-7821-4207-9).

CCIE Security (Exam 350-018) The CCIE Security exam covers IP and IP routing as well as specific security components.

CCIE Voice (Exam 351-030) The CCIE Voice exam covers those technologies and applications that make up a Cisco Enterprise VoIP solution.

Where Do You Take the Exam?

You can take the exams at any of the Sylvan Prometric or Virtual University Enterprises (VUE) testing centers around the world. For the location of a testing center near you, call Sylvan at (800) 755-3926 or VUE at (877) 404-3926. Outside of the United States and Canada, contact your local Sylvan Prometric Registration Center.

To register for a Cisco Certified Network Professional exam:

1. Determine the number of the exam you want to take. (The CIT exam number is 642-831.)

2. Register with the nearest Sylvan Prometric or VUE testing center. At this point, you will be asked to pay in advance for the exam. At the time of this writing, the exams are $125 each and must be taken within one year of payment. You can schedule exams up to six weeks in advance or as soon as one working day prior to the day you wish to take it. If something comes up and you need to cancel or reschedule your exam appointment, contact the testing center at least 24 hours in advance. Same-day registration isn't available for the Cisco tests.

3. When you schedule the exam, you'll get instructions regarding all appointment and cancellation procedures, the ID requirements, and information about the testing-center location.

Tips for Taking Your CCNP CIT Exam

The CCNP CIT test contains about 65 questions to be completed in about 90 minutes. However, understand that your test may vary somewhat from this estimate.

Many questions on the exam have answer choices that at first glance look identical—especially the syntax questions! Remember to read through the choices carefully, because "close" doesn't cut it. If you put commands in the wrong order or forget one measly character, your answer will be wrong. So, to practice, do the hands-on exercises at the end of the chapters over and over again until the solutions feel natural to you.

Unlike Microsoft or Novell tests, the exam has answer choices that are highly similar in syntax—although some syntax is dead wrong, it is usually just *subtly* wrong. Some other syntax choices may be right, but they're shown in the wrong order. Cisco does split hairs, and it is not at all averse to giving you classic trick questions. Here's an example:

`access-list 101 deny ip any eq 23` denies Telnet access to all systems.

This statement looks correct to most people because they refer to the port number (23) and think, "Yes, that's the port used for Telnet." The catch is that you can't filter IP on port numbers (only TCP and UDP can be filtered in this way). Another indicator that this command is wrong is the use of an extended access list number but with any or no destination address for the destination.

Cisco does have some simulation questions on the CIT exam. Make sure you've got hands-on skills to take this test. Practice with the hands-on labs in this book, and for further practice with routers and switches, check out the CCNP Virtual Lab from Sybex.

Also, never forget that the right answer is the Cisco answer. In many cases, more than one appropriate answer is presented, but the *correct* answer is the one that Cisco recommends.

Here are some general tips for exam success:

- Arrive early at the exam center, so you can relax and review your study materials.
- Read the questions *carefully*. Don't just jump to conclusions. Make sure that you're clear about *exactly* what each question asks.
- Don't leave any questions unanswered. They count against your score.
- When answering multiple-choice questions that you're not sure about, use the process of elimination to get rid of the obviously incorrect answers first. Doing this greatly improves your odds if you need to make an educated guess.
- As of this writing, the written exams still allow you to skip ahead and then return to previous questions. However, it is always best to check the Cisco website before taking any exam, to get the most up-to-date information.

After you complete an exam, you'll get immediate, online notification of your pass or fail status, a printed Examination Score Report that indicates your pass or fail status, and your exam results by section. (The test administrator will give you the printed score report.) Test scores are automatically forwarded to Cisco within five working days after you take the test, so you don't need to send your score to them.

What Does This Book Cover?

This book covers everything you need to pass the CCNP CIT exam. It teaches you how to document your network, and how to troubleshoot and maintain Cisco routers and switches in a large internetwork. Each chapter begins with a list of the topics covered, related to the CCNP CIT test, so make sure to read the list before working through the chapter.

- Chapter 1 discusses the complexity of today's internetworks and introduces you to the Cisco Troubleshooting Methodology. You'll study how to apply this methodology to network problems.

- Chapter 2 focuses on what goes into a network baseline, as well as how to create one. It also details two of the baseline's components: the network configuration table and the network topology diagram.

- Chapter 3 continues the discussion on documentation by explaining the end-system version of a network configuration table and network topology diagram. This chapter also takes you through the steps required to create these documents. In the second half of the chapter, various troubleshooting approaches are discussed and some end-system troubleshooting commands are reviewed.

- Chapter 4 reviews the OSI reference model and then discusses connection-oriented and connectionless protocols. Following this, the IP, ICMP, TCP, and UDP protocols are examined, and Layer 2 protocols are covered.

- Chapter 5 focuses on the skills and knowledge needed to use Cisco's built-in diagnostic tools in a TCP/IP environment. These tools include show, debug, and logging commands as well as a router core dump. This chapter also examines appropriate use of the ping and traceroute utilities. LAN and WAN problems are explored, and the chapter ends with a discussion of access lists.

- Chapter 6 is dedicated to covering IP routing protocols, specifically RIP, IGRP, EIGRP, OSPF, and BGP. The benefits and drawbacks of each are included, as well as the commands used to verify correct functionality. We also discuss the issues of redistributing these protocols.

- Chapter 7 examines serial and Frame Relay connectivity. You'll study the function of the show and debug IOS commands needed to successfully troubleshoot problems in serial and Frame Relay environments, as well as some common problem areas.

- Chapter 8 discusses ISDN and related protocols, specifically looking at what is necessary to set up an ISDN dial solution. In addition, time is spent looking at the debug output from the call setup, to show how an ISDN call is established.

- Chapter 9 details the functioning of Catalyst series switches. This chapter includes information on the architecture of the switch as well as the command syntax used to configure the switch. It also discusses the use of VLANs and trunking switch ports together.

- Chapter 10 is a summary chapter that takes the information from the previous chapters and applies it to real-world examples. These examples demonstrate combining the troubleshooting methodology with the technical skills learned in this book.

- The Glossary is a handy resource for Cisco vocabulary and is an excellent tool for understanding some of the more obscure terms used in this book.

Each chapter ends with review questions that are specifically designed to help you retain the knowledge presented. To really nail down your skills, read each question carefully.

How to Use This Book

This book can provide a solid foundation for the serious effort of preparing for the CCNP CIT exam. To best benefit from this book, use the following study method:

1. Take the Assessment Test immediately following this Introduction. (The answers are at the end of the test.) Carefully read over the explanations for any question you get wrong, and note which chapters the material comes from. This information will help you plan your study strategy.

2. Study each chapter carefully, making sure that you fully understand the information and the test topics listed at the beginning of each chapter. Pay extra-close attention to any chapter where you missed questions in the Assessment Test.

3. Note the questions that confuse you, and study those sections of the book again.

4. Before taking the exam, try your hand at the two bonus exams included on the CD that comes with this book. The questions in these exams appear only on the CD. This will give you a complete overview of what you can expect to see on the real thing.

5. Remember to use the products on the CD included with this book. The electronic flashcards and the EdgeTest exam-preparation software have all been specifically picked to help you study for and pass your exam. Study on the road with the *CCNP: Cisco Internetwork Troubleshooting Study Guide* eBook in PDF format, and test yourself with the electronic flashcards.

 The electronic flashcards can be used on your Windows computer, Pocket PC, or Palm device.

6. Make sure you review the Key Terms list at the end of each chapter. Appendix A includes all the commands used in the book, along with an explanation for each command.

To learn all the material covered in this book, you'll have to apply yourself regularly and with discipline. Try to set aside the same time every day to study, and select a comfortable and quiet place to do so. If you work hard, you'll be surprised at how quickly you learn this material. All the best!

What's On the CD?

We worked hard to provide some really valuable tools to help you with your certification process. All of these tools should be loaded on your workstation when studying for the test.

The Sybex Test Engine for Cisco CIT Test Preparation

New from Sybex, this test-preparation software prepares you to successfully pass the CIT exam. In the test engine, you'll find all the questions from the book, plus the two additional Bonus Exams that appear exclusively on the CD. You can take the Assessment Test, test yourself by chapter, or take the two Bonus Exams that appear on the CD.

Electronic Flashcards for PC, Pocket PC, and Palm Devices

After you read the *CCNP: Cisco Internetwork Troubleshooting Study Guide,* you'll of course read the review questions at the end of each chapter and study the practice exams included in the book and on the CD. But wait, there's more! Test yourself with the flashcards included on the CD. If you can get through these difficult questions and understand the answers, you'll know you'll be ready for the CCNP CIT exam.

The flashcards include 150 questions specifically written to hit you hard and make sure you are ready for the exam. Between the review questions, practice exam, and flashcards, you'll be more than prepared for the exam.

CCNP: Cisco Internetwork Troubleshooting Study Guide in PDF

Sybex offers this Cisco Certification book on the accompanying CD so that you can read the book on your PC or laptop. The eBook is in Adobe Acrobat format, and Acrobat Reader is included on the CD as well. This is extremely helpful to readers who travel and don't want to carry a book, as well as to readers who find it more comfortable reading from their computer.

How to Contact the Authors

You can reach Art Pfund by e-mailing him at `art.pfund@comcast.net`.

Assessment Test

1. Which are reasons for using a troubleshooting method? (Choose all that apply.)

    A. Problem isolation and resolution will occur more quickly.

    B. No documentation needs to be done when following a method.

    C. Due to complex topologies and technologies, a systematic method is the most efficient way to resolve network problems.

    D. All of the above.

2. What are the benefits of gathering additional facts for troubleshooting? (Choose all that apply.)

    A. Possible causes of problems may be identified.

    B. A specific problem definition may be created.

    C. Information is provided for a baseline.

    D. All of the above.

3. Which of the following are key components of creating an action plan? (Choose all that apply.)

    A. Multiple changes as long as they are documented

    B. Changes that do not compromise security

    C. Changes that have only brief network impact

    D. Back-out plans

4. How many methods of problem isolation exist?

    A. 2

    B. 3

    C. 4

    D. 6

5. Which of the following steps are part of the Cisco troubleshooting methodology? (Choose all that apply.)

    A. Observation of results

    B. Observation of changes

    C. Iteration

    D. Documentation

    E. Problem definition

    F. Problem resolution

    G. Troubleshooting

6. Which protocol attributes are associated with the Internet Protocol (IP)? (Choose all that apply.)

   A. Connection-oriented

   B. Connectionless

   C. Layer 2

   D. Layer 3

7. Select the potential attributes of a connectionless protocol.

   A. Broadcast control

   B. Sequenced PDUs

   C. Broadcast transmissions

   D. Wireless connectivity

8. Choose all protocols that operate only at Layer 3 from the following list:

   A. PPP (Point-to-Point Protocol)

   B. IP (Internet Protocol)

   C. EIGRP (Enhanced Interior Gateway Routing Protocol)

   D. SDLC (Synchronous Data Link Control)

   E. X.25

   F. BGP (Border Gateway Protocol)

9. Choose all the Layer 2 protocols from the following list:

   A. TCP

   B. Ethernet

   C. UDP

   D. IP

   E. Token Ring

   F. FDDI

   G. EIGRP

10. Choose two attributes that a connection-oriented protocol possesses.

    A. Flow control

    B. Error control

    C. Broadcast control

    D. Collision detection

11. Which of the following are parts of a network baseline? (Choose all that apply.)

    A. End-system network configuration table

    B. Network overview document

    C. Network summary document

    D. Network topology diagram

12. What Windows 2000 command shows all the IP addresses and TCP port numbers of the current connections to an end-system?

    A. `netstat`

    B. `ipconfig`

    C. `ifconfig`

    D. `route`

13. What is SNMP used for?

    A. Creating network maps

    B. Traffic analysis

    C. Statistical/environmental data collection

    D. All of the above

14. A network configuration table usually contains what kind of information?

    A. IP addresses

    B. CRCs

    C. Interface name

    D. SNMP configuration

    E. `show running-config`

    F. Interface type

    G. Interface speed

    H. VLANs

15. You are seeing incrementing interface resets on an interface. What is the most appropriate troubleshooting method to use for this situation?

    A. Bottom-up troubleshooting

    B. Top-down troubleshooting

    C. Divide-and-conquer troubleshooting

    D. Wait-and-see troubleshooting

16. What Unix command shows the IP address and subnet mask of the interface?

    A. `ipconfig`

    B. `ifconfig`

    C. `cat /etc/resolv.conf`

    D. `netstat`

17. Which of the following routing protocols is a distance vector protocol and a Cisco proprietary routing protocol?

    A. EIGRP

    B. IGRP

    C. RIP

    D. BG

18. Which commands should be used in conjunction for thorough problem isolation? (Choose two.)

    A. `ping`

    B. `show ip interface`

    C. `traceroute`

    D. `arp`

19. What command(s) can be issued on a Windows XP system to provide interface IP information?

    A. `show ip interface`

    B. `ipconfig /all`

    C. `winipcfg`

    D. `ipcfg`

20. Which protocols are used for dynamic IP address assignment? (Choose two.)

    A. AutoIP

    B. AutoARP/IP

    C. BootP

    D. DHCP

21. Choose the troubleshooting tool that is used to test for reachability and connectivity.

    A. `Traceroute`

    B. Debug

    C. `show interface`

    D. Ping

22. How many levels of `ping` and `traceroute` are there on Cisco routers?

   A. One

   B. Two

   C. Three

   D. Four

23. From the following list, choose the troubleshooting tool that is used for testing the path from a source host to a destination host.

   A. Traceroute

   B. Debug

   C. `show interface`

   D. Ping

24. When is a "default gateway" used on the router?

   A. When a packet leaves the router

   B. When no route exists in the route table

   C. When a static route has been set

   D. Only when the router is in boot mode

25. Why is a default metric setting necessary for route redistribution?

   A. It isn't necessary.

   B. The routes being injected must be assigned metrics that the parent protocol understands.

   C. A default metric setting provides better metrics when performing route redistribution.

   D. A default metric setting converts the parent protocol's metric to match the protocol being redistributed.

26. Which LMI (Local Management Interface) type is on by default on a Cisco router?

   A. LMI

   B. Cisco

   C. ANSI

   D. ITU-T

   E. IETF

27. What are the valid LMI types? (Choose all that apply.)

   A. LMI

   B. Cisco

   C. ITU-T

   D. ANSI

28. What are the valid Frame Relay encapsulation types? (Choose all that apply.)

   A. IETF

   B. ITU-T

   C. Cisco

   D. ANSI

29. Which kind of encapsulation is used by default on Cisco serial interfaces?

   A. SDLC

   B. PPP

   C. HDLC

   D. X.25

30. What type of tests are useful in testing for end-to-end serial link integrity?

   A. Ping

   B. Traceroute

   C. Loopback

   D. Loopup

31. Which channel is used by q.931 and q.921 for communication?

   A. A channel

   B. B channel

   C. D channel

   D. Both B and D channels

32. Which ISDN protocol is used for Layer 3 connection setup?

   A. CHAP

   B. PPP

   C. q.921

   D. q.931

33. Which command should be used to display the connection setup for Layer 3?

   A. `show interface bri n`

   B. `debug isdn q931`

   C. `debug interface bri`

   D. `debug isdn q92`

34. Which ISDN protocol is used for Layer 2 connection setup?

   A. CHAP

   B. PPP

   C. q.921

   D. q.931

35. Which channel does PPP use when negotiating the connection?

   A. A channel

   B. B channel

   C. D channel

   D. Both B and D channels

36. Which of the following are characteristic of extended IP access lists? (Choose all that apply.)

   A. Can be used to limit debug output

   B. Can be used to filter Layer 2 frames

   C. Can be applied to ports on a switch

   D. Filter on the TCP or UDP port

37. What does a result of P mean in the output of a `ping` command?

   A. Destination Unreachable

   B. Source Quench

   C. Protocol Unreachable

   D. Network Unreachable

   E. Unable to Fragment

38. Which of the following command outputs would most likely indicate a problem at the Data-Link layer?

   A. Serial 2/3 is up, line protocol is down

   B. Serial 2/3 is up, line protocol is up

   C. Serial 2/3 is down, line protocol is down

   D. Serial 2/3 is down, line protocol is up

39. Which of the following are guidelines for creating network documentation? (Choose all that apply.)

   A. Determine the scope.

   B. Document everything.

   C. Put as much information as possible on network documents.

   D. Keep documents accessible.

40. What command is used for displaying information about Cisco routers that are connected to a switch?

    A. show connections

    B. show vtp neighbor

    C. show ip route

    D. show cdp neighbor

41. What command on a Windows NT end-system is used to add routes to that end-system?

    A. route add

    B. ip add route

    C. ip route add

    D. add route

42. What are some of the benefits of a named access list over a numbered access list? (Choose all that apply.)

    A. A named access list can be applied to all interface types.

    B. Individual lines can be removed from a named access list.

    C. Named access lists are easier for the router to work with.

    D. Named access lists are easier for the network administrator to work with.

43. Which of these commands will verify whether an https web server, 10.7.7.7, was reachable through the network?

    A. debug https traffic

    B. telnet 10.7.7.7

    C. telnet 10.7.7.7 80

    D. telnet 10.7.7.7 443

44. You are troubleshooting a serial connection problem. After making a couple of changes, you find that the problem is still occurring. What should your next step be?

    A. Continue making changes.

    B. Back out the changes you've made up to this point and begin gathering facts again.

    C. Reload the router.

    D. Execute a shut/no shut on the interface.

45. How often should the network configuration table be updated?

    A. There is no such document.

    B. Once a week.

    C. Once a month.

    D. Once a year.

    E. Anytime there is a change in the network.

46. What are the three major roles of a router when configured with VLANs?

    A. Define the collision domain.

    B. Provide Layer 2 VLAN switching.

    C. Provide Layer 2 VLAN translation.

    D. Provide Layer 3 VLAN routing.

47. Which of the following VLAN encapsulation types do Cisco routers support? (Choose all that apply.)

    A. Inter-Switch Link (ISL)

    B. IEEE Ethernet 802.3

    C. IEEE 802.1Q

    D. IEEE 802.1Z

48. When using a router, which of the following scenarios will not work?

    A. VLAN 10 uses ISL while VLAN 20 uses 802.1q.

    B. The switch is configured to use ISL and the router uses 802.1q.

    C. VLAN 10 uses 802.1q, then tries to communicate with a remote host not on a VLAN.

    D. Both VLAN 10 and VLAN 20 use 802.1q.

49. What switch command shows VTP state information on the switch?

    A. `show vtp state`

    B. `show vtp`

    C. `show vtp domain`

    D. `show vtp status`

50. What does the term "blocking" mean with regard to a Catalyst port?

    A. An access list has been applied to the port.

    B. Packets are not allowed out of the port.

    C. Spanning tree has blocked the port to prevent a loop.

    D. The port has been shut down.

51. What router command will show the IP listing of the helper addresses applied on an interface?

    A. `show interface`

    B. `show ip interface`

    C. `show interface helper`

    D. `show helper brief`

52. After a "forklift" upgrade has been performed on a server in which the old hardware was removed and a new server put in its place, you find that the new server cannot be pinged from the directly connected subnet. The new server was given the IP address of the old server, and it has been verified that the new server is configured correctly. What could be the cause of the problem?

    A. Access list needs to be updated.

    B. Routing table on the router needs to be cleared to flush out the old entry.

    C. ARP table on the router needs to be cleared to flush out the old entry.

    D. A static route must be added to the router.

53. Which of the following are information items that will be requested when you open a TAC case? (Choose all that apply.)

    A. Output from a show tech-support

    B. Support contract number

    C. Mailing address

    D. Software versions

54. Which 6500 card provides Layer 3 capabilities to the 6500 switch?

    A. RSM

    B. RFSC

    C. MSFC

    D. PFC

55. Which command would you use to verify network connectivity to an end-system?

    A. arp

    B. tracert

    C. traceroute

    D. ping

56. What do the following lines of router output indicate? (Choose all that apply.)

```
Router_C#show int ethernet 0/1
Ethernet0/1 is up, line protocol is up
  Hardware is Lance, address is 0000.0c47.abea (bia
    0000.0c47.abea)
  Internet address is 172.16.60.1/24
  MTU 1500 bytes, BW 10000 Kbit, DLY 1000 usec, rely 255/255,
    load 46/255
  Encapsulation ARPA, loopback not set, keepalive set (10 sec)
 ARP type: ARPA, ARP Timeout 04:00:00
```

    A. The interface is up and appears to be functioning properly.

    B. This interface is in loopback.

    C. The encapsulation type for this interface is ARPA.

    D. The bandwidth metric for this interface is 100Mbps.

57. Which configuration register setting will cause the router to boot the IOS image from the boot ROM?

A. 0x2000

B. 0x2101

C. 0x1002

D. 0x2102

58. What do the following lines of router output indicate? (Choose all that apply.)

```
Router_A#show interface to0
... some output deleted ...
   MTU 4464 bytes, BW 16000 Kbit, DLY 630 usec, rely 255/255,    load 1/255
   Encapsulation SNAP, loopback not set, keepalive set (10 sec)
   ARP type: SNAP, ARP Timeout 04:00:00
   Ring speed: 16 Mbps
... output removed ...
   Last clearing of "show interface" counters never
```

A. The ring speed is 4Mbps.

B. The ring speed is 16Mbps.

C. The interface counters have never been cleared.

D. Encapsulation is SNMP.

59. Look at the following outputs from two different interfaces connected to each other. Why aren't the interfaces functioning properly?

```
Router_A#show interface to0
TokenRing0 is up, line protocol is down
   Hardware is TMS380, address is 0007.787c.e14b (bia    0007.787c.e14b)
   Internet address is 172.16.30.1, subnet mask is    255.255.255.0
   MTU 4464 bytes, BW 16000 Kbit, DLY 630 usec, rely 255/255,    load 1/255
   Encapsulation SNAP, loopback not set, keepalive set (10 sec)
   ARP type: SNAP, ARP Timeout 04:00:00
   Ring speed: 16 Mbps
   Single ring node, Source Route Transparent Bridge capable
   Ethernet Transit OUI: 0x000000
   Last input never, output never, output hang never
   Last clearing of "show interface" counters never
   Queueing strategy: fifo
   Output queue 0/40, 0 drops; input queue 0/75, 0 drops
   5 minute input rate 0 bits/sec, 0 packets/sec
   5 minute output rate 0 bits/sec, 0 packets/sec
      0 packets input, 0 bytes, 0 no buffer
```

```
          Received 0 broadcasts, 0 runts, 0 giants
          0 input errors, 0 CRC, 0 frame, 0 overrun, 0 ignored,        0 abort
          0 packets output, 0 bytes, 0 underruns
          0 output errors, 0 collisions, 0 interface resets
          0 output buffer failures, 0 output buffers swapped out
          5 transitions
Router_B#show interface to1
TokenRing0 is up, line protocol is down
   Hardware is TMS380, address is 0007.787c.e14b (bia     0007.787c.e14b)
   Internet address is 172.16.30.2, subnet mask is    255.255.255.0
   MTU 4464 bytes, BW 4000 Kbit, DLY 630 usec, rely 255/255,    load 1/255
   Encapsulation SNAP, loopback not set, keepalive set (10 sec)
   ARP type: SNAP, ARP Timeout 04:00:00
   Ring speed: 4 Mbps
   Single ring node, Source Route Transparent Bridge capable
   Ethernet Transit OUI: 0x000000
   Last input never, output never, output hang never
   Last clearing of "show interface" counters never
   Queueing strategy: fifo
   Output queue 0/40, 0 drops; input queue 0/75, 0 drops
   5 minute input rate 0 bits/sec, 0 packets/sec
   5 minute output rate 0 bits/sec, 0 packets/sec
      0 packets input, 0 bytes, 0 no buffer
      Received 0 broadcasts, 0 runts, 0 giants
      0 input errors, 0 CRC, 0 frame, 0 overrun,    0 ignored,        0 abort
      0 packets output, 0 bytes, 0 underruns
      0 output errors, 0 collisions, 0 interface resets
      0 output buffer failures, 0 output buffers swapped out
      5 transitions
```

    A. Duplicate IP addresses

    B. Lobe wire fault

    C. Ring speed mismatch

    D. Five carrier transitions

60. Which of the following factors may contribute to excessive collisions on an Ethernet interface? (Choose all that apply.)

    A. Ethernet interface

    B. Transceiver

    C. Cable

    D. Encapsulation

Answers to Assessment Test

1. C.   Quick resolution of problems is not guaranteed by using a model, and documentation should always be performed. For further explanation of the reasons for using a troubleshooting method, refer to Chapter 1.

2. A, B.   A baseline contains information taken from a normally functioning network, so gathering baseline information is not part of troubleshooting. The benefits of gathering additional facts for troubleshooting are that you identify possible causes of trouble, and that you have information to contribute to the problem definition. For further explanation of gathering facts for troubleshooting, refer to Chapter 1.

3. B, D.   Making multiple changes creates more difficulty when you have to back out of changes, and multiple changes do not allow for good observation results. Changes should not create any adverse network impact. For further explanation of creating an action plan, refer to Chapter 1.

4. B.   The three methods for isolating the source of a network problem are outside-in, inside-out, and divide-by-half. For further explanation of methods of problem isolation, refer to Chapter 1.

5. A, C, E.   In addition to observation of results, iteration, and problem definition, Cisco's troubleshooting method contains other steps not included in this question. Though not an official step in the process, documenting changes after they are complete is an important part of the overall process. For further explanation of Cisco's troubleshooting method, refer to Chapter 1.

6. B, D.   IP is a connectionless protocol and a Layer 3 protocol. For further information about IP, refer to Chapter 4.

7. C.   Connectionless protocols do not use any type of control. Sequenced PDUs are a type of control. Physical connectivity does not determine the protocol properties. For further information about connectionless protocols, refer to Chapter 4.

8. B, C, F.   IP, EIGRP, and BGP are Layer 3; PPP, SDLC, and X.25 all operate at Layer 2. Refer to Chapter 4 for further information.

9. B, E, F.   Ethernet, token Ring and FDDI are all Layer 2 technologies. For further information, refer to Chapter 4.

10. A, B.   Flow control and error control allow for complete connection and data-transfer control. For further information about connection-oriented protocols, refer to Chapter 4.

11. A, D.   The network baesline consists of network configuration tables, the network topology diagram, end-system network configuration tables and end-system topology diagrams. For additional information, refer to Chapter 2.

12. A.   The `netstat` command gives you the IP addresses and TCP port numbers of the current connections to an end-system, for both Windows- and UNIX-based systems. For further information, refer to Chapter 3.

13. C.   Simple Network Management Protocol (SNMP) is used to collect statistical/environmental data from network devices. For additional information on SNMP, refer to Chapter 4.

14. A, C, F, G, H. The network configuration table holds fundamental information about the configuration of the network. Some of the standard items included in this table are device name, flash statistics, DRAM, IOS/CATOS, interface number, MAC address, speed, duplex, VLANs, trunking, IP address, subnet, subnet mask, and routing protocol. For details about the network configuration table, refer to Chapter 2.

15. A. Interface resets are usually indicative of a physical issue in the network. Therefore, the bottom-up approach is the most appropriate. For details, refer to Chapter 3.

16. B. The `ifconfig -a` command will show information regarding Unix interface configuration. Refer to Chapter 3 for details.

17. B. Both EIGRP and IGRP are proprietary routing protocols, but EIGRP is a hybrid routing protocol and not a distance vector routing protocol like IGRP. Refer to Chapter 6 for more information.

18. A, C. Using both ping and traceroute in conjunction greatly aids problem isolation. Refer to Chapter 5 for more information.

19. B. The `ipconfig /all` command can be used on a Windows XP machine; `show ip interface` is for use on a router; `winipcfc` is used on Windows *9x* and ME; and `ipcfc` is incorrect syntax. Refer to Chapter 3 for more information on these commands.

20. C, D. BootP and DHCP (Dynamic Host Configuration Protocol) are used for IP address assignment. (The other two answers, AutoIP and AutoARP/IP, don't exist.) Refer to Chapter 5 for more information.

21. D. Ping uses ICMP (Internet Control Message Protocol) to test for connectivity of remote hosts. Refer to Chapter 5 for more details.

22. B. There are two levels, user and privileged. Refer to Chapter 5 for more details.

23. A. Traceroute tests the route or path from a source to a destination. Refer to Chapter 5 for more information.

24. B. The term "default" indicates that no other route has been specified. So instead of dropping the packet, the router forwards it out the default gateway. Refer to Chapter 6 for more information.

25. B. Routes from the incoming protocol must be assigned new metrics so they can be redistributed. Refer to Chapter 6 for more information.

26. B. Cisco LMI is on by default. Refer to Chapter 7 for more information.

27. B, C, D. Valid LMI types are Cisco, ITU-T, and ANSI. LMI stands for Local Management Interface. Refer to Chapter 7 for more information.

28. A, C. There are only two valid encapsulation types for Frame Relay: IETF and Cisco. Refer to Chapter 7 for more information.

29. C. HDLC is an enhancement over SDLC, and PPP is a protocol, not an encapsulation. X.25 is not configured by default. Refer to Chapter 7 for more information.

Chapter
1

Troubleshooting Methodology

EXAM TOPICS COVERED IN THIS CHAPTER INCLUDE:

✓ Know troubleshooting methodologies.

Troubleshooting is a skill that takes time and experience to fully develop. To be successful when diagnosing and repairing network failures, a good set of troubleshooting tools and skills is essential.

While there's no specific exam objective that maps to this chapter, the information presented here is nevertheless important to the exam. This chapter emphasizes the importance of following a specific set of troubleshooting steps when you try to diagnose and solve network problems. An effective troubleshooting methodology is needed because of the complexity of today's network environments. As a Cisco Certified Network Professional, you need to understand and know how to apply an efficient and systematic troubleshooting methodology. Otherwise, you would be required to have a very intimate understanding of the network you are troubleshooting. It is imperative that you learn troubleshooting skills and understand the information available to you while solving network problems.

The Complexity of Internetworks

When a network failure occurs, time is of the essence. When a production network goes down, several things are affected. The most important of these is the bottom line—network failures cost money. A good example is a call-center network. The company relies on the network to be available for its employees so that they can take phone orders, answer inquiries, or perform other business transactions that generate income. A failure in this environment needs to be diagnosed and repaired in a timely manner. The longer the network is down, the more money the company loses.

To minimize monetary and productivity losses, network failures must be resolved quickly. Troubleshooting is an integral part of getting this done. Intimate knowledge of a network also facilitates rapid resolution. Armed with a few troubleshooting skills and intimate knowledge of the network, you can solve most problems rather quickly, thus saving money.

Hold on a minute. What if you're new on the job and you don't yet have an intimate knowledge of the network? You can probably get up to speed quickly enough, right? Although that may have been the case in the past, getting up to speed becomes an overwhelming challenge in today's complex networks. These networks consist of many facets of routing, dial-up, switching, video, WAN (ISDN, Frame Relay, ATM, and others), LAN, and VLAN technologies. Refer to Figure 1.1 to get an idea of how these technologies intertwine. Notice that ATM, Frame Relay, Token Ring, Ethernet, and FDDI all are present. Each technology has its own properties and commands to allow for troubleshooting. Various protocols are used for each of these technologies. In addition, different applications require specific network resources. (At least the seven-layer OSI model, which you will review in Chapter 4, is used to maintain a common template when designing new technologies and protocols.) It would take you a long time to master all of the technologies implemented in the network and to be able to solve network problems, based on your knowledge of the network alone. All of these factors contribute to today's complex network environments.

There must be an easier, more logical way to efficiently and successfully troubleshoot without having to become intimately familiar with every network environment. Well, you'll be happy to know that there is an easier option—following a troubleshooting model—and it is discussed in detail in this chapter. By following a troubleshooting model, the need for intimate knowledge of the network is reduced. A troubleshooting model should be adopted to help resolve network malfunctions and reduce downtime.

Let's move on to discuss Cisco's model in detail.

FIGURE 1.1   Today's complex enterprise network

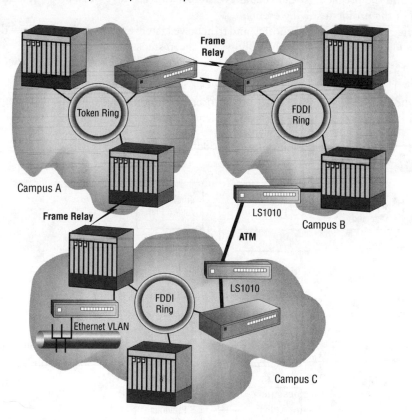

The Problem-Solving Model

Imagine trying to solve a network failure by using a different approach every time. With today's complex networks, the possible scenarios would be innumerable. Because so many different things can go wrong within a network, it would be possible to start from many different points. Not only is this an ineffective method of troubleshooting, but it is also time-consuming, and time is very valuable in a "network down" situation.

Cisco has designed an effective *troubleshooting model* that contains seven steps. A troubleshooting model is a list of troubleshooting steps or processes that can be followed to provide an efficient manner of resolving network problems. The headings in this section contain information specific to each step of the troubleshooting model. (Steps 4 and 5 are combined into one section of the chapter—creating and implementing the action plan.) After the seven steps are completed and the problem is resolved, a few more actions follow, such as completing documentation of the problem-solving events.

To be effective when troubleshooting and to achieve faster resolution times, follow the model outlined in Figure 1.2. This flow chart shows the seven steps.

The process begins when a network failure is reported to you. Following are brief descriptions of the steps to take:

1. Define the problem.   At this point in the process it is important to make a determination of the issue, identifying sets of symptoms and potential causes.

FIGURE 1.2   Cisco's troubleshooting model

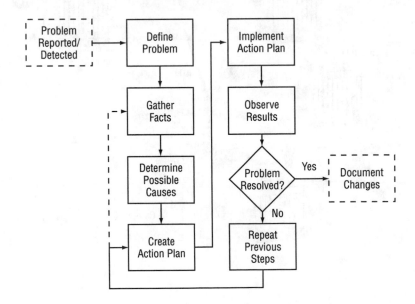

2. Gather detailed information.   These facts about the problem can be obtained from a number of sources, including key users, network management systems, output from router and switch diagnostic commands, and protocol analyzer traces.

3. Consider possible scenarios.   Brainstorm and come up with several possible or probable causes of the failure. Also, when developing this list, eliminate items that are definitely not the cause of the problem.

4. Create an action plan.   Begin with the most likely source of the trouble and devise a plan to correct this issue, changing only one variable at a time. If you change multiple items simultaneously, it is possible that the problem will be resolved without your identifying the root cause. This then leaves the potential for the problem to repeat itself in the future.

5. Implement the action plan.   As you implement each step of the action plan, carefully check to see if the problem has been resolved.

FIGURE 1.3   Example campus network

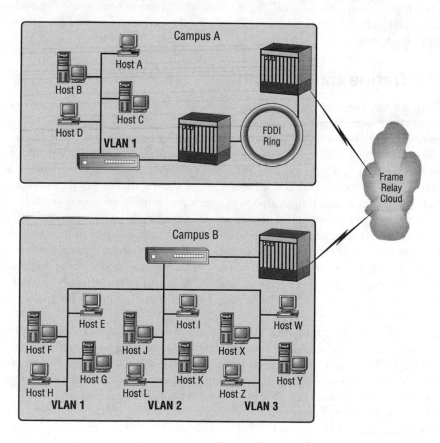

6. Observe the results of implementing the action plan.   In many instances it will be clear when the problem is resolved; however, in those cases where the problem is subtler, a more structured observation technique must be used. This technique involves many of the same tools used in the fact-gathering portion of the process, such as talking to users, employing network management tools, and checking router and switch output.

7. Repeat the process if the action plan doesn't fix the problem.   Revise your action plan to address the next most likely source of the trouble. Be sure to undo the changes that were attempted in the previous attempt. Then repeat the process starting with step 4. If there are no more potential causes for which to create an action plan, start with step 2 and repeat the process.

The best way to understand how Cisco's model works and how you should use it is by looking at an example. For this example, assume you are in charge of operational support of the network pictured in Figure 1.3. There are two campus networks, connected via a Frame Relay cloud. Within each network, VLANs are connected to a Catalyst 6500 switch and then to a core router that has a connection to the Frame Relay cloud in one way or another.

The fun begins when you get a call from a user who "can't get to Host Z." Based on this information, let's apply Cisco's troubleshooting model to solve the user's difficulty and fix the problem in the network.

Step 1: Define the Problem

As you can see, the user's problem is vague; you need more information if you are to solve the problem any time soon. This is where *problem definition* comes in. Problem definition is the step in the troubleshooting model when details are used to define what the most likely cause of a problem is. Now, while you still have the user on the line, the first step is to ask him what he means when he says he can't "get to" Host Z. The user then defines the situation by telling you that he can't FTP to Host Z. Ask the user if he experiences any other difficulties or if this is the only one. Verify where the user is currently located. After these preliminary questions, you'll have a basic idea of what is and isn't working. Unfortunately, you can't simply assume that the FTP is broken, because there are many other pieces of the network that can contribute to this problem.

It is also important to realize that you may want or need to gather facts before you actually form your problem statement. By gathering facts to help define the issue, the diagnosis of the problem or problems will be more accurate and will help you solve the trouble more quickly in the end. Problem definition and fact gathering should be used in tandem for a quick and accurate resolution.

Once you have enough information to define the problem, you should create a problem statement that is specific, concise, and an accurate description of what needs to be solved. In this case, you might have a statement that says *User A from Campus A cannot FTP to Host Z on Campus B*. With a good statement of the problem, it is easier to focus on the problem itself and not try to troubleshoot issues that do not fall within the problem definition.

Step back for a moment before you actually form your final problem statement. You need to gather more information before you can form an accurate problem statement. It's time to move on to the fact-gathering step. Keep in mind, however, that after you accumulate all the information, you have to come back and create your problem statement.

Step 2: Gather Facts

At this point, the problem is still pretty vague and needs more definition. This is where the fact-gathering step of the troubleshooting model is employed. *Fact gathering* is the process of using diagnostic tools to collect information specific to the network and network devices that are involved in a problem. Additional information should include data that excludes other possibilities and helps pinpoint the actual problem. An example of fact gathering in the case we're discussing is to verify whether you can ping, Traceroute, or Telnet to Host Z, thus reducing the number of possible causes.

Depending on the user and situation, you may or may not be able to get more detailed information. It is up to you as a network engineer or administrator to solve the problem, which means that you may have to get the information yourself.

It is important that you gain as much information as possible to actually define the problem while in the problem-definition phase of the troubleshooting model. Without a proper and specific definition of the problem, it will be much harder to isolate and resolve. Information that is useful for defining a problem is listed in Table 1.1.

TABLE 1.1   Useful Information for Defining a Problem

Information	Example
Symptoms	Can't Telnet, FTP, or get to the WWW.
Reproducibility	Is this a one-time occurrence, or does it always happen?
Timeline	When did it start? How long did it last? How often does it occur? Has the current configuration ever worked properly?
Scope	What are you able to access successfully via Telnet or FTP? Which WWW sites can you reach, if any? Who else does this affect?
Baseline Info	Were any recent changes made to the network configurations?

All of this information can be used to guide you to the actual problem and to create the problem statement. Use your network topology diagram and check each item in Table 1.1.

Identify Symptoms

First, you need to define what is working and what isn't. You can do this by identifying the symptom and defining the scope. Figure 1.4 is a picture of your network. Although the large X on the Frame Relay cloud represents that there is an FTP connectivity issue, it does not indicate the location of the failure. Right now, all you know is that a single user could not FTP to Host Z.

FIGURE 1.4   Host A cannot FTP to Host Z.

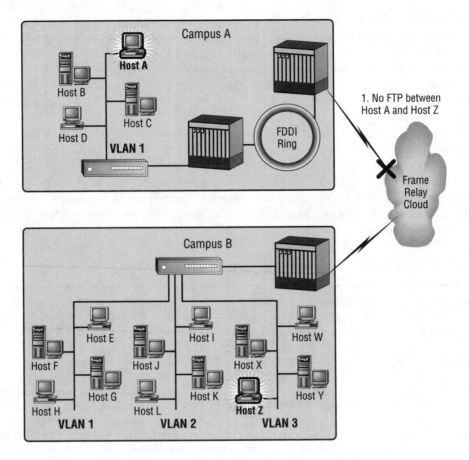

Reproduce the Problem

Before spending time and effort trying to solve this problem, verify that it is still a problem. Troubleshooting is a waste of time and resources if the problem can't be reproduced. It's just like a dog chasing its tail. If the issue is intermittent, further steps should be taken to capture as much information as possible about the event the next time it does occur. This will help narrow down the scope of items you will look at.

Understand the Timeline

In addition to verifying whether the problem is reproducible, it is important to investigate the frequency of the problem. For instance, maybe it happens only once or twice a day. By establishing a timeframe you can more readily identify any possible causes. In addition, you need to know whether this is the first time the user has attempted this function. There is a different set of variables involved with an item that worked yesterday but not today than there is with something that fails during first-time use. Obviously, if it worked yesterday, you can look at what changed overnight as well as looking for something that is broken. If the user has never used this feature before, there may be an existing access list or other security device that has only now been activated by the user's initial use of this application.

Determine the Scope of a Problem

Next, you need to find out whether anyone else is unable to FTP to Host Z. If others can FTP to Host Z (for the sake of this example, assume that they can), you can be pretty sure that the problem is specific to the user, either on their station or on the destination host. This step determines the scope of the problem and helps to differentiate between a user-specific problem and a more widely spread problem. Figure 1.5 shows that other hosts can FTP to Host Z without any problems.

Now that you have the problem narrowed down to a single user, you need to define the *boundary of dysfunctionality*. The boundary of dysfunctionality is the limit or scope of the network problem. For example, a distinction can be made between where nodes are functioning properly and where they are not. To define this boundary in our example, you need to know whether the user can successfully FTP anywhere.

FIGURE 1.5   Other hosts can FTP to Host Z

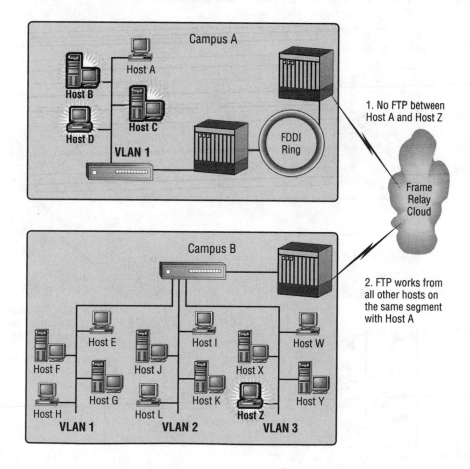

There are three methods for establishing the boundary of dysfunctionality: outside-in troubleshooting, inside-out troubleshooting, and divide-by-half troubleshooting. Each of these techniques has its own advantages and disadvantages based on the situation. The methods are explained in the following sections.

Outside-In Troubleshooting

The first method, *outside-in troubleshooting*, consists of starting the troubleshooting process at the opposite end of the connection. In this case, you would start at Campus B, VLAN 3, and work back toward the user's system (see Figure 1.6). The corresponding test would be for the user to try to FTP to another host on the same VLAN as Host Z, indicated by the X (2) on the diagram. If the result of that test is negative, then you need to come back one step. By coming back one step, you would try to FTP to a host on a different VLAN, indicated by the X (3) on the diagram. If that test failed, the only thing left to try would be to FTP to another host on the user's segment. In the example, assume that the user can FTP to other hosts that are directly connected to the same Ethernet segment. In general, outside-in troubleshooting is a good method to use when there are many hosts that cannot connect to a server or subset of servers.

FIGURE 1.6   Starting from the outside and working in

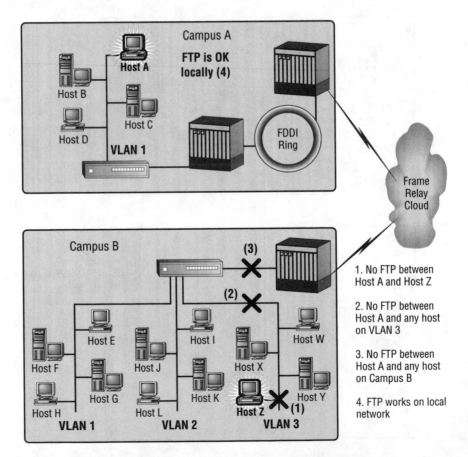

1. No FTP between Host A and Host Z

2. No FTP between Host A and any host on VLAN 3

3. No FTP between Host A and any host on Campus B

4. FTP works on local network

Inside-Out Troubleshooting

The second method of fixing the boundary of dysfunctionality is to start near the user and work your way toward the destination, Host Z in this case. This is referred to as the *inside-out troubleshooting* method. Figure 1.7 contains a diagram that describes this testing method. You see that the user can FTP to hosts within the same network, but can't FTP to any host on the Campus B network. The steps are marked by the Xs, with the step number in parentheses.

Using the second method saved you one step—three instead of four. Statistically, however, you isolate the boundary with fewer steps by using the first method. The important thing is that the boundary be established.

FIGURE 1.7   Starting from the inside and working out

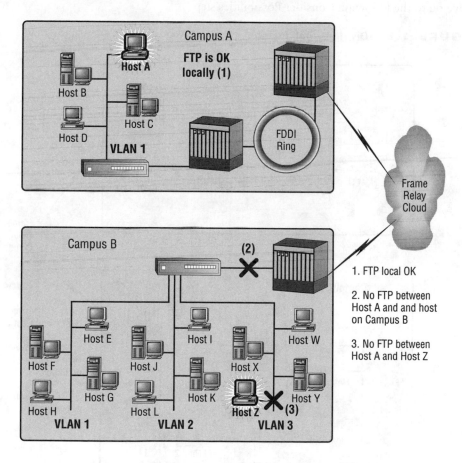

1. FTP local OK

2. No FTP between Host A and and host on Campus B

3. No FTP between Host A and Host Z

Divide-by-Half Troubleshooting

The third and final method is *divide-by-half troubleshooting,* which is depicted in Figure 1.8. Divide-by-half indicates that a point between two ends of a network problem is used as a troubleshooting reference point. Either half of the problem's scope may be investigated first. In this example, you start by trying to FTP to any host within Campus B. Depending on the results, you can divide in half again and test. If the test results in a successful FTP to any host on the Campus B network, then the new point to test is another host on VLAN 3. If the test fails, the new testing point is to try to FTP to a local host. In this case, the divide-by-half method takes three steps, just as the inside-out method does.

You now have isolated the problem to something outside the immediate network. Upon further inspection and fact gathering, you find that the user can't ping external hosts, either. With all this information in hand, you can now start to contemplate possible causes of the failure and move on to the following Consider Possibilities step.

FIGURE 1.8 Divide-by-half method

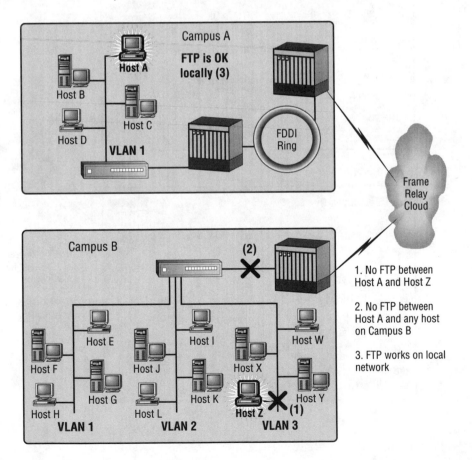

Step 3: Consider Possibilities

This step within the troubleshooting model is used to contemplate the possible causes of the failure. Obviously, it is quite easy to create a very long list of possible causes. That is why it is so important to gather as much relevant information as you can and to create an accurate problem statement. By defining the problem and assigning the corresponding boundaries, the resulting list of possible causes diminishes because the entries in the list will be focused on the actual problem and not on "possible" problems.

First, review what you know about your sample problem:

- Host A can't FTP to Host Z.
- Host A can't FTP to any host on Campus B.
- Host A can't ping to anywhere outside its own network.
- Host A can FTP to any host on its own network.
- All other hosts on Host A's network can FTP to Host Z, as well as to other hosts.

Based on what you know, you now need to list possible causes. These possible causes are as follows:

- No default gateway is configured on Host A.
- The wrong subnet mask is configured.
- There is a misconfigured access list on the router connected to the switch on Campus A.

If you had not gathered such specific information in step 2, the list could have included all possible problems with any piece of equipment between Host A and Host Z. That would have been a long list, and it would take a lot of time to eliminate all of the possible causes.

Remember that because these are only *possible* causes, you still have to create an action plan, implement it, and observe to see whether the changes made were effective. When the list of possible problems is long, it may require more iterations of the problem-solving steps to actually solve the problem. In this example, you have only four possible causes, so this is a much more manageable list. Although there may be other possible causes that you can think of (and it's great that you can do that), for this example and in the interest of simplicity, only these three are listed.

Here's where it gets interesting. You now have to check each of these possibilities and fix them if they are the cause of the problem. To do this, move on to the next step, which is to create an action plan.

Steps 4 and 5: Create and Implement the Action Plan

Creating an *action plan* is actually very easy. It entails the documentation of steps that will be taken to remedy the cause of the network problem. Most of the hard work was gathering information about the problem. The investigation gave you three leads about the source of the problem. Now it is a matter of checking out each possibility and determining which one is most likely the source of the issue.

The majority of the possibilities point directly at the host machine, so start there. The first two causes are host configuration issues. Now, assume that you've checked the TCP/IP configuration on the host and everything is configured properly. You can eliminate the host machine as the culprit.

You then move on to the remaining possible cause, which is an access list on the router. While looking at the configuration on the router, you see that an access list is applied to the Ethernet interface directly connected to the host segment. After reviewing the syntax of the access list, you determine that it is the cause of the failure.

Great—you've found the problem. Now what? Once you find the problem, you must decide what is needed to fix it. In this case, it is an access-list problem, so there are some special considerations about how to restore functionality. You must be careful in your actions here, because that list may contain other entries that provide security or other network administrative functionality. You can't just remove the list—you could cause new problems as you fix the original one.

The best thing to do in this situation is to make a copy of the access list in a text editor, and then make changes that are specific to your problem. When editing the access list, change its number. After all of the changes are made in your text editor, ensure that you have a current backup of the configuration on the router in case you need to restore the original configuration. Then paste the modified access list back into the router. Finally, go to the interface and apply the new access list. By following this procedure, the access list is never removed from the interface.

Obviously, you have now changed the access-list number that is applied to the interface, so any documentation that refers to the original number will need to be updated. If the access list that was causing the problem was applied only to Ethernet 0, you can now safely remove the old list, update this list with the corrections to address your problem, and put it back on the router. Then reapply this list to Ethernet 0. As was the case before, the access list is never removed from the interface.

When you create and implement action plans, it is important that you don't fix one problem and cause another. Before implementing an action plan, think it through or discuss it with coworkers to pick it apart, and make sure that your solution will fix the problem without doing anything to create adverse side effects.

Another good practice, when creating and implementing action plans, is to change only one thing at a time, if possible. If multiple changes must be made, it is best to make the changes in small sets. This way it is easier to keep track of what was done, what worked, and what didn't. The observation step (step 6) becomes much more effective if only a few changes are made at one time; ideally, make only one change at a time. There is nothing worse than troubleshooting your self-induced errors in addition to the original difficulties!

To summarize, follow these practices and guidelines to create a good action plan:

- Make one change or a set of related changes at a time, and then observe the results.

- Make nonimpacting changes—this means trying not to cause other problems while implementing the changes. The more transparent the change, the better.

- Do not create security holes when changing access lists, TACACS+, RADIUS, or other security-oriented configurations.

- Most importantly, make sure you can revert to the original configuration if unforeseen problems occur as a result of the change. Always have a backup or copy of the configuration.

Now that you have reviewed the process of creating and implementing changes, you need to be able to monitor the network and interpret the information to verify whether the changes implemented were effective.

Step 6: Observe Results

Observing results consists of using the exact same methods and commands that were used to obtain information to define the problem—to see whether the changes you implemented had the results you want. By making a change and then testing its effectiveness, you move toward the correct solution.

It may take one or more changes to fix the problem, but you should observe each change separately to monitor progress and to make sure that the alteration doesn't create any adverse effects. After the first change is made, you should be able to gather enough information to learn whether or not the modification was effective, even if it doesn't entirely solve the problem.

 Real World Scenario

Looks Can Be Deceiving

One common mistake when observing the results of a change is seeing symptoms go away and interpreting this as the problem's having been solved. For example, assume that users are complaining about slow response time while accessing the Internet. In the course of troubleshooting, you find and correct some non-optimally-configured interface settings on the router on the users' segment. You then go back to the user who originally reported the problem. She reports that everything is running fine now; however, she neglects to mention the fact that there was a shift change and now only two people are connecting to the Internet where there used to be 50. The next day, when all of the users are back online, the problem repeats itself. If an analysis of the observations had been done, it would have demonstrated that the traffic flow to the Internet had dropped off and that this could be a contributing factor to the improvement in response times.

As is demonstrated in this example, failure to analyze your observations creates the risk that important information can be overlooked and the problem will recur. To avoid this possibility, ensure that you look at the entire scope of the problem. Use your network management tools to help you determine whether the problem is really resolved. You can also look at your network baseline information to find out what the "normal" traffic pattern looks like. In this example, it should show a sharp drop-off in utilization when the shift changes. This would tell you that the improvement in connection speed may not be due to the interface changes you've made, but rather are due to a lower volume of traffic—and that more verification is needed.

Not until all of the changes from the action plan are implemented and the results are observed and analyzed can you verify whether the action plan has solved the problem. If it has, move on and document the modifications that were made to the network. If the changes did not work, you need to go back and either gather more information or create a new action plan. These options are explained in more detail in the next section.

Step 7: Iterate as Needed

Iterations, or repetitions of certain steps within the troubleshooting model, are simply ways of whittling away at a larger problem. By implementing action plans and monitoring the results, you can move toward solving the overall problem.

Iterations of the troubleshooting process allow you to focus with more and more detail on the possible causes of the failure. The result of focusing on the problem is your ability to identify more-specific possibilities for the failure.

The iteration process has its own set of steps: While working through the action-plan process, you might get more ideas of possible sources of the trouble. Write them down; if the current action plan doesn't work, you will have notes about some other options. If you feel that you have exhausted all of the possible causes, you should probably go back and gather more information. You will probably find additional clues.

This is also the time to undo any changes that had adverse effects or that did not fix the problem. Make sure to document what was done, so it will be easier to undo the any configuration modifications.

Document the Changes

The network problem has been officially resolved after you've implemented a change, observed that the symptoms have disappeared, and can successfully execute the tests that were used to aid in gathering information about the problem. In this example, the way to verify that the problem is solved is for Host A to try to FTP to Host Z. If this test is successful, then the problem is resolved.

In the previous sections, we have suggested that documentation is an integral part of troubleshooting. When you keep track of the alterations that were made, the routers, switches, or hosts that were changed, and when the changes occurred, you have valuable information for future reference. There is always the possibility that something you changed will have affected something else and you didn't notice it. If this happens, you will have documentation to refer to, so you can undo the changes. Or if a similar problem occurs in the future, you can refer to these documents to resolve the new problem, based on what was done the last time. More on documentation and establishing baseline information will be covered in the next chapters.

Summary

With the complexity of today's networks, it is important to adhere to a troubleshooting model to aid in efficiently and effectively isolating and resolving network problems.

Various methods of problem isolation and the troubleshooting method itself help administrators pinpoint problem areas and foresee future trouble. Troubleshooting skills are gained through experience. It is unreasonable to expect that you can jump in on your first network failure and be able to solve it quickly. Experience is the best teacher. Following a problem-solving model helps you to reach a timely solution to network failures. It helps to know your network, but the "shooting-from-the-hip" style of troubleshooting is nowhere near as effective as a methodical and logical process.

Using the seven steps of the Cisco troubleshooting model in order is a clear, calculated, and logical way to make a network run more smoothly. The three methods of problem isolation (outside-in, inside-out, and divide-by-half) are more subjective, and it is up to each individual to use the method they are comfortable with. It is important to document changes so you have a "trail" of what was done on the network. Finally, it's important to reverse any network alterations that did not correct the problem.

Exam Essentials

Know the seven steps to the Cisco troubleshooting model, as well as the function that each performs.   The seven steps to the Cisco troubleshooting model are define the problem, gather facts, determine possible causes, develop an action plan, implement the action plan, observe results, and repeat if necessary. Once a problem is resolved, documentation should be updated.

Know the troubleshooting methodologies and how to use them.   These methodologies are outside-in troubleshooting, inside-out troubleshooting, and divide-by-half troubleshooting. In addition to understanding them, know when is most appropriate to use each method.

Be able to apply the Cisco troubleshooting methodology to example situations.   Know how to apply each step of the model in real-life scenarios. You should be able to determine what step in a troubleshooting scenario is next in the series, and to correlate a task with the correct step in the process.

Key Terms

Before you take the exam, be certain you are familiar with the following terms:

action plan	iterations
boundary of dysfunctionality	observing results
divide-by-half troubleshooting	outside-in troubleshooting
fact gathering	problem definition
inside-out troubleshooting	troubleshooting model

Review Questions

1. What are valid reasons for using a troubleshooting model? (Choose all that apply.)

    A. Networks are complex and require thorough troubleshooting.

    B. Difficult problems require a systematic and logical method.

    C. Problems are always resolved more quickly by using a systematic model.

    D. Cisco equipment requires diagnostic commands to be entered in a systematic manner.

2. What are the seven steps of the Cisco troubleshooting model? (Choose all that apply.)

    A. Document the changes.

    B. Create a baseline.

    C. Create an action plan.

    D. Undo the wrong changes.

    E. Define the problem.

    F. Observe changes.

    G. Observe results.

    H. Implement an action plan.

    I. Gather facts.

    J. Consider solutions.

    K. Consider possibilities.

    L. Define the problem boundary.

    M. Iterate the process.

3. Place the seven steps of the troubleshooting model in the correct order.

    A. Define Problem, Gather Facts, Consider Possibilities, Create and Implement Action Plan, Observe Results, Iterate Process

    B. Define Problem, Gather Facts, Create and Implement Action Plan, Observe Results, Iterate Process, Consider Possibilities

    C. Consider Possibilities, Gather Facts, Define Problem, Create and Implement Action Plan, Observe Results, Iterate Process

    D. Define Problem, Create and Implement Action Plan, Gather Facts, Consider Possibilities, Observe Results, Iterate Process

4. What is the main purpose of the Define Problem step in the problem-solving model?

    A. To consider the possible causes of the problem

    B. To establish the correct troubleshooting method to be used

    C. To form a specific and concise problem statement that directs the focus of the troubleshooting effort

    D. To diagnose the problem exactly

5. What are the two major reasons for gathering facts when troubleshooting? (Choose two answers.)

    A. To isolate the possible causes of the failure.

    B. To isolate the boundary of the problem.

    C. To isolate the layer 2 from layer 3.

    D. It is required as part of the troubleshooting model.

6. Which of the following types of information are relevant while gathering facts for troubleshooting? (Choose all that apply.)

    A. Network baseline info

    B. The scope of the failure

    C. Whether the trouble is reproducible

    D. The timeline of the failure

    E. Symptoms of the failure

7. In which troubleshooting method do you start near the user and work toward the destination?

    A. Outside-in

    B. Inside-out

    C. Divide-by-half

    D. None of the above

8. Why is establishing the failure boundary important? (Choose all that apply.)

    A. Establishing the failure boundary focuses on the portion of the network or application that is failing.

    B. You know whether you can assign the task to someone else.

    C. It focuses on the relevant information.

    D. It narrows the possibilities for causes of the failure.

9. Why should you gather specific information before considering the possible causes of the failure?

    A. Gathering specific information is part of the process.

    B. It shortens the list of possible causes of failure.

    C. It provides sufficient documentation.

    D. All of the above.

10. A good action plan should follow which of the following guidelines? (Choose all that apply.)

    A. Make one change at a time.

    B. Make any changes necessary to fix the problem.

    C. Make non-service-impacting changes.

    D. Do not create security holes while implementing changes.

    E. Leave an avenue for retreat available, in case you need to back out of the changes you made.

11. During the implementation of an action plan, which of the following is true?

    A. Steps should be taken to ensure that additional problems are not caused.

    B. Network diagrams should be drawn.

    C. Traffic should be isolated to the problem area.

    D. You should gather additional facts to see if the current action plan needs to be altered.

12. What are the benefits of the iteration process? (Choose all that apply.)

    A. Iteration allows small steps toward resolving a larger network failure.

    B. It takes longer to solve the problem, but it is effective.

    C. It allows the troubleshooting process to focus on a problem with more and more detail.

    D. It allows for ineffective changes to be removed.

13. In which troubleshooting method do you start near the destination and work toward the user?

    A. Outside-in

    B. Inside-out

    C. Divide-by-half

    D. None of the above

14. What should you do after implementing the action plan? (Choose all that apply.)

    A. Call the user and tell them the problem is solved.

    B. Document the changes.

    C. Verify that the changes worked without causing additional problems.

    D. Iterate the process.

15. SNMP access to a router is no longer working. After this problem has been defined, what would be the next step in troubleshooting according to the Cisco troubleshooting model?

    A. Check the copy of the backed-up configuration.

    B. Go through the access-list changes that were implemented last night.

    C. Ping the router.

    D. Search Cisco web site for SNMP bugs.

16. Which of the following is the correct method of isolating the boundary of dysfunctionality? (Choose all that apply.)

    A. Divide-by-half

    B. Outside-in

    C. Inside-out

    D. Step-by-step

    E. Oudside-down

    F. Network-Application

17. Why should you make only one change at a time? (Choose all that apply.)

   A. Making one change at a time further isolates the problem.

   B. It makes it easier to back out if the change was ineffective.

   C. It eliminates one possible cause at a time.

   D. All of the above.

18. Which of these tasks is an important part of the iteration process? (Choose all that apply.)

   A. Creating more possible causes

   B. Gathering more information

   C. Homing in on the cause of the failure

   D. Creating a new action plan

19. You have implemented an action plan and observed the results, but the original problem still exists. What should your next step be?

   A. Repeat the problem-solving process, continuing to change more items until the problem is resolved.

   B. Determine whether there are other possibilities for the cause of the problem.

   C. Document the changes that have been made and check for bugs on CCO.

   D. Repeat the problem-solving process, undoing the changes that were made in the previous attempt.

20. Over the weekend, changes were made in your network to prepare it for an upcoming migration. On Monday, users complain of slow server-response time. What steps should be followed to correct this problem?

   A. Back out the changes one at a time.

   B. Verify utilization on the user segment.

   C. Start working from the beginning of the troubleshooting model.

   D. Verify utilization on the server segment.

Answers to Review Questions

1. A, B. Problems may not always be resolved more quickly with a troubleshooting model, but the models are still very efficient. Cisco equipment has no such requirement for troubleshooting.

2. C, E, G, H, I, K, M. Creating a baseline is a good method for identifying problems when they occur, but this is not part of the troubleshooting method. Undoing wrong changes is part of the iteration process—reversing changes is done when a new action plan is created. You can't observe changes, just the results of changes. Solutions also belong to the action-plan step of the troubleshooting method. Defining the problem boundary is part of the fact-gathering process. In addition, documentation should be updated once the changes are complete, but this is not considered part of the model.

3. A. You must create an action plan before its implementation. You cannot consider possibilities if you do not know what the problem is. You cannot create an action plan without knowing the details of the problem.

4. C. Without forming a specific problem statement, it is more difficult to identify possible solutions.

5. A, B. By isolating the possible causes and the boundary of the problem, the possible solutions can be more accurately drawn.

6. A, B, C, D, E. All of these items are very helpful when gathering information about network problems.

7. B. With inside-out troubleshooting, you start where the user or users are experiencing the problem and work toward the service they are attempting to access.

8. A, C, D. In the case of B, instead of assigning the task to someone else if the failure is outside of your jurisdiction, you should coordinate efforts to solve the problem.

9. B. To consider possible causes of failure without having specific information regarding the problem would lead to a very long list of prospects.

10. A, C, D, E. Any changes made should be included in the action plan and documentation. By doing that, you can make sure you hold to the requirements listed in the other answers.

11. A. One of the important considerations in implementing the action plan is to make sure that other users are not impacted by the changes you are making. You should already have your network diagrams, and observing and analyzing the results of the action plan will tell you whether your action plan needs modification.

12. A, C, D. The iteration process actually allows you to shorten the time it would normally take to fix a problem if you were "shooting from the hip."

13. A. Outside-in troubleshooting is a troubleshooting methodology that starts the troubleshooting process at the server side of the problem. This can be a very useful methodology when many users in various locations are having difficulty accessing one server.

14. B, C. The customer should not be told that a solution has been implemented until it has been verified. Iteration, as well, is useless without your first having observed the results of the changes.

15. C. After the problem is defined, the next step in troubleshooting is to gather facts. Determining whether or not the router responds to ping, Telnet, etc., is part of the fact-gathering process. The other three answer options are not part of the fact-gathering stage, but rather are used to determine possible causes or are tasks in creating an action plan.

16. A, B, C. All three of these methods require step-by-step execution.

17. D. These are all correct answers. When multiple changes are made, you can't be sure whether you caused any observed results or which of the changes solved the problem.

18. B, C, D. If you create more possible causes (option A) as part of the iteration process, you are doing something wrong and you need to go back to the very beginning and gather facts regarding the problem.

19. D. If an action plan does not solve the problem, the changes that were made in order to implement this plan should be backed out before proceeding. This ensures that unnecessary changes are not made to the network.

20. C. Though it is tempting to start backing out changes, the correct answer is to start the Cisco troubleshooting model. The changes from the weekend will indeed need to be looked at as the possible cause of the slowdown; however, the cause could be something totally unrelated.

Chapter

2

Network Documentation

EXAM TOPICS COVERED IN THIS CHAPTER INCLUDE:

✓ Understand the document control process and documentation standards.

✓ Establish a baseline indicative of optimal network performance.

✓ Create system topology documentation and diagrams.

When the network is down, one of your most important trouble-shooting tools can be your network documentation. Accurate and up-to-date network documentation can make the difference between a short outage and an extended one.

In this chapter we will focus on the network documentation that you need to have available, as well as how to create this documentation. We will first study a network baseline; then we'll look at the network configuration table and the network topology diagram. The documents created in this and the following chapter will allow you to effectively troubleshoot a network problem even if you are new to the network itself.

The Network Baseline

The easiest way to solve network problems is to be able to compare current configurations against previous configurations. This sounds easy enough, but it requires a lot of effort to get a system established for keeping a historical *baseline* of your network. A historical baseline is simply a collection of network settings and configurations that are maintained over time. This baseline makes it easy to locate changes, and the differences between a current configuration and a previous one.

Baseline information is actually a composite of various network and end-systems documentation. This collection includes

- Network configuration table
- Network topology diagram
- End-system network configuration table
- End-system network topology diagram

The first two items, the network configuration table and the network topology diagram, are covered in this chapter. The latter two items, the end-system network configuration table and the end-system network topology diagram, are discussed in Chapter 3, "End System Documentation and Troubleshooting."

When creating any documentation of this sort, there are several things to keep in mind.

- First, before you start, determine the scope of what the documentation should cover. Without clearly understanding what is in and out of the scope of the documentation effort, you could end up taking on more than you bargained for.

- The second rule is to be consistent. If you do not collect the same information for all the devices in the network, the documentation may have holes that will come back to haunt you later.

- Third, know your objective. When you are collecting your information, be certain you understand what the documentation will be used for, and include all relevant pieces.

- Be sure to use the documentation and ensure that it is accessible in the event of an emergency. This information was not put together just as an exercise; it is meant to be useful.

- Finally, after putting together your baseline information, you must maintain it. If the baseline is out of date, troubleshooting will be much more difficult.

After you your start using the documentation, if you are finding that you are consistently going back to the network devices to find a particular bit of information, it may be a good idea to include that information on your baseline. Likewise, if you notice that you are never using certain information, it may be best to remove that data from the baseline documentation to prevent clutter.

Network Configuration Table

The general purpose of a *network configuration table* is to give a listing of the hardware and software components used in the network. This information will be used in the course of troubleshooting to ensure that the functioning of the network is well understood. At a minimum, a network configuration table should include the name of the network device, the Layer 2 addresses and implemented feature sets, and the Layer 3 addresses and implemented features. In addition to these items, you should include any additional information about Layers 4 through 7 that is deemed important (for instance, extended access lists and application flow details). Finally, all of the specifics about the physical devices should be recorded (their location in computer room, their UPS circuit information, and so forth).

One of the most common ways to determine the specific items that will go into your network configuration table is to divide the types of information being observed into groups corresponding to the layers of the OSI model. Some items, such as name of the device, do not necessarily fall in a particular layer, but these can be incorporated in as part of the Physical layer or placed in a separate column. A sample list of items that can be included in a network configuration table is shown in Table 2.1.

TABLE 2.1   Sample List of Network Configuration Table Items

Classification	Items
Miscellaneous Information	Device name, device model, CPU type, flash memory, DRAM, interface description.
Layer 1	Media type, speed, interface numbers, connecting jack or port.

TABLE 2.1 Sample List of Network Configuration Table Items *(continued)*

Classification	Items
Layer 2	MAC address, Spanning Tree Protocol (STP) state, STP root bridge, portfast information, VLAN(s), Etherchannel configuration, encapsulation, trunking status, interface type, port security, VTP state, VTP Mode.
Layer 3	IP address, IPX address, secondary IP address, Hot Standby Routing Protocol (HSRP) address, subnet, subnet mask, routing protocol(s), access lists, tunneling information, loopback interfaces.

 Cisco technically considers the list of items under miscellaneous information as Layer 1 items.

Once you have identified the information that you will put in your network configuration table, the next step is organizing this information in a logical and repeatable sequence. When planning the organization of this information, you must take into account all the device types that are in the network as well as the needs of each of theses devices. Due to the variation in the requirements for different types of network devices, such as switches and routers, in many cases you will need a different table structure for each major classification of device. For example, in most instances there will be one set of information gathered for routers, and a separate set of information for switches. This separation prevents a lot of unnecessary fields that are left empty because they do not apply. By separating these information groups, you can simplify the overall network documentation.

 If you do decide to separate switches from routers in your network documentation, be sure to have a plan for how to account for devices that do *both* routing and switching. You might create both a routing and a switching document for such devices. Alternately, you could create a third set of documentation specifically for these types of devices.

In most cases, the preferred manner to store this information is in a spreadsheet or database. For smaller networks, a spreadsheet is usually the preferred method due to its low cost and ease of use. For large networks, a database is the preferred arrangement because of its flexibility, and it lets you better manage large volumes of data. For both of these means of storage, hard copies of the information should be maintained in addition to the electronic versions. This paper documentation may be critical during a network outage, when the information contained in the network configuration table will be most useful and you may not be able to access the online version.

Router Network Configuration Table

Now that we have discussed the basis for what goes into a network configuration table, let's go through a couple of examples. We will first create the template for what we are looking for, and then step through the gathering of the necessary information. For these examples, we will first create a separate network configuration table for routers and one for switches. The network itself in this case is a small one containing fewer than 15 routers and 20 switches.

Based on this information, we have decided to include the following list of items in our router network configuration table:

- Device Name
- Model #
- Location
- Flash
- DRAM
- IOS Version
- Interface Name
- MAC Address
- Subnet
- Subnet Mask
- IP Address
- Routing Protocol

The start of the router network configuration table is shown in Figure 2.1. As you can see in the figure, part of the information has already been input for our example. This information was gathered through a series of show commands run on each router. Specifically, the commands used were show version, show ip interface brief, show interface, show ip protocols, and show ip interface.

FIGURE 2.1   Sample network configuration table for routers

Device Name, Model	Location	Flash	DRAM	IOS	Interface	MAC Address	Subnet/ Subnet Mask	IP Address	Routing Protocol
Salmon, 2610	Seattle	16	48	12.0(2)	E0/0	0004.4d65.b9c0	10.254.254.0/24	10.254.254.1	EIGRP 200
					S0/0	NA	10.10.10.0/30	10.10.10.1	EIGRP 200
Marlin, 3640	Miami	16	48	12.1(2)	FA0/0	0060.837b.b880	10.20.20.0/24	10.20.20.1	OSPF 21
					S1/0	NA	10.10.10.0/30	10.1.10.2	EIGRP 200

Though the information in the first two columns of the sample network configuration table can be obtained through some show commands (assuming the location or snmp location options are set in the router), in our example, as well as in most real-world scenarios, they are already known by the network administrator doing the work. The next three columns in our example—Flash, DRAM, and IOS—are all obtained by using the show version command.

```
salmon>show version
Cisco Internetwork Operating System Software
IOS (tm) C2600 Software (C2600-JS-M), Version 12.0(12), RELEASE SOFTWARE (fc1)
Copyright (c) 1986-2000 by cisco Systems, Inc.
Compiled Tue 11-Jul-00 10:09 by htseng
Image text-base: 0x80008088, data-base: 0x80B1468C
ROM: System Bootstrap, Version 11.3(2)XA4, RELEASE SOFTWARE (fc1)
salmon uptime is 3 days, 20 hours, 48 minutes
System restarted power on
System image file is "flash:c2600-js-mz.120-12.bin"
cisco 2610 (MPC860) processor (revision 0x203) with 39936K/9216K bytes of memory
.
Processor board ID JAD04430NYN (832809334)
M860 processor: part number 0, mask 49
Bridging software.
X.25 software, Version 3.0.0.
SuperLAT software (copyright 1990 by Meridian Technology Corp).
TN3270 Emulation software.
Basic Rate ISDN software, Version 1.1.
1 Ethernet/IEEE 802.3 interface(s)
2 Serial(sync/async) network interface(s)
1 ISDN Basic Rate interface(s)
32K bytes of non-volatile configuration memory.
16384K bytes of processor board System flash (Read/Write)

Configuration register is 0x2102
```

The flash information is shown at the bottom of the show version output, the DRAM is in the middle, and the IOS is at the top. One item to note is that because the 2610 is a shared memory router, the DRAM information here is divided into two categories, separated by a slash character. The first number represents the local memory on the router, and the number on the other side of the slash represents the I/O memory on the router. The local memory is used for items such as holding the running IOS, whereas the I/O memory is used for buffers and similar input and output functions.

To obtain the interfaces that are active on the router, as well as the IP addresses that are assigned to these interfaces, the show ip interface brief command is used.

```
salmon#show ip interface brief
Interface    IP-Address    OK? Method Status                Protocol
Ethernet0/0  10.254.254.1  YES NVRAM  up                    up
Serial0/0    10.10.10.1    YES NVRAM  up                    up
Serial0/1    unassigned    YES unset  administratively down down
```

Once you have determined which interfaces are used on the router, you can execute the show interface command to get the MAC addresses of the interfaces and the subnet information.

```
salmon#show interface e0/0
Ethernet0/0 is up, line protocol is up
 Hardware is AmdP2, address is 0004.4d65.b9c0 (bia 0004.4d65.b9c0)
 Internet address is 10.254.254.1/24
 MTU 1500 bytes, BW 10000 Kbit, DLY 1000 usec, rely 255/255, load 1/255
 Encapsulation ARPA, loopback not set, keepalive set (10 sec)
 ARP type: ARPA, ARP Timeout 04:00:00
 Last input 00:00:00, output 00:00:00, output hang never
 Last clearing of "show interface" counters never
 Queueing strategy: fifo
 Output queue 0/40, 0 drops; input queue 0/75, 0 drops
 5 minute input rate 0 bits/sec, 0 packets/sec
 5 minute output rate 0 bits/sec, 0 packets/sec
   27067 packets input, 3624228 bytes, 0 no buffer
   Received 27067 broadcasts, 0 runts, 0 giants, 0 throttles
   0 input errors, 0 CRC, 0 frame, 0 overrun, 0 ignored, 0 abort
   0 input packets with dribble condition detected
   39804 packets output, 3815083 bytes, 0 underruns
   0 output errors, 0 collisions, 0 interface resets
   0 babbles, 0 late collision, 0 deferred
   0 lost carrier, 0 no carrier
   0 output buffer failures, 0 output buffers swapped out
```

In looking at the output of the show interface command, notice that following the MAC address is the output (bia 0004.4d65.b9c0). The bia stands for Burned in Address and is the MAC address that was assigned by Cisco to the interface. The BIA is usually, but not always, the MAC address that is used on the interface. Specifically, by using the interface-level mac-address command, a network administrator can set the MAC address used to any value considered appropriate.

The final command we'll examine that is used to populate the network configuration table is show ip protocols.

```
salmon#show ip protocols
Routing Protocol is "eigrp 200"
 Outgoing update filter list for all interfaces is
 Incoming update filter list for all interfaces is
 Default networks flagged in outgoing updates
 Default networks accepted from incoming updates
 EIGRP metric weight K1=1, K2=0, K3=1, K4=0, K5=0
```

```
EIGRP maximum hopcount 100
EIGRP maximum metric variance 1
Redistributing: eigrp 200
Automatic network summarization is in effect
Routing for Networks:
 10.0.0.0
Routing Information Sources:
 Gateway     Distance    Last Update
Distance: internal 90 external 170
```

The command shown just above tells you the routing protocol that is active on the router, as well as the networks this routing protocol is used for.

One command that was not demonstrated in our example is often used in creation of network configuration tables: the show ip interface command. In addition to the standard IP address information, this command provides a wealth of other information such as whether or not access lists are applied to the interface, the switching methodology of the interface, and whether or not there is a helper address assigned. Here is a sample output of the show ip interface command:

```
salmon#show ip interface e0/0
Ethernet0/0 is up, line protocol is up
 Internet address is 10.254.254.1/24
 Broadcast address is 255.255.255.255
 Address determined by non-volatile memory
 MTU is 1500 bytes
 Helper address is not set
 Directed broadcast forwarding is disabled
 Multicast reserved groups joined: 224.0.0.10
 Outgoing access list is not set
 Inbound access list is not set
 Proxy ARP is enabled
 Security level is default
 Split horizon is enabled
 ICMP redirects are always sent
 ICMP unreachables are always sent
 ICMP mask replies are never sent
 IP fast switching is enabled
 IP fast switching on the same interface is disabled
 IP Flow switching is disabled
 IP Fast switching turbo vector
 IP multicast fast switching is enabled
 IP multicast distributed fast switching is disabled
```

```
IP route-cache flags are Fast
Router Discovery is disabled
IP output packet accounting is disabled
IP access violation accounting is disabled
TCP/IP header compression is disabled
RTP/IP header compression is disabled
Probe proxy name replies are disabled
Policy routing is disabled
Network address translation is disabled
Web Cache Redirect is disabled
BGP Policy Mapping is disabled
```

Switch Network Configuration Table

Now that the router network configuration table is complete, let's move on to the switch version of this table. More information on switches and switch commands is provided in Chapter 9, "Troubleshooting Switched Ethernet." As stated in the preceding section, in this example we are assuming that there are about 20 switches in the network for which we are creating documentation. In addition, we are working with switches that have only Layer 2 functionality. Based on this arrangement, we have decided to include the following list of items in our switch network configuration table:

- Device Name
- Model #
- Location
- Flash
- DRAM
- CATOS Version
- Management Address
- VTP Domain
- VTP Mode
- Port Number
- Port Speed
- Port Duplex
- VLAN
- Spanning Tree Protocol (STP) State
- Portfast Status
- Trunk Status

The beginning of the switch network configuration table is shown in Figure 2.2.

As was the case with the network configuration table for routers, just a few commands are needed to populate the table produced for the switches. Specifically these commands are show version, show interface, show vtp domain, show port, show trunk, and show spantree *vlan*.

You will note that the above are CatOS commands. The IOS equivalents of these commands are: show version, show interface, show vtp status, show interface, show interfaces trunk, and show spanning-tree *vlan* respectively. More information about the differences between CatOS and IOS are covered in Chapter 9, "Troubleshooting Switched Ethernet."

FIGURE 2.2 Sample network configuration table for switches

Device Name, Model	Location	Flash	DRAM	CATOS	Mgmt IP	VTP Domain	VTP Mode	Port	Speed	Duplex	VLAN(s)	STP State (Fwd/Block)	Portfast (Yes/No)	Trunk (Yes/No)
core_switch, 6509	Dover, DE	16	64	6.4(3)	10.40.40.2	dover_core	Transparent	1/1	1000	Full	1,2,45,46	Fwd	No	Yes
								1/2	1000	Full	1,2,45,46	Block	No	Yes
								3/1	100	Full	45	Fwd	Yes	No
								3/2	10	Half	45	Fwd	Yes	No
								3/3	A-100	A-Full	45	Fwd	Yes	No

The first of these commands, show version, operates very similarly to the same command in the router. It produces a number of the elements that are needed in order to populate the switch network configuration table.

```
core_switch> (enable) show version
WS-C6509 Software, Version NmpSW: 6.4(3)
Copyright (c) 1995-2003 by Cisco Systems
NMP S/W compiled on Apr 10 2003, 17:33:25

System Bootstrap Version: 5.3(1)

Hardware Version: 2.0 Model: WS-C6509 Serial #: SCA123456F

PS1 Module: WS-CAC-1300W  Serial #: SON01234564
PS2 Module: WS-CAC-1300W  Serial #: SON01234569

Mod Port Model               Serial #    Versions
--- ---- ------------------- ----------- ---------------------------
1    2   WS-X6K-SUP1A-2GE    SAD05430RPV Hw : 3.2
                                         Fw : 5.3(1)
```

```
                                        Fw1: 5.1(1)CSX
                                        Sw : 6.4(3)
                                        Sw1: 6.4(3)
            WS-F6K-PFC          SAD05430LYJ  Hw : 1.1
3   48      WS-X6248-RJ-45      SAD04330N7Z  Hw : 1.2
                                        Fw : 5.1(1)CSX
                                        Sw : 6.4(3)
7   24      WS-X6324-100FX-MM  SAD0234523C  Hw : 1.3
                                        Fw : 5.4(2)
                                        Sw : 6.4(3)
8   8       WS-X6408A-GBIC      SAL43566W9J  Hw : 2.0
                                        Fw : 5.4(2)
                                        Sw : 6.4(3)
```

		DRAM			FLASH			NVRAM	
Module	Total	Used	Free	Total	Used	Free	Total	Used	Free
1	**65408**K	48425K	16983K	**16384**K	9568K	6816K	512K	310K	202K

```
Uptime is 55 days, 11 hours, 28 minutes
```

As you can see in the boldfaced areas of the output, the show version command provides the CATOS level of the switch, as well as the flash and DRAM information.

The next command, show vtp domain, reports both the VTP domain and the VTP mode of the switch. (VTP, VLAN Trunk Protocol, is covered in more detail in Chapter 9, "Troubleshooting Switched Ethernet.")

```
core_switch> (enable) show vtp domain
```

Domain Name	Domain Index	VTP Version	Local Mode	Password
dover_core	1	2	**Transparent**	-

Vlan-count	Max-vlan-storage	Config Revision	Notifications
13	1023	0	enabled

Last Updater	V2 Mode	Pruning	PruneEligible on Vlans
10.40.40.2	disabled	disabled	2-1000

Once you have obtained the VTP data, the next piece of information needed is the management interface IP address. This address is included as part of the output from the `show interface` command. Notice that on a switch, the command displays far less information than for routers and focuses only on the management interfaces and not on the user ports.

```
core_switch> (enable) show interface
sl0: flags=51<UP,POINTOPOINT,RUNNING>
  slip 0.0.0.0 dest 0.0.0.0
sc0: flags=63<UP,BROADCAST,RUNNING>
  vlan 2 inet 10.40.40.2 netmask 255.255.255.252 broadcast 10.40.40.3
```

By using a separate VLAN for the management VLAN we ensure that management traffic to or from the switch will not be directly affected by user traffic, and vice versa. For further protection, a separate uplink instead of a common trunk can be used for the management VLAN, as is shown in this example.

The next command that is used to populate the switch network configuration table is the `show port` command, which provides a substantial amount of fairly concise information about each port on the switch. Be aware, however, that the output can get very lengthy if there are a large number of ports on the switch. For the purpose of the switch network configuration table, the port numbers, VLAN (for nontrunked ports), duplex, and speed information can be obtained from the output.

```
core_switch> (enable) show port
```

Port	Name	Status	Vlan	Duplex	Speed	Type
1/1	core_switch_2	connected	trunk	full	1000	1000BaseSX
1/2	core_switch_2	connected	trunk	full	1000	1000BaseSX
3/1	server1	connected	45	full	100	10/100BaseTX
3/2	mgmt_tool1	connected	45	half	10	10/100BaseTX
3/3	server3	connected	45	a-full	a-100	10/100BaseTX
3/4		notconnect	45	auto	auto	10/100BaseTX
3/5		notconnect	45	auto	auto	10/100BaseTX
3/6		notconnect	45	auto	auto	10/100BaseTX

```
...
...
<Output removed>
```

The output removed from the foregoing `show port` command includes more than just additional port numbers, names, status, VLAN, duplex, speed, and type. It contains packet statistics, error rates, security parameters, and much more. This information was not shown here because it does not directly relate to the switch network configuration table.

Since the VLAN information is not included in the output of a **show port** command for a trunked port, we need to get this data in another manner. There are a couple of ways to get this information, but the usual method is via the **show trunk** command.

```
core_switch> show trunk
* - indicates vtp domain mismatch
Port     Mode         Encapsulation  Status       Native vlan
-------- ------------ -------------- ------------ -----------
 1/1     nonegotiate    dot1q        trunking        45
 1/2     nonegotiate    dot1q        trunking        45


Port     Vlans allowed on trunk
-------- ------------------------------------------------------------
 1/1     1-2,45-46
 1/2     1-2,45-46


Port     Vlans allowed and active in management domain
-------- ------------------------------------------------------------
 1/1     1-2,45-46
 1/2     1-2,45-46


Port     Vlans in spanning tree forwarding state and not pruned
-------- ------------------------------------------------------------
 1/1     1-2,45-46
 1/2     1-2,45-46
```

The VLANs that traverse the trunk are shown in the VLANs allowed on trunk section of the output. If a VLAN is not listed in this section, then it will not be permitted on the trunk.

The final command necessary to complete the information in the switch network configuration table is the show spantree *vlan* command. In our case, we need information regarding VLAN 45, the VLAN in which our servers reside.

```
core_switch> show spantree 45
VLAN 45
Spanning tree mode      PVST+
Spanning tree type      ieee
Spanning tree enabled

Designated Root            00-d0-f6-bc-aa-aa
Designated Root Priority   49152
Designated Root Cost       3004
Designated Root Port       1/1
```

```
Root Max Age  20 sec  Hello Time 2 sec  Forward Delay 15 sec

Bridge ID MAC ADDR        00-d0-f6-bc-7e-00
Bridge ID Priority        49152
Bridge Max Age 20 sec  Hello Time 2 sec  Forward Delay 15 sec
```

Port	Vlan	**Port-State**	Cost	Prio	**Portfast**	Channel_id
1/1	45	forwarding	4	32	disabled	0
1/2	45	blocking	4	32	disabled	0
3/1	45	forwarding	19	32	enabled	0
3/2	45	forwarding	100	32	enabled	0
3/3	45	forwarding	19	32	enabled	0
3/4	45	not-connected	19	32	disabled	0
3/5	45	not-connected	19	32	disabled	0
3/6	45	not-connected	19	32	disabled	0

```
...
...
<Output removed>
```

Notice that this command provides the necessary information to complete the STP State and the Portfast configuration columns of the table.

When both the router and switch network configuration tables are complete, we can move on to creating the network topology diagrams.

Network Topology Diagrams

Network configuration tables are great building blocks for your network documentation, but they are not sufficient for getting a clear picture of how devices connect and interact within the network. This is where the *network topology diagram* comes in. Simply put, a network topology diagram is nothing more than a graphical representation of the network, allowing you to easily see how components in the network are connected and how they interact. Arguably, it is the most heavily utilized piece of documentation used in network troubleshooting and maintenance.

Components of a Network Topology Diagram

Like the network configuration table, the network topology diagram can contain a number of items; its scope will depend on the complexity of the network involved. In its simplest form, a network topology diagram will only include the devices and the connections between them.

However, in most cases the diagram will contains much more information. Some common items are as follows:

- Device Name
- Connections Between Devices (which can also include circuit numbers on WAN links)
- Device Type
- Interface Name
- Speed
- Media Type
- MAC Address
- VLANs
- Trunk
- Encapsulation
- IP Address
- Subnet
- Subnet Mask
- Routing Protocols

Unlike the network configuration tables, it is quite common for the network topology diagram to depict a combination of Layer 2 and Layer 3 devices. This allows for a more complete view of the interactions in the network and a better overall view of network connectivity. Just as you do with network configuration tables, however, you need to be careful to incorporate enough information into the topology diagram without adding too much. These are working documents; if they become too overloaded with information, their maintenance will be more difficult. On the other side, you also do not want to be hunting down information in the middle of an emergency. There is a delicate balance between too much and not enough information.

Anther point of note: Unless your network is small, you are not going to be able to fit it into a single network topology diagram. Typically you will need to make multiple topology diagrams that cover separate aspects of the network. Depending on the drawing program you are using to create the diagrams, you can also link each of these separate topology diagrams together. In this manner you can double-click on a particular area to see more- or less-detailed information or move to another segment of the network.

Creating a Network Topology Diagram

Now that we have explained the purpose and suggested components for a network topology diagram, let's go through the steps to create one.

We will begin with an examination of the standard set of symbols used in such diagrams. By now, most of you will have already seen and know these symbols; they are illustrated in Figure 2.3. Employing a standard set of symbols for device types helps to ensure that any new network administrators coming into the environment will be able to easily understand the documentation.

Real World Scenario

Consistency and Simplicity Are the Keys

When creating network documentation, one goal frequently overlooked is the need to make the documentation consistent and easy to read. Make an effort to apply the same structure and methodology consistently to all the documentation. In this chapter we have discussed the need for consistency when gathering the information and setting up a document, but it is also important to maintain this uniformity from one document to the next.

One of the main purposes of your network documentation is its role in a troubleshooting effort when the network is down. Since you can't schedule when a problem will occur, it is quite possible that you will be using your documentation to solve a problem in the middle of the night when you are not completely rested and are not operating at your peak effectiveness. At such a time, you do not want to be saddled with documents that are incompatible or so cluttered with information that they are difficult to read. Keep in mind when and how the network documentation is going to be used, and take some simple steps to make it easy to comprehend.

One of the first things you should do is ensure that the symbols used on all the diagrams mean the same thing on each one. Do not use one symbol to signify a router on one diagram and a different symbol to represent the same router on another.

Next, create a template for all your network configuration tables and topology diagrams. Earlier in the chapter we discussed the template for a network configuration table, but templates for network topology diagrams can be even more useful. For example, if you have multiple branch locations, use an identical format and device-placement scheme on all the topology diagrams so that similar information is always in the same spot on each diagram. This will save you time in locating the facts you need.

Besides maintaining consistency, it is also important to avoid too much complexity. If the network documentation contains extraneous information, it can make it difficult to find the specifics that you need for your troubleshooting. The documentation should have enough information to help you understand how things are connected and what the baseline of the network is, without overwhelming you with data that may or may not be relevant.

FIGURE 2.3   Networking symbols

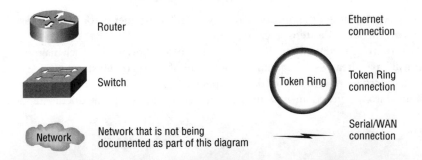

In most cases, a network topology diagram is created after the network configuration tables are set up, since the topology diagram uses much of the information contained in the configuration tables. Figure 2.4 illustrates a sample network topology diagram and its relationship to some of the information used from the router configuration table.

Similarly, there is also a direct correlation between items on the topology diagram and the switch network configuration table, as illustrated in Figure 2.5.

Since most of the information that is on the network topology diagram has already been retrieved and placed in the network configuration tables, relatively few commands are needed to generate the diagram itself. One command of great assistance is `show cdp neighbor`. The Cisco Discovery Protocol (CDP) is a proprietary protocol that identifies directly attached Cisco devices. This discovery is done at Layer 2, so there is no need to have IP connectivity to see the neighbors. The `show cdp neighbor` command shows the neighbors that have been learned via CDP and gives their summary information. More detailed information can be found by using the `show cdp neighbor detail` command.

FIGURE 2.4 Items from the router configuration table

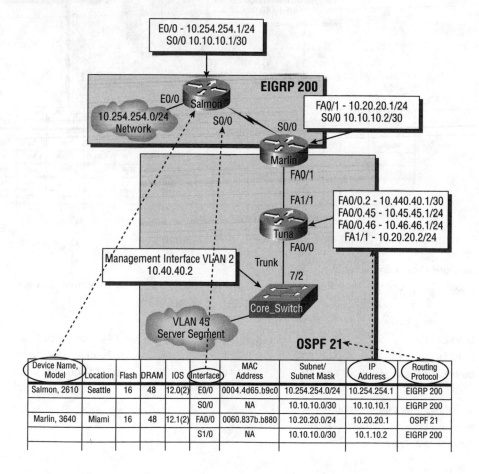

Device Name, Model	Location	Flash	DRAM	IOS	Interface	MAC Address	Subnet/ Subnet Mask	IP Address	Routing Protocol
Salmon, 2610	Seattle	16	48	12.0(2)	E0/0	0004.4d65.b9c0	10.254.254.0/24	10.254.254.1	EIGRP 200
					S0/0	NA	10.10.10.0/30	10.10.10.1	EIGRP 200
Marlin, 3640	Miami	16	48	12.1(2)	FA0/0	0060.837b.b880	10.20.20.0/24	10.20.20.1	OSPF 21
					S1/0	NA	10.10.10.0/30	10.1.10.2	EIGRP 200

FIGURE 2.5 Items from the switch configuration table

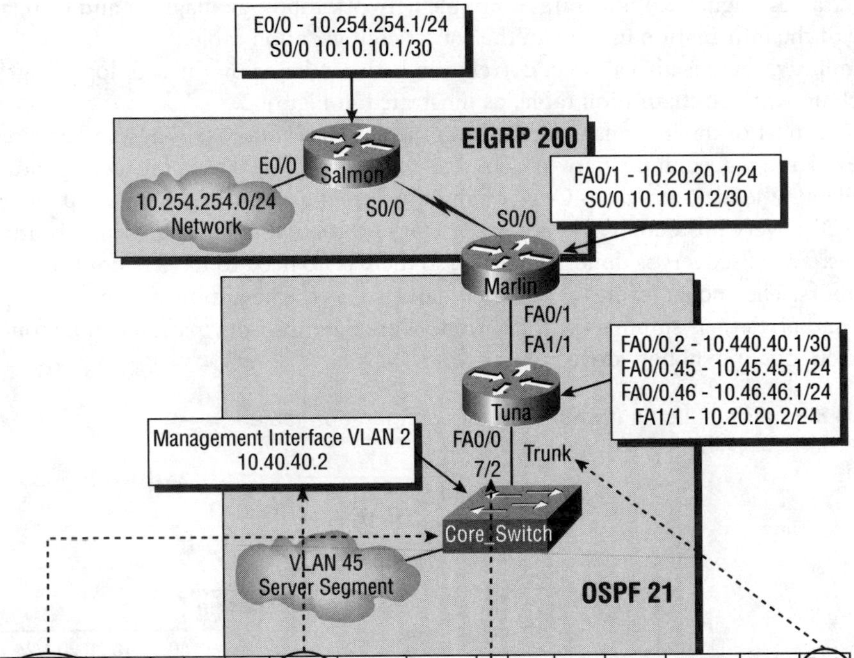

Device Name, Model	Location	Flash	DRAM	CATOS	Mgmt IP	VTP Domain	VTP Mode	Port	Speed	Duplex	VLAN(s)	STP State (Fwd/Block)	Portfast (Yes/No)	Trunk Yes/No
core_switch, 6509	Dover, DE	16	64	6.4(3)	10.40.40.2	dover_core	Transparent	1/1	1000	Full	1,2,45,46	Fwd	No	Yes
								1/2	1000	Full	1,2,45,46	Block	No	Yes
								3/1	100	Full	45	Fwd	Yes	No
								3/2	10	Half	45	Fwd	Yes	No
								3/3	A-100	A-Full	45	Fwd	Yes	No

Following are examples of the output of each command.

```
salmon#show cdp neighbor
Capability Codes: R - Router, T - Trans Bridge, B - Source Route Bridge
        S - Switch, H - Host, I - IGMP, r - Repeater

Device ID          Local Intrfce Holdtme Capability Platform Port ID
marlin             Ser 0/0       172        R        3640    Ser 0/0
069017443(switch_a) Eth 0/0      141       T B S    WS-C5500 2/13

salmon#show cdp neighbors detail
------------------------
Device ID: marlin
```

```
Entry address(es):
 IP address: 10.10.10.2
Platform: cisco 3640, Capabilities: Router
Interface: Serial0/0, Port ID (outgoing port): Serial0/0
Holdtime : 160 sec

Version :
 Cisco Internetwork Operating System Software
 IOS (tm) 3600 Software (C3640-JS56I-M), Version 12.1(2), RELEASE
  SOFTWARE (fc2)
 Copyright (c) 1986-2000 by cisco Systems, Inc.
 Compiled Thu 08-Dec-00 04:50 by phanguye

-------------------------
Device ID: 069017443(switch_a)
Entry address(es):
 IP address: 10.254.254.102
Platform: WS-C5500, Capabilities: Trans-Bridge Source-Route-Bridge
Switch
Interface: Ethernet0/0, Port ID (outgoing port): 2/13
Holdtime : 130 sec

Version :
WS-C5500 Software, Version McpSW: 4.5(5) NmpSW: 4.5(5)
Copyright (c) 1995-1999 by Cisco Systems
```

 NOTE Since these commands are available in both routers and switches, you can effectively move across the network one device at a time, documenting each neighbor along the way.

One final recommendation: Accuracy is the key to any successful documentation strategy. As things change in the network, your documents must be updated to reflect these changes. It is usually best to get in the habit of changing your documents as a normal part of changing the network, and not as an afterthought. (This applies to scheduled changes as well as after troubleshooting!) In this manner, you are less likely to get involved in other tasks and forget to update the documentation.

Summary

Documentation is essential in today's increasingly complex networks. It provides vital information that can greatly reduce network downtime. It also provides verification that the network is operating correctly.

Baseline information on a network is information about the normal operating conditions of a network. This baseline is used to determine whether a network configuration is set up in the manner expected and whether it is operating normally. Some of the specific components of the network baseline are the network configuration tables, the network topology diagrams, the end-system configuration tables, and the end-system topology diagrams.

Network configuration tables show the key configuration parameters that are in place on the network devices. Some typical items included in a network configuration table are device name, flash memory DRAM, IOS/CATOS, interface number, MAC address, speed, duplex, VLANs, trunking, IP address, subnet, subnet mask, and routing protocol. Although these are some of the standard items in a network configuration table, each table will vary based on a device's type as well as the design of the particular network. In most cases this information is stored in a spreadsheet or database format, but hard copies should be regularly printed so that information will always be available in the event of a problem or failure.

Network topology diagrams are graphical representations of the network components, and in most cases contain a subset of the data maintained in the network configuration tables. The topology diagrams are meant to make the network administrator better able to visualize the path across the network. Some standard items that go into a network topology are device name, connections between devices, interface name, VLANs, trunking, IP address, subnet mask, and routing protocols. As is true for the network configuration tables, hard copies of network topology diagrams should be regularly printed to ensure that information is always available when the network goes down.

Exam Essentials

Know what a network baseline is and the major components that go into making it.   A baseline is a set of documentation that establishes normal operating conditions on the network. Some of the key components of a baseline are the network configuration tables, the network topology diagrams, the end-system configuration tables, and the end-system topology diagrams.

Know what network configuration tables are and the information they contain.   Network configuration tables are used to record key settings of network devices, as well as other related information. Some common items included in a network configuration table are device name, flash information, DRAM, IOS/CATOS, interface number, MAC address, speed, duplex, VLANs, trunking, IP address, subnet, subnet mask, and routing protocol.

Know what network topology diagrams are and the information they contain.   Network topology diagrams are graphical representations of the network; they are usually built from many of the same components as the network configuration tables. Some common components of network topology diagrams are device name, connections between devices, interface name, VLANs, trunking, IP address, subnet mask, and routing protocols.

Commands Used in This Chapter

The following list contains a summary of all the commands used in this chapter.

Commands	Descriptions
show cdp neighbor	Can be used on either the switch or router. Based on CDP information, shows directly attached Cisco neighboring devices.
show cdp neighbor detail	Can be used on either the switch or router. Based on CDP information, shows detailed information on directly attached Cisco neighboring devices.
show interface	For routers, shows detailed information about the interfaces on the router. For switches, shows information regarding the management interface on the switch.
show ip interface	Shows information regarding the interface pertaining to IP, including address and whether any IP access lists are applied.
show ip interface brief	Shows concise information about the IP addresses assigned to each interface on the router.
show ip protocols	Shows information regarding the IP routing protocols that are running on the router.
show port	Shows port information on a switch.
show spantree *vlan*	Shows Spanning Tree Protocol (STP) information on a particular VLAN.
show trunk	Shows trunking information on a switch.
show version	Can be used on either the switch or router. Shows information regarding current IOS/CATOS code, flash, and DRAM.
show vtp domain	Shows vtp mode and domain information on a switch.

Key Terms

Before you take the exam, be certain you are familiar with the following terms:

Baseline   network topology diagram

network configuration table

Review Questions

1. What are the two items that are required as part of a network topology diagram?

   A. Contact information

   B. IP addresses

   C. Routing protocols

   D. Device names

   E. IOS version

   F. Connections between devices

2. What documentation tool is used to provide a view of the network while it is performing at an acceptable level?

   A. `show proc cpu` command

   B. Network baseline

   C. Netsys

   D. Network Analyzer

3. Which of the following guidelines will help to ensure that you have good network documentation? (Choose three.)

   A. Document everything.

   B. Be consistent.

   C. Maintain the documentation.

   D. Back up documentation regularly.

   E. Re-create all documentation yearly.

   F. Keep documentation accessible.

4. What command shows information such as the IP address of the interface and whether any IP access lists are applied?

   A. `show access list`

   B. `show ip interface`

   C. `show interface`

   D. `show cdp neighbor`

5. How often should you update your network configuration tables and network topology diagrams?

   A. Every month

   B. Whenever a change is made in the network

   C. Whenever you plan to make a change in the network

   D. There is no set time to update network configuration tables and topology diagrams

6. What command gives you information such as the amount of flash memory that is available on the router?

    A. show running-config

    B. show ip protocols

    C. show version

    D. show config

7. What router and switch command shows directly connected network devices?

    A. show cdp neighbor

    B. show connections neighbor

    C. show stp neighbor

    D. show vtp neighbor

8. When creating a network configuration table for a switch, which of the following information is relevant and should be considered for inclusion? (Choose three.)

    A. STP state

    B. HSRP state

    C. VTP mode

    D. Management IP address

    E. Routing protocols

    F. Interface IP address

9. What command shows information regarding the routing protocols running on a router?

    A. show protocols

    B. show ip protocols

    C. show version

    D. show config

10. What command shows information regarding the VLAN trunking protocol running on a router?

    A. show protocols

    B. show vtp domain

    C. show version

    D. show trunk

11. What router command shows information such as the MAC address and IP address of an interface?

    A. show ip interface

    B. show cam dynamic

    C. show arp interface

    D. show interface

12. Which of the following are *not* parts of a network topology diagram? (Choose two.)

   A. IP address

   B. Interface resets

   C. Routing protocols

   D. Device names

   E. CRCs

13. What CatOS switch command shows information regarding the management IP address?

   A. `show ip interface`

   B. `show cam dynamic`

   C. `show management IP`

   D. `show interface`

14. What CatOS switch command gives you information about the speed of an interface as well as the VLAN the interface it is in?

   A. `show port`

   B. `show cam dynamic`

   C. `show spantree vlan`

   D. `show interface`

15. What router command shows a concise listing of IP addresses and the associate interfaces?

   A. `show ip interface`

   B. `show ip interface brief`

   C. `show interface brief`

   D. `show interface`

16. What CatOS switch command shows information VLANs that are allowed to pass over a trunk port?

   A. `show port`

   B. `show cam dynamic`

   C. `show spantree vlan`

   D. `show trunk`

17. What CatOS switch command shows STP state information for a port?

   A. `show port`

   B. `show cam dynamic`

   C. `show spantree vlan`

   D. `show stp domain`

18. What network document shows a graphical view of network components?

    A. Network topology diagram

    B. Network configuration table

    C. Baseline

    D. Network logical diagram

19. Which documentation items are included as part of a baseline? (Choose two.)

    A. Network configuration table

    B. End-system logical diagram

    C. End-system topology diagram

    D. Network logical diagram

20. What CatOS command shows information such as the amount of flash memory that is available on the switch?

    A. `show running-config`

    B. `show ip protocols`

    C. `show version`

    D. `show config`

Answers to Review Questions

1. D, F. In its simplest form, a network topology diagram contains only the devices' names (representing the devices) and the connections between the devices. Additional information, such as IP addresses and IOS, is included, as well, on most network topology diagrams.

2. B. The network baseline is actually a composite of multiple network and end-system documents. This documentation tool is used to define the normal operating parameters of the network.

3. B, C, F. There are five key guidelines to ensuring good network documentation: determine the scope, know your objective, be consistent, keep the documents accessible, and maintain the documentation.

4. B. The `show ip interface` command provides the IP address of the interface as well as the access lists that are applied.

5. B. This network documentation should be updated whenever you make a change to the network, but not before the change is made.

6. C. In addition to the flash information, `show version` also gives you the DRAM information and the level of IOS that is available on the router.

7. A. The correct syntax of the command to display directly connected network devices is `show cdp neighbor`.

8. A, C, D. STP state, VTP mode, and the management IP address should always be considered for part of a switch network configuration table. The other three items, HSRP state, routing protocols, and interface IP address, should be considered when creating a network configuration table for a router.

9. B. The correct syntax of the command is `show ip protocols`.

10. B. The correct answer is `show vtp domain`; VTP stands for VLAN Trunking Protocol.

11. D. The `show interface` command provides the MAC and IP addresses of an interface.

12. B, E. Neither interface resets nor CRCs are on network topology diagrams.

13. D. The `show interface` command on the switch provides information regarding the management IP address of the switch.

14. A. For a switch, the `show port` command shows the speed of the interface and the related VLAN interface.

15. B. The `show ip interface brief` command output includes IP addresses and the associated interfaces on a router in a concise format.

16. D. The `show trunk` command output tells you the VLANs that are permitted to go over a trunk port.

17. C. The `show spantree` *vlan* command provides the Spanning Tree Protocol (STP) state of a port.

18. A. A network topology diagram shows a graphical representation of the network components.

19. A, C. In addition to the network configuration table and the end-system topology diagram, the network baseline also includes the network topology diagram and the end-system configuration table.

20. C. The `show version` command on a switch provides similar information to that produced by the same command on the router.

Chapter 3

End-System Documentation and Troubleshooting

EXAM TOPICS COVERED IN THIS CHAPTER INCLUDE:

✓ Create end-system documentation.

✓ Know troubleshooting methodologies.

✓ Verify network connectivity.

✓ Use the optimal troubleshooting approach in resolving network problems.

✓ Develop a network documentation system.

✓ Work with end users to diagnose and resolve network problems.

✓ Understand the document control process and documentation standards.

✓ Establish a baseline indicative of optimal network performance.

✓ Create a baseline monitoring methodology.

You learned in Chapter 2 that detailed network information can be an invaluable tool in troubleshooting network problems.

However, many network problems are a result of the end systems on the network, not the network itself. The purpose of this chapter is to examine the documentation for these end systems so that you can effectively address network problems in these areas. This chapter will also explore a new troubleshooting approach based on the OSI model. Finally, this chapter will end with an overview of some of the commands that can be used on end systems to assist in troubleshooting network problems.

End-System Network Configuration Table

The general purpose of an *end-system network configuration table*, also referred to as an end-system configuration table, is to give a listing of the hardware and software components on the end-systems in the network. Much like the network configuration table was a listing of network devices, the end-system network configuration table is a listing of the end-systems in the environment and key features about them. Depending on the size of your network, an end-system network configuration table may contain all devices or just the servers and network management stations.

Though it was mentioned in Chapter 2, it is worth repeating that there are five steps to ensuring that you have good, effective documentation: Determine the scope, know your objective, be consistent, keep the documents accessible, and maintain the documentation. These actions directly apply to the end-system documentation as well, so be sure to keep them in mind as you are planning for and implementing your documentation strategy.

The specific items included in your end-system network configuration table will vary depending on the purpose of the table. There will be vastly different information included if the table is going to be used only for inventory purposes, as compared with the type of table maintained as a troubleshooting tool. Therefore, in order to determine what you need to include in your end-system configuration table, you need to start by defining the role of the table and choosing items for the table that will achieve this goal. Some common items included in end-system configuration tables are shown in Table 3.1.

One of the items you will immediately notice when looking at the table is the information that is included on Layer 7, the Application layer. Because one of the primary roles for servers is to service applications, it is imperative that Layer 7 information be captured somewhere. For example, say you get a call from a user who cannot get to the XYZ database but everything else

TABLE 3.1   Sample List of Network Configuration Table Items for End Systems

Classification	Items
Miscellaneous information	System name, system manufacturer/model, CPU speed, RAM, storage, system purpose.
Layer 1 and 2	Media type, interface speed, VLAN, network jack.
Layer 3	IP address, default gateway, subnet mask, WINS, DNS.
Layer 7	Operating system (including version), network-based applications, high-bandwidth applications, and low-latency applications, special considerations.

on their system is working fine. By looking at the end-system configuration table you can see that the XYZ database exists on a single server. You have now greatly narrowed the scope of the problem and can more effectively begin the troubleshooting process.

The end-system configuration table is typically compiled in either a spreadsheet or database application. In addition to this electronic version, regular hard copies of the end-system configuration table must be made to ensure that the information is accessible in the event of a network problem.

Now that we have defined what an end-system network configuration table is, the next section will walk through the process of creating one.

Creating an End-System Network Configuration Table

The easiest way to explain how to create an end-system network configuration table is to study an example. In this example, we will look at creating the table for some servers. These servers are used companywide for such processes as e-mail, system backup, and streaming video. All of the servers are located in the Miami office of this company.

Based on this information, we have decided to include the following list of items in our end-system network configuration table:

- System Name
- System Purpose
- Operating System
- VLAN
- IP Address
- Subnet Mask
- Default Gateway
- DNS Servers

- WINS Server
- Network Applications
- High-Bandwidth Network Applications
- Low-Latency Network Applications

The start of the end-system network configuration table is shown in Figure 3.1, which shows part of the information already input for our example.

FIGURE 3.1 Sample end-system network configuration table

System Name/Purpose	OS	IP Address/Mask	Default Gateway	DNS	WINS	Network Applications	High Bandwidth Apps	Low Latency Apps
streamer/(Live Streaming Video)	Win 2000 SP4	10.45.45.8/24	10.45.45.1	10.3.3.3, 10.4.4.3	10.5.5.3, 10.6.6.3	http, iptv,ftp	NA	iptv
backup1/(Backup Server)	Unix Solaris 7	10.45.45.12/24	10.45.45.1	10.3.3.3, 10.4.4.3	NA	Backup Pro, ftp, telnet, smtp	Backup Pro	NA
web1/Web Server	LINUX Redhat Ent AS 2.1	10.45.45.25/24	10.45.45.1	10.3.3.3, 10.4.4.3	NA	http, ftp, telnet, smtp	NA	NA

Unless you have an inventory management tool that can gather this information for you, a lot of it will have to be collected manually. Depending on the system type, there are a number of commands available to gather this information. As you will see in the End-System Trouble-shooting Commands section later in this chapter, many of these same commands can also be used in troubleshooting when there is a problem in the network. Specifically, the commands that we will examine are as follows:

- For the Windows platforms: `ping`, `arp`, `telnet`, `ipconfig`, and `winipcfg`.
- For Unix, Linux, and Mac OS X systems: `ping`, `ifconfig`, and `cat /etc/resolv.conf`.

Most people are already familiar with the very useful `ping` command. This command is used to send an ICMP echo and receive an ICMP echo reply over the network. The end-system imple-mentation of the command is very similar to that on Cisco routers and switches. Run in a com-mand window on an NT/2000/XP station, four ping packets are sent out by default anytime the command is executed. Though it is primarily used for troubleshooting, `ping` can be used in the discovery phase of documentation to verify which IP addresses on the network are in use.

The options of the `ping` command can be seen by executing the command `ping /?`, as shown here:

```
C:\>ping /?
```

```
Usage: ping [-t] [-a] [-n count] [-l size] [-f] [-i TTL] [-v TOS]
            [-r count] [-s count] [[-j host-list] | [-k host-list]]
            [-w timeout] target_name
```

```
Options:
    -t              Ping the specified host until stopped.
                    To see statistics and continue - type Control-Break;
                    To stop - type Control-C.
    -a              Resolve addresses to hostnames.
    -n count        Number of echo requests to send.
    -l size         Send buffer size.
    -f              Set Don't Fragment flag in packet.
    -i TTL          Time To Live.
    -v TOS          Type Of Service.
    -r count        Record route for count hops.
    -s count        Timestamp for count hops.
    -j host-list    Loose source route along host-list.
    -k host-list    Strict source route along host-list.
    -w timeout      Timeout in milliseconds to wait for each reply.
```

In the following output, the ping command in NT/2000/XP shows not only the results of the ping but a summary of the results, as well.

```
C:\>ping 10.10.10.1

Pinging 10.10.10.1 with 32 bytes of data:

Reply from 10.10.10.1: bytes=32 time=136ms TTL=120
Reply from 10.10.10.1: bytes=32 time=136ms TTL=120
Reply from 10.10.10.1: bytes=32 time=138ms TTL=120
Reply from 10.10.10.1: bytes=32 time=137ms TTL=120

Ping statistics for 10.10.10.1:
    Packets: Sent = 4, Received = 4, Lost = 0 (0% loss),
Approximate round trip times in milli-seconds:
    Minimum = 136ms, Maximum = 138ms, Average = 136ms
```

From a Unix, Linux, or Mac OS X end-system, the default values vary somewhat, but the general concept is the same as a Windows end-system. For example, from a Sun Solaris end system, the options for ping are:

```
unix1% ping
usage: ping host [timeout]
usage: ping -s[drvRlLn] [-I interval] [-t ttl] [-i interface] host
[data size] [npackets]
```

The output of the ping command can also vary based on the particular end-system that is being used. For example, the output could be four ping packets as was the case with Windows, or just a simple message stating the end-system is alive, as is the case here:

```
unix1% ping 10.10.10.1
10.10.10.1 is alive
unix1%
```

 The help files in Unix are called man (short for manual) pages. These files can be accessed by typing **man command**. So, to get more information on the ping command, you would type **man ping**.

The arp command is used to show the current MAC-address-to-IP-address mappings on the end system. These mapping can be used to determine which other end systems were recently contacted. This can provide clues as to what applications are interdependent. The downside to the arp command is that, because it is dependant on Layer 2 information, it will only show the IP address of other end systems on the same subnet. If network communication is with a device on another subnet, the arp table will just show the IP address and MAC address of the default gateway.

Like the ping command, options for the arp command are displayed by adding a /? at the end of the command.

```
C:\>arp /?

Displays and modifies the IP-to-Physical address translation tables
   used by address resolution protocol (ARP).

ARP -s inet_addr eth_addr [if_addr]
ARP -d inet_addr [if_addr]
ARP -a [inet_addr] [-N if_addr]

   -a          Displays current ARP entries by interrogating the
               current protocol data.  If inet_addr is specified,
               the IP and Physical addresses for only the specified
               computer are displayed.  If more than one network
               interface uses ARP, entries for each ARP table are
               displayed.
   -g          Same as -a.
   inet_addr   Specifies an internet address.
   -N if_addr  Displays the ARP entries for the network interface
               specified by if_addr.
```

```
-d              Deletes the host specified by inet_addr. inet_addr may
                be wildcarded with * to delete all hosts.
-s              Adds the host and associates the Internet address
                inet_addr with the Physical address eth_addr.  The
                Physical address is given as 6 hexadecimal bytes
                separated by hyphens. The entry is permanent.
eth_addr        Specifies a physical address.
if_addr         If present, this specifies the Internet address of the
                interface whose address translation table should be
                modified. If not present, the first applicable
                interface will be used.
```
Example:
```
> arp -s 157.55.85.212    00-aa-00-62-c6-09  Adds a static entry.
> arp -a                                     Displays the arp table.
```

And here is a sample output of the arp command using the -a option to list the current translations:

```
C:\>arp -a

Interface: 10.9.9.9 --- 0x2
  Internet Address      Physical Address      Type
  10.9.9.1              00-06-22-fd-06-01     dynamic
  10.9.9.100            00-e0-18-19-a8-19     dynamic
  10.9.9.222            00-a0-cc-cb-64-c5     dynamic
```

Telnet is used for discovery of end systems in two different ways. First, telnet can be used by the network administrator to log into some of the end systems on the network remotely. This functionality is enabled by default on most Unix and LINUX servers but is not by default available on NT/2000/XP. Secondly, telnet can be used to verify that an end system is indeed listening on a particular TCP port. For example, you can telnet to a web server on TCP port 80. You will not see any meaningful data, but if a connection is established you have verified not only that the server is listening on port 80 but also that port 80 traffic is getting through the network to the server.

 WARNING   Use caution when telnetting to a port. Though it is usually not a problem, some custom applications do not respond well to these types of connections.

The options for telnet on NT/2000/XP are shown in the following command output:

```
C:\>telnet /?

telnet [-a][-e escape char][-f log file][-l user][-t term][host [port]]
```

```
-a      Attempt automatic logon. Same as -l option except uses
        the currently logged on user's name.
-e      Escape character to enter telnet client prompt.
-f      File name for client side logging
-l      Specifies the user name to log in with on the remote system.
        Requires that the remote system support the TELNET ENVIRON
        option.
-t      Specifies terminal type.  Supported term types are vt100,
        vt52, ansi and vtnt only.
host    Specifies the hostname or IP address of the remote computer
        to connect to.
port    Specifies a port number or service name.
```

The ipconfig command is the first command in the series discussed here that will go a long way toward getting the data you need in order to complete the end-system network configuration table. This command shows detailed information on the IP address, DNS servers, and WINS servers that are configured on the NT/2000/XP workstation. As is the case for all the commands covered in this section, ipconfig is run from the command prompt on the NT/2000/XP end system. Some of the other options will be covered in the End-System Troubleshooting Commands section later in this chapter, but for the documentation process the /all option is what is primarily used. The entire list of options for ipconfig are shown here:

C:\>ipconfig /?

```
USAGE:
    ipconfig [/? | /all | /renew [adapter] | /release [adapter] |
             /flushdns | /displaydns | /registerdns |
             /showclassid adapter |
             /setclassid adapter [classid] ]
where
    adapter         Connection name
                    (wildcard characters * and ? allowed, see examples)

    Options:
        /?          Display this help message
        /all        Display full configuration information.
        /release    Release the IP address for the specified adapter.
        /renew      Renew the IP address for the specified adapter.
        /flushdns   Purges the DNS Resolver cache.
        /registerdns Refreshes all DHCP leases and re-registers DNS
```

```
                      names
        /displaydns  Display the contents of the DNS Resolver Cache.
        /showclassid Displays all the dhcp class IDs allowed for
                     adapter.
        /setclassid  Modifies the dhcp class id.
```

The default is to display only the IP address, subnet mask and
default gateway for each adapter bound to TCP/IP.

For Release and Renew, if no adapter name is specified, then the IP
   address leases for all adapters bound to TCP/IP will be released or
renewed.

For Setclassid, if no ClassId is specified, then the ClassId is
removed.

```
Examples:
    > ipconfig               ... Show information.
    > ipconfig /all          ... Show detailed information
    > ipconfig /renew        ... renew all adapters
    > ipconfig /renew EL*     ... renew any connection that has its
                                  name starting with EL

    > ipconfig /release *Con* ... release all matching connections,
                                  eg. "Local Area Connection 1" or
                                      "Local Area Connection 2"
```

Following is the output of the ipconfig /all command. The IP address, subnet, gateway, DNS servers, and WINS servers are in boldface.

C:\>**ipconfig /all**

Windows IP Configuration

```
        Host Name . . . . . . . . . . . : Sever1
        Primary Dns Suffix  . . . . . . : fla.somecompany.com
        Node Type . . . . . . . . . . . : Hybrid
        IP Routing Enabled. . . . . . . : No
        WINS Proxy Enabled. . . . . . . : No
        DNS Suffix Search List. . . . . : fla.somecompany.com
                                          somecompany.com
```

```
Ethernet adapter Local Area Connection 4:

        Connection-specific DNS Suffix  . :
        Description . . . . . . . . . . : NVIDIA nForce MCP
   Networking Adapter
        Physical Address. . . . . . . . : 00-cc-47-49-F4-32
        Dhcp Enabled. . . . . . . . . . : No
        IP Address. . . . . . . . . . . : 10.9.9.9
        Subnet Mask . . . . . . . . . . : 255.255.255.0
        Default Gateway . . . . . . . . : 10.9.9.1
        DNS Servers . . . . . . . . . . : 10.3.3.3
                                          10.4.4.3
        Primary WINS Server . . . . . . : 10.5.5.3
        Secondary WINS Server . . . . . : 10.6.6.3
```

If the end-system you are working on is Windows 9x or Windows ME, a different methodology is used to discover this information. On these machines, there is a GUI tool that replaces the `ipconfig` command-line command. The executable to start this tool is `winipcfg.exe`. This utility shows all the same information as `ipconfig`, but it does so via the GUI instead of the command line.

NOTE   Both `ipconfig` and `winipcfg` are available in Windows 98.

To get the IP information from a Unix, Linux, or Mac OS X system, you use the `ifconfig -a` command. This prints out the address information for each interface on the box. Following is sample output:

```
unix1% ifconfig -a
lo0: flags=849<UP,LOOPBACK,RUNNING,MULTICAST> mtu 8232
        inet 127.0.0.1 netmask ff000000
hme0: flags=863<UP,BROADCAST,NOTRAILERS,RUNNING,MULTICAST> mtu 1500
        inet 10.7.7.58 netmask ffffff00 broadcast 10.7.7.255
```

As is the case in many routers, the loopback interface is an internal virtual interface. Since the loopback is addressed with 127.0.0.1, it is only used for internal communication inside the box. The hme0 interface is the interface that is connected to the network and is the one that goes into the end-system network configuration table.

Since Unix, Linux, and Mac OS X end-systems do not use WINS, the only remaining bit of IP information we need to get from the end-system is the DNS servers' names. This is stored in the `resolv.conf` file, which is most often found in the `/etc` directory on the system. To see the

DNS servers that are defined, all you need to do is to list the contents of the `resolv.conf` file using the `cat` command as shown here:

```
unix1% cat /etc/resolv.conf
domain fla.somecompany.com
search fla.somecompany.com somecompany.com
nameserver      10.3.3.3
nameserver      10.4.4.3
```

For the remaining information in the end-system configuration table, such as the applications on the system as well as which of these application are high- and low-bandwidth and/or low-latency applications, it is best to talk with the server administrators. They will have the best idea of what is on each server and how it is used.

End-System Network Topology Diagram

Now that the end-system network configuration table is complete, we will focus on the end-system network topology diagram. Like the topology diagram for the network, the end-system diagram is designed to give a graphical representation of the end-systems in the network, giving you a better view of traffic flow and interdependencies. This view also allows for easier identification of potential bottlenecks or significant points of failure. For example, you can easily see on the end-system network topology diagram whether your users will need to cross a slow serial connection to get to new servers that are being put in. You can also see if there is only one path available from these users to the servers and, if redundancy is required, alter the location of the servers or add another path.

In most cases, the end-system network topology diagram is just an extension of the network topology diagram, with the information gathered for the end-system network configuration table added. Because of the amount of information included in these diagrams, it is necessary to ensure that only pertinent data is added. Adding too much data can quickly clutter up the diagram and make it difficult to use.

Typical items in an end-system topology diagram are as follows:

- System Name
- Connection to the Network
- System Purpose
- VLAN
- IP Address
- Subnet Mask
- Network Applications

At a minimum, the system name and connection to the network are needed on the topology diagram. The exception to this rule is when you are including a large number of like-configured end systems that serve a common purpose and exist on the same subnet. In this arrangement, where it is impractical to include each separate machine in the diagram, they can be grouped together and represented by descriptive text. An example of this grouping is shown in Figure 3.2 in the next section.

 Real World Scenario

Windows Name Resolution

When working with Windows systems, it is important to know the process by which names are associated to IP addresses. In a Unix system this resolution is relatively straightforward and usually involves the use of cached entries, a HOSTS file, or DNS. In a Windows environment, however, there are a few other options available. All the options that are available are as follows:

- Internal cache of recently used entries

- Broadcast message to the local network

- Local LMHOSTS file

- Local HOSTS file

- WINS server

- DNS server

In addition to the local cache, HOSTS file, and DNS are three other options: broadcast, LMHOSTS, and WINS. The order in which these items are checked in a Windows system varies based on a number of factors, but in general, the internal cache and broadcast message are the first items used to try to resolve a name into an IP address.

Following this, the LMHOSTS and HOSTS files are used. Both these files are usually located in the %SystemRoot%\System32\Drivers\Etc directory of each Windows end system. They are text-based files that can be edited to provide static name-to-IP-address translation.

Next in the series is the Windows Internet Name Service (WINS) server, which is Microsoft's version of a NetBIOS name server. It dynamically updates the names of other Windows clients that are on the network. The server can then be queried in much the same manner as a DNS server for name-to-IP-address resolution.

The final item used by a Windows end system is a DNS server. As is the case with any station using DNS, a Windows station sends a query to the DNS server, and the server responds with the IP address or a notification saying it does not know the address.

Creating an End-System Network Topology Diagram

Now that an end-system network topology diagram has been explained, let's go through the steps to create one. Since most end-system network topology diagrams are built on the network topology diagrams, the standard symbols set that was used in the network diagrams will also be used here in the end-system network topology diagram. In addition, there will be symbols to indicate servers, workstations, and other network attached end systems.

The other information added to the end-system diagram is a subset of the data in the end-system network configuration table. Figure 3.2 shows how this data maps to the topology diagram.

FIGURE 3.2 Sample end-system network topology diagram

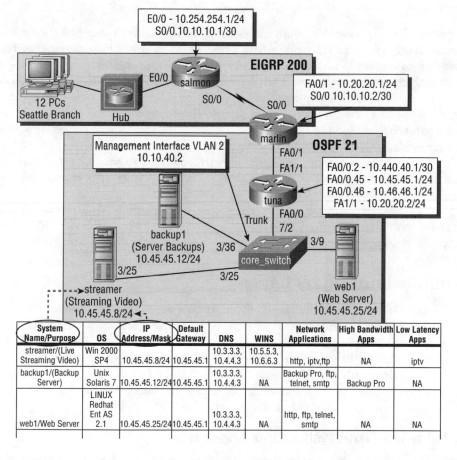

System Name/Purpose	OS	IP Address/Mask	Default Gateway	DNS	WINS	Network Applications	High Bandwidth Apps	Low Latency Apps
streamer/(Live Streaming Video)	Win 2000 SP4	10.45.45.8/24	10.45.45.1	10.3.3.3, 10.4.4.3	10.5.5.3, 10.6.6.3	http, iptv,ftp	NA	iptv
backup1/(Backup Server)	Unix Solaris 7	10.45.45.12/24	10.45.45.1	10.3.3.3, 10.4.4.3	NA	Backup Pro, ftp, telnet, smtp	Backup Pro	NA
web1/Web Server	LINUX Redhat Ent AS 2.1	10.45.45.25/24	10.45.45.1	10.3.3.3, 10.4.4.3	NA	http, ftp, telnet, smtp	NA	NA

As you can see in Figure 3.2, the servers entered in the network configuration are shown in their appropriate place in the network. Only the key information on the servers was transferred to the topology diagram to keep it from becoming too cluttered. Also, as mentioned earlier in this discussion, notice in the upper-left of the diagram that a grouping of computers was used instead of showing all 12 of the Seattle users' computers. This simplifies the drawing without sacrificing too much detail. If more detail is needed, specifically on the Seattle office, a new end-system network topology diagram could be created specifically for that office.

Well, after what seems like an eternity, you have completed your network configuration tables, network topology diagrams, end-system network configuration tables, and end-system network topology diagrams! Now you just have to make sure that you keep them accessible and update them anytime there is a change in the network. Also, remember to print hard copies regularly, so that you will still have your documentation if the network is down.

Troubleshooting End-System Problems

In a perfect world, network administrators would be free to work solely on the network components of the system, and the end-systems would be taken care of by someone else. The reality is that we do not live in such a place, so network administrators frequently must help troubleshoot problems on the end systems. Th assistance provided may be simply checking connectivity, or it may involve the complete rebuilding of the end system! We are not going to get into the rebuilding of a Windows server from scratch—here in this section we will see how to diagnose what is happening on an end system, and how to take some simple corrective actions when they are needed.

In addition to running these commands directly, you can also have the end user run many of these commands for you and tell you the results. This can be very helpful, especially when the users are located in a remote location.

Some of the commands examined in this section are variations of the ones used in creating the end-system documentation; others are new. But before we look at how to identify and correct problems, we will spend a little more time on how to approach the problem.

Troubleshooting by Layer

In Chapter 1, a couple of troubleshooting approaches were discussed. Specifically these approaches involved identifying the endpoints of the problem and working from one side or the other, or starting at a midpoint and working toward the endpoints. While this works for linear problems, system misbehavior that affects multiple people in dispersed locations doesn't necessarily fit into this troubleshooting model. Therefore, Cisco has started backing a new model of troubleshooting based on the layers of the OSI model. This model has three distinct approaches: bottom-up, top-down, and divide-and-conquer.

Bottom-Up Troubleshooting Approach

As the name implies, when you use the *bottom-up troubleshooting* approach, you start with the bottom, Physical layer of the OSI model and work your way up to the Application layer. This approach is used when you suspect the problem is at the Physical layer, or when you are troubleshooting a complex network problem. In these situations, ensuring that the core components required for networking are in place can go a long way toward isolating the problem.

The downside to bottom-up troubleshooting is that it can require the checking of each interface along the path to see if errors are occurring there. Depending on the length of the path from the endpoints of the problem, this process can be very time-consuming. In these cases, determining the most likely culprit based on the symptoms of the trouble can save a lot of time.

Top-Down Troubleshooting Approach

If you suspect that the problem lies in a piece of software, then *top-down troubleshooting* should be used. You start by testing the application and work down the OSI layers to find the source of the problem. The challenge to this type of troubleshooting is that you need to check all the user's network applications in order to find the one that is causing the errors. This is a potentially time-consuming troubleshooting method if there are a large number of applications that could be the source of the trouble.

Divide-and-Conquer Troubleshooting Approach

The *divide-and-conquer troubleshooting* approach allows you to select the specific layer (Data Link, Network, or Transport) of the OSI model in which to begin troubleshooting. You make your selection based on experience with similar problems in the past, along with the specific symptoms of the current trouble. After selecting the layer you wish to start with, the next task is to determine the direction of the problem by determining whether the problem exists at, above, or below this layer. Most commonly this is done by studying output from the IOS commands on the router or through analysis of the output of network management tools. Once the direction of the problem is determined, you continue troubleshooting through the OSI model in that direction until you isolate the difficulty.

Often you can check the first four layers (Physical through Transport) by using the traceroute command.

End-System Troubleshooting Commands

As was shown in the section "Creating an End-System Network Configuration Table," there are many occasions when you need to execute commands on the end system in order to get a clear picture of what is going on in the network. This is true not only for the discovery of network information but also for the troubleshooting of network behavior. Since the basic commands used for discovery were discussed earlier in the chapter, here in this section we will focus specifically on the troubleshooting commands. You will notice that many of the same commands are used for both troubleshooting and discovery.

In this section, the Unix versions of the commands are used for the Unix, Linux, and Mac X end-system types. There can be slight variations between the Unix and the Linux/Mac X versions of the commands. However, most are very similar and in some cases identical to their UNIX counterparts.

Ping

The `ping` command was covered in some detail earlier in the chapter, so you can refer back to the section "Creating an End-System Network Configuration Table" for the ping basics. Here we will focus on some of the options available under the `ping` command that are helpful in your troubleshooting activities.

One of the most common ping options is the continuous ping. These pings send a continuous stream of packets to the destination address. Setting up a continuous ping to an end-system that is having connectivity problems is a good way to see when the end-system is once again reachable over the network. In Windows systems, the flag to send a continuous ping is `-t`, and in the UNIX environment it is `-s`.

Another frequently used ping option used for troubleshooting is the record route option. This records the path the packet is taking through the network and stores this information in the IP header of the ping packet.

The record route option does require that the intervening routers and the end station retain this information in the packet, and the hop count is limited to nine.

In a Windows station, record route can be enabled with the `-r # of hops to record` option. In the following example, the route will be recorded for up to nine hops, which is the maximum value allowed.

```
C:\>ping -r 9 10.5.5.5

Pinging 10.5.5.5 with 32 bytes of data:

Reply from 10.5.5.5: bytes=32 time=86ms TTL=251
    Route: 10.45.45.1 ->
           10.10.10.66 ->
           10.5.5.1 ->
           10.5.5.5 ->
           10.16.16.18 ->
           10.10.9.56 ->
           10.10.7.23 ->
           10.56.21.3
Reply from 10.5.5.5: bytes=32 time=86ms TTL=251
    Route: 10.45.45.1 ->
           10.10.10.66 ->
           10.5.5.1 ->
           10.5.5.5 ->
           10.16.16.18 ->
           10.10.9.56 ->
```

```
                 10.10.7.23 ->
                 10.56.21.3
Reply from 10.5.5.5: bytes=32 time=85ms TTL=251
       Route: 10.45.45.1 ->
                 10.10.10.66 ->
                 10.5.5.1 ->
                 10.5.5.5 ->
                 10.16.16.18 ->
                 10.10.9.56 ->
                 10.10.7.23 ->
                 10.56.21.3
Reply from 10.5.5.5: bytes=32 time=83ms TTL=251
       Route: 10.45.45.1 ->
                 10.10.10.66 ->
                 10.5.5.1 ->
                 10.5.5.5 ->
                 10.16.16.18 ->
                 10.10.9.56 ->
                 10.10.7.23 ->
                 10.56.21.3


Ping statistics for 10.5.5.5:
     Packets: Sent = 4, Received = 4, Lost = 0 (0% loss),
Approximate round trip times in milli-seconds:
     Minimum = 83ms, Maximum = 86ms, Average = 85ms
```

In Unix, the similar command option for record route is as follows:

```
unix1% ping -s -nRv 10.5.5.5
PING 10.5.5.5 (10.5.5.5): 56 data bytes
64 bytes from 10.5.5.5: icmp_seq=0. time=123. ms
  IP options:  <record route> 10.45.45.1, 10.10.10.66, 10.5.5.1,
    10.5.5.5, 10.16.16.18, 10.10.9.56, 10.10.7.23,
10.56.21.3
```

Trace Route

Similar to the record route option of the ping command, the trace route command is used to determine the path that the packet is taking through the network. However, trace route uses a different approach than the ping command. Specifically, the trace route command starts by sending out a packet with a Time to Live (TTL) of 1. The TTL of this packet will expire at the first router, and therefore this device will send back a TTL expiration message. The address from which the TTL expiration comes is then recorded, and a second packet is sent out with a TTL of 2. The second-hop router then replies back with a TTL expiration message. This process continues until the destination is reached.

The trace route command operates in the Unix and Windows environment in the same manner as the `trace` command in the Cisco router.

 Though the functionality is the same, it is worthy of note that in the Cisco and the Unix versions of trace route, a UDP packet on port 33434 is used for the tracing, whereas Windows stations use an ICMP echo instead.

In Windows, the syntax for the trace route command is `tracert`. The options for the command are shown in the following output, which is followed by a sample trace.

```
C:\>tracert /?

Usage: tracert [-d] [-h maximum_hops] [-j host-list] [-w timeout] target_name

Options:
    -d                 Do not resolve addresses to hostnames.
    -h maximum_hops    Maximum number of hops to search for target.
    -j host-list       Loose source route along host-list.
    -w timeout         Wait timeout milliseconds for each reply.




C:\>tracert 10.5.5.5

Tracing route to 10.5.5.5 over a maximum of 30 hops

    1      7 ms      1 ms      1 ms   10.21.2.1
    2     84 ms     83 ms     84 ms   10.45.45.3
    3     88 ms     85 ms     83 ms   10.10.10.67
    4     87 ms     86 ms     88 ms   10.5.5.5

Trace complete.
```

When looking at the above trace, there are a couple things to note. First, Windows by default sends out three traces for each TTL value. The times listed to the left of the IP address are the times for each of the TTL expiration messages from these packets to return.

Also, when comparing the output from a recorded ping to the output of the trace route command, be aware of a couple of noteworthy differences. Ping records the exiting interface on the router, whereas trace route in general records the interface on which you enter. Another difference is that when using a trace route, you only get the path taken to the end device; you do not see the return path.

As is the case with many of the commands discussed here, there is some subtle difference between Unix and Windows in terms of both syntax and output. Here are the Unix command options and a sample output:

```
unix1% traceroute
Usage: traceroute [-dFInvx] [-f first_ttl] [-g gateway | -r] [-i iface]
        [-m max_ttl] [-p port] [-q nqueries] [-s src_addr] [-t tos]
        [-w waittime] host [packetlen]
unix1% traceroute 10.5.5.5
traceroute to 10.5.5.5 (10.5.5.5), 30 hops max, 40 byte packets
 1   10.21.2.1 (10.21.2.1)  1.046 ms  1.878 ms  1.880 ms
 2   10.45.45.3 (10.45.45.3)  82.487 ms  84.850 ms  83.378 ms
 3   10.10.10.67 (10.10.10.67)  84.196 ms  86.057 ms  84.105 ms
 4   10.5.5.5 (10.5.5.5)  89.133 ms  88.664 ms  88.597 ms
unix1%
```

The *arp* Command

Although the arp command was covered in the earlier discovery section, as well, it is being repeated here because it can be a very meaningful part of the troubleshooting process. As is the case on the routers, sometimes it is necessary to verify that the Layer-2-to-Layer-3 translation is working as expected on the end system. In both Unix and Windows NT/2000/XP systems, the command to display this information is arp -a. The command options and sample output from an XP box are as follows:

```
C:\>arp /?

Displays and modifies the IP-to-Physical address translation tables
used by address resolution protocol (ARP).

ARP -s inet_addr eth_addr [if_addr]
ARP -d inet_addr [if_addr]
ARP -a [inet_addr] [-N if_addr]

  -a          Displays current ARP entries by interrogating the
              current protocol data.  If inet_addr is specified,
              the IP and Physical addresses for only the specified
              computer are displayed.  If more than one network
              interface uses ARP, entries for each ARP table are
              displayed.
```

-g	Same as -a.
inet_addr	Specifies an internet address.
-N if_addr	Displays the ARP entries for the network interface specified by if_addr.
-d	Deletes the host specified by inet_addr. inet_addr may be wildcarded with * to delete all hosts.
-s	Adds the host and associates the Internet address inet_addr with the Physical address eth_addr. The Physical address is given as 6 hexadecimal bytes separated by hyphens. The entry is permanent.
eth_addr	Specifies a physical address.
if_addr	If present, this specifies the Internet address of the interface whose address translation table should be modified. If not present, the first applicable interface will be used.

```
Example:
  > arp -s 157.55.85.212   00-aa-00-62-c6-09  .... Adds a static entry.
  > arp -a                                    .... Displays the arp table.
```

```
C:\>arp -a

Interface: 10.12.1.11 --- 0x2
  Internet Address        Physical Address      Type
  10.12.1.1               00-06-5a-23-06-f9     dynamic
```

Similar output from a UNIX machine is shown below.

```
unix1% arp
Usage: arp hostname
       arp -a
       arp -d hostname
       arp -s hostname ether_addr [temp] [pub] [trail]
       arp -f filename
```

```
unix1% arp -a
Net to Media Table
Device  IP Address              Mask            Flags   Phys Addr
------  --------------------    ---------------  -----   ---------------
hme0    10.12.1.1               255.255.255.255          00:06:5a:23:06:f9
hme0    10.12.1.68              255.255.255.255          00:04:f2:cd:65:1f
hme0    224.0.0.0               240.0.0.0        SM      01:00:5e:00:00:00
```

In addition to displaying information about the translation from Layer 2 to Layer 3, the arp command can also be used to add and delete entries to the ARP table.

The *route* Command

If an end station has multiple interfaces, it can be useful to know which of these interfaces is being used for particular destinations. In theses cases, for both Windows NT/2000/XP stations and UNIX stations, you can use the route command. Following are the options and the syntax for displaying the routing table for NT/2000/XP:

```
C:\>route /?

Manipulates network routing tables.

ROUTE [-f] [-p] [command [destination] [MASK netmask]   [gateway]
[METRIC metric]  [IF interface]

  -f          Clears the routing tables of all gateway entries.  If
              this is used in conjunction with one of the commands,
              the tables are cleared prior to running the command.
  -p          When used with the ADD command, makes a route persistent
              across boots of the system. By default, routes are
              not preserved when the system is restarted. Ignored
              for all other commands, which always affect the
              appropriate persistent routes. This option is not
              supported in Windows 95.
  command     One of these:
                PRINT     Prints  a route
                ADD       Adds    a route
                DELETE    Deletes a route
                CHANGE    Modifies an existing route
  destination Specifies the host.
  MASK        Specifies that the next parameter is the 'netmask'
  value.
  netmask     Specifies a subnet mask value for this route entry.
              If not specified, it defaults to 255.255.255.255.
  gateway     Specifies gateway.
  interface   the interface number for the specified route.
  METRIC      specifies the metric, ie. cost for the destination.

All symbolic names used for destination are looked up in the network
Database file NETWORKS. The symbolic names for gateway are looked up in
the host name database file HOSTS.
```

If the command is PRINT or DELETE. Destination or gateway can be a wildcard, (wildcard is specified as a star '*'), or the gateway argument may be omitted.

If Dest contains a * or ?, it is treated as a shell pattern, and only matching destination routes are printed. The '*' matches any string, and '?' matches any one char. Examples: 157.*.1, 157.*, 127.*, *224*.
Diagnostic Notes:
     Invalid MASK generates an error, that is when (DEST & MASK) != DEST.
     Example> route ADD 157.0.0.0 MASK 155.0.0.0 157.55.80.1 IF 1
            The route addition failed: The specified mask parameter is
  invalid.
(Destination & Mask) != Destination.

Examples:

```
> route PRINT
> route ADD 157.0.0.0 MASK 255.0.0.0  157.55.80.1 METRIC 3 IF 2
        destination^      ^mask     ^gateway    metric^    ^
                                                     Interface^
```
     If IF is not given, it tries to find the best interface for a given gateway.
```
> route PRINT
> route PRINT 157*         .... Only prints those matching 157*
> route CHANGE 157.0.0.0 MASK 255.0.0.0 157.55.80.5 METRIC 2 IF 2
  CHANGE is used to modify gateway and/or metric only.
> route PRINT
> route DELETE 157.0.0.0
> route PRINT
```

C:\>**route print**
```
===============================================================
Interface List
0x1 ......................... MS TCP Loopback interface
0x2 ... 00 04 f2 cd 65 1f...... NVIDIA nForce MCP Networking Adapter - Packet
Scheduler Miniport
===============================================================
===============================================================
```

```
Active Routes:
Network Destination        Netmask          Gateway       Interface   Metric
          0.0.0.0          0.0.0.0        10.12.1.1      10.12.1.11     20
        127.0.0.0        255.0.0.0        127.0.0.1       127.0.0.1      1
       10.12.1.0    255.255.255.0       10.12.1.11      10.12.1.11     20
      10.12.1.11  255.255.255.255        127.0.0.1       127.0.0.1     20
     10.12.1.255  255.255.255.255       10.12.1.11      10.12.1.11     20
        224.0.0.0        240.0.0.0       10.12.1.11      10.12.1.11     20
  255.255.255.255 255.255.255.255       10.12.1.11      10.12.1.11      1
Default Gateway:           10.12.1.1
===========================================================================
```

Persistent Routes:
  None

For the Unix side of things, the options and sample printout are as follows:

```
unix1% route
usage: route [ -fnqv ] cmd [[ -<qualifers> ] args ]
unix1% route -n
Kernel IP routing table
Destination   Gateway       Genmask         Flags Metric Ref     Use Iface
10.12.1.0     0.0.0.0       255.255.255.0   U     0      0         0 hme0
127.0.0.0     0.0.0.0       255.0.0.0       U     0      0         0 lo
0.0.0.0       10.12.1.1     0.0.0.0         UG    0      0         0 hme0
```

In addition to printing out the routing table, the route command can also be used to add or delete static routes if they are needed.

The *netstat* Command

The netstat command is used to display current connections to the end system. This can be useful in a troubleshooting scenario to assist in the verification of connectivity. In addition to the IP addresses of the connections, the netstat command also shows the port the connections are using. The Windows NT/2000/XP options and sample output of the command are shown here:

C:\>**netstat /?**

```
Displays protocol statistics and current TCP/IP network connections.

NETSTAT [-a] [-e] [-n] [-o] [-s] [-p proto] [-r] [interval]

  -a          Displays all connections and listening ports.
  -e          Displays Ethernet statistics. This may be combined with
              the -s option.
```

-n   Displays addresses and port numbers in numerical form.

-o   Displays the owning process ID associated with each connection.

-p proto   Shows connections for the protocol specified by proto; proto may be any of: TCP, UDP, TCPv6, or UDPv6. If used with the -s option to display per-protocol statistics, proto may be any of: IP, IPv6, ICMP, ICMPv6, TCP, TCPv6, UDP, or UDPv6.

-r   Displays the routing table.

-s   Displays per-protocol statistics. By default, statistics are shown for IP, IPv6, ICMP, ICMPv6, TCP, TCPv6, UDP, and UDPv6; the -p option may be used to specify a subset of the default.

interval   Redisplays selected statistics, pausing interval seconds between each display. Press CTRL+C to stop redisplaying statistics. If omitted, netstat will print the current configuration information once.

```
C:\>netstat -n
```

Active Connections

```
  Proto  Local Address          Foreign Address        State
  TCP    10.12.1.11:3718        10.215.198.192:80      ESTABLISHED
  TCP    10.12.1.11:3719        10.215.198.153:80      ESTABLISHED
  TCP    10.12.1.11:3722        10.215.198.6:80        ESTABLISHED
  TCP    10.12.1.11:3724        10.12.1.100:139        ESTABLISHED
  TCP    10.12.1.11:3726        10.255.37.1:23         ESTABLISHED
```

The Unix version of the command is very similar to the Windows version. Its options and sample output are as follows:

```
unix1% netstat -help
usage: netstat [-adgimnprsDMv] [-I interface] [interval]
unix1% netstat -n
```

```
TCP
   Local Address      Remote Address    Swind Send-Q Rwind Recv-Q State
   ----------------- ----------------- ----- ------ ----- ------ ------
   10.4.132.58.32891 10.4.132.58.162   57344     0 57344     0 ESTAB
```

```
10.4.132.58.162      10.4.132.58.32891  57344      0 57344      0 ESTAB
10.4.132.58.53074    10.4.128.10.1960   24820      0 8760       0 ESTAB
10.4.132.58.38090    10.104.108.13.1960 62780      0 8760       0 ESTAB
...
...
<output removed>
```

The *ipconfig* Command

In the "Creating an End-System Network Configuration Table" section, we introduced the ipconfig command used with the /all option. While this option is useful for gathering information on a system, other options in the ipconfig command are helpful for troubleshooting purposes.

The first of these options are the /release and /renew options, which are used to release and renew DHCP addresses. Following are examples:

```
C:\>ipconfig /release

Windows IP Configuration


Ethernet adapter Local Area Connection:

        Connection-specific DNS Suffix  . :
        IP Address. . . . . . . . . . . : 0.0.0.0
        Subnet Mask . . . . . . . . . . : 0.0.0.0
        Default Gateway . . . . . . . . :

C:\WINDOWS\system32>ipconfig /renew

Windows IP Configuration


Ethernet adapter Local Area Connection:

        Connection-specific DNS Suffix  . :
        IP Address. . . . . . . . . . . : 10.22.5.3
        Subnet Mask . . . . . . . . . . : 255.255.255.0
        Default Gateway . . . . . . . . : 10.22.5.1
```

The next option useful in troubleshooting is the /displaydns option. It allows you to see the DNS-name-to-IP-address cache that is on the workstation. The following output is from an XP machine right after pinging www.cisco.com.

C:\>ipconfig /displaydns

```
Windows IP Configuration

        ns1.cisco.com
        ----------------------------------------
        Record Name . . . . . : ns1.cisco.com
        Record Type . . . . . : 1
        Time To Live  . . . . : 86227
        Data Length . . . . . : 4
        Section . . . . . . . : Answer
        A (Host) Record . . . : 128.107.241.185


        1.0.0.127.in-addr.arpa
        ----------------------------------------
        Record Name . . . . . : 1.0.0.127.in-addr.arpa.
        Record Type . . . . . : 12
        Time To Live  . . . . : 0
        Data Length . . . . . : 4
        Section . . . . . . . : Answer
        PTR Record  . . . . . : localhost


        ns2.cisco.com
        ----------------------------------------
        Record Name . . . . . : ns2.cisco.com
        Record Type . . . . . : 1
        Time To Live  . . . . : 86227
        Data Length . . . . . : 4
        Section . . . . . . . : Answer
        A (Host) Record . . . : 192.135.250.69


        www.cisco.com
```

```
-----------------------------------------
Record Name . . . . . : www.cisco.com
Record Type . . . . . : 1
Time To Live  . . . . : 86227
Data Length . . . . . : 4
Section . . . . . . . : Answer
A (Host) Record . . . : 198.133.219.25


Record Name . . . . . : ns1.cisco.com
Record Type . . . . . : 1
Time To Live  . . . . : 86227
Data Length . . . . . : 4
Section . . . . . . . : Additional
A (Host) Record . . . : 128.107.241.185


Record Name . . . . . : ns2.cisco.com
Record Type . . . . . : 1
Time To Live  . . . . : 86227
Data Length . . . . . : 4
Section . . . . . . . : Additional
A (Host) Record . . . : 192.135.250.69


localhost
-----------------------------------------
Record Name . . . . . : localhost
Record Type . . . . . : 1
Time To Live  . . . . : 0
Data Length . . . . . : 4
Section . . . . . . . : Answer
A (Host) Record . . . : 127.0.0.1
```

WARNING   In addition to the local DNS cache on the machine, Internet Explorer keeps its own name-resolution cache. By default, names are cached in Internet Explorer versions 4.0 or higher for 30 minutes, and for 24 hours in IE versions below 4.0. Shutting down Internet Explorer and restarting it will refresh this cache.

The final option for the `ipconfig` command that we will review is `/flushdns`, which is complementary to the `/displaydns` option. The `/flushdns` option clears out all entries in the DNS cache on the workstation. This works out well for troubleshooting stale DNS entries. The output of the command is shown here:

```
C:\>ipconfig /flushdns

Windows IP Configuration

Successfully flushed the DNS Resolver Cache.


C:\>
```

The *nbtstat* Command

As was touched on earlier, Windows systems can also use WINS (NetBIOS) to resolve names into IP addresses. In these cases the `ipconfig /displaydns` command will not show these associations. In order to view this information you need to use the `nbtstat` command. The options that are available for this command are:

```
C:\>nbtstat /?

Displays protocol statistics and current TCP/IP connections using NBT
(NetBIOS over TCP/IP).

NBTSTAT [ [-a RemoteName] [-A IP address] [-c] [-n]
        [-r] [-R] [-RR] [-s] [-S] [interval] ]

  -a  (adapter status) Lists the remote machine's name table given its
                name
  -A  (Adapter status) Lists the remote machine's name table given its
                        IP address.
  -c  (cache)          Lists NBT's cache of remote [machine] names and
                        their IP addresses
  -n  (names)          Lists local NetBIOS names.
  -r  (resolved)       Lists names resolved by broadcast and via WINS
  -R  (Reload)         Purges and reloads the remote cache name table
  -S  (Sessions)       Lists sessions table with the destination IP
                        addresses
  -s  (sessions)       Lists sessions table converting destination IP
                         addresses to computer NETBIOS names.
```

```
-RR   (ReleaseRefresh) Sends Name Release packets to WINS and then,
                        starts Refresh
RemoteName   Remote host machine name.
IP address   Dotted decimal representation of the IP address.
interval     Redisplays selected statistics, pausing interval seconds
             between each display. Press Ctrl+C to stop redisplaying
             statistics.
```

The two options that you will most likely use in a troubleshooting situation are the -c and -R options. The -c option is used to display the current name resolution cache and the -R option is used to clear this cache. Sample output from both of these commands is given below.

C:\>**nbtstat -c**

```
Local Area Connection:
Node IpAddress: [10.1.1.1] Scope Id: []

             NetBIOS Remote Cache Name Table

        Name           Type     Host Address   Life [sec]
    ---------------------------------------------------------
        MICHELE   <20>  UNIQUE   10.2.2.2          570
        NERMAL    <20>  UNIQUE   10.100.100.100    580
        NERMAL    <00>  UNIQUE   10.100.100.100    575
        PICASO    <42>  UNIQUE   10.8.8.8          415
        ALEX      <20>  UNIQUE   10.9.9.9          582
        LEAH      <20>  UNIQUE   10.10.10.10       492
```

```
\Device\NetBT_Tcpip_{D84EDBA9-F40F-4AFF-8409-24613C6A325B}:
C:\> nbtstat -R
    Successful purge and preload of the NBT Remote Cache Name Table.
```

Summary

End-system documentation is just as important as the network documentation in terms of the overall documentation strategy. The two main components that make up end-system documentation are the end-system network configuration table and the end-system network topology table.

End-system network configuration tables are documents that show the key configuration parameters in place on the end-systems in the network. Some of the common items in an end-system network configuration table are the system name, system manufacturer/model, CPU speed, RAM, storage, system purpose, media type, interface speed, VLAN, IP address, default gateway, subnet mask, WINS, DNS, operating system (including version), network-based applications, high-bandwidth applications, and low-latency applications. The specific items included on the end-system network configuration table depend on the purpose of the documentation. In most cases, the end-system table is kept in a spreadsheet or database format. As is the case with all the documentation covered in this book, be sure to keep hard copies of the documents to use in the event of a network outage.

End-system network topology diagrams are graphical representations of the end systems in the network. In many cases, they are just additions to the network topology diagram; however, they can be their own entity. The data included in an end-system network topology diagram is usually a small subset of that maintained in the end-system network configuration tables. The topology diagrams are meant to make the network administrator better able to visualize the path across the network. Some of the standard items that go into an end-system network topology are system name, connection to the network, system purpose, VLAN, IP address, subnet mask, and network applications.

Having a well-defined troubleshooting strategy can greatly reduce the amount of time it takes to define and fix a problem in the network end systems. One approach to accomplishing this goal is troubleshooting by OSI layer. With this method, troubleshooting is done either from the Physical layer of the OSI model up, which is the bottom-up approach; or from the Application layer down, which is the top-down approach; or by selecting a layer in the middle based on prior experience with the problem, which is the divide-and-conquer approach. Bottom-up troubleshooting is used most often when the problem is believed to be at the Physical layer, or when the problem is complex. The top-down approach is used when the problem is believed to be a software issue. The divide-and-conquer method is appropriate in instances where the troubleshooter has seen similar problems in the past and has a good idea at which OSI level the problem is occurring.

Finally, in this chapter we covered a number of commands that can be used to effectively troubleshoot problems on end-systems. These commands include `ping` and its record route option, trace route, `arp`, `route`, `nbtstat`, `netstat`, and `ipconfig`. All of these commands have Windows NT/2000/XP and UNIX equivalents, and most have a direct relationship to a Cisco IOS command.

Exam Essentials

Know what end-system network configuration tables are and the information they contain. End-system network configuration tables are used to record key settings of end systems in the network. Items commonly included in a network configuration table are system name, system manufacturer/model, CPU speed, RAM, storage, system purpose, media type, interface speed, VLAN, IP address, default gateway, subnet mask, WINS, DNS, operating system (including version), network-based applications, high-bandwidth applications, and low-latency applications.

Know what end-system network topology diagrams are and the information they contain. End-system network topology diagrams are graphical representations of the network and are usually built with many of the same components as the end-system network configuration tables. Some common components of the network topology diagram are system name, connection to the network, system purpose, VLAN, IP address, subnet mask, and network applications.

Understand the layer-based troubleshooting approach.   This troubleshooting approach is based on the layers of the OSI model. The methodologies used in this approach are known as bottom-up, top-down, and divide-and-conquer.

Know the commands to discover information and troubleshoot end systems.   There are Unix and Windows versions of the discovery and troubleshooting commands, and many of them correlate directly to Cisco IOS commands. Some of these commands are `arp`, `ifconfig`, `ipconfig`, `netstat`, `ping`, `route`, `telnet`, and the trace route command.

Commands Used in This Chapter

The following list contains a summary of all the commands used in this chapter.

Commands	Descriptions
`arp`	Can be used on Unix- and Windows-based machines. Reports the Layer-3-to-Layer-2 translations being used by the end system.
`cat /etc/ resolv.conf`	Unix-based command that displays the contents of the `resolv.conf` file. This file is used to define the DNS settings for the end system.
`ifconfig`	Unix-based command that lets you view and set interface configurations.
`ipconfig`	Windows (specifically NT/2000/XP)–based command that is used to view interface and DNS configurations.
`netstat`	Can be used on Unix- and Windows-based machines. Displays current network connection information.
`ping`	Can be used on Unix- and Windows-based machines. Verifies network connectivity with an ICMP packet.
`route`	Can be used on Unix- and Windows-based machines. Displays the current routing information on the machine.
`telnet`	Can be used on Unix- and Windows-based machines. Establishes terminal access to end systems.
`traceroute`	Unix-based trace route command.
`tracert`	Windows-based trace route command.
`winipcfg`	Windows 9x and Windows ME command that is used to view interface and DNS configurations.
`nbtstat`	Windows command that is used to view the current NetBIOS over TCP/IP name-translation table.

Key Terms

Before you take the exam, be certain you are familiar with the following terms:

bottom-up troubleshooting

divide-and-conquer troubleshooting

end-system network configuration table

end-system network topology diagram

top-down troubleshooting

Review Questions

1. What are the two items that are required as part of an end-system network topology diagram? (Choose two.)

    A. Contact information

    B. IP addresses

    C. Routing protocols

    D. Device names

    E. IOS version

    F. Connections between devices

2. An interface is incrementing CRCs and throwing FCS errors. Which troubleshooting approach would be the optimal one to use to address this issue?

    A. Bottom-up

    B. Top-down

    C. Divide-and-conquer

    D. Hunt and peck

3. What Windows NT command shows the DNS servers that are configured on the system?

    A. `ipconfig`

    B. `ipconfig /all`

    C. `ifconfig`

    D. `ifconfig /all`

4. What command on a Windows 95 system will show the default gateway the machine is using?

    A. `ipconfig`

    B. `arp -a`

    C. `winipcfg`

    D. `netstat`

5. What Unix command shows the DNS servers that are configured?

    A. `ipconfig /all`

    B. `ifconfig -a`

    C. `cat /etc/resolv.conf`

    D. `netstat`

6. What Windows XP command shows IP addresses and ports of all connections to an end system?

   A. `ipconfig /all`

   B. `ifconfig -a`

   C. `route connection`

   D. `netstat`

7. Which of these Windows 2000 commands would be most appropriate to use in order to see the network path a packet takes to get to a Unix server?

   A. `ping`

   B. `trace`

   C. `tracert`

   D. `traceroute`

8. A user is experiencing a problem with an application. All other applications on the desktop are working fine. Some of the other desktop applications use the same server as the nonfunctioning application. Which troubleshooting approach is the optimal one to use to address this issue?

   A. Bottom-up

   B. Top-down

   C. Divide-and-conquer

   D. Reboot and hope

9. What Unix command shows IP addresses and ports of all connections to an end system?

   A. `ipconfig /all`

   B. `ifconfig -a`

   C. `route connection`

   D. `netstat`

10. Which of the following are parts of an end-system network configuration table? (Choose three.)

    A. IP address

    B. System name

    C. Routing Protocols

    D. VLAN

    E. VTP State

11. What XP command shows the IP-to-MAC-addresses translation table on an end system?

    A. `show mac`

    B. `arp -a`

    C. `ipconfig`

    D. `ifconfig`

12. Which of the following are *not* parts of an end-system network topology diagram? (Choose two.)

   A. IP address

   B. Access list

   C. Interface state

   D. System names

   E. System purpose

13. What Windows NT command has an option that allows for the termination of a DHCP lease and the returning of the DHCP address to the available DHCP pool on an end-system?

   A. ifconfig

   B. ipconfig

   C. route

   D. arp

14. What Unix command allows you to gather information about the configuration of an interface?

   A. ifconfig -a

   B. ifconfig /all

   C. ipconfig -a

   D. ipconfig /all

15. What command can be used to verify that a server is listening on a given TCP port?

   A. arp

   B. route

   C. telnet

   D. traceroute

16. You have two workstations on a particular segment. One workstation is a Unix end-system, and the other is running Windows XP. You are able to ping a Windows 2000 server on another segment from both end systems, and you are able to trace route from the XP end system to the server. The trace route from the Unix machine makes it halfway to the server and then starts failing. At what OSI layer would you start troubleshooting this problem?

   A. Physical

   B. Data Link

   C. Network

   D. Transport

   E. Session

   F. Presentation

   G. Application

17. What command on a Windows 2000 end system will display the current routing information?

    A. `route print`

    B. `route -n`

    C. `print route`

    D. `route show`

18. You are working on a Unix system and want to set up a continuous ping to a server with the IP address 10.1.1.2. What command will do this?

    A. `ping -t 10.1.1.2`

    B. `ping 10.1.1.2`

    C. `ping -s 10.1.1.2`

    D. `ping -c 10.1.1.2`

19. Which command will verify Layer 4 connectivity to a server?

    A. `ping`

    B. `ipconfig`

    C. `telnet`

    D. `ifconfig`

20. How often should the end-system topology diagram be updated?

    A. Once a week

    B. Once a month

    C. Once a year

    D. Whenever there is a change in the network

Answers to Review Questions

1. D, F. In its simplest form, an end-system network topology diagram contains only the devices names (representing the devices) and the connections between them.

2. A. Cyclic Redundancy Checks (CRCs) and Frame Check Sequence (FCS) errors are usually indicative of a physical problem. Therefore, the bottom-up approach would be most appropriate in this scenario.

3. B. For a Windows NT end-system, the `ipconfig /all` command tells you about the configured DNS servers.

4. C. The `winipcfg` command brings up a GUI that will display the default gateway information.

5. C. The `cat /etc/resolv.conf` command will show the contents of the `resolv.conf` file, which is where DNS information is stored on a Unix end-system.

6. D. The `netstat` command shows the IP addresses and ports for all connections to an XP end system.

7. C. On a Windows 2000 machine, the appropriate trace route command is `tracert`. Though `ping -r` may work, `tracert` is more appropriate to get you the network path to a Unix server.

8. B. Because only a single application is experiencing difficulty, it is most likely an application problem. Therefore, the top-down approach is most appropriate.

9. D. The `netstat` command is used on both Windows and Unix systems to investigate the connections to an end system.

10. A, B, D. The routing protocol and VTP state are part of the network configuration table, but not the end-system network configuration table.

11. B. The `arp -a` command gives you shows IP-to-MAC-address translation information.

12. B, C. Neither access lists nor interface state resets are on end-system network topology diagrams.

13. B. The `ipconfig /release` command will terminate a DHCP lease and return the DHCP address to the available DHCP pool on an end-system.

14. A. The `ifconfig -a` command will show information about the interfaces configured on the end system.

15. C. The `telnet` command lets you verify whether a server is listening on a given port.

16. D. Since the ping went through successfully, you can safely assume that the Network layer and everything below it is working correctly. Since Windows end systems use ICMP for trace route and Unix uses UDP, there is a good possibility that an extended access list is limiting UDP traffic in the network path.

17. A. The `route print` command shows the current routing information on a Windows 2000 end system.

18. C. In the Unix environment, the `-s` option is used to set up a continuous ping. The `-t` option is used in a Windows environment.

19. C. Ping only verifies that there is Layer 3 connectivity. Telnet can verify up to Layer 4.

20. D. The end-system documentation should be updated at the same time the network documentation is updated, anytime there is a change in the network.

Chapter 4

Protocol Attributes

EXAM TOPICS COVERED IN THIS CHAPTER INCLUDE:

- ✓ Verify network connectivity.
- ✓ Use the optimal troubleshooting approach in resolving network problems.
- ✓ Minimize downtime during troubleshooting.
- ✓ Use Cisco IOS commands to identify problems.
- ✓ Determine the layer or layers on which a problem is occurring.

As you know, to successfully troubleshoot network problems, it is important to have a good understanding of how network components, including PCs and servers, communicate with each other. Without this basic knowledge, troubleshooting a network problem is like trying to read a book in a foreign language. The information is there, but it just isn't comprehensible. Although the troubleshooting model discussed in Chapter 1 provides the method of retrieving all the necessary information, the data is useless without an understanding of the information presented.

This chapter is a review of the protocols used by Layers 2, 3, and 4 of the OSI model. We briefly review the seven layers of the OSI model, and then discuss how they communicate with one another. We then discuss Layer 2 and Layer 3 protocols. More-specific information on some of the material covered here can be found in later chapters and is cross-referenced here where appropriate.

The OSI Reference Model

This section is a review of the OSI model, which was originally discussed in *CCNA: Cisco Certified Network Associate Study Guide, 3rd ed.,* by Todd Lammle Sybex 2002. The *OSI model* (the Open Systems Interconnection reference model) is the template used to design applications or protocols that allow nonhomogenous computers or networks to communicate with one another. The ISO (International Organization for Standardization) developed the OSI model.

The OSI model consists of seven layers. Each layer communicates directly with its adjacent layers, as well as with the corresponding layer of the destination system (depicted in Figure 4.1). Communication between layers facilitates the transfer of data up and down the OSI model. Communication between the corresponding layers of the source system and the destination system enables two heterogeneous networks or computers to understand each other.

The OSI template defines the services and roles that each layer is to provide. Because each layer provides different services and functions, the layers need to communicate so that the data can be transmitted up and down the seven layers and onto the destination system. The following list summarizes the responsibility of each of the seven layers, starting from the Physical layer and working up to the Application layer:

Physical This layer sends and receives bits with values of 1s and 0s. The Physical layer is in charge of determining how it sends these values. If the physical connection between two machines is fiber optic, then the Physical layer has to use light to transmit the 1s and 0s. If the connection is electrical, then electrical signals are sent to represent the 1s and 0s.

Data-Link   This layer takes all the data that is accumulated as packets are handed from one layer to the next, and then packages it into frames. The Data-Link layer equates the Network layer address (IP address) to a data-link address, or MAC address, of the next hop. Once the physical address is known, the frame is sent to that address. The receiving interface uses the Data-Link layer to extract the packet from the frame, discards the frame, and then sends the packet up to the Network layer.

Network   This layer defines the topology of the network through the use of logical addressing. Routing protocols use this information to route packets.

Transport   This layer takes care of end-to-end communications. It is responsible for connection to the destination system, as well as packet segmentation and assembly. The Transport layer includes both connection-oriented and connectionless protocols (for example, TCP and UDP).

Session   This layer is responsible for coordinating communication among applications, which it does through dialog-control methods.

Presentation   This layer negotiates syntax, so it is responsible for the proper method of presenting the data to the Application layer. Some of the Presentation layer functions are compression/decompression and encryption/decryption of data.

FIGURE 4.1   OSI layer communication scheme

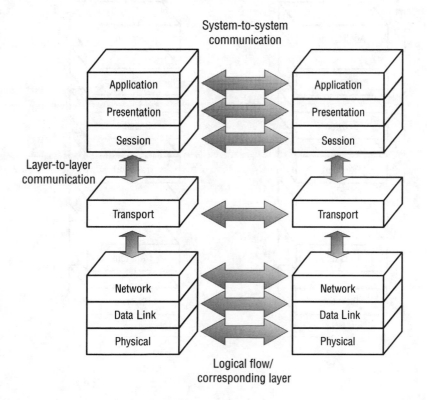

Application   This is the user and application interface. The Application layer is responsible for data exchange and job management. It also handles file, print, message, database, and application services.

You saw how the logical data flow of the OSI model works, but look at Figure 4.2, in which you can see the actual data flow. This figure depicts data that is handed from the Application layer all the way down to the Physical layer. At that point, the data is transmitted across any variety of physical media to the next hop, or destination system. Once the 1s and 0s arrive at the Physical layer of the destination system, the information is sent to Layer 2. This layer discards the frame, and then the extracted packet is handed up to the Network layer. The network packet header is stripped off, and the resulting packet is handed up to the Transport layer. This process is repeated for each layer until it arrives at the Application layer.

Now that each layer of the OSI reference model has been explained briefly, you need to focus on the functions of each layer in detail. This detail provides the necessary background and information to effectively troubleshoot network problems that occur within specific layers of the OSI model.

FIGURE 4.2   Data flow through the OSI model

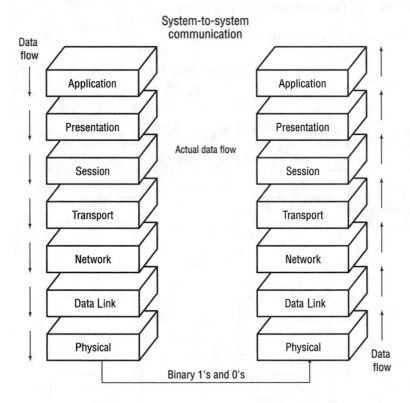

Global Protocol Classifications

As mentioned, each layer of the OSI model utilizes specific protocols that enable the layer to perform the necessary functions and communicate with adjacent layers. Each protocol has specific properties based on the functions that it needs to accomplish. Throughout all seven layers, there are two major protocol classifications: connection-oriented and connectionless.

Connection-Oriented Protocols

Connection-oriented protocols contain inherent functions that control the connection as well as data transfer. These functions are very detailed in the procedures that are followed to enable reliable and error-free data transfer. When a source open system needs to transfer data to a destination open system, the connection-oriented protocols actually establish a communication pipe. The *pipe,* as it is called here, is nothing more than a logical connection between two open systems. A great deal of information is used to establish this communication pipe, however.

In order to establish a connection, the two open systems must share certain information that allows them to negotiate terms and finally establish a link. The information includes the common protocol that will be used, required resources, and available resources. Look at Figure 4.3. This figure shows the steps taken as communication is established between two open systems when using TCP, a connection-oriented protocol.

The originating system first sends a connection request to the destination system. This request contains information that the two systems need to agree upon before the connection can be established. Some of the information includes the common protocol, protocol parameters, and required resources. *Protocol parameters* are the window sizes and other possible parameters. The *window size* is the amount of data that a station can transmit before needing an acknowledgment from the destination system that all the data was received without error, or that errors existed and part of the data will need to be retransmitted. *Required resources* can include necessary bandwidth, specific port numbers, and other network resources.

The destination system receives this connection request; if it can accommodate the common protocol, protocol attributes, and required resources, it replies with a connection accept. If, for some reason, the destination system cannot accommodate any of the requirements sent by the originating system, the destination system responds with a connection deny. A denied connection can result from a blocked port on the destination system, insufficient bandwidth between the systems, or other unavailable requested resources.

Assuming that a connection is established between the two systems, data and control information is exchanged during the life of the connection. This data exchange can be considered a *dialog.* First, the originating system sends data until the window size is reached. That system then waits for a response from the destination system. The destination system sends control information that informs the originating system what needs to happen next. The transmission can be an acknowledgment that all data in the transmission was received without error and that the originating system can send the next batch of data. In addition, the destination system can send a message informing the originating system that some of the data was missing, corrupted, or had other errors that require the data to be retransmitted.

FIGURE 4.3   Link establishment and data transfer using a connection-oriented protocol

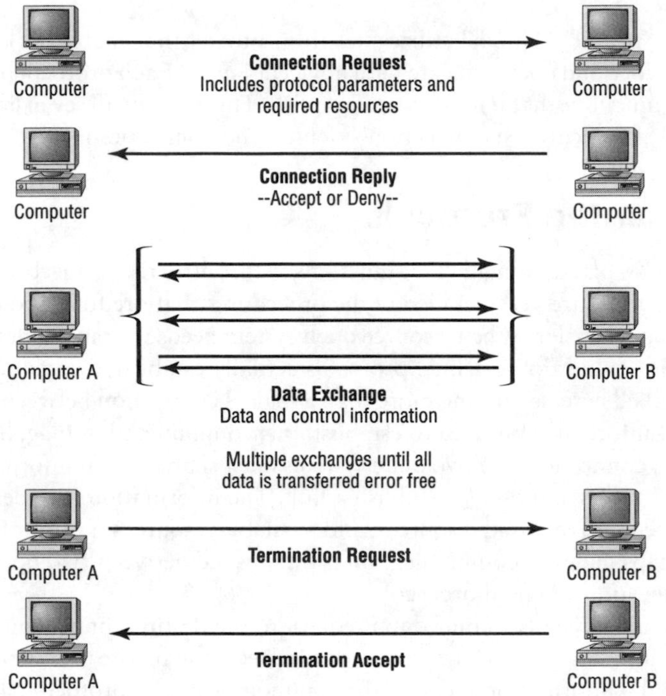

The foregoing procedure can be summarized with the description of three processes. You will learn more about each of these processes in the following sections.

Sequenced Data Transfer   Each packet of a session is assigned a sequence number.

Flow Control   Acknowledgments are required after a specified amount of data has been sent.

Error Control   Verification of contiguous and nonerroneous packets.

Sequenced Data Transfer

Systems send protocol data units (PDUs) to one another, and each level of the OSI model has its own type of PDU. Figure 4.4 shows the PDU names for all seven OSI layers. For example, the Application layer's PDU name is Layer 7 PDU. Although this convention can be used for all layers, some layers use other names as well. For instance, a Layer 3 PDU is called a *packet* and a Layer 2 PDU is called a *frame*. When a system sends data to another system, the data has to be fragmented so that it fits the MTU (maximum transmission unit). Therefore, several frames may be needed to transfer the original data. Connection-oriented protocols assign a sequence number to each outgoing and incoming PDU. This is *sequenced data transfer*.

Figure 4.5 shows you how sequencing works. There is a possibility that the destination system will receive the PDUs out of order. If this happens, the protocol on the destination system uses the sequence numbers to put the PDUs back into the correct order so that the original data is obtained.

FIGURE 4.4   OSI layer PDU names

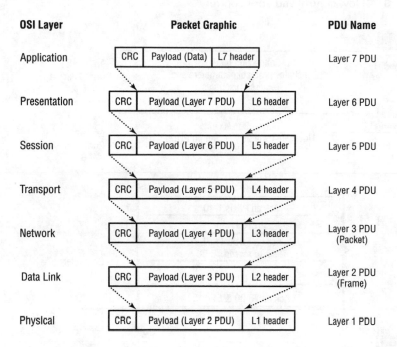

OSI Layer	Packet Graphic	PDU Name
Application	CRC | Payload (Data) | L7 header	Layer 7 PDU
Presentation	CRC | Payload (Layer 7 PDU) | L6 header	Layer 6 PDU
Session	CRC | Payload (Layer 6 PDU) | L5 header	Layer 5 PDU
Transport	CRC | Payload (Layer 5 PDU) | L4 header	Layer 4 PDU
Network	CRC | Payload (Layer 4 PDU) | L3 header	Layer 3 PDU (Packet)
Data Link	CRC | Payload (Layer 3 PDU) | L2 header	Layer 2 PDU (Frame)
Physical	CRC | Payload (Layer 2 PDU) | L1 header	Layer 1 PDU

FIGURE 4.5   Connection-oriented PDU sequencing

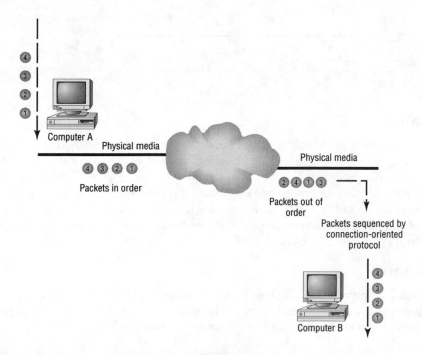

FIGURE 4.6 Flow control and error control

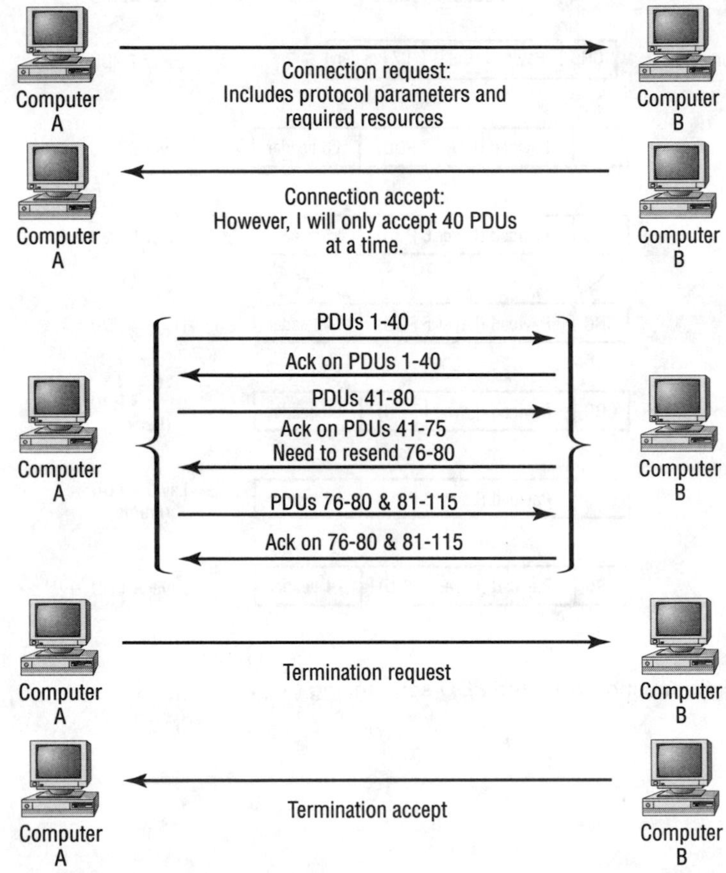

Flow Control

Although flow control was briefly described earlier, this section contains more detail. *Flow control* is responsible for ensuring that the transmitting station does not send data faster than the receiving station can process it. This is done by establishing a window size for the transportation.

Look at Figure 4.6 to see how windowing works. Notice that the originating system sends out a specified number of PDUs. Once that number is reached, the originating system waits for a response from the destination system. After the response is received, the system continues to transmit data.

Error Control

Error control is responsible for checking each transmission and verifying that all of the PDUs are contiguous and not erroneous. If there are missing or damaged PDUs, the destination will not send an ACK packet for the previous transmission. (Refer to Figure 4.6.)

Once all of the data is transferred without errors, the originating system sends a termination request, which tells the destination system that no more data needs to be transmitted. The destination system then responds with a termination acknowledgment.

As you can see, both systems do a lot of communicating, aside from the exchange of data. From the connection request to the termination acknowledgment, every exchange is accompanied with control information that keeps the data transfer reliable and error free. Table 4.1 gives examples of several connection-oriented protocols.

TABLE 4.1   Connection-Oriented Protocols

Protocol Name	Protocol Description
ATM	ATM (Asynchronous Transfer Mode) uses virtual circuits from one node to another. The permanent virtual circuits, or PVCs, are established by using connection-oriented procedures.
TCP	TCP (Transmission Control Protocol) was developed to overcome reliability problems. It uses flow control and error control extensively.
Novell SPX	Novell SPX (Sequenced Packet Exchange) is Novell's implementation of a network protocol that provides error-free and reliable data transport.
AppleTalk ATP	Apple uses ATP (AppleTalk Transaction Protocol) to provide connectivity between two socket clients. It is based on the request/response interaction of the two clients.

Connectionless Protocols

Now that connection-oriented protocols have been discussed, we'll move on to connectionless protocols. *Connectionless protocols* differ from connection-oriented protocols because they do not provide for flow control.

Figure 4.7 shows you how connectionless protocols work. This figure looks somewhat like Figure 4.3, except that there are no steps that involve a connection setup or termination. It is also missing the flow control and error control information sent by the receiving system.

Connectionless protocols do not send data relative to any other data units. The data included in the PDU must contain enough information for the PDU to get to its destination and for the receiving system to properly process it. Because there is no established connection, flow and error control cannot be implemented. Without flow and error control, the originating system has no way of knowing whether all of the transmitted data was received by the destination system without errors. Table 4.2 shows examples of connectionless protocols.

In this section, you learned the difference between connection-oriented and connectionless protocols. These protocol characteristics may be found at any level of the OSI model. The Transport layer, Layer 4 of the OSI model, is most notably known for the functions it provides by using connection-oriented or connectionless protocols. Some of the Transport layer's responsibilities are session establishment, flow control and error control, and session teardown.

FIGURE 4.7   Connectionless data transfer

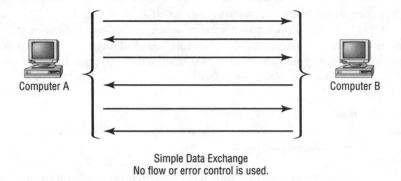

Simple Data Exchange
No flow or error control is used.

The following sections begin discussions of protocols that are specific to the Data-Link and Network layers, respectively.

TABLE 4.2   Connectionless Protocols

Protocol Name	Protocol Description
UDP	UDP (User Datagram Protocol) is a connectionless protocol used by IP.
AppleTalk DDP	DDP (Datagram Delivery Protocol) is a connectionless network protocol used for service between two network sockets.
Novell IPX	Novell IPX (Internetwork Packet Exchange) is Novell's Layer 3 protocol.

Layer 2: Data-Link Layer Protocols and Applications

This section is dedicated to Layer 2 protocols and applications. It is a very important section because it provides specific information on how the Layer 2 protocols work. What better way to be able to troubleshoot a problem than by understanding the intricacies of the protocol in question?

This section covers the following Layer 2 protocols:

- Ethernet/IEEE 802.3
- Token Ring/IEEE 802.5
- PPP
- SDLC
- Frame Relay
- ISDN

Ethernet/IEEE 802.3

These two terms actually refer to different things: *Ethernet* is a communication technology and *IEEE 802.3* is a variety of Ethernet. Ethernet, in the more specific sense, is a *carrier sense, multiple access/collision detection (CSMA/CD)* local area network. An Ethernet network uses these attributes—carrier sense, multiple access, and collision detection—to enhance communication. This definitely does *not* mean that Ethernet is the only technology that uses these attributes. In today's technical jargon, however, the term *Ethernet* is getting closer to meaning *all* CSMA/CD technologies.

Both Ethernet and IEEE 802.3 are broadcast networks. All frames that cross a given segment can be heard by all machines populating that segment. Because all machines on the segment have equal access to the physical media, each station tries to wait for a quiet spot before it transmits its data. If two machines talk at the same time, a collision occurs.

Ethernet services both the Physical and Data-Link layers, whereas IEEE 802.3 is more concerned with the Physical layer and how it talks to the Data-Link layer. Several IEEE 802.3 protocols exist; each one has a distinct name that describes how it is different from other IEEE 802.3 protocols. Table 4.3 summarizes these differences.

TABLE 4.3   IEEE 802.3 Characteristics

802.3 Values	10Base5	10Base2	1Base5	10BaseT	100Base T	10Broad 36	10Broad 36	1000Bas eT
Data rate (Mbps)	10	10	1	10	100	10	10	1000
Signaling method	Base-band	Base-band	Base-band	Base-band	Base-band	Broad-band	Broad-band	Base-band
Maximum segment length (m)	500	185	185	100	100	1800	1800	100
Media	50 Ohm coax	50 Ohm coax	Unshielded twisted pair	Unshielded twisted pair	Unshielded twisted pair	75 Ohm coax	75 Ohm coax	Unshielded twisted pair
Topology	Bus	Bus	Star	Star	Star	Bus	Bus	Star

Table 4.3 is an excerpt from Cisco documentation; for the full document, please see
`http://www.cisco.com/univercd/cc/td/doc/cisintwk/ito_doc/ethernet.htm`.

In Table 4.3 you will notice that the terms baseband and broadband are used to describe the
signaling type. In a baseband transmission, only a single frequency is used for sending data, and
therefore only a single signal can be sent over the same media. A broadband signal multiplexes
multiple signals of different frequencies together on the same physical media.

Though not specifically called out in the table, there are four different IP encapsulation types
supported by Cisco for Ethernet. These are ARPA, SNAP, Novell-Ether, and SAP. Of these,
ARPA is the default encapsulation type used.

Frame Structures

Frame formats are similar between Ethernet and IEEE 802.3. Figure 4.8 depicts the similarities
and differences between the two. The frame structures are read from right to left. Starting at the
right, you see that both frames begin with a preamble. The `Preamble` is a 7-byte field. (Notice
that we have moved from bits to bytes to specify field lengths.) The preamble consists of alternating 1s and 0s.

FIGURE 4.8   Ethernet vs. IEEE 802.3 frames

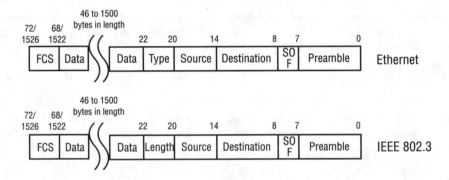

The next field is the `SOF`, the start-of-frame delimiter. It is used to synchronize the frame-
reception portions of all the machines on the segment. This field is only 1 byte long.

The two fields following the SOF are 6 bytes each; they are the `Destination` and `Source`
MAC addresses of the receiving and sending stations. Each MAC address is unique.

Up to this point, the frames are exactly the same. Starting with the next field, they are different.
The next field is a 2-byte field in both frame structures. Ethernet defines the field as a `Type` field;
IEEE 802.3 defines it as a `Length` field. Ethernet uses this field to specify which upper-layer protocol will receive the packet. IEEE 802.3 uses the field to define the number of bytes in the payload
(802.2 header and data) field. One easy method of observing the difference between an Ethernet
and 802.3 frame is to look at the `Type/Length` field. If this value is 1500 (0x05DC) or less, then
it is an IEEE 802.3 frame. If it is greater than 1500, it is an Ethernet frame.

Next is the `Data` field, in both Ethernet and 802.3 formats. The only difference between the
two versions of this field is that Ethernet uses a variable byte size, between 46 and 1500 bytes,

for data. This data is what will be handed to the upper-layer protocols. IEEE 802.3 uses a 46–1500 variable byte size, as well, but the information here contains the 802.2 header and the encapsulated data that will eventually be passed to an upper-layer protocol that is defined within the data field.

Finally, the last field is the Frame Check sequence (FCS) field. It is 4 bytes and stores information that will be used for calculating the CRC after the data has been sent or received.

Token Ring/IEEE 802.5

Token Ring and *IEEE 802.5* have the same relationship as Ethernet and IEEE 802.3. In this case, however, the IEEE 802.5 specification follows IBM's Token Ring much more closely. Both implementations specify baseband signaling, token passing, and data rates. Token Ring is IBM's token-passing LAN technology. It has bandwidth capabilities of either 4Mbps or 16Mbps in a ring topology.

Token Ring/IEEE 802.5 differs greatly from Ethernet/IEEE 802.3. Ethernet/IEEE 802.3 is CSMA/CD LANs, whereas Token Ring/IEEE 802.5 is apportioned networks. *Apportioned* means that equal time is allotted to every station on a ring. This is achieved by passing a token around the ring. The next section explains apportioned Token Ring in a little more detail.

Tokens

The physical design of Token Ring/IEEE 802.5 is just as the name indicates—a ring. Multiple stations connect to the same ring, just as Ethernet/IEEE 802.3 stations connect to the same segment.

The main idea behind Token Ring/IEEE 802.5 is that a station cannot transmit data onto the ring without first possessing the *token*. The token is just a small frame containing control information. Use Figure 4.9 as a visual reference for the following example. The frame or token is sent around the ring. Each station on the ring waits its turn to receive the token. If a station receives the token but doesn't have anything to transmit, it simply passes the token on to the next station in line. However, if the station does have information to send, it alters the frame, changing it into a start-of-frame identifier, and then appends the data to the frame. While the token frame has been changed into a start-of-frame identifier, no other station on the ring can use the token to transmit data, thus eliminating collisions.

The altered frame leaves the source station and circles the ring in search of the destination station. Based on what's in the frame, each station determines whether it is the destination host. If a station is the destination, it copies the frame and then processes it, as necessary. The frame continues to travel around the ring until it reaches the source host. Once reaching the source, the frame is removed and a new token is generated and sent out onto the ring. This way, each station has an equal opportunity to transmit data.

Fault Recovery

Token Ring/IEEE 802.5 uses several methods to help prevent and to heal network failures quickly and efficiently. An *Active Monitor* is designated by the workstations on the ring. The Active Monitor is responsible for token monitoring, token generation when the token seems to have disappeared, purging recycling frames, and other ring maintenance.

FIGURE 4.9   Token passing

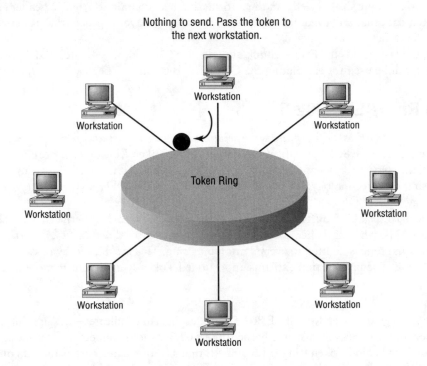

In addition, the physical connectivity of Token Ring/IEEE 802.5 is fault tolerant. If a machine on a ring becomes unreachable, the machine is electrically disconnected from the ring. The multistation access unit (MAU) in which the Token Ring/IEEE 802.5 cabling is located shuts down the port that is unreachable, thus healing the ring. Physical connectivity is tested by using *beaconing,* which locates the fault and reports back with the nearest active upstream neighbor, or NAUN. This information helps to isolate network failures and shortens troubleshooting time.

Ring Insertion

A Token Ring NIC card must go through five steps in order to be inserted into a Token Ring network. For more detail on this process, refer to the Cisco website at:

 For more detail on the insertion process, refer to the Cisco website at: http://www.cisco.com/en/US/products/hw/modules/ps2643/products_tech_note09186a0080093dc2.shtml#first

1. Lobe Media Check   This check verifies the cabling by looping the workstation's transmit signal to the receive signal at the concentrator. Once this loop is up, a lobe Media Test MAC frame is sent to verify connectivity.

2. Physical Insertion   The workstation sends a signal to the Concentrator/MAU indicating that the Lobe Media Check is complete and the workstation is connected to the ring on a physical level. This insertion actually breaks the ring, causing the Active Monitor to send a Ring Purge Frame.

3. Neighbor Notification   Once the ring has been purged, the new workstation through the normal ring startup process learns its neighbors, and its neighbors discover the new workstation's presence.

4. Address Verification   The workstation then sends several Duplicate Address Test MAC frames around the ring to verify that it has a unique MAC address.

5. Request Initialization   The final step in the ring insertion process completes the logical connection to the ring. In this step, a Request Initialization MAC frame is sent to the Ring Parameter Server to get the ring parameters and other information.

Once all of these steps are complete, the ring returns to normal functioning as describe in the previous sections.

Token Frame Format

We now look at the two frame types used by Token Ring/IEEE 802.5. Remember that we will move from right to left in the frame structure. The two principal frame types used in Token Ring and IEEE 802.5, shown in Figure 4.10, are the *token frame* and the *data* or *command frame* formats.

FIGURE 4.10   Structure of token and data/command frames

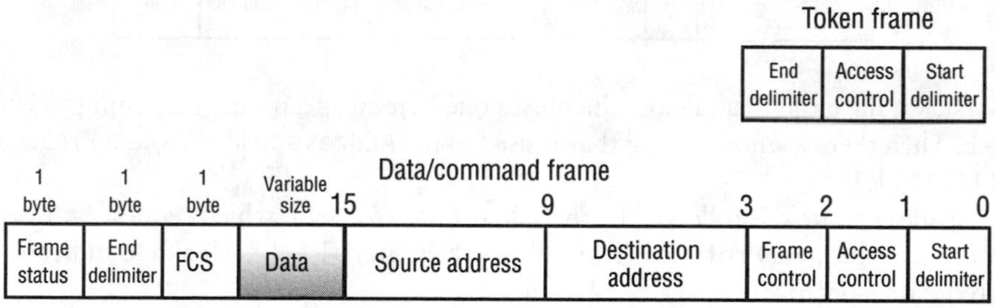

Figure 4.10 shows that both frames start with a Start Delimiter and an Access Control field. These two fields are each 1 byte long. The Start Delimiter alerts each station on the ring that the frame is a data or command frame, not a simple token frame. The Access Control field is used to assign priority to the frame and to help distinguish what frame type it is. Possible frame types are token, data/command, and monitor.

After the access control frame, the token frame and data/command frame formats are different. The data frame contains additional fields that the token frame does not have. All of the station's data is inserted into the frames following the Access Control field. The data segment commences with a 1-byte field that holds information regarding frame control. This is an indicator of whether the frame contains data or command information.

The next two fields are 6 bytes long and contain the packet's destination and source addresses. Next, the `data` field, of variable length, carries all the data that is to be encapsulated. The length of this field is determined by how long the sending station can hold a token.

Error-checking information follows the header and data fields. It is used in CRC calculation.

Now you are at the end of the data/command frame, where there are two more frames. The `End Delimiter`, which occurs in the token frame as well, is only 1 byte long and indicates the end of the frame. After that, a data/command frame has one more field. The last field, the `Frame Status`, or FS, can relay one of two values: frame-copied or address-recognized.

Point-to-Point Protocol (PPP)

Point-to-point Protocol (PPP) is used to transfer data over serial point-to-point links. It accomplishes this by using a Layer 2 serial encapsulation called *High-level Data Link Control (HDLC)*. HDLC is used for frame encapsulation on synchronous serial lines. It uses a Link Control Protocol (LCP) to manage the serial connection. Network Control Protocols (NCPs) are used to allow PPP to use other protocols from Layer 3, thus enabling PPP to assign IP addresses dynamically.

PPP uses the same frame structure as HDLC. Figure 4.11 gives you a picture of what the frame looks like. As always, we move from right to left.

FIGURE 4.11 PPP packet structure

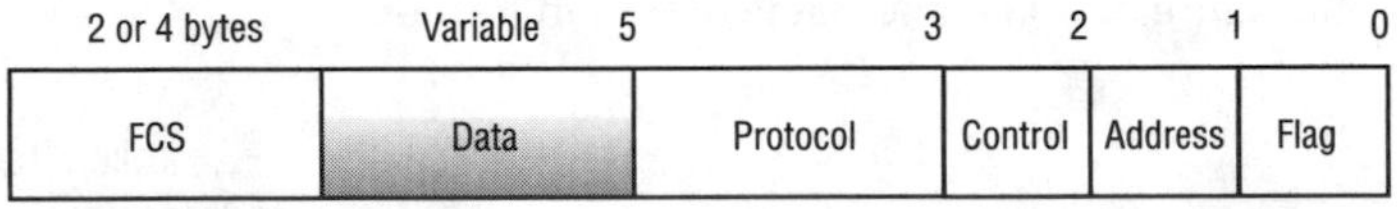

2 or 4 bytes	Variable	5	3	2	1	0
FCS	Data	Protocol	Control	Address	Flag	

First, we have the `Flag` field, which uses one byte to specify the beginning or ending of a frame. Then there is another byte that is used in the `Address` field to hold a broadcast address of 11111111.

The `Address` field is followed by the 1-byte `Control` field, which requests a transmission of user data. The 2-byte `Protocol` field follows the `Control` field. This field indicates the encapsulated data's protocol.

The `Data` field contains the information that will be handed to the upper-layer protocols. It is a variable-length field. After that is the FCS. Like the other protocols, it is used for CRC calculation.

Synchronous Data Link Control (SDLC)

Synchronous Data Link Control (SDLC) is based on a synchronous, more-efficient, faster, and flexible bit-oriented format. SDLC has several derivatives that perform similar functions with some enhancements: HDLC, LAPB (Link Access Procedure, Balanced), and IEEE 802.2, just to name a few. HDLC is the default encapsulation type on most Cisco router serial interfaces.

SDLC is used for many link types. Two node types exist within SDLC: *primary nodes* and *secondary nodes*. Primary nodes are responsible for the control of secondary stations and for link management operations such as link setup and teardown. Secondary nodes talk only to the primary node when fulfilling two requirements. First, they have permission from the primary node; second, they have data to transmit. Even if a secondary node has data to send, it cannot send the data if it does not have permission from the primary node.

Primary and secondary stations can be configured together in four different topologies:

Point-to-point   This topology requires only two nodes—a primary and a secondary.

Multipoint   This configuration uses one primary station and multiple secondary stations.

Loop   This configuration uses one primary and multiple secondary stations. The difference between the loop and multipoint setups is that in a loop the primary station is connected between two secondary stations, which makes two directly connected secondary stations. When more secondary stations are added, they must connect to the other secondary stations that are currently in the loop. When one of these stations wants to send information to the primary node, it must transit the other secondary stations before it reaches the primary.

Hub go-ahead   This configuration also uses one primary and multiple secondary stations, but it uses a different communication topology. The primary station has an outbound channel. This channel is used to communicate with each of the secondary stations. An inbound channel is shared among the secondary stations and has a single connection into the primary station.

Frame Structure

SDLC uses three different frame structures: information, supervisory, and unnumbered. Overall, the structure of the frames is similar among all three, except for the Control frame. The Control frame is varied to distinguish the type of SDLC frame that is being used. Figure 4.12 gives the structure for the different SDLC frames. Pay close attention to the bit values next to the send sequence number within the Control frame.

First, let's talk about the frame fields that are common among all three frame types. As you can see, all three frames depicted in Figure 4.12 start with a `Flag` field that is followed by an `Address` field. The `Address` field of SDLC frames is different from other frame structures because only the address of the secondary node is used, rather than a destination and source address. The secondary address is used because all communication is either originated or received by the primary node; thus, it is not necessary to specify its address within the frame.

The Control frame follows the `Address` field. Information contained within the Control frame defines the SDLC frame type. The Control frame begins with a receive sequence number. This sequence number is used to tell the protocol the number of the next frame to be received.

The `P/F` or `Poll Final` number, following the receive sequence number, is used differently by primary and secondary nodes. Primary nodes use the information to communicate to the secondary node that an immediate response is required. The secondary node uses the information to tell the primary node that the frame is the last one in the current dialog.

After the P/F bit, the Send Sequence Number is used to identify the current frame's sequence number. Following that, 1 or 2 bits are used to define the frame type. Table 4.4 specifies the bit values and the corresponding frame type.

FIGURE 4.12   SDLC frame structures

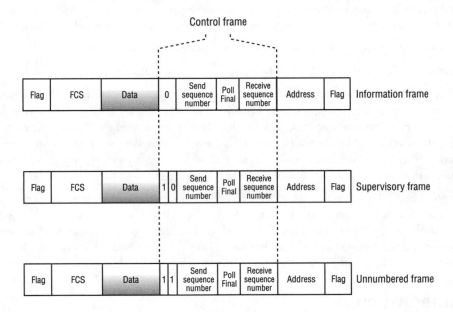

TABLE 4.4   SDLC Frame Types

Bit Value	Frame Type
0	Information
0 1	Supervisory
1 1	Unnumbered

The Data field follows the Control frame. As with other frame types, the FCS field comes next and is used to calculate the CRC. SDLC frames differ again with the last field, which is another Flag field like one at the beginning of the frame.

Now that we have discussed the frame structure, let's examine the three different frame types. Information frames carry exactly that—information destined for the upper-layer protocols. Supervisory frames control SDLC communications; they are responsible for flow control and error control for I-frame (information). Unnumbered frames provide the initialization of secondary nodes, as well as other managerial functions.

Frame Relay

Frame Relay was developed as a digital packet-switching technology, whereas older technologies such as X.25 were analog-based technologies. The technology used in Frame Relay allows it to multiplex several different data flows over the same physical media. More information on Frame Relay is presented in Chapter 7, "Troubleshooting Serial Line and Frame Relay Connectivity."

Frame Relay also uses permanent and switched virtual circuits between the data terminal equipment (DTE) (customer connection) and the data communication equipment (DCE) (service providers frame relay switch). These virtual circuits have unique identifiers that allow the Frame Relay to keep track of each logical data flow. The identifier is known as a *DLCI* (data link connection identifier). The DLCI number is used to create a logical circuit within a physical circuit. Multiple logical circuits can be created within one physical circuit.

Look at the following router-configuration excerpt:

```
interface Serial1/5
 description Physical Circuit
 no ip address
 no ip directed-broadcast
 encapsulation frame-relay
!
interface Serial1/5.1 point-to-point
 description To Building A
 ip address 172.16.1.17 255.255.255.252
 no ip directed-broadcast
 frame-relay interface-dlci 17 IETF
!
interface Serial1/5.2 point-to-point
 description To Building B
 ip address 172.16.1.25 255.255.255.252
 no ip directed-broadcast
 frame-relay interface-dlci 22 IETF
```

From this configuration, you can see that two logical circuits have been defined to communicate over one physical circuit. Notice that each subinterface or logical circuit has a unique DLCI. Each DLCI maps to another DLCI within the Frame Relay cloud. This mapping continues throughout the Frame Relay cloud until it maps to another DTE on the destination side of the virtual circuit.

Frame Structure

Frame Relay does not provide any information on flow and error control. As a result, no space is reserved within the frame for this information. These functions are left to the upper-layer protocols. Frame Relay *does* provide congestion detection and can notify the upper layers of possible problems; however, Frame Relay is primarily concerned only with the transmission and reception of data.

As a mechanism for data circuit identification, Frame Relay uses a DLCI number. Ten bits of the 2-byte `Address` field are used to define the DLCI. To a Frame Relay frame, the DLCI is the most significant address in the header. Figure 4.13 depicts a Frame Relay frame.

FIGURE 4.13 Frame Relay frame structure

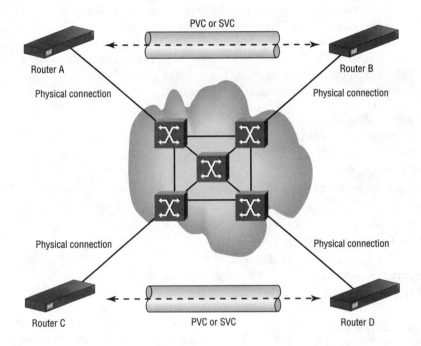

Integrated Services Digital Network (ISDN)

Integrated Services Digital Network (ISDN) is a service that allows telephone networks to carry data, voice, and other digital traffic. There are two types of ISDN interfaces: *Basic Rate Interface (BRI)* and *Primary Rate Interface (PRI)*. BRI uses two B channels and one D channel. Each of the two B channels operates at 64Kbps bidirectionally; the D channel operates at 16Kbps. The B channels are used for transmitting and receiving data. The D channel is used for protocol communications and signaling.

In contrast, PRI uses 23 B channels and 1 D channel. All 23 B channels are added to a rotary group, as well. The D channel runs at the same line speed as the B channels—64Kbps. Because of the D channel's additional line speed, PRI has the equivalent line speed of a T1 circuit (1.544Mbps). In Europe, PRI offers 30 B channels and 1 D channel, making it the equivalent of an E1 circuit.

Just as there are two types of ISDN interfaces, there are two terminal equipment types. Type 1 (TE1) is equipment that was built specifically for use on ISDN. Type 2 (TE2) is equipment that was made before the ISDN specifications, and it requires a terminal adapter to actually interface with ISDN. Terminal equipment, which is comparable to DTE as described in the Frame Relay section, includes computers or routers.

In order for terminal equipment to work, it must be able to connect to a network termination. There are three types of ISDN network terminations, known as NT devices. Type 1 (NT1) devices are treated as customer premises equipment. Type 2 (NT2) devices are more intelligent devices than NT1 and can perform concentration and switching functions. The last type is a combination of Types 1 and 2. It is known as a Type 1/2 or NT1/2.

More information about troubleshooting ISDN is covered in Chapter 8, "Troubleshooting ISDN."

Frame Structure

Look at Figure 4.14 to get a picture of the ISDN frame. As you can see, this frame is similar to the HDLC frame that you studied earlier (Figure 4.11) ISDN uses LAP (Link Access Procedure) on the D channel for Layer 2 functions. Unlike the HDLC frame, the ISDN frame is bounded by Flag fields.

FIGURE 4.14   ISDN frame format

Flag	FCS	Data	Control	EA	TEI	EA	C/R	SAPI	Flag

After the Flag field, again going from right to left, we see the Address field. The Address field contains several bits of key information:

SAPI   This field is the service access point identifier. It defines which services are provided to Layer 3.

C/R   This field designates the frame as a command or a response.

EA   This is the last bit of the first byte of the Address field. This bit defines the Address field as 1 or 2 bytes. If it is set to 1 byte, this is the last field within the Address field. If it is set to 2, then one more field follows, ending with another EA bit.

TEI   This is the terminal endpoint identifier, the Layer 2 address used to identify individual devices connecting to an ISDN network.

Layers 3 and 4: IP Routed Protocols

The Network layer is used by the Transport layer to provide the best end-to-end services and path for PDU delivery. This means that the Network layer also uses protocols to accomplish this task. This section discusses protocols that are used within Layer 3 of the OSI model. Some of these protocols use other protocols within them for finer granularity of certain functions.

There is a significant difference between *routing* protocols and *routed* protocols. Routing protocols are used to exchange route information and to create a network topology, thus enabling routing decisions to be made. The routed protocols, on the other hand, contain information regarding the end systems, how communication is established, and other information relevant to the transfer of data. The routing protocols will be covered in Chapter 6, "TCP/IP Routing Protocol Troubleshooting." or NT1/2.

Internet Protocol (IP)

It is important to distinguish between the Internet Protocol suite and the actual Internet Protocol that is used in the Network layer of the OSI model.

The IP suite consists of several discrete protocols that are implemented at different levels of the OSI model.

The *Internet Protocol (IP)* is a Network-layer protocol of the IP suite. It is used to allow routing among internetworks and heterogeneous systems. IP is a connectionless protocol, even though it can provide error reporting, and performs the segmentation and reassembly of PDUs.

IP Packet Structure

Now that you know what IP is, look at the actual packet structure in more detail. Following is an IP packet that was broken down by EtherPeek, a network analyzer. The entire header has six layers, and each layer consists of 32 bits. Look at each section of the header and get an explanation for each.

```
IP Header - Internet Protocol Datagram
   Version:              4
   Header Length:        5
   Precedence:           0
   Type of Service:      %000
   Unused:               %00
   Total Length:         60
   Identifier:           0
   Fragmentation Flags:  %000
   Fragment Offset:      0
   Time To Live:         2
   IP Type:              0x58   EIGRP
   Header Checksum:      0x10dc
```

```
Source IP Address:    205.124.250.7
Dest. IP Address:     224.0.0.10
No Internet Datagram Options
```

At this point, we will define the key fields that appear in this listing. As you can see, the packet IP header starts out with the `Version` field. Right now, the standard is IPv4. The version parameter uses 4 of the 32 bits available.

The next field is the IP `Header Length`, or IHL. This field also uses another 4 bits and it specifies the datagram header length in 32-bit words.

The `Type of Service` (TOS) follows the IHL. This field uses 8 bits and indicates datagram priority and how other OSI layers are to handle the datagram once they receive it.

Following the TOS is the `Total Length` parameter. This field indicates how long the packet is, including header and payload or data. The length is in units of bytes. The field itself uses 16 bits, which brings the total for these fields to 32 bits or four bytes.

The second field begins with the `Identifier` or `Identification` field. The `Identifier` is a 16-bit field that contains an integer value that identifies the packet. It is like a sequencing number that is used when reassembling datagram fragments.

The `Fragmentation Flags` field follows, using only 3 bits. This field is used to control fragmentation of a datagram. If the datagram can be fragmented, the first bit has a value of 0; otherwise, a value of 1 is assigned to the first bit if the datagram is not to be fragmented. The second bit is used to indicate the last fragment of a fragmented datagram. The third bit is an undefined bit and is set to 0.

`Fragment Offset` follows the Flags field. This value uses 13 bits and specifies the fragment's position in the original datagram. The position is measured from the beginning of the datagram and marked off in 64-bit increments. This again brings you to 32 bits, so you must move down to the next layer in the IP packet.

The third field begins with the `Time-to-Live` (TTL) field, which is a counter whose units are measured in hops. A starting value is given, and it counts decrements by 1 as it passes through each hop or router. Once the value of this field is 0, the packet is discarded. This field uses 8 bits.

The protocol field (`IP Type`) follows the TTL parameter. This field tells Layer 3 which upper-layer protocol is supposed to receive the packet. It uses a decimal value to specify the protocol. This field uses 8 bits.

The `Header Checksum` field finishes the third layer. The checksum is used to help verify the integrity of the IP header. This field uses 16 bits.

The next two fields are the `Source IP Address` and `Dest. IP Address respectively`. Both of these are 32 bits long.

An `Options` field occupies the final field of the header. The field needs to be 32 bits long, so any additional empty bits are padded.

Figure 4.15 gives a good visual representation of the IP packet structure.

IP Addressing Review

No review of TCP/IP networking would be complete without a review of IP addressing. In this section we will not explain the basics of IP addressing; rather, we will focus more on the application of *Variable Length Subnet Masking (VLSM)* and the calculation of networks as it pertains to troubleshooting in an IP environment. If you need a more detailed discussion, see *CCNA: Cisco Certified Network Associate Study Guide, 3rd ed.*, by Todd Lammle Sybex, 2002.

FIGURE 4.15   The IP packet structure

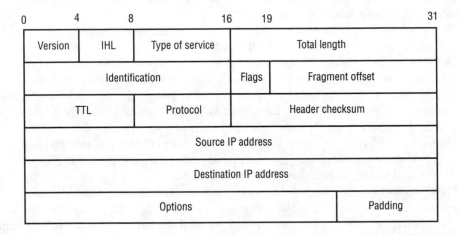

As internetworks grew and address space became more scarce, several methodologies were devised to extend the address space availability. One of these methodologies was VLSM. In older routing protocols, if you wanted to subnet a major network, you had to make all the subnets the same size. This was because the routing protocols passed only network information and did not include subnet mask information. Newer routing protocols pass subnet information along with the individual routes, allowing for the use of VLSM. This enables better use of address space because network administrators can size the subnets based on the need. For example, a point-to-point connection has only two nodes on it, and as such only needs two host addresses. Without VLSM, if your standard subnet mask was 255.255.255.0, a /24 subnet, then 256 "addresses" would be used on this point-to-point connection (though 256 addresses are used, only 254 are usable by hosts). With VLSM, this same connection could use a 255.255.255.252 mask, /30, using only four addresses—two for the hosts, one for the subnet, and one for the broadcast address. For reference, Table 4.5 shows various subnet mask information.

TABLE 4.5   Subnet Mask Information

Subnet	Mask	Total # of Addr. per Sub	# of Usable Addr. per Sub
/32	255.255.255.255	1	0
/31	255.255.255.254	2	0
/30	255.255.255.252	4	2

TABLE 4.5   Subnet Mask Information *(continued)*

Subnet	Mask	Total # of Addr. per Sub	# of Usable Addr. per Sub
/29	255.255.255.248	8	6
/28	255.255.255.240	16	14
/27	255.255.255.224	32	30
/26	255.255.255.192	64	62
/25	255.255.255.128	128	126
/24	255.255.255.0	256	254
/23	255.255.254.0	512	510
/22	255.255.252.0	1,024	1,022
/21	255.255.248.0	2,048	2,046
/20	255.255.240.0	4,096	4,094
/19	255.255.224.0	8,192	8,190
/18	255.255.192.0	16,384	16,382
/17	255.255.128.0	32,768	32,766
/16	255.255.0.0	65,536	65,534
/15	255.254.0.0	131,072	131,070
/14	255.252.0.0	262,144	262,142
/13	255.248.0.0	524,288	524,286
/12	255.240.0.0	1,048,576	1,048,574
/11	255.224.0.0	2,097,152	2,097,150
/10	255.192.0.0	4,194,304	4,194,302
/9	255.128.0.0	8,388,608	8,388,606

TABLE 4.5   Subnet Mask Information *(continued)*

Subnet	Mask	Total # of Addr. per Sub	# of Usable Addr. per Sub
/8	255.0.0.0	16,777,216	16,777,214
/7	254.0.0.0	33,554,432	33,554,430
/6	252.0.0.0	67,108,864	67,108,862
/5	248.0.0.0	134,217,728	134,217,726
/4	224.0.0.0	268,435,456	268,435,454
/3	192.0.0.0	536,870,912	536,870,910
/2	128.0.0.0	1,073,741,824	1,073,741,822
/1	0.0.0.0	2,147,483,648	2,147,483,646

One drawback to VLSM is the complexity that it adds to the network. When there was only one mask used in an environment, the network administrators could easily memorize the subnet information. With VLSM, however, subnet information needs to be calculated based on the individual situation. Miscalculation of the subnets can lead to communication problems if machines are assigned outside a subnet boundary or on a subnet or broadcast address.

 Real World Scenario

Tips for Successfully Using VLSM in a Network

As is the case with many elements of networking, planning is the key to successfully using VLSM in a network. This is especially true of VLSM implementations being put in place on existing networks. Without proper planning, a VLSM implementation can provoke serious support problems. There a numerous ways to implement VLSM; here we will only focus on two.

Divide Up a Single /24 Network   This implementation strategy is best designed for smaller remote sites connecting to one or two central locations. A single /24 network can be divided up and used for the remote sites. In this manner, summarization and problem tracking are made easier. For example, assume that the standard remote location has 60 IP-enabled devices on a single segment, 2 routers, 1 switch, and 2 point-to-point Frame Relay links, and is assigned the 10.1.1.0 /24 subnet. Using the small-site VLSM strategy, you can take this /24 and divide it up into the following.

> 10.1.1.0 /25 for the user segment
>
> 10.1.1.244 /30 for Frame Relay link 2
>
> 10.1.1.248 /30 for Frame Relay link 1
>
> 10.1.1.253 /32 for router 2 loopback
>
> 10.1.1.254 /32 for router 1 loopback
>
> As you can see, /32 subnets are being used for the router loopback addresses. This does not conform to the rules of IP addressing, but it is supported by Cisco routers. Also, though it is true that with only 60 IP-enabled devices a /26 mask could have been used, that would leave no room for future growth. The suggested arrangement, on the other hand, allows for effective use of the address range and permits some future expansion. Notice also that /30 masks were used for the Frame Relay links. In the event that these links might become point-to-multipoint links, however, a different mask should be used.
>
> **Use One Mask Size per Service**   The second tip for implementing VLSM is to try to use the same mask size for the same service type. For example, use a /32 mask for all loopback interfaces, a /30 mask for all point-to point links, a /26 mask for all server segments, and a /24 mask for all user segments. In this manner you can easily identify the general purpose of a subnet just by looking at the mask.
>
> As stated, there are various ways to implement VLSM successfully; it just takes some planning up front. This planning must take into account the current IP addressing scheme. In addition, ensure that the final implementation is consistently applied and will be scalable and adaptable as the network requirements change.

Internet Control Message Protocol (ICMP)

The *Internet Control Message Protocol (ICMP)* is used throughout IP networks. ICMP was designed to provide routing-failure information to the source system. This protocol provides four types of feedback that are used to make the IP routing environment more efficient:

Reachability   This is determined by using ICMP echo and reply messages.

Redirects   These messages tell hosts to redirect traffic or choose alternative routes.

Timeouts   These messages indicate that a packet's designated TTL is expired.

Router Discovery   These messages discover directly connected routers' IP addresses. Router discovery actually uses the ICMP Router Discovery Protocol to do this. This passive method gathers directly connected IP addresses without having to understand specific routing protocols.

Here is a look at a couple of ICMP packets (echo request and reply).

```
ICMP - Internet Control Messages Protocol
  ICMP Type:           8  Echo Request
  Code:                0
  Checksum:            0x495c
  Identifier:          0x0200
  Sequence Number:     512
  ICMP Data Area:
  abcdefghijklmnop   61 62 63 64 65 66 67 68 69 6a 6b 6c    6d 6e 6f 70
  qrstuvwabcdefghi   71 72 73 74 75 76 77 61 62 63 64 65    66 67 68 69
Frame Check Sequence:  0x342e3235
ICMP - Internet Control Messages Protocol
  ICMP Type:           0  Echo Reply
  Code:                0
  Checksum:            0x515c
  Identifier:          0x0200
  Sequence Number:     512
  ICMP Data Area:
  abcdefghijklmnop   61 62 63 64 65 66 67 68 69 6a 6b 6c    6d 6e 6f 70
  qrstuvwabcdefghi   71 72 73 74 75 76 77 61 62 63 64 65    66 67 68 69
Frame Check Sequence:  0x342e3235
```

The ICMP structure is similar to the IP structure in that it has a type, checksum, identifier, and sequence number. The field names differ a little but have the same functionality.

Transmission Control Protocol (TCP)

The *Transmission Control Protocol (TCP),* a connection-oriented protocol on the Transport layer that provides reliable delivery of data, is an integral part of the IP suite. Look at the structure of the TCP packet. The following EtherPeek frame was taken during a POP3 transaction:

```
TCP - Transmission Control Protocol
  Source Port:       110  POP3
  Destination Port: 1097
  Sequence Number:  997270908
  Ack Number:       7149472
  Offset:           5
  Reserved:         %000000
  Code:             %010000
          Ack is valid
```

```
Window:              8760
Checksum:            0x8064
Urgent Pointer:      0
No TCP Options
No More POP Command or Reply Data
```
Extra bytes (Padding):
```
UUUUUU               55 55 55 55 55 55
```
Frame Check Sequence: 0x04020000

This structure is similar to the IP packet structure. The TCP header is 32 bits long and has a minimum length of five fields, but can be six fields deep when options are specified. The first field starts with Source and Destination Port fields. Each of these fields is 16 bits long.

A Sequence Number field occupies the entire second layer, meaning that it is 32 bits long. TCP is a connection-oriented protocol, and this field is used to keep track of the various requests that have been sent.

The third layer is a 32-bit length field containing the acknowledgment sequence number that is used to track responses.

The fourth layer begins with the Offset field, which is 4 bits and specifies the number of 32-bit words present in the header. Six bits are reserved for future use (this is called the Reserved field). This field follows the Offset field.

The next field, called the Flag or Code field, is also a 6-bit field, and it contains control information. Look at Table 4.6 for an explanation of the 6 bits within the Flag field.

The Window field specifies the buffer size for incoming data. Once the buffer is filled, the sending system must wait for a response from the receiving system. This field is 16 bits long.

Layer 5 of the TCP header begins with the Checksum parameter, which also occupies 16 bits. It is used to verify the integrity of the transmitted data.

The Urgent Pointer field references the last byte of data, so the receiver knows how much urgent data it will receive. This is also a 16-bit field.

Finally, there is the Option field, which must also be 32 bits long. If the options do not occupy 32 bits, padding is added to reach the correct length.

TABLE 4.6   Flag Bit Assignments

Bit number (right to left)	Control Information	Definition
1	URG	Urgent pointer is significant.
2	ACK	Acknowledgment pointer is significant.
3	PSH	Push function.

TABLE 4.6 Flag Bit Assignments *(continued)*

Bit number (right to left)	Control Information	Definition
4	RST	Reset connection.
5	SYN	Synchronize sequence numbers.
6	FIN	No more data to transfer.

User Datagram Protocol (UDP)

The *User Datagram Protocol (UDP)* is a connectionless protocol on the Transport layer of the OSI model. The overall structure of UDP is simpler than TCP, because UDP is connectionless and therefore does not have overhead to maintain connection information. UDP is commonly used for real-time applications such as video and voice. In these time-sensitive applications, when a packet is lost or corrupted there is not enough time for the applications to recognize that a packet is missing and request that it be resent, and for this retransmitted packet to arrive. Therefore, the overhead that comes with TCP is not warranted for this type of data transfer.

The following frame snippet was taken using EtherPeek and is of a DNS request:

```
UDP - User Datagram Protocol
  Source Port:      1213
  Destination Port: 53 domain
  Length:           38
  Checksum:         0xBFBA
```

As you can see, all of the overhead that is associated with the connection-oriented nature of the TCP frame, such as sequence and acknowledgment number, has been removed in UDP. As a result, the UDP packet is condensed down to four fields.

The first two of these fields, Source and Destination Port, are both 16 bits long. The Destination Port field must be filled in with the destination port of the service that is being requested; however, the Source Port field only needs a value when the sending station needs a reply from the receiver. When the conversation is unidirectional and the source port is not used, this field should be set to 0. When a reply is needed, the receiving station will reply to the sender on the port indicated in the original packet's source field.

The last two fields in a UDP header are Length and Checksum. Like the source and destination port information, the length and checksum are both 16 bits long. The Length field shows the total number of bytes in the UDP packet, including the UDP header and user data. Checksum, though optional, allows the receiving station to verify the integrity of the UDP header as well as the data that is contained in the packet. If Checksum is not used, it should be set to a value of 0.

Summary

A great deal of information is covered in this chapter, with the focus on Network and Data-Link layer protocols. It is important to understand this information in order to facilitate your troubleshooting efforts. If you do not sufficiently understand the protocols present in Layers 2 and 3 of the OSI model, you should study them in depth. The majority of networking problems occur in these two layers.

Many encapsulation types are available at the second layer of the OSI model. The ones discussed in this chapter were Ethernet, Token Ring, PPP, SDLC, Frame Relay, and ISDN. Each has its own strengths and weaknesses that make it better suited for a particular installation.

There are two major protocol classifications: connection-oriented and connectionless. Connection-oriented protocols allow for sequenced data transfer, flow control, and error control. Examples of connection-oriented protocols include ATM and TCP. Connectionless protocols require less overhead; however, they do so at the expense of the sequenced data transfer, and the error and flow control offered by connection-oriented protocols. The connectionless protocol discussed in this chapter is UDP.

Exam Essentials

Know the differences between connectionless and connection-oriented protocols.   Connection-oriented protocols have flow-control and error-checking methodologies that are not present in connectionless protocols. Connectionless protocols offer better performance characteristics for real-time voice and video applications.

Know the Data Link protocols and technologies.   The major technologies covered in this section include Ethernet, Token Ring, PPP, SDLC (HDLC), Frame Relay, and ISDN.

Know how to calculate subnet masks.   Understand how VLSM functions, and know how to determine an appropriate address and subnet mask combination.

Key Terms

Before you take the exam, be certain you are familiar with the following terms:

Active Monitor	Internet Protocol (IP)
Basic Rate Interface (BRI)	OSI model
beaconing	packet
carrier sense, multiple access/collision detection (CSMA/CD)	pipe
Connectionless protocols	Point-to-point Protocol (PPP)
Connection-oriented protocols	primary nodes
DLCI	Primary Rate Interface (PRI)
error control	secondary nodes
Ethernet	sequenced data transfer
Flow control	Synchronous Data Link Control (SDLC)
frame	token
Frame Relay	Token Ring
High-level Data Link Control (HDLC)	Transmission Control Protocol (TCP)
IEEE 802.3	User Datagram Protocol (UDP)
IEEE 802.5	Variable Length Subnet Masking (VLSM)
Integrated Services Digital Network (ISDN)	window size
Internet Control Message Protocol (ICMP)	

Review Questions

1. Which type of global protocol provides error control and flow control?

    A. Connectionless

    B. Connection-oriented

    C. IP

    D. UDP

2. Which of the following protocols are considered connection-oriented protocols? (Choose all that apply.)

    A. ATM

    B. UDP

    C. TCP

    D. IP

3. Which of the following protocols are considered connectionless protocols? (Choose all that apply.)

    A. Frame Relay

    B. UDP

    C. PPP

    D. SDLC

    E. IP

4. Which protocol of the IP protocol suite provides environmental information regarding IP networks, such as congestion and reachability?

    A. ICMP

    B. UDP

    C. TCP

    D. SMTP

5. You have determined that a problem exists on the Transport layer. Which of the following could be the cause of the problem? (Choose two.)

    A. The end system

    B. The patch cord

    C. The hub

    D. The router

6. What advantage over connection-oriented transfers is offered by connectionless data transfers?

   A. Flow-and-error control

   B. Guarantee of data integrity

   C. A more secure transfer

   D. Less overhead and network traffic

7. Which of the following situations could indicate a Network layer problem? (Choose two.)

   A. Devices on the same subnet can communicate with one another but not with devices on another subnet.

   B. Devices on the same subnet cannot communicate with one another but can communicate with devices on another subnet.

   C. Users cannot access a server on a different subnet.

   D. Bootp is not functioning on a device connected to the subnet.

8. Assuming the following IP addresses, which hosts are assigned legal IP addresses and would be able to communicate with each other without using a router?

   ```
   Host 1 IP address 10.2.25.47 /28
   Host 2 IP address 10.2.25.48 /28
   Host 3 IP address 10.2.25.46 /28
   Host 4 IP address 10.2.25.33 /28
   ```

   A. Hosts 1 and 4

   B. Hosts 1, 2, and 3

   C. Hosts 3 and 4

   D. Hosts 1 and 2

   E. Hosts 1, 2, 3, and 4

9. How many usable addresses are in a /30 subnet?

   A. 2

   B. 4

   C. 6

   D. 8

10. In TCP, what does *window size* refer to?

    A. The duration of time a workstation can transmit data before releasing the token.

    B. After a collision, the amount of time a workstation must wait before retransmitting.

    C. The amount of data that a station can transmit before needing an acknowledgment from the destination system.

    D. The duration of time the protocol will wait before assuming the packet was lost and request a retransmission.

11. What are the functions of an Active Monitor? (Choose 3.)

    A. Determining delay after a collision

    B. Monitoring the token

    C. Purging recycling frames

    D. Generating a token

    E. Passing data from the ring to the gateway

12. Which of the following items are in a TCP frame but not a UDP frame? (Choose two.)

    A. Source port

    B. Checksum

    C. Sequence number

    D. Acknowledgment number

13. A user on a workstation is unable to connect to a web server. You are successfully able to ping between a workstation and a server and have verified that there are no access lists between them. What is the highest layer of the OSI model that has been ruled out as the cause of the problem?

    A. Physical

    B. Data-Link

    C. Network

    D. Transport

    E. Session

    F. FPresentation

    G. GApplication

14. What is the maximum segment length for 1000Base-T on UTP?

    A. 33 meters

    B. 50 meters

    C. 75 meters

    D. 100 meters

15. Which Ethernet IP encapsulation is the default for Cisco routers? Use Cisco terminology.

    A. ARPA

    B. SAP

    C. Novell-Ether

    D. SNAP

16. What features does Token Ring possess that Ethernet does not? (Choose two.)

    A. Faster speeds

    B. Token passing

    C. Fault isolation

    D. MAC addresses

17. What is CSMA/CD used for on an Ethernet segment? (Choose two.)

    A. Speed negotiation

    B. Collision detection

    C. Duplex negotiation

    D. Carrier sense

    E. Setting trunk type

18. Which interface type was PPP originally designed to use?

    A. Ethernet

    B. Token Ring

    C. Serial

    D. None of the above

19. Which node types exist within SDLC and its derivatives? (Choose two.)

    A. Master

    B. Slave

    C. Server

    D. Client

    E. Primary

    F. Secondary

20. You have eliminated the Data-Link and Physical layers as possible causes of a problem. Which of the following devices can you look at next as part of your troubleshooting? (Choose three.)

    A. User's workstation

    B. Server

    C. Hub

    D. Patch panel

    E. Switch

    F. Router

Answers to Review Questions

1. B. Connection-oriented is the type of protocol that provides error control and flow control. Connectionless protocols such as IP and UDP do not.

2. A, C. ATM and TCP are connection-oriented. UDP and IP are both connectionless protocols.

3. B, E. UDP and IP are connectionless protocols. Frame Relay, PPP, and SDLC are all connection-oriented protocols.

4. A. ICMP provides environmental statistics for IP networks. The other protocols do not.

5. A, D. Only the end system and router operate on Layer 4. The patch cord and hub only operate at layer 1.

6. D. Due to the simplicity of connectionless protocols, they create less overhead and also use less bandwidth.

7. A, C. Any *inter*subnet traffic must use a Network layer protocol, but this is not always required of *intra*subnet traffic. The situations described in answers A and C require intersubnet communication and are thus the ones that could have a Network-related issue.

8. C. Since it is a /28 mask, the subnet boundaries are at 10.2.25.32 and 10.2.25.48. Therefore, Hosts 3 and 4 are on the same subnet. Host 1 is assigned the broadcast address for the 10.2.25.32 /28 subnet, and Host 2 is assigned the network address for the 10.2.25.48 /28 subnet.

9. A. Though a /30 subnet encompasses four addresses, only two are usable.

10. C. The larger the window size, the more data that can be transmitted before an acknowledgment is required.

11. B, C, D. Under normal operation, the Active Monitor monitors the token and creates one if one does not exist on the ring. In the event that frames are not being removed from the ring, the Active Monitor will purge them from the ring.

12. C, D. Because there is no flow control in UDP, a connectionless protocol, there is no need for the sequence number or acknowledgment number fields.

13. C. Because you can ping from the workstation and the server and there are no access lists in between, this eliminates the Physical, Data-Link, and Network layers as possible problems. Of these three, the Network is the highest layer.

14. D. The maximum segment length is the same as that for 100Base-T (100 meters).

15. A. Cisco uses ARPA as its default Ethernet encapsulation. The other encapsulation types can be set via the command line, but are not on by default.

16. B, C. Ethernet does not use a token, nor does it provide fault isolation. It is possible that Ethernet can be faster than Token Ring, and Ethernet also uses MAC addresses.

17. B, D. CSMA/CD stands for carrier sense, multiple access/collision detection. This technology allows multiple Ethernet stations to verify that there is a carrier signal on the line and to access it if it is quiet. CSMA/CD also allows for detection of and recovery from a collision.

18. C. PPP uses serial connections and is primarily used on WAN links. Ethernet and Token Ring are both LAN technologies.

19. E, F. Primary and secondary are the correct terms for the node types within SDLC.

20. A, B, F. Only the workstation, server, and router have components that operate at the Network layer or above.

Chapter

5

Cisco Diagnostic Commands and TCP/IP Connectivity Troubleshooting

---

EXAM TOPICS COVERED IN THIS CHAPTER INCLUDE:

✓ Verify network connectivity.

✓ Use the optimal troubleshooting approach in resolving network problems.

✓ MInImize downtime during troubleshooting.

✓ Use Cisco IOS commands to identify problems.

✓ Rectify suboptimal performance issues at Layers 2 through 7.

The next two chapters are focused primarily on essential TCP/IP troubleshooting skills and tools. Here in Chapter 5, we will explain show and debug commands. In addition, generic commands such as ping and traceroute will be applied to network problems. Problem isolation techniques that are used in troubleshooting LANs will be outlined and implemented. Finally, the use and kinds of access lists will be examined.

The next chapter, Chapter 6, focuses on the IP routing protocols, including RIP, IGRP, EIGRP, OSPF, and BGP. In addition to an explanation of these routing protocols, the show and debug commands used specifically for them will be examined. The final part of Chapter 6 explores redistribution issues and solutions.

Many of the show and debug commands are not protocol specific. Though these commands do not deal exclusively with the TCP/IP protocol, they are used in troubleshooting many TCP/IP problems and therefore are included here in Chapter 5 for completeness. As is the case with the show and debug commands, logging and core dumps are not limited to the TCP/IP but can be used to contribute to troubleshooting TCP/IP problems and are also included in this chapter for completeness.

In addition to all the detailed problem-solving techniques presented in these two chapters, quick reference summary charts are located at the end of Chapter 6. These tables help to quickly associate a cause to many TCP/IP symptoms.

Troubleshooting Commands

We will cover several troubleshooting tools in this chapter, each of which is part of the Cisco IOS. There are many show commands that are supported by the router. In addition to show commands, a tool called debug, is used to see specific information regarding packet transfer and exchange.

Part of effectively using these tools is using them without adversely affecting the router and its many processes. Here you will learn the specifics of several troubleshooting commands, along with the information needed in order to use them without causing additional problems on your network.

We start with nonintrusive, Cisco-specific show commands. After discussing the show commands, we move on to the debug tool. To finalize this section, we discuss some non-Cisco-specific troubleshooting tools: ping and traceroute.

show Commands

A large number of show commands are supported by Cisco IOS. Explaining them all is beyond the scope of this book. The most effective and useful show commands are described in the following sections, and Table 5.1 gives you a list of the ones most frequently used. To get an idea of all of the show commands, execute the show ? command from the router prompt.

TABLE 5.1   Frequently Used show Commands

show Command	Information Produced
access-lists	List of access lists
accounting	Accounting data for active sessions
adjacency	Adjacent nodes
buffers	Buffer pool statistics
cdp	Cisco Discovery Protocol (CDP) information
cef	Cisco Express Forwarding
configuration	Contents of the NVRAM
controllers	Interface controller status
debugging	State of each debugging option
environment	Environmental monitor statistics
extended	Extended interface information
frame-relay	Frame Relay information
interfaces	Interface status and configuration
ip	IP information
line	TTY line information
logging	Contents of logging buffers
memory	Memory statistics
ppp	PPP parameters and statistics
processes	Active process statistics
protocols	Active network routing protocols
queue	Queue contents

TABLE 5.1   Frequently Used show Commands *(continued)*

show Command	Information Produced
queueing	Queuing configuration
running-config	Current operating configuration
stacks	Process stack utilization
startup-config	Contents of startup configuration
tcp	Status of TCP connections
tech-support	System information for Tech Support
version	System hardware and software version and status

The following sections describe the show commands grouped into four categories: global, interface-related, process-related, and protocol-related. Depending on the problem you are troubleshooting, you can focus on the problem by using appropriate commands. For example, if you are troubleshooting a protocol-related problem, then you will probably use the protocol family of show commands. If you notice problems on a circuit, you can use the interface family of show commands to obtain detailed information about the interface.

Global Commands

Global commands deal with global router settings. Information that does not relate to interfaces or protocols, yet has overall router information, is considered to be subject to a global show command. Table 5.2 shows useful global show commands. A detailed description of the commands as well as sample output is included after the table. (Logging is covered in its own section at the end of the chapter.)

TABLE 5.2   Global show Commands

Global show Command	Information Produced
version	System hardware and software status
running-config	Current operating configuration
startup-config	Contents of startup configuration
logging	Contents of logging buffers

TABLE 5.2   Global show Commands *(continued)*

Global show Command	Information Produced
buffers	Buffer pool statistics
stacks	Process stack utilization
tech-support	System information for Tech Support
access-lists	List of access lists
memory	Memory statistics

show version

This command is used to display the system hardware and software versions. It also provides information about how long the router was running and the reason it was last restarted. Review the output of the show version command:

```
Router_B>show version
Cisco Internetwork Operating System Software
IOS (tm) RSP Software (RSP-JSV-M), Version 12.1(16), RELEASE SOFTWARE (fc1)
Copyright (c) 1986-2002 by cisco Systems, Inc.
Compiled Tue 09-Jul-02 07:36 by kellythw
Image text-base: 0x60010958, data-base: 0x614C4000

ROM: System Bootstrap, Version 11.1(8)CA1, EARLY DEPLOYMENT RELEASE
 SOFTWARE (fc1)
BOOTLDR: RSP Software (RSP-BOOT-M), Version 12.1(16), RELEASE SOFTWARE (fc1)

Router_B uptime is 35 weeks, 1 day, 6 hours, 18 minutes
System returned to ROM by reload at 00:12:02 EST Tue Oct 8 2002
System restarted at 23:52:37 EST Mon Oct 7 2002
System image file is "slot0:rsp-jsv-mz.121-16.bin"

cisco RSP4 (R5000) processor with 131072K/2072K bytes of memory.
R5000 CPU at 200Mhz, Implementation 35, Rev 2.1, 512KB L2 Cache
Last reset from power-on
G.703/E1 software, Version 1.0.
G.703/JT2 software, Version 1.0.
X.25 software, Version 3.0.0.
SuperLAT software (copyright 1990 by Meridian Technology Corp).
```

```
Bridging software.
TN3270 Emulation software.
Chassis Interface.
5 VIP2 controllers (2 FastEthernet)(6 HSSI)(1 ATM).
1 VIP2 R5K controller (8 Serial).
2 FastEthernet/IEEE 802.3 interface(s)
8 Serial network interface(s)
6 HSSI network interface(s)
1 ATM network interface(s)
123K bytes of non-volatile configuration memory.

20480K bytes of Flash PCMCIA card at slot 0 (Sector size 128K).
8192K bytes of Flash internal SIMM (Sector size 256K).
No slave installed in slot 7.
Configuration register is 0x102

Router_B>
```

As you can see, the output contains a great deal of information. We'll move through it field by field. The first field indicates the revision of software that is actively running on the router. In this case, it is Cisco IOS 12.1(16).

The next field is the bootstrap version, which indicates the Cisco IOS that is used in case the IOS isn't found. This IOS is stored on the PROMs or flash memory of the router. The router boots by using 11.1(8)CA. This allows the router to actually boot so that you can fix software problems.

Current router status information is located in the field following the bootstrap information. This output tells you the length of time the router has been up and the last date it was reloaded. If an error caused the router to reload, the error message is included in this field. Finally, the file that was used while booting is listed.

Directly after this section is a line that tells the type of processor used and the amount of DRAM present. The DRAM is displayed in the format *value1/value2* bytes of memory. Value 1 is the amount of local memory present; Value 2 is the amount of I/O memory present. The total DRAM in the router is the sum of these two values.

The final section describes the route processor and amount of RAM. At the end of the section, all interface processors are listed, followed by the number of interfaces. The last three lines indicate the different amounts and types of memory.

show startup-config and running-config

These two commands are used to view the syntax of the router's configuration. The show startup-config command displays the contents of the configuration that was written to NVRAM. The show running-config, show config, and write term commands are all equivalent. The results of these commands display the configuration that was loaded into memory and is running on the router.

Although you should already be familiar with these two commands, here is a very good troubleshooting tip: Compare the two configurations when working on network problems. It is always possible that configuration changes were made to the running configuration but not copied to the startup configuration. There may be extra or missing commands in the configuration versions. You may be able to solve the problem of missing commands in the running configuration quickly by copying the `startup-config` to the `running-config`.

These commands provide you with global, protocol, and interface information. You can analyze them for proper configuration and then make changes, if needed. Many problems can be isolated by viewing the configuration. What usually happens is that you will see something that wasn't there before, see something that shouldn't be there, or notice that something is missing that needs to be there. For this technique to work, you must be familiar with the router and its configuration. If backups are made of the configurations, you can compare them to the `running-config` to look for differences.

show buffers

The buffers come configured with default settings. They can be modified, if necessary, but if you do this it's usually a good idea to have a Cisco TAC engineer look at the memory allocation and suggest the new buffer settings. Following is an example of the buffer settings:

```
Router_B>show buffers
Buffer elements:
     999 in free list (500 max allowed)
     2594679003 hits, 0 misses, 500 created

Public buffer pools:
Small buffers, 104 bytes (total 480, permanent 480):
     455 in free list (20 min, 1000 max allowed)
     243410950 hits, 0 misses, 0 trims, 0 created
     0 failures (0 no memory)
Middle buffers, 600 bytes (total 360, permanent 360):
     357 in free list (20 min, 800 max allowed)
     374760214 hits, 8298 misses, 5776 trims, 5776 created
     2275 failures (0 no memory)
Big buffers, 1524 bytes (total 360, permanent 360):
     358 in free list (10 min, 1200 max allowed)
     274949626 hits, 0 misses, 0 trims, 0 created
     0 failures (0 no memory)
VeryBig buffers, 4520 bytes (total 40, permanent 40):
     40 in free list (5 min, 1200 max allowed)
     12900991 hits, 173 misses, 519 trims, 519 created
     0 failures (0 no memory)
Large buffers, 5024 bytes (total 40, permanent 40):
```

```
      40 in free list (3 min, 120 max allowed)
      0 hits, 0 misses, 0 trims, 0 created
      0 failures (0 no memory)
Huge buffers, 18024 bytes (total 4, permanent 0):
      3 in free list (3 min, 52 max allowed)
      2459 hits, 2 misses, 8716 trims, 8720 created
      0 failures (0 no memory)

Interface buffer pools:
IPC buffers, 4096 bytes (total 312, permanent 312):
      312 in free list (104 min, 1040 max allowed)
      696006349 hits, 0 fallbacks, 0 trims, 0 created
      0 failures (0 no memory)

Header pools:
```

You can view six buffer distinctions in this output: small, middle, big, very big, large, and huge; and each division is allocated a particular amount of buffer space. These allocations are determined at router boot-up and vary by interface type. The show buffers output details the buffer name and size, with the buffer size following immediately after its name. The (total 120, permanent 120) for the small pool specifies that there are a total of 120 spaces allocated to the small pool. The permanent means that the 120 buffer spaces are permanently assigned to the small buffer pool. When a buffer's space is permanent, it cannot be de-allocated and given back to the system memory for other uses.

In the next field, you can see the number of free buffer spaces that are open to accepting a packet. Each pool maintains a minimum and maximum threshold, which the pool uses to decide whether more buffer space needs to be allocated to it. This is seen in the min and max allowed indicators.

The last two lines of information given for each pool describe the activity happening there. This information, which includes all hits, misses, trims, created spaces, and failures, is described in the following list:

Hits   The number of times the pool was used successfully.

Misses   The number of times a packet tried to find a space within a pool but found no available spaces. In this case, the packet is not discarded; rather, a space is created for it.

Trims   The number of spaces removed from the pool because the amount exceeded the number of allowed buffer spaces. This value is only meaningful on dynamically allocated buffer pools; static pools cannot be trimmed.

Created   The number of spaces created to accommodate requests for space when there wasn't enough at the time the request was made or if there were fewer than the min of a certain type of buffer available. Once the space is no longer needed, it will be trimmed.

Failures The number of times a buffer pool tried unsuccessfully to create space. When a failure occurs, the requesting packet is dropped.

The last field is the `no memory` field, which records the number of failures that occurred due to the lack of sufficient system memory required to create additional buffer space.

If you observe a significant increase in the number of misses while monitoring buffers with the `show buffers` command, the pool can be tuned by assigning different values to the `max-free`, `min-free`, and `permanent` parameters. Increasing the values for these parameters overrides the system defaults—instead of having to create additional spaces on demand within a pool, the spaces can be statically allocated and assigned. This helps you avoid racking up missed and failed packet statuses.

You can adjust these parameters with the following command:

```
buffers {small | middle | big | verybig | large | huge |   type number}
  {permanent | max-free | min-free |   initial} number
```

The `type` represents interface type, and `number` is the number to be assigned to the specified parameter.

Table 5.3 depicts the sizes of the buffer space within a pool. When a packet needs to be stored in a buffer, it requests space from the pool in proportion to its size requirement. For example, a full-size Ethernet packet at a 1500MTU requires one buffer space from the big buffer pool.

TABLE 5.3 Sizes of the Buffer within a Pool

Pool Name	Buffer Size (in Bytes)
Small	104
Middle	600
Big	1524
Very Big	4520
Large	5024
Huge	18,024

show stacks

The `show stacks` command is not very useful to you, but it is invaluable information for the Cisco TAC. An example of output from the command appears just below. As you can see, it won't make a lot of sense to the user. The information is sent to Cisco, and Cisco runs it through a stack decode that provides the information relevant to system problems.

Stacks are used to provide information on the router's processes and processor utilization. The output displayed is from a healthy router. If the router were to crash, the latest stack information is saved so it can be captured once the router comes back up. The data contains information regarding the reason for the reload and any errors that are attributed to the crash.

```
Router_A#show stack
Minimum process stacks:
 Free/Size   Name
10288/12000  Init
 5196/6000   Router Init
 9672/12000  Virtual Exec

Interrupt level stacks:
Level   Called Unused/Size  Name
  1     49917   8200/9000   Network Interrupt
  2         2   8372/9000   Network Status Interrupt
  3         0   9000/9000   OIR interrupt
  4         0   9000/9000   PCMCIA Interrupt
  5      2561   8652/9000   Console Uart
  6         0   9000/9000   Error Interrupt
  7  27140712   8608/9000   NMI Interrupt Handler
Router_A#
```

show tech-support

The show tech-support command is a compilation of several show commands (version, running-config, controllers, stacks, interfaces, diagbus, buffers, process memory, process cpu, context, boot, flash bootflash, ip traffic, and controllers cbus). It should be noted that, although these are the typical commands issued by show tech-support, the commands can vary depending on hardware and software levels. You can get most of the information you need by issuing the show tech-support command, instead of issuing all of the commands separately.

The show tech-support command does not allow you to scroll through its output on the router because of the enormous amount of information that is displayed. To capture the output, you need a terminal with a large line-buffer setting, or you can log the output directly to a terminal.

show access-lists

The show access-lists command is useful to view the access list configuration without sorting through the running or start-up configuration. In addition to displaying the line entries of the access list, the command uses the access list number to define what type of access list is being displayed. The output from the show access-lists command follows:

```
Router_B#show access-lists
```

```
Extended IP access-list 105
    permit ip 172.16.0.0 0.0.255.255 any (97160 matches)
    permit ip 10.0.0.0 0.255.255.255 any
    deny   ip any any (102463 matches)
Novell access-list 801
    permit 606E3000 (3245 matches)
    permit 506E3074
    permit B06F2E00 (655 matches)
    permit D06F2EFE
    permit 717B012C
    permit E06F2E67
    permit F9BE0714 (5038 matches)
    permit A054AB00
    permit 617B07C4
    permit 017B1900
```

This information gives you a summary of each access list on the router. The access list type is defined and the number assigned to it is shown. Each line of the list is displayed individually. The list also specifies match-ups between networks and wildcard masks.

show memory

This command is helpful for diagnosing memory problems such as allocation failures, low amounts of free memory, and so on. In the following output, you can see that the first field has the memory divided between processor memory and fast memory. The fields are self-explanatory; they describe the total, used, and free amounts of memory. As you will see in the Process Commands section later, the output here is very similar to the show processes memory command.

```
Router_C>show memory
        Head      Total(b)   Used(b)    Free(b)    Lowest(b)   Largest(b)
Proc  60DC38E0    52676384   34896328   17780056   15823612    14764584
Fast  60DA38E0    131072     128344     2728       27282684
Processor memory
Address   Bytes  Prev.     Next     Ref  PrevF  NextF  Alloc PC   What
60DC38E0  1056   0         60DC3D2C  1                 601342A4   List Elements
60DC3D2C  2656   60DC38E0  60DC47B8  1                 601342A4   List Headers
60DC47B8  9000   60DC3D2C  60DC6B0C  1                 60135498   Interrupt Stack
60DC6B0C  9000   60DC47B8  60DC8E60  1                 60135498   Interrupt Stack
```

Interface Commands

Interface commands deal with detailed interface settings and configurations. Because each type of interface uses particular protocols and technologies, the show interface command is capable of displaying all data related to a specified interface. Table 5.4 lists useful interface-related show commands. Here in this section we will focus on the show interface and show ip interface commands.

TABLE 5.4 show interface Commands

show interface Command	Information Produced
queuing/queue	Queuing configuration and contents
interface <interface-type> <interface-number>	Interface status and configuration
ip interface	Information specifically related to IP interfaces

show queueing and show queue

To verify the configuration and operation of the queuing system, you can issue the following two commands:

```
show queueing [fair | priority | custom]
show queue [interface-type interface-number]
```

Following are the results from these commands on Router C. Because weighted fair queuing is the only type of queuing that has been enabled on this router, it wasn't necessary to issue the optional command options fair, custom, or priority.

```
Router_C#show queueing
Current fair queue configuration:
Interface  Discard     Dynamic      Reserved
           threshold   queue count  queue count
  Serial0    96          256            0
  Serial1    64          256            0
Current priority queue configuration:
Current custom queue configuration:
Current RED queue configuration:
Router_C#
```

This command output shows that weighted fair queuing is enabled on both serial interfaces, and that the discard threshold for Serial 0 was changed from 64 to 96. There's a maximum of 256 dynamic queues for both interfaces—the default value. The lines following the interface information are empty because their corresponding queuing algorithms aren't configured yet.

The next command, show queue, displays more-detailed information pertaining to the specified interface.

```
Router_C#show queue serial0
 Input queue: 0/75/0 (size/max/drops); Total output drops: 0
 Queueing strategy: weighted fair
 Output queue: 0/1000/96/0 (size/max total/threshold/ drops)
   Conversations 0/1/256 (active/max active/max total)
   Reserved Conversations 0/0 (allocated/max allocated)
Router_C#
```

show interface

As mentioned, the show interface command has many derivatives. Table 5.5 lists many of the options that are available with this command.

 It is important to recognize that the interface processors listed are there because they are present on the router. For example, you won't see a Token Ring interface listed unless there is a Token Ring interface on the router.

TABLE 5.5   show interface Command Options

show interface Command Option	Information Produced
atm (interface type)	ATM interface
ethernet (interface type)	IEEE 802.3
serial (interface type)	Serial
hssi (interface type)	HSSI interface
accounting	Interface accounting
fair-queue	Interface Weighted Fair Queueing (WFQ) info
rate-limit	Interface rate-limit info
mac-accounting	Interface MAC accounting info

Now look at sample outputs from an Ethernet and a serial interface. After each sample, we will go through a detailed explanation.

```
Router_A#show interface Ethernet 5/4
Ethernet5/4 is up, line protocol is up
```

```
    Hardware is cxBus Ethernet, address is 009a.822e.51b6 (bia 90.323f.acdb)
    Description: Connection to Router_B
    Internet address is 172.16.1.1/24
    MTU 1500 bytes, BW 10000 Kbit, DLY 1000 usec, rely 255/
      255, load 33/255
    Encapsulation ARPA, loopback not set, keepalive set (10
      sec)
    ARP type: ARPA, ARP Timeout 04:00:00
    Last input 00:00:00, output 00:00:00, output hang never
    Last clearing of "show interface" counters never
    Queueing strategy: fifo
    Output queue 0/40, 101553 drops; input queue 0/75, 1327
      drops
    5 minute input rate 247000 bits/sec, 196 packets/sec
    5 minute output rate 1329000 bits/sec, 333 packets/sec
      421895792 packets input, 2524672293 bytes, 1 no
      buffer
      Received 453382 broadcasts, 0 runts, 0 giants
      6 input errors, 1 CRC, 5 frame, 0 overrun, 494
      ignored,        0 abort
      0 input packets with dribble condition detected
      618578101 packets output, 977287695 bytes, 0
      underruns
      0 output errors, 30979588 collisions, 1 interface
    resets
      0 babbles, 0 late collision, 0 deferred
      0 lost carrier, 0 no carrier
      0 output buffers copied, 0 interrupts, 0 failures
Router_A#
```

This output starts with the most pertinent information—the physical interface and line protocol status. In this case, both are up. There is much argument as to what constitutes an "up" interface. It is very simple—the controller sends a signal that there are electrons flowing through the physical interface. So, just doing a no shut on an interface brings it into an "up" status, even if nothing is plugged into the interface. Line protocol is up means that the interface is able to send itself a frame and receive it back.

The next fields contain the Layer 2 MAC address, the interface description, and the Layer 3 IP address. Below the interface address information, you'll find the line settings for the interface; MTU, bandwidth, delay, reliability, and load are listed. These values are used to calculate a distance-vector protocol route metric.

Default Ethernet encapsulation for Cisco is ARPA. You can see that this is true and that the keepalive is the default at 10 seconds. This line is very important when troubleshooting Ethernet problems. If the encapsulation type is not compatible with other machines on the network, you will have communication problems. In order to better demonstrate this, let's examine the example given in the following paragraph.

When the router broadcasts from an interface, it uses the encapsulation that is configured. Look at Figure 5.1. In this case, an ARPA frame (#1) is sent. If the hosts on the network do not understand ARPA, they do not respond to the broadcast. On the other hand, if a host broadcast uses a SNAP frame (#2), the router is designed to understand any incoming frame encapsulation and can respond to the broadcast. Another bit of useful information that the router adds to the ARP table is the encapsulation type of that host. Then, the next time that the router wants to speak with the given host, it uses the documented frame type instead of the type configured on the interface. Here's a look at the ARP table (notice that the **Type** field is SNAP):

```
Router_C>show arp
Protocol  Address        Age (min)  Hardware Addr   Type  Interface
Internet  172.16.1.1     -          0010.296a.a820  ARPA  Ethernet5/0
Internet  172.16.1.22    62         0010.29d1.68a0  SNAP  Ethernet5/0
Router_C>
```

FIGURE 5.1   Ethernet frame encapsulation compatibility

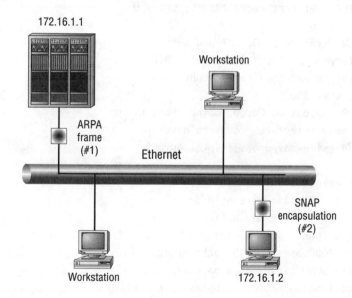

Continuing on with the output from the show interface command, you can see a great deal of statistical information. The counters for the interface have not been cleared since the router booted. Queuing type for the interface is first-in-first-out (FIFO). You should be familiar with the next few fields, since the input and output queue were previously discussed in the *show queueing* and *show queue section*. Here, you have statistical information that displays the number of drops. The interface traffic statistics follow.

Statistical information includes the number of packets that travel across the interface, and the bandwidth utilization. The following fields are dedicated to Ethernet troubleshooting. The cyclic redundancy check field counts the number of frames that were received that do not pass the CRC test. Next are frame errors and overruns. Overruns occur when the receiver on the interface receives frames faster than it can move them to the hardware buffer on the interface. The ignore signal is sent if there are buffer problems.

Output errors consist of underruns and collisions. The other fields are counters for the physical interface: resets, lost carrier, and no carrier. These are followed by more buffer error counters.

Now we'll review the output from a serial interface:

```
Router_D#sho int s1/0
Serial1/0 is up, line protocol is up
  Hardware is cxBus Serial
  Description: Connection to frame-relay cloud
  MTU 1500 bytes, BW 1544 Kbit, DLY 20000 usec, rely 255/
  255, load 1/255
  Encapsulation FRAME-RELAY, loopback not set, keepalive
  set    (10 sec)
  LMI enq sent  195167, LMI stat recvd 195165, LMI upd
  recvd     10, DTE LMI up
  LMI enq recvd 0, LMI stat sent  0, LMI upd sent  0
  LMI DLCI 1023  LMI type is CISCO  frame relay DTE
  Broadcast queue 0/64, broadcasts sent/dropped 0/0,
  interface broadcasts 908350
  Last input 00:00:00, output 00:00:00, output hang never
  Last clearing of "show interface" counters never
  Input queue: 0/75/4 (size/max/drops); Total output
  drops:    22795
  Queueing strategy: weighted fair
  Output queue: 0/64/22795 (size/threshold/drops)
     Conversations  0/59 (active/max active)
     Reserved Conversations 0/0 (allocated/max allocated)
  5 minute input rate 7000 bits/sec, 9 packets/sec
  5 minute output rate 9000 bits/sec, 8 packets/sec
     55695166 packets input, 3680326698 bytes, 1 no buffer
     Received 0 broadcasts, 0 runts, 0 giants
     1 input errors, 0 CRC, 0 frame, 0 overrun, 0 ignored,
     1 abort
     56424159 packets output, 569801054 bytes, 0 underruns
     0 output errors, 0 collisions, 2 interface resets
     8656902 output buffers copied, 0 interrupts, 0
```

```
         failures
         3 carrier transitions
         RTS up, CTS up, DTR up, DCD up, DSR up
Router_D#
```

This output has a lot of Frame Relay information that we will discuss in Chapter 7. For now, we'll just review the fields of information that are available by using this command. You can see that the first line is the interface status line. The metric values are also listed. Following the Frame Relay information, you see the interface traffic statistics. At the bottom of the output are the buffer error fields, as well as the physical interface counters. A carrier transition is counted anytime the carrier status change occurs. (We will explore this output in Chapter 7.)

show ip interface

This command provides information specific to the TCP/IP configuration of the specified interface. Information regarding the interface status, IP address, subnet mask, broadcast address, and applied access lists is all contained in the show ip interface command output. In addition, the command also provides information on proxy ARP, which will be explained in further detail later in this chapter; helper addresses, which are used for DHCP configurations; the status of network address translation (NAT); and many other items. The amount of output from the show ip interface command for a particular interface is second only to that of the show interface command. Here is a sample:

```
Router_B#show ip interface serial 0
Serial0 is up, line protocol is up
  Internet address is 172.16.30.6/30
  Broadcast address is 255.255.255.255
  Address determined by non-volatile memory
  MTU is 1500 bytes
  Helper address is not set
  Directed broadcast forwarding is enabled
  Multicast reserved groups joined: 224.0.0.10
  Outgoing access list is not set
  Inbound  access list is not set
  Proxy ARP is enabled
  Security level is default
  Split horizon is enabled
  ICMP redirects are always sent
  ICMP unreachables are always sent
  ICMP mask replies are never sent
  IP fast switching is enabled
  IP fast switching on the same interface is enabled
  IP multicast fast switching is enabled
  Router Discovery is disabled
```

```
   IP output packet accounting is disabled
   IP access violation accounting is disabled
   TCP/IP header compression is disabled
   Probe proxy name replies are disabled
   Gateway Discovery is disabled
   Policy routing is disabled
   Network address translation is disabled
Router_B#
```

Process Commands

Process commands deal directly with the processes running on the router. If the standard show processes command is issued, you get a result similar to a ps -ef executed on a Unix box. The output details each process, including process ID number (PID), time running, and stack information. This output is too general to be used effectively while troubleshooting, but there are two very important process command options that can be executed to refine this output.

The two options available with the show processes command are cpu and memory, as described in Table 5.6. Each of these options refines the processes' output and makes it more useful and user-friendly.

TABLE 5.6   show process Commands

show interface Command	Information Produced
cpu	Amount of CPU time being spent on each process.
memory	Memory statistics

show processes cpu

The output from this command, shown just below, relates the router's processes and CPU utilization. The first line of the output displays the router's CPU utilization over three periods. In addition, you will notice that the CPU utilization for the 5-second interval has two percentages, 15% and 6%. The first number is the average CPU utilization for all processes on the router over the last 5 seconds. The second number is the percentage of the CPU spent on interrupt-driven processes. In general, interrupt-driven tasks are core to the router's ability to route packets. Examples of these tasks include fast- or process-switched packets, input from the console or auxiliary ports, and corrections of memory-alignment issues. Items such as maintaining VTY sessions and responding to SNMP queries are non-interrupt-driven processes that would only show up in the first percentage.

Underneath the CPU utilization line, you can see the processes running on the router. Starting from the left, you can see the PID, followed by the runtime and other data. The three columns that deal with CPU utilization detail the percentage of CPU cycles used by the specified process. The process description is found in the far-right column.

```
Router_C>show processes cpu
CPU utilization for five seconds: 15%/6%; one minute: 7%;    five minutes: 7%
  PID  Runtime(ms)   Invoked   uSecs    5Sec    1Min    5Min   TTY  Process
    1           76   1564143       0   0.00%   0.00%   0.00%     0  Load Meter
    2            0         1       0   0.00%   0.00%   0.00%     0  LAPF Input
    3      3638844    872510    4170   0.00%   0.04%   0.00%     0  Check heaps
    4            4        28     142   0.00%   0.00%   0.00%     0  Pool Manager
    5            0         2       0   0.00%   0.00%   0.00%     0  Timers
```

. . . [output removed] . . .

When the overall CPU utilization gets high, you can identify which process is using the most CPU cycles, and then focus your attention on that process. For example, if the IP-EIGRP CPU utilization runs high, you can determine that there is a problem within EIGRP, perhaps a routing loop or some other instability.

show processes memory

The second helpful option for the show processes command is memory, which is used to associate memory utilization with the router's processes. Here is a sample output:

```
Router_D>show processes memory
Total: 52503792, Used: 45141524, Free: 7362268
  PID TTY  Allocated      Freed    Holding   Getbufs   Retbufs Process
    0   0      54400        304    8898364         0         0 *Init*
    0   0        632 3906083084        632         0         0 *Sched*
    0   0  700723436  729437084     472484   1091352         0 *Dead*
    1   0         96          0       6876         0         0 SSCOP Input
    2   0          0          0       6780         0         0 Check heaps
    3   0   17262036     152680       6916  12351248    260336 Pool Manager
```

. . . [output removed] . . .

The first line details the total, used, and free amounts of system memory. Following that, you see the PID, allocated, freed, and holding memory. This means that the processor has allocated a given amount of memory to the process; if the process does not need all of that memory, it frees some of it and retains the rest.

TCP/IP Protocol Commands

We will discuss the major TCP/IP protocol commands in this section. In addition to the TCP/IP-related commands listed here, other protocol-related commands are covered later in the book. These cover protocols including HDLC, Frame Relay, X.25, and ISDN.

Table 5.7 lists the frequently used IP options for the show command.

TABLE 5.7   Frequently Used show IP Command Options

show ip Command Option	Information Produced
access-lists	IP access lists.
accounting	The active IP accounting database.
arp	Information regarding the IP ARP entries in the ARP cache.
interface	IP interface status and configuration.
protocols	Information regarding the IP routing protocols running on a router.
route	IP routing table.
traffic	IP protocol statistics.

show ip access-list

This command provides information regarding a specified access list, or all access lists that fall within the 1–199 range. When various access lists are configured on the router, the show ip access-list command shows named IP access lists only. (Named access lists are explained later in this chapter.) From the following sample output, you can see that it lists both standard and extended lists:

```
Standard IP access list 5
    permit 172.16.14.2
    permit 172.16.91.140
    permit 172.16.10.51
    permit 172.16.1.7
    permit 172.16.155.0, wildcard bits 0.0.0.255
Extended IP access list 152
    deny ip any 172.16.91.0 0.0.0.63 log (268436 matches)
    deny ip any host 172.16.91.66 log (81058 matches)
    permit tcp any any established (8809 matches)
    permit ip host 172.16.2.55 any
    permit ip host 172.60.22.10 any (2194226 matches)
    permit ip host 172.140.64.8 any (7930443 matches)
    permit ip 172.16.10.0 0.0.255.255 any (9076 matches)
```

show ip arp

This command provides information contained in the router's ARP cache, including the IP address, MAC address, encapsulation type, and interface from which the MAC was learned. Here is a sample:

```
Router_C#show ip arp
Protocol  Address         Age (min)  Hardware Addr   Type   Interface
Internet  172.16.60.1         -       0010.7bd9.2881  ARPA   Ethernet0/1
Internet  172.16.50.2         -       0010.7bd9.2880  ARPA   Ethernet0/0
Internet  172.16.50.1         6       0000.0c09.99cc  ARPA   Ethernet0/0
Router_C#
```

show ip protocols

This command provides information about the IP routing protocols that run on the router. The sample output shown here includes only EIGRP information because that is all that is being run on the router. As you can see, global filters are not applied. Metric values are displayed for each individual routing protocol. Route redistribution information is also provided.

```
Router_B#show ip protocols
Routing Protocol is "eigrp 100"
  Outgoing update filter list for all interfaces is not
  set
  Incoming update filter list for all interfaces is not
  set
  Default networks flagged in outgoing updates
  Default networks accepted from incoming updates
  EIGRP metric weight K1=1, K2=0, K3=1, K4=0, K5=0
  EIGRP maximum hopcount 100
  EIGRP maximum metric variance 1
  Redistributing: eigrp 100
  Automatic network summarization is not in effect
  Routing for Networks:
    172.16.0.0
  Routing Information Sources:
    Gateway          Distance      Last Update
  Distance: internal 90 external 170
Router_B#
```

show ip route

This command returns information stored in the IP route table. The command can be issued as a general command, and all IP routes and corresponding information will be displayed. Additionally, you can specify a given network, and the command will return information regarding that network only.

Following are two samples. Notice that the two outputs are different. The general command provides summary information for every IP route in the route table. However, when a network is specified, the results are much more detailed. Items such as the exact routing protocol responsible for learning the route, the source interface, and the next-hop router's IP address are all included.

```
Router_A>show ip route
Codes: C - connected, S - static, I - IGRP, R - RIP, M - mobile, B - BGP
    D - EIGRP, EX - EIGRP external, O - OSPF, IA - OSPF
    inter area
    N1 - OSPF NSSA external type 1, N2 - OSPF NSSA
    external type 2
    E1 - OSPF external type 1, E2 - OSPF external type 2,
    E - EGP
     i - IS-IS, L1 - IS-IS level-1, L2 - IS-IS level-2, *
     - candidate default
U - per-user static route, o - ODR

Gateway of last resort is not set

     172.16.0.0/16 is variably subnetted, 2 subnets, 2     masks
D       172.16.50.0/24 [90/2195456] via 172.16.30.6, 00:00:19, Serial1
C       172.16.30.4/30 is directly connected, Serial1
Router_A>


Router_A>show ip route 172.16.50.0
Routing entry for 172.16.50.0/24
  Known via "eigrp 100", distance 90, metric 2195456, type  internal
  Redistributing via eigrp 100
  Last update from 172.16.30.6 on Serial1, 00:02:03 ago
  Routing Descriptor Blocks:
  * 172.16.30.6, from 172.16.30.6, 00:02:03 ago, via
  Serial1
      Route metric is 2195456, traffic share count is 1
      Total delay is 21000 microseconds, minimum bandwidth
      is 1544 Kbit
      Reliability 128/255, minimum MTU 1500 bytes
      Loading 1/255, Hops 1


Router_A>
```

show ip traffic

This command returns information pertaining to IP traffic statistics. When the command is issued, the output is organized according to the IP protocol. Here is a sample:

```
Router_B#show ip traffic
IP statistics:
  Rcvd:  400 total, 400 local destination
         0 format errors, 0 checksum errors,
         0 bad hop count
         0 unknown protocol, 0 not a gateway
         0 security failures, 0 bad options,
         0 with options
  Opts:  0 end, 0 nop, 0 basic security,
         0 loose source  route
         0 timestamp, 0 extended security, 0 record route
         0 stream ID, 0 strict source route, 0 alert,
         0 cipso
         0 other
  Frags: 0 reassembled, 0 timeouts, 0 couldn't reassemble
         0 fragmented, 0 couldn't fragment
  Bcast: 0 received, 0 sent
  Mcast: 398 received, 401 sent
  Sent:  404 generated, 0 forwarded
         0 encapsulation failed, 0 no route

ICMP statistics:
  Rcvd: 0 format errors, 0 checksum errors, 0 redirects, 0
  unreachable
         0 echo, 0 echo reply, 0 mask requests, 0 mask
         replies, 0 quench
         0 parameter, 0 timestamp, 0 info request, 0 other
         0 irdp solicitations, 0 irdp advertisements
  Sent: 0 redirects, 0 unreachable, 0 echo, 0 echo reply
         0 mask requests, 0 mask replies, 0 quench, 0
         timestamp
         0 info reply, 0 time exceeded, 0 parameter problem
         0 irdp solicitations, 0 irdp advertisements

UDP statistics:
  Rcvd: 0 total, 0 checksum errors, 0 no port
  Sent: 0 total, 0 forwarded broadcasts
```

```
TCP statistics:
  Rcvd: 0 total, 0 checksum errors, 0 no port
  Sent: 0 total

Probe statistics:
  Rcvd: 0 address requests, 0 address replies
        0 proxy name requests, 0 where-is requests, 0
        other
  Sent: 0 address requests, 0 address replies (0 proxy)
        0 proxy name replies, 0 where-is replies

EGP statistics:
  Rcvd: 0 total, 0 format errors, 0 checksum errors, 0 no
  listener
  Sent: 0 total

IGRP statistics:
  Rcvd: 0 total, 0 checksum errors
  Sent: 0 total

OSPF statistics:
  Rcvd: 0 total, 0 checksum errors
        0 Hello, 0 database desc, 0 link state req
        0 link state updates, 0 link state acks

  Sent: 0 total

IP-IGRP2 statistics:
  Rcvd: 402 total
  Sent: 406 total

PIMv2 statistics: Sent/Received
  Total: 0/0, 0 checksum errors, 0 format errors
  Registers: 0/0, Register Stops: 0/0

IGMP statistics: Sent/Received
  Total: 0/0, Format errors: 0/0, Checksum errors: 0/0
  Host Queries: 0/0, Host Reports: 0/0, Host Leaves: 00
  DVMRP: 0/0, PIM: 0/0
```

```
ARP statistics:
  Rcvd: 0 requests, 0 replies, 0 reverse, 0 other
  Sent: 1 requests, 5 replies (0 proxy), 0 reverse
Router_B#
```

debug Commands

The debug commands and options are very powerful tools. The messages produced by the debugging process give detailed information and provide insight into what is happening on a very low level.

This power does not come free of charge. In most cases, debugging requires every packet to be process-switched, meaning that the route processor has to look at every packet entering the router in order for valid information to be obtained. In addition, the router must run and manage many other processes. Debugging can cause a great deal of additional overhead on a router. Therefore, it is important to use the tool with discretion. Use it to provide additional information on an existing problem, not to monitor a router. As a rule of thumb, debug commands should not be run on a router that already has a CPU utilization greater than 50%.

Because most problems are reported while a network is in production, the last thing you want to do is crash a router or cause unnecessary overhead by using the debug tool. By focusing the application of the debug command by using various command options and access lists, you can effectively troubleshoot problems without causing additional ones.

 WARNING   Always remember to turn the debugging function off after you obtain the necessary data. If left on, it can cause another network problem.

There are two "tricks" to successfully using the debug tool. First, make sure that your router is configured to apply timestamps to all messages. This is done with the following commands:

Router_A(config)#**service timestamps debug datetime msec localtime**
Router_A(config)#**service timestamps log datetime msec localtime**

Next, make sure that you see these messages. By default, error and debug messages are sent only to the console. If you are telnetted to the router, you will not see the debug or log messages unless you issue the following command:

Router_A#**terminal monitor**

You can turn the messages off again by issuing the no form of the command:

Router_A#**terminal no monitor**

If the output messages from the debug become excessive, it becomes difficult, if not impossible, to enter commands. Should this happen, there are two commands that you can issue to stop the messages. The first one was already mentioned (terminal no monitor, or term no mon for short). In this case, you type, but you don't see anything echo back. It can get confusing. Remember that the text messages that echo to the screen are not entered on the command line of the router. You can safely type **term no mon** and press Enter, even with hundreds of messages scrolling past you on the screen. The router eventually recognizes and processes the command. That stops the messages from scrolling down the screen, but it does not stop the processor from looking at every packet.

To stop the debug process altogether, the easiest way is to type the shorthand form of undebug all, like this:

```
Router_A#un all
```

It is short and sweet, yet effective. It works especially well when the router seems to be having a runaway. This command stops all debug processes and all associated messages. It can be entered safely while messages are scrolling wildly down the screen. It may take the router a few CPU cycles to accept the command and actually stop the debug process, so don't panic.

As an alternative, you can also have the un all command ready to go if you allow multiple telnet sessions to the same router. In this instance, you would telnet to the router twice. In one of the telnet sessions, set up the terminal monitor command so that you would receive the debug output. In the other window, type in the undebug all command but do not press Enter. Then return to your first telnet session and execute the debug command you need. If the output is overwhelming, go back to your other telnet session and hit Enter. As was the case before, it may take several seconds for the router to process the command and the messages to stop appearing on the screen.

Limiting Debug Output

Because of the potential impact to the router, you should take precautions whenever you use debug commands. Be as specific as possible when entering the debug commands so that you look at only information relevant to your issue. In addition to the commands themselves, you can apply access lists to the debug commands to further limit the information you are examining.

For example, if you wanted to see ping (ICMP) packets going between stations with IP addresses of 10.20.20.20 and 10.30.30.30, you could create an access list like this:

```
access-list 100 permit icmp host 10.20.20.20 host 10.30.30.30
```

Then apply this access list to the debug command as shown here:

```
Router_C#debug ip packet detail 100
IP packet debugging is on (detailed) for access list 100
Router_C#
IP: s=10.20.20.20 (Serial0), d=10.30.30.30 (Serial1), g=10.5.30.30, len
 100, forward ICMP type=8, code=0
```

In this manner, only ICMP packets going from 10.20.20.20 to 10.30.30.30 are shown in the debug output, rather than all of the packets going through the router.

As with the show commands, there are global-, interface-, and protocol-related debugging options. Because these tools and commands are used and discussed often in upcoming chapters, they are only summarized here according to usage.

 Real World Scenario

Verify the Packet Flow without Using Debug

One question that frequently arises during troubleshooting is whether a particular packet is making it all the way through or even to a particular router. One way to verify this is by using debugging commands. The usual warning applies: Debugging commands can have a severe impact on the overall functionality of the router. Therefore, alternate solutions should be examined. In this case, one alternate solution is to use the log feature of an access list.

Assume that you want to verify that pings from 10.20.20.20 and destined to 10.30.30.30 are getting to the router. To do this, we first create an access list with two lines:

```
access-list 100 permit icmp host 10.20.20.20 host 10.30.30.30 log
access-list 100 permit ip any any
```

Notice the log at the end of the first line of the access list. This will put an entry in the log anytime a packet meeting the criteria specified in the line is seen by the router. Also notice the permit ip any any at the end. This line ensures that other traffic on the interface will not be affected.

At this point, make sure you are on the console or have your telnet session set up as a terminal monitor, and apply the access list inbound on the interface to be used by the packets to enter the router. These commands look like this:

```
Router_A(config)#interface serial0
Router_A(config-if)#ip access-group 100 in
%SEC-6-IPACCESSLOGDP: list 100 permitted icmp 10.20.20.20 -> 10.30.30.30 (0/0), 1
packet
```

By using access lists in this manner, you are able to verify that particular traffic is flowing over this router.

Although potentially safer than using debug, the log option on access lists can also create a large amount of data if substantial traffic meets the selection criteria specified in the access list. In addition, if an access list is already in place on a particular interface, modifications to accommodate this list will need to be part of the implementation. Even with these caveats, this "trick" can save you time and aggravation over using the debug commands.

Global Debugging

Some global **debug** commands are listed in Table 5.8. The table is not comprehensive; it is just a list of commonly used global **debug** commands. To obtain a comprehensive list, issue the following command:

Router_A#**debug** ?

TABLE 5.8 Common Global debug Commands

Global debug Command	Description
aaa	Enable AAA Authentication, Authorization, and Accounting debugging options
adjacency	Enable adjacency debugging options
all	Enable all debugging options
cbus	Enable debug options dealing with ciscoBus events
cdp	Enable debugging on CDP information
chat	Enable chat scripts activity debugging
dhcp	Enable debugging on DHCP client activity
dialer	Enable debugging on Dial on Demand events
domain	Enable debugging on Domain Name System (DNS) events
entry	Enable debugging on incoming queue entries
snmp	Enable SNMP debugging
tacacs	Enable TACACS authentication and authorization event debugging
tbridge	Enable debugging on transparent bridging

Interface Debugging

Interface debugging is used to obtain information that is specific to interfaces, interface signaling, and interface processes. The same caution applies to interface-related **debug** commands as it does to the global commands: The more focused the debug through the use of options, the easier it is to isolate the problem.

Interface-oriented commands are provided in Table 5.9. Again, each of these commands has additional options available. To see the related options, use the commands listed, followed by a question mark. Most of these commands will be described and applied in later chapters.

TABLE 5.9   Interface-Related debug Commands

debug Command	Description
atm	Enable debugging on ATM interface events
channel	Enable debugging on the channel interface information
ethernet-interface	Enable debugging on ethernet interface events
fastethernet	Enable debugging on fast ethernet interface events
serial	Enable debugging on serial interface events
token	Enable debugging on Token Ring interface events
tunnel	Enable debugging on the functioning of a tunnel interface

Protocol Debugging

There are two protocol classes that can be debugged: desktop (or routed) protocols and routing protocols. Several debug options exist for protocol information, and each protocol has its own associated debug options. These options can be obtained by using the command-line help on the router.

Table 5.10 is a list of the protocol-related debug commands available.

TABLE 5.10   Protocol-Related debug Commands

debug Command	Description
apple	Enable debugging on AppleTalk events
arp	Enable debugging on IP ARP and HP probe transactions
atm	Enable debugging on ATM signaling
broadcast	Enable debugging on broadcast packets

TABLE 5.10   Protocol-Related debug Commands *(continued)*

debug Command	Description
dlsw	Enable debugging on Data Link Switching (DLSw) events
eigrp	Enable debugging on the EIGRP routing protocol
frame-relay	Enable debugging on Frame Relay events
ip	Enable debugging on IP specific information
ipx	Enable debugging on Novell/IPX specific information
isis	Enable debugging on the IS-IS routing protocol
ppp	Enable debugging on PPP (Point to Point Protocol) events
spanning	Enable debugging on Spanning-tree information
telnet	Enable debugging on incoming telnet connections
translate	Enable debugging on protocol translation events
vlan	Enable VLAN related debugging

IP Debugging

Just like the show commands, numerous debug commands and options exist specifically for IP. The problem being analyzed will dictate which IP debug commands need to be used. Table 5.11 lists many of the available debug commands and options within IP. Note that the first command, arp, is not an IP-specific command, yet it provides valuable IP information.

TABLE 5.11   IP-Related debug Commands and Options

Command	Description
arp	Enable debugging of IP ARP and HP Probe transactions
bgp	Enable debugging of the BGP routing protocol
cache	Enable debugging of IP cache operations
cef	Enable debugging of IP CEF operations

TABLE 5.11   IP-Related debug Commands and Options *(continued)*

Command	Description
cgmp	Enable debugging of the CGMP protocol activity
eigrp	Enble debugging of the IP EIGRP routing protocol information
error	Enable debugging of IP errors
ftp	Enable debugging of FTP events
http	Enable debugging of HTTP connections
icmp	Enable debugging of ICMP transactions
igmp	Enable debugging of IGMP protocol activity
igrp	Enable debugging of IGRP information
mbgp	Enable debugging of the MBGP routing protocol
mcache	Enable debugging of IP multicast cache operations
mds	Enable debugging of IP distributed multicast information
mobile	Enable debugging of mobile IP protocols
mpacket	Enable debugging of IP multicast packets
mrouting	Enable debugging of IP multicast routing events
msdp	Enable debugging of Multicast Source Discovery Protocol (MSDP) events
mtag	Enable debugging of IP multicast tagswitching activity
nat	Enable debugging of NAT events
ospf	Enable debugging of OSPF routing protocol information
packet	Enable IP packet debugging and IPSO security transactions
peer	Enable debugging of IP peer address activity
pim	Enable PIM protocol activity debugging

TABLE 5.11 IP-Related debug Commands and Options *(continued)*

Command	Description
policy	Enable debugging of Policy routing events
rip	Enable IP RIP routing protocol debugging
routing	Enable routing table event
rsvp	Enable debugging on the RSVP protocol
security	Enable debugging of the IP security options
tcp	Enable debugging of TCP-based transactions
udp	Enable debugging of UDP-based transactions

The debug ip packets command contains an option to provide an access list, which narrows the scope of the debug even more. There are some prerequisites, though. In order to properly use debug ip packets, the packets must be process-switched, which means that all switching types must be turned off. Fast, optimum, and other switching types do not provide the necessary information regarding the IP transactions.

By looking at the output of these commands, you can get a sense of what is going on at each layer of the OSI model. They allow you to identify where a problem is occurring and let you focus in on that layer. Though not the first place to start in troubleshooting, debugging can be a valuable tool in the overall process.

logging Commands

The last set of commands examined here are the logging commands. Logging commands allow you to save errors and other messages for later review. This information can be sent to the console, to a terminal, to an internal buffer on the router, and/or to a syslog server.

You can view the logging information on a router by executing the show logging command that was referenced in the "show Commands" section (see Table 5.2). Following is a sample output of this command:

```
Router_B>show logging
Syslog logging: enabled (6519 messages dropped, 0 flushes, 0 overruns)
    Console logging: level debugging, 9047 messages logged
    Monitor logging: level debugging, 1256 messages logged
    Buffer logging: level debugging, 9047 messages logged
    Trap logging: level notifications, 3276 message lines logged
        Logging to 10.20.20.20, 3276 message lines logged
```

```
Log Buffer (65536 bytes):

Feb 11 01:00:45: %CLEAR-5-COUNTERS: Clear counter on all interfaces by
 user1 on vty0 (10.20.20.20)
Feb 11 19:40:26: %SYS-4-SNMP_WRITENET: SNMP WriteNet request. Writing
current configuration to 10.30.30.30
Feb 12 07:40:39: %DUAL-5-NBRCHANGE: IP-EIGRP 64700: Neighbor
10.40.40.40 (Serial1/1/1.30) is down: holding time expired
```

As you can see, the four different logging locations available—console, monitor, buffer, and trap (syslog server)—are referenced in the output. In addition to the locations, there are some logging "levels" indicated as well.

Cisco routers have eight possible logging levels. These levels or values range from 0 to 7 and are detailed in Table 5.12. The logging level, indicated after each of the locations in the show logging command, represents the level of severity that is required for a message to be logged. Any message with a severity equal to or less than the logging level will be recorded. For example, the trap level in the foregoing output was set to notifications, or 5. This means that all messages with a level of 5 or less (i.e., notifications, warnings, errors, critical, alerts, and emergencies) will be sent to the syslog server. In contrast, the console has its level set to debugging. Since debugging is the highest level, all messages, no matter what level, will be sent to the console.

TABLE 5.12   Logging Levels

Logging Level	Name	Description
0	Emergencies	System unusable messages
1	Alerts	Take immediate action
2	Critical	Critical condition
3	Errors	Error message
4	Warnings	Warning messages
5	Notifications	Normal but significant condition
6	Informational	Information messages
7	Debugging	Debug messages

The next logical question is "How do I know what level of debugging I need?" By default, the console, monitor, and buffer logging are set to the debugging level, and the trap logging is set to informational. If you want to modify these values, you can gauge the value you want to use by looking at the messages that already have been logged. Most messages include the logging level as part of the entry. For instance, in the example above, -5- in the middle of clear counters indicates a level 5 notification; and -4- between sys and SNMP indicates a level 4 warning. Also, if you look at the "Verify the Packet Flow Without Using Debug" sidebar, you will note the -6- in the log output from the access list. This message would be treated as a level 6 informational message.

Finally, it should be noted that the process of message logging does consume router CPU cycles. As with the debug tool, care must be taken with logging. If too many messages are being logged and the router is already busy, performance issues can result. In most cases, the messages that are being logged are being generated by a **debug** command. Therefore, if you know you are going to run a **debug** command that will generate a large amount of output, you can turn off some of the logging to help minimize the performance impact of this debug. However, not all of the logging types are created equal when it comes to load on the router. The logging options are as follows, from most load to least load: console, monitor, trap, and buffer. So if you are doing a debug that will produce abundant messages, you can minimize the load on the router by ensuring that only the buffer logging is enabled.

The commands used with the logging options are described in Table 5.13.

TABLE 5.13   Logging-Related Commands

logging Command	Description
Buffered	Sets buffer size, as well as the logging level for the buffer. The no form of the command disables the logging buffer.
clear logging	Clears the logging buffer.
Console	Sets the logging level for the console. The no form of the command disables logging to the console.
Monitor	Sets the logging level for the monitor. The no form of the command disables logging to the monitor.
Trap	Sets the logging level for the syslog server. The no form of the command disables logging to the syslog server.

Executing a Router Core Dump

The information contained in a core dump can be useful for diagnosing router problems. A core dump contains an exact copy of the information that currently resides in system memory. Depending on the amount of RAM and the memory utilization, the core dump file can be very large. The information provided is normally used only by Cisco engineers.

There are two general methods for capturing the information contained in memory. In the first method, a router is configured to execute a core dump when the router crashes. The second method is to use a user-privileged exec command from the command line.

exception Command

The exception command allows you to configure a router to execute a core dump if the router crashes. An integral part of the exception command is the TFTP, FTP, or RCP server. Here is a sample configuration:

```
Router_A#conf t
Enter configuration commands, one per line. End with CNTL/Z.
Router_A(config)#exception dump 172.16.10.10
Router_A(config)#^Z
Router_A#
```

The IP address in the command is the IP address of the TFTP, FTP, or RCP server. The router needs this address so it knows where to download the core dump. It uses any of these three protocols (TFTP, FTP, or RCP).

Configuration varies, depending on which type of server is used. TFTP does not require any additional configuration than the example just above. FTP and RCP, however, require additional commands in order to support the file transfer. Here is an example:

```
Router_A#conf t
Enter configuration commands, one per line. End with CNTL/Z.
Router_A(config)#exception dump 172.16.10.11
Router_A(config)#ip ftp username kevin
Router_A(config)#ip ftp password aloha
Router_A(config)#ip ftp source-interface e0
Router_A(config)#exception protocol ftp
Router_A(config)#^Z
Router_A#
```

Because FTP servers require some type of username and password combination to allow access to the file system, this information must be specified on the router. You can map the FTP server to the exiting interface on the router by using the source-interface command. This is just like a static route. If the route table did not have the route in its table, it would still know how to get to the FTP server. You must also specify which protocol is going to be used.

RCP requires configuration on the RCP server by editing the .rhosts files, as well as the router configuration. Here is a sample:

```
Router_A#conf t
Enter configuration commands, one per line. End with CNTL/Z.
Router_A(config)#exception protocol rcp
Router_A(config)#exception dump 172.16.10.12
```

```
Router_A(config)#ip rcmd remote-username kevin
Router_A(config)#ip rcmd rcp-enable
Router_A(config)#ip rcmd rsh-enable
Router_A(config)#ip rcmd remote-host kevin 172.16.10.12 kevin
Router_A(config)#^Z
Router_A#
```

The remote-host command is configured by providing the local username, followed by the IP address for the RCP server and the remote username for the RCP server. This allows the router to log in on the RCP server and commence transferring the core dump.

write core Command

The write core command allows the user to execute a core dump without crashing the router.

WARNING   It is not advisable to use this command unless it is requested by Cisco TAC. Because it is copying the contents of memory via TFTP, it could have an adverse effect on the router.

Here is a sample of the write core command:

```
Router_A#write core
Remote host? 172.16.10.10
Name of core file to write [Router_A-core]?
Write file Router_A-core on host 172.16.10.10? [confirm]
Writing Router_A-core !!!!! [OK]
Router_A#
```

The router output has been truncated in this example. You will see exclamation marks until the file is completely transferred. The more memory that needs to be copied, the longer it will take.

Again, this information will only be useful to Cisco engineers for diagnosing and resolving router problems. Be aware that this command does have limitations. In a real router crash, it is quite possible that routing will be affected and, as a result, the router will not know how to get to the exception server. Therefore, if the exception server is not on a directly connected segment, then setting up a default gateway (ip default-gateway) will correct this issue.

ping Commands

The tools discussed thus far are in-depth tools used for problems that require troubleshooting with a high level of granularity. These tools are used to provide very detailed and specific information at a very low-level view. The ping command, on the other hand is a high-level simple tool. It is used to test for reachability and connectivity throughout a network.

Ping can be used to effectively isolate network problems. If certain hosts on a network respond to the pings when others do not, this directs your efforts to focus more on the individual hosts that are not responding.

Cisco provides two implementations of the `ping` command: the user and privileged levels. On both levels, `ping` works for the following protocols:

- IP
- IPX
- AppleTalk
- CLNS
- Apollo
- VINES
- DECnet
- XNS
- VRF (now in 12.x)

For this study guide, we will specifically focus on the IP `ping` command.

User EXEC Mode

The user mode for `ping` is restricted. Only the non-verbose method is allowed for the user level. IP `ping` uses ICMP as the protocol to provide connectivity and reachability messages. It works on a simple principle: an ICMP echo message is sent to the specified IP address. If the address is reachable, the receiving station sends an ICMP echo-reply message back to the sending station.

It is important to be able to decipher the symbols that are echoed to the screen while a ping is taking place. By default and for user mode, five ICMP echo messages are sent. Here are a few samples:

```
Router_A>ping 172.16.1.10
Type escape sequence to abort.
Sending 5, 100-byte ICMP Echoes to 172.16.1.10, timeout is 2 seconds:
!!!!!
Success rate is 100 percent (5/5), round-trip min/avg/max = 1/2/4 ms
Router_A>
Router_A>ping 172.16.2.130
Type escape sequence to abort.
Sending 5, 100-byte ICMP Echoes to 172.16.2.130, timeout is    2 seconds:
.....
Success rate is 0 percent (0/5)
Router_A>
```

It looks good so far, but what do the different characters mean? Table 5.14 defines the two that we have just seen as well as the other possible outputs.

Now that the characters are defined, you can analyze the sample outputs. In the first ping, all five packets received echo-reply messages, which indicates that the host is reachable. Notice that the output gives a success percentage based on the five requests that were sent. It also gives the minimum, average, and maximum response times.

TABLE 5.14   ping Character Map

Character	Explanation
!	Received an echo-reply message
.	Timeout
U / H	Destination unreachable
N	Network unreachable
P	Protocol unreachable
Q	Source quench
M	Unable to fragment
A	Administratively denied
?	Unknown packet-type

The second ping doesn't look so good. All five requests timed out. This means that each request waited two seconds for a response. When no response was received, a . character was echoed to the screen. It is possible that a request was received, but it was after the two-second waiting period. Either way, the host cannot be considered reachable.

Privileged EXEC Mode

The privileged mode for ping is known as an *extended ping*. This mode allows many options to aid in providing additional detailed information. The functionality of the ping command is based on the same technology as for user mode. The extended ping offers options to change some of the ping settings.

The best way to understand it is to see it:

```
Router_B #ping
Protocol [ip]:
Target IP address: 172.16.12.93
Repeat count [5]:
Datagram size [100]:
Timeout in seconds [2]:
Extended commands [n]: y
Source address or interface: 172.16.1.2
Type of service [0]:
```

```
Set DF bit in IP header? [no]:
Validate reply data? [no]:
Data pattern [0xABCD]:
Loose, Strict, Record, Timestamp, Verbose[none]: r
Number of hops [ 9 ]:
Loose, Strict, Record, Timestamp, Verbose[RV]:
Sweep range of sizes [n]:
Type escape sequence to abort.
Sending 5, 100-byte ICMP Echoes to 172.16.12.93, timeout is 2 seconds:
Packet has IP options:  Total option bytes= 39, padded     length=40
 Record route: <*> 0.0.0.0 0.0.0.0 0.0.0.0 0.0.0.0
         0.0.0.0 0.0.0.0 0.0.0.0 0.0.0.0 0.0.0.0
Reply to request 0 (1 ms). Received packet has options
 Total option bytes= 40, padded length=40
 Record route: 172.16.1.2 172.16.0.13 172.16.12.1172.16.12.93
 172.16.0.14 172.16.0.21 172.16.1.2 <*> 0.0.0.0 0.0.0.0
 End of list
Reply to request 1 (4 ms). Received packet has options
 Total option bytes= 40, padded length=40
 Record route: 172.16.1.2 172.16.0.13 172.16.12.1172.16.12.93
 172.16.0.14 172.16.0.21 172.16.1.2 <*> 0.0.0.0 0.0.0.0
 End of list
Reply to request 2 (4 ms). Received packet has options
 Total option bytes= 40, padded length=40
 Record route: 172.16.1.2 172.16.0.13 172.16.12.1 172.16.12.93
 172.16.0.14 172.16.0.21 172.16.1.2 <*> 0.0.0.0 0.0.0.0
End of list
Reply to request 3 (1 ms). Received packet has options
 Total option bytes= 40, padded length=40
 Record route: 172.16.1.2 172.16.0.13 172.16.12.1 172.16.12.93
172.16.0.14 172.16.0.21 172.16.1.2 <*> 0.0.0.0 0.0.0.0
 End of list
Reply to request 4 (1 ms). Received packet has options
 Total option bytes= 40, padded length=40
 Record route: 172.16.1.2 172.16.0.13 172.16.12.1 172.16.12.93 172.16.0.14
172.16.0.21 172.16.1.2 <*> 0.0.0.0 0.0.0.0
 End of list
Success rate is 100 percent (5/5), round-trip min/avg/max = 1/2/4 ms
Router_B#
```

If present, the character echoes have the same meaning as listed for the user mode of the `ping` command. In addition, the summary information provided at the end of the extended ping is the same as that of the user mode ping. However, the dialog used in the extended ping is slightly different from that of the user ping. The extended ping mode is accessed by just typing the word **ping**. The default protocol is IP. The next field is the target IP address. The default values are located within the brackets of each dialog question. The repeat count is five ICMP requests. The next field is the datagram size, followed by the timeout.

Additional commands are available by answering **yes** to the extended commands prompt. Extended options include the source IP address (it must be an IP address that is present on the router), type of service, don't fragment bit, data pattern, and header options.

Header options enable the route processor to analyze the packet header. There are five header options:

- Loose
- Strict
- Record
- Timestamp
- Verbose

The Record option records the ICMP packet's route to the destination address; it records up to nine hops. You can see the results of using the Record packet header option in the previous output. The IP addresses are the addresses of the exiting interface. If you follow the route, you can see the packet leave the router and finally get to the destination on the fourth hop. But wait a minute—there are still more addresses. Yes, they are the addresses of the path back to the router. The path is recorded for both directions, not just to the destination.

The final option in the extended ping command allows the router to increment the packet size between 76 bytes and 18,024 bytes. Because it is an Ethernet interface, it does not exceed 1500 bytes.

traceroute Command

The `traceroute` command is used for displaying the packet's path toward its destination. The functionality of the traceroute utility works on error messages that are generated by expired TTL values in the IP packet header. When the TTL value in an IP header reaches 0, the entire packet is discarded. At the same time, the IP host responsible for discarding the packet sends an error message to the source IP address in the header, informing the source that the packet was dropped. The TTL value is decremented by 1 every time the packet transits a router or IP host.

Traceroute capitalizes on this message exchange. When the traceroute function is used, the TTL in the IP header is set to a value of 1. It then sends the packet to the specified destination. Because the next-hop decrements the TTL counter to 0, the packet is discarded and a message is sent back to the source address. The traceroute utility records the IP address from the error message and echoes it to the screen. An `nslookup` is performed on the IP address; if a result is received, the DNS name is displayed in addition to the IP address.

The TTL is then incremented to 2 and sent out. The packet transverses the first hop, the TTL is decremented to 1, and the packet is forwarded on to the next hop. When the second hop receives the packet, the TTL is decremented to 0 and the error message is sent to the source address.

This process is followed until the destination host responds or until the TTL is exceeded. By default, the maximum TTL is 30. This means that if the destination host does not respond, the traceroute utility will attempt 30 times. Multiple requests are sent at each attempt, which results in three RTT responses. In addition to the TTL error messages, Port Unreachable (P) messages provide sufficient information for a path to the destination.

Table 5.15 lists the explanation for the response characters available within the traceroute utility.

TABLE 5.15 traceroute Response Meanings

Character	Explanation
xx msec	The RTT for each packet
*	Timeout
H	Host unreachable
U	Port unreachable
N	Network unreachable
P	Protocol unreachable
A	Administratively denied
Q	Source quench
?	Unknown packet type

Successful functionality of the `traceroute` command depends on the IP configuration on each host along the path to the destination. It is possible that the IP configuration will not send error messages when the TTL expires, when TTL is not decremented, or when no port unreachable messages are sent. If any of these problems exists, you'll probably get timeout responses.

In addition, it is important to note that not all trace utilities use the same protocol. Cisco routers and some Linux stations use a UDP packet as the probe packet, whereas many Unix and Windows stations use an ICMP packet to probe. Therefore, if you are blocking UDP in a firewall but allowing ICMP, it is possible that a trace from a Cisco device will be blocked, while one from an NT station will get through without difficulty.

User EXEC Mode

The user mode of the traceroute command allows only the default options when using the command. Here is a sample output:

```
Router_B>traceroute www.netscape.com
Translating "www.netscape.com"...domain server (172.16.4.2)     [OK]
Type escape sequence to abort.
Tracing the route to www-ld1.netscape.com (207.200.75.200)
1 172.16.2.1 0 msec 0 msec 0 msec
2 172.16.4.53 [AS 209] 12 msec 8 msec 8 msec
  3 den-core-02.inet.qwest.net (205.171.16.137) [AS 209]     12 msec
    12 msec 8 msec
  4 sfo-core-02.inet.qwest.net (205.171.4.1) [AS 209]     32 msec
    36 msec 36 msec
  5 sjo-core-01.inet.qwest.net (205.171.4.101) [AS 209]     36 msec
    36 msec 40 msec
  6 sjo-core-03.inet.qwest.net (205.171.22.6) [AS 209]     36 msec
    36 msec 36 msec
  7 sjo-edge-05.inet.qwest.net (205.171.22.50) [AS 209]     36 msec
    40 msec 36 msec
  8 205.171.48.154 [AS 209] 36 msec 36 msec 36 msec
  9 h-207-200-69-241.netscape.com (207.200.69.241)  [AS 6992] 40 msec
    40 msec 36 msec
 10 www-ld1.netscape.com (207.200.75.200) [AS 6992] 36 msec     36 msec 36 msec
Router_B>
```

As you can see, the nslookup for the first two hops failed. The RTTs for the three probes follow. The times increment as the packet moves closer to the destination address. In addition to the DNS entry, IP address, and RTT, the AS number is also listed.

Here is another sample that includes timeouts and administratively denied probes:

```
Router_B>traceroute www.novell.com
Translating "www.novell.com"...domain server (172.16.4.2)     [OK]
Type escape sequence to abort.
Tracing the route to www.novell.com (137.65.2.5)
1 172.16.1.13 0 msec 0 msec 0 msec
  2 205.171.48.53 [AS 209] 8 msec 8 msec 12 msec
  3 den-core-01.inet.qwest.net (205.171.16.109) [AS 209]
12 msec 8 msec 12 msec
  4 den-brdr-01.inet.qwest.net (205.171.16.114) [AS 209]
8 msec 12 msec 12 msec
  5 s2-0-0.den-bb1.cerf.net (134.24.112.77) [AS 1740] 8
```

```
msec    16 msec 12 msec
    6 s10-0-0.slc-bb1.cerf.net (134.24.46.98) [AS 1740]
88 msec 84 msec 84 msec
    7 novell-gw.slc-bb1.cerf.net (134.24.116.54) [AS 1740]
84 msec 84 msec 84 msec
    8 134.24.116.58 [AS 1740] 84 msec 84 msec 84 msec
    9  *   *   !A
Router_B>
```

Here, the probe made it to the destination address, but instead of receiving a TTL Expired or Port Unreachable message, we get an Administratively Denied message.

Privileged EXEC Mode

The privileged mode has options that are similar to the ping privileged mode. The dialog contains several prompts that change the traceroute settings. The default settings are listed in the brackets. They can be selected by pressing Enter, or changed by substituting a new value. We'll now look at the privileged dialog, and then we can explain each of the prompts:

```
Router_B#traceroute
Protocol [ip]:
Target IP address: 137.65.2.11
Source address: 172.16.2.9
Numeric display [n]:
Timeout in seconds [3]:
Probe count [3]:
Minimum Time to Live [1]:
Maximum Time to Live [30]:
Port Number [33434]:
Loose, Strict, Record, Timestamp, Verbose[none]:
Type escape sequence to abort.
Tracing the route to www.novell.com (137.65.2.11)
1 172.16.0.1 0 msec 0 msec 0 msec
    2 205.171.48.53 [AS 209] 8 msec 8 msec 12 msec
    3 den-core-02.inet.qwest.net (205.171.16.137) [AS 209]
12 msec 8 msec 12 msec
    4 den-brdr-01.inet.qwest.net (205.171.16.142) [AS 209]
8 msec 12 msec 12 msec
    5 s2-0-0.den-bb1.cerf.net (134.24.112.77) [AS 1740]
12 msec 12 msec 12 msec
    6 s10-0-0.slc-bb1.cerf.net (134.24.46.98) [AS 1740]
84 msec 84 msec 88 msec
```

```
    7 novell-gw.slc-bb1.cerf.net (134.24.116.54) [AS 1740]
   84 msec 84 msec 84 msec
    8 134.24.116.58 [AS 1740] 84 msec 88 msec 84 msec
    9 134.24.116.58 [AS 1740] !A  *   *
Router_B#
```

Target IP address   The IP address of the destination host.

Source address   The IP address present on the router. This is used to select an address that is not directly connected to the next hop.

Numeric display   Disables nslookup on the IP address. Consequently, if this option is chosen, only the IP address is displayed.

Timeout   The threshold for response times for the returning error message.

Probe count   The number of probes sent at each TTL level.

Minimum TTL   The numerical value for the first TTL level.

Maximum TTL   The maximum TTL value; an equivalent of 30 hops is the default and is the highest value possible.

Port number   The port number used by UDP that creates a port unreachable error message.

Loose source routing   Specifies nodes that must be included in the path to the destination.

Strict source routing   Specifies the only nodes allowed in the path to the destination.

Record   Specifies the number of hops for the verbose path to display.

Timestamp   Specifies the number of timestamps to display.

Verbose   Automatically selected if any of the previous options are selected.

LAN Connectivity Problems

Troubleshooting LAN connectivity was covered in part through the discussion of troubleshooting Ethernet and Token Ring problems in Chapter 4. Those are LAN technologies. This section deals with host connectivity in relation to Cisco routers.

Obtaining an IP Address

Hosts can obtain an IP address in one of two ways: statically or dynamically. Once an IP address is configured on a host, it is assigned to that host until the administrator removes it. If the address, mask, and gateway were configured correctly, and it is not a duplicate IP address, the host will not have any problems connecting to the LAN that could be attributed to its IP address and configuration.

Two protocols are used to allow hosts to obtain their IP address dynamically: *Bootstrap Protocol (BootP)* and *Dynamic Host Configuration Protocol (DHCP)*.

FIGURE 5.2   DHCP client/server sequence

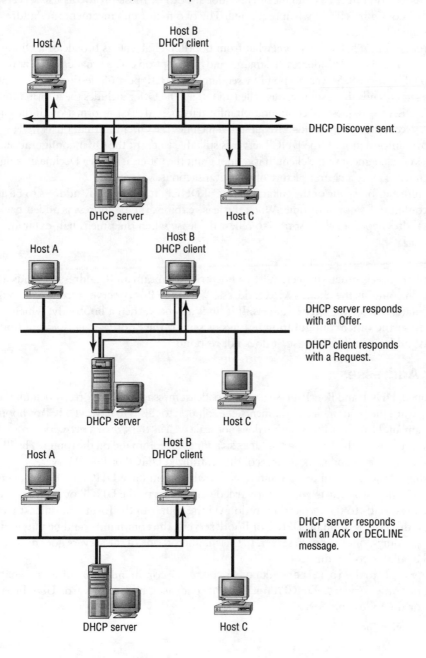

DHCP

DHCP is a superset of the Bootstrap Protocol (BootP). This means that it uses the same protocol structure as BootP, but it has enhancements added. Both of these protocols use servers that dynamically configure clients when requested. The two major enhancements are address pools and lease times.

The process for DHCP differs somewhat from BootP. DHCP clients broadcast a Discover message that contains the MAC address, hostname, and other options. The broadcast is sent from UDP port 67 to UDP port 68. Servers respond by sending from UDP port 68 destined to UDP port 67. When the server sends the response, it is called an Offer. The Offer includes the information sent in the client's Discover request, IP configuration information, and lease information. If the client chooses to accept the offer, it sends a Request that includes the Offer information as well as the original Discover information. If the DHCP server is still able to grant the Offer configuration, it will send an acknowledgment to the client. If it cannot grant the Offer, it sends a Decline message to the client. Figure 5.2 gives a clearer picture of these transactions.

Lease information is one of the enhancements of DHCP. It allows an IP address to be assigned for a preconfigured amount of time. When the lease expires, the IP address is added back to the available address pool. Each host tries to renew the lease when the time is half-expired.

BootP

The BootP process is much simpler. When a host tries to obtain an IP address, it sends a bootrequest, which contains the client's MAC address. When the BootP server receives the request, it checks its database for the MAC address. If it finds an entry, then a bootreply, which contains the IP address and other configuration settings, is sent. If the BootP server does not find the client's MAC address in its database, it does not respond.

Helper Addresses

As mentioned, DHCP and BootP messages are broadcast messages. Therefore, by default the router will not forward them. In small environments, the solution to this is to have a DHCP or BootP server on each segment. However, this solution does not scale well as the size of a network grows. In these situations, you can use the `ip helper-address <address>` command on the router. The IP address referenced in the command is the address of the centralized DHCP or BootP server.

By adding this command to each interface on which you have DHCP or BootP clients, all DHCP and BootP broadcasts will be forwarded via unicast to the DHCP or BootP server. This server then responds to the requesting station via the router in the form of a unicast packet. In addition, if there are redundant DHCP or BootP servers, the command could be put on the interface multiple times, once for each server. In this manner, if one of the servers goes down, the others is still available to handle requests.

One downside to the `ip helper-address <address>` command is that after it is enabled, by default it not only forwards DHCP/BootP UDP broadcasts, it also forwards UDP broadcasts destined for the following ports:

- Time service (port 37)
- IEN-116 Name Service (port 42)

- TACACS service (port 49)
- Domain Name System (port 53)
- Trivial File Transfer Protocol (TFTP) (port 69)
- NetBIOS Name Server (port 137)
- NetBIOS Datagram Server (port 138)

In order to only forward DHCP/BootP broadcasts, you can use the global configuration command no ip forward-protocol udp <*port*> for each of the services in the above list.

DHCP Services on a Router

Beginning with IOS 12.0(1) T, you can also configure a router as a DHCP server. In contrast to the helper address, which forwards requests to an external DHCP server, configuring a router as a DHCP server allows the router to service DHCP requests locally. The router becomes a full-featured DHCP server and can provide DHCP addresses, from separate IP address pools to any device on a connected interface.

Troubleshooting DHCP and BootP

Because these protocols are dynamic, there may be times when they fail or when an end user is unable to connect to the network. If you have a protocol analyzer, you could capture the DHCP and BootP sequences to make sure that the clients and servers are talking.

You can also use the show commands available to aid in troubleshooting DHCP on Cisco routers.

```
Router_C#show dhcp server
DHCP Proxy Client Status:
   DHCP server: ANY (255.255.255.255)
   Leases:   0
   Offers:   0      Requests: 0     Acks: 0      Naks: 0
   Declines: 0      Releases: 0     Bad:  0
Router_C#
```

If the router is configured to use DHCP, you can also get information regarding the lease by issuing the show dhcp lease command.

ARP

Address Resolution Protocol maps Layer 2 MAC addresses to Layer 3 IP addresses. An ARP table is built on the router through the exchange of ARP requests and replies. Here is a sample ARP table:

```
Router_C>show arp
Protocol  Address         Age (min)  Hardware Addr   Type   Interface
Internet  172.16.60.1     -          0010.7bd9.2881  ARPA   Ethernet0/1
```

```
Internet  172.16.50.2   -      0010.7bd9.2880  ARPA  Ethernet0/0
Internet  172.16.50.1   108    0000.0c09.99cc  ARPA  Ethernet0/0
Router_C>
```

Notice the Age field in the ARP table. ARP entries are stored or cached for future use. This allows a router to look up the MAC address, instead of having to send a broadcast to learn it again. However, the ARP entry does not stay in the table indefinitely.

Several problems could occur if a MAC address were permanently mapped to an IP address. You learned that DHCP can assign a given IP address to any requesting host, if it is available. In this scenario, the IP address could be assigned to different MAC addresses. If this were to happen, any existing entry in an ARP table would be invalidated. If a NIC is replaced on a host, the MAC address is changed as well. If the ARP cache was not cleared and updated, the IP address would still be mapped to the old MAC address. You get the picture. These mappings are not permanent, so the cache entries cannot be permanent, either.

Sometimes difficulties occur within a network because of ARP problems. The best way to troubleshoot these issues is by looking at the ARP table on the router with the show arp command and (if necessary) using the debug arp tool. Problems can fixed by simply clearing the ARP cache and allowing the router to rebuild the table.

It is also worthy of note that the last ARP reply that is received is the one that is entered in the ARP cache. Therefore, if you are looking at an ARP entry that is changing values, it could indicate a duplicate address conflict, or possibly signals that someone is trying to hack into your system by spoofing an address!

Proxy ARP

By default, Cisco router interfaces have *proxy ARP* enabled. Proxy ARP, defined in RFC 1027, aids in routing packets from workstations that have no default gateway set or that have misconfigured subnet information. Specifically, a Cisco router will reply to an ARP request with its own MAC address if the following conditions are met:

- Proxy ARP is enabled on the interface on which the ARP was seen.
- The ARP request is for an address not on the local subnet.
- The router has a route for that subnet in its routing table.
- All routes in the routing table for the requested address are out an interface other than the interface on which the ARP was seen.

The host that originated the ARP request will then send packets destined for this address to the router, which will then forward them on to their destination. If you want to disable proxy ARP on an interface, you can use the no ip proxy-arp command.

Though there are a couple uses for Proxy ARP, most are to overcome the requirement of "standard" network configurations. For example, Proxy ARP allows low for mismatched router/workstation subnet masking that may be required for the routing protocol you are using. Or it can be used as a safeguard to enable functionality to users not well versed in the world of networking.

Sample TCP Connection

In order to properly troubleshoot a connection issue, it is important to clearly understand how this connection is set up from the start. TCP is a connection-oriented protocol. As such, before data can be exchanged, a connection needs to be established. This connection is established by the *TCP three-way handshake*. To better explain exactly how this works, we'll give you an example. Figure 5.3 has a graphical representation of this example.

Assume that two computers on the same segment, Computer A and B, have just been powered on. A user on Computer A wants to initiate a telnet session to Computer B. Computer A has an IP address of 192.168.1.100 and B has an address of 192.168.1.101. To keep things simple for this example, assume that the user is telnetting to computer B by its IP address, not its name.

When the user presses Enter on the telnet request, Computer A first looks at its ARP cache and sees if it has a MAC address associated with the IP address of B, 192.168.1.101. Since this computer was just powered on, it does not. Computer A now checks to verify that Computer B is on the subnet. Since it is, Computer A sends out an ARP request for the MAC address of 192.168.1.101. If Computer B were on a different subnet, Computer A would have sent out an ARP request for the default gateway instead.

FIGURE 5.3   Sample connection scenario

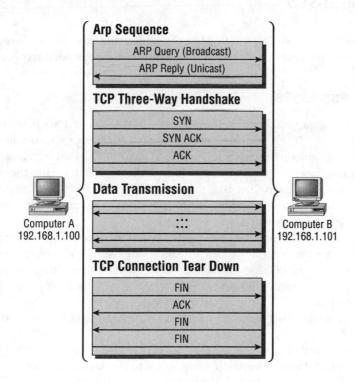

ARP requests are Layer 2 broadcasts, so all computers connected to the subnet, including Computer B, receive this ARP request. Computer B sees that the ARP is for its IP address and responds directly to Computer A with its MAC address. Computer B also gleaned Computer A's IP address and MAC information from the ARP request and added this information to its own ARP cache.

Now that Computer A has the IP and MAC information, the TCP three-way handshake can begin. The start of this process is Computer A sending a SYN (synchronize) packet to Computer B on TCP port 23, letting Computer B know that Computer A wants to set up a connection. Computer B then responds with a SYN ACK (synchronize and acknowledgment) packet. Computer A responds to the SYN ACK message from B with an ACK (acknowledgment) packet.

At this point the TCP session is set up and the telnet session data can flow normally between A and B. Once the user is done with the telnet session, the connection needs to be torn down. In order to do this, Computer A sends a FIN (Finished or Finalize) packet to Computer B, and B responds with an ACK packet. Communication from A to B has now been torn down; however, B also needs to indicate that it has finished with the connection as well. Computer B sends a FIN packet to Computer A to do this. Computer A responds with an ACK packet and the connection is terminated.

IP Access Lists

Troubleshooting access lists is a very simple task when you understand how they are written and when you are familiar with the protocols that can be managed by using extended access lists.

Standard Access Lists

A *standard access list* is a sequential list of Permit or Deny statements that are based on the source IP address of a packet. When a packet reaches a router, the packet has to follow a particular procedure, based on whether the packet is trying to enter or leave an interface. If there is an access list on the interface, the packet must go through every line in it until the packet matches the specified criteria. If the packet goes through the entire list without a match, it is dropped. For the packet to be forwarded, there has to be a Permit statement at the end of the list allowing that, or else the packet will simply be dropped.

In Cisco IOS, there's an implied Deny statement at the end of the access list, so if the purpose of your access list is to deny a few criteria but forward everything else, you must include a Permit statement as the final line of the access list. However, you do not have to end the access list with a Deny statement if the list's purpose is to permit only certain criteria and drop the rest—this is automatically understood.

Figure 5.4 shows a flowchart that describes the steps taken when a packet enters or leaves an interface.

Stepping through the flowchart, you can see that the packet arrives at the specific interface through which it must enter or leave. The router's first step is to check whether there is an access list applied to the interface. If so, router steps through each line of the access list until the packet's source address matches one of the source addresses listed. If a packet's information matches multiple lines in the access list, the first match will be the one used, whether that line is a Permit or a Deny. If the packet fails to match any of the source addresses, it is denied. However, if the packet's source address does find a match in the list, the packet is then subjected to any condition applied on that line of the access list. The two conditional possibilities are to deny the packet or permit it. When a packet is denied, it is dropped; when it is permitted, it is forwarded to the next hop.

Exiting packets are first routed to the exiting interface and then verified by the access list, which determines whether the packet will be dropped or forwarded through the interface. Incoming packets arrive from the forwarding machine or router, and are then checked against the access list. If the packet is permitted by the list, the packet is accepted through the interface and forwarded to the exit interface. This is important information to understand when troubleshooting any access list. The situation depends on whether the packet is incoming or outgoing, so you can tell which interfaces to look at and analyze access lists for.

Troubleshooting standard access lists is very simple because they are based on only one criterion, the source IP address. The basic method of troubleshooting an access list is to read it line by line and analyze it to determine whether any lines are out of order or typed incorrectly.

If, after analyzing the access list, you cannot see any problems but the problem is still occurring, you can temporarily remove the access list from the interface to see what effect this has on the problem. If the problem disappears after the access list is removed, something is wrong with the access list and it needs to be fixed. If the problem does not go away with the removal of the access list from the interface, you can eliminate the access list as a possible cause.

The commands used to view IP access lists are show running-config, show startup-config, and show ip access-list <access-list number>. These commands provide the information regarding each line of the access list. In addition to these commands, you can issue the show ip interface command, which provides you with information about which access lists are applied to the interface. Here is a sample output from the show ip interface command:

```
Router_B>show ip interface
Ethernet0 is up, line protocol is up
   Internet address is 172.16.50.1/24
   Broadcast address is 255.255.255.255
   Address determined by non-volatile memory
   MTU is 1500 bytes
   Helper address is not set
   Directed broadcast forwarding is disabled
   Multicast reserved groups joined: 224.0.0.10
   Outgoing access list is not set
   Inbound  access list is not set
   Proxy ARP is enabled
   Security level is default
   Split horizon is enabled
   ICMP redirects are always sent
```

```
ICMP unreachables are always sent
ICMP mask replies are never sent
IP fast switching is enabled
IP fast switching on the same interface is disabled
IP multicast fast switching is disabled
Router Discovery is disabled
IP output packet accounting is disabled
IP access violation accounting is disabled
TCP/IP header compression is disabled
Probe proxy name replies are disabled
Gateway Discovery is disabled
Policy routing is disabled
```

FIGURE 5.4   Flowchart process of a standard access list

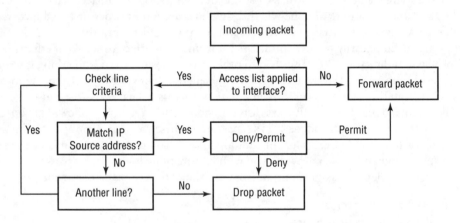

As you can see from this output, interface Ethernet0 does not have any access lists applied to it.

Extended Access Lists

Extended access lists offer filtering on port numbers, session-layer protocols, and destination addresses, in addition to filtering by source address. Although these extended filtering features make this kind of access list much more powerful, they can also make the list more difficult to troubleshoot because of the potential complexity.

A packet must follow the same basic process when arriving at an interface with an extended access list applied to it as it does when confronting an interface with an applied standard list. Figure 5.5 illustrates the procedure that a packet follows when being compared against an extended list—the only difference is the much greater scope of criteria that are specifiable.

FIGURE 5.5 Packet processing through an extended access list

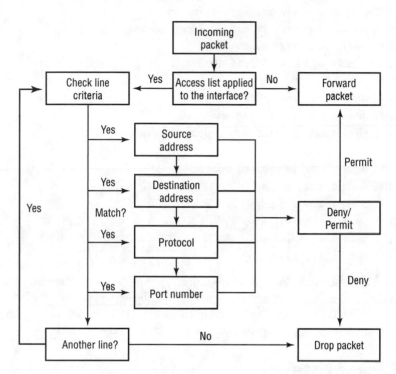

In addition to correctly analyzing the lines of the access list, you must know which way the list is applied to the interface. By conceptualizing the packet flow through an interface and the subsequent access list, you will be successful in troubleshooting access list–related problems. Here is a sample extended access list:

```
access-list 101 deny    tcp any any eq chargen
access-list 101 deny    tcp any any eq daytime
access-list 101 deny    tcp any any eq discard
access-list 101 deny    tcp any any eq echo
access-list 101 deny    tcp any any eq finger
access-list 101 deny    tcp any any eq kshell
access-list 101 deny    tcp any any eq klogin
access-list 101 deny    tcp any any eq 37
access-list 101 deny    tcp any any eq uucp
access-list 101 deny    udp any any eq biff
access-list 101 deny    udp any any eq bootpc
access-list 101 deny    udp any any eq bootps
access-list 101 deny    udp any any eq discard
```

```
access-list 101 deny    udp any any eq netbios-dgm
access-list 101 deny    udp any any eq netbios-ns
access-list 101 permit udp host 172.16.10.2 any eq snmp
access-list 101 deny    udp any any eq snmp
access-list 101 permit udp host 172.16.10.2 any eq
   snmptrap
access-list 101 deny    udp any any eq snmptrap
access-list 101 deny    udp any any eq who
access-list 101 permit udp 172.16.50.0 0.0.0.255 any eq
   xdmcp
access-list 101 deny    udp any any eq xdmcp
access-list 101 permit tcp any any
access-list 101 permit udp any any
access-list 101 permit icmp any any
access-list 101 permit igmp any any
access-list 101 permit eigrp any any
```

As you can see, there are many line options that need to be understood when troubleshooting extended access lists. Not only do you have to understand the significance of the line, but you have to be familiar with the protocol you are troubleshooting. If necessary, debug options can be used in conjunction with access lists to isolate and diagnose network failures.

Named Access Lists

Beginning with IOS 11.2, in addition to the numbered standard and extended access lists, you can also use *named access lists*. Named access lists can be either standard or extended. Though the fundamental concepts of named and numbered access lists are the same, there are a couple major differences between the two.

The first is that a named access list has a logical name, not an arbitrary number like its numbered counterpart. In addition, if you want to remove a single line from a named access list, you can. To accomplish this same function with a numbered access list, you must remove and reapply the entire list. Finally, a named access list does not have the access list name at the beginning of each line, thus making it slightly easier to read. Instead, the name is shown at the top of the access list, and then the individual Permit/Deny statements follow. For example, if the access list from the preceding "Extended Access List" section were converted to a named list, it would look like the following:

```
ip access-list extended ENGINEERING-DEPT-IN
  deny    tcp any any eq chargen
  deny    tcp any any eq daytime
  deny    tcp any any eq discard
  deny    tcp any any eq echo
  deny    tcp any any eq finger
```

```
deny    tcp any any eq kshell
deny    tcp any any eq klogin
deny    tcp any any eq 37
deny    tcp any any eq uucp
deny    udp any any eq biff
deny    udp any any eq bootpc
deny    udp any any eq bootps
deny    udp any any eq discard
deny    udp any any eq netbios-dgm
deny    udp any any eq netbios-ns
permit udp host 172.16.10.2 any eq snmp
deny    udp any any eq snmp
permit udp host 172.16.10.2 any eq snmptrap
deny    udp any any eq snmptrap
deny    udp any any eq who
permit udp 172.16.50.0 0.0.0.255 any eq xdmcp
deny    udp any any eq xdmcp
permit tcp any any
permit udp any any
permit icmp any any
permit igmp any any
permit eigrp any any
```

Note the keyword extended in the first line of the access list. This denotes the list as an extended access list. If it were a standard access list, this keyword would have been standard.

Although there are some differences between named and numbered access lists, the overall functionality remains the same. If a named list is a standard access list, the flowchart in Figure 5.4 applies to the logical flow of data. If it is an extended access list, refer to Figure 5.5. As such, the restriction on standard access lists' filtering only on source address still applies to a named list. Another important difference between a named and numbered access list is that individual lines of a named list can be removed for editing; to edit a line in a numbered list, however, the whole list needs to be removed and readded.

Summary

When used properly, the show and debug commands are powerful tools for troubleshooting a problem or just for researching the performance of a router. However, these commands, especially the debug commands, should be used with care, as they can substantially increase the load on the router. Therefore, when debugging, it is advisable to use access lists to limit the information that is being debugged.

In addition to the show and debug commands, logging is another method to determine whether there is a problem on the router. Logging information can be sent to the console, the terminal monitor, an internal buffer on the router, and/or an external syslog server. In addition to the various locations that can be used to view logging information, the logging messages can also be viewed based on the severity of the problem.

Other troubleshooting commands, such as core dumps, ping, and traceroute, can be used to further define an issue. The exception dump command causes the router to write to a file the information that is in the memory at the time of a crash. This file can later be used by TAC to help isolate the cause of the problem. The ping and traceroute commands can be used to verify the reachability of hosts as well as the path taken to get to the hosts.

In order to effectively troubleshoot network problems, an engineer needs to understand how the protocols in the network work. This includes the ARP protocol, the TCP connection and teardown sequence, as well as the functions of DHCP and BootP.

IP access lists come in multiple varieties—named, numbered, standard, and extended—and all use the same basic structure and have the same basic function. Primarily used for protecting networks from unwanted traffic, the access list is read from the top down. If at any point the packet matches a line in the list, whether this line is a Permit or a Deny, the list is exited and the associated function is performed on the packet. In addition to looking at packet flow, access lists are also used for many other tasks, such as restricting routing updates, limiting access to telnet sessions to the router, and limiting SNMP access to the router.

Exam Essentials

Know the show and debug commands that are available and how to interpret the output. The CCNP Support exam covers several show and debug commands. In addition to knowing the commands, you should also know how to limit the output of the debug command using access lists.

Know and understand the logging levels on a router. The logging levels are debugging, informational, notifications, warnings, errors, critical, alerts, and emergencies. You should be able to determine the logging levels for each logging destination on a router.

Know how to use the ping and traceroute commands. The ping command is used to test for reachability and connectivity throughout a network. The traceroute command is used for displaying the packet's path toward its destination. Knowing how to use the commands includes knowing the extended ping and traceroute options available under privileged mode.

Understand how DHCP and BootP function. DHCP and BootP are broadcast messages; DHCP is a superset of BootP. Know the specific functions of each and understand the similarities and differences between the two. Also, be familiar with the function of a helper address on a router.

Understand what an ARP broadcast is and how it is used in networking. ARP stands for Address Resolution Protocol. ARP provides a table of information that the router can look up, instead of having to broadcast for information. Be sure you also understand the proxy ARP protocol.

Understand the TCP three-way handshake.   TCP uses the three-way handshake—SYN, SYN ACK, ACK—to establish a connection. To tear down a connection, the packet sequence is FIN, ACK, FIN ACK.

Know the different types of access lists and their functions.   The two types of IP access lists are standard and extended. Both types can be used as either named or numbered lists.

Commands Used in This Chapter

The following list contains a summary of all the commands used in this chapter.

Commands	Descriptions
access-list	Can be used to limit debug output, traffic flow, or other access on a router.
clear logging	Clears the logging buffer.
Debug	Used to show more-detailed information about the router performance.
exception dump	Configures the router to perform a core dump via RCP, TFTP, or FTP if and when the router crashes.
logging buffered	Sets buffer size, as well as the logging level for the buffer. The no form of the command disables the logging buffer.
logging console	Sets the logging level for the console. The no form of the command disables logging to the console.
logging monitor	Sets the logging level for the monitor. The no form of the command disables logging to the monitor.
logging trap	Sets the logging level for the syslog server. The no form of the command disables logging to the syslog server.
Ping	Initiates an ICMP echo request. There are two levels, User and Privileged. The IP protocol is used.
show access-lists	Displays the specified access list from the configuration.
show arp	Displays the contents of the ARP table as well as status.
show buffers	Displays buffer statistics for the router.
show interface	Displays interface-specific settings and statistics.
show logging	Displays logs for the router, including traps and system errors. Can also provide logs when logging access lists.

`show memory`	Displays the statistics and status of the router's memory.
`show processes cpu`	Displays the router's processes and the percentage of CPU utilization over 5 seconds, 1 minute, and 5 minutes.
`show processes memory`	Displays the router's processes and the amount of memory allocated to each.
`show queue`	Displays interface-specific queuing information.
`show queueing`	Displays queuing information for the router.
`show running-config`	Displays the current configuration that is loaded into memory.
`show stacks`	Displays the router's stack information.
`show startup-config`	Displays the configuration version that is saved in NVRAM.
`show tech-support`	A comprehensive command that includes `show running-config`, `show version`, `show stacks`, `show processes cpu`, and `show processes memory`, along with many others.
`show version`	Displays the version of IOS, the reason for last reload, and the router's hardware configuration.
`terminal monitor`	Enables the router to echo console message to the active TTY port. This facilitates the debug tool.
`terminal no monitor`	Disables the echo.
`traceroute`	A hop-by-hop ICMP traceroute. This command has two levels, User and Privileged.
`un all`	Turns off all possible debugging.
`write core`	Initiates a core dump to the specified host.
`show queueing`	Displays queuing information for the router.

Key Terms

Before you take the exam, be certain you are familiar with the following terms:

Bootstrap Protocol (BootP)	named access lists
Dynamic Host Configuration Protocol (DHCP)	proxy ARP
extended access lists	standard access list
extended ping	TCP three-way handshake

Review Questions

1. What information is provided by the show logging command? (Choose all that apply.)
    A. Access list logs
    B. Debug messages
    C. Syslog messages
    D. Console messages
    E. None of the above

2. What information is provided by issuing the show version command? (Choose all that apply.)
    A. Hardware and software version
    B. Reason for last upgrade
    C. Reason for last reload
    D. Uptime
    E. Configuration version

3. What information is provided by issuing the show startup-config command?
    A. The current configuration
    B. The configuration held in FLASH
    C. The configuration held in NVRAM
    D. The configuration held in RAM

4. What information is provided by issuing the show running-config command?
    A. The current configuration
    B. The configuration held in FLASH
    C. The configuration held in NVRAM
    D. The configuration held in RAM

5. Which Cisco IOS show command provides comprehensive information that is sent to the Cisco TAC?
    A. show all
    B. show processes
    C. show tech-support
    D. show stacks

6. What is the default Ethernet IP encapsulation on a Cisco router?

A. SNAP

B. ARPA

C. Ethernet II

D. Novell-Ether

7. What information is provided by the `show arp` command? (Choose all that apply.)

A. Layer 3 address

B. Layer 2 address

C. Encapsulation

D. Interface MAC address

E. TTL timer

8. What configuration changes should be added to a router to provide accurate debug information? (Choose all that apply.)

A. `debug all`

B. `service timestamps debug datetime msec localtime`

C. `service timestamps log datetime msec localtime`

D. `service udp-small-servers`

E. `service tcp-small-servers`

9. What command do you issue to view messages being sent to the console?

A. `monitor terminal`

B. `terminal monitor`

C. `show console`

D. `echo terminal`

10. What command turns off all debugging?

A. `no debug all`

B. `no debug`

C. `un all`

D. `undebug all`

E. All of the above

11. In general, what is the maximum percentage utilization for a router's CPU in order to run debug commands?

   A. 25%

   B. 50%

   C. 66%

   D. 75%

12. What is the purpose of the `ping` command?

   A. Step-by-step connectivity

   B. Reachability and connectivity

   C. Test the ICMP protocol

   D. Test routing protocols

13. What is the purpose of the `traceroute` command?

   A. Step-by-step path connectivity

   B. Reachability and connectivity

   C. Test the ICMP protocol

   D. Test routing protocols

14. What are the default logging settings and levels for a Cisco router? (Choose all that apply.)

   A. Buffer, console, and trap are enabled and set to Debugging.

   B. Trap is enabled and set to Informational.

   C. Monitor is enabled and set to Informational.

   D. Buffer, console, and monitor are enabled and set to Debugging.

   E. Trap is disabled and set to Informational.

   F. Monitor is disabled and set to Informational.

15. How can you limit the amount of debug information that is displayed?

   A. Use the keyword `brief` in the `debug` command.

   B. Enable Netflow Switching.

   C. Use an access list with the `debug` command.

   D. Run the `debug` command from a telnet session.

16. What logging feature causes the most load on the router?

   A. Buffer

   B. Console

   C. Monitor

   D. Trap

17. You notice intermittent packet loss in your network and it seems to have some correlation to packet size. What option(s) in extended ping can help you diagnose this problem further? (Choose all that apply.)

A. Datagram size

B. Timeout

C. Type of service

D. DF bit

E. Validate reply data

F. Data pattern

G. Sweep range of sizes

18. A host wants to set up a new TCP connection. What type of packet is sent?

A. SYN

B. ACK

C. SYN ACK

D. ARP broadcast

19. Which debug command can be used to provide important IP information, yet is not part of the IP debug commands?

A. debug ospf

B. debug eigrp

C. debug arp

D. debug ip arp

20. You execute a show processes cpu command on the router and receive the following output. What does the 25% mean?

CPU utilization for five seconds: 75%/25%; one minute: 50%; five minutes: 45%

A. The peak CPU utilization over the past 5 seconds was 25%.

B. The average CPU utilization for non-interrupt processes over the last 5 seconds was 25%.

C. The average CPU utilization for interrupt processes over the last 5 seconds was 25%.

D. The average CPU utilization over the last 5 seconds for all processes was 25%.

Answers to Review Questions

1.   A, B, C, D. The show logging command provides access list logs, debug messages, syslog messages, and console messages.

2.   A, C, D. The show version command does not provide you with information regarding the reason for the last upgrade; nor does it provide the version of configuration that resides on the router. It does provide the uptime, hardware and software version, and the total uptime of the device.

3.   C. The start-up configuration is held in the NVRAM memory.

4.   A. The running configuration is the configuration currently being run by the router.

5.   C. show tech-support is the command that contains the information requested by TAC.

6.   B. ARPA is the default encapsulation used by Cisco. SNAP, Ethernet II, and Novell-Ether are valid encapsulation types but are not turned on by default.

7.   A, B, C, D. Of the options shown here, the TTL timer is the only statistic not shown in the show arp command.

8.   B, C. Timestamps are important to debugging so that correlations can be made when events occur. Debug all is a command that implements debugging—it has nothing to do with how accurate the information is. Options D and E are commands that enable certain UDP and TCP services to the router. They have nothing to do with debug.

9.   B. terminal monitor is the correct command; term mon can be used as a shorthand version of this command.

10.   A, C, D. un all is a shortcut command to turn off debug; the full command is undebug all. In addition, you can use no debug all to accomplish the same thing. The no debug command is incomplete.

11.   B. Some debug commands require less overhead than others; however, to be on the safe side, when a router is over 50% utilized you should try to get the information without using debug.

12.   B. The ping packets are used to test for connectivity to a remote IP address.

13.   A. Traceroute is used to map the hop-path connectivity.

14.   B, D. By default, buffer, console, monitor, and trap logging are enabled. The buffer, console, and monitor logs are set to a level of debugging, and the trap log is set to Informational. It is true that you must use the terminal monitor command to see the log information for the monitor, but it is on. Likewise, before the trap log can be used, a syslog server must be defined.

15.   C. You can limit the information that the debug command applies to by applying an access list to the command.

16.   B. The console logging takes the most overhead, followed by monitor, trap, and buffer.

17. A, D, G. Since you believe it is a problem related to packet size, setting the datagram size and sweeping a range of sizes will be of value. In addition, setting the DF (Don't Fragment) bit will also assist in this endeavor.

18. A. It is true that if a station does not have an ARP entry for the destination station, it must send an ARP. However, since the question specifically asked about a TCP connection, SYN is the correct answer.

19. C. The `debug arp` command provides important IP information even though it is not part of the IP debug set.

20. C. The first percentage is the average CPU utilization for all processes on the router; the second number is the average CPU utilization for interrupt-driven events.

Chapter 6

TCP/IP Routing Protocol Troubleshooting

EXAM TOPICS COVERED IN THIS CHAPTER INCLUDE:

✓ Verify network connectivity.

✓ Use the optimal troubleshooting approach in resolving network problems.

✓ Minimize downtime during troubleshooting.

This chapter is dedicated to covering essential skills and tools for TCP/IP routing protocol troubleshooting. Starting with a description of default gateways and the difference between static and dynamic routing, specifics on troubleshooting the different routing protocols will be discussed. These routing protocols include RIP, IGRP, EIGRP, OSPF, and BGP. In addition to examining the routing protocols themselves, we will review the subject of redistribution and how to filter information being passed from one protocol to another.

In addition to covering detailed problem-solving techniques, we have included quick-reference summary charts at the end of the chapter that summarize information provided in both this chapter and Chapter 5. These tables help to quickly associate a cause with many TCP/IP symptoms.

Default Gateways

The capability of a router to route or forward data depends on its knowledge of the world around it. This knowledge comes in the form of a route table. The route table is populated by the router's own networks, as well as by advertisements received from neighboring routers. This will be covered in detail in the upcoming section on static and dynamic routing.

What happens if a router doesn't have a route to a destination? There are two possibilities. If the router is configured to do so, it will send the packet to a neighboring router that is considered the default gateway, with the hope that the default gateway will know where to send the packet. If the router is not configured to take this action, it will simply drop the packet.

How do you configure a router to send packets to a neighbor without a route? That is where the gateway of last resort comes in. A gateway of last resort tells the router that if it doesn't have a route to a given network, it should send the packet out the specified interface, or default gateway.

The purpose of a default gateway is somewhat of a last-ditch effort to forward a packet. Look at Figure 6.1. In this example, Router A receives from Host A a packet that is destined for network 10.1.2.0. The problem is that Router A does not have a route for 10.1.2.0. The only chance of getting the packet forwarded to network 10.1.2.0 is to send it to Router B and hope that Router B has a route to network 10.1.2.0. Router A considers Router B as its default gateway and so sends the packet to Router B. For this example, assume that Router B does have the route and sends the packet on its way.

TCP/IP hosts also have default gateways set. If the default gateway for a router or a host is configured improperly, data will not be routed. Default gateways are used on TCP/IP hosts so that they don't have to keep individual route tables. All hosts need to point to a router on the same network in order to be used as the default gateway.

FIGURE 6.1 Default gateways

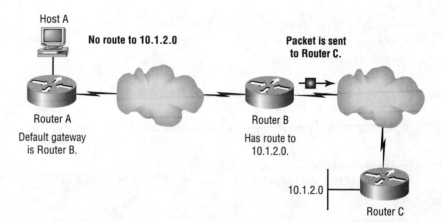

When the default gateway is not working properly, whether it is on a host or on a router, the problem is likely caused by incorrect configuration. As was covered in Chapter 3, to check for proper configuration on Windows, issue the `ipconfig /all` command from a DOS prompt. As a refresher, here is a sample output from that command:

```
1 Ethernet adapter :

        Description . . . . . . . . : ELPC3R Ethernet Adapter
        Physical Address. . . . . . : 00-A0-24-A5-06-57
        DHCP Enabled. . . . . . . . : No
        IP Address. . . . . . . . . : 172.16.50.130
        Subnet Mask . . . . . . . . : 255.255.255.0
        Default Gateway . . . . . . : 172.16.50.1
        Primary WINS Server . . . . :
        Secondary WINS Server . . . :
        Lease Obtained. . . . . . . :
        Lease Expires . . . . . . . :

C:\WINDOWS>
```

The way to check for a default gateway on a Cisco router is to use the **show ip route** command. The output follows:

```
Router_C#show ip route
Codes: C - connected, S - static, I - IGRP, R - RIP, M -    mobile, B - BGP
    D - EIGRP, EX - EIGRP external, O - OSPF, IA - OSPF
    inter area
```

```
    E1 - OSPF external type 1, E2 - OSPF external type 2,
    E - EGP
    i - IS-IS, L1 - IS-IS level-1, L2 - IS-IS level-2, *
    - candidate default
       U - per-user static route


Gateway of last resort is 172.16.50.2 to network 10.1.2.0

    172.16.0.0/16 is variably subnetted, 2 subnets, 2
    masks
C      172.16.50.0/24 is directly connected, Ethernet0/0
D      172.16.30.4/30 [90/2195456] via 172.16.50.1, 00:00:18, Ethernet0/0
Router_C#


Router_B#show ip route
Codes: C - connected, S - static, I - IGRP, R - RIP, M - mobile, B - BGP
    D - EIGRP, EX - EIGRP external, O - OSPF, IA - OSPF
       inter area
    N1 - OSPF NSSA external type 1, N2 - OSPF NSSA
    external type 2
    E1 - OSPF external type 1, E2 - OSPF external type 2,
    E - EGP
     i - IS-IS, L1 - IS-IS level-1, L2 - IS-IS level-2, *
    - candidate default
       U - per-user static route, o - ODR


Gateway of last resort is 172.16.50.2 to network 0.0.0.0

    172.16.0.0/16 is variably subnetted, 2 subnets, 2 masks
C       172.16.50.0/24 is directly connected, Ethernet0
C       172.16.30.4/30 is directly connected, Serial0
S*   0.0.0.0/0 [1/0] via 172.16.50.2
Router_B#
```

The difference between these two examples was that one was dynamically set by using the ip default-network command and the other is set by using a static route. Both methods end with the same results. If Router B does not have a route for a requested destination, it forwards the packet to the next hop of 172.16.50.2.

As stated earlier, having a default gateway configured is very important. The ping and traceroute commands can be used to isolate default gateway problems. When the router uses a dynamic method of selecting a default gateway, there is a greater possibility that it may fail.

Static and Dynamic Routing

Static routing depends solely on a manual input of routes. If you do not want to enable a routing protocol on the router, you can manually enter all the routes that you believe will be necessary; for everything else, the default gateway is used. This is a very cumbersome and poor way to configure a router. Static routes are only used locally and are not advertised to neighboring routers unless they are redistributed into a routing protocol session.

Dynamic routing is based on active routing protocols that share route information with one another. When a destination is no longer reachable, the route is removed from the routing table and the change is propagated throughout the network. If a new destination becomes available, the router adds the information into the route table and propagates the change throughout the network.

This dynamic approach is much better than static routes. When there is failure of a host that has been entered in the route table via a static route, the route can remain in the route table. If this static route is redistributed, other routers would still learn the route and send traffic there. The result is that packets reaching the router with the static address are dropped.

By issuing the show ip route command, you can tell which routes are learned dynamically and which are learned statically. Here is an example:

```
Router_B>show ip route
Codes:  C- connected, S- static, I- IGRP, R - RIP, M -    mobile, B - BGP
     D - EIGRP, EX - EIGRP external, O - OSPF, IA - OSPF
     inter area
     N1 - OSPF NSSA external type 1, N2 - OSPF NSSA
     external type 2
        E1 - OSPF external type 1, E2 - OSPF external type
        2, E - EGP
        i - IS-IS, L1 - IS-IS level-1, L2 - IS-IS level-2,
        *    - candidate default
        U - per-user static route, o - ODR

Gateway of last resort is 172.16.50.2 to network 0.0.0.0

     172.16.0.0/16 is variably subnetted, 3 subnets, 2
     masks
C       172.16.50.0/24 is directly connected, Ethernet0
D       172.16.60.0/24 [90/2195456] via 172.16.50.2, 00:31:39, Ethernet0
C       172.16.30.4/30 is directly connected, Serial0
S*      0.0.0.0/0 [1/0] via 172.16.50.2
Router_B>
```

The S indicates that the route is a static route. The other routes are either directly connected or learned via a routing protocol—in this case, EIGRP.

Troubleshooting RIP

Routing Information Protocol (RIP) was first designed for Xerox. The protocol, known as *routed*, was later used in Unix. Thereafter, RIP was implemented as a TCP/IP routing protocol. RIP is used by most versions of Novell NetWare for routing. Other protocols have been derived from RIP.

RIP is a distance-vector routing protocol. The metric used by RIP is the *hop count*, which specifies the number of steps or nodes that a packet must transit in order to reach the destination host.

RIP's major drawback is that it has a hop-count limit: the packet can travel a maximum of 15 hops. If the route to the destination exceeds 15 hops, the destination is tagged as unreachable. This is good for small networks because it helps prevent the count-to-infinity in a routing loop, but it is inefficient for today's Internet.

Now that you know a little about how RIP works, look at the packet structure in Figure 6.2. The packet is 24 bytes long. RIP uses five parameters to define packet information. The packet is divided into nine fields, and zeros are used to pad the packet to the full 24 bytes.

FIGURE 6.2   RIP packet structure

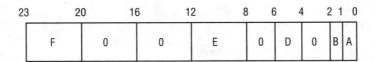

Table 6.1 shows a legend of the five parameters used within the RIP packet. As you can see in Figure 6.2, some of the fields are empty. They are just padded with zeros.

TABLE 6.1   RIP Parameters

Parameter Key	Parameter	Description
A	Command	Identifies the packet as a request (value = 1) or a response (value = 2). Requests tell the receiving router to send its route table information. Response packets include the route table information.
B	Version number	Specifies the version of RIP being used.
D	Address family identifier	Address family type. This means which protocol is carrying the RIP packet.
E	Address	The 32-bit IP address.
F	Metric	The hop count to the destination system.

RIP version 1 is a classful protocol, which means it doesn't include any subnet information about the network with route information. However, RIP version 2 is classless, allowing it to function in environments using variable length subnet masking (VLSM).

RIP-1 and RIP-2

The original version of RIP (RIP-1) had several limitations that restricted its use and scalability. Problems such as the frequent routing updates and limited hop-count needed to be overcome. RIP uses UDP broadcasts to flood route updates. Every router floods the network with its update. RIP also features split horizon and poison reverse updates to prevent routing loops. RIP updates every 30 seconds and has a hop-count limit of 16 hops.

RIP-2 functions in much the same way as RIP-1, but with a few enhancements. RIP-2 supports classless routing (CIDR), route summarization, and variable length subnet masks (VLSM). Other key enhancements in RIP-2 are that it uses a multicast (to address 224.0.0.9), instead of a broadcast for updates. In addition, RIP-2 can do triggered updates and also has the capability to use authentication if desired.

show Commands

The show commands that are useful for troubleshooting RIP-1 and RIP-2 are listed in Table 6.2.

TABLE 6.2   RIP-Related show Commands

Command	Description
show ip route rip	Displays the RIP route table.
show ip route	Displays the IP route table.
show ip interface	Displays IP interface configuration.
show running-config	Displays the running configuration.

debug Commands

As was mentioned in previous chapters, the debug command should always be used with caution and, in many circumstances, as a last resort. If the show commands described in the preceding section do not provide you with enough information to isolate and resolve the RIP problem, you can enable the debug tool.

The syntax for the debug mode in RIP is debug ip rip events. If you need even more general RIP information, use the global form of the command, debug ip rip. This command provides you with all possible RIP protocol information.

Typical RIP Problems

Because RIP uses UDP broadcasts by default, it can cause network congestion or broadcast storms if the protocol is not configured correctly. The way to avoid this problem is to configure RIP to allow unicast updates. This is done with the *neighbor* statement from within the RIP protocol configuration mode. In addition to using the `neighbor` statement, specified interfaces can be made passive by using the `passive-interface` command. This command stops routing updates from being sent out to the specified interfaces. Even if neighbor statements are used, too-frequent routing updates can also cause network congestion. This can be controlled or remedied by adjusting the various RIP timers.

Problems can also occur due to RIP version mismatches. By default, Cisco routers can understand both versions, but they advertise and forward data using RIP-1. It is possible to configure interfaces to send and receive only one version. The problem occurs when the RIP- versions on the two connected interfaces do not match.

For example, if Router A's interfaces are configured to send and receive only RIP-2, and Router B's interfaces are configured to listen to and speak RIP-1, the two routers won't be able to share RIP information. This problem can be resolved by analyzing the interface configuration on both routers and changing them so they match.

Troubleshooting IGRP

The *Interior Gateway Routing Protocol (IGRP)* is a Cisco proprietary routing protocol that uses a distance-vector algorithm because it uses a vector (a one-dimensional array) of information to calculate the best path. This vector or metric can consist of five elements:

- Bandwidth
- Delay
- Load
- Reliability
- MTU

By default, only two of the elements are used in the calculation of the metric: bandwidth and delay. Bandwidth is the minimum bandwidth over the path, and delay is the cumulative delay over the path. IGRP is intended to replace RIP and create a stable, quickly converging protocol that will scale with increased network growth.

IGRP Features and Operation

IGRP has several features included in the algorithm—these features and brief descriptions can be found in Table 6.3. The features were added to make IGRP more stable, and a few were created to deal with routing updates and make network convergence happen faster. Note also that IGRP is a classful routing protocol.

Updates in IGRP are sent out as broadcasts to everyone on the segment, much like what occurs in RIP-1. However, unlike RIP, which uses a UDP packet on port 520, Cisco decided against using TCP or UDP for IGRP and instead uses an IP datagram with protocol ID 9. This allows them to start the IGRP header information directly after the IP header, thus reducing overhead.

TABLE 6.3   IGRP Features

Feature	Description
Configurable metrics	Metrics involved in the algorithm responsible for calculating route information. They may be configured by the user.
Flash update	Updates are sent out before the default time setting. This occurs when the metrics change for a route.
Poison reverse updates	Implemented to prevent routing loops. These updates place a route in *holddown*. Holddown means that the router will not accept any new route information on a given route for a certain period.
Unequal-cost load balancing	Allows packets to be shared/distributed across multiple paths.

show Commands

The show commands that are useful for troubleshooting IGRP are listed in Table 6.4.

TABLE 6.4   IGRP-Related show Commands

Command	Description
show running-config	Displays the current configuration.
show ip route igrp	Displays IGRP routes only.
show ip route	Displays the entire route table.

debug Commands

IGRP events—as well as the protocol itself—can be analyzed by the debug tool. To watch IGRP events and protocol communications, you can enter the following debug commands:

- debug ip igrp events
- debug ip igrp transactions

Depending on the problem or the activity within IP, these commands can produce a great number of messages being logged to the console and the router's logging buffer.

Typical IGRP Problems

Because IGRP is a distance-vector protocol, you will not encounter problems with neighbor relationships or the different databases used by link-state protocols.

For IGRP, the most typical problems are caused by access lists, improper configuration, or the line to an adjacent router being down. The easiest way to tell if the router is receiving and sending IGRP information is to use the two debugging tools.

The primary symptom of a problem with IGRP is the lack of IGRP learned routes. This can be verified through the use of the show commands listed in Table 6.4.

Troubleshooting EIGRP

Enhanced IGRP (EIGRP) is a hybrid link-state and distance-vector routing protocol that was created to resolve some of the difficulties encountered with IGRP. For example, in IGRP the entire route table is sent when changes are made in the network, and there is a lack of formal neighbor relationships with connected routers. Like IGRP, EIGRP is also a proprietary Cisco routing protocol. EIGRP is a hybrid of both link-state and distance-vector routing algorithms, which brings the best of both worlds together.

EIGRP's specific features are detailed in Table 6.5. The features offered by EIGRP make it a stable and scalable protocol. Just as IGRP is proprietary to Cisco, so is EIGRP. However, unlike IRGP, EIGRP uses a multicast for communication. This multicast address, 224.0.0.10, is used for all EIGRP packets.

TABLE 6.5 EIGRP Features

Feature	Description
Route tagging	Distinguishes routes learned via different EIGRP sessions.
Formal neighbor relationships	Uses the Hello protocol to establish peering.
Incremental routing updates	Only changes are advertised, rather than the entire route table.
Classless routing	EIGRP supports subnet and VLSM information.
Configurable metrics	Metric information can be set through configuration commands.
Equal-cost load balancing	Allows traffic to be sent equally across multiple connections.

To aid in calculating the best route and in load sharing, EIGRP utilizes several databases of information:

- The route database, where the best routes are stored
- The topology database, where all route information resides
- A neighbor table, which is used to house information concerning other EIGRP neighbors

Neighbor Formation

The manner in which EIGRP establishes and maintains *neighbor relationships* is derived from its link-state properties. EIGRP uses the Hello protocol (similar to OSPF) to establish and maintain peering relationships with directly connected routers. Hello packets are sent between EIGRP routers to determine the state of their connection. Once the neighbor relation is established via the Hello protocol, the routers can exchange route information.

Each router establishes a *neighbor table*, in which it stores important information regarding the neighbors that are directly connected. The information consists of the neighbor's IP address, holdtime interval, smooth round-trip timer (SRTT), and queue information. These data are used to help determine when the link state changes.

When two routers initialize communication, their entire route tables are shared. Thereafter, only changes to the route table are propagated. These changes are shared with all directly connected EIGRP-speaking routers. Here is a summary of these steps:

1. Hello packets are multicast out all of the router's interfaces.
2. Replies to the Hello packets include all routes in the neighbor router's topology database, including the metrics. Routes that are learned from the originating router are not included in the reply.
3. The originating router acknowledges the update to each neighbor via an ACK packet.
4. The topology database is then updated with the newly received information.
5. Once the topology database is updated, the originating router then advertises its entire table to all the new neighbors.
6. Neighbor routers acknowledge the receipt of the route information from the originating router by sending back an ACK packet.

These steps are used in the initialization of EIGRP neighbors and change only slightly when updates are sent to existing neighbors.

Route Calculation and Updates

Because EIGRP uses distance-vector and link-state information when calculating routes by using the DUAL algorithm, convergence is much faster than with IGRP. The trick behind the convergence speed is that EIGRP calculates new routes only when a change in the network directly affects the routes contained in its route table.

Like IGRP, EIGRP's metric can be based on bandwidth, delay, load, reliability, and/or MTU. By default, only bandwidth and delay together are used; however, the user has the option to use the remaining items if they wish. To make that a little clearer, look at Figure 6.3, in which you see three routers meshed, *and* each router has an Ethernet segment connected as well.

FIGURE 6.3 Route updating vs. calculation of new route

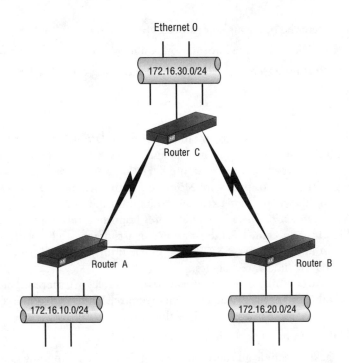

It is important to understand the difference between *accepting* a routing update and *calculating* a new route. If a change occurs to a network that is directly connected to a router, all of the relevant information is used to calculate a new metric and route entry for it. After the router calculates the new route, it is advertised to the neighbors.

Using Figure 6.3 as the example, assume that Ethernet 0 on Router C is very congested because of high traffic volumes. Also assume that load has been added to the metric calculation for all routers in this mesh. Router C then uses the distance and link information to calculate a new metric for network 172.16.30.0. With the new metric in place, the change is propagated to Routers A and B. To understand completely, you need to recognize that the other routers don't do any calculation—they just receive the update. Routers A and B don't need to calculate a new route for network 172.16.30.0 because they learn it from Router C.

On the other hand, if the link between Router A and Router C becomes congested, both routers have to calculate a new route metric. The change is then advertised to Router B by both Routers A and C.

Topology and Route State Information

The topology database stores all routes and metrics known via adjacent routers. By default, six routes can be stored for each destination network. If there are multiple routes to the destination, the router chooses the route with the best (lowest) metric and installs this into the routing table. It is possible for multiple routes to a destination to have the same metric. In these cases, assuming these routes have the best metric, they all will be installed in the routing table, and traffic destined to this network will be load-shared across them. The remaining routes will then serve as backups for the primary route if they meet the feasibility condition. While the best route is being chosen for a destination, the route is considered to be in an active state. After the route is chosen, the route status changes to passive.

Information given in Table 6.6 represents closely, though not exactly, that contained in an actual topology table. The Status field shows whether a new route is being calculated or whether a primary route has been selected. In our example, the route is in passive state because it has already selected the primary route.

TABLE 6.6   Topology Table Information

Status:	P
Route—Adjacent Router's Address (Metrics)	10.10.10.0/24 via 10.1.2.6 (*3611648*/3609600) via 10.5.6.6 (4121600/3609600) via 10.6.7.6 (5031234/ 3609600)
Number of Successors:	1 (Router C)
Feasible Distance:	3611648

Updates and Changes

EIGRP also has link-state properties. One of these properties is that it propagates only changes in the route table instead of sending an entire new route table to its neighbors. When changes occur in the network, a regular distance-vector protocol sends the entire route table to neighbors. By avoiding sending the entire route table, less bandwidth is consumed. Neighboring routers don't have to re-initialize the entire route table, which would cause convergence issues. The neighbors just have to insert the new route changes. This is one of the principal enhancements over IGRP.

Updates can follow two paths. If a route update contains a better metric or a new route, the routers simply exchange the information. If the update contains information that a network is unavailable or if the metric is worse than before, an alternate path must be found. The flowchart in Figure 6.4 describes the steps that must be taken to choose a new route.

The router first searches the topology database for feasible successors. If no feasible successors are found, a multicast request is sent to all adjacent routers. Each router then responds to the query. Depending on how the router answers, different paths are taken. After the intermediate steps are taken, two final actions can occur. If route information is eventually found, the route is added to the route table and an update is sent. If the responses from the adjacent routers do not contain any route information, the route is removed from the topology and route tables. After the route table is updated, the new information is sent to all adjacent routers via a multicast.

FIGURE 6.4 Handling route changes

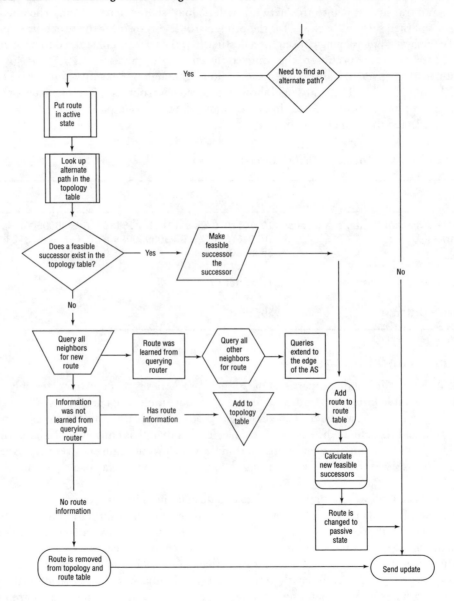

show Commands

Due to the complexity of EIGRP, there are several more show commands available to aid in troubleshooting EIGRP problems. The majority of the commands are listed in Table 6.7.

TABLE 6.7   EIGRP-Related show Commands

Command	Description/Output
show running-config	Displays the current configuration.
show ip route	Displays the full IP route table.
show ip route eigrp	Displays the EIGRP routes.
show ip eigrp interfaces	Displays EIGRP peer information for that interface.
show ip eigrp neighbors	Displays all EIGRP neighbors, along with summary information about each neighbor.
show ip eigrp topology	Displays the contents of the EIGRP topology table.
show ip eigrp traffic	Displays a summary of EIGRP routing statistics, such as the number of Hellos and routing updates.
show ip eigrp events	Displays a log of the most recent EIGRP protocol events. This information includes the insertion and removal of routes from the route table, updates, and neighbor status.

debug Commands

Several debug commands within EIGRP allow you to specify what processes you want to debug. Here is a list of commands:

- debug ip eigrp <AS number>
- debug ip eigrp neighbor
- debug ip eigrp notifications
- debug ip eigrp summary
- debug ip eigrp

Here is a sample of the information that can be obtained by using these commands:

```
Router_C#debug ip eigrp
IP-EIGRP Route Events debugging is on
IP-EIGRP: Processing incoming QUERY packet
```

```
IP-EIGRP: Int 172.16.30.4/30 M 4294967295 - 0 4294967295 SM
   4294967295 - 0 4294967295
IP-EIGRP: 172.16.30.4/30 routing table not updated
IP-EIGRP: 172.16.30.4/30, - do advertise out Ethernet0/0
IP-EIGRP: Int 172.16.30.4/30 metric 4294967295 - 1657856 4294967295
IP-EIGRP: Processing incoming UPDATE packet
IP-EIGRP: Int 172.16.30.4/30 M 2195456 - 1657856 537600 SM
   2169856 - 1657856 512000
IP-EIGRP: Int 172.16.30.4/30 metric 2195456 - 1657856 537600
IP-EIGRP: Processing incoming QUERY packet
IP-EIGRP: Int 172.16.30.4/30 M 4294967295 - 0 4294967295 SM
   4294967295 - 0 4294967295
IP-EIGRP: 172.16.30.4/30 routing table not updated
IP-EIGRP: 172.16.30.4/30, - do advertise out Ethernet0/0
IP-EIGRP: Int 172.16.30.4/30 metric 4294967295 - 1657856 4294967295
IP-EIGRP: Processing incoming UPDATE packet
IP-EIGRP: Int 172.16.30.4/30 M 2195456 - 1657856 537600 SM
   2169856 - 1657856 512000
IP-EIGRP: Int 172.16.30.4/30 metric 2195456 - 1657856 537600
```

You can see in this information when routes are removed from the route table and no longer advertised. Once the route is advertised to the router, it inserts the route back into the route table and commences advertisement.

Typical EIGRP Problems

Some of the typical problems with EIGRP are the loss of neighbor adjacencies, lost routes in earlier versions of IOS, stuck in active and lost default gateways.

Neighbor failures can be attributed to link failures just as much as they can be attributed to software problems. If a neighbor relation has problems establishing, use the proper debug command to see what is occurring between both routers.

When troubleshooting an EIGRP problem, it is always a good idea to get a picture of the network. The most relevant picture is provided by the show ip eigrp neighbors command. This command shows all adjacent routers that share route information within a given autonomous system. If neighbors are missing, check the configuration and link status on both routers to verify that the protocol has been configured correctly.

If all neighbors are present, verify the routes learned. By executing the show ip route eigrp command, you gain a quick picture of the routes in the route table. If the route does not appear in the route table, verify the source of the route. If the source is functioning properly, check the topology table.

The topology table is displayed by using the show ip eigrp topology command. If the route is in the topology table, it is safe to assume that there is a problem between the topology database and the route table. You need to find the reason why the topology database is not injecting the route into the route table.

Other commands, such as `show ip eigrp traffic`, can be used to see whether updates are being sent. If the counters for EIGRP input and output packets don't increase, no EIGRP information is being sent between peers.

The `show ip eigrp events` command is an undocumented command. It displays a log of every EIGRP event—when routes are injected and removed from the route table, and when EIGRP adjacencies reset or fail. This information can be used to see whether there are routing instabilities in the network.

Stuck in Active

Another problem that you will see quite often in larger EIGRP implementations is routers that are stuck in active (SIA). In EIGRP, when a route is removed, the router sends a query to each neighbor for new route. If the neighbor doesn't have the route, they in turn send a query to all their neighbors (except the one that sent them the initial query.) This process then continues until the edge of the EIGRP network is reached, or until a summary boundary is reached (summary boundaries are explained in more detail below). A route becomes stuck in active when a router does not receive a reply to all of the queries it sent out within a set time interval (three minutes by default). This occurs most often in larger networks as queries traverse from one side of the network to the other and then replies to queries must be sent back. This all happens one router at a time, and any single router in the network can cause the problem.

One of the most common ways to address the SIA problem is to limit the size of your EIGRP query domain. This can be done through the use of another routing protocol to create a query boundary, which is self-explanatory. Or, more commonly, you can use summaries. Let's see how this works.

If EIGRP receives a query for a route that is an exact match for a route in its routing table, EIGRP will send a query to all of its EIGRP neighbors asking about this route. However, if a query is received for a route *not* in the routing table, EIGRP sends a negative response to the query but does not send a query to its neighbors. Since a summary restricts the more specific routes from being advertised and causes EIGRP to only send the summary route, the more specific routes are never in the routing table of any router past the point of summarization. Therefore, when routers past this point get a query for one of the specific routes, they look for it in their routing table. Finding only the summary route, they send a negative response to the query and do not send a query their neighbors, thus creating a query boundary and lessening the probability of having a SIA problem.

Troubleshooting OSPF

Open Shortest Path First (OSPF) differs from IGRP and Enhanced IGRP because it is a pure link-state routing technology. Also, it is an open standard routing protocol, which means that it was not developed solely by Cisco. OSPF was designed and developed by the IETF to provide a scalable, quickly converging, and efficient routing protocol that can be used by all routing equipment. Complete details for OSPF are found in RFC 2178.

Areas are used within OSPF to define a group of routers and networks belonging to the same OSPF session. Links connect routers, and the information about each link is defined by its link state. On each broadcast or multi-access network segment, two routers must be assigned the responsibilities of designated router (DR) and backup designated router (BDR).

Like EIGRP, OSPF maintains three databases: adjacency, topology, and route. The adjacency database is similar to the neighbor database used by EIGRP. It contains all information about OSPF neighbors and the links connecting them. The topology database maintains all route information. The best routes from the topology database are placed in the route database, or route table.

Neighbor and Adjacency Formation

The Hello protocol is used to establish peering sessions among routers. Hello packets are multicast out every interface. The information that is multicast includes the router ID, timing intervals, existing neighbors, area identification, router priority, designated and backup router information, authentication password, and stub area information. All this information is used when establishing new peers. Descriptions of each element can be found in Table 6.8.

TABLE 6.8 OSPF Multicast Information

Information	Description
Router ID	Highest active IP address on the router.
Time intervals	Intervals between Hello packets, and the allowed dead time interval.
Existing neighbors	Addresses for any existing OSPF neighbors.
Area identification	OSPF area number and link information, which must be the same for a peering session to be established.
Router priority	Value assigned to a router and used when choosing the DR and BDR.
DR and BDR	If these routers have already been chosen, their Router ID and address are contained in the Hello packet.
Authentication password	All peers must have the same authentication password if authentication is enabled.
Stub area flag	This is a special area—two routers must share the same stub information. This information is not necessary to initiate a regular peering session with another OSPF router.

Figure 6.5 is a flowchart that depicts each step of the initialization process. The process starts by sending out Hello packets. Every listening router then adds the originating router to the adjacency database. The responding routers reply with all of their Hello information so that the originating router can add them to its adjacency table.

FIGURE 6.5   OSPF peer initialization

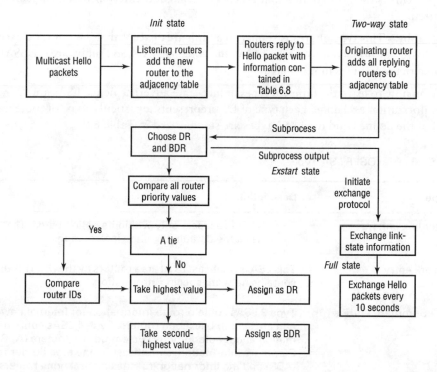

After adjacencies are established, the DR and BDR must be chosen before route information and link-state information can be exchanged. Once the DR and BDR are chosen, route information is exchanged, and the OSPF peers continue to multicast Hello packets every 10 seconds to determine whether neighbors are still reachable.

Before we go any further with peer initialization, we need to discuss several terms specific to OSPF. These terms are key to your understanding of OSPF and how it functions.

OSPF Area Types

The easiest way to understand OSPF areas is to build from what you already know about EIGRP. You learned that EIGRP uses autonomous system numbers to specify routing processes and the routing process to which individual routers belong. OSPF uses areas in place of an autonomous system. An OSPF area consists of a group of routers or interfaces on a router that is assigned to a common area. When deploying OSPF, there must be a backbone area. Standard and stub areas connect to the backbone area. Following are brief descriptions of each router type.

Backbone   This area accepts all link-state advertisements (LSAs) and is used to connect multiple areas.

Stub   This area does not accept any external routing update, but it accepts summary LSAs.

Totally Stub   These areas are closed off from accepting external or summary advertisements.

Standard   This is the normal area that accepts internal and external LSAs, and summary information.

Not So Stubby   This type of area is similar to a Stub area except that Type 5 LSAs (see Table 6.9) are not flooded into the area from the core. The Not So Stubby area (NSSA) can import external AS routes into the area.

Move on now to learn the different types of link-state advertisements. LSAs are the heart of OSPF's information exchange. Each type of LSA represents a particular type of route information. All of the defined and used LSA types are summarized in Table 6.9.

TABLE 6.9   OSPF LSA Types

LSA Type	Description
1 - Router link entry	This LSA is broadcast only within its defined area. The LSA contains all the default link-state information.
2 - Network entry	This LSA is multicast to all area routers by the DR. This update contains network-specific information.
3 and 4 - Summary entries	Type 3 LSAs contain route information for internal networks and are sent to backbone routers. Type 4 LSAs contain information about autonomous system border routers (ASBRs). Summary information is multicast by the area border router (ABR) and the information reaches all backbone routers (see Table 6.10).
5 - Autonomous System entry	Originating from the ASBR, these packets contain information about external networks.
7 - Not So Stubby Area	Not So Stubby Area (NSSA) permits Type 7 AS external routes to be imported inside the NSSA area by redistribution.

The LSA types represent the types of route being advertised and assist in restricting the number and type of routes that are accepted by a given area. As is shown in Table 6.9, an LSA of Type 5 is sent only by the Autonomous System Border Router. This brings you to the point where you need to understand the router types that belong to the various OSPF areas.

Multiple router types can exist within an OSPF area. Table 6.10 lists all of the OSPF router types and the role that each plays within the area.

TABLE 6.10   OSPF Router Types

Router Type	Responsibility
Internal	All interfaces are defined on the same area. All internal routers have an identical link-state database.
Backbone	Has at least one interface assigned to area 0.
Area border router (ABR)	Interfaces are connected to multiple OSPF areas. Information specific to each area is stored on this type of router.
Autonomous system boundary router (ASBR)	This type of router has an interface connected to an external network or to a different AS.

In addition to the responsibilities explained previously, a router can also be assigned other responsibilities. These additions are assumed when a router is assigned the role of DR or BDR.

show Commands

Because of the complexity of OSPF, several show commands are available to provide information regarding the configuration and functionality of OSPF on a router. Table 6.11 lists most of the available OSPF-related show commands. These commands provide you with substantial information valuable for troubleshooting OSPF routing problems.

TABLE 6.11   OSPF-Related show Commands

Command	Description / Output
show running-config	Displays the current router configuration.
show ip route	Displays the entire IP route table.
show ip route ospf	Displays OSPF routes.
show ip ospf	Displays information for OSPF.
show ip ospf *process-id*	Displays information relevant to the specified process ID.
show ip ospf border-routers	Displays the routers that join different areas, or border routers.
show ip ospf database	Provides an OSPF database summary.

TABLE 6.11 OSPF-Related show Commands *(continued)*

Command	Description / Output
show ip ospf interface	Displays OSPF information on a interface.
show ip ospf neighbor	Displays OSPF neighbor information.
show ip ospf request-list	Displays the link-state request list.
show ip ospf retransmission list	Displays the link-state retransmission list.
show ip ospf summary-address	Displays summary-address redistribution information.
show ip ospf virtual-links	Displays virtual link information.
show ip interface	Displays IP interface settings.

debug Commands

OSPF runs many processes to maintain all its databases, routing updates, and peering connections. Most of these processes use link-state advertisements (LSAs) to share information. LSAs are the heart of OSPF's information exchange. These types were highlighted in Table 6.9.

Here are the available debug options for OSPF:

debug ip ospf adj   Provides debug information about events concerning adjacency relationships with other OSPF routers.

debug ip ospf events   Provides debug information for all OSPF events.

debug ip ospf flood   Provides information about OSPF flooding. Flooding is the way that an OSPF router sends updates. It broadcasts a change in its route table, and all other members of the OSPF area receive the update.

debug ip ospf lsa-generation   Gives detailed information regarding the generation of LSA messages.

debug ip ospf packet   Gives detailed information regarding OSPF packets.

debug ip ospf retransmission   If OSPF has to retransmit information, it triggers a retransmission event that **debug** captures and echoes to the console.

debug ip ospf spf   Provides debug information for all SPF transactions. By enabling SPF debugging, OSPF events debugging is also turned on.

debug ip ospf tree   Provides information for the OSPF database tree.

Following is a debug ip ospf trace. Notice that OSPF event debugging was turned on as well (second and third lines of the output). SPF is an algorithm used to select the best route to each destination.

```
Router_A#debug ip ospf spf
OSPF spf intra events debugging is on
OSPF spf inter events debugging is on
OSPF spf external events debugging is on
Router_A#
%LINEPROTO-5-UPDOWN: Line protocol on Interface Serial1, changed state to down
%LINK-3-UPDOWN: Interface Serial1, changed state to down
OSPF: running SPF for area 0
OSPF: Initializing to run spf
 It is a router LSA 172.16.40.1. Link Count 1
   Processing link 0, id 172.16.30.4, link data 255.255.255.252, type 3
    Add better path to LSA ID 172.16.30.7, gateway 172.16.30.4, dist 64
    Add path fails: no output interface to 172.16.30.4,
    next hop 0.0.0.0
OSPF: Adding Stub nets
OSPF: Path left undeleted to 172.16.30.4
OSPF: Entered old delete routine
OSPF: No ndb for STUB NET old route 172.16.60.0, mask /24, next hop 172.16.30.6
OSPF: No ndb for STUB NET old route 172.16.30.4, mask /30, next hop 172.16.30.5
OSPF: No ndb for NET old route 172.16.50.0, mask /24, next hop 172.16.30.6
OSPF: delete lsa id 172.16.60.255, type 0, adv rtr 172.16.60.1 from delete list
OSPF: delete lsa id 172.16.30.7, type 0, adv rtr 172.16.40.1 from delete list
OSPF: delete lsa id 172.16.50.1, type 2, adv rtr 172.16.50.1 from delete list
OSPF: running spf for summaries area 0
OSPF: sum_delete_old_routes area 0
OSPF: Started Building Type 5 External Routes
OSPF: ex_delete_old_routes
OSPF: Started Building Type 7 External Routes
OSPF: ex_delete_old_routes
%LINK-3-UPDOWN: Interface Serial1, changed state to up
%LINEPROTO-5-UPDOWN: Line protocol on Interface Serial1, changed state to up
OSPF: running SPF for area 0
OSPF: Initializing to run spf
 It is a router LSA 172.16.40.1. Link Count 1
   Processing link 0, id 172.16.30.4, link data 255.255.255.252, type 3
    Add better path to LSA ID 172.16.30.7, gateway 172.16.30.4, dist 64
    Add path: next-hop 172.16.30.5, interface Serial1
```

```
OSPF: Adding Stub nets
OSPF: insert route list LS ID 172.16.30.7, type 0, adv rtr 172.16.40.1
OSPF: Entered old delete routine
OSPF: running spf for summaries area 0
OSPF: sum_delete_old_routes area 0
OSPF: Started Building Type 5 External Routes
OSPF: ex_delete_old_routes
OSPF: Started Building Type 7 External Routes
OSPF: ex_delete_old_routes
```

This is a lot of information over a very short period. You can get an idea of what the CPU goes through when there is a link-state change in a OSPF network.

Typical OSPF Problems

Because of the great number of processes and calculations that must be made by the CPU when changes occur in an OSPF network, the router can become overwhelmed with all the processing that has to be done. The bigger the OSPF network, the more calculations that occur, not to mention the greater probability of changes that are propagated throughout the network.

A general rule of thumb is to not add more than 100 routers per area, and to not have more than 700 routers throughout the network. It is possible to have smaller or larger networks, but the numbers here are given simply as a guideline. As links are added to a network, the likelihood of instability also increases. When a large network experiences instability, the routers have to spend a great deal of time and CPU cycles processing link and route updates. Proper route summarization can go along way to correcting the issues noted above.

Another problem common to OSPF is wrongly configured wildcard masks in the OSPF network statements. OSPF uses wildcard bits to specify the networks that should be advertised, instead of using multiple network statements. Both approaches work, but be aware of potential problems with the wildcard mask.

It is not always convenient for all areas to connect back to area 0; Therefore, in many cases virtual links are used. A virtual link allows for a remote area to connect to area 0 by "tunneling" through another area. Though this will allow for OSPF to function, there can be issues with this configuration if the virtual connection takes an unreliable path, causing flapping of the area. Consequently, virtual links should be used sparingly.

At times the most difficult challenge with OSPF is just getting the neighbors to come up. A common issue in getting a neighbor relationship up is the occurrence of a mismatch in OSPF settings (Hello interval, dead interval, authentication, and so on). If all of these are configured correctly, make sure that the OSPF interface network types match. These interface network types are broadcast, point-to-point, NBMA, point-to-multipoint, and virtual link.

Troubleshooting BGP

You are now familiar with several IGPs (Interior Gateway Protocols), including IGRP, EIGRP, and OSPF. For enterprise networks to communicate with other autonomous systems or ISPs, the IGP information has to be injected into BGP, which is used by all network entities that compose the Internet.

Border Gateway Protocol (BGP) is an open-standard protocol that was developed and defined in several RFCs: 1163, 1267, 1654, and 1655, to name a few. The two types of BGP are iBGP and eBGP. There are several differences between the two. Primarily, iBGP (internal BGP) is used to share BGP information with routers within the same AS, whereas eBGP (external BGP) is used to share route information between two separate autonomous systems. More details will be given as we discuss each type separately.

Neighbor Relationship

The key to BGP configuration is the neighbor relationship. Unlike many of the previously discussed protocols, BGP uses TCP to establish neighbor relationships. Specifically, a TCP connection on port 179 is set up when the neighbor relationship is formed, and remains up as long as the relationship exists. This connection is used to send routing updates, notifications, and keepalives between the routers.

BGP is an Exterior Gateway Protocol (EGP), and as such, its design assumes it will be used to connect many different companies with varying configurations and levels of trust. Because of this design assumption, there are numerous configuration options for each neighbor relationship. You can set up BGP to prefer one neighbor's routes over another (all the time or only some of the time), to update the next-hop information to one neighbor but not another, to advertise a route only if another route is in the routing table, to update the path information for some but not all routes from a neighbor, and to perform many other manipulations on the routes that are entered into the routing table. In addition, most of these attributes can be assigned based on groups of neighbors as well as on an individual neighbor-by-neighbor basis.

The cost of this flexibility is complexity. A simple BGP configuration, with a couple of neighbors and little or no manipulation of the routes, is no harder to manage and maintain than any IGP, such as OSPF or EIGRP. However, if significant route manipulation and neighbor relationship management is needed in your implementation, troubleshooting any issue can become a major undertaking. Therefore, whenever possible create groups for neighbors and simplify any route manipulation to adjust a minimum number of terms.

eBGP vs. iBGP

The distinguishing characteristic between an iBGP neighbor and an eBGP neighbor is that an iBGP neighbor is in the same autonomous system and an eBGP neighbor is in a different autonomous system. Treatment of iBGP and eBGP peers differs greatly. In general, eBGP neighbors share a common subnet, while iBGP neighbors can be anywhere within the same AS. In addition, an eBGP route has an administrative distance of 20 by default, compared with 200 for an iBGP route.

It is not a requirement for eBGP neighbors to share a common subnet. If they do not—for example, if you are using loopbacks—the path to the neighbor's loopback must be known by a means other than BGP, such as a static route, and be no more than 255 hops away. Once this is complete, add a neighbor *ip address* ebgp-multihop command for that neighbor into the BGP configuration.

In iBGP, route information learned from one iBGP peer is not advertised to another iBGP peer. Therefore, per the RFCs, all routers connected via iBGP should be in a logical mesh. This avoids inconsistent route information and routing loops. By default, when routes are exchanged between iBGP peers, the "next hop" attribute is not updated. This goes back to the assumption that there is a logical mesh of all iBGP peers. With this mesh, it is assumed that every device in the mesh knows how to get to all the same networks, and therefore the next hop does not need to be updated because the iBGP peers should know about it. As is the case with most things in BGP, this behavior can be changed if your needs dictate.

The purpose of eBGP is to inject routes owned by the enterprise network into another AS. Two prerequisites must be met in order for internal routes to be propagated via BGP:

- The route to be advertised must be present in the router's IGP route table. You can fulfill this condition by injecting the routes into a router's route table via one of these three methods: an IGP, a static route, or directly connected networks. BGP has a synchronization option that requires BGP and the IGP routes to synchronize before BGP will advertise IGP-learned networks. The no synchronization command indicates that BGP and the IGP do not have to synchronize before BGP advertises the routes.

- BGP must learn the route. You also have three ways to accomplish this second prerequisite. BGP learns of networks that it needs to advertise through other BGP advertisements, network statements, and redistribution of an IGP into BGP.

show Commands

There are numerous show commands available for BGP. Many are similar to ones that were issued for other routing protocols. Table 6.12 describes the principal show commands for BGP.

TABLE 6.12 BGP-Related show Commands

Command	Description
show ip bgp	Shows information about BGP learned routes, including indicating which ones will be in the routing table.
show ip bgp *network*	Shows BGP information on a specific network.
show ip bgp neighbors	Shows information on BGP neighbors.

TABLE 6.12   BGP-Related show Commands *(continued)*

Command	Description
show ip bgp neighbors *ip address* advertised-routes	Shows all routes being advertised to a particular neighbor.
show ip bgp neighbors *ip address* received-routes	Shows all routes being received from a particular neighbor.
show ip bgp peer-group	Shows information about BGP peer groups.
show ip bgp summary	Shows a summary of all BGP connections.
show ip route bgp	Displays the BGP route table.
show ip route	Displays the IP route table.
show ip interface	Displays IP interface configuration.
show running-config	Displays the running configuration.

debug Commands

Despite the overall complexity of BGP, there are relatively few debug commands. Those that do exist are very focused as to the information that they show. This does mean you need to know specifically what you are looking for, but it also makes the debug commands less of a burden on the router to run. Therefore, the debug commands that are available are usable in most real-life installations.

As with all debug commands, you need to take care when using the BGP debug options. Even though they are focused, significant load can be placed on the processor if there are a large number of routes in the routing table. Some of the frequently used commands are as follows:

- debug ip bgp <*ipaddress*> updates
- debug ip bgp dampening
- debug ip bgp events
- debug ip bgp keepalives
- debug ip bgp updates

Here is an example of the output from debug ip bgp *ip address* updates:

```
Router_B#debug ip bgp 172.16.20.6 updates
BGP updates debugging is on for neighbor 172.16.20.6
BGP: 172.16.20.6 computing updates, neighbor version 0, table
   version 2, starting at 0.0.0.0
```

```
BGP: 172.16.20.6 send UPDATE 10.0.0.0/8, next 172.16.20.5, metric 0, path 100
BGP: 172.16.20.6 1 updates enqueued (average=50, maximum=50)
BGP: 172.16.20.6 update run completed, ran for 0ms, neighbor version 0,
   start version 2, throttled to 2, check point net 0.0.0.0
BGP: 172.16.20.6 rcv UPDATE w/ attr: nexthop 172.16.20.6, origin ?,
   metric 0, path 200
BGP: 172.16.20.6 rcv UPDATE about 19.0.0.0/8
BGP: 172.16.20.6 rcv UPDATE about 100.100.0.0/16
BGP: 172.16.20.6 rcv UPDATE about 100.200.0.0/14
BGP: 172.16.20.6 rcv UPDATE about 199.199.0.0/16
BGP: 172.16.20.6 rcv UPDATE about 200.200.1.0/24
BGP: 172.16.20.6 rcv UPDATE about 200.200.64.0/18
BGP: 172.16.20.6 computing updates, neighbor version 2, table
   version 8, starting at 0.0.0.0
BGP: 172.16.20.6 update run completed, ran for 0ms, neighbor version 2,
   start version 8, throttled to 8, check point net 0.0.0.0
Router_B#
```

Typical BGP Problems

Most problems with BGP are a result of the complexity of the implementation. These problems will most likely occur during the implementation itself. Once BGP is set up and running, it is a very stable protocol that can effectively manage the routing table for the entire Internet.

Many of the typical problems that occur in BGP affect the areas in which BGP differs from other routing protocols. For example, in other routing protocols when a route is learned from a neighbor and there is no other route in the routing table for this network, the route is installed in the network. In BGP, certain other conditions may need to be met before this occurs. In addition, BGP's network statements work differently from other routing protocols'. For example, in EIGRP a `network 10.0.0.0` command would tell EIGRP to route out any network between `10.0.0.0` and `10.255.255.255`. In BGP, this same statement means to send the `10.0.0.0 / 8` network if it is in the routing table. If the `10.2.2.0 /24` network is in the table, in BGP this will not be sent (assuming the auto-summary feature of BGP has been disabled).

Another common BGP difficulty concerns the default manner in which iBGP distributes routes. Because iBGP is built on the concept that all iBGP neighbors have the same routes in their routing table, the `next-hop` attribute of a route is left as the address of the eBGP peer and is not updated when routes are sent to iBGP peers. If an iBGP peer's routing table does not contain the external peer's address, traffic for this destination will be dropped. To overcome this, the `next-hop-self` command can be used to tell the router to advertise itself rather than the external peer as the next hop.

Redistribution of Routing Protocols

When multiple routing protocols are used within a network and they need to be redistributed into one another, it is important that it be done correctly by assigning the proper metrics through the redistribution. If protocols are redistributed without metric adjustment, many networking problems can occur.

Although redistribution allows multiple protocols to share routing information, it can result in routing loops, slow convergence, and inconsistent route information. This is caused by the differing algorithms and methods used by each protocol. It is not good practice to redistribute bidirectionally (if, for example, you have both IGRP 100 and RIP routing sessions running on your router). Bidirectional redistribution occurs if you enter redistribution commands under each protocol session. Here is an example:

```
Router_A#config t
Enter configuration commands, one per line. End with CNTL/Z.
Router_A(config)#router igrp 100
Router_A(config-router)#redistribute RIP
Router_A(config-router)#router RIP
Router_A(config-router)#redistribute igrp 100
Router_A(config-router)#^Z
Router_A#
```

When a route from RIP, IGRP, or OSPF is injected into another routing protocol, the route loses its identity and its metrics are converted from the original format to the other protocol's format. This can cause confusion within the router. Ensuring that the metric is converted properly is done through metric commands. In most cases, the specific command used is `default-metric`.

Dealing with Routing Metrics

The router in which multiple protocols or sessions meet is called the *autonomous system boundary router (ASBR)*. When routes from one protocol or session are injected or redistributed into another protocol or session, the routes are tagged as external routes. Following is a simple example of a route table that has external routes:

```
Router_X#show ip route eigrp
     172.16.0.0/16 is variably subnetted, 301 subnets, 10
     masks
D EX    172.16.27.230/32
             [170/24827392] via 172.16.131.82, 02:33:32,
             ATM6/0/0.3114
```

```
D EX     172.16.237.16/29
                [170/40542208] via 172.16.131.82, 23:40:32,
                ATM6/0/0.3114
                [170/40542208] via 172.16.131.74, 23:40:32,
                ATM6/0/0.3113
D EX     172.16.237.24/29
                [170/40542208] via 172.16.131.82, 23:40:32,
                ATM6/0/0.3114
                [170/40542208] via 172.16.131.74, 23:40:32,
                ATM6/0/0.3113
D EX     172.16.52.192/26
                [170/2202112] via 172.16.131.82, 23:40:27,
                ATM6/0/0.3114
D EX     172.16.41.216/29
                [170/46232832] via 172.16.131.82, 23:40:28,
                ATM6/0/0.3114
D EX     172.16.38.200/30
                [170/2176512] via 172.16.131.82, 23:40:27,
                ATM6/0/0.3114
D EX     172.16.237.0/29
                [170/40542208] via 172.16.131.82, 23:40:32,
                ATM6/0/0.3114
                [170/40542208] via 172.16.131.74, 23:40:32,
                ATM6/0/0.3113
D        172.16.236.0/24
                [90/311808] via 172.16.131.82, 23:40:32,
                ATM6/0/0.3114
                [90/311808] via 172.16.131.74, 23:40:32,
                ATM6/0/0.3113
D        172.16.235.0/24
                [90/311808] via 172.16.131.82, 23:40:32,
                ATM6/0/0.3114
```

Most of the information in this example is self-explanatory, but there are a couple of points that need discussion. As you can see, in this route table all of the routes are prefaced with a D, meaning that they are EIGRP routes. Routes that originated outside EIGRP and were redistributed into it are denoted with the EX (external) tag. The numbers inside the brackets (for instance, [90/311808]) represent the administrative distance/metric of the route, respectively. In this case, the router is using the default administrative distances of 90 for internal and 170 for external EIGRP routes.

IGRP and EIGRP Metrics

Each protocol has its own method of route redistribution. You must be familiar with each protocol's implementation of route redistribution and default-metric settings.

IGRP and EIGRP use the same command to adjust metrics: the `default-metric` command. Here is an example:

```
default-metric bandwidth delay reliability load MTU
```

This command takes the metrics for the protocol being injected into IGRP or EIGRP, and converts them directly to values that IGRP or EIGRP can use. The *bandwidth* is the capacity of the link; *delay* is the time in microseconds; *reliability* and *load* are values from 1 to 255; and *MTU* is the maximum transmission unit in bytes. If you are looking for some possible values for the default metric, you can just examine the output of a `show interface` command.

Finally, you can also change the distance values that are assigned to EIGRP (90 internal; 170 external). The administrative distance value tells the router which protocol to believe. The lower the distance value, the more believable the protocol. The administrative distance values for EIGRP are changed with the following command from within the EIGRP session:

```
distance eigrp internal-distance external-distance
```

Internal-distance and *external-distance* both have a range of values from 1 to 255.

> **WARNING** Remember that a value of 255 tells the router to ignore the route. So, unless you want the routes from the protocol to be ignored, never use the value of 255.

You may find the distance setting to be a source of trouble when you're troubleshooting routing problems. If multiple protocols advertise the same routes, it is possible that differences in the administrative distance may cause the route to be learned by the wrong protocol, and thus it is not propagated correctly throughout the network.

Metrics used by EIGRP are essentially equal to 256 times the IGRP metrics. As with IGRP, metrics decide how the routes are selected. The higher the metric associated with a route, the less desirable the route is. The specific formula for determining the EIGRP metric is the following:

Metric = $256 * [K1 * Bandwidth + (K2 * Bandwidth)/(256-load) + K3 * Delay] * [K5/(reliability + K4)]$ where the values $K1$ through $K5$ are configurable constants. By default, $K2$, $K4$ and $K5$ are set equal to 0, and $K1$ and $K3$ are set equal to 1. If $K5$ is set to 0, the last section of the formula ($K5/(reliability + K4)$) is not used. Because, $K2$, $K4$, and $K5$ are set to 0 by default, the default formula reduces down to:

Metric = $256 * [Bandwidth + Delay]$

> **NOTE** Remember that the Bandwidth as referred to in the formula is the minimum bandwidth on the network path and the Delay is actually the sum of the delays on the network path.

OSPF Metrics

The metrics associated with OSPF are different from those associated with IGRP and EIGRP. OSPF uses bandwidth as the main metric in selecting a route. The cost is calculated by using the bandwidth for the link. The equation is 100,000,000 (10 to the 8th power) divided by the bandwidth. You can change bandwidth on the individual interface.

The cost is manipulated by changing the value to a number within the range of 1 to 65,535. Because the cost is assigned to each link, the value must be changed on each interface. The command to do this is ip ospf *cost*

> Cisco bases link cost on bandwidth. Other vendors may use other metrics to calculate the link's cost. When connecting links between routers from different vendors, you may have to adjust the cost to match the other router. Both routers must assign the same cost to the link for OSPF to work.

You can configure the OSPF distance with the following command:

```
distance ospf [external | Intra-area | Inter-area] distance
```

This command allows the distance metric to be defined for external OSPF, and intra-area and inter-area routes. As the names imply, intra-area routes are routes that exist in a particular OSPF area and inter-area routes are routes that come from other OSPF areas. Distance values range from 1 to 255—and the lower the distance, the better.

Other values important to OSPF's operation are not actually metrics, but can be configured as well. Values such as the router ID and router priority are important in router initialization and for DR and BDR selection. You can change these values with some minor configuration changes.

To change the router priority, use the following command on the desired interface:

```
ip ospf priority number
```

The *number* can range from 0 to 255—a higher value indicates a higher priority when choosing the DR and BDR for the area.

Just as with EIGRP, new metrics must be assigned to route information that is injected into the OSPF session. The command in this case is much simpler than the command used when assigning metrics for EIGRP or IGRP—it is almost the same, but only one metric is assigned. The value of the metric is the cost for the route.

```
default-metric cost
```

Distribute Lists

Distribute lists are access lists applied to an interface from within a routing protocol. The purpose of a distribute list is to control which routes are advertised to adjacent routers. As of IOS 12.0(3)T, you can also use a *prefix list* in place of the access list. A prefix list, specified by the `ip prefix-list` command, allows greater flexibility in specifying the networks that should be allowed. For example, with a prefix list you can tell the routing protocol to accept all routes as long as the mask length for the route is between /8 and /24, as in the following command:

`ip prefix-list MASK-SIZE permit 0.0.0.0/0 ge 8 le 24`

Problems can occur if distribute lists are missing or improperly configured. Figure 6.6 shows three meshed routers. Here, undesired routing can occur if the advertised routes are not controlled through the use of distribute lists.

FIGURE 6.6   Distribute lists to prevent routing loops

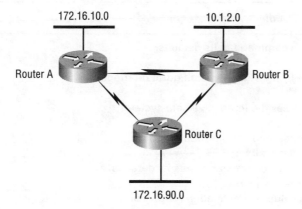

Routers A and B are core-level routers. Router C is a small access router. The potential problem is that Router A could learn about network `10.1.2.0` via Router C instead of Router B, if no distribute lists are used to control what routes are advertised from Router C.

If all of Router A's traffic destined for `10.1.2.0` were routed through Router C, it could easily overwhelm the small router. In this scenario, you'd only want Router C to have redundant links to the core, and not let the core transit an access router to reach another core router.

The problem can be solved or avoided by configuring an access list that permits only networks connected to Router C. The access list would be applied outbound to the interfaces connecting Routers A and B with the `distribute-list` command. The command is issued from within the routing protocol configuration mode.

Distribute lists can solve problems as well as cause them. When the downstream routers are configured to learn their default gateway dynamically, the router must have the default network in the route table. If the route is not present, the router will lose the gateway of last resort. When a distribute list is applied, you must verify that it allows route advertisement of the default network, as well as any other crucial routes.

Route Maps

Route maps are used to manipulate routing. They are small scripts that can contain multiple instances and multiple conditions for each instance. Route maps are somewhat like access lists if you specify that the packet must match an access list. In addition to the capability of permitting or denying the packet, you can define what is done before the packet is forwarded.

Route maps can be used to set metrics for route updates, to set a command to its default value, and so on. Table 6.13 gives a list of what a route map can do.

TABLE 6.13   Route Map Configuration Commands

Command	Description
default	Sets a command to its defaults.
exit	Exits from route-map configuration mode.
help	Describes the interactive help system.
match	Matches values from routing table.
no	Negates a command or sets its defaults.
set	Sets values in destination routing protocol.

Here is a sample route map:

```
route-map test permit 10
 match ip address 1
 set metric-type type-2
!
route-map test permit 20
 match ip address 2
 set metric-type type-1
!
route-map test permit 30
 set metric 100
```

The router runs through this route map, just as it runs through an access list. The only difference is that the router performs some commands instead of simply forwarding or dropping the packet. In this example, any packet matching the addresses listed in the IP access list 1 has its metric set as an OSPF type-2 metric. Any packet matching the addresses specified in access list 2 has its OSPF metric set to type-1. The final instance of the route map "test" is to set the metric of the route update to 100.

Real World Scenario

Managing Access Lists and Route Maps

This chapter discusses how access lists and route maps are used to assist in route control. As is the case with many router control elements, managing these items in a smaller environment is not a problem. However, as the environment gets larger and more components are added, an effective management plan can save administrative overhead and potentially eliminate some problems before they occur. The first item that needs attention in this plan is *naming*.

Whenever possible, use named access lists. Some commands, such as `snmp-server community` and `access-class`, accept only numbered lists; however, in most instances you can use the named lists. By using named lists, you will be able to easily determine the use of the access list as well as, potentially, the direction in which it is applied.

When naming your access lists and route maps, be sure to use descriptive names. Also, if the access list will be used to filter traffic on an interface, indicate in the name of the list whether it will be applied inbound or outbound on the interface. If they are to be used in a route map, name the route map and access list similarly. All of these naming suggestions will allow for easier correlation during troubleshooting. Since the named access list and route map are case sensitive, it is a good practice to use either all capital or all lowercase letters. This makes it easier to spot whether a letter is out of place.

For example, if your naming standard used all capital letters for named access lists, the access list that would be applied inbound on the interface connecting to the engineering department could be ENGINEERING-DEPT-IN.

If you are running a code level above 12.0(2)T, you can also use remarks to assist in documenting the role for a particular access-list line. Following are examples of the remark command for both named and numbered lists:

Numbered List:

```
access-list 100 remark Do not allow Sales Dept subnet to telnet out
access-list 100 deny tcp 10.30.30.0 0.0.0.255 any eq telnet
```

Named List:

```
ip access-list extended SALES-DEPT-IN
  remark Do not allow Sales Dept subnet to telnet out
  deny tcp 10.30.30.0 0.0.0.255 any eq telnet
```

One final suggestion: If the same access list or route map is used on multiple routers, be sure to name them the same on all the routers. This will avoid confusion and allow for easier documentation and updating. For example, if you have a standard numbered access list that is used to limit SNMP read-only traffic on the routers, always use the same number on every router. By using these simple procedures, life with access lists and route maps will be that much more bearable.

TCP/IP Symptoms and Problems: Summary Sheet

Table 6.14 lists several common TCP/IP symptoms and their probable causes.

TABLE 6.14 TCP/IP Symptoms and Causes

Symptom	Problems
Local host cannot communicate with a remote host	(a) DNS not working properly (b) No route to remote host (c) Missing default gateway (d) Administrative denial (access lists)
Certain applications won't work properly	(a) Administrative denial (access lists) (b) Network not configured to handle the application
Booting failures	(a) BootP server did not have an entry for the MAC address (b) Missing IP helper-address (c) Access lists (d) Change in the NIC or MAC address (e) Duplicate IP address (f) Improper IP configuration
Can't ping a remote station	(a) Access lists (b) No route to host (c) No default gateway set (d) Remote host down
Missing routes	(a) Improper routing protocol configuration (b) Distribute lists (c) Passive interface (doesn't receive updates) (d) Neighbor not advertising routes (e) Protocol version mismatch (f) Neighbor relation not established
Adjacencies not forming	(a) Improper routing protocol configuration (b) Improper IP configuration (c) Misconfigured network or neighbor statements (d) Mismatched Hello timers (e) Mismatched area ID
High CPU utilization	(a) Several routing updates due to instabilities (b) Debug wasn't turned off (c) A process gone amok

TABLE 6.14   TCP/IP Symptoms and Causes *(continued)*

Symptom	Problems
Route stuck in active mode	(a) Misconfigured timers (b) Hardware problems (c) Unstable link

TCP/IP Symptoms and Action Plans: Summary Sheet

Table 6.15 contains action plans for each of the problems outlined in Table 6.15.

TABLE 6.15   Action Plans for Common TCP/IP Problems

Problem	Action Plan
DNS not working properly	Check the DNS configuration on host and DNS server. May use the nslookup utility to verify functionality of the DNS server.
No route to remote host	This can be caused by several different things: 1. Check the default gateway using the ipconfig /all or winipcfg command if you are on a Windows machine. 2. Using the show ip route command, check to see whether the router has a route. 3. If the router doesn't have a route, use the show ip route command to see whether a gateway of last resort is set. 4. If there is a gateway, check the next hop in the path toward the destination. If there is no gateway, fix the problem or investigate why the router does not have a route.
Access lists	If you isolate the problem to an access list, you must analyze the list, rewrite it correctly, and then apply the new access list.
Network not configured to handle the application	When applications use NetBIOS, NetBEUI, IPX, or other non-IP applications, verify that the routers involved are configured to properly handle the applications by using transparent bridging, SRB, tunneling, and so on.

TABLE 6.15   Action Plans for Common TCP/IP Problems *(continued)*

Problem	Action Plan
Booting failures	1. Check the DHCP or BootP server, and verify that it has an entry for the MAC address of the problem station.
	2. Use debug ip udp to verify that packets are being received from the host.
	3. Verify that the helper addresses are correctly configured.
	4. Check for access lists that might be denying the packets.
	5. Make the necessary changes.
Missing routes	1. Look on the first router to see what routes are being learned. Issue the show ip route command.
	2. Depending on the routing protocol, verify that adjacencies have been formed with neighboring routers.
	3. Using the show running-config command, look at the router's configuration and verify that the routing protocol has the proper network or neighbor statements.
	4. When troubleshooting OSPF, verify that the wildcard mask permits the correct routes.
	5. Check the distribute lists that are applied to the interfaces. Analyze the inbound filters.
	6. Verify that both neighbors have the correct IP configuration.
	7. If routes are being redistributed, verify the metric.
	8. Verify that the routes are being redistributed properly.
Adjacencies not forming	1. Perform a show ip *protocol* neighbors command to list the adjacencies that have formed.
	2. Look at the protocol configuration to confirm which adjacencies have not formed.
	3. Check the network statements in the protocol configuration.

TABLE 6.15   Action Plans for Common TCP/IP Problems *(continued)*

Problem	Action Plan
	4. Show the ip *protocol* interface to obtain interface-specific information such as Hello timers.
	5. Once you have isolated the problem, make the necessary changes.

Summary

Before the advent of the routing protocol, the only way to get packets from point A to point B was to use static routes. As internetworks grew in size, it became impractical to keep adding new routes manually. Engineers began creating and using dynamic routing protocols. One of the first of these, RIP, provided dynamic updates as well as automatic failover in the event of a failure. However, RIP did not have many of the other features common in routing protocols today. As new routing protocols were created, they offered more features and capabilities. With each generation, engineers gained more flexibility in determining how packets were routed through the network.

Today, a number of protocols can be used to route TCP/IP traffic. These include the ones studied in this chapter—RIP, IGRP, EIGRP, OSPF, and BGP. Each of these protocols has its own strengths and weaknesses and is best suited for particular environments. Problems can arise, however, when one routing domain must redistribute its routes into another. This redistribution can cause suboptimal routing or routing loops.

To prevent these issues, special steps should be taken at the redistribution points. Specifically, distribute lists, prefix lists, and/or route maps should be used. These tools allow for the filtering of the routes being redistributed, as well as filtering of the routes that are sent to or received from a neighbor. In addition to the distribution lists, prefix lists, and/or route maps, engineers also can employ a wide array of show and debug commands to determine exactly what a routing protocol is doing. These commands vary in granularity. Some show information about the general routing characteristics on a router; others show detailed information about a singular route learned from a particular protocol. By using these commands together, you can effectively troubleshoot routing problems of any type and severity.

Exam Essentials

Know the concept of the default gateway and how it is used.   The default gateway can be either dynamically learned or statically defined. In either case, the default gateway is used as the destination path for any packet for which there is no specific route in the routing table.

Know the difference between static and dynamic routing.   Static routing allows the administrator to define routes on a router-by-router basis. However, the cost of this flexibility is a high amount of overhead any time there is a change in the network. Dynamic routing, using one of the routing protocols mentioned in this chapter, automatically distributes routing tables to all participating routers. Dynamic routing also allows automatic updates to all routers when there is a change in the network.

Know the routing protocols and the show **and** debug **commands that can be used with them.** The routing protocols covered in this chapter are RIP, IGRP, EIGRP, OSPF, and BGP. Be sure to review the tables showing the show and debug commands available for each protocol.

Know the issues surrounding the redistribution of one routing protocol into another.   Redistribution, if not done properly, can cause routing loops. Special care is needed when bidirectional redistribution takes place. In addition to routing loops, using multiple routing protocols with different administrative distances can cause suboptimal routing.

Know how to use distribute lists, prefix lists, and route maps to filter routing information. Distribute lists, prefix lists, and route maps can be used to filter and manipulate routing updates in various ways. Though all three are similar in function, distribute lists are really nothing more than access lists that are applied to routing updates. Prefix lists add the ability to filter based on the address as well as the subnet mask of the route. Route maps allow for the manipulation as well as the filtering of routing updates.

Commands Used in This Chapter

The following list contains a summary of all the commands used in this chapter.

Commands	Descriptions
debug ip bgp *ip address updates*	Debugs BGP update packets from the neighbor specified in the command.
debug ip bgp dampening	Debugs neighbor-dampening activities for BGP.
debug ip bgp events	Debugs major BGP events.
debug ip bgp keepalives	Debugs BGP keepalive packets.
debug ip bgp updates	Debugs BGP update packets from all neighbors.
debug ip eigrp	Causes a general debug to be performed on all EIGRP.
debug ip eigrp *AS number*	Debugs EIGRP for the specified AS.
debug ip eigrp neighbor	Debugs the transactions and exchanges among EIGRP neighbors.

`debug ip eigrp notifications`	Provides detailed information about neighbor notifications.
`debug ip eigrp summary`	Provides summarized information during a debug.
`debug ip igrp events`	Provides information regarding IGRP events (protocol-related).
`debug ip igrp transactions`	Provides more-detailed information regarding IGRP events (protocol-related).
`debug ip ospf adj`	Provides debug information about events concerning adjacency relationships with other OSPF routers.
`debug ip ospf events`	Provides debug information for all OSPF events.
`debug ip ospf flood`	Provides information about OSPF flooding. (Flooding is the way that OSPF router sends updates.) It broadcasts a change in its route table and all other members of the OSPF area receive the update.
`debug ip ospf lsa-generation`	Gives detailed information regarding the generation of LSA messages.
`debug ip ospf packet`	Gives detailed information regarding OSPF packets.
`debug ip ospf retransmission`	When OSPF has to retransmit information, this command triggers a retransmission event that the debug tool captures and echoes to the console.
`debug ip ospf spf`	Provides debug information for all SPF transactions. By enabling SPF debugging, OSPF events debugging is also turned on.
`debug ip ospf tree`	Provides information for the OSPF database tree.
`debug ip rip`	Provides you with all possible RIP protocol information.
`debug ip rip events`	Provides output regarding RIP protocol events.
`default-metric`	Sets the metric value used when redistributing one routing protocol into another.
`show ip bgp`	Shows information about BGP learned routes, including indicating which ones will be in the routing table.
`show ip bgp neighbors`	Shows information on BGP neighbors.

`show ip bgp neighbors` *ip address* `advertised-routes`	Shows all routes being advertised to a particular neighbor.
`show ip bgp neighbors` *ip address* `receivedroutes`	Shows all routes being received from a particular neighbor.
`show ip bgp peer-group`	Shows information about BGP peer groups.
`show ip bgp summary`	Shows a summary of all BGP connections.
`show ip eigrp events`	Displays a log of the most recent EIGRP protocol events. This information includes the insertion and removal of routes from the route table, updates, and neighbor status.
`show ip eigrp interfaces`	Displays EIGRP peer information for that interface.
`show ip eigrp neighbors`	Displays all EIGRP neighbors, along with summary information about each neighbor.
`show ip eigrp topology`	Displays the contents of the EIGRP topology table.
`show ip eigrp traffic`	Displays a summary of EIGRP routing statistics, such as the number of Hellos and routing updates.
`show ip interface`	Displays the status, IP configuration, and settings for the interface.
`show ip ospf`	Displays information for OSPF.
`show ip ospf` *process-id* `\`	Displays information relevant to the specified process ID.
`show ip ospf borderrouters`	Displays the routers that join different areas, or border routers.
`show ip ospf database`	Provides an OSPF database summary.
`show ip ospf interface`	Displays OSPF information on a interface.
`show ip ospf neighbor`	Displays OSPF neighbor information.
`show ip ospf request-list`	Displays link-state request list.
`show ip ospf retransmission list`	Displays link-state retransmission list.
`show ip ospf summary-address`	Displays summary-address redistribution information.
`show ip ospf virtual-links`	Displays virtual link information.
`show ip protocols`	Provides information about the IP routing protocols that run on the router.

`show ip route`	Displays the contents of the IP route table as well as the default gateway for the router.
`show ip route bgp`	Displays the BGP route table.
`show ip route eigrp`	Displays the EIGRP routes.
`show ip route igrp`	Displays IGRP routes only.
`show ip route ospf`	Displays the OSPF routes.
`show ip route rip`	Displays the RIP route table.

Key Terms

Before you take the exam, be certain you are familiar with the following terms:

areas	neighbor
autonomous system boundary router (ASBR)	neighbor relationships
Border Gateway Protocol	neighbor table
distribute lists	Open Shortest Path First (OSPF)
Enhanced IGRP (EIGRP)	prefix list
holddown	route maps
hop count	Routing Information Protocol (RIP)
Interior Gateway Routing Protocol (IGRP)	

Review Questions

1. Choose four common IP show commands.

    A. show ip route

    B. show ip interface

    C. show running-config

    D. show ip access-lists

    E. show ip default-gateway

    F. show ip mrm

2. What is the function of a default gateway?

    A. The default gateway is a default next hop if the router or host does not know a route to the destination.

    B. It is used to provide the default network.

    C. It provides the method of returning network management information to a router.

    D. None of the above.

3. What are the methods of setting the gateway of last resort on a Cisco router? (Choose two.)

    A. Configure ip default-route.

    B. Configure ip default neighbor.

    C. Configure a static route.

    D. Configure an IP default-network.

4. Match each command with its corresponding output. The output choices are as follows: (1) Displays IP; (2) Displays the current configuration; (3) Displays the RIP route table; (4) Displays the IP route table.

    A. show ip route rip

    B. show ip route

    C. show ip interface

    D. show running-config

5. Match each command with its corresponding output. The output choices are as follows: (1) Displays IGRP routes only; (2) Displays the entire route table; (3) Displays the current configuration.

    A. show running-config

    B. show ip route igrp

    C. show ip route

6. Match each command with its corresponding output. The output choices are as follows: (1) Displays EIGRP peer information for that interface; (2) Displays a summary of EIGRP routing statistics, such as the number of Hellos and routing updates; (3) Displays the contents of the EIGRP topology table; (4) Displays the EIGRP routes; (5) Displays a log of most recent EIGRP protocol events (including the insertion and removal of routes from the route table, updates, and neighbor status); (6) Displays all EIGRP neighbors, along with summary information about each neighbor.

A. `show ip route eigrp`

B. `show ip eigrp interfaces`

C. `show ip eigrp neighbors`

D. `show ip eigrp topology`

E. `show ip eigrp traffic`

F. `show ip eigrp events`

7. Match each command with its corresponding output. The output choices are as follows: (1) Displays OSPF routes; (2) Displays the routers that join different areas or border routers; (3) Displays OSPF neighbor information; (4) Displays summary-address redistribution information; (5) Displays information for OSPF; (6) Displays process ID number that displays information relevant to the specified process ID; (7) Displays link-state request list; (8) Displays link-state retransmission list; (9) Provides an OSPF database summary; (10) Displays virtual link information; (11) Displays OSPF information on an interface.

A. `show ip route ospf`

B. `show ip ospf`

C. `show ip ospf process-id`

D. `show ip ospf border-routers`

E. `show ip ospf database`

F. `show ip ospf interface`

G. `show ip ospf neighbor`

H. `show ip ospf request-list`

I. `show ip ospf retransmission list`

J. `show ip ospf summary-address`

K. `show ip ospf virtual-links`

8. Where are distribute lists applied?

A. Directly to the interface

B. To the interface via the routing protocol

C. To the routing protocol

D. None of the above

9. What command(s) is/are used to see the contents of a route map? (Choose all that apply.)

   A. show running-config

   B. show ip route-map

   C. show route-map

   D. show ip interface

10. What is the difference between a route map and an access list?

    A. There is no difference between a route map and an access list.

    B. Access lists have greater impact on the router's CPU.

    C. The route map allows actions other than forwarding or dropping the packet.

    D. None of the above.

11. Why should metrics be set properly when redistributing routing protocols?

    A. To avoid confusion.

    B. So the protocol receiving the injected routes can propagate the correct information.

    C. Routing will not work without them.

    D. None of the above.

12. You are doing bidirectional redistribution of routes between EIGRP and OSPF. All of the EIGRP routes are showing up in OSPF; however, none of the OSPF routes are showing up in EIGRP. What are the possible causes for this problem? (Choose all that apply.)

    A. Distribute lists are configured incorrectly.

    B. Route-maps are set up incorrectly.

    C. There is a physical connectivity issue.

    D. Router IOS levels do not match.

    E. Default metric is not configured for EIGRP.

    F. OSPF and EIGRP have different AS numbers.

13. What are the administrative distances for an eBGP and iBGP route by default?

    A. 90 for eBGP and 170 for iBGP

    B. 200 for eBGP and 20 for iBGP

    C. 20 for both

    D. 20 for eBGP and 200 for iBGP

    E. 170 for eBGP and 90 for iBGP

    F. 90 for both

14. What are the administrative distances for an internal and external EIGRP route default?

   A. 90 for internal and 170 for external

   B. 90 for both

   C. 170 for internal 90 for external

   D. 70 for internal 190 for external

   E. 190 for internal 70 for external

   F. 70 for both

15. What are the administrative distances for RIP-1 and a RIP-2 route by default?

   A. 120 for RIP-1 110 for RIP-2

   B. 110 for RIP-1 120 for RIP-2

   C. 120 for both

   D. 110 for both

   E. 15 for both

   F. 16 for both

16. Match each command with its corresponding output. The output choices are as follows: (1) Displays BGP routes; (2) Shows information on BGP neighbors; (3) Shows all routes being received from a particular neighbor; (4) Shows all routes being advertised to a particular neighbor; (5) Shows information about BGP learned routes, including indicating which ones will be in the routing table; (6) Shows a summary of all BGP connections; (7) Shows information about BGP peer groups.

   A. `show ip bgp`

   B. `show ip bgp neighbors`

   C. `show ip BGP neighbors` *ip address* `advertised-routes`

   D. `show ip BGP neighbors` *ip address* `received-routes`

   E. `show ip bgp peer-group`

   F. `show ip bgp summary`

   G. `show ip route bgp`

17. You want to change the AS path information of a BGP route that you learn from an eBGP neighbor. What command type will be used in the BGP configuration to accomplish this?

   A. Route map

   B. Prefix list

   C. Distribute list

   D. BGP AS list

   E. Access list

18. You issue a show IP route command and receive the following output:

B 10.20.20.0/24 [20/0] via 10.30.30.1, 3w0d

What does the 20 in [20/0] mean?

A. The next Hello will be sent in 20 seconds.

B. The metric of this route is 20.

C. There are 20 hops to the destination network.

D. The administrative distance of this route is 20.

19. You issue a show IP route command and receive the following output:

D EX 172.16.38.200/30
        [170/2176512] via 172.16.131.82, 23:40:27,   ATM6/0/0.3114

What does the EX mean?

A. The route is a candidate default route.

B. This is an external route.

C. The route is in holddown.

D. The route is being redistributed into BGP.

20. You issue a show IP route command and receive the following output:

S*   0.0.0.0/0 [1/0] via 172.16.50.2

What does the * mean?

A. The route is a candidate default route.

B. This is an external route.

C. The static route is pointed to a destination that does not exist.

D. The route redistributed.

Answers to Review Questions

1. A, B, C, D. `show ip default-gateway` is not a valid command, and `show ip mrm` is only used when working with multicast issues.

2. A. The default gateway indicates the next hop for packets with no route to the destination address.

3. C, D. Answer C, configuring a static route, and D, configuring an IP default-network, are the valid methods, though not stated here in their exact syntax. Answers A and B are invalid as to both method and syntax.

4. A (3), B (4), C (1), D (2). IP-related information for an interface is given by the `show ip interface` command.

5. A (3), B (1), C (2). The current configuration is also known as the running configuration.

6. A (4), B (1), C (6), D (3), E (2), F (5). These are all EIGRP-related commands. They can be verified by logging on to the router and experimenting with the output of each of the commands.

7. A (1), B (5), C (6), D (2), E (9), F (11), G (3), H (7), I (8), J (4), K (10). These are all OSPF-related commands and can be verified by logging on to a router and experimenting with the output of each of the commands.

8. B. The list must be applied to an interface from within the routing protocol.

9. A, C. Route maps are not IP specific.

10. C. Route maps use access lists to match a packet. After a match is made, many different actions may be taken.

11. B. Different protocols do not share the same metric values. A translation has to occur for the injected routes to be understood by the new protocol. This is done by setting default metrics.

12. A, B, E. Answers A and B should be obvious, but E is not as obvious. If a default metric is not configured, the redistribution will not occur.

13. D. Because BGP is an EGP, it gives a better administrative distance for external routes.

14. A. As an IGP, EIGRP prefers internal routes to those learned from another protocol.

15. C. There are differences between RIP versions 1 and 2, but administrative distance is not one of them.

16. A (5), B (2), C (4), D (3), E (7), F (6), G (1). These are all BGP-related commands and can be verified by logging on to a router and experimenting with the output of each of the commands.

17. A. In the BGP configuration, a route map will be specified. The route map will most likely use an access list or prefix list to define the traffic that will be affected, but these will not show up in the BGP configuration.

18. D. The first number in the brackets is the administrative distance; the second number is the metric.

19. B. The EX indicates that it is an external route in EIGRP. You can also tell this by looking at the metric of the route, which is 170.

20. A. In the routing table the candidate for the default route is indicated by the *. In addition, notice that the administrative distance of a static route is 1.

Chapter

7

Troubleshooting Serial Line and Frame Relay Connectivity

EXAM TOPICS COVERED IN THIS CHAPTER INCLUDE:

- ✓ Verify network connectivity.
- ✓ Use the optimal troubleshooting approach in resolving network problems.
- ✓ Minimize downtime during troubleshooting.
- ✓ Use Cisco IOS commands to identify problems.
- ✓ Work with external providers to diagnose and resolve network problems.

Many of the commands that are available to troubleshoot serial and Frame Relay problems are similar. This chapter first discusses topics relating to troubleshooting serial lines. After those topics have been covered in detail, the **show** and **debug** commands relating to Frame Relay are discussed.

Summaries of troubleshooting symptoms and solutions are provided at the end of each section. These summaries will be valuable as quick-reference guides when you are isolating and diagnosing problems on serial lines and Frame Relay interfaces.

Troubleshooting Serial Lines

There are numerous commands available to aid in troubleshooting serial lines. Some of them are **show** commands; others are **debug** commands. Here is a list of the commands that are discussed in this section, along with advice about the information they provide for troubleshooting:

- `clear counters serial`
- `show interface serial`
- `show controllers serial`
- `show buffers`
- `debug serial interface`

An integral part of serial connections is the hardware involved. Look at Figure 7.1. In this graphic, you see Router A connected to a channel service unit/digital service unit (CSU/DSU), through a serial cable that is connected to another CSU/DSU, and then connected to Router B. Please refer to this figure as you go through the rest of the discussion.

FIGURE 7.1   Serial line setup

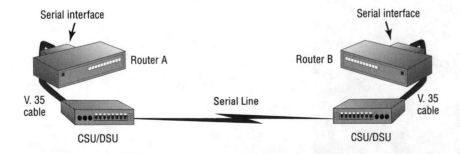

HDLC Encapsulation

High-level Data Link Control (HDLC) is an encapsulation method used by serial links. HDLC provides a 32-bit checksum and three different transfer modes: normal, asynchronous response, and asynchronous balanced.

HDLC is used by default on Cisco serial interfaces. The first important point of troubleshooting serial line problems is to verify that both sides of the link are using the same encapsulation type. Here is a look at a serial interface from a Cisco 2501. Notice that the encapsulation type is HDLC:

```
Router_A>show interface serial0
Serial0 is administratively down, line protocol is down
  Hardware is HD64570
  Internet address is 172.16.20.6/30
  MTU 1500 bytes, BW 1544 Kbit, DLY 20000 usec, rely 255/
  255, load 1/255
  Encapsulation HDLC, loopback not set, keepalive set (10
  sec)
  Last input never, output never, output hang never
  Last clearing of "show interface" counters never
  Input queue: 0/75/0 (size/max/drops); Total output
  drops: 0
  Queueing strategy: weighted fair
  Output queue: 0/1000/64/0 (size/max total/threshold/
drops)
     Conversations  0/0/256 (active/max active/max total)
     Reserved Conversations 0/0 (allocated/max allocated)
  5 minute input rate 0 bits/sec, 0 packets/sec
  5 minute output rate 0 bits/sec, 0 packets/sec
     0 packets input, 0 bytes, 0 no buffer
     Received 0 broadcasts, 0 runts, 0 giants, 0 throttles
     0 input errors, 0 CRC, 0 frame, 0 overrun, 0 ignored,
     0 abort
     0 packets output, 0 bytes, 0 underruns
     0 output errors, 0 collisions, 1 interface resets
     0 output buffer failures, 0 output buffers swapped
     out
     0 carrier transitions
     DCD=down  DSR=down  DTR=down  RTS=down  CTS=down
Router_A>
```

Other encapsulations may be used on serial interfaces, but HDLC is used for synchronous data link control. In addition Cisco's version of HDLC is slightly different from that of "generic" HDLC.

show interface serial Command

The show interface serial commands provide you with a great deal of helpful information when you troubleshoot problems related to serial lines and other serial interfaces such as Frame Relay. However, in order to get correct information, you should first clear the counters for the interface of interest.

Before you do so, look at the output of the show interface serial 1 command:

```
Router_A>show interface serial 1
Serial1 is up, line protocol is up
  Hardware is HD64570
  Internet address is 172.16.30.5/30
  MTU 1500 bytes, BW 1544 Kbit, DLY 20000 usec, rely 255/  255, load 1/255
  Encapsulation HDLC, loopback not set, keepalive set (10   sec)
  Last input 00:00:08, output 00:00:07, output hang never
  Last clearing of "show interface" counters never
  Input queue: 0/75/0 (size/max/drops);
Total output drops: 0
  Queueing strategy: weighted fair
  Output queue: 0/1000/64/0 (size/max total/threshold/drops)
    Conversations  0/1/256 (active/max active/max total)
    Reserved Conversations 0/0 (allocated/max allocated)
  5 minute input rate 0 bits/sec, 0 packets/sec
  5 minute output rate 0 bits/sec, 0 packets/sec
    1307 packets input, 85380 bytes, 0 no buffer
    Received 695 broadcasts, 0 runts, 0 giants, 0 throttles
    0 input errors, 0 CRC, 0 frame, 0 overrun, 0 ignored,
    0 abort
    1308 packets output, 85652 bytes, 0 underruns
    0 output errors, 0 collisions, 116 interface resets
    0 output buffer failures, 0 output buffers swapped
    out
    238 carrier transitions
    DCD=up  DSR=up  DTR=up  RTS=up  CTS=up
Router_A>
```

First note that the output tells you the interface is up and the line protocol is also up. The information contained in the `show interface serial` command will be discussed in more detail in just a moment. For now, it is important to recognize that many of the counters have elevated numbers. Also, notice that the seventh line of the output declares that the counters were never cleared.

You cannot effectively troubleshoot if you do not have accurate data returned through the many diagnostic commands. One way to ensure that the data you are analyzing is accurate and directly applies to the problem at hand is to perform the `clear counters serial` *number* command, which resets the interface counters to zero. This ensures that the data retrieved from the `interface` command is representative of what is happening at that moment on the network.

Here is how it is done and what the interface looks like after the command has been issued:

 NOTE   Line numbers added to the output below for ease of reading.

```
Router_A#clear counters serial 1
Clear "show interface" counters on this interface [confirm]
%CLEAR-5-COUNTERS: Clear counter on interface Serial1 by console
Router_A#show interface serial 1
 1. Serial1 is up, line protocol is up
 2.   Hardware is HD64570
 3.   Internet address is 172.16.30.5/30
 4.   MTU 1500 bytes, BW 1544 Kbit, DLY 20000 usec, rely 255/255, load
 5.   51/255
 6.   Encapsulation HDLC, loopback not set,
 7.   keepalive set (10  sec)
 8.   Last input 00:00:00, output 00:00:00, output hang never
 9.   Last clearing of "show interface" counters 00:28:48
10.   Input queue: 1/75/0 (size/max/drops);
11. Total output drops: 0
12. Queueing strategy: weighted fair
13.   Output queue: 0/1000/64/0 (size/max total/threshold/drops)
14.      Conversations  0/2/256 (active/max active/max total)
15.      Reserved Conversations 0/0 (allocated/max allocated)
16.   5 minute input rate 321000 bits/sec, 48 packets/sec
17.   5 minute output rate 320000 bits/sec, 48 packets/sec
18.      12439 packets input, 13257786 bytes, 0 no buffer
19.      Received 202 broadcasts, 0 runts, 0 giants, 0 throttles
20.      0 input errors, 0 CRC, 0 frame, 0 overrun, 0 ignored,
21.      0 abort
22.      12438 packets output, 13256434 bytes, 0 underruns
23.      0 output errors, 0 collisions, 0 interface resets
```

```
24.     0 output buffer failures, 0 output buffers swapped
25.     out
26.     0 carrier transitions
27.     DCD=up  DSR=up  DTR=up  RTS=up  CTS=up
Router_A#
```

Notice the ninth line of the output. It says that the counters were cleared 28 minutes before. Once the counters are cleared, you can associate any new data with current network events. If you try to associate current network events with inaccurate data, you will never find the problem. In addition to clearing the individual interface, you can execute the clear counters command without specifying an interface to clear all the counters on the router.

Now we'll go through the available data provided by the show interface serial command. Refer to the output 1 listed.

The first line provides information regarding the status of the interface and the line protocol:

```
Serial1 is up, line protocol is up
```

In this case, both are up and functional. If the interface is down, the line protocol must also be down.

Cabling problems, carrier problems, or hardware problems can all be reasons for a serial interface to report as down. These problems can be addressed by verifying proper cable connectivity, replacing hardware (including cables), and checking the CSU/DSU for carrier signal. If you cannot resolve the problem by using these techniques, you can and should contact the local carrier, who can verify the carrier service.

Another possibility for the interface status is that the interface is up but the line protocol is down. When this happens, it can be due to one or more of a variety of problems, as follows:

- Failed CSU/DSU
- Router interface problems
- Mismatched timing on CSU/DSU or carrier network
- Misconfigured interface
- Keepalive signals not received from remote router
- Carrier problem

You should verify that the local interface and the remote interface are properly configured. *Loopback tests* can be performed. These tests will be discussed in the CSU/DSU section of the chapter.

Continuing with the description of the output of the show interface serial command, notice that the second line of the output displays the hardware type of the interface:

```
Hardware is HD64570
```

The third line shows the Layer 3 IP address with the associated subnet mask:

```
Internet address is 172.16.30.5/30
```

Line 4 and 5 contains all of the information needed to create a route metric for the interface. The data includes MTU, bandwidth, delay, reliability, and load. Note that the load and reliability values are in fractional form (out of 255).

```
MTU 1500 bytes, BW 1544 Kbit, DLY 20000 usec, rely 255/255, load 51/255
```

Line 6 and 7 indicate the type of encapsulation that is being used on the line, as well as loopback and keepalive information:

```
Encapsulation HDLC, loopback not set, keepalive set (10 sec)
```

The eighth line displays the last time the interface saw any traffic:

```
Last input 00:00:00, output 00:00:00, output hang never
```

Again, the ninth line shows the time that transpired since the last time the interface counters were cleared:

```
Last clearing of "show interface" counters 00:28:48
```

Lines 10 through 15 contain information regarding the queuing on the interface:

```
Input queue: 1/75/0 (size/max/drops);
Total output drops: 0
  Queueing strategy: weighted fair
  Output queue: 0/1000/64/0 (size/max total/threshold/
  drops)
    Conversations  0/2/256 (active/max active/max total)
    Reserved Conversations 0/0 (allocated/max allocated)
```

Lines 16 and 17 display the five-minute average for input and output bits per second, and packets per second on the interface:

```
5 minute input rate 321000 bits/sec, 48 packets/sec
5 minute output rate 320000 bits/sec, 48 packets/sec
```

Beginning with line 18 and until line 21, the output displays interface input information. The first line is a counter that keeps track of the number of incoming packets on the interface. The next line displays information for broadcast, runt, giant, and throttled packets. The last lines (lines 20 and 21) displays any input, CRC, frame, overrun, ignored, or abort errors:

```
12439 packets input, 13257786 bytes, 0 no buffer
    Received 202 broadcasts, 0 runts, 0 giants,
    0 throttles
    0 input errors, 0 CRC, 0 frame, 0 overrun, 0 ignored,
    0 abort
```

The output interface statistics begin with line 22 and end on line 26. This data reflects the number of output packets, underruns, output errors, collisions, interface resets, output buffer failures, swapped output buffers, and carrier transitions:

```
12438 packets output, 13256434 bytes, 0 underruns
    0 output errors, 0 collisions, 0 interface resets
    0 output buffer failures,
    0 output buffers swapped out
    0 carrier transitions
```

Input and output information contain 32-bit counters for the packet and byte counts. As soon as each count increments over roughly 4.2 billion, the counter resets at zero.

Interface resets should be considered warning flags. If you see a large number of interface resets after clearing the counter, you should be concerned. Interface resets are caused by the following:

- Queued packets not sent for several seconds
- Problems with hardware (for example, router interface, cable, or CSU/DSU)
- Mismatched clocking signals
- Looped interface
- Interface shut down
- Line protocol down and the interface resetting periodically

The next warning flag to note is the carrier transitions statistic. This counts the number of times that the DCD (data carrier detect) signal changes state. If the carrier keeps fluctuating, you do not have a stable circuit. This is often a carrier problem, and the local carrier must be contacted.

The final line of the show interface serial command displays carrier-specific information:

```
DCD=up  DSR=up  DTR=up  RTS=up  CTS=up
```

show controllers Command

The show controllers command is used to display interface status and tells you whether a cable is connected to the interface. Following are a couple of different outputs from the show controllers command.

The first output is from interface serial 0. There is no cable attached to the interface:

```
Router_A#show controllers serial 0
HD unit 0, idb = 0x94AEC, driver structure at 0x99870
buffer size 1524  HD unit 0, No cable, clockrate 4000000
cpb = 0x41, eda = 0x4940, cda = 0x4800
RX ring with 16 entries at 0x414800
```

```
.
.   {some output omitted}
.
TX ring with 2 entries at 0x415000
.
.   {some output omitted}
.
0 missed datagrams, 0 overruns
0 bad datagram encapsulations, 0 memory errors
0 transmitter underruns
0 residual bit errors

Router_A#
```

The second output is from interface serial 1, which does have a cable connected, V.35 DCE, and is functioning properly:

```
Router_A#show controllers serial 1
HD unit 1, idb = 0x9D4E0, driver structure at 0xA2260
buffer size 1524  HD unit 1, V.35 DCE cable, clockrate 4000000
cpb = 0x42, eda = 0x3104, cda = 0x3118
RX ring with 16 entries at 0x423000
.
.   {some output omitted}
.
TX ring with 2 entries at 0x423800
.
.   {some output omitted}
.
0 missed datagrams, 0 overruns
0 bad datagram encapsulations, 0 memory errors
0 transmitter underruns
0 residual bit errors

Router_A#
```

The basic information provided by this command is the interface status regarding missed datagrams, overruns, bad encapsulation, memory errors, underruns, and bit errors. In addition, it indicates the interface clock rate, as well as the type of cable connected to the interface.

If you don't see a cable connected to the interface, verifying that a cable is properly connected is a good item to include in a troubleshooting action plan. Excessive errors on the interface can be an indication of faulty hardware.

show buffers Command

The show buffers command can be used to look at system buffer pools, but it also provides information regarding interface buffers. Look at the sample output from a 2514 router:

```
Router_B>show buffers
Buffer elements:
     500 in free list (500 max allowed)
     52587626 hits, 0 misses, 0 created

Public buffer pools:
Small buffers, 104 bytes (total 50, permanent 50):
     50 in free list (20 min, 150 max allowed)
     7709985 hits, 0 misses, 0 trims, 0 created
     0 failures (0 no memory)
Middle buffers, 600 bytes (total 25, permanent 25):
     24 in free list (10 min, 150 max allowed)
     2045756 hits, 0 misses, 0 trims, 0 created
     0 failures (0 no memory)
Big buffers, 1524 bytes (total 50, permanent 50):
     50 in free list (5 min, 150 max allowed)
     2541768 hits, 774 misses, 217 trims, 217 created
     24 failures (0 no memory)
VeryBig buffers, 4520 bytes (total 10, permanent 10):
     10 in free list (0 min, 100 max allowed)
     52464 hits, 0 misses, 0 trims, 0 created
     0 failures (0 no memory)
Large buffers, 5024 bytes (total 0, permanent 0):
     0 in free list (0 min, 10 max allowed)
     0 hits, 0 misses, 0 trims, 0 created
     0 failures (0 no memory)
Huge buffers, 18024 bytes (total 0, permanent 0):
     0 in free list (0 min, 4 max allowed)
     0 hits, 0 misses, 0 trims, 0 created
     0 failures (0 no memory)

Interface buffer pools:
Ethernet0 buffers, 1524 bytes (total 32, permanent 32):
    5 in free list (0 min, 32 max allowed)
    255684 hits, 64696 fallbacks
    8 max cache size, 5 in cache
```

```
Ethernet1 buffers, 1524 bytes (total 32, permanent 32):
     0 in free list (0 min, 32 max allowed)
     300993 hits, 1024384 fallbacks
     8 max cache size, 6 in cache
Serial0 buffers, 1524 bytes (total 32, permanent 32):
     7 in free list (0 min, 32 max allowed)
     25 hits, 0 fallbacks
     8 max cache size, 8 in cache
Serial1 buffers, 1524 bytes (total 32, permanent 32):
     7 in free list (0 min, 32 max allowed)
     25 hits, 0 fallbacks
     8 max cache size, 8 in cache
```

Notice that the interface buffers are listed at the end of the output. This information can be useful to troubleshoot serial interface problems. It is important to look at the number of free buffers. These numbers indicate the memory that is available on the interface for buffering incoming and outgoing packets.

debug serial interface Command

As always with debug tools, you must exercise caution. When executing a serial debug or Frame Relay debug, the router can generate large amounts of data that can encumber the router. Make sure that the specific command is used when possible. You can use **debug** in conjunction with access lists to focus the application of the debug tool.

The debug of a serial interface displays HDLC or Frame Relay communication messages. A sample follows that includes Frame Relay information. It is important to understand that the output of this command varies with the encapsulation type used on the interface.

```
Router_A#debug serial interface
Serial network interface debugging is on
Serial0(out): StEnq, myseq 135, yourseen 134, DTE up
Serial0(in): Status, myseq 135
Serial1(out): StEnq, myseq 2, yourseen 8, DTE up
Serial1(in): Status, myseq 2
Serial2(out): StEnq, myseq 247, yourseen 247, DTE up
Serial2(in): Status, myseq 247
Serial3(out): StEnq, myseq 30, yourseen 28, DTE up
Serial3(in): Status, myseq 30
Serial0(out): StEnq, myseq 136, yourseen 135, DTE up
Serial0(in): Status, myseq 136
Serial1(out): StEnq, myseq 3, yourseen 9, DTE up
Serial1(in): Status, myseq 3
```

```
Serial2(out): StEnq, myseq 248, yourseen 248, DTE up
Serial2(in): Status, myseq 248
Serial3(out): StEnq, myseq 31, yourseen 29, DTE up
Serial3(in): Status, myseq 31
Serial0(out): StEnq, myseq 137, yourseen 136, DTE up
Serial0(in): Status, myseq 137
Serial1(out): StEnq, myseq 4, yourseen 10, DTE up
Serial1(in): Status, myseq 4
Serial2(out): StEnq, myseq 249, yourseen 249, DTE up
Serial2(in): Status, myseq 249
Serial3(out): StEnq, myseq 32, yourseen 30, DTE up
Serial3(in): Status, myseq 32
```

This sample includes output from many interfaces. The boldface type is used to highlight the data for interface serial 0. Here are definitions of what you see:

StEnq   An LMI (Local Management Interface) status inquiry sent from the router to the Frame Relay switch. (LMIs are discussed further in the sections on troubleshooting Frame Relay later in the chapter.)

Status   Reply sent to the router from the Frame Relay switch.

myseq   The local keepalive number. The value is the sequence identifier.

yourseen   The keepalive sent by the other side of the serial connection. This value is the actual sequence number last received, incremented by 1. It indicates expectation of the next sequence number to be sent.

DTE   The data-termination equipment status. In this example, it is up.

The in and out specify the directions in which the packets are sent. Outbound packets are keepalives sent by the local side; inbound packets are the keepalives sent from the other end.

If the sequence numbers for a given interface don't increment, then there is probably a timing or line problem at one or the other end of the connection. The line will reset if two out of six consecutive keepalive packets fail to increment. Although the Layer 3 protocol considers the line protocol to be down, the Layer 2 protocol continues to send keepalive messages.

Here is a sample of HDLC communication:

```
Router_A#debug serial interface
Serial network interface debugging is on
Serial0: HDLC myseq 172188, mineseen 172188*, yourseen 172326, line up
Serial0: HDLC myseq 172189, mineseen 172189*, yourseen 172327, line up
Serial0: HDLC myseq 172190, mineseen 172190*, yourseen 172328, line up
Serial0: HDLC myseq 172191, mineseen 172191*, yourseen 172329, line up
Router_A#
```

The field values are very similar to the field values in the Frame Relay output. Here are the field definitions:

myseq The local keepalive number. The value is the sequence identifier.

yourseen The keepalive sent by the other side of the serial connection, incremented by 1.

mineseen This is the other side's sent **yourseen**, or the expectation of what will be sent next. If everything is working properly, this should equal the **myseq**.

CSU/DSU Loopback Tests

Loopback tests aid in physically isolating serial line and Frame Relay problems. Four different loopback tests can be performed to troubleshoot the circuit. You can perform two of them, and the local provider has access to perform the other two. Here is a list of the four loopback tests:

- Local loopback on the local CSU/DSU
- Local loopback on the remote CSU/DSU
- Remote loopback from the local NIU to the remote CSU/DSU
- Remote loopback from the remote NIU to the local CSU/DSU

 Though it is possible to perform a subset of these loopback commands on certain interface types on a router, they are more commonly performed on the CSU/DSU. Therefore, it is the CSU/DSU variation of the loopbacks that is focused on in this chapter.

Look at Figure 7.2 to see how the tests are performed.

The tests that you can perform are the two local loopback tests. You can perform these tests because you have access to the equipment. The local provider has to perform the remote loopback tests because it has access to the equipment within the cloud.

FIGURE 7.2 CSU/DSU loopback tests

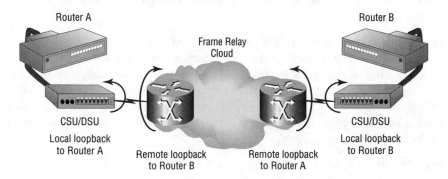

When using loopback tests for troubleshooting, you should follow these steps:

1. Perform the local loopback test for the local router (Router A in this example).

2. Verify the line status. This means to check for LMI status when using Frame Relay on the interface.

3. Perform the local loopback test for the remote router, Router B.

4. Verify the line status. This means to check for LMI status when using Frame Relay on the interface.

5. If you see LMI but cannot get remote connectivity, contact your local service provider, which can run the remote loopback tests.

Remember that LMI stands for Local Management Interface. (See "Troubleshooting Frame Relay" later in the chapter for more on LMIs.)When you see LMI up on a router interface during a loopback test, it means that the protocol is working locally but not necessarily remotely. By putting a CSU/DSU into loopback, the signal is sent back to the interface, so the line protocol shows up. For end-to-end connectivity, both end sites must have LMI up status. In addition, all of the Frame Relay switches that participate in the permanent virtual circuit (PVC) must be working properly. Remote loopback tests confirm the functionality of the circuit.

 Real World Scenario

Troubleshooting Red, Yellow, and Blue

When troubleshooting a serial connection, many times you need the assistance of your local telephone company or carrier in order to resolve the problem. Though it is tempting to call and open a ticket with them at the first sign of trouble, I have found that in many cases you can assist them in finding the problem, or solve it yourself, with some testing on your own.

The first thing that I do when a circuit is down is to perform the loopback tests described in this chapter to ensure that my router, in-house wiring, and CSU/DSU are working correctly. Assuming that these items test correctly, I put a DS-1/DS-3 test on the circuit and look at the signal coming to and from the carrier. In most cases I will get either a red, yellow, or blue alarm coming from them.

If I get a red alarm on the signal from the carrier, this means I am not receiving any signal on the link. I may or may not be transmitting information correctly. If I see a yellow alarm, it means the far-end device is not receiving any information. However, since I am receiving the yellow alarm signal that it is sending, I know that my receive path is fine, and therefore the problem lies on the transmitting path somewhere between my current location and the destination device. Finally, a blue alarm is an all-ones signal. This usually is generated by one of the carrier's systems that needs to be reset or reconfigured.

With this information in hand, I then can open a trouble ticket with the carrier and help them isolate where to start looking for the problem, thus decreasing the time it takes to correct the problem.

Serial Line Summary

Several encapsulations and protocols may be used over serial lines. Because of this variety, many different problems can occur. Again here, it is important to realize that the output of show commands may differ depending on the interface configuration.

To aid you in diagnosing and resolving serial line problems, this section includes two quick reference tables: one with symptoms and problems, and one with suggested action plans.

Symptoms and Problems

Table 7.1 lists several common serial line conditions and their related possible problems.

TABLE 7.1   Serial Line Symptoms and Problems

Symptom or Condition	Associated Problems
Interface is administratively down; line protocol is down	(a) The interface has been placed in shutdown via a configuration command. (b) Duplicate IP addresses are not allowed and one of the two interfaces with the same IP address will be shut down.
Interface is down; line protocol is down	(a) Improper cabling. (b) No carrier signal from local provider. (c) Hardware failure (interface or CSU/DSU; cabling). (d) Clocking (or lack thereof).
Interface is up; line protocol is down	(a) Misconfigured interface, local or remote. (b) Local provider problem. (c) Keepalive sequencing not incrementing. (d) Hardware failures (local or remote interfaces and CSU/DSU). (e) Noisy line. (f) Timing mismatches. (g) L2 issues such as LMI.
Interface is up; line protocol is up (looped)	The circuit is in loopback somewhere.
Incrementing carrier transition counter	(a) Unstable signaling coming from the local provider. (b) Faulty cabling. (c) Failing hardware (for example, interface or CSU/DSU).
Incrementing interface resets	(a) Faulty cabling, causing the loss of the CD signal. (b) Hardware failure. (c) Line congestion.

TABLE 7.1   Serial Line Symptoms and Problems *(continued)*

Symptom or Condition	Associated Problems
Input drops, errors, CRC, and framing errors	(a) Line speed oversubscribes the router interface capacity. (b) Local provider problem. (c) Noisy line. (d) Faulty cabling. (e) Improper cabling. (f) Failing hardware.
Output drops	The interface is capable of transmitting at higher than line speed.

Problems and Action Plans

Now that you have seen the list of symptoms with their associated problems, you need a quick reference for resolving the problems. Table 7.2 provides summary action plans for handling the listed serial line problems.

TABLE 7.2   Action Plans for Common Serial Line Problems

Problem	Resolution Action Plan
Local provider problems	1. Check the CSU/DSU for a CD signal. Check for other signals, such as RX and TX clocking, to see if the circuit is transmitting and receiving information. 2. If you do not get a CD signal or have other problems, contact the local service provider to troubleshoot and fix the problem.
Improper or faulty cabling	1. Make sure that you are using the proper cable for the equipment being used. 2. Use a breakout box to check the control leads. 3. Swap faulty cables.
Misconfigured interface	1. View the interface configuration using the show running-config command. 2. Make sure that the same encapsulation type is used at both ends of the circuit by using the show interface command.
Keepalive problems	1. Verify that keepalives are being sent. You can check this via the router configuration or by using the show interface command.

TABLE 7.2   Action Plans for Common Serial Line Problems *(continued)*

Problem	Resolution Action Plan
	2. If the configuration says that keepalives are being sent, you may want to enable debug serial interface for the interface.
	3. Verify that the sequence numbers are incrementing.
	4. If the sequences don't increment, run loopback tests on the local and remote sites.
	5. If the sequences don't increment even when the CSU/DSU is in loopback, you have a hardware problem. Replace faulty hardware.
Hardware failure	1. Replace the hardware.
Interface is in loopback mode	1. Check the interface configuration.
	2. If there is a loopback entry in the interface configuration, remove it with the no form of the command.
	3. If the interface configuration is clean, check the CSU/DSU to see if it is placed in loopback.
	4. If CSU/DSUit is in loopback, remove itthe CSU/DSU from loopback mode.
	5. If the CSU/DSU is not in loopback mode, contact the local provider; it may have placed the circuit in loopback.
Interface is administratively down	1. Check the configuration. Verify that the IP address is not a duplicate.
	2. Enter the configuration mode and issue the no shutdown command within the interface.
Line speed is larger than the interface capacity	1. Reduce input queue size by using the hold-queue in command.
	2. Increase output queues on exiting interfaces.
Interface speed is larger than the line speed	1. Reduce broadcast traffic.
	2. Increase output queue.
	3. Implement queuing algorithms, if necessary.

Troubleshooting Frame Relay

Frame Relay is a popular WAN solution in many networks. Frame Relay supports PVCs and switched virtual circuits (SVCs). These virtual circuits are built by using *DLCI num-bers*. A *Data-Link Connection Identifier (DLCI)* is used to identify the virtual circuits in a Frame Relay cloud. Figure 7.3 depicts a Frame Relay network. Notice the DLCI numbers assigned to the interfaces throughout the network.

FIGURE 7.3   Frame Relay network

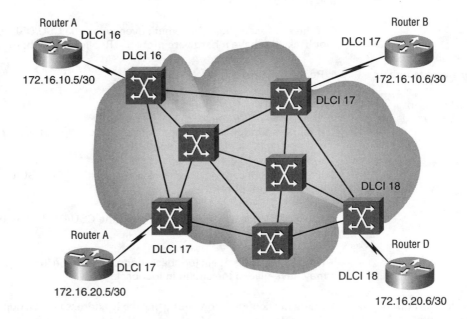

It is important to remember that the DLCI is significant only locally. The DLCI maps to Layer 3 IP addresses, as shown in Figure 7.3. The IP addresses given on the diagram suggest the PVCs that exist through the Frame Relay cloud.

When Frame Relay problems occur, follow this troubleshooting checklist:

1. Check Layer 1, the Physical layer, for any cabling or interface problems.

2. Check the interface encapsulation.

3. Check the LMI type.

4. Verify the DLCI-to-IP address mapping.

5. Verify the Frame Relay PVCs.

6. Verify the Frame Relay LMI.

7. Verify the Frame Relay map.

8. Verify the loopback tests, as described in the "CSU/DSU Loopback Tests" section earlier in the chapter.

   The following sections describe the commands to execute each of these steps.

Frame Relay *show* Commands

The following show commands are covered in this section:

- show interface
- show frame-relay lmi
- show frame-relay pvc
- show frame-relay map

Notice that the second command listed here contains the term *LMI (Local Management Interface)*. LMI provides support for keepalive devices to verify data flow. As mentioned in the earlier sections on serial line troubleshooting, this part of the chapter includes many references to LMI. You will see this term a great deal when dealing with Frame Relay troubleshooting.

show interface

The show interface command is used to provide information on serial lines. In addition to normal serial line information, Frame Relay information is included in the output if the interface is configured for Frame Relay.

Line-by-line detail has already been given in this chapter for a normal serial interface. Only the fields relating to Frame Relay are listed here. Following is a sample of a Frame Relay interface output:

```
Router_A#show interface serial0
Serial0 is up, line protocol is up
  Hardware is HD64570
  MTU 1500 bytes, BW 1544 Kbit, DLY 20000 usec, rely 255/255, load 1/255
  Encapsulation FRAME-RELAY, loopback not set, keepalive set (10 sec)
  LMI enq sent  823406, LMI stat recvd 823403, LMI upd recvd 507, DTE LMI up
  LMI enq recvd 0, LMI stat sent  0, LMI upd sent  0
  LMI DLCI 1023  LMI type is CISCO  frame relay DTE
  Broadcast queue 0/64, broadcasts sent/dropped 0/0, interface
broadcasts 36752578
  Last input 00:00:00, output 00:00:00, output hang never
  Last clearing of "show interface" counters never
  Input queue: 0/75/0 (size/max/drops); Total output drops: 0
  Queueing strategy: weighted fair
  Output queue: 0/64/0 (size/threshold/drops)
```

```
     Conversations  0/20 (active/max active)
     Reserved Conversations 0/0 (allocated/max allocated)
  5 minute input rate 5000 bits/sec, 6 packets/sec
  5 minute output rate 5000 bits/sec, 6 packets/sec
     134880248 packets input, 102288228 bytes, 0 no buffer
     Received 823910 broadcasts, 0 runts, 0 giants
     1 input errors, 1 CRC, 0 frame, 0 overrun, 0 ignored,
     1 abort
     136835759 packets output, 3397101778 bytes, 0 underruns
     0 output errors, 0 collisions, 14 interface resets
     0 output buffer failures, 0 output buffers swapped
     out
     2 carrier transitions
     DCD=up  DSR=up  DTR=up  RTS=up  CTS=up
Router_A#show interface serial 0.2
Serial0.2 is up, line protocol is up
  Hardware is HD64570
  Internet address is 172.16.30.6/30
  MTU 1500 bytes, BW 1544 Kbit, DLY 20000 usec, rely 255/  255, load 1/255
  Encapsulation FRAME-RELAY
Router_A#
```

Here are the relevant Frame Relay terms:

Encapsulation Frame Relay encapsulation type used; either Cisco (default) or IETF.

LMI enq sent Number of LMI enquiries (alternative spelling of *inquiries*) sent.

LMI stat recvd Number of LMI status packets received.

LMI upd recvd Number of LMI updates received.

DTE LMI Status of the DTE (data-termination equipment) Local Management Interface.

LMI enq recvd Number of LMI enquiries received.

LMI stat sent Number of LMI status packets sent.

LMI upd sent Number of LMI updates sent.

LMI DLCI The DLCI number used for LMI. Cisco LMI type uses DLCI 1023. When ANSI is used, the LMI DLCI is 0.

LMI type The LMI type used by the interface. Default is Cisco. The other two types are ANSI and ITU-T (aka Q933a). The LMI types on the router and the Frame Relay switch must match. Simply put, LMI type must match on the DTE and DCE equipment.

show frame-relay lmi

The show frame-relay lmi command displays LMI-relevant information. The output contains the LMI type, inquiry, update, and status information:

```
Router_B#show frame-relay lmi
LMI Statistics for interface Serial0 (Frame Relay DTE) LMI TYPE = CISCO
  Invalid Unnumbered info 0    Invalid Prot Disc 0
  Invalid dummy Call Ref 0    Invalid Msg Type 0
  Invalid Status Message 0    Invalid Lock Shift 0
  Invalid Information ID 0    Invalid Report IE Len 0
  Invalid Report Request 0    Invalid Keep IE Len 0
  Num Status Enq. Sent 823406    Num Status msgs Rcvd 823403
  Num Update Status Rcvd 507    Num Status Timeouts 3
```

show frame-relay pvc

When you issue the show frame-relay pvc command, you get output that contains the LMI status of every DLCI on the router, or you may be more specific and enter a command to check only certain PVCs.

There are two types of DLCI usage: local DTE and switched. Things to check for in the output of the command include dropped frames, congestion notifications, and discard-eligible packets.

Here is a sample output. The data provided includes PVC information. It has the input and output packets for the interface, as well as FECN and BECN packet information. These statistics are available for every PVC on the router. Here, only two PVCs are shown:

```
Router_A#show frame-relay pvc

PVC Statistics for interface Serial0 (Frame Relay DTE)

DLCI = 18, DLCI USAGE = LOCAL, PVC STATUS = ACTIVE, INTERFACE = Serial0.4

input pkts 37515875 output pkts 38589330 in bytes 4113557032
out bytes 2755391175 dropped pkts 16 in FECN pkts 0
in BECN pkts 0 out FECN pkts 0 out BECN pkts 0
in DE pkts 315420 out DE pkts 0
pvc create time 13w4d, last time pvc status changed 06:40:12

DLCI = 19, DLCI USAGE = UNUSED, PVC STATUS = ACTIVE, INTERFACE = Serial0

input pkts 38 output pkts 0 in bytes 8372
out bytes 0 dropped pkts 0 in FECN pkts 0
in BECN pkts 0 out FECN pkts 0 out BECN pkts 0
```

```
in DE pkts 0 out DE pkts 0
pvc create time 13w4d, last time pvc status changed 7w4d
Num Pkts Switched 0
```

Problems can be detected by watching the number of FECN or BECN packets increase, which indicates line congestion. If these values are increasing rapidly compared to the overall number of frames going across the network, there could be an issue. Forward explicit congestion notification, FECN, notifies the receiving station (DTE) that congestion was experienced en route to the destination. Backward explicit congestion notification, BECN, notifies the sending station that congestion was experienced. FECN messages are sent in the direction of the congestion, and BECN messages are sent in the opposite direction of the congestion.

show frame-relay map

The show frame-relay map command provides information about the DLCI numbers and the encapsulation of all Frame Relay interfaces. The status of the interface is indicated with the up or down state found within the parentheses. The next field indicates the type of interface: point-to-point or multipoint. The DLCI for the interface and the encapsulation type are also included in the output.

Here is a sample:

```
Router_B#show frame-relay map
Serial0.10 (down): point-to-point dlci, dlci 24(0x18,0x480), broadcast,
 IETF, BW = 1024000 status defined, inactive
Serial0.7 (down): point-to-point dlci, dlci 21(0x15,0x450), broadcast,
 IETF, BW = 1024000 status defined, inactive
Serial0.5 (up): point-to-point dlci, dlci 20(0x14,0x440), broadcast,
 IETF, BW = 1024000 status defined, active
Serial0.6 (up): point-to-point dlci, dlci 30(0x1E,0x4E0), broadcast,
 IETF, BW = 48000 status defined, active
Serial0.4 (up): point-to-point dlci, dlci 18(0x12,0x420), broadcast,
 IETF, BW = 1024000 status defined, active
Serial0.2 (up): point-to-point dlci, dlci 27(0x1B,0x4B0), broadcast,
 IETF, BW = 48000 status defined, active
Serial0.11 (up): point-to-point dlci, dlci 31(0x1F,0x4F0), broadcast,
 IETF, BW = 48000 status defined, active
Serial0.9 (up): point-to-point dlci, dlci 29(0x1D,0x4D0), broadcast,
 IETF, BW = 48000 status defined, active
Serial0.12 (up): point-to-point dlci, dlci 32(0x20,0x800), broadcast,
 IETF, BW = 48000 status defined, active
Serial0.8 (up): point-to-point dlci, dlci 28(0x1C,0x4C0), broadcast,
 IETF, BW = 48000 status defined, active
Serial1.1 (up): point-to-point dlci, dlci 16(0x10,0x400), broadcast,
 IETF, BW = 1024000 status defined, active
```

Frame Relay *debug* Commands

As always, you must exercise caution when using **debug** commands, due to the amount of output they can generate. The more traffic that exists on an interface, the more output will be generated on the router. The commands discussed in this section are:

- debug frame-relay lmi
- debug frame-relay events

debug frame-relay lmi

An LMI Frame Relay debug displays LMI exchange information. The exchange consists of LMI status inquiries and responses, including sequencing numbers. Here is a sample:

```
Router_B#debug frame-relay lmi
Frame Relay LMI debugging is on
Displaying all Frame Relay LMI data
Serial0(out): StEnq, myseq 142, yourseen 141, DTE up
datagramstart = 0x40081DA0, datagramsize = 13
FR encap = 0xFCF10309
00 75 01 01 01 03 02 8E 8D
Serial0(in): Status, myseq 142
RT IE 1, length 1, type 1
KA IE 3, length 2, yourseq 142, myseq 142
Serial1(out): StEnq, myseq 9, yourseen 15, DTE up
datagramstart = 0x40000528, datagramsize = 13
FR encap = 0xFCF10309
00 75 01 01 01 03 02 09 0F

Serial1(in): Status, myseq 9
RT IE 1, length 1, type 1
KA IE 3, length 2, yourseq 16, myseq 9
Serial2(out): StEnq, myseq 254, yourseen 254, DTE up
datagramstart = 0x40000528, datagramsize = 13
FR encap = 0xFCF10309
00 75 01 01 01 03 02 FE FE
```

The StEnq, myseq, and yourseen data are similar to the data provided by the serial debug command, explained earlier. Following are definitions of the fields introduced here:

RT IE   Report Type Information Element

KA IE   Keepalive Information Element

This **debug** command does not generate a great deal of output, as you can see. Therefore, it can be used even during high-traffic times. Some outputs will include more information than the sample displayed previously. Additional information includes clocking, PVC, and Committed Information Rate detail.

debug frame-relay events

Data provided by this command is useful because it gives details about protocols and applications using the DLCI. A sample follows. The (i) and (o) specify inbound and outbound traffic:

```
Router_A#debug frame-relay events
Serial3(i): dlci 1023(0xFCF1), pkt type 0x309, datagramsize 13
Serial3.6(o): dlci 1023(0xFCF1), pkt type 0x309, datagramsize 13
Serial3(i): dlci 1023(0xFCF1), pkt type 0x309, datagramsize 13
Serial3.6(o): dlci 1023(0xFCF1), pkt type 0x309, datagramsize 13
Serial0.2(o): dlci 1023(0xFCF1), pkt type 0x309, datagramsize 13
Serial3(i): dlci 1023(0xFCF1), pkt type 0x309, datagramsize 13
```

The pkt type is used to distinguish the packet type that transits the DLCI. The packet type tells you which applications are on the circuit. Several different packet types may appear in the pkt type field.

Frame Relay Summary

This summary section includes tables that can be used for quick reference when you are diagnosing, isolating, and resolving Frame Relay problems.

Symptoms and Problems

Table 7.3 includes Frame Relay symptoms and their related problems.

TABLE 7.3   Frame Relay Symptoms and Problems

Symptom or Condition	Associated Problem(s)
Frame Relay link is down	(a) Faulty cabling
	(b) Faulty hardware
	(c) Local service provider problem
	(d) LMI type mismatch
	(e) Keepalives not being sent

TABLE 7.3   Frame Relay Symptoms and Problems *(continued)*

Symptom or Condition	Associated Problem(s)
	(f) Encapsulation type
	(g) DLCI mismatch
Cannot ping remote host across a Frame Relay network	(a) DLCI assigned to wrong subinterface
	(b) Encapsulation mismatch
	(c) Access list problem
	(d) Interface misconfiguration

Problems and Action Plans

Table 7.4 includes the resolution action plans for the problems listed in Table 7.3.

TABLE 7.4   Action Plans for Common Frame Relay Problems

Problem	Resolution Action Plan
Faulty cabling	1. Check the cabling and use a breakout box to test the control leads.
	2. Replace cabling as needed.
Faulty hardware	1. Isolate hardware problems by performing loopback tests.
	2. Change the cable to a new interface on the router, and configure the new interface to match the configuration of the old interface. If the link comes up, you know that you must replace the hardware.
Local service provider problem	1. If loopback tests bring the LMI state up, but you cannot connect to the remote site, contact the local carrier.
	Problems can include carrier problems as well as Frame Relay misconfiguration, such as DLCI mismatch or encapsulation mismatch.
LMI type mismatch	1. Verify that the LMI type on the router matches the LMI type for every device in the PVC.
	2. If you're using a public provider network, you won't have access to the LMI information; contact the carrier.

TABLE 7.4 Action Plans for Common Frame Relay Problems *(continued)*

Problem	Resolution Action Plan
Keepalive problems	1. Use the show interface command to see whether keepalives are disabled or to verify that they are configured properly. 2. If the keepalive is not set, enter the configuration mode and specify the keepalive interval on the proper interface.
Encapsulation type	1. Verify that the encapsulation type is the same on both routers. If non-Cisco equipment is used, the encapsulation must be set for IETF. You can display this information by using the show frame-relay map command. 2. To change the encapsulation, use the encapsulation frame-relay ietf command.
DLCI mismatch	1. Use the show running-config command to display the DLCI number assigned to the proper interface. The show frame-relay pvc command can also display the DLCI assigned to the interface. 2. If the correct DLCI number is configured on the proper interface, contact the local carrier to verify that it has the same DLCI configured on the Frame Relay switch.
Access list problem	1. Use the show ip interface command to display the access list applied to the interface. 2. Analyze the access list, and then remove and modify it, if necessary.

Summary

Though the protocols involved are different, troubleshooting WAN connectivity uses the same basic problem-solving techniques that were used to troubleshoot LAN connectivity issues earlier in the book. These techniques will continue to be applied, as well, for functions explained through the rest of the book.

Although there are several different types of interfaces, some form of a serial interface will most often be used to create the WAN connection. This serial interface may or may not have a built-in CSU/DSU. In either case, there are numerous show and debug commands for examining the health of this interface as well as the connection or connections it supports. Many of these same commands, such as show interface and show controllers, are used to examine LAN interfaces as well. In addition to the show and debug commands, loopbacks can also be set up on the Cisco routers or, more commonly, on the CSU/DSU used in the circuit path.

Various encapsulation types can be used on a WAN circuit. By default, a Cisco serial interface uses High-level Data Link Control (HDLC) as the encapsulation type. This encapsulation type is used for synchronous data link control. Another common encapsulation type is Frame Relay. Frame Relay allows for multiple locations to be connected on a single physical interface. This is done through the use of virtual circuits, either permanent or switched, and via Data-Link Connection Identifiers or DLCIs.

Exam Essentials

Know how to determine the encapsulation type of an interface.   By looking at the output of a show interface command, you can determine the encapsulation type of an interface. You should also know the major characteristics of the encapsulation used and how to identify these characteristics.

Know the show and debug commands that are used to troubleshoot serial line problems.   Among the show and debug commands that can be used to troubleshoot serial line problems are show interface serial, debug serial interface, and debug serial packet. You should know the show and debug commands for the interfaces as well as the protocol being used. Also, you need to understand the buffer information that is displayed as part of the output from some of these commands.

Know how HDLC functions and how to troubleshoot issues.   HDLC is a point-to-point protocol. It is also the default protocol used on Cisco router serial interfaces. The show interface command as well as the serial debug command provides detailed information about the functioning of HDLC.

Know how Frame Relay functions and how to troubleshoot issues.   Frame Relay can be used as a point-to-point, point-to-multipoint, or multipoint-to-multipoint protocol. It provides this functionality through the use of one or multiple Virtual Circuits (VCs) per physical circuit. The commands show frame-relay pvc, show frame-relay map, show frame-relay lmi, show interface, debug frame-relay lmi, and debug frame-relay events can be used to diagnose Frame Relay issues.

Understand DLCI and LMI information and how these interfaces are used in Frame Relay. DLCIs are only significant locally and represent the VC, either switched or permanent. LMI is used for management of the Frame Relay link.

Know the purposes of loopbacks and how they can be applied.   Loopbacks are used to help isolate a problem to a specific section of the circuit. They are most often applied on the local or remote CSU/DSU.

Commands Used in This Chapter

The following list contains a summary of all the commands used in this chapter.

Commands	Descriptions
`clear counters serial`	Clears the statistical counters on the interface.
`debug frame-relay events`	Gives details about protocols and applications using the DLCI.
`debug frame-relay lmi`	Displays LMI exchange information. The exchange consists of LMI status inquiries and responses, including sequencing numbers.
`debug serial interface`	Displays signaling information for the interface.
`debug serial packet`	Displays information regarding serial packets.
`show buffers`	Displays buffer statistics for the router.
`show controllers serial`	Shows specific hardware information regarding the serial controller.
`show frame-relay lmi`	Displays LMI-relevant information. The output contains the LMI type, inquiry, update, and status information.
`show frame-relay map`	Contains information about the DLCI numbers and the encapsulation of all Frame Relay interfaces. The status of the interface is indicated with the up or down state.
`show frame-relay pvc`	Provides the LMI status of every DLCI on the router; or you may specify only certain PVCs.
`show interface serial`	The `show interface` command executed on a serial interface. Provides important information regarding serial interfaces, including IP, encapsulation, and line statistics.

Key Terms

Before you take the exam, be certain you are familiar with the following terms:

Data-Link Connection Identifier (DLCI)   Local Management Interface (LMI)

High-level Data Link Control (HDLC)   loopback tests

Review Questions

1. What is the output of the `clear counters` command?

   A. The `clear counters` command displays all counters for the specified interface, and then resets the counters.

   B. It displays the value of the counters before the last time the interface was reset.

   C. There is no output from `clear counters`.

   D. It clears the statistical counter on the specified interface.

2. Which of the following elements are displayed by using the `show interface serial` command? (Choose all that apply.)

   A. Frame Relay information

   B. Encapsulation type

   C. Interface error information

   D. IOS version number

3. Which of the following elements are displayed by using the `show controller serial` command? (Choose all that apply.)

   A. Encapsulation type

   B. LMI type

   C. Clock rate

   D. Cable type

   E. Cable connection status

   F. Error information

4. Which of the following elements are displayed by using the `show buffers` command? (Choose all that apply.)

   A. Interface buffers (on low-level routers)

   B. Very huge buffers

   C. Huge buffers

   D. Tiny buffers

5. Which of the following information fields are displayed by using the `debug serial interface` command? (Choose all that apply.)

   A. `myseq`

   B. `yourseen`

   C. `mineseen`

   D. `StEnq`

6. What are two of the four CSU/DSU loopback tests? (Choose two.)

    A. Local loopback at local site

    B. Remote loopback from remote site

    C. Local remote loopback from local site

    D. Remote local loopback from remote site

7. Below is the output of a show controllers command. What is the interface type for this router?

```
Router_A#show controllers serial 0
HD unit 0, idb = 0x94AEC, driver structure at 0x99870
buffer size 1524  HD unit 0, No cable, clockrate 4000000
cpb = 0x41, eda = 0x4940, cda = 0x4800
RX ring with 16 entries at 0x414800
.
.  {some output omitted}
.
TX ring with 2 entries at 0x415000
.
.  {some output omitted}
.
0 missed datagrams, 0 overruns
0 bad datagram encapsulations, 0 memory errors
0 transmitter underruns
0 residual bit errors
```

    A. DTE

    B. DCE

    C. Frame Relay

    D. Not enough information provided

8. On a Frame Relay interface, what is the default LMI type?

    A. Cisco

    B. ANSI

    C. IEEE

    D. ITU-T

9. Which of the following fields are Frame Relay/LMI-related, indicated in output from the `show interface serial` command? (Choose all that apply.)

   A. LMI enq sent

   B. LMI stat recvd

   C. RESTARTs

   D. LMI encapsulation

10. Which of the following fields are Frame Relay/LMI-related, indicated in output from the `show interface serial` command? (Choose all that apply.)

    A. LMI upd recvd

    B. DTE LMI

    C. LMI enq recvd

    D. Frame Relay enq sent

11. Which of the following fields are Frame Relay/LMI-related, indicated in output from the `show interface serial` command? (Choose all that apply.)

    A. LMI stat sent

    B. LMI upd sent

    C. LMI DLCI

    D. LMI type

12. Which command(s) display the LMI type? (Choose all that apply.)

    A. `show interface serial`

    B. `show frame-relay map`

    C. `show frame-relay pvc`

    D. `show frame-relay lmi`

13. Which of the following information fields are displayed by the `show frame-relay pvc` command? (Choose all that apply.)

    A. BECN statistics

    B. FECN statistics

    C. Configuration register setting

    D. VPI number

14. Which of the following commands provide the DLCI number of the serial interface? (Choose all that apply.)

    A. `show running-config`

    B. `show frame-relay map`

    C. `show serial dlci`

    D. `show frame-relay lmi`

15. What property must the DLCI number have?

    A. The DLCI number must match the DLCI on the other end of the PVC.

    B. It must be between 0 and 16.

    C. It has only local significance.

    D. All of the above.

16. Which of the following statements is/are true of the LMI type on the router? (Choose all that apply.)

    A. The LMI type on the router must match that on the remote end.

    B. It must have the same DLCI as the other end.

    C. It can be set to Cisco.

    D. It can be set to ANSI.

17. Which of the following statements is/are true regarding the encapsulation used when connecting a Cisco router to a non-Cisco router?

    A. It must be Cisco.

    B. It must be ANSI.

    C. It must be IETF.

    D. It must be ITU.

18. Which statements are true regarding the encapsulation on the router's interface? (Choose all that apply.)

    A. Both sides of the PVC must be using the same type.

    B. Encapsulation is local to the router.

    C. ITU-T is a valid encapsulation type.

    D. IETF is a valid encapsulation type.

19. Which of the following `debug` commands can be detrimental to router performance?

    A. `frame-relay packets`

    B. `frame-relay events`

    C. `frame-relay lmi`

    D. None of the above

20. The `debug frame-relay lmi` command does not generate a large amount of output. Why?

    A. Infrequent LMI exchanges between the router and switch

    B. Small amounts of data in each LMI packet

    C. Nondetailed information is provided

    D. None of the above

Answers to Review Questions

1. C. Other than the dialog of the command, `clear counters` produces no output.

2. A, B, C. Frame Relay information, the encapsulation type, and interface error information are all three displayed using the `show interface serial` command. You can determine the IOS version number with the `show version` command.

3. C, D, E, F. The `show controller serial` command gives clock rate, cable type, cable connection status, and error information. The encapsulation and LMI types are displayed using the `show interface serial` command.

4. A, C. B, very huge buffers, and D, tiny buffers, are not valid names for the buffer pools. There are other buffers in addition to interface buffers and huge buffers, but they are not listed here.

5. A, B, C, D. All of these fields—`myseq`, `yourseen`, `mineseen`, and `StEnq`—are available via the output from the `debug serial interface` command.

6. A, B. A loopback test is either local or remote.

7. D. The interface can be either DTE or DCE, depending on the cable type attached. Since the output indicates no cable is attached, there is not enough information to determine the interface type.

8. A. The default LMI type is ANSI.

9. A, B. Answers A and B, `LMI enq sent` and `LMI stat recvd`, are the Frame Relay/LMI-related fields. There are more, but they are not listed here.

10. A, B, C. `LMI upd recvd`, `DTE LMI`, and `LMI enq recvd` are also valid Frame Relay/LMI fields.

11. A, B, C, D. As you can see, a great number of fields are related to Frame Relay/LMI via the `show interface serial` command. In this case, all the answers are correct: `LMI stat sent`, `LMI upd sent`, `LMI DLCI`, and `LMI type`.

12. A, D. Show `interface serial` and `show frame-relay lmi` are the two commands that can provide information regarding the LMI type.

13. A, B. BECN statistics and FECN statistics, along with other statistics, can be found via the `show frame-relay pvc` command.

14. A, B. The two commands that provide DLCI number information are `show running-config` and `show frame-relay map`. There are additional commands, but they are not shown here.

15. C. The DLCI does have a limit in values, but it is of local significance only. It does not need to match the other end.

16. A, C, D. It doesn't matter what type is set for the router, as long as both ends of the PVC are configured to use the same type.

17. C. Encapsulation must be IETF, because non-Cisco equipment will not understand Cisco-specific encapsulation.

18. A, D. IETF and Cisco are valid encapsulations. They must be the same on both sides of the connection.

19. A. The `frame-relay packets debug` can be very detrimental to performance because every packet would be analyzed by the debug process.

20. A. The data provided by the `debug` command is summarized, and exchanges do not occur as frequently as Frame Relay packets.

Chapter

8

Troubleshooting ISDN

EXAM TOPICS COVERED IN THIS CHAPTER INCLUDE:

✓ Verify network connectivity.

✓ Use Cisco IOS commands to identify problems.

✓ Determine the layer or layers on which a problem is occurring.

✓ Rectify sub-optimal performance issues at Layers 2 through 7.

✓ Work with external vendors to diagnose and resolve network problems.

"It Still Does Nothing."

   "Yes, this is the phone company. May I please speak with Mr. Isdn?"

The jokes and stories about ISDNs (Integrated Services Digital Network) have been merciless and, in some cases, more prevalent than the service itself.

Although it is true that ISDN is difficult to order and configure, ISDN is an important option for administrators to consider when designing networks. Frame Relay and xDSL are strong contenders, but ISDN's availability and cost advantages in certain situations are difficult to ignore. In addition, the configuration challenges have been removed to a large degree as the service becomes better known.

This chapter will cover the basics of how ISDN operates as well as how to troubleshoot common problems. Specifically, ISDN switch types will be covered, as well as PPP, and features such as dialer lists and restricting traffic over an ISDN interface. The chapter will finish up discussing the debugging options that are available for ISDN.

Some of the commands listed in this chapter are unavailable on certain Cisco routers because of hardware and software considerations. The Cisco 804 router with internal ISDN BRI was used to provide the screen output for this chapter.

ISDN Fundamentals

ISDN was developed in large part from the phone company's conversion to digital networks from analog switches. This conversion, which started in the 1960s, resulted in the following features:

- Clearer, cleaner signals
- Compressible voice, resulting in better trunk utilization
- Longer distances between switching devices
- Value-added features, including caller ID and three-way calling
- Greater bandwidth—a single connection to the phone company can service more than one phone number
- Elimination of load coils and amplifiers in the network

The concept of ISDN was originally conceived as a means to move the digital network into the home, where a single ISDN connection would provide two standard phone lines and digital services for data. This migration from the analog phone would continue to use the existing copper wire plant, while adding services that would ultimately increase revenues.

Unfortunately, users failed to accept ISDN in the numbers desired. This was especially true in the United States, where installation problems, service availability, and high pricing all conspired to hinder acceptance.

In the late 1990s, ISDN was finding a new marketplace. Always On ISDN uses the D channel to replace legacy X.25 networks, especially in point-of-sale transactions. (A description of the B and D channels is included in the "Physical Layer Connections" section, later in this chapter.) Standard ISDN service is popular for videoconferencing and as a residential connection to the Internet. However, cable modems and DSL technologies have replaced much of this market in today's environment.

Common ISDN Problems

Like problems that affect other protocols and networking devices, ISDN difficulties occur in certain common areas. Some frequently encountered problems are presented in this section for administrators to consider when evaluating real-world issues. Later in this chapter, the commands that are appropriate for troubleshooting these problems with Cisco routers will be presented.

ISDN problems can be divided into three general categories: misconfigured routers, physical wiring and ISDN protocol issues, and misconfigured switches.

Misconfigured Routers

The router configuration is one of many areas that can require attention when researching ISDN problems. Misconfiguration issues can happen due to a variety of reasons, including typographical errors, erroneous information from service providers, and failure to correctly configure the router itself. The following sections discuss several aspects of router configuration that often contribute to router misbehavior, with suggestions for troubleshooting those problems.

Service Profile Identifiers (SPIDs)

The *Service Profile Identifiers,* or *SPIDs*, can be compared to phone numbers in the analog phone environment. The SPID numbers usually include the telephone number with area code and, occasionally, extra digits used by the switch. So a SPID like this one, 41555512340101, corresponds to phone number 415-555-1234, with additional parameters of 0101. The local service provider should document these numbers for the administrator.

In some cases, the service provider will also assign a Local Directory Number (LDN). The LDN is not required to make outgoing calls, but if it's not present and is required by the service provider, its absence can create problems for connecting on both B channels.

ISDN is unique in that the local device must learn its identifying number. This is in contrast to analog phones, which remain unaware of their actual phone number—relying on a switch to trigger the ringer. If this does not happen or if the SPIDs or LDNs are misconfigured, you can have problems with your ISDN connection.

SPIDs are used only in North America, and the integration of the phone number into the SPID is most applicable for public ISDN installations.

It is surprisingly common for administrators to assign IP addresses within two different subnets on ISDN interfaces that connect to each other. It is important to consider each end of an ISDN DDR connection to be part of a single subnet. From a Layer 3 perspective, they are the same as any other point-to-point WAN connection.

Challenge Handshake Authentication Protocol (CHAP)

ISDN provides the capability to control access by requiring authentication, which helps to make public network usage more acceptable from a business/security perspective.

The inner workings of the *Challenge Handshake Authentication Protocol (CHAP)* are beyond the scope of this chapter; basically, CHAP is used to provide a layer of security on inbound connections. When troubleshooting, it is important to confirm that the CHAP configurations on both routers match. As noted in the ppp command output that follows, Cisco also supports the Microsoft CHAP and PAP protocols. MS-CHAP was added in IOS 12.0.

CHAP authentication requires the point-to-point protocol (PPP). This is enabled on the interface with the command encapsulation ppp.

```
Top(config-if)#ppp auth ?
  chap     Challenge Handshake Authentication Protocol    (CHAP)
  ms-chap  Microsoft Challenge Handshake Authentication    Protocol (MS-CHAP)
  pap      Password Authentication Protocol (PAP)
```

When troubleshooting, remember that it is quite common for the username parameters that define the passwords to be set incorrectly, by including a typo in the password itself or omitting a username. With encrypted passwords, this is more difficult to research. If a password problem is suspected, an administrator should enable the debug ppp authentication function. As shown in the output that follows (the lines in italic), the authentication failed due to an incorrect password.

In PPP, both the username and password are case sensitive. So be careful when
entering both of these values.

```
Bottom#debug ppp authentication
PPP authentication debugging is on
Bottom#ping 10.1.1.1
Type escape sequence to abort.
Sending 5, 100-byte ICMP Echos to 10.1.1.1, timeout is 2    seconds:
01:54:14: %LINK-3-UPDOWN: Interface BRIO:1, changed state    to up.
01:54:14: BRO:1 PPP: Treating connection as a callout
01:54:14: BRO:1 PPP: Phase is AUTHENTICATING, by both
01:54:14: BRO:1 CHAP: O CHALLENGE id 7 len 27 from    "Bottom"
01:54:14: BRO:1 CHAP: I CHALLENGE id 7 len 24 from "Top"
01:54:14: BRO:1 CHAP: O RESPONSE id 7 len 27 from "Bottom"
01:54:14: BRO:1 CHAP: I FAILURE id 7 len 25 msg is "MD/DES compare failed"
01:54:15: %ISDN-6-DISCONNECT: Interface BRIO:1 disconnected from
 18008358661 , call lasted 1 seconds
01:54:15: %LINK-3-UPDOWN: Interface BRIO:1, changed state to down.
01:54:18: %LINK-3-UPDOWN: Interface BRIO:1, changed state to up.
01:54:18: BRO:1 PPP: Treating connection as a callout
01:54:18: BRO:1 PPP: Phase is AUTHENTICATING, by both
01:54:18: BRO:1 CHAP: O CHALLENGE id 8 len 27 from    "Bottom"
01:54:18: BRO:1 CHAP: I CHALLENGE id 8 len 24 from "Top"
01:54:18: BRO:1 CHAP: O RESPONSE id 8 len 27 from "Bottom"
01:54:18: BRO:1 CHAP: I FAILURE id 8 len 25 msg is "MD/DES compare failed"
01:54:19: %ISDN-6-DISCONNECT: Interface BRIO:1 disconnected from
 18008358661 , call lasted    1 seconds
01:54:19: %LINK-3-UPDOWN: Interface BRIO:1, changed state to down.
01:54:22: %LINK-3-UPDOWN: Interface BRIO:1, changed state to up.
```

 Real World Scenario

One-Way Chap Authentication

In many businesses today, ISDN lines no longer fill just one specific role. They are being used
to connect remote locations back to the corporate network; they are being used for dial-backup,
for connecting to the Internet, and in many more scenarios. I have also seen the same line being
used for multiple purposes simultaneously.

When all of these connections are made within like company devices, bidirectional CHAP does not create a problem, since all of the devices can be configured to use this authentication methodology. However, when using the same router for incoming calls and to connect to an ISP or an ISDN device made by a company other than Cisco, CHAP can become an issue. In many of these instances, CHAP is not configured on the called device. In other cases, the far-end device does not support CHAP challenges from the calling device. However, you still want to use CHAP authentication when your router is called.

In these problematic situations, the simplest solution that I have found is to use the Cisco IOS command ppp authentication chap callin to enable *one-way* CHAP authentication. This command is used at the interface level and will send a CHAP challenge only when the router is called, not when it calls out. This allows you to connect to devices that don't support bidirectional CHAP authentication or are not configured for CHAP, without giving up the security that CHAP provides when you receive an incoming call.

Note, too, that a similar command also exists for PAP if you are running PAP in your environment. As is the case with CHAP, this configuration goes on the calling router.

Dialer Map Entries

Dialer map statements relate upper-layer addresses to their associated phone numbers. Therefore, it is critical that dialer map entries contain valid IP addresses and numbers. If they are not valid, you could cause the ISDN line to come up when it is not supposed to, or worse yet, not come up at all. Note that an individual dialer map statement is needed for each protocol, as follows:

```
dialer map ip 10.11.3.20 name Top broadcast 18005551212
dialer map appletalk 310.10 name Top broadcast 18005551212
```

In certain cases you can run DDR without using dialer maps. But for ease of troubleshooting and consistency, maps should be used whenever possible.

Some ISDN switches require the area code and escape character, even when the phone numbers are in the same area code.

Access Lists

Access lists are commonly used in ISDN connections to prevent certain types of traffic from triggering a connection and to bring up the link only when "interesting traffic" is seen. Most frequently, this is done to save money, because ISDN is often tariffed on a per-minute, per-B-channel basis. However, Frame Relay and other technologies commonly provide the same or greater bandwidth at lower cost. This is usually true after approximately 40 hours per month of utilization on the B channels. The xDSL technologies are quickly gaining market share at an unlimited usage tariff, as well.

To control usage, administrators frequently configure an access list based on permitted functions only, and all other services are denied. This sometimes causes problems when a new service is added to the system without being explicitly added to the access list. Troubleshooting any ISDN configuration that worked in the past should include a thorough review of all access lists, including the dialer lists.

```
Bottom(config)#dialer-list 1 protocol ip ?
  deny    Deny specified protocol
  list    Add access list to dialer list
  permit  Permit specified protocol
```

A dialer list to provide IP, IPX, and AppleTalk services is shown as follows:

```
dialer-list 1 protocol ip permit
dialer-list 1 protocol appletalk permit
dialer-list 1 protocol ipx permit
```

The above list is just a sample of a dialer list. As written, it will cause the ISDN line to be brought up for any IP, IPX, or AppleTalk traffic. Although this is useful for demonstrations and in the lab, a more-restrictive list is more appropriate for real-world installations.

Point-to-Point Protocol

Although the point-to-point protocol (PPP) is recommended for ISDN connectivity, there are other options available, including the default HDLC. PPP is recommended in large part to provide security via CHAP, as described previously in this section.

For troubleshooting, PPP provides additional information regarding the connection, including the protocol type. This information rarely presents itself in a manner that is usable to administrators, however. Often more helpful to the administrator will be an understanding of the protocol and its capability to provide useful functions, including CHAP. Note that the PPP protocol is the same for analog or ISDN connections, so the configuration of PPP on a workstation using an analog modem requires PPP encapsulation on an ISDN host router. PPP also supports compression.

PPP contains protocol field values that document the upper-layer information included in the datagram. Table 8.1 provides a list of some protocol field values.

TABLE 8.1   Point-to-Point Protocol Field Values

Hex Value of Field	Protocol
0021	IP
0029	AppleTalk
002B	IPX
003D	Multilink
0201	802.1d Hellos
0203	Source Route Bridging Bridge Protocol Data Units
8021	IPCP
8029	ATCP
802B	IPXCP
C223	CHAP
C023	PAP

Physical Layer Connections

It is important to consider the Physical layer when troubleshooting ISDN, especially in new installations. Wiring is particularly important when connecting ISDN videoconferencing equipment to internal PBX equipment. Some administrators use Category 5 wiring for internal ISDN connections, although Category 3 is acceptable. This chapter focuses on the Basic Rate Interface (BRI), which operates over standard copper pairs.

The Basic Rate Interface

Most installations of ISDN in the field are BRI. This differs from the available Primary Rate Interface (PRI), which uses a T1 as the conduit. The primary rate of telecommunications connections is usually measured in DS-1 increments. A DS-1, or T1, is equivalent to 24 T1 voice channels. The basic rate for a voice connection is referred to as a DS-0, or a single 64Kbit channel of the T1. In ISDN, this refers to the single B-channel capacity of the circuit. The formal description of BRI is specified in I.430; the I.431 specification addresses PRI ISDN.

ISDN BRI was designed to provide digital services over existing pairs of copper. The service is used for videoconferencing, voice services, data, and out-of-band management. In addition, in many cases, the D-channel function of BRI is used for replacement of legacy X.25 networks.

The ISDN BRI Channels

ISDN BRI is a 192Kbps circuit that is divided into three distinct channels. The two primary data channels are the B channels. Each B channel provides 64Kbps. The third channel provides 16Kbps of bandwidth for commands and signaling and is referred to as the D channel. The remaining bandwidth of 48Kbps is overhead.

The physical frame in ISDN BRI is 48 bits, and the circuit sends 4000 frames per second.

The Local Loop

Although the majority of administrators troubleshoot only the local side of the ISDN circuit, there is a remote side that is critical to the successful operation of ISDN.

The *local loop* refers to the circuit between the customer premises and the central office (CO). This may include an access layer, referred to as an RT, which permits digital connections to be greater distances from the central office. The local loop interconnects the ISDN device to an ISDN switch—a DMS-100, for example. Note that all digital services are sensitive to the distance between the switch and end device.

The Physical Layer

In order to properly troubleshoot ISDN, it is very important that you have a good understanding of its technology, terminology, architecture, and functionality. Figure 8.1 shows the ISDN components and where these components' points fit into the ISDN installation. In addition to the components, the illustration also shows the reference points that are commonly used in troubleshooting ISDN issues. Following are descriptions of the components and reference points in Figure 8.1.

FIGURE 8.1   ISDN components and reference points

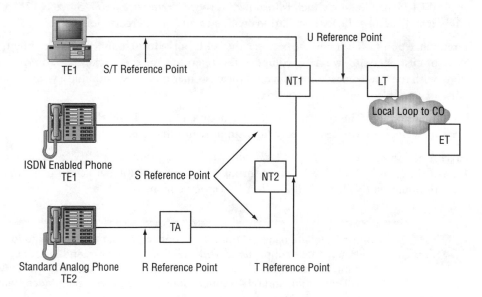

LT/ET   The line termination and exchange termination points are called *LT* and *ET* respectively. They handle the termination of the local loop and switching functions.

NT1   The *NT1* is the network termination point. It is often the demarcation point (demarc) where the provider terminates their portion of the circuit. It connects the four-wire subscriber line to the two-wire local loop and acts as an entry point for the ISDN circuit. In North America, the NT1 is provided by the customer and is considered Customer Premise Equipment. However, in most other parts of the world this device is provided and managed by the carrier.

NT2   The *NT2* is primarily seen only in larger companies that are using PBXs. The NT2 is used to perform Layer 2 and 3 protocol functions and as a concentration point.

TA   The *TA* is the Terminal Adapter. This device is used to connect non-ISDN-enabled devices, TE2, to the ISDN network. A TA may be added to the device itself or may be a stand-alone unit.

TE1   A device with a four-wire, twisted-pair digital interface is referred to as *terminal equipment type one (TE1)*. Most modern ISDN devices are of this type.

TE2   *Terminal equipment type two (TE2)* devices do not contain ISDN interfaces. A TA is required.

R reference point   Devices without internal ISDN functions are called TE2s and require a connection to a TA for operation in ISDN networks. There is no standard connection between these devices, however—the connection is referred to as the *R reference point*.

S reference point   The *S reference point* is the interface between the ISDN router (or other user equipment) and the NT2 or NT1. Note that the user equipment is referred to as the TE1 or TA.

S/T reference point   If no NT2 is installed, the connection between the NT1 and either the TA or the TE1, depending on which is installed, is the *S/T reference point*. Since NT2 devices are rarely installed, most ISDN installations will have an S/T reference point.

T reference point   The interface between the NT1, or the local loop termination point, and the NT2, or customer-site switching equipment, is referred to as the *T reference point*. This point, along with the S reference point, is within the customer premises, and faulty wiring may be the cause of a problem within this context.

U reference point   The *U reference point* is between the NT1 and the LT. It is normally serviced on a single pair to reduce costs and simplify installations.

Layer 1 S/T interface   The *Layer 1 S/T interface* connection uses a physical connector of RJ-45, as defined in ISO 8877. A straight-through pin configuration connects the TE to the network termination (NT). Table 8.2 reflects the specific pinning.

NOTE   Some installers use RJ-11 or RJ-14 connections for ISDN terminations. Although these connections work, RJ-45 is the recommended connection in all circumstances. Wires 1, 2, 7, and 8 may be used for alternate mark inversion (AMI) encoding, and RJ-45 connections provide a visual variance from standard phone jacks.

TABLE 8.2   The RJ-45 ISDN S/T Interface

Pin	Terminal End-Point (TE)	Network Termination (NT)
1	Power +	Power +
2	Power −	Power −
3	Transmit +	Receive +
4	Receive +	Transmit +
5	Receive −	Transmit −
6	Transmit −	Receive −
7	Power −	Power −
8	Power +	Power +

Misconfigured Phone Switches

Administrators must consider the possibility that the service provider failed to properly configure the ISDN switch. Although this is a very rare occurrence, the possibility exists and should be considered, especially in new installations.

An understanding of ISDN as it relates to the OSI model can greatly assist the network troubleshooter in locating causes of problems with the phone switches. In addition, administrators must be aware of the ISDN switch types and their impact on connectivity.

Troubleshooting Layer 2

There are two Layer 2 troubleshooting targets that should be identified and analyzed when working on ISDN networks: the q.921 protocol and PPP.

q.921

ISDN maps well with the OSI reference model. Layer 2 is defined in *q.921*.

The q.921 signaling is carried over the D channel by using *Link Access Procedure protocol*, or LAPD. This connection between the central office switch (the Teltone ILS-2000 in the test network discussed here) and the router must occur and complete before connections are possible.

Troubleshooting q.921 problems is most frequently handled with the **debug isdn q921** command. Often, problems are related to the *terminal endpoint identifier*, or *TEI*. This value uniquely identifies each terminal in the network, and a TEI of 127 represents a broadcast. TEIs 64 through 126 are reserved for assignment during the activation of a Layer 2 ISDN connection. This assignment is dynamic.

TEI has a variety of message types that allow the engineer to identify what type of information is being exchanged, thus identifying any failures in the TEI process. Refer to Table 8.3 for descriptions of these types. By using these references, you will be able to understand the exchanges during the TEI process.

TABLE 8.3   TEI Message Types

TEI Message Type	Type Description
1	ID Request
2	ID Assigned
3	ID Denied
4	ID Check Request
5	ID Check Response
6	ID Remove
7	ID Verify

Administrators may also need to review the *SAPI*, or *service access point identifier*. This field may include a SAPI of 0, which represents that Layer 3 signaling is present. Such signaling is provided by the q.931 protocol (see the later section "Troubleshooting Layer 3"). Other values may include 63, which is a management SAPI for the assignment of the TEI values, and 64, which is used for call control.

One last target to check while troubleshooting the q.921 with the `debug isdn q.921` command is the SABME (Set Asynchronous Balanced Mode Extended) message. The SABME is exchanged along with the ID verify messages. If the SABME fails and sends a disconnect response, no further link establishment will occur, and you should investigate the reason for the SABME failure. If the SABME succeeds, an acknowledgment is sent and the Layer 2 connection is complete, and the TE will begin to send INFO frames.

Sample outputs for the `show interface` and `debug isdn q921` commands are discussed later in the chapter. The outputs are long and cover multiple pages. However, you should look through the output carefully and try to follow what is happening using the information you have learned thus far.

PPP

Troubleshooting targets within the PPP protocol is also important when trying to isolate and resolve ISDN BRI problems. *LCP, or Link Control Protocol,* is the protocol used by PPP to set up and maintain links. It also assists in setting the PPP options. Before getting into the sequence used to set up PPP, let's look at some of the LCP options. The primary ones are detailed in Table 8.4.

TABLE 8.4   LCP Type Options

LCP Type Number	LCP Type	Description
0	Reserved	Not used.
1	Maximum Receive Unit (MRU)	Sets the maximum packet size. Default is 1500 bytes.
3	Authentication Protocol	Sets the Authentication protocol to be used (CHAP or PAP).
4	Quality Protocol	Sets the protocol to use for Link Quality Monitoring, which is disabled by default.
5	Magic Number	Used to detect loopback links and other Layer 2 issues.
7	Protocol Field Compression	Used to negotiate compression of the PPP Protocol field.
8	Address and Control Field Compression	Used to negotiate compression of the Data-Link layer address and control fields.

In addition to LCP for link control, PPP also uses *Network Control Protocol (NCP)* for configuring and establishing Network layer protocols. Administrators also need to review the steps in PPP and CHAP negotiation. Let's look at the steps taken by PPP to establish a link.

1. LCP at the router (TE) sends a configuration request known as a CONFREQ. Options are specified by the requesting router.

2. The request is either accepted or denied. If it is accepted, an acknowledgment, CONFACK, is returned to the TE. If the request is denied, a negative CONFACK is returned. The difference between a normal and a negative CONFACK is the acceptance or denial of the request. If the CONFREQ was not recognized by the remote TE, a configuration reject message, CONFREJ, is sent to the requesting TE.

3. If the CONFREQ was recognized and accepted and CHAP is being used for authentication, the process continues with the three-way handshake.

   A. Challenge is sent to the remote TE.

   B. The remote TE responds.

   C. If the values match, authentication is given.

The troubleshooting targets in this process are the request/response sequence between the peers, as well as all of the CHAP targets.

Troubleshooting Layer 3

The third layer of ISDN is addressed in the ITU-T I.451 specification, also called *q.931*. (An easy way to remember the difference between q.921 and q.931 is to look at the tens digit of the number. q.921 corresponds to Layer 2, and q.931 corresponds to Layer 3.) The q.931 protocol includes several message commands, which are viewed with the `debug isdn q931` command. These commands include `call setup`, `connect`, `release`, `cancel`, `status`, `disconnect`, and `user information`.

The output of the `show` and `debug` commands will be covered later in the chapter.

It is important to identify the troubleshooting targets that exist in Layer 3 for ISDN BRI. Understand that the Layer 3 connection is between the local router (TE) and the remote ISDN switch (ET). Just as the q.931 operates on the D channel, so does all debugging. Troubleshooting targets include the call reference flag, message types, and information elements. Tables 8.5, 8.6, and 8.7 provide summaries for the messages and their meaning.

TABLE 8.5   Call Reference Flag Definitions

Field Value	Definition
0	From call originator
1	To call originator

TABLE 8.6   q.931 Message Types

Field Value	Definition
0x05	Setup
0x45	Disconnect
0x7d	Status

TABLE 8.7   q.931 Information Elements

Field Value	Definition
0x04	Bearer capability
0x2c	Keypad facility
0x6c	Calling party number

TABLE 8.7   q.931 Information Elements *(continued)*

Field Value	Definition
0x70	Called party number
0x3a	SPID

Again, all of this information is provided by the debug isdn q931 command. A sample output is provided later, in the "Debugging ISDN" section. The easiest way to keep track of the various calls is with the call reference number indicated in the output of the debug command. This way you will be able to follow the same call all the way through the process.

Note that these messages are carried on the D channel and are not end-to-end. Rather, they are for connections and setup between the central office switch and the router. The B channel is then available for data transfer.

ISDN calls are established between the router and the local switch over the D channel. The local switch establishes a separate connection to the remote switch, which is responsible for the call setup to the remote router or other ISDN device.

Now let's discuss the call setup on Layer 3 via q.931. It will aid you in troubleshooting and isolating ISDN BRI network problems. This is the process that must be followed. You can use the output of the debug isdn q931 to verify that the process is happening correctly.

1. SETUP: The SETUP process sends information elements; this occurs between the local TE and the remote TE.

2. CALL_PROC: The call proceeding signal is given; this occurs between the ET and the TE.

3. ALERT: The remote TE alerts the local TE via a ring-back.

4. CONNECT: The remote TE answers, thus stopping the local ring-back.

5. CONNECT_ACK: A message from the remote ET to the remote TE is sent, acknowledging that the setup is complete.

Switch Types

Recall that ISDN is a connection between the ISDN router and the phone company's central office switch. Therefore, it is important to define the type of switch in use to the router. This is configured with the isdn switch-type command. The isdn switch ? command reports the available switch types and their usual country or continent for the Cisco router.

```
Top(config)#isdn switch-type ?
  basic-1tr6    1TR6 switch type for Germany
```

```
basic-5ess      AT&T 5ESS switch type for the U.S.
basic-dms100    Northern DMS-100 switch type
basic-net3      NET3 switch type for UK and Europe
basic-ni        National ISDN switch type
basic-ts013     TS013 switch type for Australia
ntt             NTT switch type for Japan
vn3             VN3 and VN4 switch types for France
```

In North America, if the switch type is unknown, an administrator may wish to use the auto-configuration command; this command is isdn autodetect. If the SPID is unknown, the command isdn spidn 0 can be used. Some administrators prefer to specify the switch type and SPID information manually. Please be advised that these autoconfiguration options are not available on many routers; however, it is available on the Cisco 804 router, and it may be helpful in new installations. It is likely that Cisco will add this function to new products.

It is important to note that the switch type is specific to the local loop switch, and not to the remote connection or entire connection. For example, when connecting a router in North America to use for connections to Europe, the North American router is likely to be set to basic-dms100. The European router is set to basic-net3.

ISDN Troubleshooting Commands

The Cisco IOS provides a broad range of troubleshooting commands to assist administrators in the deployment and configuration of ISDN, including the common problems noted in the foregoing sections. Although many of these troubleshooting commands are common to other topologies and protocols (ping, for example), other commands are specific to ISDN, including debug isdn q931.

Figure 8.2 diagrams the network used for this chapter.

FIGURE 8.2   ISDN Troubleshooting network design

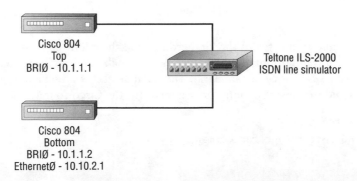

Some switch types and configurations may set each B channel at 56Kbps, instead of the potentially available 64Kbps, due to constraints in the carriers networks. Failure to match speeds causes connectivity problems.

ping

As with non-dial-on-demand (DDR) connections, the ping command is one of the most useful troubleshooting tools. ping verifies routes and other connections; in DDR, the command triggers a call.

```
Bottom#ping 10.1.1.1
Type escape sequence to abort.
Sending 5, 100-byte ICMP Echos to 10.1.1.1, timeout is    2 seconds:
.
00:37:12: %LINK-3-UPDOWN: Interface BRI0:1, changed state   to up
00:37:13: %LINEPROTO-5-UPDOWN: Line protocol on Interface BRI0:1 changed state
to up.!!!
Success rate is 60 percent (3/5), round-trip min/avg/max =    32/38/48 ms
Bottom#
00:37:14: %LINK-3-UPDOWN: Interface BRI0:2, changed state   to up
00:37:15: %LINEPROTO-5-UPDOWN: Line protocol on Interface BRI0:2,
 changed state to up
```

Notice that the five pings generated by the router completed before the second B channel came up.

It is quite common for up to the first three pings to fail in DDR ISDN connections. This is due to the two- to three-second delay in establishing the connection. It is usually not an indication of a problem. Also, be sure to ensure that ICMP is defined as "interesting traffic" for this interface, or the link will not come up at all.

clear interface bri n

The clear interface bri n command resets the various counters that are available on the interface and terminates a connection on the interface. The n value should equal the port, or port and slot, of the interface. This command is most useful for clearing a call that was activated by a dialer map or other catalyst, which may be desired when configuring and testing new access lists and other call triggers.

```
Bottom#clear int bri0
Bottom#
00:26:158913789951: %ISDN-6-DISCONNECT: Interface BRI0:2
    disconnected from 8358663 , call lasted 104 seconds
00:26:154624128828: %LINK-3-UPDOWN: Interface BRI0:2,
  changed state to down
00:26:36: %ISDN-6-LAYER2UP: Layer 2 for Interface BR0, TEI
  92 changed to up
00:26:36: %ISDN-6-LAYER2UP: Layer 2 for Interface BR0, TEI
  93 changed to up
00:26:37: %LINEPROTO-5-UPDOWN: Line protocol on Interface
  BRI0:2, changed state to down
```

show interface bri n

Information regarding the ISDN BRI D channel is available with the show interface bri
n command.

```
Bottom#show int bri0
BRI0 is up, line protocol is up (spoofing)
  Hardware is BRI with U interface and POTS
  Internet address is 10.1.1.2/24
  MTU 1500 bytes, BW 64Kbit, DLY 20000 usec,
    reliability 255/255, txload 1/255, rxload 1/255
  Encapsulation HDLC, loopback not set
  Last input 00:00:05, output 00:00:05, output hang never
  Last clearing of "show interface" counters never
  Input queue: 0/75/0 (size/max/drops); Total output   drops: 0
  Queueing strategy: weighted fair
  Output queue: 0/1000/64/0 (size/max total/threshold/   drops)
    Conversations  0/1/256 (active/max active/max total)
    Reserved Conversations 0/0 (allocated/max allocated)
  5 minute input rate 0 bits/sec, 0 packets/sec
  5 minute output rate 0 bits/sec, 0 packets/sec
    85 packets input, 791 bytes, 0 no buffer
    Received 4 broadcasts, 0 runts, 0 giants, 0 throttles
    0 input errors, 0 CRC, 0 frame, 0 overrun, 0 ignored,    0 abort
    92 packets output, 701 bytes, 0 underruns
    0 output errors, 0 collisions, 4 interface resets
    0 output buffer failures, 0 output buffers swapped    out
    1 carrier transitions
```

Note in the output that the command reports the D channel's status, as well as spoofing on the interface. This is due to the dynamic nature of DDR connections—they are up only when necessary. In addition, note that the interface was not configured for point-to-point protocol (PPP) but is using the default encapsulation of HDLC.

It is important for administrators to review the output of the show interface command, especially when researching user reports of slow performance. For example, the txload and rxload parameters provide a strong indication of bandwidth loads. Observe the (spoofing) tag in the following output as well. This indicates that the router is maintaining the link as though it was always active, even though ISDN is dynamic.

show interface bri n 1 2

The show interface bri *n* 1 2 command is used to display a single B channel of the BRI interface. In this example, the circuit is down.

```
Bottom#show interface bri0 1
BRIO:1 is down, line protocol is down
  Hardware is BRI with U interface and POTS
  MTU 1500 bytes, BW 64Kbit, DLY 20000 usec,
     reliablility 255/255, txload 1/255, rxload 1/255
  Encapsulation PPP, loopback not set, keepalive set (10      sec)
  LCP Closed, multilink Closed
  Closed: BACP, CDPCP, IPCP
  Last input 00:02:09, output 00:02:09, output hang never
  Last clearing of "show interface" counters never
  Queueing strategy: fifo
  Output queue 0/40, 0 drops; input queue 0/75, 0 drops
  5 minute input rate 0 bits/sec, 0 packets/sec
  5 minute output rate 0 bits/sec, 0 packets/sec
     219 packets input, 3320 bytes, 0 no buffer
     Received 219 broadcasts, 0 runts, 0 giants, 0    throttles
     146 input errors, 9 CRC, 59 frame, 0 overrun, 0           ignored, 78 abort
     279 packets output, 16195 bytes, 0 underruns
     0 output errors, 0 collisions, 0 interface resets
     0 output buffer failures, 0 output buffers swapped    out
     15 carrier transitions
```

Although the show interface bri *n* 1 2 command can be important when isolating an individual B channel problem, the show interface bri *n* command usually suffices for the majority of troubleshooting processes.

show controller bri

The interface hardware controller information is displayed with the show controller bri command. This command is most useful for troubleshooting with Cisco's TAC, but some information can assist the administrator as well. Most importantly, the status of the interface, in this case a U type connection is available in this show command.

```
Bottom#show controller bri
BRI unit 0:BRI unit 0 with U interface and POTS:
Layer 1 internal state is ACTIVATED
Layer 1 U interface is ACTIVATED.
ISDN Line Information:
    Current EOC commands:
        RTN - Return to normal
    Received overhead bits:
        AIB=1, UOA=1, SCO=1, DEA=1, ACT=1, M50=1,    M51=1, M60=1, FEBE=1
    Errors:  [FEBE]=0, [NEBE]=0
    Errors:  [Superframe Sync Loss]=0, [IDL2 Data       Transparency Loss]=0
             [M4 ACT 1 -> 0]=0
BRI U MLT Timers:  [TPULSE]=0, [T75S]=0
. . . some output omitted . . .
  0 missed datagrams, 0 overruns
  0 bad datagram encapsulations, 0 memory errors
  0 transmitter underruns
```

show isdn status

The show isdn status command is one of the more significant troubleshooting commands because the output reports not only the status of the interface, but a breakdown of each layer. As shown in the first output example, the router has established a connection at Layer 1, but Layer 2 either remains in a negotiation mode or has failed to negotiate due to an improperly set switch or router.

```
Top#show isdn status
Global ISDN Switchtype = basic-ni
ISDN BRI0 interface
dsl 0, interface ISDN Switchtype = basic-ni
    Layer 1 Status:
ACTIVE
    Layer 2 Status:
TEI = 79, Ces = 1, SAPI = 0, State = MULTIPLE_FRAME_     ESTABLISHED Spid
Status:
```

```
TEI 79, ces = 1, state = 8(established)
    spid1 configured, no LDN, spid1 NOT sent, spid1 NOT      valid
TEI Not Assigned, ces = 2, state = 1(terminal down)
    spid2 configured, no LDN, spid2 NOT sent, spid2 NOT      valid
    Layer 3 Status:
0 Active Layer 3 Call(s)
    Activated dsl 0 CCBs = 1
CCB:callid=0x0, sapi=0x0, ces=0x1, B-chan=0 calltype =       INTERNAL
Total Allocated ISDN CCBs = 1
```

The following display reports a correctly configured router and switch. Note that the SPIDs are confirmed and all layers are active on both B channels.

```
Top#show isdn status
Global ISDN Switchtype = basic-ni
ISDN BRI0 interface
dsl 0, interface ISDN Switchtype = basic-ni
    Layer 1 Status:
ACTIVE
    Layer 2 Status:
TEI = 83, Ces = 1, SAPI = 0, State = MULTIPLE_FRAME_       ESTABLISHED
TEI = 84, Ces = 2, SAPI = 0, State = MULTIPLE_FRAME_       ESTABLISHED
    Spid Status:
TEI 83, ces = 1, state = 5(init)
    spid1 configured, no LDN, spid1 sent, spid1 valid
    Endpoint ID Info: epsf = 0, usid = 1, tid = 1
TEI 84, ces = 2, state = 5(init)
    spid2 configured, no LDN, spid2 sent, spid2 valid
    Endpoint ID Info: epsf = 0, usid = 3, tid = 1
    Layer 3 Status:
0 Active Layer 3 Call(s)
    Activated dsl 0 CCBs = 0
Total Allocated ISDN CCBs = 0
```

Although show isdn status is most frequently used for new installations, field installations and SOHO (small office, home office) installations frequently find the ISDN device turned off when not in use. This is usually because the router has been plugged into a power strip attached to a PC.

When the router is disconnected from the ISDN circuit, the D channel (which is always "on") suddenly disconnects. Some phone companies view this as an error and disconnect the circuit on the central office switch. When the user returns power to the circuit, connectivity doesn't occur and the switch no longer expects a connection. The show isdn status command provides an indication of problems that require contacting the phone company. If there is a problem with an ISDN connection and the user has disconnected the power or the ISDN phone cable one potential problem could be that the phone company has disabled the circuit. To help prevent this problem, it is recommended that administrators instruct users that the cable or power is never to be disconnected.

show dialer

The show dialer command reports information regarding the DDR connections, including the number dialed, the success of the connection, the idle timers that control the duration of a DDR connection without data packets, and the number of calls that were screened or rejected due to administrative policy.

This command is useful for verifying a previous connection or checking the number called. Note that dialer map statements, which link network addresses to ISDN numbers, can be implemented incorrectly—for example, IP address 1 might be linked to number B instead of A. Although the router dials and the ISDN connection may succeed, the router cannot pass packets due to Layer 3 mismatches. Notice the Idle timer (120 secs) notation, which reflects the default Idle timer of two minutes for each B channel. The Idle timer shuts down the connection when no "interesting" packets have traversed the link.

```
Bottom#show dialer
BRI0 - dialer type = ISDN
Dial String      Successes    Failures    Last called  Last status
18008358661              2           0    00:02:49     successful
0 incoming call(s) have been screened.
0 incoming call(s) rejected for callback.
BRI0:1 - dialer type = ISDN
Idle timer (120 secs), Fast idle timer (20 secs)
Wait for carrier (30 secs), Re-enable (15 secs)
Dialer state is idle
BRI0:2 - dialer type = ISDN
Idle timer (120 secs), Fast idle timer (20 secs)
Wait for carrier (30 secs), Re-enable (15 secs)
Dialer state is idle
```

show ppp multilink

Multilink is an extended portion of the point-to-point protocol. As shown in italic in the following output, the service is configured with the ppp multilink bap and ppp bap commands. PPP multilink allows for the combining of both B channels in a connection to allow 128Kbps of throughput.

```
interface BRI0
```

```
ip address 10.1.1.2 255.255.255.0
no ip directed-broadcast
encapsulation ppp
dialer map ip 10.1.1.1 name Top broadcast 18008358661
dialer-group 1
isdn switch-type basic-ni
isdn spid1 0835866201
isdn spid2 0835866401
ppp multilink
dialer load-threshold 128 either
hold-queue 75 in
```

WARNING   The debug command is assigned a high CPU priority and can generate a high processor load. Always use caution when using a debug command. The resulting processor load and output can degrade router performance or render the system unusable.

TIP   It is recommended that routers be configured with timestamps for debug and log output. To provide debug time information, use the command service timestamps debug datetime msec and show-timezone localtime.

Debugging ISDN

The debug commands in ISDN are extremely helpful for researching problem causes and resolving them. This section addresses the commands and provides some useful methods for employing them. In addition, scenarios are described in which such commands may be needed.

debug bri

The debug bri command gives you information about the B channels of the BRI. An example of the command's output is provided here; note that bandwidth information is included.

The B channels of the BRI are the data-carrying channels; therefore, an error in the activation of a B channel prevents data flow. It is also possible for the router to command one B channel to connect while the other B channel fails, which may be due to a misconfigured SPID or configuration error. The command provides some insight into this potential problem.

```
Bottom#debug bri
Basic Rate network interface debugging is on
Bottom#ping 10.1.1.1
Type escape sequence to abort.
Sending 5, 100-byte ICMP Echos to 10.1.1.1, timeout is 2        seconds:
00:29:48: BRI: enable channel B1
00:29:48: BRI0:MC145572 state handler current state 3
  actions 1 next state 3
00:29:48: BRI0:Starting activation
00:29:48: %LINK-3-UPDOWN: Interface BRI0:1, changed state   to up.
00:29:49: BRI 0 B1: Set bandwidth to 64Kb
00:29:50: %LINEPROTO-5-UPDOWN: Line protocol on Interface
  BRI0:1, changed state to up
00:29:50: BRI 0 B2: Set bandwidth to 64Kb
00:29:50: BRI: enable channel B2
00:29:50: BRI0:MC145572 state handler current state 3
  actions 1 next state 3
00:29:50: BRI0:Starting activation
00:29:50: %LINK-3-UPDOWN: Interface BRI0:2, changed state   to up.!!!
Success rate is 60 percent (3/5), round-trip min/avg/max =     36/41/52 ms
00:29:50: BRI: enable channel B2
00:29:50: BRI0:MC145572 state handler current state 3
  actions 1 next state 3
00:29:50: BRI0:Starting activation
00:29:50: BRI 0 B2: Set bandwidth to 64Kb
00:29:51: %LINEPROTO-5-UPDOWN: Line protocol on Interface
  BRI0:2, changed state to up
```

debug isdn q921

The q.921 protocol addresses Layer 2 of the OSI model and its relationship to ISDN. Information regarding the D channel interface is available via the debug isdn q921 command.

The D channel is always connected in ISDN, and the channel is used for signaling between the switch and local ISDN device. Connections over the B channels cannot occur without signaling commands on the D channel. Administrators should use the debug isdn q921 command to monitor the proper flow of messages when calls do not connect. It is recommended that a baseline debug be performed and recorded to compare against the suspected problem debug output.

```
Bottom#debug isdn q921
ISDN Q921 packets debugging is on
00:19:15: ISDN BR0: TX -> RRp sapi = 0  tei = 92 nr = 12
```

```
00:19:64424550400: ISDN BR0: RX <-  RRf sapi = 0   tei = 92        nr = 12
Bottom#ping 10.1.1.1
Type escape sequence to abort.
Sending 5, 100-byte ICMP Echos to 10.1.1.1, timeout is 2      seconds:
.
00:19:23: ISDN BR0: TX ->  INFOc sapi = 0   tei = 92    ns = 12
  nr = 12   i = 0x080
10305040288901801832C0B3138303038333538363631
00:19:98789554100: ISDN BR0: RX <-  INFOc sapi = 0    tei = 92
  ns = 12   nr = 13
i =    0x08018302180189952A1B809402603D8307383335383636318E0B2
   054454C544F4E45203120
00:19:23: ISDN BR0: TX ->  RRr sapi = 0  tei = 92  nr = 13
00:19:103079256064: ISDN BR0: RX <-  INFOc sapi = 0    tei = 92  ns = 13
  nr = 13
 i = 0x08018307
00:19:24: ISDN BR0: TX ->  RRr sapi = 0   tei = 92  nr = 14
00:19:24: %LINK-3-UPDOWN: Interface BRI0:1, changed state   to up
00:19:24: ISDN BR0: TX ->  INFOc sapi = 0  tei = 92    ns = 13  nr = 14
  i = 0x080
1030F
00:19:103079215104: ISDN BR0: RX <-  RRr sapi = 0    tei = 92        nr = 14
00:19:25: %LINEPROTO-5-UPDOWN: Line protocol on Interface
  BRI0:1, changed state to up
00:19:107379488692: ISDN BR0: RX <-  UI sapi = 0    tei = 127
  i = 0x08010A05040288
9018018A3401403B0282816C094181383335383636337008C138333538    36    3632
00:19:25: %LINK-3-UPDOWN: Interface BRI0:2, changed state      to up.!!!
Success rate is 60 percent (3/5), round-trip min/avg/max =      32/38/48 ms
00:19:25: ISDN BR0: TX ->  INFOc sapi = 0  tei = 92    ns = 14
  nr = 14   i = 0x080
18A0718018A
00:19:107374223360: ISDN BR0: RX <-  INFOc sapi = 0    tei = 92  ns = 14  nr = 15
 i = 0x08010A0F
00:19:25: ISDN BR0: TX ->  RRr sapi = 0   tei = 92  nr = 15
00:19:27: %LINEPROTO-5-UPDOWN: Line protocol on Interface
  BRI0:2, changed state to up
00:19:36: ISDN BR0: TX ->  RRp sapi = 0  tei = 93 nr = 0
00:19:154618822656: ISDN BR0: RX <-  RRf sapi = 0    tei = 93        nr = 0
```

debug dialer

The debug dialer command tells you about the cause of a dialing connection and the status of the connection. Note in the following output that an IP packet caused the dial to occur. This information can provide assistance for tuning connections. Administrators frequently do this to limit the use of an ISDN circuit when charged on distance and per-minute tariffs.

```
Bottom#debug dialer
Dial on demand events debugging is on
Bottom#ping 10.1.1.1
Type escape sequence to abort.
Sending 5, 100-byte ICMP Echos to 10.1.1.1, timeout is 2      seconds:
00:27:26: BRIO: Dialing cause ip (s=10.1.1.2, d=10.1.1.1)
00:27:26: BRIO: Attempting to dial 18008358661
00:27:27: %LINK-3-UPDOWN: Interface BRIO:1, changed state   to up.
00:27:27: dialer Protocol up for BR0:1
00:27:28: %LINEPROTO-5-UPDOWN: Line protocol on Interface
 BRIO:1, changed state to up
00:27:29: %LINK-3-UPDOWN: Interface BRIO:2, changed state   to up.!!!
Success rate is 60 percent (3/5), round-trip min/avg/max =     32/37/48 ms
Bottom#
00:27:29: dialer Protocol up for BR0:2
00:27:30: %LINEPROTO-5-UPDOWN: Line protocol on Interface
  BRIO:2, changed state to up
```

debug isdn q931

The q.931 specification addresses Layer 3 of the OSI model for ISDN. Events occurring at Layer 3 can be monitored with the debug isdn q931 command. In the following output, the two B channels are disconnected.

The output from this command is best compared to a baseline debug captured on a working connection. However, administrators can use the output to verify acknowledgments and messages without a complete understanding of the protocol. There is a great deal of information provided by the following command. Among other valuable uses, this abundance of information can be used to verify the Layer 3 (q.931) setup.

```
Bottom#debug isdn q931
ISDN Q931 packets debugging is on
00:15:184683593728: ISDN BRO: RX <-  STATUS_ENQ pd = 8      callref = 0x82
00:15:43: ISDN BRO: TX -> STATUS pd = 8  callref = 0x02
00:15:43:         Cause i = 0x809E - Response to STATUS
```

```
   ENQUIRY or number unassigned
00:15:43:          Call State i = 0x0A
00:15:188978601984: ISDN BR0: RX <-  STATUS_ENQ pd = 8          callref = 0x06
00:15:44: ISDN BR0: TX ->  STATUS pd = 8  callref = 0x86
00:15:44:          Cause i = 0x809E - Response to STATUS
   ENQUIRY or number unassigned
00:15:44:          Call State i = 0x0A
00:16:55834615808: ISDN BR0: RX <-  STATUS_ENQ pd = 8     callref = 0x82
00:16:13: ISDN BR0: TX ->  STATUS pd = 8  callref = 0x02
00:16:13:          Cause i = 0x809E - Response to STATUS
   ENQUIRY or number unassigned
00:16:13:          Call State i = 0x0A
00:16:60129583104: ISDN BR0: RX <-  STATUS_ENQ pd = 8          callref = 0x06
00:16:14: ISDN BR0: TX ->  STATUS pd = 8  callref = 0x86
00:16:14:          Cause i = 0x809E - Response to STATUS
   ENQUIRY or number unassigned
00:16:14:          Call State i = 0x0A
00:16:188978601984: ISDN BR0: RX <-  DISCONNECT pd = 8          callref = 0x82
00:16:188978561024:          Cause i = 0x8290 - Normal call      clearing
00:16:188978601984:          Signal i = 0x3F - Tones off
00:16:44: %ISDN-6-DISCONNECT: Interface BRI0:1    disconnected    from
 18008358661 To p, call lasted 120    seconds
00:16:44: %LINK-3-UPDOWN: Interface BRI0:1, changed state   to down
00:16:44: ISDN BR0: TX ->  RELEASE pd = 8  callref = 0x02
00:16:188978601984: ISDN BR0: RX <-  RELEASE_COMP pd = 8          callref = 0x82
00:16:188978561024: %ISDN-6-DISCONNECT: Interface BRI0:2
      disconnected from 8358 663 , call lasted 120 seconds
00:16:44: ISDN BR0: TX ->  DISCONNECT pd = 8  callref =    0x86
00:16:44:          Cause i = 0x8090 - Normal call clearing
00:16:188978561024: ISDN BR0: RX <-  RELEASE pd = 8     callref = 0x06
00:16:44: %LINK-3-UPDOWN: Interface BRI0:2, changed state   to down
00:16:44: ISDN BR0: TX ->  RELEASE_COMP pd = 8  callref =     0x86
00:16:45: %LINEPROTO-5-UPDOWN: Line protocol on Interface
 BRI0:1, changed state to down
00:16:45: %LINEPROTO-5-UPDOWN: Line protocol on Interface
 BRI0:2, changed state to down
```

debug ppp negotiation

When the router is configured for point-to-point protocol, the debug ppp negotiation command provides real-time information about the establishment of a session. This is useful if connections are possible with the HDLC protocol but failures are occurring with the PPP protocol.

Substantial information is produced by the following command. Apart from that, it can be used to verify the PPP negotiation described earlier in the chapter. You should use this output to verify the troubleshooting targets in PPP negotiation.

```
Bottom#debug ppp negotiation
PPP protocol negotiation debugging is on
Bottom#ping 10.1.1.1
Type escape sequence to abort.
Sending 5, 100-byte ICMP Echos to 10.1.1.1, timeout is 2     seconds:
00:22:28: %LINK-3-UPDOWN: Interface BRIO:1, changed state   to up
00:22:28: BRO:1 PPP: Treating connection as a callout
00:22:28: BRO:1 PPP: Phase is ESTABLISHING, Active Open
00:22:28: BRO:1 LCP: O CONFREQ [Closed] id 3 len 10
00:22:28: BRO:1 LCP:    MagicNumber 0x50239604      (0x050650239604)
00:22:28: BRO:1 LCP: I CONFREQ [REQsent] id 13 len 10
00:22:28: BRO:1 LCP:    MagicNumber 0x5023961F      (0x05065023961F)
00:22:28: BRO:1 LCP: O CONFACK [REQsent] id 13 len 10
00:22:28: BRO:1 LCP:    MagicNumber 0x5.023961F      (0x05065023961F)
00:22:28: BRO:1 LCP: I CONFACK [ACKsent] id 3 len 10
00:22:28: BRO:1 LCP:    MagicNumber 0x50239604      (0x050650239604)
00:22:28: BRO:1 LCP: State is Open
00:22:28: BRO:1 PPP: Phase is UP
00:22:28: BRO:1 CDPCP: O CONFREQ [Closed] id 3 len 4
00:22:28: BRO:1 IPCP: O CONFREQ [Closed] id 3 len 10
00:22:28: BRO:1 IPCP:    Address 10.1.1.2 (0x03060A010102)
00:22:28: BRO:1 CDPCP: I CONFREQ [REQsent] id 3 len 4
00:22:28: BRO:1 CDPCP: O CONFACK [REQsent] id 3 len 4
00:22:28: BRO:1 IPCP: I CONFREQ [REQsent] id 3 len 10
00:22:28: BRO:1 IPCP:    Address 10.1.1.1 (0x03060A010101)
00:22:28: BRO:1 IPCP: O CONFACK [REQsent] id 3 len 10
00:22:28: BRO:1 IPCP:    Address 10.1.1.1 (0x03060A010101)
00:22:28: BRO:1 CDPCP: I CONFACK [ACKsent] id 3 len 4
00:22:28: BRO:1 CDPCP: State is Open
00:22:28: BRO:1 IPCP: I CONFACK [ACKsent] id 3 len 10
00:22:28: BRO:1 IPCP:    Address 10.1.1.2 (0x03060A010102)
00:22:28: BRO:1 IPCP: State is Open
00:22:28: BRO IPCP: Install route to 10.1.1.1
00:22:2.!!!
Success rate is 60 percent (3/5), round-trip min/avg/max =     32/38/48 ms
Bottom#9: %LINEPROTO-5-UPDOWN: Line protocol on Interface
   BRIO:1, changed state to up
```

```
00:22:29: %LINK-3-UPDOWN: Interface BRI0:2, changed state   to up
00:22:29: BR0:2 PPP: Treating connection as a callin
00:22:29: BR0:2 PPP: Phase is ESTABLISHING, Passive Open
00:22:29: BR0:2 LCP: State is Listen
00:22:30: BR0:2 LCP: I CONFREQ [Listen] id 3 len 10
00:22:30: BR0:2 LCP:    MagicNumber 0x50239CC8     (0x050650239CC8)
00:22:30: BR0:2 LCP: O CONFREQ [Listen] id 3 len 10
00:22:30: BR0:2 LCP:    MagicNumber 0x50239CDA     (0x050650239CDA)
00:22:30: BR0:2 LCP: O CONFACK [Listen] id 3 len 10
00:22:30: BR0:2 LCP:    MagicNumber 0x50239CC8     (0x050650239CC8)
00:22:30: BR0:2 LCP: I CONFACK [ACKsent] id 3 len 10
00:22:30: BR0:2 LCP:    MagicNumber 0x50239CDA     (0x050650239CDA)
00:22:30: BR0:2 LCP: State is Open
00:22:30: BR0:2 PPP: Phase is UP
00:22:30: BR0:2 CDPCP: O CONFREQ [Closed] id 3 len 4
00:22:30: BR0:2 IPCP: O CONFREQ [Closed] id 3 len 10
00:22:30: BR0:2 IPCP:    Address 10.1.1.2 (0x03060A010102)
00:22:30: BR0:2 CDPCP: I CONFREQ [REQsent] id 3 len 4
00:22:30: BR0:2 CDPCP: O CONFACK [REQsent] id 3 len 4
00:22:30: BR0:2 IPCP: I CONFREQ [REQsent] id 3 len 10
00:22:30: BR0:2 IPCP:    Address 10.1.1.1 (0x03060A010101)
00:22:30: BR0:2 IPCP: O CONFACK [REQsent] id 3 len 10
00:22:30: BR0:2 IPCP:    Address 10.1.1.1 (0x03060A010101)
00:22:30: BR0:2 CDPCP: I CONFACK [ACKsent] id 3 len 4
00:22:30: BR0:2 CDPCP: State is Open
00:22:30: BR0:2 IPCP: I CONFACK [ACKsent] id 3 len 10
00:22:30: BR0:2 IPCP:    Address 10.1.1.2 (0x03060A010102)
00:22:30: BR0:2 IPCP: State is Open
00:22:31: %LINEPROTO-5-UPDOWN: Line protocol on Interface
  BRI0:2, changed state to up
00:21:22: BR0:1 LCP: O ECHOREQ [Open] id 12 len 12 magic    0x5020C645
00:21:22: BR0:1 LCP: echo_cnt 1, sent id 12, line up
00:21:22: BR0:1 PPP: I pkt type 0xC021, datagramsize 16
00:21:22: BR0:1 LCP: I ECHOREP [Open] id 12 len 12 magic    0x5020C654
00:21:22: BR0:1 LCP: Received id 12, sent id 12, line up
00:21:22: BR0:2 LCP: O ECHOREQ [Open] id 12 len 12 magic    0x5020CD1B
00:21:22: BR0:2 LCP: echo_cnt 1, sent id 12, line up
00:21:22: BR0:2 PPP: I pkt type 0xC021, datagramsize 16
00:21:22: BR0:2 LCP: I ECHOREP [Open] id 12 len 12 magic    0x5020CD0D
00:21:22: BR0:2 LCP: Received id 12, sent id 12, line up
```

```
00:21:23: BR0:1 PPP: I pkt type 0xC021, datagramsize 16
00:21:23: BR0:1 LCP: I ECHOREQ [Open] id 12 len 12 magic      0x5020C654
00:21:23: BR0:1 LCP: O ECHOREP [Open] id 12 len 12 magic      0x5020C645
00:21:23: BR0:2 PPP: I pkt type 0xC021, datagramsize 16
00:21:23: BR0:2 LCP: I ECHOREQ [Open] id 12 len 12 magic      0x5020CD0D
00:21:23: BR0:2 LCP: O ECHOREP [Open] id 12 len 12 magic      0x5020CD1B
00:21:24: BR0:2 PPP: I pkt type 0x0207, datagramsize 15
00:21:25: BR0:2 PPP: I pkt type 0x0207, datagramsize 312
00:21:25: %ISDN-6-DISCONNECT: Interface BRI0:1    disconnected from
  18008358661 To p, call lasted 120    seconds
00:21:25: %LINK-3-UPDOWN: Interface BRI0:1, changed state   to down
00:21:107379488949: %ISDN-6-DISCONNECT: Interface BRI0:2
    disconnected from 8358 663 , call lasted 120 seconds
00:21:25: %LINK-3-UPDOWN: Interface BRI0:2, changed state   to down
00:21:26: %LINEPROTO-5-UPDOWN: Line protocol on Interface
  BRI0:1, changed state to down
00:21:26: %LINEPROTO-5-UPDOWN: Line protocol on Interface
  BRI0:2, changed state to down
```

debug ppp packet

The debug ppp packet command reports real-time PPP packet flow, including the type of packet and the specific B channel used. Although this command generates a significant amount of output, it is quite useful for locating errors that involve upper-layer protocols.

As with other debug packet commands, debug ppp packet records each packet that moves through the router using PPP. The administrator can thus monitor traffic flows as if a protocol analyzer were attached to the interface. This can be useful for troubleshooting Application layer problems, but a formal protocol analyzer is highly recommended.

```
Bottom#debug ppp packet
PPP packet display debugging is on
Bottom#ping 10.1.1.1
Type escape sequence to abort.
Sending 5, 100-byte ICMP Echos to 10.1.1.1, timeout is 2     seconds:
00:24:49: %LINK-3-UPDOWN: Interface BRI0:1, changed state   to up.
00:24:50: BR0:1 LCP: O CONFREQ [Closed] id 4 len 10
00:24:50: BR0:1 LCP:    MagicNumber 0x5025BF23     (0x05065025BF23)
00:24:50: BR0:1 PPP: I pkt type 0xC021, datagramsize 14
00:24:50: BR0:1 PPP: I pkt type 0xC021, datagramsize 14
00:24:50: BR0:1 LCP: I CONFREQ [REQsent] id 14 len 10
00:24:50: BR0:1 LCP:    MagicNumber 0x5025BF46     (0x05065025BF46)
```

```
00:24:50: BRO:1 LCP: O CONFACK [REQsent] id 14 len 10
00:24:50: BRO:1 LCP:    MagicNumber 0x5025BF46      (0x05065025BF46)
00:24:50: BRO:1 LCP: I CONFACK [ACKsent] id 4 len 10
00:24:50: BRO:1 LCP:    MagicNumber 0x5025BF23      (0x05065025BF23)
00:24:50: BRO:1 PPP: I pkt type 0x8207, datagramsize 8
00:24:50: BRO:1 PPP: I pkt type 0x8021, datagramsize 14
00:24:50: BRO:1 CDPCP: O CONFREQ [Closed] id 4 len 4
00:24:50: BRO:1 PPP: I pkt type 0x8207, datagramsize 8
00:24:50: BRO:1 IPCP: O CONFREQ [Closed] id 4 len 10
00:24:50: BRO:1 IPCP:    Address 10.1.1.2 (0x03060A010102)
00:24:50: BRO:1 CDPCP: I CONFREQ [REQsent] id 4 len 4
00:24:50: BRO:1 CDPCP: O CONFACK [REQ.!!!
Success rate is 60 percent (3/5), round-trip min/avg/max =      36/41/52 ms
. . . some output omitted . . .
00:25:03: BRO:2 LCP: O ECHOREP [Open] id 2 len 12 magic
      0x5025C605undebug all
All possible debugging has been turned off
Bottom#
```

Summary

Though originally designed to bring digital networking to the home environment, ISDN has evolved into a commonly used business tool. It allows small offices to connect to multiple disparate locations without the need for a dedicated circuit. This connectivity includes connecting back to the corporate office, to other businesses, to an ISP, and to many other locations. In addition, ISDN has also been used to provide backup services when a primary link fails.

Numerous component and connection types are used in ISDN. Acronyms have been assigned and used to better describe how each major component interacts with the other major ISDN components. Commonly used connections between major components were given abbreviations called reference points. The specific component acronyms and reference points are detailed in Figure 8.1 and textually explained in the section that follows this figure.

An ISDN BRI channel is made up of two 64Kbps B channels used for carrying traffic and a single 16Kbps D channel used for signaling. The signaling that is used over the D channel for call setup is q.921 for Layer 2, and q.931 for Layer 3. In addition, the most common protocol used for encapsulation on an ISDN link is PPP. With negotiation occurring over the B channels, PPP supports multiple Layer 3 protocols, such as IP, IPX, and AppleTalk. PPP also supports CHAP and PAP security.

When troubleshooting ISDN, numerous show and debug commands can be used. These commands allow for detailed analysis of the interface, q.921, q.931, and PPP. Some common commands are show interface, show ISDN status, show dialer, debug isdn q921, debug ISDN q931, and debug ppp authentication.

Exam Essentials

Know the basics of how ISDN operates.   Know that ISDN is a digital service. Also know the number and size of B channels and D channels and the use of SPIDs.

Know the ISDN components.   The components used in ISDN are TE1, TE2, TA, NT2, NT1, LT, and ET. In North America, the NT1 is the last component that is considered Customer Provided Equipment (CPE), whereas in most other locations the NT1 is carrier provided and maintained.

Know the ISDN reference points.   The reference points used in an ISDN connection are R, S, T, and U. If no NT2 is used, the S and T reference points combine to make an S/T reference point.

Understand how ISDN calls are set up.   Access lists are used in conjunction with dialer maps to define the traffic type that will bring up a link, as well as to specify the number that is dialed. In addition, authentication can be set up to ensure the validity of an incoming call.

Know the function of q.921.   The q.921 protocol in combination with LAPD is used to set up the Layer 2 connection over the D channel. The `debug ISDN q921` command allows for the debugging of specific q.921 information.

Know the function of q.931.   The q.931 protocol is used to set up the Layer 3 connection over the D channel. The `debug ISDN q931` command allows for the debugging of specific q.931 information.

Know how PPP is used and how it is set up.   LCP is used as the Layer 2 protocol for link establishment and maintenance. NCP performs similar functions for Layer 3 protocols. PPP also has the capability to use authentication. The `debug ppp negotiation` command can be used to look specifically at the PPP setup.

Know the function of CHAP and PAP.   CHAP and PAP are both authentication protocols used with PPP. These protocols allow for verification of both the calling and called devices. The `debug ppp authentication` command can be used to look at the CHAP or PAP authentication process.

Commands Used in This Chapter

The following list contains a summary of all the commands used in this chapter.

Commands	Descriptions
`clear interface bri` *n*	Resets the various counters that are available on the Basic Rate Interface (BRI) and terminates a connection on the interface.
`debug bri`	Provides information regarding the B channels of the interface.

`debug dialer`	Provides information regarding the cause of a dialing connection and the status of the connection.
`debug isdn q921`	Gives details regarding the Layer 2 connection sequence for ISDN.
`debug isdn q931`	Gives details regarding the Layer 3 connection sequence for ISDN.
`debug ppp authentication`	Gives details regarding the PPP/CHAP authentication connection sequence.
`debug ppp negotiation`	Provides real-time information about the establishment of a session.
`debug ppp packet`	Reports real-time PPP packet flow, including the type of packet and the specific B channel used.
`ping`	Initiates an ICMP echo request. There are two levels, User and Privileged. The IP protocol is used.
`show controller bri`	Displays the interface status and the superframe error counter.
`show dialer`	Reports information regarding the DDR connections, including the number dialed, the success of the connection, the idle timers that control the duration of a DDR connection without data packets, and the number of calls that were screened or rejected due to administrative policy.
`show interfacebri n`	Reports the B channel's status, as well as spoofing on the interface.
`show interfacebri n 1 2`	Displays a single B channel of the BRI interface.
`show isdn status`	Reports the status of the interface, as well as a breakdown of each layer.
`show ppp multilink`	Displays configuration settings for PPP multilink.

Key Terms

Before you take the exam, be certain you are familiar with the following terms:

Access lists	S reference point
Challenge Handshake Authentication Protocol (CHAP)	SAPI
Dialer map	service access point identifier
ET	Service Profile Identifiers
ISDN BRI (Basic Rate Interface)	SPIDs
Layer 1 S/T interface	S/T reference point
Link Access Procedure protocol	T reference point
local loop	TA
LT	TE1
NT1	TE2
NT2	TEI
q.921	terminal endpoint identifier
q.931	U reference point

Review Questions

1. Where does the q.931 signaling operate?

    A. At Layer 3 of the OSI model on the B channel

    B. At Layer 2 of the OSI model on the B channel

    C. At Layer 3 of the OSI model on the D channel

    D. At Layer 2 of the OSI model on the D channel

    E. On all channels of the BRI

2. What does the Basic Rate Interface (BRI) provide?

    A. 64Kbps of bandwidth in each direction

    B. 192Kbps of user bandwidth

    C. Two 64Kbps data channels and one management channel of 16Kbps

    D. Two 64Kbps data channels

    E. 128Kbps for user data

3. The remote router is connected to a DMS-100 switch using the `basic-dms100` setting. The local router would be configured with what command?

    A. `isdn switch-type basic-dms100`

    B. `isdn switch-type basic-basic-ni1`

    C. `isdn switch basic dms100`

    D. The answer cannot be determined from the information given.

4. Challenge Handshake Authentication Protocol (CHAP) requires which of the following? (Choose all that apply.)

    A. ISDN

    B. PPP

    C. A defined username

    D. Encrypted passwords on the router

    E. An external server running TACACS+

5. Router_A is configured for ISDN BRI and PPP, with an IP address of 192.168.10.1 and a subnet mask of 255.255.255.252. Router_B would be configured with which of the following?

    A. 192.168.10.254

    B. 192.168.10.2

    C. 192.168.10.3

    D. `ip unnumbered`

    E. The answer cannot be determined from the information given.

6.   An ISDN call initially succeeds, but pings and other packets fail. What is the likely cause? (Choose all that apply.)

   A. A faulty cable

   B. A misconfiguration of CHAP

   C. Incorrect speeds between the switch and router

   D. An incorrect route or missing route

7.   An administrator finds that an ISDN router does not dial. What are the possible causes? (Choose all that apply.)

   A. A misconfigured dialer map

   B. A dialer list filter

   C. An incorrect switch type

   D. Incorrect SPIDs

8.   What does the `clear interface bri` *n* command accomplish? (Choose 2)

   A. Clears the interface counters for interface *n*

   B. Disconnects all calls on the router

   C. Disconnects the active calls on interface *n*

   D. None of the above

9.   What are the advantages of CHAP? (Choose all that apply.)

   A. Password authentication

   B. Compression

   C. Encryption of data packets

   D. Encryption of the authentication process

10.   Which of the following command(s) restrict dialing on an ISDN router?

   A. `dialer-list 1 protocol ip list 101`

   B. `dialer list 1 protocol ip list 110`

   C. `access-list 200 permit ip any any`

   D. `dialer-map deny packet bri0`

11.   Which of the following is required for CHAP services?

   A. TCP/IP

   B. PPP

   C. PAP

   D. TACACS+

   E. Radius

12. Which channels must be active in order for ISDN BRI to send packets?

    A. Both B channels

    B. One B channel and the D channel

    C. Both B channels and the D channel

    D. All 24 B channels

13. Which of the following commands provide information regarding the status of the interface? (Choose two.)

    A. `show interface bri`

    B. `show controller bri`

    C. `show isdn sync`

    D. `show isdn controller`

14. In North America, a SPID might appear as which of the following?

    A. 10.1.1.1

    B. e415.5551.2120

    C. 41555512120101

    D. 5551212

15. To verify all three layers of an ISDN circuit prior to dialing, an administrator should use which of the following commands?

    A. `show ppp multilink`

    B. `show dialer`

    C. `debug bri`

    D. `show isdn status`

16. How long is the default ISDN Idle timer for each B channel?

    A. 30 seconds

    B. 60 seconds

    C. 90 seconds

    D. 120 seconds

    E. 300 seconds

17. Layer 3 of ISDN (q.931) is responsible for which of the following?

    A. Determining the switch type

    B. Call setup and disconnect

    C. Assignment of the TEI

    D. Encapsulation of packets on the B channel

18. What is the D channel used for? (Choose all that apply.)

    A. q.921 messages

    B. q.931 messages

    C. TCP/IP

    D. AppleTalk

19. If the switch type is unknown, which command can the administrator use to determine it?

    A. `isdn switch type 0`

    B. `isdn auto switch`

    C. `isdn autodetect`

    D. `isdn switch generic`

    E. None of the above

20. An administrator has a non-ISDN device (TE2). Which of the following is required to connect the device to the ISDN network?

    A. A terminal adapter (TA)

    B. Category 5 wiring

    C. Category 3 wiring

    D. A codec

    E. This device cannot be connected

Answers to Review Questions

1. C. q.931 runs on the D channel and is located at Layer 3.

2. C. Answers D and E are partially correct, but the correct answer is C: the BRI includes both B channels and the D channel.

3. D. Because ISDN switch type is only locally significant, it's possible that the remote end of a connection could use a different switch. Therefore, more information is needed before `switch-type` is configured.

4. B, C. PPP is required for CHAP to work on ISDN. Usernames must be defined on the routers for authentication purposes. The other options are not required for proper CHAP operation.

5. B. The subnet mask indicates only two hosts on the network. The only other host allowed is 192.168.10.2.

6. B, D. The possibility of a faulty cable can be eliminated because the call would not succeed if there were a cable fault. Speeds are default, so C is not a possible cause. If CHAP is misconfigured the call could succeed, only to be immediately torn down once CHAP authentication fails. And, an incorrect or missing route could cause traffic to be routed in a manner that is not intended.

7. A, B, C, D. Any of these situations can be the cause of the router's inability to dial.

8. A, C. The `clear interface bri n` command clears all active calls on a particular interface as well as clears the counters for that interface. It does not clear all the calls on the router. The interface must be specified to clear the call.

9. A, D. CHAP is intended for password authentication and encryption.

10. A. The correct syntax requires a hyphen between `dialer` and `list`.

11. B. PPP is a required protocol for CHAP to function.

12. B. One B channel can be used without the other. The D channel must be active to handle the call.

13. A, B. Both the `show interface bri` and the `show controller bri` commands provide information about the ISDN interface.

14. C. The SPID is appended to the 10-digit phone number.

15. D. The `status` parameter provides the necessary information.

16. D. The timer is set for 2 minutes idle time by default.

17. B. q.931 is responsible for the call setup and disconnect, since this occurs on Layer 3.

18. A, B. The D channel is used for administration and not data (payload) transfers.

19. C. The `isdn autodetect` command tells the router to listen for the switch type and set it accordingly.

20. A. A terminal adapter (TA) is required for a non-ISDN device.

Chapter

9

Troubleshooting Switched Ethernet

EXAM TOPICS COVERED IN THIS CHAPTER INCLUDE:

✓ Use Cisco IOS commands to identify problems.

✓ Rectify suboptimal performance issues at Layers 2 through 7.

✓ Rectify Layer 1 connectivity problems.

✓ Restore services back to baseline conditions.

Switching and virtual networking became the Holy Grail of manufacturers and customers alike in the 1990s. High-speed, low-latency bridging at Layer 2 provided the first inducement for administrators to purchase and install switches. By the late 1990s, switches were no longer restricted to Layer 2, and route- and port-based switching at Layers 3 and 4 were becoming commonplace.

Switching provides many significant advantages, including greater aggregate bandwidth at lower cost with collision (full-duplex) control. The downside of switching frequently includes a forklift upgrade in the wiring closet and slightly modified troubleshooting procedures. For example, it is not possible to simply plug a protocol analyzer into a port and see all traffic on the segment.

The Cisco Catalyst product line includes Ethernet, FDDI, Token Ring, and ATM switching. Although this section focuses primarily on the Catalyst 6500 product line, other Catalyst products are available and possibly better suited for some implementations.

Switches, Bridges, and Hubs

An understanding of switches and their functions requires an understanding of the differences between broadcast and collision domains.

The *broadcast domain* defines the scope of broadcasts within the network. Usually this is equal to the diameter of the subnet, because most upper-layer protocols rely on broadcasts to function. As such, the broadcast domain is usually controlled by routers.

Collision domains are defined by the scope of impact that a collision may have. With hubs, this scope is equal to all stations connected to the shared media; as the number of nodes and traffic load increases, collisions become a more significant problem for administrators and designers. Switches reduce this scope to two stations: the switch port and the end node. By using full-duplex Ethernet, which is an option available on most switches and newer NICs, collisions are no longer a factor.

On an Ethernet hub, the collision domain and the broadcast domain are the same—all ports receive all frames, and the receivers are required to analyze the destination address. If the frame is a broadcast or a unicast to the station (omitting multicasts), the frame will be processed further. The negative to this is unnecessary processing at all the workstations for which the frames were not intended. The collision domain on a hub is inclusive of all ports and stations on that hub. The broadcast domain on a hub is identical to the collision domain, although this assumes that a single hub represents the entire network or that a single hub is the only device connected to the router port. Technically, routers contain the broadcast domain. All other stations will hear any frame sent from a station on the hub.

The collision domain on a switch is limited to the individual port on the switch and its directly connected resource (workstation or other device). This greatly reduces workstation overhead because the frames received by the workstation should be intended for that station. In addition, the switch can provide a dedicated pipe to the workstation. Thus, a 10Mb network interface card can provide 10Mb, rather than sharing that bandwidth with all other stations. A small 12-port Ethernet switch provides a theoretical 120Mb of bandwidth, compared to the 10Mb provided by a standard Ethernet hub or the 20 Mb provided by a 2 port bridge.

Table 9.1 compares the differences between switches and hubs.

TABLE 9.1   Comparison of Switches and Hubs

Type	Switch	Hub
Unicasts	Sent only to destination port.	Sent to all ports.
Broadcasts	Sent to all ports defined to the same VLAN.	Sent to all ports.
Aggregate bandwidth	Equal to bandwidth of each port times number of ports. A 12-port Ethernet switch is capable of providing a total bandwidth of 120Mbit. (Note that backplane, processor, and other factors may change this simplification.)	Equal to speed of medium—an Ethernet hub would provide a total of 10Mbit.
Full/half-duplex	Full-duplex connections available.	Half-duplex only.
Support for mixed media:Token Ring, Ethernet, FDDI, and so on	Depending on the switch, translations may occur between frame types or physical media.	Supports single media.

Table 9.2 contrasts the differences between switches and bridges.

TABLE 9.2   Comparison of Switches and Bridges

Specification	Switches	Bridges
Support for mixed media	Usually.	Depends on bridge configuration.
Processing of frames	Hardware (ASIC).	Software or generic hardware.
Number of ports	From 4 to over 100.	Usually under 16; sometimes only two.
Frame type translation	Usually.	Depends on bridge configuration.

Catalyst Troubleshooting Tools

The Catalyst system provides significant diagnostic and administrative tools in the CLI (command-line interface). Troubleshooting switched networks frequently includes correlating Layer 2 addressing to Layer 3, and researching Physical layer problems. Although this section focuses primarily on the tools and commands themselves, a review of standards and typical problems will be presented later in the chapter.

Catalyst Command-Line Interfaces

Many administrators prefer the command-line interface (CLI), especially if they are already experienced with the Cisco IOS. Although the GUI applications can simplify many functions, and (in some cases) address functions not available from the CLI, they fail to provide the speed and simplicity of CLI.

In the case of Cisco switches, you may encounter two different CLI types, depending on the switch and the code running on the switch. These two variations of code that are available to run on the switch are called *Native* mode and *Hybrid* mode. Native mode syntax very closely resembles router configuration commands that have been covered up to this point in this study guide. This variation of command syntax is the only one available on switches such as the 1900 series, 3550 series and 2950 series. On switches in the 4500 and 6500 series, there is an option to run in either Native mode or Hybrid mode.

One major difference between running in Native mode and Hybrid mode is in how Layer 3 functionality, if present, is handled in the switch. In Native mode, the configuration for items such as the MSFC (Multilayer Switch Feature Card) in a 6500 is combined with that of the Layer 2 capabilities of the switch. In this manner, any configuration that is done on the switch, regardless of the layer, can be done via the same CLI. In Hybrid mode, Layer 2 switching functionality is controlled by one CLI, and the routing functionality is controlled by a separate CLI. The switching CLI of the Hybrid mode is also referred to as set-based because many of the configuration statements begin with the word set.

Though the focus of this chapter is on the Hybrid-mode switching CLI, you'll find a table, Table 9.6, at the end that shows the Native mode equivalents to some common Hybrid mode commands.

To avoid confusion, and unless specifically stated otherwise, the term *CLI* in this chapter refers to the Hybrid-mode switching CLI.

Hybrid Mode Catalyst CLI

The CLI provides a wealth of configuration and diagnostic tools for the administrator. Commands include the set and clear options that are used to configure the switch, and the show commands to monitor the current settings.

The show commands, displayed in enable mode with the show ? command, include the following:

accounting	Show accounting information
alias	Show aliases for commands
arp	Show ARP table
authentication	Show authentication information
authorization	Show authorization information
banner	Show system banner
boot	Show booting environment variables
cam	Show CAM table
cdp	Show Cisco Discovery Protocol Information
channel	Show channel information
config	Show system configuration
cops	Show COPS information
counters	Show port counters
default	Show default status
dot1q-all-tagged	Show dot1q tag status
dot1x	Show dot1x port capability & version
dvlan	Show dynamic vlan statistics
environment	Show environment information
errdisable-timeout	Show err-disable timeout config
errordetection	Show errordetection settings
fabric	Show fabric information
file	Show contents of file
flash	Show file information on flash device
garp	Show GARP information
gmrp	Show GMRP information
gvrp	Show GVRP information
ifindex	Show information for this Ifindex
igmp	Show IGMP information
imagemib	Show image mib information
interface	Show network interfaces
ip	Show IP Information
kerberos	Show kerberos configuration information
lcperroraction	Show action on lcp errors
log	Show log information
logging	Show system logging information
mac	Show MAC information
microcode	Show microcode versions
mls	Show multilayer switching information

module	Show module info
msfcautostate	Show MSFC derived interface state enabled/disabled
msmautostate	Show MSM derived interface state enabled/disabled
multicast	Show multicast information
netstat	Show network statistics
ntp	Show ntp statistics
pbf	Show PBF information
port	Show port information
proc	Show cpu and processes utilization
protocolfilter	Show protocolfilter information
pvlan	Show Private Vlan Information
qos	Show QOS information
radius	Show RADIUS information
rcp	Show rcp information
reset	Show schedule reset information
rgmp	Show RGMP information
rspan	Show remote switch port analyzer information
running-config	Show system runtime configuration
security	Show Security ACL information
snmp	Show SNMP information
span	Show switch port analyzer information
spantree	Show spantree information
startup-config	Show system startup configuration
summertime	Show state of summertime information
system	Show system information
tacacs	Show TACACS information
tech-support	Show system information for Tech-Support
test	Show results of diagnostic tests
time	Show time of day
timezone	Show the current timezone offset
top	Show TopN report
traffic	Show Traffic information
trunk	Show trunk ports
udld	Show Uni-directional Link Detection information
users	Show active Admin sessions
version	Show version information
vlan	Show Virtual LAN information
vmps	Show VMPS information
vtp	Show VTP Information

show system

The show system command provides high-level summary information regarding the switch, including the status of power supplies, uptime and administrative settings, and the percentage of traffic on the backplane.

```
Switch_A> (enable) show system
PS1-Status PS2-Status
---------- ----------
ok         ok


Fan-Status Temp-Alarm Sys-Status Uptime d,h:m:s Logout
---------- ---------- ---------- -------------- ---------
ok         off        ok         331,09:58:18   20 min


PS1-Type             PS2-Type
-------------------- --------------------
WS-CAC-1300W         WS-CAC-1300W


Modem   Baud  Backplane-Traffic Peak Peak-Time
------- ----- ----------------- ---- -------------------------
disable 9600  0%                11%  Thu Jul 10 2003, 01:30:06


PS1 Capacity: 1153.32 Watts (27.46 Amps @42V)
PS2 Capacity: 1153.32 Watts (27.46 Amps @42V)
PS Configuration : PS1 and PS2 in Redundant Configuration.


System Name            System Location          System Contact           CC
---------------------- ------------------------ ------------------------ ---
Switch_A               Dover, DE                Network Support


No active fabric module in the system.

Core Dump              Core File
---------------------- ----------------------
disabled               slot0:crashinfo


Switch_A-> (enable)
```

show port

The show port commands give you specific information about ports or all ports on a module. This includes commands that are available from other show commands, including show mac, for example.

```
Switch_A> (enable) show port ?
Usage: show port
       show port <mod_num>
       show port <mod_num/port_num>
Show port commands:
show port broadcast      Show port broadcast information
show port cdp            Show port CDP information
show port channel        Show port channel information
show port counters       Show port counters
show port fddi           Show port FDDI information
show port filter         Show Token Ring port filtering
                            information
show port help           Show this message
show port mac            Show port MAC counters
show port multicast      Show port multicast information
show port security       Show port security information
show port spantree       Show port spantree information
show port status         Show port status
show port trap           Show port trap information
show port trunk          Show port trunk information
```

The show port command output appears as follows. Note that VLAN membership, port speed and configuration, and error statistics are available.

```
Switch_A-> (enable) show port 3/3
Port  Name                 Status     Vlan       Duplex Speed Type
----- -------------------- ---------- ---------- ------ ----- ---------
 3/3  Switch_B 2/7 MxC     connected  980        full   1000  1000-LX/LH


Port  Security Violation Shutdown-Time Age-Time Max-Addr Trap     IfIndex
----- -------- --------- ------------- -------- -------- -------- -----
 3/3  disabled shutdown              0        0        1 disabled      13

Port  Num-Addr Secure-Src-Addr   Age-Left Last-Src-Addr     Shutdown/Time-Left
----- -------- ----------------- -------- ----------------- -----------
 3/3         0                 -        -                 -         -         -
```

```
Port      Broadcast-Limit Multicast Unicast Total-Drop
--------  --------------- --------- ------- --------------------
3/3                     -         -       -                    0


Port  Send FlowControl   Receive FlowControl   RxPause     TxPause
      admin    oper       admin     oper
----- -------- --------   --------- ---------   ----------  ----------
3/3   desired  off        off       off                0           0


Port  Status      Channel               Admin Ch
                  Mode                  Group Id
----- ----------  -------------------   ----- -----
3/3   connected   auto silent               7     0


Port  Align-Err  FCS-Err     Xmit-Err    Rcv-Err     UnderSize
----- ---------- ----------  ----------  ----------  ---------
3/3            0          0           0           0           0


Port  Single-Col Multi-Coll Late-Coll   Excess-Col Carri-Sen Runts     Giants
----- ---------- ---------- ----------  ---------- --------- --------- ---------
3/3            0          0          0           0         0         0         0


Port  Last-Time-Cleared
----- -------------------------
3/3   Mon Jul 7 2003, 05:56:31
```

show log

The show log command does not report events the same way that a Cisco router does. The command reports significant events, including reboots of all modules, traps, and power supply failures. Note that the following output reports power supply failures, along with module reset information in the period that may be useful information for the administrator if users report intermittent connectivity problems.

```
Switch_A-> (enable) show log

Network Management Processor (ACTIVE NMP) Log:
  Reset count:   13
  Re-boot History:   Aug 17 2002 04:11:13 0, Aug 16 2002 16:59:51 0
                     Aug 16 2002 16:56:42 0, Aug 16 2002 12:54:29 0
                     Aug 13 2002 19:37:45 0, Jun 13 2002 10:46:28 0
```

```
                    Jun 12 2002 16:06:00 0, Jun 12 2002 16:03:16 0
                    Jun 12 2002 15:58:29 0, Jun 12 2002 15:40:03 0
   Bootrom Checksum Failures:      0   UART Failures:              0
   Flash Checksum Failures:        0   Flash Program Failures:     0
   Power Supply 1 Failures:        1   Power Supply 2 Failures:    0
   Swapped to CLKA:                0   Swapped to CLKB:            0
   Swapped to Processor 1:         0   Swapped to Processor 2:     0
   DRAM Failures:                  0


   Exceptions:                     0


   Loaded NMP version:          6.3(5)
   Reload same NMP version count: 10


   Last software reset by user: 8/16/2002,16:59:30


   EOBC Exceptions/Hang:            0

Heap Memory Log:
Corrupted Block = none


NVRAM log:


Module 3 Log:
   Reset Count:   2
   Reset History: Sat Aug 17 2002, 04:13:04
                  Tue Aug 13 2002, 19:39:37


Module 4 Log:
   Reset Count:   2
   Reset History: Sat Aug 17 2002, 04:13:10
                  Tue Aug 13 2002, 19:39:42


Module 15 Log:
   Reset Count:   15
   Reset History: Sat Aug 17 2002, 04:12:25
                  Fri Aug 16 2002, 17:01:01
                  Fri Aug 16 2002, 16:57:52
                  Fri Aug 16 2002, 12:55:39
```

show logging buffer

The equivalent to the show log command on a router is the show logging buffer command on a switch. Depending on the logging level, show logging buffer can report on port up, port down, or spanning tree issues as well as just about anything else that is happening on the switch. The output of this command is as follows:

```
Switch_A> show logging buffer
2002 May 04 13:42:55 EST -04:00 %MLS-5-ROUTERADD:Route Processor
    10.4.0.254 added
2002 May 04 13:44:32 EST -04:00 %SNMP-5-MODULETRAP:Module 2 [Down] Trap
2002 May 04 13:44:32 EST -04:00 %SPANTREE-5-PORTDEL_FAILNOTFOUND:2/1 in
vlan 1 not found (RedundantTask)
2002 May 04 13:44:32 EST -04:00 %SPANTREE-5-PORTDEL_FAILNOTFOUND:2/2 in
 vlan 1 not found (RedundantTask)
2002 May 04 13:44:34 EST -04:00 %SYS-5-SUP_MODSBY:Module 2 is in standby mode
2002 May 04 13:44:34 EST -04:00 %SNMP-5-MODULETRAP:Module 2 [Up] Trap
2002 May 04 13:45:01 EST -04:00 %SYS-5-SUP_IMGSYNCSTART:Active
 supervisor is synchronizing the NMP image
2002 May 04 13:45:09 EST -04:00 %SYS-5-SUP_IMGSYNCFINISH:Active
 supervisor has synchronized the NMP image
```

show interface

The show interface command reports the IP configuration of the Supervisor module. Although the SLIP (Serial Line Internet Protocol) connection is configured on sl0, most installations use the in-band sc0 connection. As shown here, it belongs to VLAN 1, which always exists on the switch.

```
Switch_A> (enable) show interface
sl0: flags=51<UP,POINTOPOINT,RUNNING>
        slip 0.0.0.0 dest 0.0.0.0
sc0: flags=63<UP,BROADCAST,RUNNING>
        vlan 1 inet 10.11.10.1 netmask 255.255.255.0 broadcast 10.11.10.255
```

show cdp

Cisco Discovery Protocol (CDP) is an extraordinarily powerful troubleshooting tool. Available on all Cisco routers and switches, the protocol operates between Cisco devices on media that support SNAP. CDP has been available since IOS 10.3.

NOTE   CDP packets are sent as a multicast and are not forwarded by the router or switch. Specifically, they are sent to the destination MAC address of 01:00:0c:cc:cc:cc.

Following is a sample of the CDP report on a Catalyst 6506 switch with three neighbors:

```
Switch_A> (enable) show cdp neighbor detail
Device-ID: Router_A.domain.com
Device Addresses:
  IP Address: 10.1.1.1
Holdtime: 142 sec
Capabilities: ROUTER
Version:
  Cisco Internetwork Operating System Software
  IOS (tm) 4500 Software (C4500-J-M), Version 11.2(15a)P, P RELEASE
    SOFTWARE (fc1)
  Copyright (c) 1986-1998 by cisco Systems, Inc.
Platform: cisco 4700
Port-ID (Port on Device): FastEthernet0
Port (Our Port): 2/1
```

```
Device-ID: Router_B.domain.com
Device Addresses:
  IP Address: 10.1.2.1
Holdtime: 130 sec
Capabilities: ROUTER
Version:
  Cisco Internetwork Operating System Software
  IOS (tm) 4500 Software (C4500-J-M), Version 11.2(15a)P, P
    RELEASE SOFTWARE (fc1)
  Copyright (c) 1986-1998 by cisco Systems, Inc.
Platform: cisco 4700
Port-ID (Port on Device): FastEthernet0
Port (Our Port): 2/2
```

```
Device-ID: Router_C.domain.com
Device Addresses:
  IP Address: 10.10.1.1
Holdtime: 177 sec
Capabilities: ROUTER SR_BRIDGE
Version:
  Cisco Internetwork Operating System Software
  IOS (tm) C2600 Software (C2600-JS-M), Version 12.0(2a), RELEASE
   SOFTWARE (fc1)
  Copyright (c) 1986-1999 by cisco Systems, Inc.
```

Platform: cisco 2612
Port-ID (Port on Device): Ethernet1/0
Port (Our Port): 2/17

A CDP datagram decodes with EtherPeek, as follows:

Packet 3 captured at 05/22/2003 09:08:57 AM; Packet size is   302(0x12e)bytes
      Relative time: 000:00:01.473
      Delta time: 0.042.868
Ethernet Protocol
      Address: 00-00-0C-1B-63-97 --->01-00-0C-CC-CC-CC
      Length: 288
Logical Link Control
      SSAP Address: 0xAA, CR bit = 0 (Command)
      DSAP Address: 0xAA, IG bit = 0 (Individual address)
      Unnumbered frame: UI
SubNetwork Access Protocol
      Organization code: 0x00000c
      Type: Custom Defined
Flags: 0x80   802.3
  Status: 0x00
  Packet Length:339
  Timestamp: 16:40:23.689000 03/16/2002
802.3 Header
  Destination: 01:00:0c:cc:cc:cc
  Source: 00:00:0c:17:b6:f2
  LLC Length: 321
802.2 Logical Link Control (LLC) Header
  Dest. SAP: 0xaa   SNAP
  Source SAP: 0xaa   SNAP
  Command: 0x03   Unnumbered Information
  Protocol: 00-00-0c-20-00
  Packet Data:
  . _'....Router_A 01 b4 9e 27 00 01 00 0c 52 6f 75 74 65 72 5f 41
  ...6............ 00 02 00 36 00 00 00 03 01 01 cc 00 04 0a 02 01
  ... ._7.....   01 02 08 aa aa 03 00 00 00 81 37 00 0a 00 00 00
  ...._ 0b 00 00 0c 17 b6 f2 02 08 aa aa 03 00 00 00 80
  ....o....Ethern   9b 00 03 00 02 6f 00 03 00 0d 45 74 68 65 72 6e
  et1.......... C   65 74 31 00 04 00 08 00 00 00 01 00 05 00 d0 43
  isco Internetwor 69 73 63 6f 20 49 6e 74 65 72 6e 65 74 77 6f 72
  k Operating Syst 6b 20 4f 70 65 72 61 74 69 6e 67 20 53 79 73 74

```
  em Software .IOS    65 6d 20 53 6f 66 74 77 61 72 65 20 0a 49 4f 53
   (tm) 4000 Softw    20 28 74 6d 29 20 34 30 30 30 20 53 6f 66 74 77
  are (XX-J-M), Ve    61 72 65 20 28 58 58 2d 4a 2d 4d 29 2c 20 56 65
  rsion 11.0(17),     72 73 69 6f 6e 20 31 31 2e 30 28 31 37 29 2c 20
  RELEASE SOFTWARE    52 45 4c 45 41 53 45 20 53 4f 46 54 57 41 52 45
   (fc1).Copyright    20 28 66 63 31 29 0a 43 6f 70 79 72 69 67 68 74
   (c) 1986-1997 b    20 28 63 29 20 31 39 38 36 2d 31 39 39 37 20 62
  y cisco Systems,    79 20 63 69 73 63 6f 20 53 79 73 74 65 6d 73 2c
   Inc..Compiled T    20 49 6e 63 2e 0a 43 6f 6d 70 69 6c 65 64 20 54
  hu 04-Sep-97 14:    68 75 20 30 34 2d 53 65 70 2d 39 37 20 31 34 3a
  44 by richv....c    34 34 20 62 79 20 72 69 63 68 76 00 06 00 0e 63
  isco 4000           69 73 63 6f 20 34 30 30 30
Frame Check Sequence:   0x00000000
```

show config

The show config command is similar to the show running-config command on Cisco routers. The command provides all configuration settings on the switch for all modules, with a few exceptions for certain modules such as the MSFC (Multilayer Switch Feature Card). One difference is that show config only shows the nondefault configuration. If you want to see all the configuration on a switch, execute the command show config all.

Here is the output of show config:

```
Switch_A-> (enable) show config
This command shows non-default configurations only.
Use 'show config all' to show both default and non-default configurations.
..............
................
................
...................
..

begin
!
# ***** NON-DEFAULT CONFIGURATION *****
!
!
#time: Mon Jul 14 2003, 08:28:01 EST
!
#version 6.3(5)
!
set password Dsasdf84nsmth;dHRkt@#sdf.sdfgg
```

```
set enablepass $safgP$PO921asfdgIOUPIUKLJKJh1
set prompt Switch_A->
set banner motd ^C

                    NOTICE:

Legal warning - Only use for legitement purposes.

^C

!
#system
set system name  Switch_A
set system location Dover, DE
set system contact  Net Support
!
#!
#snmp
set snmp community read-only       public
set snmp community read-write      private
set snmp community read-write-all secret
set snmp rmon enable
set snmp trap enable  module
set snmp trap enable  chassis
set snmp trap enable  repeater
set snmp trap enable  vtp
set snmp trap enable  auth
set snmp trap enable  ippermit
set snmp trap 10.1.1.1 snmp port 162 owner CLI index 1
set snmp trap 10.2.2.2 snmp port 162 owner CLI index 2
!
#tacacs+
set tacacs server 10.8.8.8 primary
set tacacs server 10.9.9.9
set tacacs key good_key
!
#authentication
set authentication login tacacs enable console primary
set authentication login tacacs enable telnet primary
set authentication login tacacs enable http primary
set authentication enable tacacs enable console primary
```

```
set authentication enable tacacs enable telnet primary
set authentication enable tacacs enable http primary
!
#vtp
set vtp domain Switches_1
set vtp mode transparent
set vlan 1 name default type ethernet mtu 1500 said 100001 state active
set vlan 222 name Management type ethernet mtu 1500 said 10
0222 state active
set vlan 300 name Segment1 type ethernet mtu 1500 said 1009
66 state active
set vlan 301 name Crossconnect2 type ethernet mtu 1500 said 1009
68 state active
set vlan 302 name Accounting type ethernet mtu 1500 said 1009
70 state active
set vlan 303 name Travel type ethernet mtu 1500 said 1
00303 state active
set vlan 304 name Manufacturing1 type ethernet mtu 1500 said 1
00304 state active
set vlan 305 name Manufacturing2 type ethernet mtu 1500 said 1
00305 state active
set vlan 306 name Manufacturing3 type ethernet mtu 1500 said 1
00306 state active
set vlan 307 name Backoffice type ethernet mtu 1500 said 1009
80 state active
set vlan 308 name Network Support type ethernet mtu 1500 said 1009
83 state active
set vlan 309 name Finance type ethernet mtu 1500 said 1009
84 state active
set vlan 310 name Customer_Service type ethernet mtu 1500 said 1009
86 state active
set vlan 311 name Customer_Service2 type ethernet mtu 1500 said 1009
88 state active
set vlan 312 name Customer_Service3 type ethernet mtu 1500 said 100311
state active
set vlan 1002 name fddi-default type fddi mtu 1500 said 101002 state active
set vlan 1004 name fddinet-default type fddinet mtu 1500 said 101004
state active stp ieee
set vlan 1005 name trnet-default type trbrf mtu 1500 said 101005 state
active stp ibm
set vlan 1003 name token-ring-default type trcrf mtu 1500 said 101003
```

```
state active mode srb aremaxhop 7 stemaxhop 7 backupcrf off
!
#ip
set interface sc0 222 10.10.10.10/255.255.255.0 10.10.10.255

set ip route 0.0.0.0/0.0.0.0          10.10.10.1
!
#dns
set ip dns server 10.3.3.3 primary
set ip dns server 10.4.4.4
set ip dns server 10.5.5.5
set ip dns enable
set ip dns domain test.test-ap.com
!
#spantree
#vlan                    <VlanId>
set spantree fwddelay 15     1003
set spantree maxage   20     1003
set spantree disable  1005
set spantree fwddelay 15     1005
set spantree maxage   20     1005
!
#syslog
set logging server enable
set logging server 10.1.1.1
set logging server 10.2.2.2
set logging level cdp 5 default
set logging level earl 5 default
set logging level ip 5 default
set logging level pruning 5 default
set logging level snmp 5 default
set logging level spantree 5 default
set logging level tac 5 default
set logging level tcp 5 default
set logging level telnet 5 default
set logging level tftp 5 default
set logging level vtp 5 default
set logging level ld 2 default
set logging level privatevlan 2 default
!
#ntp
```

```
set ntp client enable
set ntp server 10.1.1.1
set ntp server 10.2.2.2
set timezone EST -5 0
set summertime enable EST
!
#set boot command
set boot config-register 0x102
set boot system flash bootflash:cat6000-sup2_6-3-5.bin
!
#cdp
set cdp version v1
!
#port channel
set port channel 1/2 5
set port channel 1/1 49
!
# default port status is enable
!
!
#module 1 : 2-port 1000BaseX Supervisor
set module name      1
set vlan 301  1/2
set vlan 302  1/1
set port name        1/1  Switch_A0 p1/1
set port name        1/2  Router_4 2/1
set trunk 1/1  off negotiate 1-1005,1025-4094
set trunk 1/2  off negotiate 1-1005,1025-4094
set port channel 1/1-2 mode off
!
#module 2 empty
!
#module 3 : 8-port 1000BaseX Ethernet
set module name      3
set vlan 300  3/7
set vlan 303  3/5
set vlan 304  3/6
set vlan 305  3/2
set vlan 306  3/1
set vlan 307  3/3
set vlan 308  3/4
```

```
set vlan 309   3/8
set port name        3/1   Switch_D Port 3/1
set port name        3/2   Switch_C Port 3/2
set port name        3/3   Switch_B 2/7 MxC
set port name        3/4   Switch_E 2/8 MxC
set port name        3/5   Router_1 Port 3/1
set port name        3/6   Router_2 Port 3/1
set port name        3/7   Router_3 2/1
set port name        3/8   Test_Net
set trunk 3/1   off negotiate 1-1005,1025-4094
set trunk 3/2   off negotiate 1-1005,1025-4094
set trunk 3/3   off negotiate 1-1005,1025-4094
set trunk 3/4   off negotiate 1-1005,1025-4094
set trunk 3/5   off negotiate 1-1005,1025-4094
set trunk 3/6   off negotiate 1-1005,1025-4094
set trunk 3/7   off negotiate 1-1005,1025-4094
set trunk 3/8   off negotiate 1-1005,1025-4094
set port channel 3/7 mode off
!
#module 4 empty
!
#module 5 empty
!
#module 6 empty
!
#module 7 empty
!
#module 8 empty
!
#module 9 empty
!
#module 15 : 1-port Multilayer Switch Feature Card
!
#module 16 empty
!
#cam
set cam agingtime 1     20000
set cam agingtime 222   20000
set cam agingtime 302   20000

end
```

show test

The status of the switch, including interface cards, power supplies, and memory, is available by using the show test command.

Observe that the first show test output reports only the status of the Supervisor module and no information specific to the other modules.

```
Switch_A-> (enable) show test

Diagnostic mode: minimal    (mode at next reset: minimal)

Environmental Status (. = Pass, F = Fail, U = Unknown, N = Not Present)
  PS1: .      PS2: .      PS1 Fan: .      PS2 Fan: .
  Chassis-Ser-EEPROM: .     Fan: .
  Clock(A/B): A           Clock A: .      Clock B: .
  VTT1: .    VTT2: .    VTT3: .

Module 1 : 2-port 1000BaseX Supervisor
Network Management Processor (NMP) Status: (. = Pass, F = Fail, U = Unknown)
  ROM:  .   Flash-EEPROM: .   Ser-EEPROM: .   NVRAM: .   EOBC Comm: .

Line Card Status for Module 1 : PASS

Port Status :
  Ports 1  2
  -----------
        .  .


Line Card Diag Status for Module 1  (. = Pass, F = Fail, N = N/A)

 Module 1
  Earl VI Status :
        NewLearnTest:            .
        IndexLearnTest:          .
        DontForwardTest:         .
        DontLearnTest:           .
        ConditionalLearnTest:    .
        BadBpduTest:             .
        TrapTest:                .
        MatchTest:               .
        Ingress/EgressSpanTest:  .
        CaptureTest:             .
```

```
        ProtocolMatchTest:         .
        ChannelTest:               .
        IpFibScTest:               .
        IpxFibScTest:              .
        L3DontScTest:              .
        L3Capture2Test:            .
        L3VlanMetTest:             .
        AclPermitTest:             .
        AclDenyTest:               .
        InbandEditTest:            .
        ForwardingEngineTest:      .

Loopback Status [Reported by Module 1] :
  Ports 1  2
  -----------
          .  .


InlineRewrite Status :
        InlineRewrite Test skipped as Minimal diagnostics selected
```

The following output provides the test results from module three of a Catalyst 6509. The module has eight ports providing 1000Mbit Ethernet. As a result of the show test 3 command, the switch reports the test results of the entire card.

```
Switch_A-> (enable) show test 3

Diagnostic mode: minimal    (mode at next reset: minimal)


Module 3 : 8-port 1000BaseX Ethernet

Line Card Status for Module 3 : PASS

Port Status :
  Ports 1  2  3  4  5  6  7  8
  ----------------------------
         .  .  .  .  .  .  .  .

Line Card Diag Status for Module 3  (. = Pass, F = Fail, N = N/A)

  Loopback Status [Reported by Module 1] :
```

```
Ports 1  2  3  4  5  6  7  8
----------------------------
        .  .  .  .  .  .  .

InlineRewrite Status :
     InlineRewrite Test skipped as Minimal diagnostics selected
```

show mac

The following output is from the show mac command. Because it is quite long, it was truncated from the original capture. For highly populated switches, this command requires a capturing program for later analysis. Note that numerous counters are maintained in normal operation, including the frame traffic per port; the total number of incoming frames, including discards; and the total number of transmits and aborts due to excessive deferral or MTU violations. Broadcast counters are also maintained in addition to discards. In some cases, an administrator may find the show port command more helpful in troubleshooting. Also, don't confuse this command with the show cam command explained later in this chapter. The show cam command shows the MAC to ports relationships on the switch, whereas, the show mac command provides port statistics.

The following output has been slightly modified for space considerations. RCV-M is representative of RCV-Multi. Xmit-M is used in place of Xmit-Multi, and Dcrd is used for Discard.

```
Switch_A> (enable) show mac
```

MAC	Rcv-Frms	Xmit-Frms	Rcv-M	Xmit-M	Rcv-Broad	Xmit-Broad
1/1	0	0	0	0	0	0
1/2	0	0	0	0	0	0
2/1	1840	1997	53	136	8	91
2/2	941	1026	56	133	4	95
2/3	6001	6489	0	187	26	73
2/4	776	1179	0	187	1	98
2/5	4951	6115	0	187	0	99
2/6	0	0	0	0	0	0
2/7	26	301	0	187	1	98
2/8	246	524	0	187	0	99
2/9	0	0	0	0	0	0

```
. . . some output omitted . . .
```

MAC	Dely-Exced	MTU-Exced	In-Dcrd	Lrn-Dcrd	In-Lost	OutLost
1/1	0	0	0	0	0	0

Port					
1/2	0	0	0	0	0	0
2/1	0	0	0	0	0	0
2/2	0	0	0	0	0	0
2/3	0	0	0	0	0	0
2/4	0	0	0	0	0	0
2/5	0	0	0	0	0	0
2/6	0	0	0	0	0	0
2/7	0	0	0	0	0	0
2/8	0	0	0	0	0	0
2/9	0	0	0	0	0	0

. . . some output omitted . . .

Port	Rcv-unicast	Rcv-Multicast	Rcv-Broadcast
1/1	0	0	0
1/2	0	0	0
2/1	1814	56	8
2/2	882	58	8
2/3	5996	0	26
2/4	793	0	2
2/5	5099	0	0
2/6	0	0	0
2/7	26	0	1
2/8	252	0	0
2/9	0	0	0

. . . some output omitted . . .

Port	Xmit-Unicast	Xmit-Multicast	Xmit-Broadcast
1/1	0	0	0
1/2	0	0	0
2/1	1819	141	97
2/2	798	140	101
2/3	6260	195	83
2/4	921	195	107
2/5	6104	195	109
2/6	0	0	0
2/7	16	195	08
2/8	242	195	109
2/9	0	0	0

. . . some output omitted . . .

Port	Rcv-Octet	Xmit-Octet
1/1	0	0
1/2	0	0

```
 2/1                    445231                405059
 2/2                    208680                300413
 2/3                   2935182               2876636
 2/4                     61427                114408
 2/5                    716265                601719
 2/6                         0                     0
 2/7                      3125                 53564
 2/8                     36993                 96826
 2/9                         0                     0
. . . some output omitted . . .


Last-Time-Cleared
-------------------------
Fri Jul 11 2003, 12:14:38
```

show vtp domain

The VLAN Trunk Protocol (VTP) is designed to simplify the introduction of VLANs in multi-switch networks. Within the management domain, a new VLAN is only specified once, and the configuration is propagated throughout the network. The configuration information includes the parameters needed for differing topologies within the switched network.

The show vtp domain command provides the following status information. Note that VTP updates are sent over VLAN 1 when troubleshooting VTP issues.

```
Switch_A> (enable)  show vtp domain
Domain Name          Domain Index VTP Version Local Mode   Password
-------------------- ------------ ----------- ------------ --------
Global                1            2           Transparent  -


Vlan-count Max-vlan-storage Config Revision Notifications
---------- ---------------- --------------- -------------
5          1023             0               enabled


Last Updater    V2 Mode  Pruning  PruneEligible on Vlans
--------------- -------- -------- -------------------------
10.1.2.20       disabled disabled 2-1000
```

show cam

Switches operate at Layer 2 of the OSI model, so MAC addresses are the basis for forwarding decisions. Although VLANs are typically assigned on Layer 3 boundaries, the switch directs unicast frames in the same manner as a bridge.

The show cam command reports the MAC address associated with the ports of the switch, as follows. Note the specifications that must be included with the command in the first output, followed by the actual MAC list in the second.

```
Switch_A> (enable) show cam
Usage: show cam [count] <dynamic|static|permanent|system> [vlan]
       show cam <dynamic|static|permanent> <mod_num/port_num>
       show cam <mac_addr> [vlan]
       show cam agingtime
```

```
Switch_A> (enable) show cam dynamic 1
VLAN   Dest MAC/Route Des   Destination Ports or VCs
1      00-80-2f-9f-54-5f    2/3
1      00-08-27-ca-c9-cd    3/18
1      00-08-27-ca-cd-da    3/23
1      00-08-27-ca-d1-20    3/27
1      00-08-27-29-89-80    3/44
1      00-08-27-29-88-a7    4/41
1      00-08-27-d2-ce-43    4/1
1      00-08-27-9a-0e-e9    3/13
1      00-08-27-ca-db-5e    4/38
1      00-08-27-ca-db-70    4/30
1      00-08-27-29-82-5d    2/22
1      00-08-27-8c-fd-e5    3/7
1      00-08-27-8c-fc-c0    3/32
1      00-08-27-d2-f8-10    4/43
1      00-08-27-ca-e0-47    4/29
1      00-08-27-ca-e0-6c    2/20
1      00-08-27-d2-fd-ab    3/2
1      00-08-27-d2-fe-4a    4/36
1      00-08-27-d2-fe-f5    2/24
1      00-08-27-d2-ff-c7    2/23
1      00-08-27-d2-ff-dd    4/45
1      00-08-27-d2-f1-87    2/8
Total Matching CAM Entries Displayed = 21
```

Duplicate MAC Addresses

Some network devices may be configured with the same MAC address on each interface, including certain dual-homed Unix workstations. This is a common event that can create substantial problems in the network. The show cam command is one of the best methods for finding this issue, although prevention via communication and change control can be more beneficial. If the administration of workstations and network services is divided in an administrator's organization, it is recommended that this issue be reviewed and that duplicate MAC addresses be used only when required. Documentation of the installation should accompany such a decision.

show spantree

Although the spanning tree process is covered later in this chapter, the use of spanning trees is crucial to the successful running of switched networks where loops may occur. The show spantree command reports the status of the spanning tree process for each VLAN, when enabled as follows:

```
Switch_A> (enable) show spantree
VLAN 1
Spanning tree enabled
Spanning tree type        ieee

Designated Root           00-90-86-fc-48-00
Designated Root Priority  32768
Designated Root Cost      0
Designated Root Port      1/0
Root Max Age   20 sec   Hello Time 2  sec   Forward Delay  15 sec

Bridge ID MAC ADDR        00-90-86-fc-48-00
Bridge ID Priority        32768
Bridge Max Age 20 sec    Hello Time 2  sec   Forward Delay  15 sec

Port    Vlan  Port-State      Cost   Priority  Fast-Start   Group-method
------- ----  --------------  -----  --------  ----------   -----------
 1/1    1     not-connected    19        32    disabled
 1/2    1     not-connected    19        32    disabled
 2/1    1     forwarding       19        32    disabled
 2/2    1     forwarding       19        32    disabled
 2/3    1     forwarding       19        32    disabled
 2/4    1     forwarding       19        32    disabled
 2/5    1     forwarding       19        32    disabled
 2/6    1     not-connected    19        32    disabled
 2/7    1     forwarding       19        32    disabled
 2/8    1     forwarding       19        32    disabled
 2/9    1     not-connected   100        32    disabled
. . . some output omitted . . .
```

show version

The show version command provides hardware and software version numbers, in addition to memory and system uptime statistics. The output of the command appears as follows:

```
Switch_A-> (enable) show version
WS-C6509 Software, Version NmpSW: 6.3(5)
Copyright (c) 1995-2002 by Cisco Systems
NMP S/W compiled on Feb  7 2002, 19:33:49

System Bootstrap Version: 7.1(1)

Hardware Version: 2.0  Model: WS-C6509  Serial #: SCA041603LL

PS1  Module: WS-CAC-1300W    Serial #: ACP04060383
PS2  Module: WS-CAC-1300W    Serial #: ACP04081148

Mod Port Model               Serial #    Versions
--- ---- ------------------- ----------- -------------------------------
1   2    WS-X6K-S2U-MSFC2     SAD061503TJ Hw : 3.5
                                          Fw : 7.1(1)
                                          Fw1: 6.1(3)
                                          Sw : 6.3(5)
                                          Sw1: 6.3(5)
         WS-F6K-PFC2          SAD061506DS Hw : 3.2
3   8    WS-X6408-GBIC        SAD041009YA Hw : 2.4
                                          Fw : 5.1(1)CSX
                                          Sw : 6.3(5)
15  1    WS-F6K-MSFC2         SAD061505U8 Hw : 2.2
                                          Fw : 12.1(2)
                                          Sw : 12.1(2)

        DRAM                    FLASH                    NVRAM
Module Total   Used    Free    Total   Used    Free    Total Used  Free
------ ------- ------- ------- ------- ------- ------- ----- ----- -----
1      262016K 69444K 192572K 32768K  7136K  25632K  512K  270K  242K

Uptime is 331 days, 10 hours, 44 minutes
```

RMON

Modern network devices provide greater visibility into the functioning of the network. Simple Network Management Protocol (SNMP) and *Remote Monitoring (RMON)* provide much of this visibility. RMON is another method for obtaining environmental and statistical information from devices. Much of the RMON technology implementation is based on the deployment of RMON probes that gather the information from the circuit (physical media) because the router or switch may not support all levels of RMON information.

Catalyst 6500 series switches provide internal support for four of the nine RMON groups defined in RFC 1757. These groups include port utilization and error statistics, historical statistics, alarm notification, and event logging. Additional monitoring may use the Switched Port Analyzer (SPAN) function, which is also referred to as *port mirroring*. Cisco's SwitchProbe product line can provide access to the other five layers of RMON in addition to the RMON2 groups. Examples of the commands used to configure a SPAN port appear later in this chapter.

Indicator Lights

In addition to what is supplied by the CLI, the Catalyst switch provides diagnostic information via LEDs on the line modules and the Supervisor engine.

The Supervisor engine includes load LEDs that indicate the current utilization of the switch. A high load (over 60%) may indicate a network problem, including a broadcast storm or the need for review of the network design. This set of lights is useful when troubleshooting in the main equipment room or wiring closet.

Following start-up, during which the LEDs will flash, the LEDs should appear steady green. An orange LED may indicate a problem; a red LED may indicate a failure.

Controlling Recurring Paths with Spanning Tree

Although there are differences, switches share many common positives and negatives with bridges. For example, bridges frequently hide larger network problems and are invisible to the administrator. This differs significantly from routers, which are visible through increments in hop counters and MAC address changes in each frame. Bridges do not modify the frame in any way, so a frame may traverse multiple bridges with no changes to the frame. A changing frame provides indications that facilitate troubleshooting.

One common problem in bridged networks involves loops, or a situation in which a single frame can continuously traverse the network. Note again that a bridge does not increment a counter—specifically, a time-to-live (TTL) value—in the packet to differentiate frame A from frame A the seventh time crossing the bridge. Such recurring paths can and should be controlled. The most typical method of control is called *spanning tree*. The spanning-tree algorithm is defined in 802.1D and is used to control recurring paths among multiple switches, thus avoiding loops in the network.

Should switches fail to prevent multiple forwardings of the same packet, and an administrator interconnects multiple switches (or bridges) between two segments, a loop can occur. This loop could theoretically take a single broadcast packet, which a bridge would automatically forward, and resend it hundreds of times. Refer to Figure 9.1. Station A sends a broadcast, Switch One forwards the packet to the yellow cable, and Switch Two sends the broadcast back to the blue cable. Switch One then receives a forwarded broadcast packet that is in turn forwarded to the yellow cable. This continues infinitely without some type of intervention or control built into the software on the switch.

FIGURE 9.1   A simple bridge/switch loop configuration

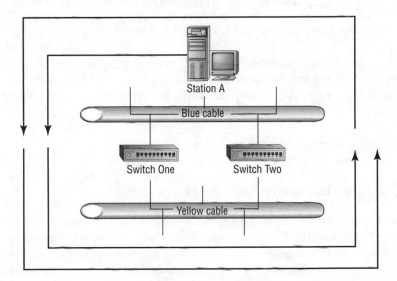

Station A

Blue cable

Switch One   Switch Two

Yellow cable

Notice that Figure 9.1 denotes a single flow of packets that move counterclockwise; however, in a real loop, the initial broadcast is also forwarded clockwise. Although different cable colors have been used in this example, both cables are within the same VLAN.

Although Figure 9.1 reflects shared media connected to switches, a switch/bridge loop can occur in an all-switched network. This diagram simplifies the physical connections involved by moving them "outside the box."

Logically, an administrator could avoid the entire loop issue by removing one of the two bridges/switches. Because only one path would exist, no loop is created. However, there are advantages to installing multiple switches or bridges. With multiple switches/bridges, the network can incorporate some degree of fault tolerance.

Troubleshooting Spanning Tree Problems

There are several troubleshooting targets for isolating and resolving problems relating to the Spanning-Tree Protocol (STP) in a switched network. The most essential aspect of troubleshooting spanning tree problems is to understand the protocol itself. It is also important to pay attention to indicators that there may be loops in the network. One simple indicator is the LED on the Supervisor engine: If the LED shows around 60% load, this may be a signal that loops are occurring.

Proper spanning tree functionality requires that there is only one unique bridge ID for each VLAN. You must also be aware that trunk ports on the Catalyst 6500 may belong to multiple spanning trees. This can cause the problem that if loops occur on one, the other spanning trees may be adversely affected. The show spantree command will display this information.

Spanning tree has many more implementation option than are listed here. If you would like more detailed information on Spanning Tree please see the *CCNP: Building Cisco Multilayer Switched Networks Study Guide, 3rd Ed.*

When the Cisco port-fast and uplink-fast modes are enabled on ports, some of the transitions of the spanning tree algorithm are skipped. This could add to the potential of loops in the network. The show spantree command also reports whether the fast-start option has been enabled on a port-by-port basis.

 Real World Scenario

Eliminating Boot-Up Errors in a Switched Environment

Though the controls put in place to prevent spanning tree loops are necessary in order to ensure a stable network, they can have unintended side effects. If an operating system manufacturer has optimized its operating system to immediately start using the network connection, the length of delay caused by the spanning tree loop-detection process, usually around 35 seconds, can generate an error. These errors can manifest as "No Domain Controller Found" messages in an NT environment, or even a "No DHCP Server Available."

To avoid these problems, we have found it best to set up user and server ports on the switch differently from the setup for ports that connect to other routers, switches, and hubs. Specifically, on user and server ports, we enable spantree portfast, and disable EtherChannel negotiation and trunk negotiation. In addition, we also hard-code the speed and duplex settings on the port. In this manner, the switch port starts forwarding any packets seen from this port immediately after a link is detected. This effectively eliminates the errors caused by detection delays.

There are a couple of drawbacks to this arrangement. The first and most obvious is that more manual configuration is required anytime there is a move, add, or change in the environment. The second drawback is that ports are not checked when they come up to see if there is a spanning tree loop. Note that spanning tree is still running on the port even with spantree portfast enabled. Therefore, a loop will be detected if it's there, and the appropriate port put into blocking mode. However, this loop will not be detected before traffic from the port is allowed through. Thus there is potential for a broadcast storm after the port is brought up but before the spanning tree protocol detects and eliminates the loop. Even with these drawbacks, I have found that the overall benefit to configuring user and server ports in this manner outweighs the risks.

Virtual LANs

In their simplest form, *virtual LANs* (or *VLANs*) are no different from traditional LANs. The virtual component comes from the capability to define memberships based on individual ports, as administered by either a physical port or a dynamic relationship to the MAC address.

VLANs can potentially reduce the costs associated with moves, adds, and changes, in addition to reducing the costs for unused ports on non-VLAN hubs and switches. However, VLAN technology adds to the initial costs and may require additional training. It is not uncommon to find a single switch serving more than one subnetwork. This logical segmentation of ports can create its own set of troubleshooting issues. However, the VLAN's increased port utilization and other cost savings will more than offset these issues.

Administrators unaccustomed to segmented switches may find VLANs confusing. With hubs, all ports are part of the same network, and most networks are configured with a separate hub for each subnet—even if that subnet contains as few as two devices. Switches with VLAN capabilities, with their higher port cost and necessary management systems, may have three or four subnets connected into the same chassis. In troubleshooting, it is important to have an accurate understanding of the current switch configuration and of VLAN definitions, and—more importantly— to have verification that the end nodes match those definitions. It is not uncommon for a port to be defined to VLAN 1, where the workstation is configured with an IP address and default gateway matching VLAN 5. Under such circumstances, the workstation support staff will incorrectly believe that the configuration is correct, and the network administrator will document that the port is correct. In addition to the `show port` command, it is important to have valid documentation of all VLANs and the associated network configurations for each VLAN.

Inter-Switch Link (ISL)

It is not possible for a switch to forward datagrams from one VLAN to another without a router or routing function. Recall that switches operate at Layer 2 of the OSI model, and although switches are available with routing engines and even Layer 4 processors, this section will retain a definition limited to Layer 2.

Inter-Switch Link (ISL) is a Cisco proprietary method of interconnecting two devices that support VLANs. These connections provide the administrator with a cost-effective option in deploying switches and VLANs in the network. For example, a normal switch installation requires that a single port in each VLAN be connected to the corresponding router interface, assuming a typical installation in which each VLAN is a logical extension of a subnet. This requires *n* ports on the router, in addition to the same number of ports on the switch.

Although this solution is easy to install and provides each VLAN with a dedicated 10Mb or 100Mb port on the router, it also greatly increases the costs and fails to account for differences in local and remote traffic. Recall that networks were historically designed with 80% of the traffic remaining on the local subnet. Although the percentage of local traffic is significantly lower today, it is still unlikely that you would find all traffic leaving the subnet.

What would happen if *n* VLANs on the switch could share a single 100Mb connection to the router? The number of ports used for connectivity would equal two, as opposed to (*n**2), and the available number of ports for servers and workstations would increase substantially.

In this section, the use of ISL was defined with a switch-to-router connection. ISL should also be considered when the administrator wishes to connect multiple switches that are members of the same VLAN.

Administrators must keep the following issues in mind when considering ISL:

- ISL is available only on products that support ISL. Although a number of other vendors have licensed ISL technology (including Intel), the standard is proprietary to Cisco, and fewer vendors support the ISL standard compared to IEEE 802.1Q. In addition, with the release of 802.1Q and gigabit interfaces, Cisco has altered the default trunk encapsulation in favor of 802.1Q. Gigabit EtherChannel trunk links default to 802.1Q, whereas non-EtherChannel gigabit ports negotiate ISL or 802.1Q. Fast Ethernet ports, as of this writing, continue to default to ISL.

- ISL links must be point-to-point.

- ISL should only be used on 100Mb full-duplex or greater connections. Although it is possible to use ISL on 10Mb links, the limited bandwidth and other considerations make such a plan impractical.

- ISL may require an upgrade of the IOS or memory on the router.

- ISL can encapsulate Token Ring. This is referred to as ISL+.

- ISL adds 30 octets to the original frame (26 bytes in the header and an additional 4 byte CRC), which is encapsulated without modification.

- ISL includes a CRC value at the end of the frame.

Because ISL is an encapsulation of the original frame, an administrator must consider the overhead generated to support the encapsulation. Frequently, the available bandwidth is more than sufficient to cover this additional load. ISL adds 30 octets to the length of the original frame. In the case of Ethernet, this results in a frame 1548 octets long.

The ISL frame is shown in Figure 9.2.

FIGURE 9.2   The ISL encapsulation

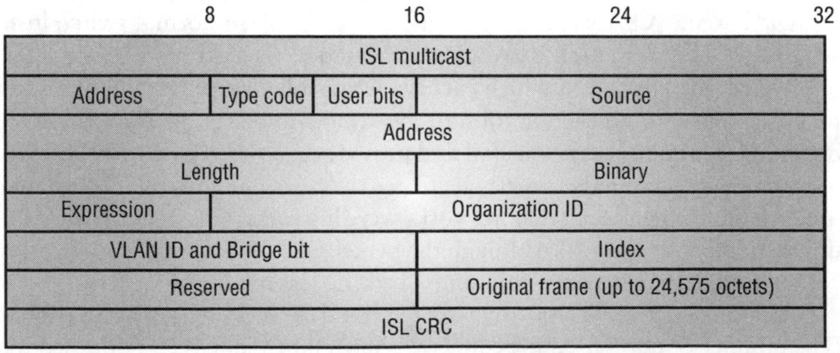

	8		16		24		32
ISL multicast							
Address		Type code	User bits		Source		
Address							
Length				Binary			
Expression			Organization ID				
VLAN ID and Bridge bit				Index			
Reserved				Original frame (up to 24,575 octets)			
ISL CRC							

Figure 9.2 is indexed in Table 9.3.

TABLE 9.3   Key for Figure 9.2

Figure Symbol	Definition
ISL multicast address	The ISL multicast address of 01:00:0C:00:00. *Note that this is a 40-bit value.*
Type code	The encapsulated frame's type code. For Ethernet, this is 0000. Token Ring frames are defined with 0001, and FDDI is marked with 0010. Type code 0011 is reserved for ATM.
User bits	The user-defined bits are used to mark the encapsulated frame's priority. Frames marked 0000 are processed as normal priority; 0011 marks the frame as high priority.
Source address	This is the 48-bit MAC address of the source port.
Length	The length field defines the length of the ISL frame minus the multicast address, the type and user-defined bits, and the source address of the ISL packet. The length field also omits its own length and the CRC from the 16-bit value. Thus, the length is always equal to the length of the ISL frame minus 18 octets.
Binary expression	ISL frames use SNAP LLC, and the binary expression decodes to AA:AA:03, which is the same as the SNAP header.
Organization ID	The Organization ID bits provide the unique organization identifier of the source address. This is equal to the first three octets of the MAC address.
VLAN ID; Bridge bit	The VLAN identifier is a 15-bit value that identifies the VLAN membership of the frame. Cisco uses only 10 bits in this header to support up to 1024 virtual LANs. The bridge bit is set for all encapsulated bridge protocol frames, including spanning tree updates, in addition to Cisco's CDP and VTP (VLAN Trunking Protocol) packets.
Index	Useful for troubleshooting and contains the source port value of the frame.
Reserved	The reserved bits are set to zero for Ethernet frames. However, when ISL encapsulates Token Ring, the access control (AC) and frame information (FC) octets are duplicated here. When encapsulating FDDI, the frame control octet is prefixed with 0x00 and copied in this field.

TABLE 9.3   Key for Figure 9.2 *(continued)*

Figure Symbol	Definition
Original frame	This field may be 24,575 octets long and includes Ethernet, Token Ring, or FDDI frames—along with the original CRC value for the encapsulated frame.
ISL CRC	This field is a new 32-bit CRC that is calculated for the entire ISL frame. It is calculated using the entire ISL frame, including the original frame.

802.1Q Trunking

Although the *IEEE 802.1Q* standard is similar to the Cisco proprietary ISL protocol in terms of function, as a standard it may be used to connect non-Cisco trunks to Cisco equipment. Note that the 802.1Q encapsulation is accessed with the command `encapsulation dot1Q`, which is available in IOS versions 12.0.1(t) and higher on routers and in CatOS 4.1 on the Catalyst 6500 switches.

ISL provides additional functions, when compared with 802.1Q. For example, spanning trees are handled somewhat better in ISL. Nevertheless, 802.1Q should be recommended in any network that does not adhere to a strict Cisco-only policy, given the proprietary concerns.

From a troubleshooting perspective, 802.1Q requires the same understanding of the VLAN's relationships to the subnets that are beneficial in all switching diagnostics. The 802.1Q header differs from the ISL header, in that only 4 octets are added to the frame, as compared to the 30 added in ISL. Also, the 802.1Q information is not wrapped around the original packet—the VLAN information is inserted into the frame, following the destination and source addresses in the original packet. This lack of overhead is another benefit of 802.1Q.

Most protocol analyzers provide decode filters for 802.1Q in their current releases, but administrators should check with their vendor to ensure this functionality is supported. It is rare that the problem is directly related to the tag information itself (although administrators should consider this in researching trunk problems). Rather, most trunking problems, along with 802.1Q, result from misconfiguration of the VLANs or mismatches between two sides of the trunk. Though they serve similar functions, ISL cannot connect to 802.1Q on the same link.

VLAN Trunking Protocol (VTP)

The *VLAN Trunking Protocol (VTP)* uses multicast messages to inform all other switches in the VTP domain about the VLANs within the domain. This domain is a management domain that allows control of the VTP multicast updates. A switch can be configured with three different VTP settings.

VTP Server   The server maintains the VLAN information for the VTP domain. If you are operating with a VTP server to which clients are connecting, all VLAN modifications, additions, and deletions must be done on the VTP server. These changes will then be propagated down to all the VTP clients in the domain. Trunk ports are then reconfigured to allow traffic from the new VLAN.

VTP Client   The client also maintains a copy of the VLAN information for the domain and will transmit any changes received from the VTP server to other VTP clients in the same domain that are connected to the client. When a change is detected, the trunk ports are then reconfigured to allow traffic from the new VLAN.

VTP Transparent   When a switch is in transparent mode, changes made on the VTP server do not affect VLANs on this switch. The switch does, however, continue to forward VTP advertisements if you are running VTP version 2. If you need to modify, add, or delete VLAN from a switch in transparent mode, it must be done on the switch itself.

Cabling Issues

Today's networks operate at higher speeds than ever before. Bandwidth is measured in gigabits, with individual workstations accessing 100Mb connections or faster. Only recently it was still common to find a hundred stations sharing a 10Mb segment.

Higher speeds bring added complexity at the Physical layer of the network. Installations must adhere to strict tolerances regarding distance, cable type, and installation to permit proper operation. This creates new troubleshooting issues for the administrator.

Frequently, an administrator will convert a workstation to 100Mb (Fast) Ethernet, and will find an excessive number of errors that degrade performance so much that the link becomes unusable. The type of cable or the distance between the switch and workstation may cause this. For example, perhaps the original installation used Category 3 cable. Although satisfactory for 10Mb Ethernet, 100Mb Ethernet requires the higher-capacity Category 5. Also, though the distance for both 10Mb and 100Mb Ethernet on copper media is 100 meters, it is possible to use longer lengths for 10Mb without degradation. When converting to 100Mb, problems may become evident. Consideration of the Physical layer is imperative when troubleshooting switched networks. Table 9.4 presents the Physical layer limitations.

TABLE 9.4   Physical Layer Standards

Cable	10Mb	100Mb
Distance with Category 3 copper	100 meters	Not available, per 100BaseTX standard
Distance with Category 5 copper	100 meters	100 meters
Distance with Multi Mode fiber	2000 meters	2000 meters
Distance with Single Mode fiber	Up to 100 km	Up to 100 km

Half-duplex Fast Ethernet implementations limit the Multi Mode fiber distance to 400 meters to allow for the round-trip time of the packet transmission.

Cable Problems

Cable problems may appear as intermittent issues or as a single failure. Clearly, the intermittent issues provide greater challenges, especially if the problem is of very short duration. An intermittent cable problem may appear as slow performance or failure of the workstation. In most cases the port to which the workstation is attached will show an increasing number of interfaces errors. These could be in the form of runts, CRCs (cyclic redundancy checks), and/or FCS (frame check sequence) errors. In addition cabling runs that are longer than allowed by Ethernet specifications can also cause late collisions. However, it should be noted that these errors could be caused by a misconfigured or malfunctioning NIC as well.

An analyzer may be the best method for finding cable problems, and administrators should be familiar with the operation of an available cable tester, time domain reflectometer (TDR), or handheld analyzer. Even when certified by the cable installer, cables can break or develop problems during subsequent activity in the conduit or at the jack. In addition to a tester, it is a good idea to have spare cables on hand, and a crimp set to quickly reterminate circuits when troubleshooting.

Multimeters and Cable Testers

There is a large variety of physical media testing equipment. The most basic tools are multimeters and cable testers.

Both *volt-ohm meters* and *multimeters* measure voltage (AC and DC), resistance, and current. In addition, these devices can also be used to verify the continuity of a cable run from end to end. As is alluded to above, these devices deal with electrical signals. Therefore, they can only be used to test copper (or other electrically based) wiring, and cannot be used to test any fiber optic wiring.

Cable testers can be very general or they can be made for a specific type of cable. Some cable testers have adapters that allow them to test a wide range of cables such as unshielded twisted pair (UTP), shielded twisted pair (STP), or coaxial (coax) cable. Cable testers are made for electrical and optical cable.

Different from multimeters, cable testers can give the user much more information regarding the cable being tested. Cable testers come in varieties that can test both electrical and optical cables. Below are some examples of the attributes that are reported by an electrical cable tester:

- Electrical connectivity
- Open pairs
- Crossed pairs
- Out of distance specification
- Cross talk

- Attenuation
- Noise/interference
- Wiring maps
- MAC information
- Line utilization

Optical cable testers verify the same sort of information as electrical; however, they obviously use optical signals in place of electrical. In general, there are three different wavelengths that are predominantly used by optical cable testers: 850 nm, 1300 nm, and 1550 nm. Through the use of these wavelengths and by transmitting at a known power level, optical cable testers are able to measure attenuation and return loss on the fiber.

> **NOTE** It is important to realize that not all cable testers provide all of this information. A given tester may provide only some of these attributes.

Time Domain Reflectors (TDRs) and Optical TDRs (OTDRs)

Time domain reflectors (TDRs) are complex cable testers. They are used to locate physical problems in a cable. They can detect where an open circuit, short circuit, crimped wire, or other abnormality is located in a cable.

TDRs and optical TDRs (OTDRs) work on the same principle: a signal is sent down the cable and the unit waits for the reflected signal to come back. Different abnormalities in cabling cause this signal to be reflected at different signal strengths, or amplitudes. Based on the amplitude, the meter distinguishes between opens, shorts, crimps, or other failures in the cable. These meters measure the time between the sending of the signal and the arrival of the reflected signal at the unit. This time interval is used to calculate where the failure is occurring in the cable. Optical TDRs can also provide information on conditions such as signal attenuation, fiber breaks, and losses through connectors.

Crossover Cables

A surprising number of network administrators have not used crossover cables, particularly when their previous experience is from the workstation installation and configuration segments of Information Services or other Information Technology departments. In other companies, such cables are used only when absolutely necessary and with a great deal of documentation, including highly recommended color-coding.

Normally, a workstation is connected to a hub that does not require the crossover of the transmit and receive pairs in the wire. However, there are times when a connection is needed and the pairs must be crossed. This occurs when connecting two 10BaseT workstations together without a hub, or when connecting two network devices. Note that some devices provide a button or other administrator-selectable setting to enable or disable the function. Small hubs frequently provide this with an "uplink" port.

Connectivity problems can occur when the wrong type of cable is installed or when a selectable port is set incorrectly. This error may be masked by link lights and other indications that the connection is correct. The only way to isolate this problem is to look at the colors in the cube (the RJ-45 connector) and verify that they are correct.

Figure 9.3 shows the appropriate pinout for an Ethernet crossover cable. It may be appropriate when troubleshooting to swap the original cable for another of the opposite type. This provides a quick check of the cable, and substituting a straight-through cable for a crossover cable may lead to evidence of equipment that is mislabeled or misconfigured. Note that Ethernet uses wires 1, 2, 3, and 6, while T1 circuits on RJ-45 use wires 1, 2, 4, and 5. Swapping crossover cables will also lead to problems—for example, if a T1 crossover is used for an Ethernet connection.

FIGURE 9.3   Ethernet crossover pinout

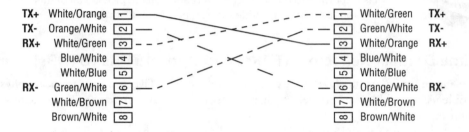

Troubleshooting Switched Connections

Switched networks incorporate a number of unique problems for administrators, including the use of port mirroring for protocol analysis, and routing and trunking. Routing and trunking within the Catalyst system may include an MSFC for routing. Trunking may incorporate one of many protocols, including ISL, 802.10, 802.1Q, and ATM LANE. The effect of trunking is the same, however. A single physical medium can be used to connect multiple VLANs (or ELANs) between switches and routers.

One of the most frequently occurring problems occuring on a switched network is a mismatch in speed or duplex settings between the switch port and the end-system NIC. If the speed of a port is set wrong, no traffic will be successfully sent; this problem is therefore relatively easy to identify and correct. However, mismatched duplex settings can be tougher to find. This is because the resulting problems will occur intermittently and most often during times of heavy load. When a duplex mismatch does occur, the user will often report slow response time and intermittent applications failures. In addition, on the side of the connection that is configured as half-duplex, there will be a steady increase in the number of late collisions reported.

The Switched Port Analyzer

This chapter previously noted that one of the difficulties in troubleshooting switched networks is the port isolation inherent in switches. Such isolation prevents the use of a protocol analyzer in a switched environment, without connecting directly to the wire between the switch and workstation. Also, such a connection cannot be full-duplex, as a general rule.

Cisco addresses this problem with SPAN, or the *Switched Port Analyzer*. You may also see this refered to as *port mirroring*. Effectively, the switch is commanded to copy all packets that would be sent to the workstation interface to another port as well. This port is not assigned a VLAN—it takes on the identity of the original port.

To configure the switch for SPAN, use the following commands:

```
set span enable|disable
set span <src_module/src_port> <dest_module/dest_port>       [rx|tx|both]
set span <src_VLAN> <dest_module/dest_port> [rx|tx|both]
```

Note that traffic may be monitored on the receive or transmit channels, or both. The administrator may select to mirror a single port within the VLAN or have all traffic within the VLAN copied onto the mirroring port. It is important for the administrator to understand the isolation problem's scope and the network topology before attempting to troubleshoot the SPAN function.

The Multilayer Switch Feature Card and Catalyst Routing

The MSFC, is a Cisco router on a daughter card within the Catalyst chassis. This card is physically attached to the Supervisor module and therefore does not take an extra slot in the chassis. The MSFC can be configured to provide routing between VLANs. With an external router, companies often incur additional expense and complexity—the MSFC virtually attaches to VLANs, and as such does not occupy a port as would an ISL or 802.1Q-linked external router. Of course, there are times when an external router is required. The performance of the MSFC is faster than a 7513, and with the advent of the FlexWAN module many of the same interface types are now supported on the 6500 series platform and the 7200 series routers.

Configuration of the MSFC is very similar to that of the Cisco router platform. As shown in the following output, the router module supports IOS features, including password encryption and HSRP. Note that the interfaces are defined as VLAN1 and VLAN2. Unlike the router, the MSFC is virtually connected to the VLANs via the backplane, which speeds up the overall router throughput.

To connect to the MSFC, administrators typically connect to the Supervisor engine CLI and then use the `session` command to attach to the MSFC. Since the MSFC does not occupy a slot in the chassis to itself, it is always shown in slot 15. For example, if the MSFC card were in slot 15, the command would read `session 15`.

 If there is a redundant supervisor/MSFC combination, the redundant MSFC would show in slot 16. You can see this, by using the `show module` command.

Following is the output from a `show running-config` command executed on the MSFC:

```
Building configuration...



Current configuration:

!

version 12.1
service timestamps debug uptime
service timestamps log uptime
no service password-encryption


!

hostname MSFC_A
!
interface Vlan1
 description Admin VLAN
 ip address 10.1.1.3 255.255.255.0
 no ip redirects
 standby 1 timers 5 15
 standby 1 priority 10
 standby 1 preempt
 standby 1 ip 10.1.1.1
!
interface Vlan2
 description User VLAN
 ip address 10.1.2.1 255.255.255.0
! ...output omitted...
```

The `show port` command provides the following information regarding the MSFC:

```
15/1 MSFC_A connected  trunk        full  1000 Route Switch
```

As noted previously, an external router may be used to connect VLANs on the Catalyst switch. This usually occurs through a single connection configured for ISL or another trunking protocol. Fast Ethernet and Gigabit Ethernet connections are common for this configuration.

When configuring the router for this type of connection, each VLAN must be defined to a subinterface, and the main interface must be configured without a configuration. This usually appears as follows.

```
interface fastethernet 0/0
no ip address
full-duplex
interface fastethernet 0/0.1
description vlan1
ip address 10.1.1.1 255.255.255.0
encapsulation isl 1
```

The encapsulation isl 1 command defines that VLAN1 is using this physical interface and is trunked via ISL. This command is placed on each subinterface. Use the set trunk and clear trunk commands on the switch to configure the switch side of the connection.

VLANs across Routers and Switches

So far in this chapter, VLAN implementation has been described on Catalyst switches and Catalyst switches with MSFCs. One VLAN implementation is left: using a router and a switch.

The router plays many important roles in the implementation of VLANs throughout a network. The overall role of a router is to provide communication among VLANs. Also, routers are able to perform many functions that add to the flexibility and scalability of VLAN deployment. Primary among these functions are broadcast management, routing, policy control, VLAN switching, and VLAN translation. Others include QoS management, redundancy, hierarchical design, and traffic shaping and management.

Broadcast Management

Simply put, routers will not forward broadcasts. Switches also control broadcasts by forwarding only to ports that are members of the source VLAN. This property allows routers to lower broadcast traffic on the network backbone.

Policy Control

Switches do not have the capability to apply policy control to individual ports or VLANs on the switch. Use of a router provides the means to implement security and policy control to and from connected VLANs. Access lists can be written and applied to the VLAN subinterface on the router to provide this capability.

VLAN Switching

VLAN switching occurs when a packet destined for the same VLAN on a different interface crosses the router. The header remains intact, and the frame is switched at Layer 2 to the destination interface where the VLAN resides.

VLAN Translation

Translation must occur in two scenarios. The first scenario occurs when VLAN A uses a different VLAN protocol than VLAN B. For example, VLAN A uses ISL for its VLAN protocol, whereas VLAN B uses 802.1Q. In order for communication to take place between end-systems on these VLANs, the router must perform protocol translation. This occurs at Layer 2; the frame headers are changed to accommodate the change in protocol.

The second scenario is when a VLAN protocol must be translated into a non-VLAN Layer 2 protocol. An example of this is when VLAN A (using ISL or 802.1Q) needs to communicate with a Layer 2 destination that does not use any VLAN protocol. The router then translates the VLAN header into a header such as 802.10 so the two can communicate.

Routing

To enable communication between different VLANs or non-VLAN networks (Layer 3), routing must occur. The router maintains routes for the subnets/networks that belong to each VLAN. When VLAN A needs to reach VLAN B, a route lookup is performed and the packets are routed on Layer 3.

When a machine on a VLAN wants to communicate to a host on any other destination not on a local VLAN, routing is performed as well. It is important to realize that there is a difference between translation and routing. Routing is a Layer 3 function, whereas translation occurs at Layer 2.

Troubleshooting VLANs on Routers

Some commands are similar across the IOS for the routers and the software running on the switches. It is important, however, to know which commands provide unique output and should be executed on a router rather than on a switch.

From the router, the following commands provide additional information regarding the VLANs. The **debug** commands provide debug information with respect to VLAN packets and the spanning tree protocol.

- `show vlans`
- `show arp`
- `show interface`
- `show cdp neighbor`
- `debug vlan packet`
- `debug spantree`

Some of these commands have been covered in previous chapters and will not be repeated here. The commands that have not been discussed are described in the following sections.

show vlans

This command is executed from the router; it displays the details about the VLANs configured on the router. The detail includes the VLAN name, the interface, and the IP address used. It also includes the VLAN protocol (encapsulation) and the interface protocol, such as IP or IPX. Here is a sample:

```
Router_A#show vlans
```

```
Virtual LAN ID:  1 (Inter Switch Link Encapsulation)

   vLAN Trunk Interface:    FastEthernet1/0.1

   Protocols Configured:    Address:          Received:      Transmitted:
        IP                  172.16.1.1        4236441842     854332923

Virtual LAN ID:  2 (Inter Switch Link Encapsulation)

   vLAN Trunk Interface:    FastEthernet1/0.2

   Protocols Configured:    Address:          Received:      Transmitted:
        IP                  172.16.2.1        3002644583     2325942305


Router_A#
```

debug vlan packet

This debug command can be useful in determining which VLANs are being sent over a trunk to a router. When debug vlan packet is enabled and a packet comes in for a VLAN that is not defined on the router, the router will note the VLAN and the interface on which the packet was seen. As with all debug commands, be careful when using this command, as it can place a load on the router if there are a lot of packets coming in the interface for an unknown VLAN.

```
Router_A#debug vlan packet

Virtual LAN packet information debugging is on

Router_A #
vLAN: ISL packet received bearing colour ID 10 on  FastEthernet1/0
 which has no subinterface configured  to route or bridge ID 10.
vLAN: ISL packet received bearing colour ID 102 on  FastEthernet1/0
 which has no subinterface configured  to route or bridge ID 102.
vLAN: ISL packet received bearing colour ID 23 on  FastEthernet1/0
 which has no subinterface configured  to route or bridge ID 23.
vLAN: ISL packet received bearing colour ID 10 on  FastEthernet1/0
which has no subinterface configured  to route or bridge ID 10.
```

VLAN Design Issues and Troubleshooting

Although VLANs must adhere to most of the basic network design rules, there are a number of new issues for administrators to consider with Catalyst switches.

First, the network diameter should be less than eight switches. This limitation is mostly related to spanning tree concerns; however, it is also a good rule of thumb for manageability.

Second, VLANs must be numbered within certain limitations, and each VLAN needs to adhere to MTU considerations. Although a large MTU is desirable for FDDI and Token Ring, the Ethernet MTU limitation of 1500 is recommended for all interfaces. This is partly due to the Catalyst backplane and the conversions that are needed between different Physical layers.

The default configuration of the switch includes the VLANs shown in Table 9.5.

TABLE 9.5 The Default Switch VLAN Configuration

VLAN Name	Type of VLAN	MTU	ISL VLAN ID	802.1Q VLAN ID (SAID)
Default	ethernet	1500	0001	100001
FDDI-default	fddi	1500	1002	101002
Token Ring default	token-ring	4472	1003	101003
FDDInet-default	fddi-net	1500	1004	101004
Trnet-default	tr-net	4472	1005	101005

When troubleshooting switches and routers, administrators should consider each element in the network by using a layered approach. For example, configuring a bridge to link two ISL trunks could cause spanning tree problems. In addition, there are two spanning tree protocols available on the switch: IEEE and DEC. Failure to use the same protocol will again cause spanning tree issues.

General routing rules apply to VLANs and the MSFC. For instance, a default router is still required on all devices, and all VLANs must have a router to go from one VLAN to another.

As an example, to display the physical interfaces, the administrator would use show port on the switch, as opposed to show interface, which is used on the router. The show interface command on the switch is used to check the SL0 and SC0 interfaces.

Remember that most troubleshooting is actually an exercise in isolation. View the network from each layer and work through the system. For example, is there a link light denoting Layer 1 connectivity? Is the port configured for the same speed and duplex on each end? These basic questions, along with the Cisco debug and show commands, frequently provide the proper clues to isolate problems.

Although they are available, the use of automatic speed and duplex configuration settings is not recommended. Most administrators prefer the control and manageability that is available from manually configuring these settings. Administrators should familiarize themselves with the proper commands on various platforms. For example, NT usually permits the modification of this setting from the network control panel, but some installations may require registry modification. On Solaris, the /kernel/drv/hme.conf file is modified when using that type of NIC.

Hybrid/Native Command Conversion

As was discussed at the beginning of the chapter, similar switch-related commands for the Hybrid and Native modes have a somewhat different syntax. Table 9.6 compares some of the common Hybrid commands to their Native mode equivalents. As is the case with configuring routers, the show command are entered in user/exec mode and the configuration commands are entered in either global configuration mode or interface level configuration mode.

TABLE 9.6   Hybrid/Native Mode Command Comparison

Hybrid Command	Native Command	Explanation
clear vlan	no vlan	Removes a VLAN from the configuratuion.
set cam agingtime	mac-address-table aging-time	Sets the timeout values for retaining MAC address information.
set port dulex	duplex	Interface command that sets the duplex on a particular port.
set port name	description	Interface command that sets the name on a port.
set port speed	speed	Interface command that sets the speed of a given port.
set span	monitor session	Sets up a SPAN port.
set spantree	spanning-tree	Sets Spanning-Tree Protocol information.

TABLE 9.6   Hybrid/Native Mode Command Comparison *(continued)*

Hybrid Command	Native Command	Explanation
set vlan	switchport access vlan	Assigns a particular interface to a given VLAN.
show cam dynamic	show mac-address-table dynamic	Shows the MAC address to port relationships. This information is stored in the CAM table.
show port	Show interface	Shows port information.
show span	show monitor	Shows the span port.
show test	show diagnostic	Shows boot-up test results.
show version	show version	Shows IOS version information for the switch.
show vlan	show vlan	Shows VLAN information.
show vtp domain	show vtp status	Shows VTP information.

Summary

In today's network environment, switching has become an integral component. It allows for greater throughput and it better utilizes existing hardware. In the Cisco switching offering, one of the main switches used is the Catalyst 6500 series. Thanks to the number of different modules available in this series, they are versatile enough to be used in almost any network.

Like the Cisco routers that were examined earlier, the Cisco switches also come with a fully featured command line interface (CLI) that allows for configuration as well as verification of the current functionality of the switch. For the switches, this CLI comes in two different formats—set-based Hybrid mode, or router-like Native mode. Although each has its strength, we focused on the set-based Hybrid mode commands in this chapter. Central to both CLIs is the show command. This command, along with the keywords available for use with it, allows for the display of nearly all the switch's characteristics.

Another important aspect of a switched environment is loop detection and elimination. This is done through the Spanning-Tree Protocol. Spanning tree sends probing packets to all neighboring devices and uses these packets to determine whether there is a loop in the network. If a loop is detected, all except one of the paths that made the loop are put in blocking mode. Once a port is placed in blocking mode, it will not forward user data. By doing this, spanning tree ensures that there is only one path to a destination at a time. If that path were to go down or be removed, then one of the "blocked" paths would be unblocked, or changed to a forwarding state, and used for user data.

One of the largest advantages of switches over the typical hub is the ability of the switch to create VLANs. A switch can have multiple VLANs defined, and each port can be put in a separate VLAN. Because of this capability, there is no longer a need for specific hardware to separate subnets. All of the subnets can be created on a single device and logically separated into VLANs.

Any new software feature needs a method for controlling and configuring it. For VLANs this is VTP, or VLAN Trunking Protocol. VTP allows VLAN configuration information to be changed in one location—a VTP server—and for this information to propagate automatically to all of the VTP clients in the VTP domain, thus easing the administrative overhead of a switched environment. If there is a concern about one change taking down the entire switched area, discrete VTP domains can be set up, or switches can be set to transparent mode. In transparent mode, each switch must be manually configured any time there is a change in the VLAN structure.

To better take advantage of the switches' ability to use VLANs, Cisco has manufactured a routing card for the 6500 series switches. Called the Multilayer Switch Feature Card (MSFC), this card provides full routing functionality to the switch. Because this card is connected to the switch's backplane, it has immediate access to any of the VLANs created on the switch. Alternatively, you can also uplink to an external router to get this functionality. This uplink can be done for a specific VLAN or for a range of VLANs if trunking is used.

One of the items that can be easily overlooked in the network is the cabling. As 100Mb Ethernet is now the standard for most new Ethernet installations, many of the Cat 3 cable plants that were installed for 10Mb Ethernet need to be replaced with Cat 5 or better cabling. In addition, as switching allows for larger Layer 2 domains and Layer 3 functionality is added to the switches, it is becoming more common to use the crossover cable to connect two switches directly.

Exam Essentials

Know the differences among switches, bridges, and hubs.   A hub can only run in half-duplex mode and has a broadcast-and-collision domain that includes all ports. Bridges do not generally have hardware ASICs and have a lower port density. Switches can operate in full- or half-duplex mode and have a collision domain of a single port and a broadcast domain of a single VLAN.

Know the show commands available for a switch.   Switch show commands include but are not limited to show cdp, show config, show flash, show log, show mac, show port, show span, show system, show test, and show version.

Know how spanning tree is used in a switch.   Spanning tree controls loops in a Layer 2 environment. The switch does this automatically.

Understand the function of a VLAN.   A VLAN is used to logically separate traffic on a switch. This allows a switch to have multiple individual subnets terminating on it.

Understand trunking and how it works.   Trunking on a Cisco switch can be done by using either ISL or 802.1Q. It allows for multiple VLANs to share the same uplink.

Understand how VTP works.   Virtual Trunking Protocol allows for easy administration of VLANs in a large switched environment. VLAN changes performed on a VTP server are automatically updated on all the VTP clients in the VTP domain. If a switch is in transparent mode, it will pass along any VTP changes sent by the server but will not make any modifications to its own VLANs.

Know how to troubleshoot cabling problems and when to use a crossover cable.   A crossover cable is used anytime like network devices are directly connected together (e.g., router to router, switch to switch, or workstation to workstation). A straight-through cable is used to connect workstations or routers to switches. Cable Testers and TDRs are among the tools that are available for testing physical cabling issues.

Commands Used in This Chapter

The following list contains a summary of all the commands used in this chapter.

Commands	Descriptions
debug span	Debugs spanning tree.
debug vlan packet	On a router connected to a trunk port on a switch, will show errors in encapsulation and packets destined for an unknown VLAN. Debugs VLAN packets.
show arp	Displays the ARP information for the router.
show bridge {vlan number}	Shows which bridging encapsulations are enabled.
show cam	Reports the MAC address associated with the ports of the switch. These addresses are stored in the CAM table; this command accesses that table.
show cdp	Displays the Cisco neighbors.
show config	Similar to the **show running-config** command on Cisco routers. Provides all configuration settings on the switch for all modules, with a few exceptions for certain modules such as the MSFC.
show interface	Reports the IP configuration of the supervisor module.
show log	Reports significant events, including reboots of all modules, traps, and power-supply failures.
show logging buffer	Shows logging information on a switch.

`show mac`	Maintains numerous counters in normal operation, including the frame traffic per port; the total number of incoming frames, including discards; and the total number of transmits and aborts due to excessive deferral or MTU violations. Broadcast counters are also maintained in addition to discards.
`show port`	Provides information about specific ports or all ports on a module. VLAN membership, port speed and configuration, and error statistics are available.
`show span`	Shows spanning tree information from the router. Very different from a `show span` command on a switch.
`show spantree`	Reports the status of the spanning tree process for each VLAN, when spanning tree has been enabled on the switch.
`show system`	Provides high-level summary information regarding the switch, including the status of power supplies, uptime, and administrative settings, as well as the percentage of traffic on the backplane.
`show test`	The status of the switch, including interface cards, power supplies, and available memory.
`show version`	Provides hardware and software version numbers, in addition to memory and system uptime statistics.
`show vlans`	Provides VLAN information and status from the router.
`show vtp domain`	Provides status information for the VTP domain configured on the switch. Note that VTP updates are sent over VLAN 1 when troubleshooting.

Key Terms

Before you take the exam, be certain you are familiar with the following terms:

broadcast domain

Cable testers

Cisco Discovery Protocol (CDP)

Collision domains

debug vlan packet

IEEE 802.1Q

Inter-Switch Link (ISL)

multimeters

port mirroring

port mirroring

Remote Monitoring (RMON)

show cam

show cdp

show config

show interface

show log

show logging buffer

show mac

show port

show spantree

show test

show version

show vlans

show vtp domain

SNAP

spanning tree

Switched Port Analyzer

Time domain reflectors (TDRs)

Unnumbered Information

virtual LANs

VLAN Trunking Protocol (VTP)

VLANs

volt-ohm meters

Review Questions

1. Which of the following is/are characteristics of Catalyst 6500 switches?

   A. Devices that operate at Layer 2 of the OSI model

   B. Limited to 16 ports

   C. Limited to only one physical media

   D. Available for Ethernet only

   E. Available for ATM only

2. 100BaseTX requires which of the following?

   A. Category 1 cables

   B. Category 3 cables

   C. Category 5 cables

   D. Fiber cables

3. A user is complaing of slow response time and you note that the switch port they are connected to indicates a number of late collisions. What is a possible cause of the problem?

   A. Collision domain too large

   B. Speed mismatch on the port

   C. CAM aging time set too long

   D. Duplex mismatch on the port

4. Which of the following is true about VLANs?

   A. VLANs define the broadcast domain.

   B. They define the collision domain.

   C. They are unique to each workstation.

   D. They are available only on Ethernet.

   E. They require the use of ISL or 802.1Q.

   F. They require the use of 802.1D or spanning tree.

5. ISL is useful for which one of the following?

   A. Trunking between non-Cisco switches

   B. Trunking between Cisco switches

   C. Configuring VLANs

   D. Quadrupling the bandwidth between switches

6. Which of the following are the same encapsulation type? (Choose all that apply.)

    A. 802.1Q

    B. ISL

    C. 802.3

    D. 802.1D

    E. None of the above

7. The Catalyst command to display information on neighboring Cisco devices is which of the following?

    A. `show neighbors cdp`

    B. `display cisco neighbors`

    C. `show cdp neighbors all`

    D. `show cdp neighbors detail`

    E. `show neighboring cdp details`

8. Spanning-Tree Protocol provides which one of the following?

    A. A single path through multiple subnets

    B. Redundant paths while preventing loops

    C. Trunking multiple VLANs onto FDDI interfaces

    D. MAC layer address translation

9. In order to connect the Marketing VLAN to the Payroll VLAN, which one of the following must be true about a packet?

    A. The packet must use ISL.

    B. It must be forwarded at least once by a router.

    C. It must be longer than 1024 octets.

    D. The packet cannot go from the Marketing VLAN to the Payroll VLAN.

    E. It must be converted into ATM cells.

10. Which of the following commands provides system uptime?

    A. `show version`

    B. `show config`

    C. `uptime`

    D. `show flash`

11. Switch utilization is available from which of the following?

    A. LEDs on the supervisor module

    B. Cisco WAN Manager

    C. CLI

    D. `show snmp utilization`

12. VLANs control the scope of which one of the following?

   A. The collision domain

   B. The broadcast domain

   C. Conversion from half- to full-duplex

13. What command would be issued to determine information on directly connected neighbors?

   A. `show neighbors`

   B. `show cdp all`

   C. `show cdp neighbors`

   D. `show cdp-neighbors`

14. Cisco Discovery Protocol (CDP) provides which of the following?

   A. Ping services for Cisco devices

   B. Automatic VLAN configuration services

   C. VLAN security by controlling the ARP discovery process

   D. Network management information regarding Cisco products

   E. Automatic ISL and 802.1Q services

15. A router connected to a 6500 series switch is experiencing a number of CRC (cyclic redundancy check) and FCS (frame check sequence) errors. At what layer(s) is the problem most likely occurring? (Choose two.)

   A. Layer 1

   B. Layer 2

   C. Layer 3

   D. Layer 4

   E. Layer 5

   F. Layer 6

   G. Layer 7

16. Which of the following commands provides information regarding individual ports on the switch?

   A. `show all ports`

   B. `show port <mod/port>`

   C. `show port detail <mod/port>`

   D. `show switch port <port/mod>`

17. An administrator adds a VLAN to Switch_A, a VTP server. Which of the following will be true about the VLAN?

    A. This VLAN must be added manually to each switch in the network.

    B. It must be added manually to each switch in the network that participates in the VLAN, but no others.

    C. It will automatically be added to each switch in the subnet.

    D. It will automatically be added to each switch in the VTP domain.

    E. It will automatically be added via the TrafficDirector tool.

18. How many VLANs can be active on a single nontrunk port?

    A. Two

    B. One

    C. Multiple

    D. None

19. How many VLANs can be present on an ISL port?

    A. Multiple

    B. Only one

    C. None

    D. Two

20. Collisions are possible on which of the following connections?

    A. FDDI

    B. Token Ring

    C. Fast Ethernet

    D. Full-duplex Ethernet

Answers to Review Questions

1. A. Switches operate at Layer 2 of the OSI model. The Catalyst 6500 has a variety of interfaces and media configurations.

2. C. Category 5 cables are required to ensure sufficient pairs of copper for the transmit and receive signals, as well as to provide the electrical characteristics needed. 100BaseFX would use fiber cables.

3. D. Duplex mismatches on ports are often characterized by slow user-response time and by late collisions on the half-duplex side of the connection, or because the cable was exceeding length specifications.

4. A. The collision domain is controlled by the switch port. A VLAN can exist on multiple machines. ISL and 802.1Q are both trunking protocols that can be used but are not required. 802.1D extends the concept of MAC bridging, and spanning tree ensures a loop-free Layer 2 environment, but neither is required to make a VLAN function.

5. B. Because ISL is a Cisco-proprietary encapsulation, it does not work with non-Cisco switches.

6. E. None of these encapsulations is of the same type, and 802.1D is not a real frame-encapsulation type.

7. D. The correct syntax is `show cdp neighbors detail`.

8. B. The main function of spanning tree is to prevent loops in a switched network.

9. B. In order for different VLANs to communicate, the packets must be routed.

10. A. The `show version` command displays the system's uptime.

11. A, C. LEDs on the supervisor module, as well as the command-line interface, allow the user to check the switch utilization.

12. B. VLANs control broadcast domains. Collisions, duplex, and mirroring are all done by the switch.

13. C. `show cdp neighbors` is the correct syntax for thegetting information on directly connected neighbors.

14. D. CDP discovers and retains information regarding directly connected Cisco devices.

15. A, B. The CRC and FCS errors are most likely occurring at the Physical or Data Link layer.

16. B. The correct syntax for the command that provides port information is `show port <mod/port>`.

17. D. VLAN information is automatically propagated via the VTP protocol within the domain. Each switch can belong to only one domain.

18. B. There can be only one VLAN per nontrunking port. When a port is a trunk port, it handles all VLANs.

19. A. An ISL port has the same function as a trunking port.

20. C. Collisions are possible on Fast Ethernet when there are multiple workstations on a switched port, or when the port is configured to half-duplex rather than full-duplex.

Chapter

10

Applying Cisco's Diagnostic Tools

EXAM TOPICS COVERED IN THIS CHAPTER INCLUDE:

- ✓ Verify network connectivity.
- ✓ Use Cisco IOS commands to identify problems.
- ✓ Rectify Layer 1 connectivity problems.
- ✓ Rectify sub-optimal performance issues at Layers 2 through 7.
- ✓ Restore services back to baseline conditions.

In the previous chapters, you learned a great deal about Layer 2 and Layer 3 technologies and protocols. With this knowledge, you'll be able to better interpret the information provided by the troubleshooting tools and commands.

The time has come to implement all that you've learned, including applying the troubleshooting methodology from Chapter 1. Once you have the technical knowledge base, you must apply it by using a troubleshooting template if you are to efficiently and successfully troubleshoot network problems.

This chapter's format will be different from what you have seen up to now. Different types of network problems will be outlined in detail, and each will then be solved. The intent is for you to take the provided information and do the troubleshooting. You'll see substantial router output and packet decodes from a protocol analyzer. The information is there for your reference and at times may not have a great deal of explanation. You must look at the output carefully in order to determine what is happening on the router or network.

For each scenario, follow the steps outlined in Chapter 1 by listing observations, gathering facts, and proposing solutions. Because the book cannot be interactive, the scenarios are intended to help you get accustomed to using the methodology, but you'll not go so far as to actually verify that the proposed solution solved the network problem. Let's begin.

Identifying and Resolving Generic Router Problems

This section deals with Cisco routers and some simple generic problems that can be remedied easily, once they are identified. Each scenario is accompanied by outputs from relevant diagnostic tools. The focus is on the router itself, because many other scenarios involve additional network equipment.

Scenario #1

You are installing a Cisco 2600 series router that was sent to you after company headquarters entered the preliminary configuration.

List Observations

You are connected to the console port. You power on the router, and this is what you see as the router boots:

```
System Bootstrap, Version 11.3(2)XA3, PLATFORM SPECIFIC   RELEASE SOFTWARE (fc1)
Copyright (c) 1998 by cisco Systems, Inc.
TAC:Home:SW:IOS:Specials for info
C2600 platform with 24576 Kbytes of main memory
program load complete, entry point: 0x80008000, size:   0x37b090
Self decompressing the image :
#######################################################################
#######################################################################
#######################################################################
#######################################################################
################################### [OK]
Restricted Rights Legend
Use, duplication, or disclosure by the Government is
subject to restrictions as set forth in subparagraph
(c) of the Commercial Computer Software - Restricted
Rights clause at FAR sec. 52.227-19 and subparagraph
(c) (1) (ii) of the Rights in Technical Data and Computer
Software clause at DFARS sec. 252.227-7013.


        cisco Systems, Inc.
        170 West Tasman Drive
        San Jose, California 95134-1706
Cisco Internetwork Operating System Software
IOS (tm) C2600 Software (C2600-D-M), Version 11.3(4)T1,    RELEASE
 SOFTWARE (fc1)
Copyright (c) 1986-1998 by cisco Systems, Inc.
Compiled Wed 01-Jul-98 11:42 by phanguye
Image text-base: 0x80008084, data-base: 0x8066A278


Cisco 2611 (MPC860) processor (revision 0x202) with   18432K/6144K
            bytes of memory.
Processor board ID JAB023601NE (1537311773)
M860 processor: part number 0, mask 32
Bridging software.
X.25 software, Version 3.0.0.
2 Ethernet/IEEE 802.3 interface(s)
1 Serial network interface(s)
```

```
32K bytes of non-volatile configuration memory.
8192K bytes of processor board System flash (Read/Write)



Press RETURN to get started!



%LINK-3-UPDOWN: Interface Ethernet0/0, changed state to down
%LINK-3-UPDOWN: Interface Ethernet0/1, changed state to up
%LINK-3-UPDOWN: Interface Serial0/0, changed state to down
Cisco Internetwork Operating System Software
IOS (tm) C2600 Software (C2600-D-M), Version 11.3(4)T1,     RELEASE
   SOFTWARE (fc1)
Copyright (c) 1986-1998 by cisco Systems, Inc.
Compiled Wed 01-Jul-98 11:42 by phanguye


%LINK-5-CHANGED: Interface Serial0/0, changed state to  administratively down
%FR-5-DLCICHANGE: Interface Serial0/0 - DLCI 324 state   changed to DELETED
```

List Observations

Well, it looks like two interfaces on the router are down—so much for the preconfigured router. You change to the privileged level by entering the enable password. Here is where you need to start listing observations. The first one is that two of the interfaces on the router are down.

Before you look at the configuration or show commands, you check the cabling connections. Assuming that the connections check out, you should check the lights in the back of the router. Figure 10.1 shows the back of a 2611 router. The router comes with two Ethernet ports, a console port, an aux port, and a serial port. Each of the network interface ports (both Ethernet ports and the serial port) has a light next to it that indicates whether there is a physical connection. If any of these lights is not lit, there is a connectivity problem. In this example, assume that two of the three lights are lit. The light next to Ethernet 0/0 is not lit.

FIGURE 10.1   Rear view of a Cisco 2611

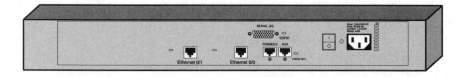

Now that you've observed the connectivity, you need to gather more information about the router's configuration. Go back to the console. You know that the problem involves two interfaces, Ethernet 0/0 and Serial 0/0. For this example, don't use show running-config or show startup-config. Instead, use the interface-specific show commands.

The first command issued is show interface ethernet 0/0. Here are the results:

```
Router_A#show interface ethernet 0/0
Ethernet0/0 is down, line protocol is down
  Hardware is AmdP2, address is 0010.7bd9.2880 (bia 0010.7bd9.2880)
  MTU 1500 bytes, BW 10000 Kbit, DLY 1000 usec, rely 255/255, load 1/255
  Encapsulation ARPA, loopback not set, keepalive set (10 sec)
  ARP type: ARPA, ARP Timeout 04:00:00
  Last input never, output never, output hang never
  Last clearing of "show interface" counters never
  Queueing strategy: fifo
  Output queue 0/40, 0 drops; input queue 0/75, 0 drops
  5 minute input rate 0 bits/sec, 0 packets/sec
  5 minute output rate 0 bits/sec, 0 packets/sec
     0 packets input, 0 bytes, 0 no buffer
     Received 0 broadcasts, 0 runts, 0 giants, 0 throttles
     0 input errors, 0 CRC, 0 frame, 0 overrun, 0 ignored,
        0 abort
     0 input packets with dribble condition detected
     0 packets output, 0 bytes, 0 underruns
     0 output errors, 0 collisions, 0 interface resets
     0 babbles, 0 late collision, 0 deferred
     0 lost carrier, 0 no carrier
     0 output buffer failures, 0 output buffers swapped out
Router_A#
```

The following outputs are from the show interface Ethernet 0/1 and show interface Serial 0/0 commands, respectively:

```
Ethernet0/1 is up, line protocol is up
  Hardware is AmdP2, address is 0010.7bd9.2881 (bia 0010.7bd9.2881)
  Internet address is 172.16.20.5/24
  MTU 1500 bytes, BW 10000 Kbit, DLY 1000 usec, rely 255/255, load 1/255
  Encapsulation ARPA, loopback not set, keepalive set (10 sec)
  ARP type: ARPA, ARP Timeout 04:00:00
  Last input never, output 00:00:02, output hang never
  Last clearing of "show interface" counters never
  Queueing strategy: fifo
  Output queue 0/40, 0 drops; input queue 0/75, 0 drops
  5 minute input rate 983450 bits/sec, 875 packets/sec
  5 minute output rate 435097 bits/sec, 357 packets/sec
```

```
     0 packets input, 0 bytes, 0 no buffer
     Received 0 broadcasts, 0 runts, 0 giants, 0 throttles
     0 input errors, 0 CRC, 0 frame, 0 overrun, 0 ignored,
        0 abort
     0 input packets with dribble condition detected
     274 packets output, 17062 bytes, 0 underruns
     0 output errors, 0 collisions, 11 interface resets
     0 babbles, 0 late collision, 0 deferred
     0 lost carrier, 0 no carrier
     0 output buffer failures, 0 output buffers swapped out
Router_A# show interface serial 0/0
Serial0/0 is administratively down, line protocol is down
   Hardware is PowerQUICC Serial
   Internet address is 172.16.20.5/30
   MTU 1500 bytes, BW 1544 Kbit, DLY 20000 usec, rely 255/255, load 1/255
   Encapsulation FRAME-RELAY, loopback not set, keepalive set (10 sec)
   LMI enq sent  0, LMI stat recvd 0, LMI upd recvd 0, DTE LMI down
   LMI enq recvd 0, LMI stat sent  0, LMI upd sent  0
   LMI DLCI 1023  LMI type is CISCO  frame relay DTE
   FR SVC disabled, LAPF state down
   Broadcast queue 0/64, broadcasts sent/dropped 0/0, interface broadcasts 0
   Last input never, output never, output hang never
   Last clearing of "show interface" counters never
   Input queue: 0/75/0 (size/max/drops); Total output drops: 0
   Queueing strategy: weighted fair
   Output queue: 0/1000/64/0 (size/max total/threshold/drops)
      Conversations  0/1/256 (active/max active/max total)
      Reserved Conversations 0/0 (allocated/max allocated)
   5 minute input rate 0 bits/sec, 0 packets/sec
   5 minute output rate 0 bits/sec, 0 packets/sec
      0 packets input, 0 bytes, 0 no buffer
      Received 0 broadcasts, 0 runts, 0 giants, 0 throttles
      0 input errors, 0 CRC, 0 frame, 0 overrun, 0 ignored, 0 abort
      0 packets output, 0 bytes, 0 underruns
      0 output errors, 0 collisions, 0 interface resets
      0 output buffer failures, 0 output buffers swapped out
      0 carrier transitions
      DCD=up  DSR=up  DTR=down  RTS=down  CTS=up
Router_A#
```

What are your observations? Check your list against the following:

- No IP address is configured on Ethernet 0/0.
- No indicator light is lit for Ethernet 0/0.
- The number of lost carrier errors is the same as the number of output errors.
- Serial 0/0 is administratively shut down.
- DLCI 324 on Serial 0/0 is in a deleted state.
- Serial 0/0 is a Frame Relay link.
- Ethernet 0/1 is up and up.

In other situations, this list can contain more information regarding the interfaces, such as encapsulation types and so on. For clarity and simplicity, only the observations relevant to this scenario are listed here.

After observations and fact-gathering are completed, it's time to formulate a problem description. Initially, from what you saw while the router booted, the problem description was vague. It could have been written something like this: "Interfaces Ethernet 0/0 and Serial 0/0 are down."

This is a good start, but it lacks detail. If this were a complicated problem, you would be troubleshooting for a long time because the description lacks focus. Based on the listed observations in this case, you know exactly what the problem description is. A focused and detailed problem statement or description for this scenario is as follows: "Ethernet 0/0 is down because it doesn't have a link, and Serial 0/0 is down because it was administratively shut down. Since Serial 0/0 is shut down, the DLCI is in a deleted state." With this problem statement, it should be obvious what needs to be done to fix the problems.

Propose Solutions

How did you do with your problem statement? Now that you've observed the problems, what will be the solutions? This step relates to the "creating an action plan" part of the troubleshooting process. The more specific the problem statement, the more easily the solutions can be defined.

In this first scenario, there appear to be a few problems that need resolution, and they all probably have simple solutions:

- Check the cable for the Ethernet port for a possible physical problem.
- Configure an IP address on Ethernet 0/0.
- Turn up interface Serial 0/0.

With the proposed solutions, the only thing left is to implement them and see if they work. You replace the cable going to Ethernet 0/0, and modify the configuration of the router as follows:

```
Router_A#conf t
Enter configuration commands, one per line. End with CNTL/Z.
Router_A(config)#interface ethernet 0/0
Router_A(config-if)#ip address 172.16.10.1 255.255.255.0
```

```
Router_A(config-if)#interface serial 0/0
Router_A(config-if)#no shut
172.16.20.5 overlaps with Ethernet0/1
Serial0/0: incorrect IP address assignment
Router_A(config-if)#^Z
Router_A#
```

List Observations—Take 2

Now let's check the interface status:

```
Ethernet0/0 is up, line protocol is up
Hardware is AmdP2, address is 0010.7bd9.2880 (bia 0010.7bd9.2880)
  MTU 1500 bytes, BW 10000 Kbit, DLY 1000 usec, rely 255/255, load 1/255
  Encapsulation ARPA, loopback not set, keepalive set (10 sec)
  ARP type: ARPA, ARP Timeout 04:00:00
  Last input never, output 00:00:05, output hang never
  Last clearing of "show interface" counters never
  Queueing strategy: fifo
  Output queue 0/40, 0 drops; input queue 0/75, 0 drops
  5 minute input rate 509000 bits/sec, 215 packets/sec
  5 minute output rate 1167000 bits/sec, 315 packets/sec
     12900 packets input, 10324500 bytes, 0 no buffer
     Received 235 broadcasts, 0 runts, 0 giants, 0 throttles
      0 input errors, 0 CRC, 0 frame, 0 overrun, 0 ignored,
         0 abort
     0 input packets with dribble condition detected
     18903 packets output, 15198309 bytes, 0 underruns
     0 output errors, 0 collisions, 1 interface resets
     0 babbles, 0 late collision, 0 deferred
     0 lost carrier, 0 no carrier
     0 output buffer failures, 0 output buffers swapped out
```

What happened to Serial 0/0? The console message stated that there was an address overlap with interface Ethernet 0/1, which means a duplicate IP address. The IP address on Ethernet 0/1 overlaps with the IP address on Serial 0/0. Let's look at the interface settings once more.

```
Router_A#show interface serial 0/0
Serial0/0 is administratively down, line protocol is down
  Hardware is PowerQUICC Serial
  Internet address is 172.16.20.5/30
  MTU 1500 bytes, BW 1544 Kbit, DLY 20000 usec, rely 255/255, load 1/255
  Encapsulation FRAME-RELAY, loopback not set, keepalive set (10 sec)
```

```
    LMI enq sent  0, LMI stat recvd 0, LMI upd recvd 0, DTE   LMI down
    LMI enq recvd 0, LMI stat sent  0, LMI upd sent  0
    LMI DLCI 1023  LMI type is CISCO  frame relay DTE
    FR SVC disabled, LAPF state down
    Broadcast queue 0/64, broadcasts sent/dropped 0/0, interface broadcasts 0
    Last input never, output never, output hang never
    Last clearing of "show interface" counters never
    Input queue: 0/75/0 (size/max/drops); Total output drops: 0
    Queueing strategy: weighted fair
    Output queue: 0/1000/64/0 (size/max total/threshold/ drops)
      Conversations  0/1/256 (active/max active/max total)
      Reserved Conversations 0/0 (allocated/max allocated)
    5 minute input rate 0 bits/sec, 0 packets/sec
    5 minute output rate 0 bits/sec, 0 packets/sec
      0 packets input, 0 bytes, 0 no buffer
      Received 0 broadcasts, 0 runts, 0 giants, 0 throttles
      0 input errors, 0 CRC, 0 frame, 0 overrun, 0 ignored, 0 abort
      0 packets output, 0 bytes, 0 underruns
      0 output errors, 0 collisions, 0 interface resets
      0 output buffer failures, 0 output buffers swapped out
      0 carrier transitions
      DCD=up  DSR=up  DTR=down  RTS=down  CTS=up
Router_A#
```

This output indicates that the interface is still administratively down. You saw the no shut command issued in the previous series of configuration commands, so why is it still in shutdown? Here is the answer: If an interface has a configuration conflict with another interface, it will not initialize. In this case, because the serial interface was configured with a duplicate IP address, it wouldn't initialize. It remains in its previous state, shutdown. In order to activate the serial link we must do some more analysis.

Referring to the show interface results for Ethernet 0/1, you see that it does have the same address as Serial 0/0. This problem can easily be resolved, as long as you know which interface should have the 172.16.20.5 address. In this scenario, we'll assume that Ethernet 0/1 has the incorrect IP address.

In essence, you've made these additional observations.

- Serial 0/0 is configured with IP address 172.16.20.5/30.

- Ethernet 0/1 is configured with IP address 172.16.20.5/24.

- You cannot change administrative state for Serial 0/0 because of the IP address overlap with Ethernet 0/1.

Propose Solutions—Take 2

Now, with these additional observations, new solutions must be proposed. Once the decision is made as to which IP address should be assigned to each interface, the problem should be resolved. The action plan is as follows:

- Leave IP address 172.16.20.5/30 assigned to interface Serial 0/0.
- Assign IP address 172.16.30.1/24 to interface Ethernet 0/1.
- Remove the administrative shutdown from interface Serial 0/0.

Here is the configuration. Following the configuration, you see the show interface output for each interface. This is done to verify that all the changes to the router have fixed the problems that were observed.

```
Router_A#conf t
Enter configuration commands, one per line. End with CNTL/Z.
Router_A(config-if)#interface ethernet 0/1
Router_A(config-if)#ip address 172.16.30.1 255.255.255.0
Router_A(config)#interface serial 0/0
Router_A(config-if)#no shutdown
Router_A(config-if)#^Z
%LINK-3-UPDOWN: Interface Serial0/0, changed state to up
%FR-5-DLCICHANGE: Interface Serial0/0 - DLCI 324 state changed to ACTIVE
%FR-5-DLCICHANGE: Interface Serial0/0 - DLCI 368 state changed to ACTIVE
%FR-5-DLCICHANGE: Interface Serial0/0 - DLCI 324 state changed to DELETED
%LINEPROTO-5-UPDOWN: Line protocol on Interface Serial0/0, changed state to up
Router_A#
Router_A#show interface ethernet 0/0
Ethernet0/0 is up, line protocol is up
  Hardware is AmdP2, address is 0010.7bd9.2880    (bia 0010.7bd9.2880)
  Internet address is 172.16.10.1/24
  MTU 1500 bytes, BW 10000 Kbit, DLY 1000 usec, rely 255/255, load 29/255
  Encapsulation ARPA, loopback not set, keepalive set (10  sec)
  ARP type: ARPA, ARP Timeout 04:00:00
  Last input 00:00:00, output 00:00:00, output hang never
  Last clearing of "show interface" counters never
  Queueing strategy: fifo
  Output queue 0/40, 0 drops; input queue 1/75, 0 drops
  5 minute input rate 509000 bits/sec, 215 packets/sec
  5 minute output rate 1167000 bits/sec, 315 packets/sec
     25800 packets input, 20685400 bytes, 0 no buffer
     Received 3235 broadcasts, 0 runts, 0 giants
     6 input errors, 1 CRC, 5 frame, 0 overrun, 640 ignored, 0 abort
```

```
      0 input packets with dribble condition detected
      37800 packets output, 30249800 bytes, 0 underruns
      283 output errors, 4 collisions, 2 interface resets
      0 babbles, 0 late collision, 0 deferred
      283 lost carrier, 0 no carrier
      0 output buffers copied, 0 interrupts, 0 failures
Router_A#show interface serial 0/0
Serial0/0 is up, line protocol is up
   Hardware is PowerQUICC Serial
   Internet address is 172.16.20.5/30
   MTU 1500 bytes, BW 1544 Kbit, DLY 20000 usec, rely 255/255, load 1/255
   Encapsulation FRAME-RELAY, loopback not set, keepalive set (10 sec)
   LMI enq sent  5, LMI stat recvd 6, LMI upd recvd 0, DTE LMI up
   LMI enq recvd 0, LMI stat sent  0, LMI upd sent  0
   LMI DLCI 1023  LMI type is CISCO  frame relay DTE
   FR SVC disabled, LAPF state down
   Broadcast queue 0/64, broadcasts sent/dropped 0/0, interface broadcasts 1
   Last input 00:00:03, output 00:00:03, output hang never
   Last clearing of "show interface" counters never
   Input queue: 0/75/0 (size/max/drops); Total output   drops: 0
   Queueing strategy: weighted fair
   Output queue: 0/1000/64/0 (size/max total/threshold/   drops)
      Conversations  0/1/256 (active/max active/max total)
      Reserved Conversations 0/0 (allocated/max allocated)
   5 minute input rate 0 bits/sec, 0 packets/sec
   5 minute output rate 0 bits/sec, 0 packets/sec
      6 packets input, 94 bytes, 0 no buffer
      Received 0 broadcasts, 0 runts, 0 giants, 0 throttles
      0 input errors, 0 CRC, 0 frame, 0 overrun, 0 ignored, 0 abort
      9 packets output, 129 bytes, 0 underruns
      0 output errors, 0 collisions, 3 interface resets
      0 output buffer failures, 0 output buffers swapped out
      0 carrier transitions
      DCD=up  DSR=up  DTR=up  RTS=up  CTS=up
Router_A#show interface ethernet 0/1
Ethernet0/1 is up, line protocol is up
   Hardware is AmdP2, address is 0010.7bd9.2881 (bia 0010.7bd9.2881)
   Internet address is 172.16.30.1/24
   MTU 1500 bytes, BW 10000 Kbit, DLY 1000 usec, rely 128/255, load 1/255
   Encapsulation ARPA, loopback not set, keepalive set (10 sec)
```

```
    ARP type: ARPA, ARP Timeout 04:00:00
    Last input never, output 00:00:07, output hang never
    Last clearing of "show interface" counters never
    Queueing strategy: fifo
    Output queue 0/40, 0 drops; input queue 0/75, 0 drops
 5 minute input rate 488000 bits/sec, 164 packets/sec
 5 minute output rate 1473000 bits/sec, 297 packets/sec
        9840 packets input, 7815720 bytes, 0 no buffer
        Received 0 broadcasts, 0 runts, 0 giants, 0 throttles
        0 input errors, 0 CRC, 0 frame, 0 overrun, 0 ignored,
          0 abort
        0 input packets with dribble condition detected
        17820 packets output, 14352560 bytes, 0 underruns
        0 output errors, 0 collisions, 0 interface resets
        0 babbles, 0 late collision, 0 deferred
        0 lost carrier, 0 no carrier
        0 output buffer failures, 0 output buffers swapped out
Router_A#
```

List Observations—Take 3

From what you can see in the interface outputs, it appears that all interfaces are working properly. However, there are three messages of concern, regarding the DLCI information in messages that were displayed after the Serial 0/0 interface was brought up. To be on the safe side, let's try to ping the router at the headquarters location.

```
Router_A#ping 172.16.20.6

Type escape sequence to abort.
Sending 5, 100-byte ICMP Echos to 172.16.20.6, timeout is 2 seconds:
.....
Success rate is 0 percent (0/5)
Router_A#
```

As suspected, there is still another issue that needs to be resolved. From the show interface command we can see that the router is receiving LMI messages and that the circuit itself appears fine. Let's take a look at the PVCs and the Frame Relay mappings that are on the router.

```
Router_A#show frame-relay pvc

PVC Statistics for interface Serial0/0 (Frame Relay DTE)

DLCI = 324, DLCI USAGE = LOCAL, PVC STATUS = DELETED,   INTERFACE = Serial0/0
```

```
    input pkts 0            output pkts 0            in bytes 0
    out bytes 0             dropped pkts 0           in FECN pkts 0
    in BECN pkts 0          out FECN pkts 0          out BECN pkts 0
    in DE pkts 0            out DE pkts 0
    out bcast pkts 0        out bcast bytes 0
    pvc create time 00:31:25, last time pvc status changed 00:31:25


DLCI = 368, DLCI USAGE = UNUSED, PVC STATUS = ACTIVE, INTERFACE = Serial0/0

    input pkts 0            output pkts 0            in bytes 0
    out bytes 0             dropped pkts 0           in FECN pkts 0
    in BECN pkts 0          out FECN pkts 0          out BECN pkts 0
    in DE pkts 0            out DE pkts 0
    out bcast pkts 0        out bcast bytes 0            Num Pkts Switched 0
    pvc create time 00:31:25, last time pvc status changed 00:31:25
Router_A#show frame-relay map
Serial0/0 (up): ip 172.16.20.6 dlci 324(0x144,0x5040),
  static,broadcast, CISCO, status deleted
Router_A#
```

Based on this output, there are two PVCs that are known to the router. One, 324, is in a deleted state and the other, 368, is in an active state. In addition, according to the show frame-relay map command, the IP address of the Headquarters router is statically mapped to the deleted DLCI 324.

With this information in hand, let's restate our observations of conditions at this point.

- Ethernet 0/0 and Ethernet 0/1 are working fine.

- Serial 0/0 is up and running without errors.

- Pinging the Headquarters router is unsuccessful.

- LMI is being sent and received successfully on Serial 0/0.

- There are two PVCs known by the router: 324 and 368.

- Only one PVC will be used at this location.

- The IP address of the headquarters router is statically mapped to DLCI 324.

Propose Solutions—Take 3

Based on these new observations, the most likely scenario is that when the router was precon-figured, the IP address was mapped to the incorrect DLCI. When a static IP-to-DLCI mapping is made, an entry for that DLCI is put in the router's PVC table. If the router doesn't receive an LMI message indicating that the frame switch knows about that DLCI, or if the interface on which this DLCI is assigned is down, the DLCI will go into a deleted state. In addition, when a router actively receives updates for a DLCI via LMI, the router will add this DLCI to its table in an active state. This appears to be what has occurred with DLCI 368. Therefore, we're assuming that DLCI 368 is the correct DLCI for this location.

Based on this information, our plan is to change the DLCI-to-IP mappings and map 172.16.20.6 to DLCI 368. It looks like this:

```
Router_A#conf t
Enter configuration commands, one per line. End with CNTL/Z.
Router_A(config)#interface serial 0/0
Router_A(config-if)#no frame-relay map ip 172.16.20.6 324 broadcast
Router_A(config-if)#frame-relay map ip 172.16.20.6 368 broadcast
Router_A(config-if)#^Z
Router_A#
Router_A#show frame-relay map
Serial0/0 (up): ip 172.16.20.6 dlci 368(0x170,0x5C00), static,
  broadcast, CISCO, status defined, active
Router_A#
Router_A#ping 172.16.20.6

Type escape sequence to abort.
Sending 5, 100-byte ICMP Echos to 172.16.20.6, timeout is   2 seconds:
!!!!!
Success rate is 100 percent (5/5), round-trip min/avg/max   = 28/30/32 ms
Router_A#
```

The changes made were effective, and they did not cause other network problems. The final step is to document what was done:

- We added 172.16.10.1/24 to Ethernet 0/0.
- We left 172.16.20.5/30 on Serial 0/0.
- We changed administrative status for interface Serial 0/0 with the no shutdown command.
- We changed the DLCI used for the Frame Relay connection.
- We changed the IP address for interface Ethernet 0/1 from 172.16.20.5/30 to 172.16.30.1/24.

All of the necessary troubleshooting steps were taken to solve the observed problems. The first step was to record observations. Then a problem statement was written. Based on the problem statement, an action plan was devised to resolve the problems. After the first changes were made, interface Ethernet 0/0 came up. You saw that the router would not allow Serial 0/0 to be removed from administrative shutdown, because of the duplicate IP address. The address conflicted with an IP address assigned to Ethernet 0/1. A new address was assigned to Ethernet 0/1, and Serial 0/0 was changed to an active state. After this, the DLCI used for the Frame Relay connection was changed and complete connectivity was achieved.

Real World Scenario

Frame Relay and Subinterfaces

In the Scenario #1 example with the Cisco 2600 router, the entire Frame Relay configuration was done on the main interface, and Frame Relay inverse ARP was turned off. This was done in order to make this example more interesting in terms of troubleshooting. Under this configuration, the interface would stay in an up/up state as long as it received LMI messages from the Frame Relay switch.

Although there are reasons to configure an interface in this manner (e.g., point-to-multipoint, multipoint-to-multipoint, consistency of configuration), using subinterfaces and the `frame-relay interface-dlci` command may have been more appropriate in this instance. Suppose that in our scenario, a subinterface (Serial 0/0.1, for example) had been configured specifically for the connection back to Headquarters. That would have made troubleshooting the DLCI problem easier. In that case, the main interface, Serial 0/0, would still have been in an up/up state, but the subinterface, Serial 0/0.1, would have been down/down until the DLCI issue was corrected. This correction would involve changing the `frame-relay interface-dlci` command to refer to DLCI 368 rather than to the originally configured value of 324. Using subinterfaces would have made it easier to spot the DLCI issue, as well as to verify when the problem had been corrected.

Scenario #2

This next scenario is a little more challenging. Look at Figure 10.2 to get a picture of the network that you'll troubleshoot.

What's happening is that Host Z is trying to ftp a file to Host A, but Host Z is unable to do so. Let's move through the troubleshooting method to solve this problem. Start by listing your observations.

FIGURE 10.2   Network diagram for scenario #2

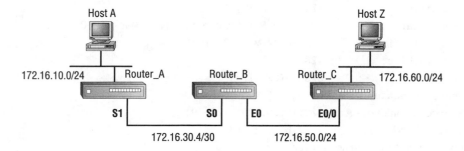

List Observations

As discussed in Chapter 1, you should define the boundary of dysfunctionality, which can be done in several ways. In this scenario, you test by attempting to ftp to Host A while observing the results.

The first test is an actual ftp attempt, the results of which are shown in Figure 10.3. The software gives you a host unreachable error message, which is an ICMP response. EtherPeek was used to capture packets in this exchange. The first packet decode is Host Z sending an ftp connection request.

FIGURE 10.3 An ftp attempt failure

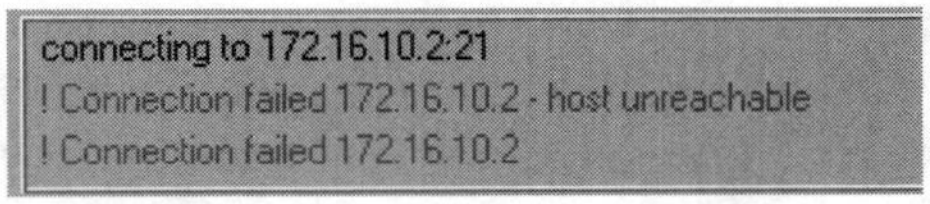

```
connecting to 172.16.10.2:21
! Connection failed 172.16.10.2 - host unreachable
! Connection failed 172.16.10.2
```

```
Flags:            0x00
Status:           0x00
Packet Length:66
Timestamp:        22:11:39.486000 04/18/2003
Ethernet Header
  Destination:    00:10:7b:d9:28:81   [0-5]
  Source:         00:a0:24:a5:06:57   [6-11]
  Protocol Type:08-00   IP   [12-13]
IP Header - Internet Protocol Datagram
  Version:              4   [14 Mask 0xf0]
  Header Length:        5   [14 Mask 0xf]
  Precedence:           0   [15 Mask 0xe0]
  Type of Service:    %000   [15 Mask 0x1c]
  Unused:             %00   [15 Mask 0x3]
  Total Length:       48   [16-17]
  Identifier:         17152   [18-19]
  Fragmentation Flags: %010 Do Not Fragment   [20  Mask 0xe0]
  Fragment Offset:    0   [20-22 Mask 0x1fffff]
  Time To Live:       128
  IP Type:            0x06  TCP   [23]
  Header Checksum:    0x1923   [24-25]
  Source IP Address:  172.16.60.130   [26-29]
  Dest. IP Address:   172.16.10.2   [30-33]
  No Internet Datagram Options
  TCP - Transport Control Protocol
```

```
Source Port:        1038  [34-35]
Destination Port: 21  FTP Control - File Transfer    Protocol  [36-37]
Sequence Number:  6198340  [38-41]
Ack Number:         0   [42-45]
Offset:             7   [46 Mask 0xf0]
Reserved:           %000000  [46 Mask 0xfc0]
Code:               %000010  [47 Mask 0x3f]
            Synch Sequence
Window:             8192  [48-49]
Checksum:           0x2bb5  [50-51]
Urgent Pointer:     0   [52-53]
TCP Options:  [54]
   Option Type:     2  Maximum Segment Size  [55]
        Length:     4
        MSS:        1460  [56-58]
   Option Type:     1  No Operation  [59]
   Option Type:     1  No Operation  [60]
   Option Type:     4  [61]
        Length:     2
No More FTP Command or Reply Data
Frame Check Sequence:   0x00000000
```

Everything looks fine with this packet. Now, look at the ICMP message received.

```
Flags:        0x00
   Status:        0x00
   Packet Length:74
   Timestamp:    22:11:39.489000 04/18/2003
Ethernet Header
   Destination:  00:a0:24:a5:06:57  [0-5]
   Source:       00:10:7b:d9:28:81  [6-11]
   Protocol Type:08-00  IP  [12-13]
IP Header - Internet Protocol Datagram
   Version:            4  [14 Mask 0xf0]
   Header Length:      5  [14 Mask 0xf]
   Precedence:         0  [15 Mask 0xe0]
   Type of Service:    %000  [15 Mask 0x1c]
   Unused:             %00  [15 Mask 0x3]
   Total Length:       56  [16-17]
   Identifier:         2815  [18-19]
   Fragmentation Flags: %000  [20 Mask 0xe0]
```

```
Fragment Offset:        0  [20-22 Mask 0x1fffff]
Time To Live:           255
IP Type:                0x01  ICMP  [23]
Header Checksum:        0xe021  [24-25]
Source IP Address:      172.16.60.1  [26-29]
Dest. IP Address:       172.16.60.130  [30-33]
No Internet Datagram Options
ICMP - Internet Control Messages Protocol  [34]
ICMP Type:              3  Destination Unreachable  [35]
Code:                   1  Host Unreachable
Checksum:               0x6439  [36-37]
Unused (must be zero):0x00000000  [38-41]
```

Notice that the source IP address in the ICMP packet is from 172.16.60.1. That's the gateway address for Host Z. Here is the header of the packet that caused the error:

```
IP Header - Internet Protocol Datagram
Version:                4  [42 Mask 0xf0]
Header Length:          5  [42 Mask 0xf]
Precedence:             0  [43 Mask 0xe0]
Type of Service:        %000  [43 Mask 0x1c]
Unused:                 %00  [43 Mask 0x3]
Total Length:           48  [44-45]
Identifier:             17152  [46-47]
Fragmentation Flags:    %010  Do Not Fragment   [48 Mask     0xe0]
Fragment Offset:        0  [48-50 Mask 0x1fffff]
Time To Live:           127
IP Type:                0x06  TCP  [51]
Header Checksum:        0x1a23  [52-53]
Source IP Address:      172.16.60.130  [54-57]
Dest. IP Address:       172.16.10.2  [58-61]
No Internet Datagram Options
TCP - Transport Control Protocol
Source Port:       1038  [62-63]
Destination Port: 21  FTP Control - File Transfer  Protocol      [64-65]
Sequence Number:   6198340  [66-69]
Ack Number:        0
```

The key information for your observation is provided under the ICMP header section. Notice the ICMP type of 3, Destination Unreachable—the code specifies that the host is not reachable. You might issue the ping command at this point, but it will render the same information—host unreachable.

What other tool might be used to aid in defining the border of dysfunctionality? There are a couple of different directions that may be taken. One method is to try to ftp a file to hosts that don't reside on the 172.16.10.0/24 network. Another option is to run a traceroute to see where the path to Host A is failing.

Let's try the latter. Following are the results of a traceroute to Host A:

```
C:\WINDOWS>tracert 172.16.10.2
Tracing route to 172.16.10.2 over a maximum of 30 hops
1     5 ms     2 ms     4 ms   172.16.60.1
2   172.16.60.1   reports: Destination host unreachable.
Trace complete.
```

These results indicate that Router C does not have a route to Host A. This allows you to draw the line of dysfunctionality to the boundary between Router C and Router B.

To further troubleshoot this problem, diagnostics must be executed from Router C. Let's bring up a console on Router C. The first command that should be issued is a show ip route. The results are as follows:

```
Router_C#show ip route
Codes: C - connected, S - static, I - IGRP, R - RIP, M - mobile, B -
 BGP D - EIGRP, EX - EIGRP external, O - OSPF, IA - OSPF inter area N1
 - OSPF NSSA external type 1, N2 - OSPF NSSA external type 2 E1 - OSPF
 external type 1, E2 - OSPF external type 2, E - EGPi - IS-IS, L1 - IS-
 IS level-1, L2 - IS-IS level-2, * - candidate default U - per-user
 static route, o - ODR
Gateway of last resort is not set
172.16.0.0/24 is subnetted, 2 subnets
C       172.16.60.0 is directly connected, Ethernet0/1
C       172.16.50.0 is directly connected, Ethernet0/0
Router_C#
```

Router C knows only routes for networks that are directly connected. This points to problems with routing updates or routing protocols between Routers B and C. Let's take a look at the configuration on both routers:

```
Router_C#show running-config
Building configuration...
Current configuration:
!
version 11.3
no service password-encryption
!
hostname Router_C
```

```
!
enable password aloha
!
interface Ethernet0/0
 ip address 172.16.50.2 255.255.255.0
!
interface Serial0/0
 no ip address
 shutdown
!
interface Ethernet0/1
 ip address 172.16.60.1 255.255.255.0
!
router eigrp 100
 network 172.16.0.0
 no auto-summary
!
ip classless
!
line con 0
line aux 0
line vty 0 4
 password aloha
 login
!
end
Router_C#
```

The show interface results should be reviewed before the configuration of Router B is displayed. The only interface of concern here is the one that connects the two routers—interface Ethernet 0/0. In the following results, notice that interface Ethernet 0/0 is up and functioning. This is proved by using the ping command.

```
Router_C>show interface ethernet0/0
Ethernet0/0 is up, line protocol is up
   Hardware is AmdP2, address is 0010.7bd9.2880 (bia 0010.7bd9.2880)
   Internet address is 172.16.50.2/24
   MTU 1500 bytes, BW 10000 Kbit, DLY 1000 usec, rely 255/255, load 1/255
   Encapsulation ARPA, loopback not set, keepalive set (10 sec)
   ARP type: ARPA, ARP Timeout 04:00:00
   Last input 02:54:40, output 00:00:00, output hang never
   Last clearing of "show interface" counters never
```

```
Queueing strategy: fifo
Output queue 0/40, 0 drops; input queue 0/75, 0 drops
5 minute input rate 0 bits/sec, 0 packets/sec
5 minute output rate 0 bits/sec, 0 packets/sec
    1006 packets input, 90611 bytes, 0 no buffer
    Received 990 broadcasts, 0 runts, 0 giants, 0 throttles
    0 input errors, 0 CRC, 0 frame, 0 overrun, 0 ignored,
        0 abort
    0 input packets with dribble condition detected
    4935 packets output, 402703 bytes, 0 underruns
    0 output errors, 0 collisions, 2 interface resets
    0 babbles, 0 late collision, 0 deferred
    0 lost carrier, 0 no carrier
    0 output buffer failures, 0 output buffers swapped out
Router_C>ping 172.16.50.1
Type escape sequence to abort.
Sending 5, 100-byte ICMP Echos to 172.16.50.1, timeout is   2   seconds:
.!!!!
Success rate is 80 percent (4/5), round-trip min/avg/max =    1/3/4 ms
Router_C>ping 172.16.50.1
Type escape sequence to abort.
Sending 5, 100-byte ICMP Echos to 172.16.50.1, timeout is   2   seconds:
!!!!!
Success rate is 100 percent (5/5), round-trip min/avg/max   =   4/4/4 ms
Router_C>
```

This output reveals that the routers are not sharing routing information. Something is causing the routing protocol to fail, but it's not because the interface is down. Before moving on, let's review our observations and make sure that the correct path is being followed.

- Host Z cannot FTP to Host A.

- Host Z cannot ping to Host A.

- Host Z cannot traceroute to Host A.

- ICMP Destination Unreachable responses were returned from the FTP request.

- Router C does not have a route to the destination network.

- Ethernet 0/0 is up and functioning.

- There is capability to ping Router B.

Before a problem definition statement can be devised, more information must be gathered from Router B. Let's telnet to Router B:

```
Router_C>172.16.50.1
```

```
Trying 172.16.50.1 ... Open
User Access Verification
Password:
Router_B(boot)>
```

Something looks wrong. Instead of coming up with the normal prompt, the router is in boot mode, which explains why no routing is taking place. When a router is in boot mode, routing protocols do not work. This is the last key observation needed, and it allows you to define the problem.

Here is the problem statement: "Router B is in boot mode, it does not route in this state, so Host Z cannot FTP to Host A." This statement lists the actual problem as well as the reported problem.

Propose Solutions

With a detailed and focused problem statement made based on your observations, you can now move on to formulate possible solutions to the problem. It's still important to consider the observations when determining the next action.

You know that the router is in boot mode, but what is causing this? There are two simple reasons for a router's being in boot mode: There is a lack of IOS on the system flash, or the router is not looking in the right location for the IOS.

Let's look at the contents of Router B's flash. Then we'll look at the router's version information.

```
Router_B(boot)#show flash
System flash directory:
File  Length    Name/status
  1   4287696   c2500-i-l.112-15.bin
[4287760 bytes used, 4100848 available, 8388608 total]
8192K bytes of processor board System flash (Read/Write)
Router_B(boot)#
```

This shows one IOS image on the system flash. Now, you need to determine which version of IOS is running on the router:

```
Router_B(boot)#show version
Cisco Internetwork Operating System Software
IOS (tm) 3000 Bootstrap Software (IGS-BOOT-R), Version 11.0(10c)XB1,
 PLATFORM SPECIFIC RELEASE SOFTWARE (fc1)
Copyright (c) 1986-1996 by cisco Systems, Inc.
Compiled Wed 10-Sep-97 13:06 by phester
Image text-base: 0x01010000, data-base: 0x00001000
ROM: System Bootstrap, Version 11.0(10c)XB1, PLATFORM SPECIFIC
 RELEASE SOFTWARE
```

```
(fc1)
Router_B uptime is 3 hours, 11 minutes
System restarted by reload
Running default software
cisco 2500 (68030) processor (revision A) with 4096K/2048K bytes of memory.
Processor board ID 01229726, with hardware revision 00000000
X.25 software, Version 2.0, NET2, BFE and GOSIP compliant.
Cisco-ET Extended Temperature platform.
1 Ethernet/IEEE 802.3 interface.
2 Serial network interfaces.
32K bytes of non-volatile configuration memory.
8192K bytes of processor board System flash (Read/Write)
Configuration register is 0x2101
Router_B(boot)#
```

The response displayed in the first few fields is that it is running a bootstrap version of IOS. Now, from these two outputs on Router B, it can be deduced that the IOS contained in flash memory was not used to boot the router.

As previously mentioned, reasons for a router's being in boot mode are that the IOS image could be corrupt, or the router is looking for the IOS in the wrong place. The router uses a configuration register to point to the location of the IOS image that it should load during the boot process.

The config-register is a 16-bit number that controls the router's boot sequence. The lowest 4 bits indicate the location from where the system image, or IOS, will be loaded. If the value is 0000, then the router enters into ROM monitor mode. If the register is set to 0001, then the IOS will be loaded from the boot ROM. (For a full description of config-register settings, refer to CCO.)

In this case, the configuration register was set to the hex value of 0x2101, which tells the router to look for the system image on the boot ROM. Remember that only the first 4 bits indicate the system image location.

The action plan for this scenario is to change the configuration register on Router B to load the image from system flash. The configuration changes are as follows. After the router reloads, a quick check can be made by issuing a show version command.

```
Router_B(boot)#conf t
Enter configuration commands, one per line. End with CNTL/Z.
Router_B(boot)(config)#config
Router_B(boot)(config)#config-register 0x2102
Router_B(boot)(config)#^Z
Router_B(boot)#
Router_B(boot)#reload
Proceed with reload? [confirm]
```

```
[Connection to 172.16.50.1 closed by foreign host]
Router_C>172.16.50.1
Trying 172.16.50.1 ... Open
User Access Verification
Password:
Router_B>enable
Password:
Router_B#show version
Cisco Internetwork Operating System Software
IOS (tm) 2500 Software (C2500-I-L), Version 11.2(15), RELEASE SOFTWARE (fc1)
Copyright (c) 1986-1998 by cisco Systems, Inc.
Compiled Tue 07-Jul-98 21:51 by tmullins
Image text-base: 0x03022F80, data-base: 0x00001000
ROM: System Bootstrap, Version 11.0(10c)XB1, PLATFORM SPECIFIC
 RELEASE SOFTWARE(fc1)
BOOTFLASH: 3000 Bootstrap Software (IGS-BOOT-R), Version
 11.0(10c)XB1, PLATFORM
SPECIFIC RELEASE SOFTWARE (fc1)
Router_B uptime is 2 minutes
System restarted by reload
System image file is "flash:c2500-i-l.112-15.bin", booted via flash
cisco 2500 (68030) processor (revision A) with 4096K/2048K bytes of memory.
Processor board ID 01229726, with hardware revision 00000000
Bridging software.
X.25 software, Version 2.0, NET2, BFE and GOSIP compliant.
Cisco-ET Extended Temperature platform.
1 Ethernet/IEEE 802.3 interface(s)
2 Serial network interface(s)
32K bytes of non-volatile configuration memory.
8192K bytes of processor board System flash (Read ONLY)
Configuration register is 0x2102
Router_B#
```

This time, the system image file is "flash:c2500-i-l.112-15.bin" booted from flash. This means it is running the proper IOS. Now look at the route table:

```
Router_B#show ip route
Codes: C - connected, S - static, I - IGRP, R - RIP, M - mobile, B -
 BGP, D - EIGRP, EX - EIGRP external, O - OSPF, IA - OSPF inter area N1
 - OSPF NSSA external type 1, N2 - OSPF NSSA external type 2 E1 - OSPF
 external type 1, E2 - OSPF external type 2, E - EGPi - IS-IS, L1 - IS-
```

```
IS level-1, L2 - IS-IS level-2, * - candidate default
U - per-user static route, o - ODR
Gateway of last resort is not set
172.16.0.0/16 is variably subnetted, 2 subnets, 2 masks
D       172.16.60.0/24 [90/307200] via 172.16.50.2, 00:00:16, Ethernet0
D       172.16.10.0/24 [90/300200] via 172.16.30.5, 00:00:19, Serial0
C       172.16.50.0/24 is directly connected, Ethernet0
C       172.16.30.4/30 is directly connected, Serial0
Router_B#
```

Now the route to 172.16.10.0/24 is present in the route table. The next step is to look at the route table on Router C.

```
Router_C>show ip route
Codes: C - connected, S - static, I - IGRP, R - RIP, M - mobile, B -
BGP, D - EIGRP, EX - EIGRP external, O - OSPF, IA - OSPF inter area N1
- OSPF NSSA external type 1, N2 - OSPF NSSA external type 2 E1 - OSPF
external type 1, E2 - OSPF external type 2, E - EGPi - IS-IS, L1 - IS-
IS level-1, L2 - IS-IS level-2, * - candidate defaultU - per-user
static route, o - ODR
Gateway of last resort is not set
172.16.0.0/16 is variably subnetted, 3 subnets, 2 masks
C       172.16.60.0/24 is directly connected, Ethernet0/1
C       172.16.50.0/24 is directly connected, Ethernet0/0
D       172.16.30.4/30 [90/2195456] via 172.16.50.1,   00:02:59, Ethernet0/0
D       172.16.10.0/24 [90/3295676] via 172.16.50.1,   00:02:59, Ethernet0/0
Router_C>
```

Everything looks to be in place, but the ultimate test is to ftp from Host Z to Host A. The connection is successful.

```
C:\WINDOWS>ftp 172.16.10.2
> ftp: connect :10061
ftp>
```

Let's review the steps taken. The observation was that Host Z could not ftp to Host A. The problem was isolated by using the ping and traceroute commands. After the problem was isolated, the correct observations were made that enabled a problem statement to be made. The problem was that Router B was in boot mode. This happened because the IOS image was loaded from the ROM instead of flash. The problem was remedied by changing the configuration register to indicate that the image should be loaded from the system flash.

The effect of the configuration changes was validated by showing the routes present on each router, as well as establishing an ftp session with Host A.

Scenario #3

The final scenario in this chapter involves WAN connectivity problems but is slightly different from Scenario #1. In this situation, a facility has been moved, just yesterday afternoon, and the existing network equipment was reconfigured and reused in the new location. This move was also used as an opportunity to clean up the location's assigned IP address ranges, to match the current addressing standard. Following the move, everything was verified and the users at the new site were able to get to internal and external resources successfully. Overnight, however, there was a power outage at the new site, and this morning the users cannot get to any internal or external resources other than ones on their own segment. To make matters worse, there is no network administrator on site—the installation had been considered successful and the network administrator who did the installation has already left.

Figure 10.4 shows the network topology for this troubleshooting scenario.

FIGURE 10.4   Network diagram for scenario #3

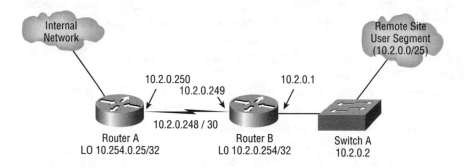

List Observations

The first thing that you can do is ensure that Router_B is reachable, by pinging both the loopback interface and the other side of the serial connection:

```
Router_A#ping 10.2.0.254
Type escape sequence to abort.
Sending 5, 100-byte ICMP Echos to 10.2.0.254, timeout is 2 seconds:
.....
Success rate is 0 percent (0/5)
Router_A#ping 10.2.0.249
Type escape sequence to abort.
Sending 5, 100-byte ICMP Echos to 10.2.0.249, timeout is 2 seconds:
.....
Success rate is 0 percent (0/5)
Router_A#
```

Because the ping tests failed, we need to look deeper into the connectivity between Router_ A and Router_B:

```
Router_A#show interface s0/0
Serial0/0 is up, line protocol is up
  Hardware is QUICC with integrated T1 CSU/DSU
  Internet address is 10.2.0.250/30
  MTU 1500 bytes, BW 1544 Kbit, DLY 20000 usec, rely 255/255, load 1/255
  Encapsulation HDLC, loopback not set, keepalive set (10 sec)
  Last input 00:00:02, output 00:00:00, output hang never
  Last clearing of "show interface" counters never
  Queueing strategy: fifo
  Output queue 0/40, 0 drops; input queue 0/75, 0 drops
  5 minute input rate 0 bits/sec, 0 packets/sec
  5 minute output rate 0 bits/sec, 0 packets/sec
     354 packets input, 31947 bytes, 0 no buffer
     Received 145 broadcasts, 0 runts, 0 giants, 0 throttles
     0 input errors, 0 CRC, 0 frame, 0 overrun, 0 ignored, 0 abort
     369 packets output, 27286 bytes, 0 underruns
     0 output errors, 0 collisions, 8 interface resets
     0 output buffer failures, 0 output buffers swapped out
     5 carrier transitions
     DCD=up  DSR=up  DTR=up  RTS=up  CTS=up

Router_A#
```

We observe that the interface is in an up/up state and that some traffic appears to be going across the interface. So at this point, Layers 1 and 2 appear to be okay. Let's see if there is anything in Router_A's log that could be of some assistance:

```
Router_A#show logging
Syslog logging: enabled (0 messages dropped, 0 flushes, 0 overruns)
    Console logging: disabled
    Monitor logging: level debugging, 0 messages logged
    Buffer logging: level debugging, 97 messages logged
    Trap logging: level informational, 32 message lines logged

Log Buffer (4096 bytes):
Jul 20 06:37:05.995: IP-EIGRP: Neighbor 10.100.0.249 not on common
 subnet for Serial0/0
Jul 20 06:37:19.603: IP-EIGRP: Neighbor 10.100.0.249 not on common
 subnet for Serial0/0
```

```
Jul 20 06:37:34.215: IP-EIGRP: Neighbor 10.100.0.249 not on common
 subnet for Serial0/0
Jul 20 06:37:48.439: IP-EIGRP: Neighbor 10.100.0.249 not on common
 subnet for Serial0/0
...
...
<output removed>
...
...
Jul 20 06:46:36.875: IP-EIGRP: Neighbor 10.100.0.249 not on common
 subnet for Serial0/0
Jul 20 06:46:50.015: IP-EIGRP: Neighbor 10.100.0.249 not on common
 subnet for Serial0/0
Jul 20 06:47:03.651: IP-EIGRP: Neighbor 10.100.0.249 not on common
 subnet for Serial0/0
Jul 20 06:47:17.791: IP-EIGRP: Neighbor 10.100.0.249 not on common
 subnet for Serial0/0
Jul 20 06:47:31.799: IP-EIGRP: Neighbor 10.100.0.249 not on common
 subnet for Serial0/0
Router_A#
```

The log indicates that the neighbor on Serial 0 is not on the same subnet and is using the IP address 10.100.0.249. Let's see if we can confirm this by checking the CDP information:

```
Router_A#show cdp neighbors serial0/0 detail
-------------------------
Device ID: Router_B
Entry address(es):
  IP address: 10.100.0.249
Platform: cisco 3640,  Capabilities: Router
Interface: Serial0/0,  Port ID (outgoing port): Serial0/0
Holdtime : 179 sec
Version :
Cisco Internetwork Operating System Software
IOS (tm) 3600 Software (C3640-JS56I-M), Version 12.0(7)T,  RELEASE SOFTWARE
(fc2)
Copyright (c) 1986-1999 by cisco Systems, Inc.
Compiled Wed 08-Dec-99 04:50 by phanguye


Router_A#
```

A `show CDP neighbors xx detail` confirms that Router B is using `10.100.0.249` as its IP address. In looking at your old documentation, you see that this is the address the router had when it was in the old location. Let's list the facts that you have gathered up to this point:

- Users in the remote location can only get to resources on their directly attached segment.
- Router A cannot ping the serial or loopback interface of Router B.
- Interface Serial 0/0 is up and the line protocol is up.
- There are EIGRP error messages in Router A's log, indicating a neighbor on an incorrect subnet.
- According to CDP, Router B is using the address `10.100.0.249` on its serial interface.
- `10.100.0.249` was the address that was used on Router B's serial interface in the old location.

The problem statement is that Router B is using an incorrect address on its serial interface. No statements about the Ethernet interface can be made at this time because Router B is not accessible.

Based on the data so far, the possible reasons for an incorrect address on the interface are as follows:

- The configuration was changed.
- The new configuration was never saved to NVRAM, and the old configuration was brought up when the router was reloaded.

The second possibility is the most likely because it would also explain why users are not able to get to any services outside their subnet.

Propose Solutions

Unfortunately, since Router B is remote and there is no one at the location who can assist, the change to the IP address must be done remotely if at all possible. To do this, we'll change the IP address of Router A's Serial 0/0 to be on the same subnet as Router B's. This will allow us to connect to Router B and correct its configuration.

Because we know that the IP address space has not yet been reassigned, in this particular scenario, we don't have to worry about creating another problem by accidentally duplicating IP addresses in the network. In your network, however, always be sure to verify that the IP address space you are using has not already been assigned elsewhere.

```
Router_A#configure terminal
Enter configuration commands, one per line.  End with CNTL/Z.
Router_A(config)#interface Serial0/0
Router_A(config-if)#ip address 10.100.0.250 255.255.255.252
```

Next, we make sure that we can ping the other side and see the EIGRP neighbor:

```
Router_A#ping 10.100.0.249
Type escape sequence to abort.
Sending 5, 100-byte ICMP Echos to 10.100.0.249, timeout is 2 seconds:
!!!!!
Success rate is 100 percent (5/5), round-trip min/avg/max = 1/3/4 ms
Router_A#
Router_A#show ip eigrp neighbors serial0/0
IP-EIGRP neighbors for process 3
H   Address             Interface    Hold Uptime    SRTT   RTO   Q  Seq
                                     (sec)          (ms)         Cnt Num
0   10.100.0.249        Se0/0          14 00:02:11 1018  5000   0  2
Router_A#
```

We can now telnet over to Router B and see how the interfaces are configured:

```
Router_B#show ip interface brief
Interface       IP-Address      OK? Method    Status              Protocol
Ethernet0/0     unassigned      YES NVRAM  administratively down   down
Serial0/0       10.100.0.249    YES NVRAM  up                      up
Serial0/1       unassigned      YES NVRAM  administratively down   down
FastEthernet1/0 10.100.0.1      YES NVRAM  up                      up
Ethernet2/0     unassigned      YES NVRAM  administratively down   down
TokenRing2/0    unassigned      YES NVRAM  administratively down   down
Loopback0       10.100.0.254    YES NVRAM  up                      up
Router_B#
```

In looking at the interfaces, we can see that all of them are set to their old values. Therefore, we need to update these values to the new correct ones.

```
Router_B#configure terminal
Enter configuration commands, one per line.  End with CNTL/Z.
Router_B(config)#interface loopback0
Router_B(config-if)#ip address 10.2.0.254 255.255.255.255
Router_B(config-if)#interface FastEthernet1/0
Router_B(config-if)#ip address 10.2.0.1 255.255.255.128
Router_B(config-if)#interface Serial0/0
Router_B(config-if)#ip address 10.2.0.249 255.255.255.252
```

Since the address you connected to the router is on Serial 0/0, when this address is changed, your telnet session will be dropped. To reconnect, we will need to change the address on Serial 0/0 on Router A back to the correct value. This is done as follows:

```
Router_A#configure terminal
```

```
Enter configuration commands, one per line.  End with CNTL/Z.
Router_A(config)#interface Serial0/0
Router_A(config-if)#ip address 10.2.0.250 255.255.255.252
```

With Serial 0/0 correctly set up on both routers, we are once again able to telnet to Router B normally. From Router A, we need to verify connectivity to the loopback and serial addresses of Router B:

```
Router_A#ping 10.2.0.249
Type escape sequence to abort.
Sending 5, 100-byte ICMP Echos to 10.2.0.249, timeout is 2 seconds:
!!!!!
Success rate is 100 percent (5/5), round-trip min/avg/max = 1/3/4 ms
Router_A#ping 10.2.0.254
Type escape sequence to abort.
Sending 5, 100-byte ICMP Echos to 10.2.0.254, timeout is 2 seconds:
!!!!!
Success rate is 100 percent (5/5), round-trip min/avg/max = 1/3/4 ms
Router_A#
```

After this we need to verify with the users that they are able to connect to their resources. And finally, we execute a `copy running-config startup-config` command on Router B so that this problem does not happen again.

 Real World Scenario

Using *reload* during Remote Configuration

It's not uncommon that a network administrator will need to work on a remote router. In many of these cases, a wrong step can sever network connectivity to the remote site, creating the need for someone to go out to the location and correct the problem. This is where the `reload` command can come in handy.

Before you start your work at the remote site, ensure that the current configuration is saved to NVRAM by executing the `copy running-config startup-config` command. Following this, assuming you only have minor alterations to make, execute the `reload in 15` command and begin your changes. This command tells the router to reload in 15 minutes. If your changes do cause the router to lose connectivity, in 15 minutes it will reset to the last saved configuration before the change started, allowing access once again. While you're doing the modifications, you can monitor the amount of time remaining before the reload by executing the `show reload` command. And, after your change is successful and everything is working as expected, you can execute the `reload cancel` command, which will cancel the scheduled reload.

Troubleshooting Ethernet Problems

This section presents troubleshooting scenarios for Ethernet-related dysfunction. The examples are simple, and you need to use only Ethernet-related commands to solve these problems.

Scenario #1

The difficulty in this first scenario is that Host A cannot telnet to Host Z. Figure 10.5 depicts the network you're working with. Troubleshooting will begin after the establishment of the boundary of dysfunctionality. You know that the problem exists between Router C and Host Z. Because this is an Ethernet environment, you know what to look for.

FIGURE 10.5   Network diagram for Ethernet scenario #1

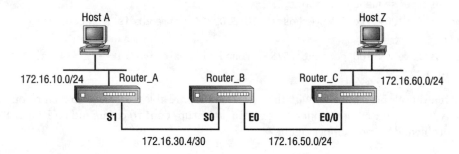

List Observations

The first thing to do is verify that Host Z is still unreachable. Let's look at the results of a ping test:

```
Router_C#ping 172.16.60.130
Type escape sequence to abort.
Sending 5, 100-byte ICMP Echos to 172.16.60.130, timeout is 2 seconds:
.....
Success rate is 0 percent (0/5)
Router_C#
```

Because the ping test failed, the cause needs to be isolated. Let's look at the interface:

```
Router_C#show interface ethernet0/1
Ethernet0/1 is up, line protocol is up
  Hardware is AmdP2, address is 0010.7bd9.2881 (bia 0010.7bd9.2881)
  Internet address is 172.16.60.1/24
  MTU 1500 bytes, BW 10000 Kbit, DLY 1000 usec, rely 255/255, load 1/255
  Encapsulation ARPA, loopback not set, keepalive set (10 sec)
```

```
ARP type: ARPA, ARP Timeout 04:00:00
Last input 00:41:42, output 00:00:00, output hang never
Last clearing of "show interface" counters never
Queueing strategy: fifo
Output queue 0/40, 0 drops; input queue 0/75, 0 drops
5 minute input rate 0 bits/sec, 0 packets/sec
5 minute output rate 0 bits/sec, 0 packets/sec
   147 packets input, 9568 bytes, 0 no buffer
   Received 5 broadcasts, 0 runts, 0 giants, 0 throttles
   0 input errors, 0 CRC, 0 frame, 0 overrun, 0 ignored, 0 abort
   0 input packets with dribble condition detected
   2009 packets output, 162455 bytes, 0 underruns
   0 output errors, 0 collisions, 2 interface resets
   0 babbles, 0 late collision, 0 deferred
   0 lost carrier, 0 no carrier
   0 output buffer failures, 0 output buffers swapped out
Router_C#
```

Everything looks good, except for the fact that no traffic is being sent across the interface. That can be another indication that there is a problem between the router and Host Z. Now, examine the ARP table:

```
Router_C>show arp
Protocol  Address    Age (min) Hardware Addr Type Interface
Internet  172.16.60.1  -     0010.7bd9.2881 ARPA  Ethernet0/1
Internet  172.16.50.2  -     0010.7bd9.2880 ARPA  Ethernet0/0
Internet  172.16.50.1  0     0000.0c09.99cc ARPA  Ethernet0/0
Router_C>
```

The address of interest is not listed in the ARP table, which means that Router C does not know where to send the Layer 2 PDU. A trace using EtherPeek shows the router sending out an ARP broadcast:

```
Flags:        0x00
  Status:       0x00
  Packet Length:64
  Timestamp:    11:30:42.713000 04/19/2003
Ethernet Header
  Destination:  ff:ff:ff:ff:ff:ff Ethernet Brdcast  [0-5]
  Source:       00:10:7b:d9:28:81  [6-11]
  Protocol Type:08-06  IP ARP  [12-13]
ARP - Address Resolution Protocol
  Hardware:               1 Ethernet (10Mb) [14-15]
```

```
Protocol:                 08-00  IP  [16-18]
Hardware Address Length:  6  [19]
Protocol Address Length:  4
Operation:                1  ARP Request  [20-21]
Sender Hardware Address:  00:10:7b:d9:28:81  [22-27]
Sender Internet Address:  172.16.60.1  [28-31]
Target Hardware Address:  00:00:00:00:00:00  (ignored) [32-37]
Target Internet Address:  172.16.60.130  [38-41]
Extra bytes (Padding):
...............  00 00 00 00 00 00 00 00 00 00 00 00 00   00 00 00   [42-57]
..               00 00   [58-59]
Frame Check Sequence:  0x00000000
```

No response was received from this broadcast. Let's list the facts that you have gathered:

- Router C cannot ping Host Z.

- Interface Ethernet 0/1 is up and line protocol is up.

- There are no collisions on the Ethernet interface.

- No traffic is transiting the Ethernet 0/1 interface.

- There is no listing for Host Z in the ARP table.

- An ARP broadcast was sent out Ethernet 0/1, but no response was received from Host Z.

The problem statement is that "Ethernet 0/1 is functioning properly, but it cannot communicate with Host Z. There is no listing for Host Z in the ARP table."

Focusing on the ARP table makes it simpler to decide the possible causes and create an action plan. What possible reasons are there for Host Z not to be listed in the ARP table? Here are some candidates:

- Failed host

- Cabling failures

- Bad Ethernet NIC on Host Z

- Mismatching frame encapsulation type

Propose Solutions

You verified that the host is not down. No traffic is transiting the Ethernet interface on the router. This indicates that the Ethernet card is not starting to fail, but could have completely failed. Cabling is probably not the issue because you would see interface resets or carrier transitions, and none of those symptoms are indicated on the interface. This leaves us with mismatching encapsulation type as the probable culprit.

The easiest way to test it is to ping Router C from Host Z.

```
C:\WINDOWS>ping 172.16.60.1
Pinging 172.16.60.1 with 32 bytes of data:
```

```
Reply from 172.16.60.1: bytes=32 time=7ms TTL=255
Reply from 172.16.60.1: bytes=32 time=1ms TTL=255
Reply from 172.16.60.1: bytes=32 time=2ms TTL=255
Reply from 172.16.60.1: bytes=32 time=4ms TTL=255
Ping statistics for 172.16.60.1:
    Packets: Sent = 4, Received = 4, Lost = 0 (0% loss),
Approximate round trip times in milli-seconds:
    Minimum = 1ms, Maximum =  7ms, Average =  3ms
C:\WINDOWS>
```

The ping was successful. Why is it that Router C can ping Host Z, but Host Z cannot ping Router C? Let's go back to the router. Look at the ARP table now.

```
Router_C>show arp
Protocol  Address       Age (min) Hardware Addr  Type  Interface
Internet  172.16.60.130 1    00a0.24a5.0657  SNAP  Ethernet0/1
Internet  172.16.60.1   -    0010.7bd9.2881  ARPA  Ethernet0/1
Internet  172.16.50.2   -    0010.7bd9.2880  ARPA  Ethernet0/0
Internet  172.16.50.1   111  0000.0c09.99cc  ARPA  Ethernet0/0
Router_C>
```

Wait a minute! Host Z is listed in the table now. How did that happen? You must remember that although Cisco understands several different encapsulation types, its default is ARPA. When the router sent the ARP request, it was sent using ARPA. Host Z does not understand ARPA, and so it did not respond to the ARP request.

The process works differently on a Cisco router, however. When Host Z sent an ARP broadcast, it was sent with SNAP encapsulation. The difference is that the router understood the broadcast, recorded the encapsulation type, and entered it into the router's ARP table. The type allows the router to override the default encapsulation. Now, when the router needs to send a frame to Host Z, it uses SNAP encapsulation. Let's test it:

```
Router_C#ping 172.16.60.130
Type escape sequence to abort.
Sending 5, 100-byte ICMP Echos to 172.16.60.130, timeout   is 2 seconds:
!!!!!
Success rate is 100 percent (5/5), round-trip min/avg/max   = 4/4/8 ms
Router_C#
```

It worked just fine because the router now knows which encapsulation type must be used when communicating with Host Z.

This problem has been resolved temporarily. To solve it permanently, you must manually change the encapsulation type used for the interface to which Host Z connects, or create a static ARP entry. Now let's move on to the next scenario.

Scenario #2

This is another simple Ethernet problem. Using the example network depicted in Figure 10.6, you will attempt to solve a less tangible network misbehavior. The user at Host A complains of very slow throughput to Host Z. He is able to ping and traceroute to the destination, but file transfers are experiencing very slow transfer times.

FIGURE 10.6   Network diagram for Ethernet scenario #2

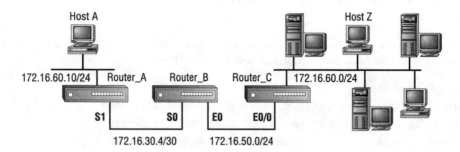

List Observations

List the observations given you by the user, and then move on to other fact-gathering procedures:

- Long transfer times
- Slow throughput
- Can ping and traceroute to host

The fact that ping and traceroute work indicates that the routing between Host A and Host Z is intact. Something else is causing latency somewhere along the line. Again, start at the far end of the problem.

The following are several show interface outputs of the same interface over an extended period of time. Look at them all and see if you can spot the problem.

```
Router_C#show int ethernet 0/1
Ethernet0/1 is up, line protocol is up
  Hardware is Lance, address is 0000.0c47.abea (bia 0000.0c47.abea)
  Internet address is 172.16.60.1/24
  MTU 1500 bytes, BW 10000 Kbit, DLY 1000 usec, rely 255/255, load 46/255
  Encapsulation ARPA, loopback not set, keepalive set (10 sec)
  ARP type: ARPA, ARP Timeout 04:00:00
  Last input 00:00:00, output 00:00:00, output hang never
  Last clearing of "show interface" counters 00:00:05
  Queueing strategy: fifo
  Output queue 0/40, 0 drops; input queue 0/75, 0 drops
```

```
  5 minute input rate 1259000 bits/sec, 629 packets/sec
  5 minute output rate 1822000 bits/sec, 486 packets/sec
     3476 packets input, 455808 bytes, 0 no buffer
     Received 2 broadcasts, 0 runts, 0 giants
     0 input errors, 0 CRC, 0 frame, 0 overrun, 0 ignored,
        0 abort
     0 input packets with dribble condition detected
     1165 packets output, 1667097 bytes, 0 underruns
     0 output errors, 175 collisions, 0 interface resets
     0 babbles, 0 late collision, 182 deferred
     0 lost carrier, 0 no carrier
     0 output buffer failures, 0 output buffers swapped out
Router_C#show int ethernet 0/1
Ethernet0/1 is up, line protocol is up
  Hardware is Lance, address is 0000.0c47.abea (bia 0000.0c47.abea)
  Internet address is 172.16.60.1/24
  MTU 1500 bytes, BW 10000 Kbit, DLY 1000 usec, rely 255/255, load 46/255
  Encapsulation ARPA, loopback not set, keepalive set (10 sec)
  ARP type: ARPA, ARP Timeout 04:00:00
  Last input 00:00:00, output 00:00:00, output hang never
  Last clearing of "show interface" counters 00:00:16
  Queueing strategy: fifo
  Output queue 0/40, 0 drops; input queue 0/75, 0 drops
  5 minute input rate 1243000 bits/sec, 627 packets/sec
  5 minute output rate 1826000 bits/sec, 484 packets/sec
     9872 packets input, 1760499 bytes, 0 no buffer
     Received 4 broadcasts, 0 runts, 0 giants
     0 input errors, 0 CRC, 0 frame, 0 overrun, 0 ignored,
        0 abort
     0 input packets with dribble condition detected
     2858 packets output, 3943213 bytes, 0 underruns
     0 output errors, 443 collisions, 0 interface resets
     0 babbles, 0 late collision, 471 deferred
     0 lost carrier, 0 no carrier
     0 output buffer failures, 0 output buffers swapped out
Router_C#show int ethernet 0/1
Ethernet0/1 is up, line protocol is up
  Hardware is Lance, address is 0000.0c47.abea (bia 0000.0c47.abea)
  Internet address is 172.16.60.1/24
  MTU 1500 bytes, BW 10000 Kbit, DLY 1000 usec, rely 255/255, load 46/255
```

```
     Encapsulation ARPA, loopback not set, keepalive set (10 sec)
     ARP type: ARPA, ARP Timeout 04:00:00
     Last input 00:00:00, output 00:00:00, output hang never
     Last clearing of "show interface" counters 00:00:37
     Queueing strategy: fifo
     Output queue 0/40, 0 drops; input queue 0/75, 0 drops
     5 minute input rate 1209000 bits/sec, 620 packets/sec
     5 minute output rate 1819000 bits/sec, 477 packets/sec
        21386 packets input, 3979009 bytes, 0 no buffer
        Received 9 broadcasts, 0 runts, 0 giants
        0 input errors, 0 CRC, 0 frame, 0 overrun, 0 ignored, 0 abort
        0 input packets with dribble condition detected
        5590 packets output, 8237684 bytes, 0 underruns
        0 output errors, 889 collisions, 0 interface resets
        0 babbles, 0 late collision, 1006 deferred
        0 lost carrier, 0 no carrier
        0 output buffer failures, 0 output buffers swapped out
Router_C#show int ethernet 0/1
Ethernet0/1 is up, line protocol is up
   Hardware is Lance, address is 0000.0c47.abea (bia 0000.0c47.abea)
   Internet address is 172.16.60.1/24
   MTU 1500 bytes, BW 10000 Kbit, DLY 1000 usec, rely 255/255, load 46/255
   Encapsulation ARPA, loopback not set, keepalive set (10 sec)
   ARP type: ARPA, ARP Timeout 04:00:00
   Last input 00:00:00, output 00:00:00, output hang never
   Last clearing of "show interface" counters 00:00:50
   Queueing strategy: fifo
   Output queue 0/40, 0 drops; input queue 0/75, 0 drops
   5 minute input rate 1209000 bits/sec, 620 packets/sec
   5 minute output rate 1819000 bits/sec, 477 packets/sec
        21386 packets input, 3979009 bytes, 0 no buffer
        Received 9 broadcasts, 0 runts, 0 giants
        0 input errors, 0 CRC, 0 frame, 0 overrun, 0 ignored, 0 abort
        0 input packets with dribble condition detected
        6000 packets output, 8237684 bytes, 0 underruns
        0 output errors, 1020 collisions, 0 interface resets
        0 babbles, 0 late collision, 1006 deferred
        0 lost carrier, 0 no carrier
        0 output buffer failures, 0 output buffers swapped out
```

So, what do you think? What are your observations? This exercise was designed specifically to educate you about Ethernet capabilities. The principal observation that you should have made was the increasing number of collisions on the interface.

Collisions are a normal occurrence for CSMA/CD protocols. The fact that a connection is not full-duplex creates the opportunity for collisions. Although collisions are normal, excessive collisions can be detrimental to a network. Though there is some debate over the exact value, when collisions exceed five to eight percent of the output packets, the interface becomes very ineffective. The higher the collision rate, the more packets have to be retransmitted.

The output queue for the Ethernet interface doesn't stop filling up just because of collisions on the line. Therefore, not only does the interface have to transmit the normal queue of packets, it has to retransmit all the frames that were lost due to collisions. The number of packets that must be transmitted can grow exponentially. Let's calculate the collision percentage for the four show interface outputs you've just examined:

- 175 collisions / 1165 output packets = 15.02% collisions
- 443 collisions / 2858 output packets = 15.5% collisions
- 889 collisions / 5590 output packets = 15.9% collisions
- 1020 collisions / 6000 output packets = 17.0% collisions

All of these values are well in excess of five to eight percent. It looks like a key observation has been made, and now the problem statement can be written. "The collision percentage on Ethernet 0/1 exceeds healthy values and can be blamed for causing slow network throughput."

Propose Solutions

The hard part now is to determine what is causing the collisions. In this scenario, we will consider solutions from Layer 1 up to Layer 2. Following are possible solutions:

- Replace a faulty cable.
- Replace a faulty transceiver.
- Replace a faulty interface by changing the router.

First we'll test the cable—if the cable passes, then we'll change the transceiver. If that doesn't help, we'll assume that the interface on the router has gone bad. If the latter is the problem, we may be able to solve it by moving the connection to another interface on the same router or to a different interface on a different router.

Figure 10.7 depicts the physical hardware involved in this scenario. The cable connects to the hub and to a transceiver that is connected to the router's AUI interface.

You tested the cable and it passed, so you then change transceivers, execute a clear counters command to reset the interface counters, and look at the interface status again.

```
Router_C#show interface ethernet 0/1
Ethernet0/1 is up, line protocol is up
  Hardware is Lance, address is 0000.0c47.abea (bia 0000.0c47.abea)
  Internet address is 172.16.60.1/24
```

```
    MTU 1500 bytes, BW 10000 Kbit, DLY 1000 usec, rely 255/255, load 28/255
    Encapsulation ARPA, loopback not set, keepalive set (10 sec)
    ARP type: ARPA, ARP Timeout 04:00:00
    Last input 00:00:00, output 00:00:00, output hang never
    Last clearing of "show interface" counters 00:00:11
    Queueing strategy: fifo
    Output queue 0/40, 0 drops; input queue 0/75, 0 drops
    5 minute input rate 1381000 bits/sec, 723 packets/sec
    5 minute output rate 1126000 bits/sec, 418 packets/sec
       8291 packets input, 1933415 bytes, 0 no buffer
       Received 3 broadcasts, 0 runts, 0 giants
       0 input errors, 0 CRC, 0 frame, 0 overrun, 0 ignored,
          0 abort
       0 input packets with dribble condition detected
       7172 packets output, 1446188 bytes, 0 underruns
       0 output errors, 251 collisions, 0 interface resets
       0 babbles, 0 late collision, 265 deferred
       0 lost carrier, 0 no carrier
       0 output buffer failures, 0 output buffers swapped out
Router_C#
Router_C#show interface ethernet 0/1
Ethernet0/1 is up, line protocol is up
  Hardware is Lance, address is 0000.0c47.abea (bia 0000.0c47.abea)
  Internet address is 172.16.60.1/24
  MTU 1500 bytes, BW 10000 Kbit, DLY 1000 usec, rely 255/255, load 28/255
  Encapsulation ARPA, loopback not set, keepalive set (10 sec)
  ARP type: ARPA, ARP Timeout 04:00:00
  Last input 00:00:00, output 00:00:00, output hang never
  Last clearing of "show interface" counters 00:00:49
  Queueing strategy: fifo
  Output queue 0/40, 0 drops; input queue 0/75, 0 drops
  5 minute input rate 1392000 bits/sec, 735 packets/sec
  5 minute output rate 1114000 bits/sec, 425 packets/sec
     39411 packets input, 8957876 bytes, 0 no buffer
     Received 14 broadcasts, 0 runts, 0 giants
     0 input errors, 0 CRC, 0 frame, 0 overrun, 0 ignored,
        0 abort
     0 input packets with dribble condition detected
     38944 packets output, 6409017 bytes, 0 underruns
     0 output errors, 1556 collisions, 0 interface resets
```

```
      0 babbles, 0 late collision, 1368 deferred
      0 lost carrier, 0 no carrier
      0 output buffer failures, 0 output buffers swapped out
Router_C#
Router_C#show interface ethernet 0/1
Ethernet0/1 is up, line protocol is up
  Hardware is Lance, address is 0000.0c47.abea (bia 0000.0c47.abea)
  Internet address is 172.16.60.1/24
  MTU 1500 bytes, BW 10000 Kbit, DLY 1000 usec, rely 255/255, load 28/255
  Encapsulation ARPA, loopback not set, keepalive set (10  sec)
  ARP type: ARPA, ARP Timeout 04:00:00
  Last input 00:00:00, output 00:00:00, output hang never
  Last clearing of "show interface" counters 00:01:16
  Queueing strategy: fifo
  Output queue 0/40, 0 drops; input queue 0/75, 0 drops
  5 minute input rate 1396000 bits/sec, 742 packets/sec
  5 minute output rate 1110000 bits/sec, 434 packets/sec
     60752 packets input, 13691996 bytes, 0 no buffer
     Received 22 broadcasts, 0 runts, 0 giants
     0 input errors, 0 CRC, 0 frame, 0 overrun, 0 ignored,
        0 abort
     0 input packets with dribble condition detected
     65212 packets output, 10035669 bytes, 0 underruns
     0 output errors, 2466 collisions, 0 interface resets
     0 babbles, 0 late collision, 2163 deferred
     0 lost carrier, 0 no carrier
     0 output buffer failures, 0 output buffers swapped out
Router_C#
Router_C#show interface ethernet 0/1
Ethernet0/1 is up, line protocol is up
  Hardware is Lance, address is 0000.0c47.abea (bia 0000.0c47.abea)
  Description: 10BaseT to Core3
  Internet address is 172.16.60.1/24
  MTU 1500 bytes, BW 10000 Kbit, DLY 1000 usec, rely 255/255, load 28/255
  Encapsulation ARPA, loopback not set, keepalive set (10 sec)
  ARP type: ARPA, ARP Timeout 04:00:00
  Last input 00:00:00, output 00:00:00, output hang never
  Last clearing of "show interface" counters 00:01:42
  Queueing strategy: fifo
  Output queue 0/40, 0 drops; input queue 0/75, 0 drops
```

```
5 minute input rate 1415000 bits/sec, 753 packets/sec
5 minute output rate 1135000 bits/sec, 442 packets/sec
   81784 packets input, 18845458 bytes, 0 no buffer
   Received 29 broadcasts, 0 runts, 0 giants
   0 input errors, 0 CRC, 0 frame, 0 overrun, 0 ignored,
      0 abort
   0 input packets with dribble condition detected
   97408 packets output, 14297058 bytes, 0 underruns
   0 output errors, 3498 collisions, 0 interface resets
   0 babbles, 0 late collision, 2986 deferred
   0 lost carrier, 0 no carrier
   0 output buffer failures, 0 output buffers swapped out
Router_C#
```

Collision percentage calculations result in an average of 3.72% collisions. This is much better than the 15% you saw previously. In this scenario, a bad transceiver was to blame for the excessive collisions. In addition to the transmitting and receiving of data on the LAN, the transceiver is also responsible for collision detection.

FIGURE 10.7   Ethernet physical hardware

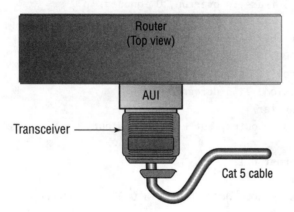

Troubleshooting Token Ring Problems

The problems described in this section's Token Ring scenarios can be effectively solved by using generic Cisco troubleshooting commands.

Scenario #1

Figure 10.8 displays the Token Ring network that is used for this scenario. You can see Routers A and B connected via Token Ring interfaces.

FIGURE 10.8 Network diagram for Token Ring scenarios #1 and #2

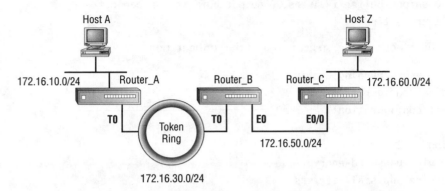

You are connecting Router A to Router B via the Token Ring interfaces, and you cannot get the interfaces to come up. You have console access to both routers.

List Observations

First you gather information from both routers that will help you to create a problem statement. Start by gathering information from Router A.

```
Router_A#show interface tokenring 0
TokenRing0 is up, line protocol is down
  Hardware is TMS380, address is 0007.787c.e14b (bia 0007.787c.e14b)
  Internet address is 172.16.30.1, subnet mask is 255.255.255.0
  MTU 4464 bytes, BW 4000 Kbit, DLY 630 usec, rely 255/255, load 1/255
  Encapsulation SNAP, loopback not set, keepalive set (10 sec)
  ARP type: SNAP, ARP Timeout 04:00:00
  Ring speed: 4 Mbps
  Single ring node, Source Route Transparent Bridge capable
  Ethernet Transit OUI: 0x000000
  Last input never, output never, output hang never
  Last clearing of "show interface" counters never
  Queueing strategy: fifo
  Output queue 0/40, 0 drops; input queue 0/75, 0 drops
  5 minute input rate 0 bits/sec, 0 packets/sec
  5 minute output rate 0 bits/sec, 0 packets/sec
     0 packets input, 0 bytes, 0 no buffer
     Received 0 broadcasts, 0 runts, 0 giants
     0 input errors, 0 CRC, 0 frame, 0 overrun, 0 ignored,
        0 abort
     0 packets output, 0 bytes, 0 underruns
```

```
   0 output errors, 0 collisions, 0 interface resets
   0 output buffer failures, 0 output buffers swapped out
   1 transition
```

Nothing looks wrong, so get a copy of the configuration.

```
Router_A#show running-config
Building configuration...
Current configuration:
!
version 11.2
no service password-encryption
no service udp-small-servers
service tcp-small-servers
!
hostname Router_A
!
enable password aloha
!
interface Ethernet0
 no ip address
 shutdown
!
interface Serial0
 ip address 172.16.20.6 255.255.255.252
 shutdown
 clockrate 4000000
 dce-terminal-timing-enable
!
interface Serial1
 no ip address
 shutdown
!
interface TokenRing0
 ip address 172.16.30.1 255.255.255.0
 ring-speed 4
!
router eigrp 100
 network 172.16.0.0
!
ip classless
```

```
!
line con 0
line aux 0
 transport input all
line vty 0 4
 password aloha
 login
!
end
Router_A#
```

Everything seems to be configured properly. Now, move on to the console of Router B. First, issue a show interface command:

```
Router_B#show interface tokenring 0
TokenRing0 is up, line protocol is down
  Hardware is TMS380, address is 0007.787c.e1cb (bia 0007.787c.e1cb)
  Internet address is 172.16.30.2, subnet mask is 255.255.255.0
  MTU 4464 bytes, BW 16000 Kbit, DLY 630 usec, rely 255/255, load 1/255
  Encapsulation SNAP, loopback not set, keepalive set (10  sec)
  ARP type: SNAP, ARP Timeout 04:00:00
  Ring speed: 16 Mbps
  Single ring node, Source Route Transparent Bridge capable
  Ethernet Transit OUI: 0x000000
  Last input never, output never, output hang never
  Last clearing of "show interface" counters never
  Queueing strategy: fifo
  Output queue 0/40, 0 drops; input queue 0/75, 0 drops
  5 minute input rate 0 bits/sec, 0 packets/sec
  5 minute output rate 0 bits/sec, 0 packets/sec
     0 packets input, 0 bytes, 0 no buffer
     Received 0 broadcasts, 0 runts, 0 giants
     0 input errors, 0 CRC, 0 frame, 0 overrun, 0 ignored,
        0 abort
     0 packets output, 0 bytes, 0 underruns
     0 output errors, 0 collisions, 0 interface resets
     0 output buffer failures, 0 output buffers swapped out
     2 transitions
```

Now you should be able to distinguish some differences and pinpoint the problem. There are two fields within this output that differ from the output from Router A. We'll give you two hints: The first is to look at the interface metrics. The second hint is to look at the ring speed.

Now, list the observations:

- The Token Ring interfaces on Routers A and B are in an up/down state.
- Router A ring speed is set to 4Mbps.
- Router B ring speed is set to 16Mbps.

The problem statement is "The ring speeds for Routers A and B are different."

Propose Solutions

The solution for this case is straightforward. Change the ring speed on Router A to match the ring speed on Router B.

```
Router_A(config)#interface tokenring 0
Router_A(config-if)#ring-speed 16
Router_A(config-if)#^Z
Router_A#
```

Now, verify the interface status. The interface should be in an up and up state.

```
Router_A#show interface tokenring 0
TokenRing0 is up, line protocol is up
  Hardware is TMS380, address is 0007.787c.e14b (bia 0007.787c.e14b)
  Internet address is 172.16.30.1, subnet mask is 255.255.255.0
  MTU 4464 bytes, BW 16000 Kbit, DLY 630 usec, rely 255/255, load 1/255
  Encapsulation SNAP, loopback not set, keepalive set (10 sec)
  ARP type: SNAP, ARP Timeout 04:00:00
  Ring speed: 16 Mbps
  Single ring node, Source Route Transparent Bridge capable
  Ethernet Transit OUI: 0x000000
  Last input never, output never, output hang never
  Last clearing of "show interface" counters never
  Queueing strategy: fifo
  Output queue 0/40, 0 drops; input queue 0/75, 0 drops
  5 minute input rate 0 bits/sec, 0 packets/sec
  5 minute output rate 0 bits/sec, 0 packets/sec
     0 packets input, 0 bytes, 0 no buffer
     Received 0 broadcasts, 0 runts, 0 giants
     0 input errors, 0 CRC, 0 frame, 0 overrun, 0 ignored,
        0 abort
     0 packets output, 0 bytes, 0 underruns
     0 output errors, 0 collisions, 0 interface resets
     0 output buffer failures, 0 output buffers swapped out
     3 transitions
```

The interface is now up, and you can ping the interface on Router B:

```
Router_A#ping 172.16.30.2
Type escape sequence to abort.
Sending 5, 100-byte ICMP Echos to 172.16.30.2, timeout is 2 seconds:
!!!!!
Success rate is 100 percent (5/5)
```

Opening a Case with the Technical Assistance Center

No matter how good your troubleshooting skills, if you work with Cisco routers long enough, at some point you're going to need to open a case with the Cisco Technical Assistance Center (TAC). This can be done either online at www.cisco.com, or via the telephone. In the United States, the number is (800) 553-2447. For overseas numbers, please see the Cisco web page.

Regardless of how the case is opened, you should be prepared to provide the following five items to the TAC when the case is opened:

1. Service and Support Contract number, and the serial number of the product for which the case is being opened

2. Network topology and explanation

3. Output from a show tech-support command as well as any other relevant output

4. Description of problem.

5. Software versions and types of equipment involved in the problem.

Summary

You will encounter several common problems with routers in general, as well as more-specific issues with Ethernet and Token Ring protocols when you are troubleshooting network issues. Most of these problems are found to be on Layer 2 and Layer 1, and occasionally Layer 3. Often these typical misbehaviors have simple solutions. For instance, you may be able to solve a problem by verifying that the correct IP address is assigned, that the correct DLCI is used, or that the Frame Relay DLCI-to-IP address mapping is correct, or by removing the administrative shutdown on an interface.

The boot mode on a router contains no routing functionality. Therefore, when a router comes up in boot mode, either by error or due to a problem, you need to take steps to return it to normal operation. Specifically, make sure you have the correct image in flash, change the configuration register to indicate that the system image should be loaded from flash, and then reload the router.

A couple of problems are common in the Ethernet environment. An encapsulation mismatch on a segment will preclude the mismatched devices from communicating with each other. When there is an Ethernet frame encapsulation mismatch, an easy way to determine the host's encapsulation type is to allow the host machine to ARP for the router. The router then records the frame type in the ARP table. Another issue in Ethernet is a high number of collisions. When this occurs on a segment that is not being heavily utilized, a hardware problem is usually the culprit. In many of these cases, replacing the transceiver will correct the situation. Note that collisions are not excessive until they are over five to eight percent.

A common issue with Token Ring is ring speed mismatches. Once they are isolated, you can easily correct ring speed mismatches in the configuration of the router or offending device.

At some point, almost every network administrator will need to open a case with Cisco TAC. This can be accomplished via the website or by phone. Cisco requires certain information when opening a case, including contract number, network topology, output of a `show tech-support` command, and the version numbers of the hardware and software involved in the problem.

Exam Essentials

Know the `show` commands and how to interpret the output.   Specifically in this chapter, we focused on `show arp`, `show cdp neighbors`, `show flash`, `show frame-relay pvc`, `show frame-relay map`, `show interface`, `show ip eigrp neighbors`, `show logging`, and `show version`.

Know the seven steps to the Cisco troubleshooting model and the function that each performs.   The Cisco troubleshooting steps are: define the problem, gather detailed information, consider possible scenarios, create an action plan, implement the action plan, observe the results of the implementation, and repeat if necessary. These steps define an effective step-by-step methodology for troubleshooting any problem.

Be able to apply the Cisco troubleshooting methodology to example situations.   You should know how to apply each step of the model in real-life scenarios. You should be able to determine what step in a troubleshooting scenario is next in the series, and to correlate a task with the correct step in the process.

Know how to use the `ping` and `traceroute` commands.   This includes the extended ping and traceroute options available under privileged mode.

Know the general steps required to identify and rectify a Physical layer issue.   Using the output of `show` commands, know what symptoms are characteristic of a physical dysfunction and what possible components can be causing the problem.

Know what information is required to open a Cisco TAC case.   To open a TAC case you need the contract number, network topology, output of a `show tech-support` command, and the version numbers of the hardware and software involved in the problem.

Commands Used in This Chapter

The following list contains a summary of all the commands used in this chapter.

Command	Description
clear counters	Clears the interface counters for easier viewing of new interface statistics.
frame-relay map	Statically maps DLCI information to a Layer 3 address.
ping	Executes the ICMP reachability test.
show arp	Displays the contents of the ARP table.
show cdp neighbors	Shows directly connected Cisco devices.
show ip arp	Displays only IP information in the ARP table.
show ip eigrp neighbors	Displays the router's EIGRP neighbors.
show flash	Displays the contents of the system flash, such as the IOS and any other files that may be present.
show frame-relay pvc	Shows information about the Frame Relay PVC on a router.
show frame-relay map	Shows the DLCI-to-Layer-3 mappings, both static and dynamic, on a router.
show interface	Lists the configuration details, status, and statistics for the interface.
show ip route	Displays the contents of the IP route table as well as the default gateway for the router.
show logging	Displays the logging buffer on the router.
show running-config	Displays the contents of the running configuration of the router.
show version	Displays the current IOS, hardware configuration, reason for last reload, and system uptime.
tracert	The **trace** command used in the Windows operating system. Provides a step-by-step ICMP trace from source to destination.

Review Questions

1. What do the following lines mean?

   ```
   Router_A#show interface ethernet 0/0
   Ethernet0/0 is up, line protocol is down
   ```

   A. The physical interface is receiving keepalive packets from the transceiver.

   B. The interface is actually down because the line protocol is down.

   C. The interface will work on Layer 2.

   D. None of the above.

2. What command would check for a missing host when troubleshooting a TCP connection?

   A. show user

   B. show ip route

   C. show ip arp

   D. show host <ip address>

3. What command is used to display the ARP table? (Choose all that apply.)

   A. show ip arp

   B. show Ethernet arp

   C. show interface arp

   D. show arp

4. Which generic troubleshooting tool is used to test for reachability and connectivity?

   A. Traceroute

   B. Debug

   C. Ping

   D. None of the above

5. What does it mean when the router is in "boot" mode?

   A. The IOS system image was loaded from the boot ROM or from BootFLASH.

   B. The IOS system image was loaded from RAM.

   C. The IOS system image was loaded from flash.

   D. The IOS system image was loaded from a BootP server.

6. How can the router be removed from boot mode?

   A. Reboot it.

   B. Change the configuration register so the system image is loaded from a source other than the boot ROM.

   C. Change the configuration by adding the `no system boot` command.

   D. None of the above.

7. Which of the following statements is accurate about a router that is in boot mode?

   A. It will route traffic as usual.

   B. It will not route traffic.

   C. It will not allow you to change the configuration register.

   D. Only traffic with high priority and established flows will be routed.

8. Which ARP types does a Cisco router recognize? (Choose all that apply.)

   A. ARPA

   B. SNAP

   C. HP

   D. LMI

9. What information is required by Cisco when opening a TAC case? (Choose two.)

   A. Output of a `show running-config` command

   B. Network topology

   C. Output of a `show logging` command

   D. Output of a `show interface` command

   E. Contract number

10. How do you calculate the collision percentage for an Ethernet interface?

   A. (collisions/input packets) * 100

   B. (collisions/interface resets) * 100

   C. (collisions/output packets) * 100

   D. (collisions/output rate bps) * 100

11. What physical device can be the source of excessive collisions? (Choose all that apply.)

   A. Transceiver

   B. CSU/DSU

   C. Ethernet interface

   D. None of the above

12. What are the two ring speeds allowed for Token Ring? (Choose two.)

    A. 2Mbps

    B. 4Mbps

    C. 8Mbps

    D. 16Mbps

13. How is the ring speed changed on the token ring interface?

    A. By issuing the global command `ring speed <4 or 16>`

    B. By issuing the interface command `ring speed <4 or 16>`

    C. By issuing the global command `ring-speed <4 or 16>`

    D. By issuing the interface command `ring-speed <4 or 16>`

14. You execute several `show interface` commands on a particular interface and see the number of overruns incrementing. What does this mean?

    A. Packets larger than the MTU size are arriving at the interface.

    B. The interface is receiving data faster than it can send it to the hardware buffer.

    C. The interface is transmitting packets faster than it receives them from the hardware buffer.

    D. The hardware buffers are full.

15. What troubleshooting tool is used to test for step-by-step path connectivity?

    A. Debug

    B. Ping

    C. Traceroute

    D. CDP

16. What is the purpose of listing observations? (Choose all that apply.)

    A. To define the problem

    B. To create an action plan

    C. To diagnose the problem

    D. To resolve the problem

17. What is the purpose of proposing solutions?

    A. It is equivalent to considering possibilities.

    B. It is equivalent to creating an action plan.

    C. It is equivalent to defining the problem.

    D. It is equivalent to the iteration process.

18. Why should you clear the counters on an interface that you are troubleshooting?

    A. By clearing the counters, you may also clear the problem that you are investigating.

    B. Clearing the counters flushes any corrupt packets from the interface.

    C. Clearing the counters creates a reference point.

    D. The `show interface` command will not work if the interface isn't cleared first.

19. What command tells you the last time the counters on a router were cleared?

    A. `show cdp neighbor`

    B. `show counters`

    C. `show interface`

    D. `show running-config`

20. You are troubleshooting a memory problem on a router and you execute the `show memory` command. What information from the output are you specifically looking for? (Choose two.)

    A. Total bytes

    B. Free bytes

    C. Used bytes

    D. Lowest bytes

    E. Largest bytes

Answers to Review Questions

1. B. Even though the interface appears to be up, if the line protocol is down, the interface will not function and therefore is actually down.

2. C. The `show ip arp` command will tell you whether the Layer-2-to-Layer-3 correlation has been made for a host. You could also use `show arp`.

3. A, D. Both `show ip arp` and `show arp` can be used to display the ARP table.

4. C. Ping is the tool that is used specifically to test for reachability and connectivity.

5. A. Boot mode is activated when the image has to be loaded from the boot ROM and no other images are available, or when the configuration register was set to read only from the boot ROM.

6. B. To get a router out of boot mode, rebooting will not help as long as the configuration register is still set to tell the router to boot only from the boot ROM. Option C, `no system boot`, is invalid syntax and would result in an error message if entered.

7. B. No routing protocols run on the boot image for a router; therefore, a router in boot mode is unable to route traffic.

8. A, B. The valid ARP types are ARPA, SNAP. HP and LMI are not a valid ARP types.

9. B, E. The output of `show running-config`, `show logging`, and `show interface` are included in the output of the `show tech-support` command (which is required to open a TAC case). Therefore, these specific commands are not required. The other items required by Cisco TAC are a description of a problem, and the version numbers of the hardware and software involved in the problem.

10. C. Collisions are based on output packets. Take the number of collisions, divide by the number of output packets and multiply by 100 to get the collision percentage.

11. A, C. Collisions are characteristics of the Ethernet protocol. Any devices involved in an Ethernet connection can contribute to collisions.

12. B, D. The two valid ring speeds for Token Ring are 4Mbps and 16Mbps.

13. D. The command `ring-speed` <4 or 16> represents the correct syntax for changing the ring speed.

14. B. This activity means that the interface is receiving data faster than it can send to the buffer. Answer C, the interface transmitting faster than it is receiving, is an underrun. Answer D, full hardware buffers, is an ignore.

15. C. Traceroute is the tool used to test for each hop in the path to the destination.

16. A. Listing observations is similar to gathering facts. Fact gathering is done to aid in the formation of a problem statement, thereby defining the problem.

17. B. Proposing solutions is the same as creating an action plan of possible solutions.

18. C. It is easier to watch for incrementing counters when they have been reset to zero. In addition, you are able to verify that any errors on the interface are new and not left over from another issue.

19. C. There is a line in the `show interface` output that shows the last time the counters for that interface were cleared—specifically, `Last clearing of "show interface" counters 00:01:42`.

20. B, D. When looking at a potential memory issue, the two most important statistics to look at first are the lowest bytes and free bytes. This information will tell you if the router is or has been running out of memory.

Glossary

10BaseT   Part of the original IEEE 802.3 standard, 10BaseT is the Ethernet specification of 10Mbps baseband that uses two pairs of twisted-pair, Category 3, 4, or 5 cabling—using one pair to send data and the other to receive. 10BaseT has a distance limit of about 100 meters per segment. *See also: Ethernet, IEEE 802.3.*

100BaseT   Based on the IEEE 802.3u standard, 100BaseT is the Fast Ethernet specification of 100Mbps baseband that uses UTP wiring. 100BaseT sends link pulses (containing more information than those used in 10BaseT) over the network when no traffic is present. *See also: 10BaseT, Fast Ethernet, IEEE 802.3.*

100BaseTX   Based on the IEEE 802.3u standard, 100BaseTX is the 100Mbps baseband Fast Ethernet specification that uses two pairs of UTP or STP wiring. The first pair of wires receives data; the second pair sends data. To ensure correct signal timing, a 100BaseTX segment cannot be longer than 100 meters.

1000Base-T   Based on the IEEE 802.3ab standard, 1000BaseT is the 1000Mbps baseband Ethernet specification. To ensure correct signal timing, a 1000BaseT segment cannot be longer than 100 meters

802.1D   IEEE spanning tree protocol that is used to prevent loops in a Layer 2 environment. It specifies a single spanning tree instance per switch.

802.1Q   *See IEEE 802.1.*

802.1s   IEEE spanning tree protocol that is used to prevent loops in a Layer 2 environment. It specifies multiple spanning tree instances per switch.

802.1w   Rapid Spanning tree protocol. This is a modification to the 802.1D standard that allows for more rapid convergence after a topology change. *See also: 802.1D.*

A&B bit signaling   Used in T1 transmission facilities and sometimes called "24th channel signaling." Each of the 24 T1 subchannels in this procedure uses one bit of every sixth frame to send supervisory signaling information.

AAL   ATM Adaptation Layer: A service-dependent sublayer of the Data-Link layer that accepts data from other applications and brings it to the ATM layer in 48-byte ATM payload segments. CS and SAR are the two sublayers that form an AAL. Currently, the four types of AAL recommended by the ITU-T are AAL1, AAL2, AAL3/4, and AAL5. AALs are differentiated by the source-destination timing they use, whether they are CBR or VBR, and whether they are used for connection-oriented or connectionless mode data transmission. *See also: AAL1, AAL2, AAL3/4, AAL5, ATM, ATM layer.*

AAL1   ATM Adaptation Layer 1: One of four AALs recommended by the ITU-T, it is used for connection-oriented, time-sensitive services that need constant bit rates, such as isochronous traffic and uncompressed video. *See also: AAL.*

AAL2   ATM Adaptation Layer 2: One of four AALs recommended by the ITU-T, it is used for connection-oriented services that support a variable bit rate, such as voice traffic. *See also: AAL.*

AAL3/4   ATM Adaptation Layer 3/4: One of four AALs (a product of two initially distinct layers) recommended by the ITU-T, supporting both connectionless and connection-oriented links. Its primary use is in sending SMDS packets over ATM networks. *See also: AAL.*

AAL5   ATM Adaptation Layer 5: One of four AALs recommended by the ITU-T, it is used to support connection-oriented VBR services primarily to transfer classical IP over ATM and LANE traffic. This least complex of the AAL recommendations uses SEAL (Simple Efficient ATM Layer), offering lower bandwidth costs and simpler processing requirements but also providing reduced bandwidth and error-recovery capacities. *See also: AAL.*

AARP   AppleTalk Address Resolution Protocol: The protocol in an AppleTalk stack that maps Data-Link addresses to Network addresses.

AARP probe packets   Packets sent by the AARP to determine whether a given node ID is being used by another node in a nonextended AppleTalk network. If the node ID is not in use, the sending node appropriates that node's ID. If the node ID is in use, the sending node will select a different ID and then send out more AARP probe packets. *See also: AARP.*

ABM   Asynchronous Balanced Mode: When two stations can initiate a transmission, ABM is an HDLC (or one of its derived protocols) communication technology that supports peer-oriented, point-to-point communications between both stations.

ABR   Area Border Router: An OSPF router that is located on the border of one or more OSPF areas. ABRs are used to connect OSPF areas to the OSPF backbone area.

access layer   One of the layers in Cisco's three-layer hierarchical model. The access layer provides users with access to the internetwork.

access link   A link used with switches; it is only part of one Virtual LAN (VLAN). Trunk links carry information from multiple VLANs.

access list   Access lists are used for filtering traffic going trough a router. This filtering can be on the traffic itself or can be used to limit access to certain services (e.g. telnet access, or SNMP) on the router. In addition they can also be used as a set of test conditions kept by routers; it determines "interesting traffic" to and from the router for various services on the network.

access method   The manner in which network devices approach gaining access to the network itself.

access server   Also known as a network access server; a communications process connecting asynchronous devices to a LAN or WAN through network and terminal-emulation software, providing synchronous or asynchronous routing of supported protocols.

acknowledgment   Verification sent from one network device to another signifying that an event has occurred. May be abbreviated as ACK. *See also: NAK.*

ACR   Allowed cell rate: A designation defined by the ATM Forum for managing ATM traffic. Dynamically controlled using congestion control measures, the ACR varies between the minimum cell rate (MCR) and the peak cell rate (PCR). *See also: MCR, PCR.*

action plan A list of steps or procedures used to resolve a network problem. This plan should possess four characteristics: Make one change at a time, make nonimpacting changes, do not compromise security, and have a procedure to back out of any changes made.

Active Monitor The mechanism used to manage a Token Ring. The network node with the highest MAC address on the ring becomes the Active Monitor and is responsible for management tasks such as preventing loops and ensuring that tokens are not lost.

address learning Used with transparent bridges to learn the hardware addresses of all devices on an internetwork. The switch then filters the network with the known hardware (MAC) addresses.

address mapping By translating network addresses from one format to another, this methodology permits different protocols to operate interchangeably.

address mask A bit combination descriptor identifying which portion of an address refers to the network or subnet and which part refers to the host. Sometimes simply called the mask. *See also: subnet mask.*

address resolution The process used for resolving differences between computer addressing schemes. Address resolution typically defines a method for tracing Network layer (Layer 3) addresses to Data-Link layer (Layer 2) addresses. *See also: address mapping.*

adjacency The relationship made between defined neighboring routers, using a common media segment, to exchange routing information.

adjacency table A table that contains all active/existing adjacencies of neighboring routers.

administrative distance A number between 0 and 255 that expresses the value of trustworthiness of a routing information source. The lower the number, the higher the integrity rating.

administrative weight A value designated by a network administrator to rate the preference given to a network link. It is one of four link metrics exchanged by PTSPs to test ATM network resource availability.

ADSU ATM Data Service Unit: The terminal adapter used to connect to an ATM network through an HSSI-compatible mechanism. *See also: DSU.*

advertising The process whereby routing or service updates are transmitted at given intervals, allowing other routers on the network to maintain a record of viable routes.

AEP AppleTalk Echo Protocol: A test for connectivity between two AppleTalk nodes; one node sends a packet to another and receives an echo, or copy, in response.

AFI Authority and Format Identifier: The part of an NSAP ATM address that delineates the type and format of the IDI section of an ATM address.

AFP AppleTalk Filing Protocol: A Presentation-layer protocol, supporting AppleShare and Mac OS File Sharing, that permits users to share files and applications on a server.

AIP   ATM Interface Processor: Supporting AAL3/4 and AAL5, this interface for Cisco 7000 series routers minimizes performance bottlenecks at the UNI. *See also: AAL3/4, AAL5.*

algorithm   A set of rules or a process used to solve a problem. In networking, algorithms are typically used for finding the best route for traffic from a source to its destination.

alignment error   An error occurring in Ethernet networks, in which a received frame has extra bits—that is, a number not divisible by eight. Alignment errors are generally the result of frame damage caused by collisions.

all-routes explorer packet   An explorer packet that can move across an entire SRB network, tracing all possible paths to a given destination. Also known as an all-rings explorer packet. *See also: explorer packet, local explorer packet, spanning explorer packet.*

AM   Amplitude Modulation: A modulation method that represents information by varying the amplitude of the carrier signal. *See also: modulation.*

AMI   Alternate Mark Inversion: A line-code type on T1 and E1 circuits that shows 0s as "01" during each bit cell, and 1s as "11" or "00," alternately, during each bit cell. The sending device must maintain ones density in AMI but not independently of the data stream. Also known as binary-coded, alternate mark inversion. *See also: B8ZS, ones density.*

amplitude   An analog or digital waveform's highest value.

analog transmission   Signal messaging whereby information is represented by various combinations of signal amplitude, frequency, and phase.

ANSI   American National Standards Institute: The organization of corporate, government, and other volunteer members that coordinates standards-related activities, approves U.S. national standards, and develops U.S. positions in international standards organizations. ANSI assists in the creation of international and U.S. standards in disciplines such as communications, networking, and a variety of technical fields. It publishes over 13,000 standards for engineered products and technologies ranging from screw threads to networking protocols. ANSI is a member of the IEC and ISO.

anycast   An ATM address that can be shared by more than one end system, allowing requests to be routed to a node that provides a particular service.

API   Application Programming Interface: A standardized connection point for use by applications on a system. This connection point allows multiple different applications on a system to access data in a controlled manner that does not affect the overall functioning of the system.

AppleTalk   Currently in two versions, the group of communication protocols designed by Apple Computer for use in Macintosh environments. The earlier Phase 1 protocols support one physical network with only one network number that resides in one zone. The later Phase 2 protocols support more than one logical network on a single physical network, allowing networks to exist in more than one zone. *See also: zone, AARP.*

Application layer   Layer 7 of the OSI reference network model, supplying services to application procedures (such as e-mail or file transfer) that are outside the OSI model. This layer chooses and determines the availability of communicating partners along with the resources necessary to make the connection, coordinates partnering applications, and forms a consensus on procedures for controlling data integrity and error recovery.

ARA AppleTalk Remote Access: A protocol for Macintosh users establishing their access to resources and data from a remote AppleTalk location.

area A logical, rather than physical, set of segments (based on CLNS, DECnet, or OSPF) along with their attached devices. Areas are commonly connected using routers to create a single autonomous system. *See also: autonomous system.*

ARM Asynchronous Response Mode: An HDLC communication mode using one primary station and at least one additional station, in which transmission can be initiated from either the primary unit or one of the secondary units.

ARP Address Resolution Protocol: Defined in RFC 826, the protocol that traces IP addresses to MAC addresses. *See also: RARP.*

ASBR Autonomous System Boundary Router: An area border router placed between an OSPF autonomous system and a non-OSPF network that operates both OSPF and an additional routing protocol, such as RIP. ASBRs must be located in a non-stub OSPF area. *See also: ABR, non-stub area, OSPF.*

ASCII American Standard Code for Information Interchange: An 8-bit code for representing characters, consisting of 7 data bits plus 1 parity bit.

ASICs Application-Specific Integrated Circuits: Used in Layer 2 switches to make filtering decisions. The ASIC looks in the filter table of MAC addresses and determines which port the destination hardware address of a received hardware address is destined for. The frame will be allowed to traverse only that one segment. If the hardware address is unknown, the frame is forwarded out all ports.

ASN.1 Abstract Syntax Notation One: An OSI language used to describe types of data. ASN.1 is independent of computer structures and depicting methods. Described by ISO International Standard 8824.

ASP AppleTalk Session Protocol: A protocol employing ATP to establish, maintain, and tear down sessions, as well as sequence requests. *See also: ATP.*

AST Automatic Spanning Tree: A function that supplies one path for spanning explorer frames traveling from one node in the network to another, supporting the automatic resolution of spanning trees in SRB networks. AST is based on the IEEE 802.1 standard. *See also: IEEE 802.1, SRB.*

asynchronous transmission Digital signals sent without precise timing, usually with different frequencies and phase relationships. Asynchronous transmissions generally enclose individual characters in control bits (called start and stop bits) that show the beginning and end of each character. *See also: isochronous transmission, synchronous transmission.*

ATCP   AppleTalk Control Program: The protocol for establishing and configuring AppleTalk over PPP, defined in RFC 1378. *See also: PPP.*

ATDM   Asynchronous Time-Division Multiplexing: A technique for sending information, it differs from normal TDM in that the time slots are assigned when necessary rather than preassigned to certain transmitters. *See also: FDM, statistical multiplexing, TDM.*

ATG   Address Translation Gateway: The mechanism within Cisco DECnet routing software that enables routers to route multiple, independent DECnet networks and to establish a user-designated address translation for chosen nodes between networks.

ATM   Asynchronous Transfer Mode: The international standard, identified by fixed-length 53-byte cells, for transmitting cells in multiple service systems such as voice, video, or data. Transit delays are reduced because the fixed-length cells permit processing to occur in the hardware. ATM is designed to maximize the benefits of high-speed transmission media such as SONET, E3, and T3.

ATM ARP server   A device that supplies logical subnets running classical IP over ATM with address-resolution services.

ATM endpoint   The initiating or terminating connection in an ATM network. ATM endpoints include servers, workstations, ATM-to-LAN switches, and ATM routers.

ATM Forum   The international organization founded jointly by Northern Telecom, Sprint, Cisco Systems, and NET/ADAPTIVE in 1991 to develop and promote standards-based implementation agreements for ATM technology. The ATM Forum broadens official standards developed by ANSI and ITU-T and creates implementation agreements before official standards are published.

ATM layer   A sublayer of the Data-Link layer in an ATM network that is service independent. To create standard 53-byte ATM cells, the ATM layer receives 48-byte segments from the AAL and attaches a 5-byte header to each. These cells are then sent to the Physical layer for transmission across the physical medium. *See also: AAL.*

ATM user-user connection   A connection made by the ATM layer to supply communication between at least two ATM service users, such as ATMM processes. These communications can be uni- or bidirectional, using one or two VCCs, respectively. *See also: ATM layer, ATMM.*

ATMM   ATM Management: A procedure that runs on ATM switches, managing rate enforcement and VCI translation. *See also: ATM.*

ATP   AppleTalk Transaction Protocol: A transport-level protocol that enables reliable transactions between two sockets, where one requests the other to perform a given task and to report the results. ATP fastens the request and response together, ensuring a loss-free exchange of request-response pairs.

attenuation   In communication, weakening or loss of signal energy, typically caused by distance.

AURP AppleTalk Update-based Routing Protocol: A technique for encapsulating AppleTalk traffic in the header of a foreign protocol that allows the connection of at least two noncontiguous AppleTalk internetworks through a foreign network (such as TCP/IP) to create an AppleTalk WAN. The connection made is called an AURP tunnel. By exchanging routing information between exterior routers, the AURP maintains routing tables for the complete AppleTalk WAN. *See also: AURP tunnel.*

AURP tunnel A connection made in an AURP WAN that acts as a single, virtual link between AppleTalk internetworks separated physically by a foreign network such as a TCP/IP network. *See also: AURP.*

authority zone A portion of the domain-name tree associated with DNS for which one name server is the authority. *See also: DNS.*

auto duplex A setting on Layer 1 and 2 devices that sets the duplex of a switch port automatically.

automatic call reconnect A function that enables automatic call rerouting away from a failed trunk line.

autonomous confederation A collection of self-governed systems that depend more on their own network accessibility and routing information than on information received from other systems or groups.

autonomous switching The ability of Cisco routers to process packets more quickly by using the ciscoBus to switch packets independently of the system processor.

autonomous system (AS) A group of networks under mutual administration that share the same routing methodology. Autonomous systems are subdivided by areas and must be assigned an individual 16-bit number by the IANA. *See also: area.*

autoreconfiguration A procedure executed by nodes within the failure domain of a Token Ring, wherein nodes automatically perform diagnostics, trying to reconfigure the network around failed areas.

auxiliary port The console port on the back of Cisco routers that allows you to dial the router and make console configuration settings.

B8ZS Binary 8-Zero Substitution: A line-code type, interpreted at the remote end of the connection, that uses a special code substitution whenever 8 consecutive 0s are transmitted over the link on T1 and E1 circuits. This technique assures ones density independent of the data stream. Also known as bipolar 8-zero substitution. *See also: AMI, ones density.*

B channel Bearer channel: A full-duplex, 64Kbps channel in ISDN that transmits user data. *See also: D channel, E channel, H channel.*

back end A node or software program supplying services to a front end. *See also: server.*

backbone The basic portion of the network that provides the primary path for traffic sent to and initiated from other networks.

bandwidth   The gap between the highest and lowest frequencies employed by network signals. More commonly, it refers to the rated throughput capacity of a network protocol or medium.

baseband   A feature of a network technology that uses only one carrier frequency—for example, Ethernet. Also named "narrowband." *See also: broadband.*

baseline   Baseline information includes historical data about the network and routine utilization information. This information can be used to determine whether there were recent changes made to the network that may contribute to the problem at hand.

Basic Management Setup   Used with Cisco routers when in setup mode. Only provides enough management and configuration to get the router working so someone can telnet in to the router and configure it.

baud   Synonymous with bits per second (bps), if each signal element represents one bit. It is a unit of signaling speed equivalent to the number of separate signal elements transmitted per second.

beacon, beaconing   An FDDI device or Token Ring frame that points to a serious problem with the ring, such as a broken cable. The beacon frame carries the address of the station thought to be down. *See also: failure domain.*

BECN   Backward Explicit Congestion Notification: BECN is the bit set by a Frame Relay network in frames moving away from frames headed into a congested path. A DTE that receives frames with the BECN may ask higher-level protocols to take necessary flow-control measures. *See also: FECN.*

BGP4   Border Gateway Protocol Version 4: Version 4 of the interdomain routing protocol most commonly used on the Internet. BGP4 supports CIDR and uses route-counting mechanisms to decrease the size of routing tables. *See also: CIDR.*

binary   A two-character numbering method that uses 1s and 0s. The binary numbering system underlies all digital representation of information.

BIP   Bit Interleaved Parity: A method used in ATM to monitor errors on a link, sending a check bit or word in the link overhead for the preceding block or frame. This allows bit errors in transmissions to be found and delivered as maintenance information.

BISDN   Broadband ISDN: ITU-T standards created to manage high-bandwidth technologies such as video. BISDN presently employs ATM technology along SONET-based transmission circuits, supplying data rates between 155Mbps and 622Mbps and beyond. *See also: BRI, ISDN, N-ISDN, PRI.*

bit-oriented protocol   Class of Data-Link layer communication protocols that transmits frames regardless of frame content. Bit-oriented protocols, as compared with byte-oriented, supply more efficient and trustworthy, full-duplex operation. *See also: byte-oriented protocol.*

blue alarm   A blue alarm on a T1 or E1 indicates a total absence of signal. The signal keeps the circuit synchronized by sending all 1s.

Boot ROM   Used in routers to put the router into bootstrap mode. Bootstrap mode then boots the device with an operating system. The ROM can also hold a small Cisco IOS.

bootstrap protocol   A protocol used to dynamically assign IP address and gateway to requesting clients.

border gateway   A router that facilitates communication with routers in different autonomous systems.

Border Gateway Protocol   Routing protocol designed for external use. It is the primary routing protocol used on the Internet.

bottom-up troubleshooting   Troubleshooting methodology based on the OSI model. With bottom-up troubleshooting, the process starts with the physical layer and moves up the OSI protocol stack. *See also: divide-and-conquer troubleshooting and top-down troubleshooting.*

boundary of dysfunctionality   The limit or scope of the network problem. This boundary lies between the areas where the network is functioning properly and where it has ceased to function.

BPDU   Bridge Protocol Data Unit: A Spanning-Tree Protocol initializing packet that is sent at definable intervals for the purpose of exchanging information among bridges in networks.

breakout boxes   These items are used to verify pin-outs (e.g., TD—transmit data, RD—receive data, CTS—clear to send) for all types of serial and parallel connections.

BRI   ISDN Basic Rate Interface: ISDN BRI was designed to provide digital services over existing pairs of copper. The service is used for videoconferencing, voice services, data, and out-of-band management. In addition, the D-channel function of BRI is used for replacement of legacy X.25 networks. ISDN BRI is a 192Kbps circuit that is divided into three distinct channels. The two primary data channels are the B channels. Each B channel provides 64Kbps. The third channel provides 16Kbps of bandwidth for commands and signaling, and is referred to as the D channel. *See also: BISDN, PRI.*

bridge   A device for connecting two segments of a network and transmitting packets between them. Both segments must use identical protocols to communicate. Bridges function at the Data-Link layer, Layer 2 of the OSI reference model. The purpose of a bridge is to filter, send, or flood any incoming frame, based on the MAC address of that particular frame.

broadband   A transmission methodology for multiplexing several independent signals onto one cable. In telecommunications, broadband is classified as any channel with bandwidth greater than 4kHz (typical voice grade). In LAN terminology, it is classified as a coaxial cable on which analog signaling is employed. Also known as wideband. *See also: baseband.*

broadcast   A data frame or packet that is transmitted to every node on the local network segment (as defined by the broadcast domain). Broadcasts are known by their broadcast address, which is a destination network and host address with all the bits turned on. Also called "local broadcast." *See also: directed broadcast.*

broadcast domain A group of devices receiving broadcast frames initiating from any device within the group. Because they do not forward broadcast frames, broadcast domains are generally surrounded by routers.

broadcast storm An undesired event on the network caused by the simultaneous transmission of a large number of broadcasts across the network segment. Such an occurrence can overwhelm network bandwidth, resulting in time-outs.

browsing In a Windows environment, available resources are shown in the Network Neighborhood through the use of browsing. The browser structure is hierarchical in nature, with one device per segment, called a master browser, that serves as an authoritative resource for that segment. In addition, there can also be a domain master browser configured for a domain that collects all information for the NT domain and distributes this as necessary to the master browsers. Browsing is designed to be automatic and not require administrative support. *See also: domain master browser, master browser, Network Neighborhood.*

buffer A storage area dedicated to handling data while in transit. Buffers are used to receive/store sporadic deliveries of data bursts, usually received from faster devices, compensating for the variations in processing speed. Incoming information is stored until everything is received prior to sending data on. Also known as an information buffer.

bus topology A linear LAN architecture in which transmissions from various stations on the network are reproduced over the length of the medium and are accepted by all other stations. *Compare with: ring topology, star topology.*

bus Any physical path, typically wires or copper, through which a digital signal can be used to send data from one part of a computer to another.

BUS Broadcast and Unknown Server: In LAN emulation, these servers are the hardware or software responsible for resolving all broadcasts and packets with unknown (unregistered) addresses into the point-to-point virtual circuits required by ATM. *See also: LANE, LEC, LECS, LES.*

BX.25 AT&T's use of X.25. *See also: X.25.*

bypass mode An FDDI and Token Ring network operation that deletes an interface.

bypass relay A device that enables a particular interface in the Token Ring to be closed down and effectively taken off the ring.

byte-oriented protocol Any type of data-link communication protocol that, in order to mark the boundaries of frames, uses a specific character from the user character set. These protocols have generally been superseded by bit-oriented protocols. *See also: bit-oriented protocol.*

cable range In an extended AppleTalk network, the range of numbers allotted for use by existing nodes on the network. The value of the cable range can be anywhere from a single to a sequence of several touching network numbers. Node addresses are determined by their cable range value.

cable testers   A family of apparatus used to verify media integrity and connectivity. Several different devices can be considered cable testers.

CAC   Connection Admission Control: The sequence of actions executed by every ATM switch while connection setup is performed in order to determine if a request for connection is violating the guarantees of QoS for established connections. Also, CAC is used to route a connection request through an ATM network.

call admission control   A device for managing traffic in ATM networks, determining the possibility of a path containing adequate bandwidth for a requested VCC.

call priority   In circuit-switched systems, the defining priority given to each originating port; it specifies in which order calls will be reconnected. Additionally, call priority identifies the calls that are allowed during a bandwidth reservation.

call set-up time   The length of time necessary to effect a switched call between DTE devices.

CBR   Constant Bit Rate: An ATM Forum QoS class created for use in ATM networks. CBR is used for connections that rely on precision clocking to guarantee trustworthy delivery. *See also: ABR, VBR.*

CCO   Cisco Connection Online: The Cisco website, CCO, is the repository for information regarding Cisco products, networking technology, configuration examples, troubleshooting tools, and network planning. CCO has two access levels. The first is guest privilege, which does not require a login account. This level provides general product and company information. The second level is for registered Cisco users who have purchased a Cisco support contract or are sponsored by a Cisco Authorized Partner. This level provides all information available to the guest level, in-depth detailed technical documentation, access to download Cisco IOS images, trouble-ticket queries, and so on.

CD   Carrier Detect: A signal indicating that an interface is active or that a connection generated by a modem has been established.

CDP   Cisco Discovery Protocol: Cisco's proprietary protocol that is used to tell a neighbor Cisco device about the type of hardware, software version, and active interfaces that the Cisco device is using. It uses a SNAP frame between devices and is not routable.

CDVT   Cell Delay Variation Tolerance: A QoS parameter for traffic management in ATM networks specified when a connection is established. The allowable fluctuation levels for data samples taken by the PCR in CBR transmissions are determined by the CDVT. *See also: CBR, PCR.*

CEF   Cisco Express Forwarding: A modern switching methodology developed by Cisco to speed up the switching of packets in network devices.

cell   In ATM networking, the basic unit of data for switching and multiplexing. Cells have a defined length of 53 bytes, including a 5-byte header that identifies the cell's data stream, and 48 bytes of payload. *See also: cell relay.*

cell payload scrambling   The method by which an ATM switch maintains framing on some medium-speed edge and trunk interfaces (T3 or E3 circuits). Cell payload scrambling rearranges the data portion of a cell to maintain the line synchronization with certain common bit patterns.

cell relay   A technology that uses small packets of fixed size, known as cells. Their fixed length enables cells to be processed and switched in hardware at high speeds, making this technology the foundation for ATM and other high-speed network protocols. *See also: cell.*

Centrex   A local exchange carrier service, providing local switching that resembles that of an onsite PBX. Centrex has no onsite switching capability. Therefore, all customer connections return to the CO. *See also: CO.*

CER   Cell Error Ratio: The ratio in ATM of transmitted cells having errors to the total number of cells sent in a transmission within a certain span of time.

channelized E1   Operating at 2.048Mpbs, an access link that is sectioned into 29 B channels and one D channel, supporting DDR, Frame Relay, and X.25. *See also: channelized T1.*

channelized T1   Operating at 1.544Mbps, an access link that is sectioned into 23 B channels and 1 D channel of 64Kbps each, where individual channels or groups of channels connect to various destinations, supporting DDR, Frame Relay, and X.25. *See also: channelized E1.*

CHAP   Challenge Handshake Authentication Protocol: Supported on lines using PPP encapsulation, CHAP is a security feature that identifies the remote end, helping keep out unauthorized users. After CHAP is performed, the router or access server determines whether a given user is permitted access. It is a newer, more secure protocol than PAP. *See also: PAP.*

checksum   A test for ensuring the integrity of sent data. It is a number calculated from a series of values taken through a sequence of mathematical functions, typically placed at the end of the data from which it is calculated, and then recalculated at the receiving end for verification. *See also: CRC.*

choke packet   When congestion exists, a choke packet is sent to inform a transmitter that it should decrease its sending rate.

CIDR   Classless Interdomain Routing: A method supported by classless routing protocols such as OSPF and BGP4, based on the concept of ignoring the IP class of address. This permits route aggregation and VLSM, enabling routers to combine routes in order to minimize the routing information that needs to be conveyed by the primary routers. It allows a group of IP networks to appear to other networks as a unified, larger entity. In CIDR, IP addresses and their subnet masks are written as four dotted octets, followed by a forward slash and the numbering of masking bits (a form of subnet notation shorthand). *See also: BGP4.*

CIP   Channel Interface Processor: A channel attachment interface for use in Cisco 7000 series routers. The CIP connects a host mainframe to a control unit. This device eliminates the need for a front-end processor (FEP) to attach channels.

CIR   Committed Information Rate: Averaged over a minimum span of time and measured in bps, CIR is a Frame Relay network's agreed-upon minimum rate of transferring information.

circuit switching   Used with dial-up networks such as PPP and ISDN. Passes data, but needs to set up the connection first—just like making a phone call.

Cisco Connection Documentation CD-ROM   The CD is the collection of technical documentation, available on CCO as well as the Documentation CD, that accompanies new Cisco equipment purchases. Both forms of the technical documentation are very helpful for providing critical information regarding Cisco products, networking technologies, and configuration examples.

Cisco Connection Family   The Cisco Connection Family is a collection of interactive electronic media that is intended to provide technical assistance and support for Cisco products and networking technologies. There are five members of the Cisco Connection family: Cisco Connection Online (CCO), Cisco Technical Assistance and Software Center, Cisco Connection Consultant Tools CD-ROM, Cisco Commerce Agents, and Cisco MarketPlace.

Cisco Express Forwarding   Cisco Express Forwarding (CEF) is a switching function, designed for high-end backbone routers. It functions on Layer 3 of the OSI model, and its biggest asset is the capability to remain stable in a large network. However, it's also more efficient than both the fast and optimum default switching paths.

Cisco FRAD   Cisco Frame-Relay Access Device: A Cisco product that supports Cisco IPS Frame Relay SNA services, connecting SDLC devices to Frame Relay without requiring an existing LAN. Can be upgraded to a fully functioning multiprotocol router. Can activate conversion from SDLC to Ethernet and Token Ring, but does not support attached LANs. *See also: FRAD.*

CiscoFusion   Cisco's name for the internetworking architecture under which its Cisco IOS operates. CiscoFusion is designed to "fuse" together the capabilities of its disparate collection of acquired routers and switches.

Cisco IOS software   Cisco Internet Operating System software: The kernel of the Cisco line of routers and switches that supplies shared functionality, scalability, and security for all products under its CiscoFusion architecture. *See also: CiscoFusion.*

CiscoSecure   Cisco's AAA tool. It works with both RADIUS and TACACS clients and can authenticate using an authentication database, NT credentials, or token passthrough.

Cisco Technical Assistance Center   The TAC provides support for Cisco contract holders, gives warranty service, and can even bill you directly if you do not have a Cisco maintenance contract.

CiscoView   GUI-based management software for Cisco networking devices, enabling dynamic status, statistics, and comprehensive configuration information. Displays a physical view of the Cisco device chassis and provides device-monitoring functions and fundamental troubleshooting capabilities. May be integrated with a number of SNMP-based network management platforms.

CiscoWorks   CiscoWorks combines several different Cisco management tools into one consolidated package. It can be used for monitoring, managing, and troubleshooting in a Cisco internetwork.

Class A network   Part of the Internet Protocol hierarchical addressing scheme. Class A networks have only 8 bits for defining networks and 24 bits for defining hosts on each network.

Class B network   Part of the Internet Protocol hierarchical addressing scheme. Class B networks have 16 bits for defining networks and 16 bits for defining hosts on each network.

Class C network   Part of the Internet Protocol hierarchical addressing scheme. Class C networks have 24 bits for defining networks and only 8 bits for defining hosts on each network.

classical IP over ATM   Defined in RFC 1577, the specification for running IP over ATM that maximizes ATM features. Also known as CIA.

classless routing   Routing that sends subnet mask information in the routing updates. Classless routing allows Variable-Length Subnet Mask (VLSM) and supernetting. Routing protocols that support classless routing are RIP version 2, EIGRP, and OSPF.

CLI   Command-line interface: Allows you to configure Cisco routers and switches with maximum flexibility.

CLP   Cell Loss Priority: The area in the ATM cell header that determines the likelihood of a cell's being dropped during network congestion. Cells with CLP = 0 are considered insured traffic and are not apt to be dropped. Cells with CLP = 1 are considered best-effort traffic that may be dropped during congested episodes, delivering more resources to handle insured traffic.

CLR   Cell Loss Ratio: The ratio of discarded cells to successfully delivered cells in ATM. CLR can be designated a QoS parameter when establishing a connection.

CO   Central Office: The local telephone company office where all loops in a certain area connect and where circuit switching of subscriber lines occurs.

collapsed backbone   A nondistributed backbone where all network segments are connected to each other through an internetworking device. A collapsed backbone can be a virtual network segment at work in a device such as a router, hub, or switch.

collision   The effect of two nodes sending transmissions simultaneously in Ethernet. When they meet on the physical media, the frames from each node collide and are damaged. *See also: collision domain.*

collision domain   The network area in Ethernet over which frames that have collided will spread. Collisions are propagated by hubs and repeaters, but not by LAN switches, routers, or bridges. *See also: collision.*

composite metric   Used with routing protocols such as IGRP and EIGRP that use more than one metric to find the best path to a remote network. IGRP and EIGRP both use bandwidth and delay of the line by default. However, Maximum Transmission Unit (MTU), load, and reliability of a link can be used as well.

configuration register A 16-bit configurable value stored in hardware or software that determines how Cisco routers function during initialization. In hardware, the bit position is set using a jumper. In software, it is set by specifying specific bit patterns used to set start-up options, configured using a hexadecimal value with configuration commands.

congestion Traffic that exceeds the network's ability to handle it.

congestion avoidance To minimize delays, an ATM network uses congestion avoidance to control traffic entering the system. Lower-priority traffic is discarded at the edge of the network when indicators signal it cannot be delivered, thus using resources efficiently.

congestion collapse The situation that results from the retransmission of packets in ATM networks where little or no traffic successfully arrives at destination points. It usually happens in networks made of switches with ineffective or inadequate buffering capabilities combined with poor packet discard or ABR congestion feedback mechanisms.

connection ID Identification given to each telnet session into a router. The show sessions command will give you the connections that a local router will have to a remote router. The show users command will show the connection IDs of users telnetted into your local router.

connectionless Data transfer that occurs without the creating of a virtual circuit. No overhead, best-effort delivery, not reliable. *See also: connection-oriented, virtual circuit.*

connection-oriented Data transfer method that sets up a virtual circuit before any data is transferred. Uses flow and error control for reliable data transfer. *See also: connectionless, virtual circuit.*

console port Typically an RJ-45 port on a Cisco router and switch that allows command-line interface capability.

control direct VCC One of three control connections defined by Phase 1 LAN emulation; a bidirectional virtual control connection (VCC) established in ATM by an LEC to an LES. *See also: control distribute VCC.*

control distribute VCC One of three control connections defined by Phase 1 LAN emulation; a unidirectional virtual control connection (VCC) set up in ATM from an LES to an LEC. Usually, the VCC is a point-to-multipoint connection. *See also: control direct VCC.*

convergence The process required for all routers in an internetwork to update their routing tables and create a consistent view of the network, using the best possible paths. No user data is passed during a convergence time.

core layer Top layer in the Cisco three-layer hierarchical model that helps you design, build, and maintain Cisco hierarchical networks. The core layer passes packets quickly to distribution-layer devices only. No packet filtering should take place at this layer.

cost An arbitrary value, based on hop count, bandwidth, or other calculation, that is typically assigned by a network administrator and used by the routing protocol to compare different routes through an internetwork. Routing protocols use cost values to select the best path to a certain destination; the lowest cost identifies the best path. Also known as path cost. *See also: routing metric.*

count to infinity   A problem occurring in routing algorithms that are slow to converge, where routers keep increasing the hop count to particular networks. To avoid this problem, various solutions have been implemented into each of the different routing protocols. Some of those solutions include defining a maximum hop count (defining infinity), route poisoning, poison reverse, and split horizon.

CPCS   Common Part Convergence Sublayer: One of two AAL sublayers that is service dependent, it is further segmented into the CS and SAR sublayers. The CPCS prepares data for transmission across the ATM network; it creates the 48-byte payload cells that are sent to the ATM layer. *See also: AAL, ATM layer.*

CPE   Customer Premises Equipment: Items such as telephones, modems, and terminals installed at customer locations and connected to the telephone company network.

crankback   In ATM, a correction technique used when a node somewhere on a chosen path cannot accept a connection setup request, blocking the request. The path is rolled back to an intermediate node, which then uses GCAC to attempt to find an alternate path to the final destination.

CRC   Cyclic redundancy check: An error-detection methodology. The frame recipient makes a calculation by dividing frame contents with a prime binary divisor and compares the remainder to a value stored in the frame by the sending node. *See also: checksum.*

CSMA/CD   Carrier Sense Multiple Access with Collision Detection: A technology defined by the Ethernet IEEE 802.3 committee. Each device senses the cable for a digital signal before transmitting. Also, CSMA/CD allows all devices on the network to share the same cable, but one at a time. If two devices transmit at the same time, a frame collision will occur and a jamming pattern will be sent; the devices will stop transmitting, wait a predetermined amount of time, and then try to transmit again.

CSU   Channel Service Unit: A digital mechanism that connects end-user equipment to the local digital telephone loop. Frequently referenced along with the data service unit as CSU/DSU. *See also: DSU.*

CTD   Cell Transfer Delay: For a given connection in ATM, the time period between a cell exit event at the source user-network interface (UNI) and the corresponding cell entry event at the destination. The CTD between these points is the sum of the total inter-ATM transmission delay and the total ATM processing delay.

cut-through frame switching   A frame-switching technique that flows data through a switch so that the leading edge exits the switch at the output port before the packet finishes entering the input port. Frames will be read, processed, and forwarded by devices that use cut-through switching as soon as the destination address of the frame is confirmed and the outgoing port is identified.

D channel   (1) Data channel: A full-duplex, 16Kbps (BRI) or 64Kbps (PRI) ISDN channel. *See also: B channel, E channel*, and *H channel*. (2) In SNA, anything that provides a connection between the processor and main storage with any peripherals.

data direct VCC   A bidirectional point-to-point virtual control connection (VCC) set up between two LECs in ATM and one of three data connections defined by Phase 1 LAN emulation. Because data-direct VCCs do not guarantee QoS, they are generally reserved for UBR and ABR connections. *See also: control distribute VCC, control direct VCC.*

data frame   Protocol Data Unit encapsulation at the Data-Link layer of the OSI reference model. Encapsulates packets from the Network layer and prepares the data for transmission on a network medium.

datagram   A logical collection of information transmitted as a Network layer unit over a medium without a previously established virtual circuit. IP datagrams have become the primary information unit of the Internet. At various layers of the OSI reference model, the terms *cell, frame, message, packet*, and *segment* also define these logical information groupings.

data link control layer   Layer 2 of the SNA architectural model, it is responsible for the transmission of data over a given physical link and compares somewhat to the Data-Link layer of the OSI model.

Data-Link layer   Layer 2 of the OSI reference model, it ensures the trustworthy transmission of data across a physical link and is primarily concerned with physical addressing, line discipline, network topology, error notification, ordered delivery of frames, and flow control. The IEEE has further segmented this layer into the MAC sublayer and the LLC sublayer. Also known as the Link layer. Can be compared somewhat to the data link control layer of the SNA model. *See also: Application layer, LLC, MAC, Network layer, Physical layer, Presentation layer, Session layer, Transport layer.*

DCC   Data Country Code: Developed by the ATM Forum, one of two ATM address formats designed for use by private networks. *See also: ICD.*

DCE   Data communications equipment (as defined by the EIA) or data circuit-terminating equipment (as defined by the ITU-T): The mechanisms and links of a communications network that make up the network portion of the user-to-network interface, such as modems. The DCE supplies the physical connection to the network, forwards traffic, and provides a clocking signal to synchronize data transmission between DTE and DCE devices. *See also: DTE.*

DDP   Datagram Delivery Protocol: Used in the AppleTalk suite of protocols as a connectionless protocol that is responsible for sending datagrams through an internetwork.

DDR   Dial-on-demand routing: A technique that allows a router to automatically initiate and end a circuit-switched session, per the requirements of the sending station. By mimicking keepalives, the router fools the end station into treating the session as active. DDR permits routing over ISDN or telephone lines via a modem or external ISDN terminal adapter.

DE   Discard Eligibility: Used in Frame Relay networks to tell a switch that a frame can be discarded if the switch is too busy. The DE is a field in the frame that is turned on by transmitting routers when the Committed Information Rate (CIR) is oversubscribed or set to 0.

debug   The Cisco IOS command that provides the administrator with low-level, detailed information about processes that run on the router.

default route   The static routing table entry used to direct frames whose next hop is not spelled out in the dynamic routing table.

delay   The time elapsed between a sender's initiation of a transaction and the first response they receive. Also, the time needed to move a packet from its source to its destination over a path. *See also: latency.*

demarc   The demarcation point between the customer premises equipment (CPE) and the telco's carrier equipment.

demodulation   A series of steps that returns a modulated signal to its original form. When receiving, a modem demodulates an analog signal to its original digital form (and, conversely, modulates the digital data it sends into an analog signal). *See also: modulation.*

demultiplexing   The process of converting a single multiplex signal, comprising more than one input stream, back into separate output streams. *See also: multiplexing.*

designated bridge   This is the bridge with the lowest path cost in the process of forwarding a frame from a segment to the route bridge.

designated port   Used with the Spanning-Tree Protocol (STP) to designate forwarding ports. If there are multiple links to the same network, STP will shut a port down to stop network loops.

designated router   An OSPF router that creates LSAs for a multi-access network and is required to perform other special tasks in OSPF operations. Multi-access OSPF networks that maintain a minimum of two attached routers identify one router that is chosen by the OSPF Hello protocol, which makes possible a decrease in the number of adjacencies necessary on a multi-access network. This in turn reduces the quantity of routing-protocol traffic and the physical size of the database.

destination address   The address for the network devices that will receive a packet.

DHCP   Dynamic Host Configuration Protocol: DHCP is a superset of the BootP protocol. This means it uses the same protocol structure as BootP, but it has enhancements added. Both of these protocols use servers that dynamically configure clients when requested. The two major enhancements are address pools and lease times. *See also: BootP.*

dialer map statements   Configuration statements that link network addresses to ISDN numbers.

directed broadcast   A data frame or packet that is transmitted to a specific group of nodes on a remote network segment. Directed broadcasts are known by their broadcast address, which is a destination subnet address with all the bits turned on.

discovery mode   Also known as dynamic configuration, the discovery mode technique is used by an AppleTalk interface to gain information from a working node about an attached network. The information is subsequently used by the interface for self-configuration.

distance-vector routing algorithm   In order to find the shortest path, this group of routing algorithms repeats on the number of hops in a given route, requiring each router to send its complete routing table with each update, but only to its neighbors. Routing algorithms of this type tend to generate loops, but they are fundamentally simpler than their link-state counterparts. *See also: link-state routing algorithm, SPF.*

distribute lists   These lists are references to access-lists and are applied to a routing protocol via interfaces.

distributed switching   Distributed switching happens on the VIP (Versatile Interface Processor) cards (which have a switching processor onboard), so it's very efficient. All required processing is done right on the VIP processor, which maintains a copy of the router's routing cache.

distribution layer   Middle layer of the Cisco three-layer hierarchical model, which helps you design, install, and maintain Cisco hierarchical networks. The distribution layer is the point where access-layer devices connect. Routing is performed at this layer.

divide-and-conquer troubleshooting   Troubleshooting methodology based on the OSI model. This troubleshooting method is based on experience with similar problems in the past. Based on this experience, troubleshooting begins a one of the middle layers of the OSI model and progresses either up or down the model depending on what is found at the original layer. *See also: bottom-up troubleshooting and top-down troubleshooting.*

divide-by-half troubleshooting   Troubleshooting method in which a point between two ends of a network problem is used as a troubleshooting reference point. Either half may be investigated first, thus narrowing down the trouble location.

DLCI   Data-Link Connection Identifier: Used to identify virtual circuits in a Frame Relay network. DLCI only has local significance.

DNS   Domain Name Service: Used to resolve host names to IP addresses.

domain master browser   Browser that collects and disseminates information from the master browsers in the domain. This information is used to identify resources in the domain and can be used with Windows networks. *See also: browsing, master browser, Network Neighborhood.*

DSAP   Destination Service Access Point: The service access point of a network node, specified in the destination field of a frame. *See also: SSAP, SAP.*

DSR   Data Set Ready: When a DCE is powered up and ready to run, this EIA/TIA-232 interface circuit is also engaged.

DSU   Data Service Unit: This device is used to adapt the physical interface on a data terminal equipment (DTE) mechanism to a transmission facility such as T1 or E1; the DSU is also responsible for signal timing. It is commonly grouped with the channel service unit and referred to as the CSU/DSU. *See also: CSU.*

DTE   Data terminal equipment: On a user-network interface serving as a destination, a source, or both, the DTE is any device located at the user end of that interface. DTE includes devices such as multiplexers, protocol translators, and computers. The connection to a data network is made through data channel equipment (DCE) such as a modem, using the clocking signals generated by that device. *See also: DCE.*

DTR   Data terminal ready: An activated EIA/TIA-232 circuit communicating to the DCE the state of preparedness of the DTE to transmit or receive data.

DUAL   Diffusing Update Algorithm: Used in Enhanced IGRP, this convergence algorithm provides loop-free operation throughout an entire route's computation. DUAL grants routers involved in a topology revision the ability to synchronize simultaneously, while routers unaffected by this change are not involved. *See also: Enhanced IGRP.*

DVMRP   Distance Vector Multicast Routing Protocol: Based primarily on the Routing Information Protocol (RIP), this Internet gateway protocol implements a common, condensed-mode IP multicast scheme, using IGMP to transfer routing datagrams between its neighbors. *See also: IGMP.*

DXI   Data Exchange Interface: Described in RFC 1482, DXI defines the effectiveness of a network device such as a router, bridge, or hub to act as an FEP to an ATM network by using a special DSU that accomplishes packet encapsulation.

dynamic entries   Used in Layer 2 and 3 devices to create a table of either hardware addresses or logical addresses dynamically.

dynamic routing   Also known as adaptive routing, this technique automatically adapts to traffic or physical network revisions.

dynamic VLAN   An administrator will create an entry in a special server with the hardware addresses of all devices on the internetwork. The server will then assign dynamically used VLANs.

E1   Generally used in Europe, a wide-area digital transmission scheme carrying data at 2.048Mbps. E1 transmission lines can be leased from common carriers for private use.

E.164   (1) Evolved from standard telephone numbering system, the standard recommended by ITU-T for international telecommunication numbering, particularly in ISDN, SMDS, and BISDN. (2) Label of field in an ATM address containing numbers in E.164 format.

EARL   Encoded Address Recognition Logic ASIC: This chip works with the bus arbitration system to control access to the data-switching bus. EARL also controls the destination ports of packet transfers.

edge device   A device that enables packets to be forwarded between legacy interfaces (such as Ethernet and Token Ring) and ATM interfaces, based on information in the Data-Link and

Network layers. An edge device does not take part in the running of any Network layer routing protocol; it merely uses the route description protocol in order to get the forwarding information required.

EEPROM Electronically Erasable Programmable Read-Only Memory: Programmed after their manufacture, these nonvolatile memory chips can be erased if necessary using electric power and reprogrammed. *See also: EPROM, flash, flash memory, PROM.*

EFCI Explicit Forward Congestion Indication: A congestion feedback mode permitted by ABR service in an ATM network. The EFCI may be set by any network element that is in a state of immediate or certain congestion. The destination end-system is able to carry out a protocol that adjusts and lowers the cell rate of the connection based on value of the EFCI. *See also: ABR.*

EIGRP *See Enhanced IGRP.*

EIP Ethernet Interface Processor: An interface processor card in Cisco 7000 series routers, supplying 10Mbps AUI ports to support Ethernet Version 1 and Ethernet Version 2 or IEEE 802.3 interfaces with a high-speed data path to other interface processors.

ELAN Emulated LAN: An ATM network configured using a client/server model in order to emulate either an Ethernet or Token Ring LAN. Multiple ELANs can exist at the same time on a single ATM network and are made up of a LAN emulation client (LEC), a LAN Emulation Server (LES), a Broadcast and Unknown Server (BUS), and a LAN Emulation Configuration Server (LECS). ELANs are defined by the LANE specification. *See also: LANE, LEC, LECS, LES.*

ELAP EtherTalk Link Access Protocol: In an EtherTalk network, the link-access protocol constructed above the standard Ethernet Data-Link layer.

encapsulation The technique used by layered protocols in which a layer adds header information to the protocol data unit (PDU) from the layer above. As an example, in Internet terminology, a packet would contain a header from the Physical layer, followed by a header from the Network layer (IP), followed by a header from the Transport layer (TCP), followed by the application protocol data.

encryption The conversion of information into a scrambled form that effectively disguises it to prevent unauthorized access. Every encryption scheme uses some well-defined algorithm, which is reversed at the receiving end by an opposite algorithm in a process known as decryption.

end-system network configuration table It is a table that contains information about the end systems in the network. This table is used during troubleshooting to help identify the purpose of an end system as well as where it is located in the environment. *See also: end-system network topology diagram, network configuration table, and network topology diagram.*

end-system network topology diagram This is a diagram used to show the physical connections of the end system in the environment. This diagram is used during troubleshooting to help identify the interrelationship between end systems as well as to determine the relevant pieces of hardware that are in a given network path. *See also: end-system network configuration table, network configuration table, and network topology diagram.*

Enhanced IGRP   Enhanced Interior Gateway Routing Protocol: An advanced routing protocol created by Cisco, combining the advantages of link-state and distance-vector protocols. Enhanced IGRP has superior convergence attributes, including high operating efficiency. *See also: IGP, IGRP, OSPF, RIP.*

enterprise network   A privately owned and operated network that joins most major locations in a large company or organization.

EPROM   Erasable Programmable Read-Only Memory: Programmed after their manufacture, these nonvolatile memory chips can be erased if necessary using high-power light and repro-grammed. *See also: EEPROM, flash, flash memory, PROM.*

error control   The control mechanism for verification of contiguous and non-erroneous packets.

ESF   Extended Superframe: Made up of 24 frames with 192 bits each, with the 193rd bit providing other functions including timing. An enhanced version of SF. *See also: SF.*

Ethernet   A baseband LAN specification created by the Xerox Corporation and then improved through joint efforts of Xerox, Digital Equipment Corporation, and Intel. Ethernet is similar to the IEEE 802.3 series standard and, using CSMA/CD, operates over various types of cables at 10Mbps. Also called DIX (Digital/Intel/Xerox) Ethernet. *See also: 10BaseT, Fast Ethernet, IEEE.*

EtherTalk   A data-link product from Apple Computer that permits AppleTalk networks to be connected by Ethernet.

excess rate   In ATM networking, traffic exceeding a connection's insured rate. The excess rate is the maximum rate less the insured rate. Depending on the availability of network resources, excess traffic can be discarded during congestion episodes. *See also: maximum rate.*

expansion   The procedure of directing compressed data through an algorithm, restoring information to its original size.

expedited delivery   An option that can be specified by one protocol layer, communicating either with other layers or with the identical protocol layer in a different network device, requiring that identified data be processed faster.

explorer packet   An SNA packet transmitted by a source Token Ring device to find the path through a source-route-bridged network.

extended addressing   The technique used by AppleTalk Phase 2 to assign multiple network addresses to a single segment.

extended IP access list   IP access list that filters the network by logical address, the protocol field in the Network layer header, and even the port field in the Transport layer header.

extended IPX access list   IPX access list that filters the network by logical IPX address, the protocol field in the Network layer header, and even the socket number in the Transport layer header.

Extended Setup   Used in Setup mode to configure the router with more detail than Basic Setup mode. Allows multiple-protocol support and interface configuration.

extended ping   The enhanced version of ping that allows user interaction to choose options when executing the ping command. This resource requires enabled access to the router.

fact gathering   The process of using diagnostic tools to collect information specific to the network and network devices involved in a problem. Additional information should include data that excludes other possibilities and helps pinpoint the actual problem.

failure domain   The region in which a failure has occurred in a Token Ring network. When a station gains information that a serious problem, such as a cable break, has occurred with the network, it sends a beacon frame that includes the station reporting the failure, its Nearest Active Upstream Neighbor (NAUN), and everything between. This defines the failure domain. Beaconing then initiates the procedure known as autoreconfiguration. *See also: autoreconfiguration, beacon, beaconing.*

fallback   In ATM networks, this mechanism is used for scouting a path if one cannot be located using customary methods. The device relaxes requirements for certain characteristics, such as delay, in an attempt to find a path that meets a certain set of the most important requirements.

Fast Ethernet   Any Ethernet specification with a speed of 100Mbps. Fast Ethernet is 10 times faster than 10BaseT, while retaining qualities such as MAC mechanisms, MTU, and frame format. These similarities make it possible for existing 10BaseT applications and management tools to be used on Fast Ethernet networks. Fast Ethernet is based on an extension of IEEE 802.3 specification (IEEE 802.3u). *See also: 100BaseT, 100BaseTX, Ethernet, IEEE.*

fast switching   A Cisco feature that uses a route cache to speed packet switching through a router. *See also: process switching.*

FDM   Frequency-Division Multiplexing: A technique that permits information from several channels to be assigned bandwidth on one wire based on frequency. *See also: TDM, ATDM, statistical multiplexing.*

FDDI   Fiber Distributed Data Interface: A LAN standard, defined by ANSI X3T9.5, that can run at speeds up to 200Mbps and uses token-passing media access on fiber-optic cable. For redundancy, FDDI can use a dual-ring architecture.

FECN   Forward Explicit Congestion Notification: A bit set by a Frame Relay network that informs the DTE receptor that congestion was encountered along the path from source to destination. A device receiving frames with the FECN bit set can ask higher-priority protocols to take flow-control action as needed. *See also: BECN.*

FEIP   Fast Ethernet Interface Processor: An interface processor employed on Cisco 7000 series routers, supporting up to two 100Mbps, 100BaseT ports.

FIB   Forwarding Information Base: The FIB consists of information duplicated from the IP route table. Every time the routing information changes, the changes are propagated to the FIB.

firewall   A barrier purposely erected between a private network and any connected public networks, made up of a router or access server or several routers or access servers. The firewall uses access lists and other methods to ensure the security of the private network.

flash   The term used to represent EEPROM (Electronically Erasable Programmable Read-Only Memory). Flash is used to hold the Cisco IOS in a router by default. *See also: EPROM, EEPROM, flash memory.*

flash memory   Developed by Intel and licensed to other semiconductor manufacturers, flash memory is nonvolatile storage that can be erased electronically and reprogrammed, physically located on an EEPROM chip. Flash memory permits software images to be stored, booted, and rewritten as needed. Cisco routers and switches use flash memory to hold the IOS by default. *See also: EPROM, EEPROM, flash.*

flat network   A network that is one large collision domain and one large broadcast domain.

flooding   Occurs when traffic is received on an interface and is then transmitted to every interface connected to that device with the exception of the interface from which the traffic originated. This technique is often used for traffic transfer by bridges, hubs, and switches throughout the network.

flow control   A methodology used to ensure that receiving units are not overwhelmed with data from sending devices. *Pacing*, as it is called in IBM networks, means that when buffers at a receiving unit are full, a message is transmitted to the sending unit to temporarily halt transmissions until all the data in the receiving buffer has been processed and the buffer is again ready for action.

FRAD   Frame Relay Access Device: Any device affording a connection between a LAN and a Frame Relay WAN. *See also: Cisco FRAD, FRAS.*

fragment   Any portion of a larger packet that has been segmented into smaller pieces. A packet fragment can be intentional and does not necessarily indicate an error. *See also: fragmentation.*

fragmentation   The process of intentionally segmenting a packet into smaller pieces when sending data over an intermediate network medium that cannot support the larger packet size.

FragmentFree   LAN switch type that reads into the data section of a frame to make sure fragmentation did not occur. Sometimes called modified cut-through.

frame   A logical unit of information sent by the Data-Link layer over a transmission medium. The term often refers to the header and trailer, employed for synchronization and error control, that surround the data contained in the unit.

Frame Relay   A more efficient replacement of the X.25 protocol (an unrelated packet-relay technology that guarantees data delivery). Frame Relay is an industry-standard, shared-access, best-effort, switched Data-Link layer encapsulation that services multiple virtual circuits and protocols among connected mechanisms.

Frame Relay bridging   Defined in RFC 1490, this bridging method uses the same spanning-tree algorithm as other bridging operations but permits packets to be encapsulated for transmission across a Frame Relay network.

framing   Encapsulation at the Data-Link layer of the OSI model. It is called framing because the packet is encapsulated with both a header and a trailer.

FRAS   Frame Relay Access Support: A feature of Cisco IOS software that enables SDLC, Ethernet, Token Ring, and Frame Relay–attached IBM devices to be linked with other IBM mechanisms on a Frame Relay network. *See also: FRAD.*

frequency   The number of cycles of an alternating current signal per time unit, measured in hertz (cycles per second).

FSIP   Fast Serial Interface Processor: The Cisco 7000 routers' default serial interface processor, it provides four or eight high-speed serial ports.

FTP   File Transfer Protocol: The TCP/IP protocol used for transmitting files between network nodes. Supports a broad range of file types and is defined in RFC 959. *See also: TFTP.*

full-duplex   The capacity to simultaneously send and receive data between two network devices. *See also: half-duplex.*

full mesh   A type of network topology where every node has either a physical or a virtual circuit linking it to every other network node. A full mesh supplies a great deal of redundancy but is typically reserved for network backbones because of its expense. *See also: partial mesh.*

GNS   Get Nearest Server: On an IPX network, a request packet sent by a client for determining the location of the nearest active server of a given type. An IPX network client launches a GNS request to get either a direct answer from a connected server or a response from a router disclosing the location of the service on the internetwork. GNS is part of IPX and SAP. *See also: IPX, SAP.*

GRE   Generic Routing Encapsulation: A tunneling protocol created by Cisco with the capacity for encapsulating a wide variety of protocol packet types inside IP tunnels, thereby generating a virtual point-to-point connection to Cisco routers across an IP network at remote points. IP tunneling using GRE permits network expansion across a single-protocol-backbone environment by linking multiprotocol subnetworks.

guard band   The unused frequency area found between two communications channels, furnishing the space necessary to avoid interference between the two.

H channel   High-speed channel: A full-duplex, ISDN primary rate channel operating at a speed of 384Kbps. *See also: B, D,* and *E channels.*

half-duplex   The capacity to transfer data in only one direction at a time between a sending unit and receiving unit. *See also: full-duplex.*

handshake   Any series of transmissions exchanged between two or more devices on a network to ensure synchronized operations.

HDLC High-level Data Link Control: Using frame characters, including checksums, HDLC designates a method for data encapsulation on synchronous serial links and is the default encapsulation for Cisco routers. HDLC is a bit-oriented synchronous Data-Link layer protocol created by ISO and derived from SDLC. However, most HDLC vendor implementations (including Cisco's) are proprietary. *See also: SDLC.*

helper address The unicast address specified, which instructs the Cisco router to change the client's local broadcast request for a service into a directed unicast to the server.

hierarchical addressing Any addressing plan employing a logical chain of commands to determine location. IP addresses are made up of a hierarchy of network numbers, subnet numbers, and host numbers to direct packets to the appropriate destination.

HIP HSSI Interface Processor: An interface processor used on Cisco 7000 series routers, providing one HSSI port that supports connections to ATM, SMDS, Frame Relay, or private lines at speeds up to T3 or E3.

holddown The state a route is placed in so that routers can neither advertise the route nor accept advertisements about it for a defined time period. Holddown is used to surface bad information about a route from all routers in the network. A route is generally placed in holddown when one of its links fails.

hop The movement of a packet between any two network nodes. *See also: hop count.*

hop count A routing metric that calculates the distance between a source and a destination. RIP employs hop count as its sole metric. *See also: hop, RIP.*

host address Logical address configured by an administrator or server on a device. Logically identifies this device on an internetwork.

HSCI High-Speed Communication Interface: Developed by Cisco, a single-port interface that provides full-duplex synchronous serial communications capability at speeds up to 52Mbps.

HSRP Hot Standby Router Protocol: A protocol that provides high network availability and provides nearly instantaneous hardware failover without administrator intervention. It generates a Hot Standby router group, including a lead router that lends its services to any packet being transferred to the Hot Standby address. If the lead router fails, it will be replaced by any of the other routers—the standby routers—that monitor it.

HSSI High-Speed Serial Interface: A network standard physical connector for high-speed serial linking over a WAN at speeds of up to 52Mbps.

hub A Physical layer device that is really just a multi-port repeater. When an electronic digital signal is received on a hub port, the signal is re-amplified or regenerated and forwarded out all segments except the segment from which the signal was received.

hybrid mode Hybrid mode is the mode on a Cisco multi-layered switches in which the routing and switching components and commands are separate from one another. *See also: native mode.*

ICD International Code Designator: Adapted from the subnetwork model of addressing, this assigns the mapping of Network layer addresses to ATM addresses. HSSI is one of two ATM formats for addressing created by the ATM Forum to be utilized with private networks. *See also: DCC.*

ICMP Internet Control Message Protocol: Documented in RFC 792, it is a Network layer Internet protocol for the purpose of reporting errors and providing information pertinent to IP packet procedures.

IEEE Institute of Electrical and Electronics Engineers: A professional organization that, among other activities, defines standards in a number of fields within computing and electronics, including networking and communications. IEEE standards are the predominant LAN standards used today throughout the industry. Many protocols are commonly known by the reference number of the corresponding IEEE standard.

IEEE 802.1 The IEEE committee specification that defines the bridging group. The specification for STP (Spanning-Tree Protocol) is IEEE 802.1D. The STP uses STA (spanning-tree algorithm) to find and prevent network loops in bridged networks. The specification for VLAN trunking is IEEE 802.1Q.

IEEE 802.3 The IEEE committee specification that defines the Ethernet group, specifically the original 10Mbps standard. Ethernet is a LAN protocol that specifies Physical layer and MAC sublayer media access. IEEE 802.3 uses CSMA/CD to provide access for many devices on the same network. FastEthernet is defined as 802.3u, and Gigabit Ethernet is defined as 802.3q. *See also: CSMA/CD.*

IEEE 802.5 The IEEE committee specification that defines Token Ring media access.

IGMP Internet Group Management Protocol: Employed by IP hosts, the protocol that reports their multicast group memberships to an adjacent multicast router.

ignore A Cisco IOS error, which can be caused in three ways: the hardware buffer fills up and it signals to the transmitting interface to throttle down; the interface is receiving frames faster than the SP can pull them off; the bus is so busy that the interface processor is unable to copy the packet from the hardware buffer to the SP buffers.

IGP Interior Gateway Protocol: Any protocol used by the Internet to exchange routing data within an independent system. Examples include RIP, IGRP, and OSPF.

IGRP Interior Gateway Routing Protocol: A Cisco proprietary routing protocol that uses a distance-vector algorithm. It uses a vector (a one-dimensional array) of information to calculate the best path. This vector consists of four elements: bandwidth, delay, load, reliability.

ILMI Integrated (or Interim) Local Management Interface: A specification created by the ATM Forum, designated for the incorporation of network-management capability into the ATM UNI. Integrated Local Management Interface cells provide for automatic configuration between ATM systems. In LAN emulation, ILMI can provide sufficient information for the ATM end station to find an LECS. In addition, ILMI provides the ATM NSAP (Network Service Access Point) prefix information to the end station.

in-band management   Management of a network device "through" the network. Examples include using Simple Network Management Protocol (SNMP) or telnet directly via the local LAN. *See also: out-of-band management.*

input queues   These queues reside on the RP, and they are used to link the SP buffers to the RP buffers. The queue reserves RP buffer space for a packet that was forwarded from the SP/SSP. If the Router Processor doesn't process the queued packets at the same rate, the queue fills up and the incoming packets are dropped.

inside-out troubleshooting   This method of troubleshooting directs the troubleshooter to start near the user and work toward the far end of the area of dysfunctionality.

insured burst   In an ATM network, this is the largest temporarily permitted data burst exceeding the insured rate on a PVC and not tagged by the traffic policing function for being dropped if network congestion occurs. This insured burst is designated in bytes or cells.

inter-area routing   Routing between two or more logical areas. *See also: area, intra-area routing.*

interface buffer   A buffer used for intermediate storage. Packets from all the hardware buffers are copied to the interface buffers. The switch processor houses the intermediate buffers by using 512KB for the SP board memory. This memory is also shared with the autonomous switching cache.

interface processor   Any of several processor modules used with Cisco 7000 series routers. *See also: AIP, CIP, EIP, FEIP, HIP, MIP, TRIP.*

Internet   The global "network of networks" whose popularity has exploded in the last few years. Originally a tool for collaborative academic research, it has become a medium for exchanging and distributing information of all kinds. The Internet's need to link disparate computer platforms and technologies has led to the development of uniform protocols and standards that have also found widespread use within corporate LANs. *See also: TCP/IP, MBONE.*

internet   Before the rise of the Internet, this lowercase form was shorthand for "internetwork" in the generic sense. Now rarely used. *See also: internetwork.*

Internet protocol   Any protocol belonging to the TCP/IP protocol stack. *See also: TCP/IP.*

internetwork   Any group of private networks interconnected by routers and other mechanisms, typically operating as a single entity.

internetworking   Broadly, anything associated with the general task of linking networks. The term encompasses technologies, procedures, and products. When you connect networks to a router, you are creating an internetwork.

intra-area routing   Routing that occurs within a logical area. *See also: area, inter-area routing.*

Inverse ARP   Inverse Address Resolution Protocol: A technique by which dynamic mappings are constructed in a network, allowing a device such as a router to locate the logical network address and associate it with a permanent virtual circuit (PVC). Commonly used in Frame

Relay to determine the far-end node's TCP/IP address by sending the Inverse ARP request to the local DLCI.

IP   Internet Protocol: Defined in RFC 791, IP is a Network-layer protocol that is part of the TCP/IP stack and allows connectionless service. IP furnishes an array of features for addressing, type-of-service specification, fragmentation and reassembly, and security.

IP address   Often called an Internet address; an address uniquely identifying any device (host) on the Internet (or any TCP/IP network). Each address consists of four octets (32 bits), represented as decimal numbers separated by periods (a format known as "dotted-decimal"). Every address is made up of a network number, an optional subnetwork number, and a host number. The network and subnetwork numbers together are used for routing, while the host number addresses an individual host within the network or subnetwork. The network and subnetwork information is extracted from the IP address using the subnet mask. There are five classes of IP addresses (A–E), which allocate specific numbers of bits to the network, subnetwork, and host portions of the address. *See also: CIDR, IP, subnet mask.*

IPCP   IP Control Program: The protocol used to establish and configure IP over PPP. *See also: IP, PPP.*

IP multicast   A technique for routing that enables IP traffic to be reproduced from one source to several endpoints or from multiple sources to many destinations. Instead of transmitting only one packet to each individual point of destination, one packet is sent to a multicast group specified by only one IP endpoint address for the group.

IPX   Internetwork Packet Exchange: Network-layer protocol (Layer 3) used in Novell NetWare networks for transferring information from servers to workstations. Similar to IP and XNS.

IPXCP   IPX Control Program: The protocol used to establish and configure IPX over PPP. *See also: IPX and PPP.*

IPXWAN   Protocol used for new WAN links to provide and negotiate line options on the link using IPX. After the link is up and the options have been agreed upon by the two end-to-end links, normal IPX transmission begins.

ISDN   Integrated Services Digital Network: Offered as a service by telephone companies, a communication protocol that allows telephone networks to carry data, voice, and other digital traffic. *See also: BISDN, BRI, and PRI.*

ISDN BRI   *See BRI.*

ISL   Inter-Switch Link: Cisco proprietary switching protocol that allows multiple VLANs to traverse the same trunk link.

ISL routing   Inter-Switch Link routing: A Cisco proprietary method of frame tagging in a switched internetwork. Frame tagging is a way to identify the VLAN membership of a frame as it traverses a switched internetwork.

isochronous transmission   Asynchronous data transfer over a synchronous data link, requiring a constant bit rate for reliable transport. *See also: asynchronous transmission, synchronous transmission.*

iteration   The repetition of certain steps within the troubleshooting model. Certain steps may need to be repeated in order to solve the problem at hand.

ITU-T   International Telecommunication Union Telecommunication Standardization Sector: A group of engineers that develops worldwide standards for telecommunications technologies.

LAN   Local Area Network: Broadly, any network linking two or more computers and related devices within a limited geographical area (up to a few kilometers). LANs are typically high-speed, low-error networks within a company. Cabling and signaling at the Physical and Data-Link layers of the OSI are dictated by LAN standards. Ethernet, FDDI, and Token Ring are among the most popular LAN technologies. *See also: MAN, WAN.*

LAN switch   A high-speed, multiple-interface transparent bridging mechanism that transmits packets between segments of data links, usually referred to specifically as an Ethernet switch. A LAN switch transfers traffic based on MAC addresses. *See also: multilayer switch, store-and-forward packet switching.*

LANE   LAN emulation: The technology that allows an ATM network to operate as a LAN backbone. To do so, the ATM network is required to provide multicast and broadcast support, address mapping (MAC-to-ATM), SVC management, and an operable packet format. Additionally, LANE defines Ethernet and Token Ring ELANs. *See also: ELAN.*

LAPB   Link Accessed Procedure, Balanced: A bit-oriented Data-Link layer protocol that is part of the X.25 stack and has its origin in SDLC. *See also: SDLC, X.25.*

LAPD   Link Access Procedure on the D channel. The ISDN Data-Link layer protocol used specifically for the D channel and defined by ITU-T Recommendations Q.920 and Q.921. LAPD evolved from LAPB and is created to comply with the signaling requirements of ISDN basic access.

latency   Broadly, latency is the time it takes for a data packet to get from one location to another. In specific networking contexts, latency can mean either (1) the time elapsed (delay) between the execution of a request for access to a network by a device and the time the mechanism actually is permitted transmission, or (2) the time elapsed between a mechanism's receipt of a frame and the time that frame is forwarded out of the destination port.

Layer 1 S/T Interface   This connection uses a physical connector of RJ-45, as defined in ISO 8877. A straight-through pin configuration connects the terminal end point (TE) to the network termination (NT).

Layer-3 switch   *See multilayer switch.*

layered architecture   Industry standard way of creating applications to work on a network. Layered architecture allows the application developer to make changes in only one layer instead of the whole program.

LCP   Link Control Protocol: The protocol designed to establish, configure, and test data-link connections for use by PPP. *See also: PPP.*

leaky bucket   An analogy for the basic cell rate algorithm (GCRA) used in ATM networks for checking the conformance of cell flows from a user or network. The bucket's "hole" is understood to be the prolonged rate at which cells can be accommodated, and the "depth" is the tolerance for cell bursts over a certain time period.

learning bridge   A bridge that transparently builds a dynamic database of MAC addresses and the interfaces associated with each address. Transparent bridges help to reduce traffic congestion on the network.

LE ARP   LAN Emulation Address Resolution Protocol: The protocol providing the ATM address that corresponds to a MAC address.

leased lines   Permanent connections between two points leased from the telephone companies.

LEC   LAN Emulation Client: Software providing the emulation of the link layer interface that allows the operation and communication of all higher-level protocols and applications to continue. The LEC client runs in all ATM devices, which include hosts, servers, bridges, and routers. The LANE client is responsible for address resolution, data transfer, address caching, interfacing to the emulated LAN, and driver support for higher-level services. *See also: ELAN, LES.*

LECS   LAN Emulation Configuration Server: An important part of emulated LAN services, providing the configuration data that is furnished upon request from the LES. These services include address registration for Integrated Local Management Interface (ILMI) support, configuration support for the LES addresses and their corresponding emulated LAN identifiers, and an interface to the emulated LAN. *See also: LES, ELAN.*

LES   LAN Emulation Server: The central LANE component that provides the initial configuration data for each connecting LEC. The LES typically is located on either an ATM-integrated router or a switch. Responsibilities of the LES include configuration and support for the LEC, address registration for the LEC, database storage and response concerning ATM addresses, and interfacing to the emulated LAN. *See also: ELAN, LEC, LECS.*

link-state routing algorithm   A routing algorithm that allows each router to broadcast or multicast information regarding the cost of reaching all its neighbors to every node in the internetwork. Link-state algorithms provide a consistent view of the network and are therefore not vulnerable to routing loops. In general, the link-state algorithm provides for faster convergence than the distance-vector algorithm. However, this is achieved at the cost of somewhat greater difficulty in computation and greater complexity (compared with distance-vector routing algorithms). *See also: distance-vector routing algorithm.*

LLAP   LocalTalk Link Access Protocol: In a LocalTalk environment, LLAP is the Data-Link layer protocol that manages node-to-node delivery of data. This protocol provides node addressing and management of bus access, and it also controls data sending and receiving to assure packet length and integrity.

LLC   Logical Link Control: Defined by the IEEE, LLC is the higher of two Data-Link layer sub-layers. LLC is responsible for error detection (but not correction), flow control, framing, and software-sublayer addressing. The predominant LLC protocol, IEEE 802.2, defines both connectionless and connection-oriented operations. *See also: Data-Link layer, MAC.*

LMI   Local Management Interface: An enhancement to the original Frame Relay specification. Among the features it provides are a keepalive mechanism, a multicast mechanism, global addressing, and a status mechanism.

LNNI   LAN Emulation Network-to-Network Interface: In the Phase 2 LANE specification, LNNI is an interface that supports communication between the server components within one ELAN.

local explorer packet   In a Token Ring SRB network, a packet generated by an end system to find a host linked to the local ring. If no local host can be found, the end system will produce one of two solutions: a spanning explorer packet or an all-routes explorer packet.

local loop   Connection from a demarcation point to the closest switching office.

LocalTalk   Utilizing CSMA/CD, in addition to supporting data transmission at speeds of 230.4Kbps, LocalTalk is Apple Computer's proprietary baseband protocol, operating at the Data-Link and Physical layers of the OSI reference model.

loopback tests   These tests aid in physically isolating serial line and Frame Relay problems. Four different loopback tests can be performed to troubleshoot the circuit: local loopback on the local CSU/DSU, local loopback on the remote CSU/DSU, remote loopback from the local NIU to the remote CSU/DSU, and remote loopback from the remote NIU to the local CSU/DSU.

LSA   Link-state advertisement: Contained inside of link-state packets (LSPs), the LSA advertisements are usually multicast packets containing information about neighbors and path costs, employed by link-state protocols. Receiving routers use LSAs to maintain their link-state databases and, ultimately, routing tables.

LT/ET   The line termination and exchange termination points are called LT and ET, respectively. They handle the termination of the local loop and switching functions.

LUNI   LAN Emulation User-to-Network Interface: Defining the interface between the LAN Emulation Client (LEC) and the LAN Emulation Server, LUNI is the ATM Forum's standard for LAN emulation on ATM networks. *See also: LES, LECS.*

MAC   Media Access Control: The lower sublayer in the Data-Link layer, MAC is responsible for hardware addressing, media access, and error detection of frames. *See also: Data-Link layer, LLC.*

MAC address   A Data-Link layer hardware address that every port or device needs in order to connect to a LAN segment. These addresses are used by various devices in the network for accurate location of logical addresses. MAC addresses are defined by the IEEE standard and their length is 6 characters, typically using the burned-in address (BIA) of the local LAN interface. Variously called hardware address, physical address, burned-in address, or MAC-layer address.

MacIP   In AppleTalk, the Network-layer protocol encapsulating IP packets in Datagram Delivery Protocol (DDP) packets. MacIP also supplies substitute ARP services.

MAN   Metropolitan-Area Network: Any network that encompasses a metropolitan area—that is, an area typically larger than a LAN but smaller than a WAN. *See also: LAN, WAN.*

Manchester encoding   A method for digital coding in which a mid-bit-time transition is employed for clocking, and a 1 is denoted by a high voltage level during the first half of the bit time. This scheme is used by Ethernet.

master browser   Browser that collects and disseminates resource information in Windows networks. There is one master browser per segment. This browser is automatically elected when the stations on a segment come online. *See also: browsing, domain master browser, Network Neighborhood.*

maximum burst   Specified in bytes or cells, this is the largest burst of information exceeding the insured rate that will be permitted on an ATM permanent virtual connection for a short time and not be dropped even if it goes over the specified maximum rate. *See also: insured burst, maximum rate.*

maximum rate   The maximum permitted data throughput on a particular virtual circuit, equal to the total of insured and uninsured traffic from the traffic source. Should traffic congestion occur, uninsured information may be deleted from the path. Measured in bits or cells per second, the maximum rate represents the highest throughput of data the virtual circuit is ever able to deliver and cannot exceed the media rate. *See also: excess rate, maximum burst.*

MBS   Maximum Burst Size: In an ATM signaling message, this metric, coded as a number of cells, is used to convey the burst tolerance.

MBONE   Multicast backbone: The multicast backbone of the Internet, it is a virtual multicast network made up of multicast LANs, including point-to-point tunnels interconnecting them.

MCDV   Maximum Cell Delay Variation: The maximum two-point CDV objective across a link or node for the identified service category in an ATM network. The MCDV is one of four link metrics that are exchanged using PTSPs to verify the available resources of an ATM network. Only one MCDV value is assigned to each traffic class. *See also: PTSP*

MCLR   Maximum Cell Loss Ratio: The maximum ratio of cells in an ATM network that fail to transit a link or node, compared with the total number of cells that arrive at the link or node. MCDV is one of four link metrics that are exchanged using PTSPs to verify the available resources of an ATM network. The MCLR applies to cells in VBR and CBR traffic classes whose CLP bit is set to zero. *See also: CBR, CLP, VBR.*

MCR   Minimum Cell Rate: A parameter determined by the ATM Forum for traffic management of the ATM networks. MCR is specifically defined for ABR transmissions and specifies the minimum value for the allowed cell rate (ACR). *See also: ACR, PCR.*

MCTD   Maximum Cell Transfer Delay: In an ATM network, the total of the maximum cell delay variation and the fixed delay across the link or node. MCTD is one of four link metrics that are exchanged using PNNI topology state packets to verify the available resources of an ATM network. There is one MCTD value assigned to each traffic class. *See also: MCDV.*

metrics   These measurements are associated with each route that is present in the route table. Metrics are calculated by the routing protocol to define a cost of getting to the destination address. Some algorithms use hop count (the number of routers between it and the destination address), whereas others use a vector of values.

MIB   Management Information Base: Used with SNMP management software to gather information from remote devices. The management station can poll the remote device for information, or the MIB running on the remote station can be programmed to send information on a regular basis.

MIP   Multichannel Interface Processor: The resident interface processor on Cisco 7000 series routers, providing up to two channelized T1 or E1 connections by serial cables connected to a CSU. The two controllers are capable of providing 24 T1 or 30 E1 channel groups, with each group being introduced to the system as a serial interface that can be configured individually.

mips   Millions of instructions per second: A measure of processor speed.

MLP   Multilink PPP: A technique used to split, recombine, and sequence datagrams across numerous logical data links.

MMP   Multichassis Multilink PPP: A protocol that supplies MLP support across multiple routers and access servers. MMP enables several routers and access servers to work as a single large dial-up pool with one network address and ISDN access number. MMP successfully supports packet fragmenting and reassembly when the user connection is split between two physical access devices.

modem   Modulator-demodulator: A device that converts digital signals to analog and vice versa so that digital information can be transmitted over analog communication facilities, such as voice-grade telephone lines. This is achieved by converting digital signals at the source to analog for transmission, and reconverting the analog signals back into digital form at the destination. *See also: modulation, demodulation.*

modem eliminator   A mechanism that makes possible a connection between two DTE devices without modems by simulating the commands and physical signaling required.

modulation   The process of modifying some characteristic of an electrical signal, such as amplitude (AM) or frequency (FM), in order to represent digital or analog information.

MOSPF   Multicast OSPF: An extension of the OSPF unicast protocol that enables IP multicast routing within the domain. *See also: OSPF.*

MPOA   Multiprotocol over ATM: An effort by the ATM Forum to standardize the running of existing and future Network-layer protocols such as IP, IPv6, AppleTalk, and IPX over an ATM network with directly attached hosts, routers, and multilayer LAN switches.

MPLS Multiprotocol Label Switching: Switching methodology that uses short labels to describe how packets should be forwarded through the network.

MSFC Multilayer Switch Feature Card: A daughter card that goes on the supervisor module of a 6500 series switch providing routing capabilities to the switch.

MTU Maximum transmission unit: The largest packet size, measured in bytes, that an interface can handle.

multicast Broadly, multicast is any communication between a single sender and multiple receivers. Unlike broadcast messages, which are sent to all addresses on a network, multicast messages are sent to a defined subset of the network addresses; this subset has a group multicast address, which is specified in the packet's destination address field. *See also: broadcast, directed broadcast.*

multicast address An IP address whose binary representation of its first octet begins with the pattern 1110. In decimal notation, this range is defined as any address between 224.0.0.0 and 239.255.255.255. Multicast addresses are used for the purpose of identifying recipients of multicast transmissions. Identical to group address. *See also: multicast.*

multicast send VCC A two-directional point-to-point virtual control connection (VCC) arranged by an LEC to a BUS; one of the three types of informational link specified by Phase 1 LANE. *See also: control distribute VCC, control direct VCC.*

multilayer switch A highly specialized, high-speed, hardware-based type of LAN router, the multilayer switch filters and forwards packets based on their Layer 2 MAC addresses and Layer 3 network addresses. It's possible that even Layer 4 can be read. Sometimes called a Layer 3 switch. *See also: LAN switch.*

multimeter Hardware used to measure voltage, resistance, and current. It works with electrical-based cabling and can be used to test for physical connectivity.

multiplexing The process of converting several logical signals into a single physical signal for transmission across one physical channel. *See also: demultiplexing.*

native mode Native mode is the mode on a Cisco multi-layerd switches in which the routing and switching components and commands combined into one interface. *See also: hybrid mode.*

NAK Negative acknowledgment: A response sent from a receiver, telling the sender that the information either was not received or contained errors. *See also: acknowledgment.*

NAT Network Address Translation: An algorithm instrumental in minimizing the requirement for globally unique IP addresses. NAT permits an organization whose addresses are not all globally unique to connect to the Internet regardless, by translating those addresses into globally routable address space.

NBP Name Binding Protocol: In AppleTalk, the transport-level protocol that interprets a socket client's name, entered as a character string, into the corresponding DDP address. NBP gives AppleTalk protocols the capacity to discern user-defined zones and names of mechanisms by showing and keeping translation tables that map names to their corresponding socket addresses.

neighboring routers   Two routers in OSPF that have interfaces to a common network. On networks with multi-access, these neighboring routers are dynamically discovered using the Hello protocol of OSPF.

NetBEUI   NetBIOS Extended User Interface: An improved version of the NetBIOS protocol used in a number of network operating systems including LAN Manager, Windows NT, LAN Server, Windows 2000 and Windows XP, implementing the OSI LLC2 protocol. NetBEUI formalizes the transport frame not standardized in NetBIOS and adds more functions. *See also: OSI.*

NetBIOS   Network Basic Input/Output System: Applications residing on an IBM LAN use the NetBIOS API to ask for services, such as session termination or information transfer, from lower-level network processes. *See also: API.*

Netflow switching   Collects detailed data for use with circuit accounting and application-utilization information. Because of all the additional data that Netflow collects (and may export), expect an increase in router overhead—possibly as much as a 5% increase in CPU utilization.

NetView   A mainframe network product from IBM, used for monitoring SNA (Systems Network Architecture) networks. It runs as a VTAM (Virtual Telecommunications Access Method) application.

NetWare   A widely used NOS created by Novell, providing a number of distributed network services and remote file access.

network address   Used with the logical network addresses to identify the network segment in an internetwork. Logical addresses are hierarchical in nature and have at least two parts: network and host. An example of a hierarchical address is 172.16.10.5, where 172.16 is the network and 10.5 is the host address.

network analyzer   Also known as protocol analyzer. A device that collects and analyzes data on a connected broadcast domain. The information provided is a packet decode of data transiting the network and is used to troubleshoot network problems.

network configuration table   It is a table that contains information about the network devices in the network. This table is used during troubleshooting to help identify the purpose and configuration of the network components. *See also: end-system network configuration table, end-system network topology diagram, and network topology diagram.*

Network layer   Layer 3 of the OSI reference model. Routing is implemented in the Network layer, enabling connections and path selection between two end systems. *See also: Application layer, Data-Link layer, Physical layer, Presentation layer, Session layer, Transport layer.*

Network Monitor   This software-based tool simply monitors the network. It can do this in several ways, including via the Simple Network Management Protocol (SNMP) and the Internet Control Message Protocol (ICMP).

Network Neighborhood A Windows tool that allows users to see the resources that are available in the network. The information is displayed by domain to allow for easier viewing and is populated through the use of browsing. *See also: Browsing, Domain Master Browser, Master Browser.*

network topology diagram It is a diagram that contains information about the network devices in the network. This diagram is used during troubleshooting to help identify relationships between network devices as well as determine the network devices that are involved in a particular flow. *See also: end-system network configuration table, end-system network topology diagram, and network configuration table.*

NFS Network File System: One of the protocols in Sun Microsystems's widely used file-system protocol suite, allowing remote file access across a network. The name is loosely used to refer to the entire Sun protocol suite, which also includes RPC, XDR (External Data Representation), and other protocols.

NHRP Next Hop Resolution Protocol: In a nonbroadcast multi-access (NBMA) network, NHRP is the protocol employed by routers in order to dynamically locate MAC addresses of various hosts and routers. It enables systems to communicate directly without requiring an intermediate hop, thus facilitating increased performance in ATM, Frame Relay, X.25, and SMDS systems.

NHS Next Hop Server: Defined by the NHRP protocol, this server maintains the next-hop resolution cache tables, listing IP-to-ATM address maps of related nodes and nodes that can be reached through routers served by the NHS.

NIC Network interface card: An electronic circuit board placed in a computer. The NIC provides network communication to a LAN.

NLSP NetWare Link Services Protocol: Novell's link-state routing protocol, based on the IS-IS model.

NMP Network Management Processor: A Catalyst 5000 switch processor module used to control and monitor the switch.

NMS Network Management Systems: A software/hardware package used to monitor availability, network performance, security, services, and policies.

node address Identifies a specific device in an internetwork. Can be a hardware address, which is burned into the network interface card, or a logical network address, which an administrator or server assigns to the node.

nondesignated port The Spanning-Tree Protocol tells a port on a Layer-2 switch to stop transmitting and creating a network loop. Only designated ports can send frames.

non-stub area In OSPF, a resource-consuming area carrying a default route, intra-area routes, inter-area routes, static routes, and external routes. Non-stub areas are the only areas that can have virtual links configured across them and exclusively contain an autonomous system boundary router (ASBR). *See also: ASBR, OSPF, stub area.*

NRZ   Nonreturn to Zero: One of several encoding schemes for transmitting digital data. NRZ signals sustain constant levels of voltage with no signal shifting (no return to zero-voltage level) during a bit interval. If a series of bits with the same value (1 or 0) occur, there will be no state change. The signal is not self-clocking. *See also: NRZI.*

NRZI   Nonreturn to Zero Inverted: One of several encoding schemes for transmitting digital data. A transition in voltage level (either from high to low or vice versa) at the beginning of a bit interval is interpreted as a value of 1; the absence of a transition is interpreted as a 0. Thus, the voltage assigned to each value is continually inverted. NRZI signals are not self-clocking. *See also: NRZ.*

NT1   Network termination 1: An ISDN designation to devices that understand ISDN standards.

NT2   Network termination 2: An ISDN designation to devices that do not understand ISDN standards. To use an NT2, you must use a terminal adapter (TA).

NVRAM   Non-Volatile RAM: Random-access memory that keeps its contents intact while power is turned off.

observing results   Using the exact same methods and commands that were used to obtain information in order to define the problem and see whether the changes implemented were effective.

OC   Optical carrier: A series of physical protocols, designated as OC-1, OC-2, OC-3, and so on, for SONET optical signal transmissions. OC signal levels place STS frames on a multimode fiber optic line at various speeds, of which 51.84Mbps is the lowest (OC-1). Each subsequent protocol runs at a speed divisible by 51.84. *See also: SONET.*

octet   Base-8 numbering system used to identify a section of a dotted decimal IP address. Also referred to as a byte.

ones density   Also known as pulse density; a method of signal clocking. The CSU/DSU retrieves the clocking information from data that passes through it. For this scheme to work, the data needs to be encoded to contain at least one binary 1 for each 8 bits transmitted. *See also: CSU, DSU.*

optimum switching   Switching method that replaced fast switching on higher-end Cisco routers. Switching is done by comparing incoming packets against the optimum switching cache.

OSI   Open System Interconnection: International standardization program designed by ISO and ITU-T for the development of data networking standards that make multivendor equipment interoperability a reality.

OSI reference model   Open System Interconnection reference model: A conceptual model defined by the International Organization for Standardization (ISO), describing how any combination of devices can be connected for the purpose of communication. The OSI model divides the task into seven functional layers, forming a hierarchy with the applications at the top and the physical medium at the bottom, and it defines the functions each layer must provide. *See also: Application layer, Data-Link layer, Network layer, Physical layer, Presentation layer, Session layer, Transport layer.*

OSPF   Open Shortest Path First: A link-state, hierarchical IGP routing algorithm derived from an earlier version of the IS-IS protocol. Features include multipath routing, load balancing, and least-cost routing. OSPF is the suggested successor to RIP in the Internet environment. *See also: Enhanced IGRP, IGP, IP.*

OTDR   Optical Time Domain Reflectors: An optical cable tester used to locate physical problems in the cable. *See also: TDR*

OUI   Organizationally Unique Identifier: Assigned by the IEEE to an organization that makes network interface cards. The organization then puts this OUI on each and every card they manufacture. The OUI is 3 bytes (24 bits) long. The manufacturer then adds a 3-byte identifier to uniquely identify the host on an internetwork. The total length of the address is 48 bits (6 bytes) and is called a hardware address or MAC address.

out-of-band management   Management "outside" the network's physical channels—for example, using a console connection not directly interfaced through the local LAN or WAN or a dial-in modem. *See also: in-band management.*

out-of-band signaling   Within a network, any transmission that uses physical channels or frequencies separate from those ordinarily used for data transfer. For example, the initial configuration of a Cisco Catalyst switch requires an out-of-band connection via a console port.

output queue   This queue resides on the RP and is used to hold the packet until the packet can be copied to the buffers on the SP/SSP. From there, it is forwarded to the specified interface processor.

outside-in troubleshooting   Troubleshooting method that consists of choosing the opposite end of the connection and working back toward you or the user that reported the problem.

overrun   Phenomenon that occurs when the receiver receives packets faster than it can transfer them to the hardware buffer.

packet   In data communications, the basic logical unit of information transferred. A packet consists of a certain number of data bytes, wrapped or encapsulated in headers and/or trailers that contain information about where the packet came from, where it's going, and so on. The various protocols involved in sending a transmission add their own layers of header information, which the corresponding protocols in receiving devices then interpret.

packet switch   A physical device that makes it possible for a communication channel to share several connections. Its functions include finding the most efficient transmission path for packets.

packet switching   A networking technology based on the transmission of data in packets. Dividing a continuous stream of data into small units—packets—enables data from multiple devices on a network to share the same communication channel simultaneously but also requires the use of precise routing information.

PAP   Password Authentication Protocol: In Point-to-Point Protocol (PPP) networks, a method of validating connection requests. The requesting (remote) device must send an authentication request, containing a password and ID, to the local router when attempting to connect. Unlike the more secure CHAP (Challenge Handshake Authentication Protocol), PAP sends the password unencrypted and does not attempt to verify whether the user is authorized to access the requested resource; it merely identifies the remote end. *See also: CHAP.*

parity checking   A method of error-checking in data transmissions. An extra bit (the parity bit) is added to each character or data word so that the sum of the bits will be either an odd number (in odd parity) or an even number (even parity).

partial mesh   A type of network topology in which some network nodes form a full mesh (where every node has either a physical or a virtual circuit linking it to every other network node), but others are attached to only one or two nodes in the network. A typical use of partial-mesh topology is in peripheral networks linked to a fully meshed backbone. *See also: full mesh.*

path cost   *See cost.*

path determination   Condition in which the router is aware of a route that leads to the desired destination address.

PCR   Peak Cell Rate: As defined by the ATM Forum, PCR is the parameter that specifies, in cells per second, the maximum rate at which a source may transmit.

PDN   Public Data Network: Generally for a fee, a PDN offers the public access to computer communication network operated by private concerns or government agencies. Small organizations can take advantage of PDNs for help creating WANs without having to invest in long-distance equipment and circuitry.

PGP   Pretty Good Privacy: A popular public-key/private-key encryption application offering protected transfer of files and messages.

Physical layer   The lowest layer—Layer 1—in the OSI reference model. The Physical layer is responsible for converting data packets from the Data-Link layer (Layer 2) into electrical signals. Physical-layer protocols and standards define, for example, the type of cable and connectors to be used, including their pin assignments and the encoding scheme for signaling 0 and 1 values. *See also: Application layer, Data-Link layer, Network layer, Presentation layer, Session layer, Transport layer.*

physical test equipment   A genre of testing equipment including multimeters, cable testers, TDRs, and OTDRs. Used for testing cable integrity and end-to-end physical connectivity.

ping   Packet Internet groper: A Unix-based Internet diagnostic tool consisting of a message sent to test the accessibility of a particular device on the IP network. The acronym (from which the "full name" was formed) reflects the underlying metaphor of submarine sonar. Just as the sonar operator sends out a signal and waits to hear it echo ("ping") back from a submerged object, the network user can ping another node on the network and wait to see if it responds.

pleisochronous   Nearly synchronous, except that clocking comes from an outside source instead of being embedded within the signal as in synchronous transmissions.

PLP   Packet Level Protocol: Occasionally called X.25 Level 3 or X.25 Protocol, a Network-layer protocol that is part of the X.25 stack.

PNNI Private Network-Network Interface: An ATM Forum specification for offering topology data used for the calculation of paths through the network, among switches and groups of switches. It is based on well-known link-state routing procedures and allows for automatic configuration in networks whose addressing scheme is determined by the topology.

point-to-multipoint connection In ATM or frame relay, a communication path going only one way, connecting a single system at the starting point, called the "root node," to systems at multiple points of destination, called "leaves." *See also: point-to-point connection.*

point-to-point connection In ATM or frame relay, a channel of communication that can be directed either one way or two ways between two ATM end systems. *See also: point-to-multipoint connection.*

poison reverse updates These update messages are transmitted by a router back to the originator (thus ignoring the split-horizon rule) after route poisoning has occurred. Typically used with DV routing protocols in order to overcome large routing loops and offer explicit information when a subnet or network is not accessible (instead of merely suggesting that the network is unreachable by not including it in updates). *See also: route poisoning.*

polling The procedure of orderly inquiry, used by a primary network mechanism, to determine whether secondary devices have data to transmit. A message is sent to each secondary, granting the secondary the right to transmit.

POP (1) Point Of Presence: The physical location where an interexchange carrier has placed equipment to interconnect with a local exchange carrier. (2) Post Office Protocol (currently at version 3): A protocol used by client e-mail applications for recovery of mail from a mail server.

port mirroring On a switch, the process by which the data going to and from one port is replicated on another for the purpose of monitoring and troubleshooting.

port security Used with Layer-2 switches to provide some security. Not typically used in production because it is difficult to manage. Allows only certain frames to traverse administrator-assigned segments.

PDU Protocol Data Unit: The name of the processes at each layer of the OSI model. PDUs at the Transport layer are called segments; PDUs at the Network layer are called packets or datagrams; and PDUs at the Data-Link layer are called frames. The Physical layer uses bits.

PPP Point-to-Point Protocol: The protocol most commonly used for dial-up Internet access, superseding the earlier SLIP. Its features include address notification, authentication via CHAP or PAP, support for multiple protocols, and link monitoring. PPP has two layers: the Link Control Protocol (LCP) establishes, configures, and tests a link; and then any of various Network Control Programs (NCPs) transport traffic for a specific protocol suite, such as IPX. *See also: CHAP, PAP, SLIP.*

prefix list Much like an access list, a prefix list is used for specifying which address ranges are allowed to access certain services. Prefix lists are primarily used for filtering routing updates. *See also: access list.*

Presentation layer   Layer 6 of the OSI reference model, it defines how data is formatted, presented, encoded, and converted for use by software at the Application layer. *See also: Application layer, Data-Link layer, Network layer, Physical layer, Session layer, Transport layer.*

PRI   Primary Rate Interface: A type of ISDN connection between a PBX and a long-distance carrier, made up of a single 64Kbps D channel in addition to 23 (T1) or 30 (E1) B channels. *See also: ISDN.*

primary nodes   SDLC protocol nodes that are responsible for the control of secondary stations and for link management, such as link setup and teardown.

priority 1   Production network down situation. The highest priority when opening a ticket with the Cisco TAC.

priority 2   Production network performance seriously degraded. The second highest priority when opening a ticket with the Cisco TAC.

priority 3   Network performance degraded. The third highest priority when opening a ticket with the Cisco TAC.

priority 4   Information needed on Cisco products. Priority associated with cases that do not require immediate troubleshooting support.

priority queueing   A routing function in which frames temporarily placed in an interface output queue are assigned priorities based on traits such as packet size or type of interface.

problem definition   The step in the troubleshooting model where details are used to define the most likely cause of a problem. This should be a concise yet accurate description of the problem at hand.

process switching   The procedure that occurs when a packet arrives on a router to be forwarded and is copied to the router's process buffer, and then the router performs a lookup on the Layer 3 address. Using the route table, an exit interface is associated with the destination address. The processor forwards the packet with the added new information to the exit interface, while the router initializes the fast-switching cache. Subsequent packets bound for the same destination address follow the same path as the first packet.

PROM   Programmable read-only memory: ROM that is programmable only once, using special equipment. *See also: EPROM.*

propagation delay   The time it takes data to traverse a network from its source to its destination.

protocol   In networking, the specification of a set of rules for a particular type of communication. The term is also used to refer to the software that implements a protocol.

protocol analyzer   Also known as network analyzer. A device that collects and analyzes data on a connected broadcast domain. The information provided is a packet decode of data transiting the network. This also includes a protocol analysis of the traffic that is captured from the network. This data is used to troubleshoot network problems.

protocol parameters   The options that are passed with connection setup within many connection-oriented protocols. An example would be the TCP window size.

protocol stack   A collection of related protocols.

proxy ARP   A variation of the ARP protocol in which the router responds to an ARP request for a station that is on a different subnet. In this manner , even when a workstation is misconfigured it can still talk on the network.

PSE   Packet Switch Exchange: The X.25 term for a switch.

PSN   Packet-switched network: Any network that uses packet-switching technology. Also known as packet-switched data network (PSDN). *See also: packet switching.*

PSTN   Public Switched Telephone Network: Colloquially, "plain old telephone service" (POTS). A term that describes the assortment of telephone networks and services available globally.

PTSP   PNNI Topology State Packet: A type of packet used in PNNI routing to send updates to local nodes.

PVC   Permanent virtual circuit: In a Frame-Relay network, a logical connection, defined in software, that is maintained permanently. *See also: SVC, VC.*

PVP   Permanent virtual path: A virtual path made up of PVCs. *See also: PVC.*

PVP tunneling   Permanent virtual path tunneling: A technique that links two private ATM networks across a public network using a virtual path, wherein the public network transparently trunks the complete collection of virtual channels in the virtual path between the two private networks.

q.921   The q.921 is the Layer 2 protocol used by ISDN, on the D channel. It establishes a connection between the central office switch and the router.

q.931   The third layer of ISDN is addressed in the ITU-T I.451 specification, which is also called q.931. This protocol includes several message commands, which are viewed with the `debug isdn q931` command. These commands include call setup, connect, release, cancel, status, disconnect, and user information.

QoS   Quality of Service: A set of metrics used to measure the quality of transmission and service availability of any given transmission system.

queue   Broadly, any list of elements arranged in an orderly fashion and ready for processing, like a line of people waiting to enter a movie theater. In routing, it refers to a backlog of information packets waiting in line to be transmitted over a router interface.

R reference point   Used with ISDN networks to identify the connection between a TE2 and a TA device.

RAM   Random access memory: Used by all computers to store information. Cisco routers use RAM to store packet buffers and routing tables, along with the hardware addresses cache.

RARP   Reverse Address Resolution Protocol: The protocol within the TCP/IP stack that maps MAC addresses to IP addresses. *See also: ARP.*

rate queue   A value assigned to one or more virtual circuits, which specifies the speed at which an individual virtual circuit will transmit data to the remote end. Every rate queue identifies a segment of the total bandwidth available on an ATM link. The sum of all rate queues should not exceed the total available bandwidth.

RCP   Remote Copy Protocol: A protocol for copying files to or from a file system that resides on a remote server on a network, using TCP to guarantee reliable data delivery.

red alarm   A red alarm on a T1 or E1 indicates that the incoming signal is corrupted. The equipment in red alarm will be sending out a yellow alarm on its outbound signal. *See also: yellow alarm.*

redistribution   Command used in Cisco routers to inject the paths found from one type of routing protocol into another type of routing protocol. For example, networks found by RIP can be inserted into an IGRP network.

redundancy   In internetworking, the duplication of connections, devices, or services that can be used as a backup in the event that the primary connections, devices, or services fail.

reload   An event or command that causes Cisco routers to reboot.

RIF   Routing Information Field: In source-route bridging, a header field that defines the path direction of the frame or token. If the Route Information Indicator (RII) bit is not set, the RIF is read from source to destination (left to right). If the RII bit is set, the RIF is read from the destination back to the source (right to left). It is defined as part of the Token Ring frame header for source-routed frames, which contains path information.

ring   Two or more stations connected in a logical circular topology. In this topology, which is the basis for Token Ring, FDDI, and CDDI, information is transferred from station to station in sequence.

ring topology   A network logical topology comprising a series of repeaters that form one closed loop by connecting unidirectional transmission links. Individual stations on the network are connected to the network at a repeater. Physically, ring topologies are generally organized in a closed-loop star. *See also: bus topology, star topology.*

RIP   Routing Information Protocol: One of the most commonly used interior gateway protocols in the Internet. RIP employs hop count as a routing metric. *See also: Enhanced IGRP, IGP, OSPF, hop count.*

RJ connector   Registered Jack connector: Used with twisted-pair wiring to connect the copper wire to network interface cards, switches, and hubs.

RMON   Remote Monitoring: Another method for obtaining environmental and statistical information from devices. Much of the RMON technology implementation is based on the deployment of RMON probes that gather the information from the circuit (physical media) because the router or switch may not support all levels of RMON information.

ROM   Read-only memory: Chip used in computers to help boot the device. Cisco routers use a ROM chip to load the bootstrap, which runs a power-on self test, and then find and load the IOS in flash memory by default.

root bridge   Used with the Spanning-Tree Protocol to stop network loops from occurring. The root bridge is elected by having the lowest bridge ID. The bridge ID is determined by the priority (32,768 by default on all bridges and switches) and the main hardware address of the device. The root bridge determines which of the neighboring Layer-2 devices' interfaces become the designated and nondesignated ports.

routed protocol   Routed protocols (such as IP and IPX) are used to transmit user data through an internetwork. By contrast, routing protocols (such as RIP, IGRP, and OSPF) are used to update routing tables between routers.

route maps   Small scripts used to manipulate routing; can contain multiple instances and multiple conditions for each instance. Route maps are somewhat like access lists if you specify that the packet must match an access list. In addition to permitting or denying the packet, you can define what is done before the packet is forwarded. Route maps can be used to set metrics for route updates, set a command to its default value, and so on.

route poisoning   Used by various DV routing protocols in order to overcome large routing loops and offer explicit information about when a subnet or network is not accessible (instead of merely suggesting that the network is unreachable by not including it in updates). Typically, this is accomplished by setting the hop count to one more than maximum. *See also: poison reverse updates.*

route summarization   In various routing protocols, such as OSPF, EIGRP, and IS-IS, route summarization is the consolidation of publicized subnetwork addresses so that a single summary route is advertised to other areas by an area border router.

router   A Network-layer mechanism, either software or hardware, using one or more metrics to decide on the best path for transmission of network traffic. Sending packets between networks by routers is based on the information provided on Network layers. Historically, this device has sometimes been called a gateway.

routing   The process of forwarding logically addressed packets from their local subnetwork toward their ultimate destination. In large networks, the numerous intermediary destinations a packet might travel before reaching its destination can make routing very complex.

routing domain   Any collection of end systems and intermediate systems that operate under an identical set of administrative rules. Every routing domain contains one or several areas, each individually given a certain area address.

routing metric   Any value that is used by routing algorithms to determine whether one route is superior to another. Metrics include such information as bandwidth, delay, hop count, path cost, load, MTU, reliability, and communication cost. Only the best possible routes are stored in the routing table, while all other information may be stored in link-state or topological databases. *See also: cost.*

routing protocol   Any protocol that defines algorithms to be used for updating routing tables between routers. Examples include IGRP, RIP, and OSPF.

routing table   A table, kept in a router, that maintains a record of only the best possible routes to certain network destinations and the metrics associated with those routes.

RP   Route Processor: Also known as a supervisory processor; a module on Cisco 7000 series routers that holds the CPU, system software, and most of the memory components used in the router.

RSP   Route/Switch Processor: A processor module combining the functions of RP and SP used in Cisco 7500 series routers. *See also: RP, SP.*

RTMP   Routing Table Maintenance Protocol: Protocol responsible for AppleTalk routing tables and their information. AppleTalk's proprietary method of maintaining route tables on AppleTalk-enabled machines.

RTS   Request To Send: An EIA/TIA-232 control signal requesting permission to transmit data on a communication line.

S reference point   ISDN reference point that works with a T reference point to convert a 4-wire ISDN network to the two-wire ISDN network needed to communicate with the ISDN switches at the network provider.

S/T reference point   If no NT2 is installed, the S/T reference point is the connection between the NT1 and either the TA or the TE1, depending on which is installed. Installation of NT2 devices is rare, so most ISDN installations will have an S/T reference point.

SAGE   Synergy Advanced Gate-Array Engine: A chip used for non-Ethernet applications— including FDDI, ATM LANE, Token Ring, and the Network Management Processor on the supervisor engine. *See also: supervisor module.*

SAINT   Synergy Advanced Interface and Network Termination: The SAINT handles Ethernet switching on the Catalyst 5000 platform, and it also handles ISL encapsulation.

SAMBA ASIC   Synergy Advanced Multipurpose Bus Arbiter ASIC located on line modules and the supervisor modules. On the line cards, this chip is responsible for broadcast suppression, based on thresholds established by the administrator. This ASIC also maintains statistics on packets. *See also: supervisor module.*

sampling rate   The rate at which samples of a specific waveform amplitude are collected within a specified period of time.

SAP   (1) Service Access Point: A field specified by IEEE 802.2 that is part of an address specification. (2) Service Advertising Protocol: The Novell NetWare protocol that supplies a way to inform network clients of resource and service availability on the network, using routers and servers. *See also: IPX.*

SAPI   Service access point identifier: A Layer 2 address used to manage different data types destined for the same device on an ISDN network.

SCR Sustainable Cell Rate: An ATM Forum parameter used for traffic management, SCR is the long-term average cell rate for VBR connections that can be transmitted.

SDLC Synchronous Data Link Control: A protocol used in SNA Data-Link layer communications. SDLC is a bit-oriented, full-duplex serial protocol that is the basis for several similar protocols, including HDLC and LAPB. *See also: HDLC, LAPB.*

secondary nodes Nodes as designated by the SDLC protocol. Secondary nodes talk only to the primary node when they fulfill two requirements: first, they have permission from the primary node; second, they have data to transmit.

seed device A root device specified in an NMS configuration, from which the network discovery begins. The seed device's neighbors are discovered, and the continuing process spreads out starting at the seed device.

seed router In an AppleTalk network, the router that is equipped with the network number or cable range in its port descriptor. The seed router specifies the network number or cable range for other routers in that network section and answers to configuration requests from non-seed routers on its connected AppleTalk network, permitting those routers to affirm or modify their configurations accordingly. Every AppleTalk network needs at least one seed router physically connected to each network segment.

sequenced data transfer The process of assigning sequence numbers to every PDU that leaves a host, so that it may be resequenced after all of the PDUs in a transmission reach the destination host.

server Hardware and software that provide network services to clients.

set-based Set-based routers and switches use the set command to configure devices. Cisco is moving away from set-based commands and is using the command-line interface (CLI) on all new devices.

Session layer Layer 5 of the OSI reference model, responsible for creating, managing, and terminating sessions between applications and overseeing data exchange between Presentation layer entities. *See also: Application layer, Data-Link layer, Network layer, Physical layer, Presentation layer,* and *Transport layer.*

setup mode Mode that a router will enter if no configuration is found in nonvolatile RAM when the router boots. Allows the administrator to configure a router step-by-step. Not as robust or flexible as the command-line interface.

SF Superframe: A superframe (also called a D4 frame) consists of 12 frames with 192 bits each, with the 193rd bit providing other functions including error checking. SF is frequently used on T1 circuits. A newer version of the technology is Extended Super Frame (ESF), which uses 24 frames. *See also: ESF.*

signaling packet An informational packet created by an ATM-connected mechanism that wants to establish connection with another such mechanism. The packet contains the QoS parameters needed for connection, and the ATM NSAP address of the endpoint. The endpoint responds with a message of acceptance if it is able to support the desired QoS, and the connection is established. *See also: QoS.*

silicon switching A type of high-speed switching used in Cisco 7000 series routers, based on the use of a separate processor (the Silicon Switch Processor, or SSP). *See also: SSE.*

simplex The mode at which data or a digital signal is transmitted. Simplex is a way of transmitting in only one direction. Half-duplex transmits in two directions but only one direction at a time. Full-duplex transmits both directions simultaneously.

sliding window The method of flow control used by TCP, as well as several Data-Link layer protocols. This method places a buffer between the receiving application and the network data flow. The "window" indicates the amount of data that will be sent before an acknowledgment of the data is expected. The window size will grow larger in stable networks and smaller in less stable ones. The window will also get smaller in the event the receiving station is having trouble processing all of the information that is coming in.

SLIP Serial Line Internet Protocol: An industry standard serial encapsulation for point-to-point connections that supports only a single routed protocol, TCP/IP. SLIP is the predecessor to PPP. *See also: PPP.*

SMDS Switched Multimegabit Data Service: A packet-switched, datagram-based WAN networking technology offered by telephone companies that provides high speed.

SMTP Simple Mail Transfer Protocol: A protocol used on the Internet to provide electronic mail services.

SNA System Network Architecture: A complex, feature-rich, network architecture similar to the OSI reference model but with several variations; created by IBM in the 1970s and essentially composed of seven layers.

SNAP Subnetwork Access Protocol: SNAP is a frame used in Ethernet, Token Ring, and FDDI LANs. Data transfer, connection management, and QoS selection are three primary functions executed by the SNAP frame.

SNMP Simple Network Management Protocol: This protocol polls SNMP agents or devices for statistical and environmental data. This data can include device temperature, name, performance statistics, and much more. SNMP works with MIB objects that are present on the SNMP agent. This information is queried and then sent to the SNMP server.

socket (1) A software structure that operates within a network device as a destination point for communications. (2) In AppleTalk networks, an entity at a specific location within a node; AppleTalk sockets are conceptually similar to TCP/IP ports.

software test equipment *See Network Monitor.*

SONET Synchronous Optical Network: The ANSI standard for synchronous transmission on fiber optic media, developed at Bell Labs. It specifies a base signal rate of 51.84Mbps and a set of multiples of that rate, known as Optical Carrier levels, up to 10 Gbps.

SP Switch Processor: Also known as a ciscoBus controller, it is a Cisco 7000 series processor module acting as governing agent for all bus activities.

SPAN Switched Port Analyzer: A feature of the Catalyst 5000 switch, offering freedom to manipulate within a switched Ethernet environment by extending the monitoring ability of the existing network analyzers into the environment. At one switched segment, the SPAN mirrors traffic onto a predetermined SPAN port, while a network analyzer connected to the SPAN port is able to monitor traffic from any other Catalyst switched port.

spanning explorer packet Sometimes called limited-route or single-route explorer packet, the spanning explorer packet pursues a statically configured spanning tree when searching for paths in a source-route bridging network. *See also: all-routes explorer packet, explorer packet, local explorer packet.*

spanning tree A subset of a network topology within which no loops exist. When bridges are interconnected into a loop, the bridge, or switch, cannot identify a frame that has been forwarded previously, so there is no mechanism for removing a frame as it passes the interface numerous times. Without a method of removing these frames, the bridges continually forward them—consuming bandwidth and adding overhead to the network. Spanning trees prune the network to provide only one path for any packet. *See also: Spanning-Tree Protocol, spanning-tree algorithm.*

spanning-tree algorithm (STA) An algorithm that creates a spanning tree using the Spanning-Tree Protocol (STP). *See also: spanning tree, Spanning-Tree Protocol.*

Spanning-Tree Protocol (STP) The bridge protocol (IEEE 802.1D) that enables a learning bridge to dynamically avoid loops in the network topology by creating a spanning tree using the spanning-tree algorithm. Spanning-tree frames called bridge protocol data units (BPDUs) are sent and received by all switches in the network at regular intervals. The switches participating in the spanning tree don't forward the frames; instead, they're processed to determine the spanning-tree topology itself. Cisco Catalyst series switches use STP 802.1D to perform this function. *See also: BPDU, learning bridge, MAC address, spanning tree, spanning-tree algorithm.*

SPF Shortest Path First algorithm: A routing algorithm used to decide on the shortest-path spanning tree. Sometimes called Dijkstra's algorithm and frequently used in link-state routing algorithms. *See also: link-state routing algorithm.*

SPID Service Profile Identifier: A number assigned by service providers or local telephone companies and assigned by administrators to a BRI port. SPIDs are used to determine subscription services of a device connected via ISDN. ISDN devices use SPID when accessing the telephone company switch that initializes the link to a service provider.

split horizon Useful for preventing routing loops, a type of distance-vector routing rule where information about routes is prevented from leaving the router interface through which that information was received.

spoofing (1) In dial-on-demand routing (DDR), where a circuit-switched link is taken down to save toll charges when there is no traffic to be sent, spoofing is a scheme used by routers. It causes a host to treat an interface as if it were functioning and supporting a session. The router sends "spoof" replies to keepalive messages from the host in an effort to convince the host that the session is up and running. *See also: DDR. (2)* The illegal act of sending a packet labeled with a false address, in order to deceive network security mechanisms such as filters and access lists.

spooler   A management application that processes requests submitted to it for execution in a sequential fashion from a queue. A good example is a print spooler.

SPX   Sequenced Packet Exchange: A Novell NetWare transport protocol that augments the datagram service provided by Network layer (Layer 3) protocols; derived from the Switch-to-Switch Protocol of the XNS protocol suite.

SQE   Signal Quality Error: In an Ethernet network, a message sent from a transceiver to an attached machine indicating that the collision-detection circuitry is working.

SRB   Source-Route Bridging: Created by IBM, SRB is the bridging method used in Token Ring networks. The source determines the entire route to a destination before sending the data and includes that information in route information fields (RIFs) within each packet. *See also: transparent bridging.*

SRT bridging   Source-Route Transparent bridging: A bridging scheme developed by IBM, merging source-route and transparent bridging. SRT takes advantage of both technologies in one device, fulfilling the needs of all end nodes. Translation between bridging protocols is not necessary. *See also: SR/TLB.*

SR/TLB   Source-Route Translational Bridging: A bridging method that allows source-route stations to communicate with transparent bridge stations aided by an intermediate bridge that translates between the two bridge protocols. Used for bridging between Token Ring and Ethernet. *Compare with: SRT.*

SSAP   Source Service Access Point: The SAP of the network node identified in the Source field of the frame. *See also: DSAP and SAP.*

SSE   Silicon Switching Engine: The software component of Cisco's silicon switching technology, hard-coded into the Silicon Switch Processor (SSP). Silicon switching is available only on the Cisco 7000 with an SSP. Silicon-switched packets are compared to the silicon-switching cache on the SSE. The SSP is a dedicated switch processor that offloads the switching process from the route processor, providing a fast-switching solution, but packets must still traverse the backplane of the router to get to the SSP and then back to the exit interface.

standard IP access list   IP access list that uses only the source IP addresses to filter a network.

standard IPX access list   IPX access list that uses only the source and destination IPX address to filter a network.

star topology   A LAN physical topology with endpoints on the network converging at a common central switch (known as a hub) using point-to-point links. A logical ring topology can be configured as a physical star topology using a unidirectional closed-loop star rather than point-to-point links. That is, connections within the hub are arranged in an internal ring. *See also: bus topology, ring topology.*

startup range If an AppleTalk node does not have a number saved from the last time it was booted, then the node selects from the startup range of values from 65280 to 65534.

static route A route whose information is purposely entered into the routing table and that takes priority over those chosen by dynamic routing protocols.

static VLANs VLANs on a switch that were manually configured as opposed to dynamically learned. In most cases, static VLANs are used in environments where there are few VLANs defined on a switch and/or these VLANs do not change often.

statistical multiplexing Multiplexing in general is a technique that allows data from multiple logical channels to be sent across a single physical channel. Statistical multiplexing dynamically assigns bandwidth only to input channels that are active, optimizing available bandwidth so that more devices can be connected than with other multiplexing techniques. Also known as statistical time-division multiplexing or stat mux.

STM-1 Synchronous Transport Module Level 1. In the European SDH standard, one of many formats identifying the frame structure for the 155.52Mbps lines that are used to carry ATM cells.

store-and-forward packet switching A technique in which the switch first copies each packet into its buffer and performs a cyclic redundancy check (CRC). If the packet is error free, the switch then looks in its filter table for the destination address, determines the appropriate exit port, and sends the packet.

STP (1) Shielded Twisted Pair: A two-pair wiring scheme, used in many network implementations, which has a layer of shielded insulation to reduce EMI. (2) Spanning-Tree Protocol.

stub area An OSPF area carrying a default route, intra-area routes, and inter-area routes, but no external routes. Configuration of virtual links cannot be achieved across a stub area, and stub areas are not allowed to contain an ASBR. *See also: non-stub area, ASBR, OSPF.*

stub network A network having only one connection to a router.

STUN Serial Tunnel: A technology used to connect an HDLC link to an SDLC link over a serial link.

subarea A portion of an SNA network made up of a subarea node and its attached links and peripheral nodes.

subarea node An SNA communications host or controller that handles entire network addresses.

subchannel A frequency-based subdivision that creates a separate broadband communications channel.

subinterface One of many virtual interfaces available on a single physical interface.

subnet *See subnetwork.*

subnet address The portion of an IP address that is specifically identified by the subnet mask as the subnetwork. *See also: IP address, subnetwork, subnet mask.*

subnet mask   Also known simply as mask, this is a 32-bit address mask used in IP to identify the bits of an IP address that are used for the subnet address. With a mask, the router does not need to examine all 32 bits, only those selected by the mask. *See also: address mask, IP address.*

subnetwork   (1) Any network that is part of a larger IP network and is identified by a subnet address. A network administrator segments a network into subnetworks in order to provide a hierarchical, multilevel routing structure, and at the same time protect the subnetwork from the addressing complexity of networks that are attached. Also known as a subnet. *See also: IP address, subnet mask,* and *subnet address.* (2) In OSI networks, the term specifically refers to a collection of ESs and ISs controlled by only one administrative domain, using a solitary network connection protocol.

supervisor module   A module on Cisco switches that holds the CPU, system software, and most of the memory components used in the switch.

SVC   Switched virtual circuit: A dynamically established virtual circuit, created on demand and dissolved as soon as transmission is over and the circuit is no longer needed. In ATM terminology, the SVC is a switched virtual connection. *See also: PVC, VC.*

switch   (1) In networking, a device responsible for multiple functions such as filtering, flooding, and sending frames. The switch works using the destination address of individual frames. Switches operate at the Data-Link layer of the OSI model. (2) Broadly, any electronic/mechanical device allowing connections to be established as needed, and terminated if no longer necessary.

switch fabric   Term used to identify a Layer 2 switched internetwork with many switches.

switched LAN   Any LAN implemented using LAN switches. *See also: LAN switch.*

switching path   The logical path followed by a packet when it's switched through a router. Some examples are process switching, fast switching, optimum switching, CEF, dCEF, and distributed switching.

synchronous transmission   Signals transmitted digitally with precision clocking. These signals have identical frequencies and contain individual characters encapsulated in control bits (called start/stop bits) that designate the beginning and ending of each character. *See also: asynchronous transmission, isochronous transmission.*

T1   Digital WAN transmission faciltity that can carry a DS-1 signal that uses 24 DS0s at 64K each to create a bandwidth of 1.536Mbps, minus clocking overhead, providing 1.544Mbps of usable bandwidth.

T3   A digital WAN that can provide bandwidth of 44.763Mbps. A T3 is composed of 28 T1s.

tag switching   Based on the concept of label swapping, in which packets or cells are designated to defined-length labels that control the manner in which data is to be sent. Tag switching is a high-performance technology used for forwarding packets. It incorporates Data-Link layer (Layer 2) switching and Network layer (Layer 3) routing and supplies scalable, high-speed switching in the network core. *See also: MPLS.*

tagged traffic   ATM cells with their cell loss priority (CLP) bit set to 1. Also referred to as discard-eligible (DE) traffic. Tagged traffic can be eliminated in order to ensure trouble-free delivery of higher priority traffic, if the network is congested. *See also: CLP.*

TCP   Transmission Control Protocol: A connection-oriented protocol that is defined at the Transport layer of the OSI reference model. Provides reliable delivery of data.

TCP/IP   Transmission Control Protocol/Internet Protocol. The suite of protocols underlying the Internet. TCP and IP are the most widely known protocols in that suite. *See also: IP, TCP.*

TCP threeway handshake   Term referring to the connection sequence for a TCP connection. This sequence consists of three steps, a SYN packet replied to by a SYN-ACK packet from the receiving end-system, which in turn is replied to with and ACK packet by the originating end-system.

TDM   Time division multiplexing: A technique for assigning bandwidth on a single wire, based on assigned time slots, to data from several channels. Bandwidth is allotted to each channel regardless of a station's ability to send data. *See also: ATDM, FDM, multiplexing.*

TDR   Time domain reflectors: Complex cable testers, used to locate physical problems in a cable. They can detect where an open circuit, short circuit, crimped wire, or other abnormality is located in a cable. *See also: OTDR.*

TE   Terminal equipment: Any peripheral device that is ISDN compatible and attached to a network, such as a telephone or computer. TE1s are devices that are ISDN-ready and understand ISDN signaling techniques. TE2s are devices that are not ISDN-ready and do not understand ISDN signaling techniques. A terminal adapter must be used with a TE2.

TE1   Terminal equipment type 1: A device with a four-pair, twisted-pair digital interface. Most modern ISDN devices are of this type.

TE2   Terminal equipment type 2: A device with no native ISDN capabilities. In order for TE2 devices to use ISDN, a terminal adapter must be used to convert the ISDN signaling into a format understood by the device.

telco   A common abbreviation for the telephone company.

Telnet   The standard terminal emulation protocol within the TCP/IP protocol stack. Method of remote terminal connection, enabling users to log in on remote networks and use those resources as if they were locally connected. Telnet is defined in RFC 854.

terminal adapter   A hardware interface between a computer without a native ISDN interface and an ISDN line. In effect, a device to connect a standard async interface to a non-native ISDN device, emulating a modem.

terminal emulation   The use of software, installed on a PC or LAN server, that allows the PC to function as if it were a "dumb" terminal directly attached to a particular type of mainframe.

TFTP   Conceptually a stripped-down version of FTP, it's the protocol of choice if you know exactly what you want and where it's to be found. TFTP doesn't provide the abundance of functions that FTP does. In particular, it has no directory browsing abilities; it can do nothing but send and receive files.

Thicknet   Also called 10Base5. Bus network that uses a thick cable and runs Ethernet up to 500 meters.

Thinnet   Also called 10Base2. Bus network that uses a thin coax cable and runs Ethernet media access up to 185 meters.

three-way handshake   *See: TCP threeway handshake.*

token   A frame containing only control information. Possessing this control information gives a network device permission to transmit data onto the network. *See also: token passing.*

token bus   LAN architecture that is the basis for the IEEE 802.4 LAN specification. Employs token-passing access over a bus topology. *See also: IEEE.*

token passing   A method used by network devices to access the physical medium in a systematic way based on possession of a small frame called a token. *See also: token.*

Token Ring   IBM's token-passing LAN technology. It runs at 4Mbps or 16Mbps over a ring topology. Defined formally by IEEE 802.5. *See also: ring topology, token passing.*

toll network   WAN network that uses the Public Switched Telephone Network (PSTN) to send packets.

top-down troubleshooting   Troubleshooting methodology based on the OSI model. With top-down troubleshooting, the process starts with the application layer and moves down the OSI protocol stack. *See also: bottom-up troubleshooting, and divide-and-conquer troubleshooting.*

T reference point   Used with an S reference point to change a four-wire ISDN network to a two-wire ISDN network.

trace   IP command used to trace the path a packet takes through an internetwork.

transparent bridging   The bridging scheme used in Ethernet and IEEE 802.3 networks; it passes frames along one hop at a time, using bridging information stored in tables that associate end-node MAC addresses within bridge ports. This type of bridging is considered transparent because the source node does not know it has been bridged, because the destination frames are sent directly to the end node. *See also: SRB.*

Transport layer   Layer 4 of the OSI reference model, used for reliable communication between end nodes over the network. The Transport layer provides mechanisms used for establishing, maintaining, and terminating virtual circuits, transport fault detection and recovery, and controlling the flow of information. *See also: Application layer, Data-Link layer, Network layer, Physical layer, Presentation layer, Session layer.*

TRIP   Token Ring Interface Processor: A high-speed interface processor used on Cisco 7000 series routers. The TRIP provides two or four ports for interconnection with IEEE 802.5 and IBM media with ports set independently to speeds of either 4Mbps or 16 Mbps.

Troubleshooting Assistant Part of the Online Technical Support menu. This tool can be used to help isolate and diagnose many networking problems, based on user input and the Cisco database.

troubleshooting model A series of steps or procedures that can be methodically executed or followed to effectively troubleshoot and resolve network failures or outages.

trunk link Link used between switches and from some servers to the switches. Trunk links carry information about many VLANs. Access links are used to connect host devices to a switch and carry only information about VLANs of which the device is a member.

TTL Time To Live: A field in an IP header, indicating the length of time a packet is valid.

TUD Trunk Up-Down: A protocol used in ATM networks for the monitoring of trunks. Should a trunk miss a given number of test messages being sent by ATM switches to ensure trunk line quality, TUD declares the trunk down. When a trunk reverses direction and comes back up, TUD recognizes that the trunk is up and returns the trunk to service.

tunneling A method of avoiding protocol restrictions by wrapping packets from one protocol in another protocol's packet and transmitting this encapsulated packet over a network that supports the wrapper protocol. *See also: encapsulation.*

U reference point Reference point between a NT1 and an ISDN network. The U reference point understands ISDN signaling techniques and uses a two-wire connection.

UDP User Datagram Protocol: A connectionless Transport layer protocol in the TCP/IP protocol stack that allows datagrams to be simply exchanged without acknowledgments or delivery guarantees, requiring other protocols to handle error processing and retransmission. UDP is defined in RFC 768.

underrun Occurs when the transmitter runs at a higher rate than that of the packets sent from the hardware buffer.

unnumbered frames HDLC frames used for control-management purposes, such as link start-up and shutdown or mode specification.

UTP Unshielded twisted-pair: Copper wiring used in small-to-large networks, for connecting host devices to hubs and switches. Also used for connecting switch to switch or hub to hub.

VBR Variable Bit Rate: A QoS class, as defined by the ATM Forum, for use in ATM networks. VBR is subdivided into the real-time (RT) class and non-real-time (NRT) class. RT is employed when connections have a fixed-time relationship between samples. Conversely, NRT is employed when connections do not have a fixed-time relationship between samples, but still need an assured QoS.

VC Virtual circuit: A logical circuit devised to assure reliable communication between two devices on a network. Defined by a virtual path connection (VPC)/virtual path identifier (VCI) pair, the virtual circuit can be permanent (PVC) or switched (SVC). Virtual circuits are used in Frame Relay and X.25. Known as virtual channel in ATM. *See also: PVC, SVC.*

VCC   Virtual Channel Connection: A logical circuit that is created by Virtual Channel Links (VCL). VCCs carry data between two endpoints in an ATM network. Sometimes called a virtual circuit connection.

VIP   (1) Versatile Interface Processor: An interface card for Cisco 7000 and 7500 series routers, providing multilayer switching and running the Cisco IOS software. The most recent version of VIP is VIP2. (2) Virtual IP: A function making it possible for logically separated, switched IP workgroups to run Virtual Networking Services across the switch ports of a Catalyst 5000.

virtual circuit   *See VC.*

virtual ring   In an SRB network, a logical connection between physical rings, either local or remote.

VLAN   Virtual LAN: A group of devices on one or more logically segmented LANs (configured by use of management software), enabling devices to communicate as if attached to the same physical medium, when they are actually located on numerous disparate LAN segments. VLANs are based on logical rather than physical connections and thus are tremendously flexible.

VLSM   Variable-length subnet mask: Helps optimize available address space and specify a different subnet mask for the same network number on various subnets. Also commonly referred to as "subnetting a subnet."

volt-ohm meter   A tool that is used to measure connectivity and resistance on a metallic cable.

VTP   VLAN Trunk Protocol: Used to update switches in a switch fabric around VLANs configured on a VTP server. VTP devices can be a VTP server, client, or transparent device. Servers update clients. Transparent devices are only local devices and do not share information with VTP clients. VTPs send VLAN information down trunked links only.

WAN   Wide area network: The network components and infrastructure that are used to connect LANs together across a DCE (data communications equipment) network. Typically, a WAN is a leased line or dial-up connection across a PSTN network. Examples of WAN protocols include Frame Relay, PPP, ISDN, and HDLC.

wildcard   Used with access-list, supernetting, and OSPF configurations. Wildcards are designations used to identify a range of subnets.

window size   The amount of data that a station can transmit before needing an acknowledgment from the destination system. The acknowledgment confirms that all the data was received without error, or that errors existed and part of the data will need to be retransmitted.

windowing   Flow-control method used with TCP at the Transport layer of the OSI model.

WinSock   Windows Socket Interface: A software interface that makes it possible for an assortment of applications to use and share an Internet connection. The WinSock software consists of a Dynamic Link Library (DLL) with supporting programs such as a dialer program that initiates the connection.

workgroup switching   A switching method that supplies high-speed (100Mbps) transparent bridging between Ethernet networks as well as high-speed translational bridging between Ethernet and CDDI or FDDI.

X.25   An ITU-T packet-relay standard that defines communication between DTE and DCE network devices. X.25 uses a reliable Data-Link layer protocol called LAPB. X.25 also uses PLP at the Network layer. X.25 has for the most part been replaced by Frame Relay.

yellow alarm   A yellow alarm on a T1 or E1 indicates that the far end of the circuit has a corrupted incoming signal. *See also: red alarm.*

ZIP   Zone Information Protocol: A Session-layer protocol used by AppleTalk to map network numbers to zone names. NBP uses ZIP in the determination of networks containing nodes that belong to a zone. *See also: ZIP storm, zone.*

ZIP storm   A broadcast storm occurring when a router running AppleTalk reproduces or transmits a route for which there is no corresponding zone name at the time of execution. The route is then forwarded by other routers downstream, thus causing a ZIP storm. *See also: broadcast storm, ZIP.*

zone   A logical grouping of network devices in AppleTalk. *See also: ZIP.*

Index

Note to the Reader: Throughout this index **boldfaced** page numbers indicate primary discussions of a topic. *Italicized* page numbers indicate illustrations.

O

-o option in netstat, 76
objectives in documentation, 27
observations in case studies
  2600 series router, 377–383, 386–387
  file transfers, **410–413**
  ftp, 390–396
  telnet, 406–408
  Token Ring, **417–420**
  WAN connectivity, 400–403
observe results step, **15–16**, 469
OCs (Optical Carriers), 469
octets, 469
Offer messages, 174
Offset field, 119
100BaseT standard, 432
100BaseTX standard, 432
1000Base-T standard, 432
ones density method, 469
Open Shortest Path First. *See* OSPF (Open Shortest Path First)
Open Systems Interconnection (OSI) reference model
  defined, 469
  layers in, *92–94*, *93–94*
opening TAC cases, **421**
Optical Carriers (OCs), 469
optical TDRs (OTDRs), 355
optimum switching, 469
Option field in TCP, 119
Options field in IP packets, 113
Organization IDs, 351
Organizationally Unique Identifiers (OUIs), 470
Original frame field, 352
OSI reference model
  defined, 469
  layers in, *92–94*, *93–94*
OSPF (Open Shortest Path First), 209–210
  areas in, **210–213**
  debug commands for, 214–216
  defined, 470
  metrics in, **224**

neighbor and adjacency formation in, 210–211, *211*
problems in, **216**
show commands for, **213–214**
ospf option in debug, 159
OTDRs (optical TDRs), 355
OUIs (Organizationally Unique Identifiers), 470
out-of-band management, 470
out-of-band signaling, 470
output queues, 470
outside-in troubleshooting
  defined, 470
  operation of, **10**, *10*
overruns field, 144

P

P character
  in ping character maps, 166
  in traceroute, 169
P (Port Unreachable) messages, 169
P/F (Poll Final) bit, 107
-p option
  in netstat, 76
  in route, 73
Packet Internet groper program. *See* ping (Packet Internet groper) program
Packet Level Protocol (PLP), 471
packet option in debug, 159
Packet Switch Exchange (PSE), 474
packet-switched networks (PSNs), 474
packet switches, 470
packet switching, 470
packets
  defined, 470
  flow verification, **155**
  in IP, **112–113**, *114*
  in PPP, 106
  in RIP, 198
  in sequenced data transfer, 96
  in TCP, **118–120**

PAP (Password Authentication Protocol), 470–471
parameters in connection-oriented protocols, 95
parity checking, 471
partial mesh topology, 471
passive-interface command, 200
Password Authentication Protocol (PAP), 470–471
passwords in OSPF, 210
path determination, 471
PCR (Peak Cell Rate), 471
PDNs (Public Data Networks), 471
PDUs (protocol data units)
  defined, 472
  in sequenced data transfer, *96*, *97*
Peak Cell Rate (PCR), 471
peer option in debug, 159
periods (.) in ping character maps, 166
permanent buffer setting, 136
permanent field for buffer pools, 137
permanent virtual circuits (PVCs)
  defined, 474
  in Frame Relay, 260
permanent virtual paths (PVPs), 474
Permit statements, 178–179
PGP (Pretty Good Privacy), 471
phone switches in ISDN, **289–294**
physical insertion in Token Ring, 105
Physical layer
  defined, 471
  in ISDN, **286–289**, *287*
  in OSI model, 92, *93–94*
physical test equipment, 471
pim option in debug, 159
ping (Packet Internet groper) program
  in case studies
    ftp, 395, 399
    router, 386
    telnet, 406
  for default gateways, 196
  defined, 471

The Official
Juniper™ Networks Certification Study Guides
From Sybex

The Juniper Networks Technical Certification Program offers a four-tiered certification program that validates knowledge and skills related to Juniper Networks technologies:

- JNCIA (Juniper Networks Certified Internet Associate)
- JNCIS (Juniper Networks Certified Internet Specialist)
- JNCIP (Juniper Networks Certified Internet Professional)
- JNCIE (Juniper Networks Certified Internet Expert)

The JNCIA and JNCIS certifications require candidates to pass written exams, while the JNCIP and JNCIE certifications require candidates to pass one-day hands-on laboratory exams.

The Only OFFICIAL Juniper Networks Study Guides Are From Sybex

Written and reviewed by Juniper employees, the Juniper Networks Study Guides are the only official Study Guides for the Juniper Networks Technical Certification Program. Each book provides in-depth coverage of all exam objectives and detailed perspectives and insights into working with Juniper Networks technologies in the real world.

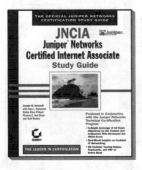

JNCIA: Juniper Networks Certified Internet Associate Study Guide
ISBN: 0-7821-4071-8

JNCIS: Juniper Networks Certified Internet Specialist Study Guide
ISBN: 0-7821-4072-6

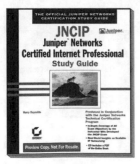

JNCIP: Juniper Networks Certified Internet Professional Study Guide
ISBN: 0-7821-4073-4

JNCIE: Juniper Networks Certified Internet Expert Study Guide
ISBN: 0-7821-4069-6

Security Certification Study Guides From Sybex

Security+™ Study Guide
by Michael Pastore • ISBN: 0-7821-4098-X • US $49.99

The Security+ certification is a new certification developed by CompTIA in response to both corporate and government requests for a certification that validates foundation-level IT security skills. Topics covered include access control, authentication, intrusion detection, malicious code, cryptography, physical security, disaster recovery, policies and procedures, and more.

CISSP: Certified Information Systems Security Professional Study Guide
by Ed Tittel, Mike Chapple, James Michael Stewart • ISBN: 0-7821-4175-7 • US $69.99

The CISSP Study Guide can give you the skills you need to pursue a successful career as an IT security professional. Written by IT security experts with years of real-world security experience, this book provides in-depth coverage of all official exam domains and includes hundreds of challenging review questions, electronic flashcards, and a searchable electronic version of the entire book.

MCSE: Windows® 2000 Network Security Design Study Guide
by Gary Govanus and Robert King • ISBN: 0-7821-2952-8 • US $59.99

This is the book needed to prepare for Exam 70-220, Designing Security for a Microsoft Windows 2000 Network. It contains comprehensive and in-depth coverage of every exam objective and practical information on designing a secure Windows 2000 network.

CCSA™ NG: Check Point™ Certified Security Administrator Study Guide
by Justin Menga • ISBN: 0-7821-4115-3 • US $59.99

CCSA (Check Point Certified Security Administrator) is the most highly recognized and respected vendor-specific security certification available. CCSA was recently selected as one of the "10 Hottest Certifications of 2003" by CertCities.com.

CCSP™: Managing Cisco Network Security Study Guide
by Todd Lammle and Carl Timm • ISBN: 0-7821-4231-1 • US $49.99

The Managing Cisco Network Security (MCNS) exam (#640-100) is the first, and most critical, in a series of five exams required for a new professional-level certification, Cisco Certified Security Professional (CCSP). Written for everyone pursuing a career as a Cisco security professional, this guide is packed with real world scenarios and exam essentials that take you beyond the basics, and reinforce key subject areas.

SYBEX®

www.sybex.com

TELL US WHAT YOU THINK!

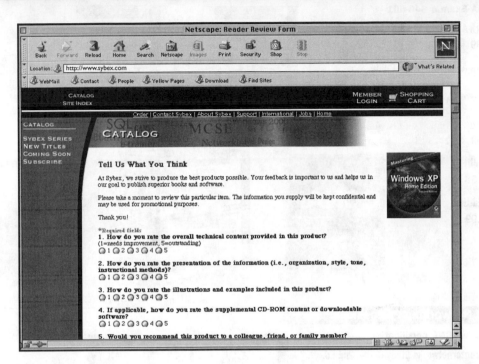

Your feedback is critical to our efforts to provide you with the best books and software on the market. Tell us what you think about the products you've purchased. It's simple:

1. Go to the Sybex website.
2. Find your book by typing the ISBN or title into the Search field.
3. Click on the book title when it appears.
4. Click **Submit a Review.**
5. Fill out the questionnaire and comments.
6. Click **Submit.**

With your feedback, we can continue to publish the highest quality computer books and software products that today's busy IT professionals deserve.

www.sybex.com

SYBEX Inc. • 1151 Marina Village Parkway, Alameda, CA 94501 • 510-523-8233

SYBEX®

The Complete Cisco Certification Solution

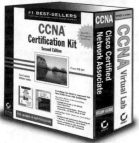